Under the Sky of My Africa

Northwestern University Press
Studies in Russian Literature and Theory

Founding Editor
  Gary Saul Morson

General Editor
  Caryl Emerson

Consulting Editors
  Carol Avins
  Robert Belknap
  Robert Louis Jackson
  Elliott Mossman
  Alfred Rieber
  William Mills Todd III
  Alexander Zholkovsky

Under the Sky of My Africa

ALEXANDER PUSHKIN AND BLACKNESS

*Edited by Catharine Theimer Nepomnyashchy,
Nicole Svobodny, and Ludmilla A. Trigos*

Foreword by Henry Louis Gates Jr.

NORTHWESTERN UNIVERSITY PRESS / EVANSTON, ILLINOIS
STUDIES OF THE HARRIMAN INSTITUTE

Northwestern University Press
Evanston, Illinois 60208-4170

Copyright © 2006 by Northwestern University Press.
Foreword copyright 2006 by Henry Louis Gates Jr.
Published 2006. All rights reserved.

Printed in the United States of America

10 9 8 7 6 5 4 3 2 1

ISBN 0-8101-1970-6 (cloth)
ISBN 0-8101-1971-4 (paper)

Library of Congress Cataloging-in-Publication Data

Under the sky of my Africa : Alexander Pushkin and blackness / edited by Catharine Theimer Nepomnyashchy, Nicole Svobodny, and Ludmilla A. Trigos ; foreword by Henry Louis Gates Jr.

    p. cm.—(Studies in Russian literature and theory) (Studies of the Harriman Institute)

    Includes bibliographical references and index.

    ISBN 0-8101-1971-4 (pbk. : alk. paper)—ISBN 0-8101-1970-6 (cloth : alk. paper)

    1. Pushkin, Aleksandr Sergeevich, 1799–1837—Knowledge—Race awareness. 2. Pushkin, Aleksandr Sergeevich, 1799–1837—Family. 3. Racially mixed people—Race identity—Russia. 4. Blacks in literature. 5. Race awareness in literature. 6. Pushkin family. 7. Russia—Ethnic relations. I. Nepomnyashchy, Catharine Theimer. II. Svobodny, Nicole. III. Trigos, Ludmilla A. IV. Series. V. Series: Studies of the Harriman Institute.
PG3358.R33.U53 2005
891.71'3—dc22   2005016715

♾ The paper used in this publication meets the minimum requirements of the American National Standard for Information Sciences—Permanence of Paper for Printed Library Materials, ANSI Z39.48-1992.

Contents

List of Illustrations	vii
Foreword	xi
Acknowledgments	xv
Editors' Note	xvii
Introduction: Was Pushkin Black and Does It Matter? *Catharine Theimer Nepomnyashchy and Ludmilla A. Trigos*	3
A. P. Gannibal: On the Occasion of the Three Hundredth Anniversary of the Birth of Alexander Pushkin's Great-Grandfather *N. K. Teletova*	46
Pushkin on His African Heritage: Publications during His Lifetime *J. Thomas Shaw*	79
Ruslan and Ludmila: Pushkin's Anxiety of Blackness *Richard F. Gustafson*	99
How Black Was Pushkin? Otherness and Self-Creation *David M. Bethea*	122
The Telltale Black Baby, or Why Pushkin Began *The Blackamoor of Peter the Great* but Didn't Finish It *Catharine Theimer Nepomnyashchy*	150
Making a True Image: Blackness and Pushkin Portraits *Richard C. Borden*	172

Pushkin and *Othello* 196
    Catherine O'Neil

The Pushkin of *Opportunity* in the Harlem Renaissance 226
    Olga P. Hasty

"Bound by Blood to the Race": Pushkin in African American Context 248
    Anne Lounsbery

Tsvetaeva's "Blackest of Black" (*Naicherneishii*) Pushkin 279
    Liza Knapp

"Sometimes I Feel Like a Motherless Child": Paul Robeson and
the 1949 Pushkin Jubilee 302
    Alexandar Mihailovic

Artur Vincent Lourié's *The Blackamoor of Peter the Great:* Pushkin's
Exotic Ancestor as Twentieth-Century Opera 332
    Caryl Emerson

Appendix A: Creativity and Blackness—a Note on Yury Tynianov's
"The Gannibals" 369

Appendix B: Introduction to "The Gannibals" by Yury Tynianov 377

Appendix C: Excerpt from "My Pushkin" by Marina Tsvetaeva 384

Appendix D: Excerpt from *Strolls with Pushkin* by Abram Tertz
(Andrei Sinyavsky) 393

Index 399

Contributors 415

Illustrations

Gallery follows page 174.

1. E. I. Geitman, *Pushkin*, 1822
2. Pushkin's inkwell
3. A. S. Pushkin, self-portrait from Elizaveta Ushakov's album, September or October 1829
4. A. S. Pushkin, self-portrait as a horse, among drawings of horses' heads; on the manuscript of the poem "André Chenier," 1825
5. A. S. Pushkin, self-portrait as a blackamoor (*arap*), in a manuscript of the novel *The Blackamoor of Peter the Great* (chapter 3), 1827
6. A. S. Pushkin, self-portrait as Dante, with the inscription in Italian "il gran Padre AP," 1835–36
7. Artist unknown, *A. S. Pushkin* (no date)
8. I. Linev, *Pushkin*, 1836–37?
9. A. S. Pushkin's death mask, January 29, 1837
10. A. A. Kozlov, *Pushkin in His Coffin*, 1837
11. F. A. Bruni, *Pushkin in His Coffin*, 1837
12. A. N. Mokritsky, *Pushkin on His Deathbed*, January 29, 1837
13. V. A. Zhukovsky, *Pushkin in His Coffin*, January 30, 1837
14. Artist unknown (S. G. Chirikov?), *A. S. Pushkin*, c. 1810s
15. K. Somov, *Pushkin at Work*, 1899
16. I. Repin, I. Aivazovsky, *Farewell, Free Elements!* 1887
17. I. Repin, *Pushkin at the Lycée Examination*, 1911
18. A. M. Opekushin, model of Pushkin's head for the Pushkin monument, 1880
19. N. P. Ul'ianov, *Pushkin and His Wife before the Mirror at a Court Ball*, 1936

Illustrations

20a. G. Chernetsov, detail from *Pushkin, Krylov, Zhukovsky, and Gnedich in the Summer Garden*, 1832
20b. G. Chernetsov, *Pushkin, Krylov, Zhukovsky, and Gnedich in the Summer Garden*, 1832
21. S. Gal'berg, *Pushkin*, 1837
22. I. P. Vitali, *A. S. Pushkin*, 1837
23. P. F. Sokolov, *A. S. Pushkin*, 1836
24. T. Wright, *A. S. Pushkin*, 1836–37
25. P. Chelishchev, *Pushkin Taking a Stroll*, 1830
26a. Artist of the Venetsianov school, detail from *A Saturday Gathering at Zhukovsky's*, 1837–39
26b. Artist of the Venetsianov school, detail from *A Saturday Gathering at Zhukovsky's*, 1837–39
27. Unknown artist, *A. S. Pushkin*, 1831
28. J. de Vivien, *A. S. Pushkin*, 1826–27
29. G. A. Gippius, *A. S. Pushkin*, 1827
30. Xavier de Maistre(?), *Pushkin as a Child*, 1800–02
31. V. A. Tropinin, *A. S. Pushkin*, 1827
32. V. A. Tropinin, sketch, 1827
33. V. A. Tropinin, study, 1827
34a. A. P. Elagina, *Portrait of Alexander Pushkin*, copy from the original by V. A. Tropinin, 1827
34b. A. P. Elagina, detail from *Portrait of Alexander Pushkin*, 1827
35. I. Repin, *A. S. Pushkin*, copy from the original by V. A. Tropinin, 1913
36. O. A. Kiprensky, *A. S. Pushkin*, 1827
37. N. I. Utkin, gravure from the original by O. A. Kiprensky, 1827
38. V. V. Mathé, *Pushkin*, 1899
39. A. Bezliudnyi, lithograph from the original by O. A. Kiprensky, 1830
40. A. I. Kravchenko, *Pushkin*, 1936
41. K. F. Iuon, *Pushkin*, 1950
42. A. P. Briullov, *Pushkin at the Housewarming Party at Smirdin's Bookshop*, 1832
43. S. F. Galaktionov, *Pushkin at the Housewarming Party at Smirdin's Bookshop*, engraving after A. Briullov's drawing, 1833
44. A. M. Opekushin, Pushkin monument in Moscow, 1875

Illustrations

45. M. K. Anikushin, model of the Pushkin monument in St. Petersburg, 1950
46. V. V. Kozlov, model of the Pushkin monument in St. Petersburg, 1936
47. I. D. Shadr, model of the Pushkin monument in St. Petersburg, 1940
48. B. Z. Zelensky, poster, 1949
49. V. I. Shukhaev, *A. S. Pushkin*, 1960
50. R. R. Bakh, *Pushkin*, 1886
51. N. Gogol, *Pushkin*, 1837
52. V. A. Favorsky, *Pushkin as a Boy at the Lycée*, 1935
53. V. A. Serov, *Pushkin in the Park*, 1899
54. V. F. Shtein, *Pushkin as a Boy*, 1910
55. N. P. Ul'ianov, *Pushkin in the Lyceum Gardens*, 1935
56. E. F. Belashova, *Pushkin as a Boy*, 1959
57. A. Z. Itkin, *Pushkin-Lycéeist*, 1968
58. A. Z. Itkin, *Pushkin-Lycéeist*, 1968
59. A. M. Nenasheva, *Pushkin-Lycéeist*, 1961
60. G. B. Dodonova, *Pushkin-Lycéeist*, 1969
61. E. A. Gendel'man, *Pushkin-Lycéeist*, 1962
62. G. S. Stolbov, *Africa*, 1961
63. I. Aivazovsky, *Pushkin on the Black Sea Coast*, 1868
64. I Aivazovsky, detail from *Pushkin on the Black Sea Coast*, 1868
65. M. Dobuzhinsky, *Pushkin and the Decembrists*, 1924
66. J. de Vivien(?), detail from miniature portrait of Pushkin, 1826
67. V. Taburin, cover design for the book *Pushkin for Children*, 1899
68. M. Skudnov, medal, *Pushkin*, 1899
69. P. P. Trubetskoi, *Pushkin*, 1899
70. N. V. Kuz'min, *Pushkin and Kaverin*, illustration to *Eugene Onegin*, 1928–33
71. N. V. Kuz'min, *Pushkin*, illustration for the poem "To Chaadaev," 1959
72. V. N. Masiutin, *Pushkin*, 1918
73. Iu. L. Obolenskaia, *Pushkin*, 1925
74. P. Ia. Pavlinov, *Pushkin*, 1924
75. A. A. Naumov, *Pushkin's Duel with d'Anthès*, 1884

Foreword

Scholars believe that as many African slaves were sold across the Sahara Desert, the Red Sea, and the Indian Ocean as crossed the Atlantic Ocean. Think of it as the "other slave trade." One of these slaves—who would be named Abram Gannibal by his new master—was born in the country today called Cameroon, sold into slavery, and taken across the desert to Constantinople. In 1704, when he was about seven or eight, he was purchased by Peter the Great. Under Peter's protection and tutelage, Gannibal became a broadly educated and well-traveled man; Voltaire himself called him "the dark star of the Enlightenment." Despite exile to Siberia—and, later, forced retirement under Peter III—Gannibal would ultimately rise to the rank of chief military engineer in the Russian Army, along the way fathering eleven children with Christina Regina von Schöberg, of German and Swedish extraction. In 1799, their granddaughter, Nadezhda, would give birth to a son she called Alexander.

For over a century and a half, Alexander Pushkin has been a shadowy if dramatic presence in African American letters, a resonant symbol of all that a person of African descent could achieve if his or her talents were unfettered by the confining strictures of racism, and simultaneously an abidingly potent sign of the sheer absurdity of America's bizarre "one-drop rule." The great artist Quincy Jones has announced plans to make a film about Pushkin for this very reason. Pushkin has enjoyed pride of place in every textbook of "the world's great men of color," as the journalist and historian J. A. Rogers put it.

Had Pushkin, the great-grandson of a black African, been born in the United States rather than in Russia, he would most likely have been a slave or, at best, a second-class citizen. His great-grandfather, accompanying Peter the Great to Paris, became friends with Montesquieu, Diderot, and Voltaire, but one is forced to wonder how the father of the American Enlightenment, Thomas Jefferson, would have regarded him? Would Jefferson have encouraged a Monticello-born Pushkin to write, to excel, indeed to found America's national literature based on a rich and emerging vernacular? Pushkin would

Foreword

have become Jefferson's house servant at most, perhaps learning how to keep books, sort the mail, and select and pour the wine.

"What proportion of America's collective artistic and intellectual genius," black thinkers since Frederick Douglass have exclaimed, "has been lost or underdeveloped, because even the slightest touch of the tar brush trumps talent every time?"

Elevated to the status of a black icon by the American abolitionist John Greenleaf Whittier in 1847, Pushkin was heralded as a beacon of hope in the long dark night of slavery, the shining star of "The Negro Can Be Elevated" movement, which excavated and held high "key noble specimens" of Negro achievement in the antislavery version of the great man and great woman school of black history. In 1940, when no less a skeptic than W. E. B. DuBois decided to publish an ostensible entry from his ill-fated *Encyclopedia of the Negro,* he chose "Alexander Pushkin" for the topic of his article.

Pushkin demonstrated all that a Negro could be: a cultured aristocrat, a man of letters, indeed the father of a national literature. By the time of the Harlem Renaissance, a veritable kitchen cabinet of superstar mulattoes and impeccable black Africans and Americans could be summoned whenever someone needed to show that persons of African descent could achieve at the highest levels in the arts. Think of it as the "Beethoven was black" school of history, even if Beethoven, sadly, did not really make the cut. (Nor, for the record, did Cleopatra or Hannibal.) But Juan Latino; Beethoven's sometime friend and rival, George Bridgetower; and Alexander Dumas did. And of this group, no one informed the African American imagination more than Pushkin, the tragic Romantic hero of the American abolitionist movement.

Pushkin's great-grandfather first appears in the African American popular imagination in 1828, in an article published in *Freedom's Journal,* the first African American newspaper. Whittier's longer, widely cited essay (with and without attribution) appeared in the *National Era* in 1847, two years following the publication of Frederick Douglass's genre-defining autobiographical slave narrative. The timing was not accidental; as Anne Lounsbery suggests in an exceptionally fascinating essay, Pushkin was Douglass's *doppelganger,* the handsome, dashing man of letters, whose personal development, unlike Douglass's, had not been proscribed. Whittier dared America to imagine Douglass as the New Man, as the progenitor of a truly new, truly *national* literature. Pushkin was far more than the abolitionists could ask for, and far more than even sympathetic white Americans could possibly imagine. But there he strode, nonetheless: a Russian national treasure, the father of Russian literature, in black—or brown—face.

Pushkin adopted a variety of stances toward his black ancestry: at times he embraced his "exoticism" and his African "hot-bloodedness"; at other times he brooded that the traces of his African lineage that showed in his face

Foreword

and his hair made him "ugly." But there is no doubt that, whatever his attitude toward it, Pushkin's African ancestry was a source of ongoing fascination for him. It made him different from all other Russians; it is thought by a number of the authors who appear in this collection of essays that this difference is what enabled Pushkin to become the great chronicler of Russian life and the Russian people. That he stood a little apart from his countrymen gave Pushkin a clear-eyed vantage point from which to view his fellow Russians.

The essays in this collection make much of the literary traces of Africa in Pushkin's work (such as his declaration in a note to *Eugene Onegin* that it is "under the sky of my Africa" that his imagination was freest, or his unfinished narrative *The Blackamoor of Peter the Great*, an adaptation of his great-grandfather's life) and also of his Romantic sympathies with Russian serfs and American slaves (to whom he once referred as "my brothers"). Many are concerned with passing, and one essay is concerned entirely with Pushkin's physical appearance in portraits, which show varying degrees of "blackness," a variation rooted not in his own relationship to his African ancestry but rather in the cultural moments in which these portraits appeared.

The essays also track the historical course followed by literary reactions to Pushkin's connection to Africa and to African Americans. Romantics celebrated Pushkin as a free and at times "uncivilized" genius who drew on his "wild" African blood to break the literary chains of his native land. Pushkin appeared several times in the abolitionist press in the United States as the example of what happens when "race prejudice" is not a factor in national life: according to John Greenleaf Whittier, a man with "African blood" could rise to the greatest artistic heights and even become a shaper of the national aesthetic only in the absence of the American brand of prejudice and racism (my word, not Whittier's). More generally, Pushkin's sympathy with slaves (whom many abolitionist writers compared to Russian serfs) won acclaim among antislavery groups.

Writers in the Harlem Renaissance seized on Pushkin because of his embrace of his African lineage (they seemed to overlook his less loving references to it) and also because he drew on a vernacular language rooted in the "low" culture of Russia to shape a national literature. Pushkin served in the Harlem Renaissance as a successful example of the movement's literary-national aspirations. A Soviet-era writer such as Marina Tsvetaeva or a composer like Lourié embraced Pushkin's "hybridity," internationalism, and cosmopolitanism as the ideals that communism (with its suppression of many artists) was falling short of.

Many critics and writers, most famously Nabokov, dismissed Pushkin's "Africanness" as a quirk of biographical fate, as a factor to be acknowledged only barely, if at all, and to be dismissed as irrelevant to his artistic life. But these essays make a convincing case for the merits of a sustained exploration

Foreword

of the role his African ancestry played in Pushkin's creative life, in his perception of himself, and in his perception and interpretation of Russia. This brilliantly edited collection is at once a major contribution to Pushkin studies, to Russian literary criticism, and to African American studies. It deserves the widest possible readership.

Henry Louis Gates Jr.

Acknowledgments

This project originated out of a conversation with Susan Harris, formerly at Northwestern University Press, at the national meeting of the American Association for the Advancement of Slavic Studies in 1997, and we would like to express our heartfelt gratitude to Susan for her encouragement and support throughout. It then developed further as the result of a series of Modern Language Association panels on Alexander Pushkin and his African heritage in 1999. As with any ongoing and long-gestating project, there are a number of people who were instrumental in helping bring it to completion. The editors would first of all like to thank our readers Marcus Levitt and Josephine Wohl for their valuable feedback during the review process. We also thank Irina Reyfman for her many suggestions and thorough reading of the manuscript; and Alla Rachkov, Kevin Laney, Ronald Meyer, and Larisa Kirichenko for their valiant efforts on our behalf and their unflagging support in all aspects, large and small. Jared Ingersoll and Clint Walker were especially helpful to us in our numerous bibliographic queries. Deborah Martinsen, Kathleen Parthé, Donia Allen, Robert Coles, and Allison Blakely provided us with useful suggestions and source materials; Souleymane Ndiaye gave us firsthand information on the experiences of African exchange students in Moscow; and Kara Lynch graciously shared the prerelease version of her documentary *Black Russians* with us. Finally, we are grateful for the research assistance of Douglas Greenfield, Eric Roston, Cate Huetter, and Tench Coxe.

The editors express appreciation to the University Seminars at Columbia University for their help in publication. Material in this work was presented to the University Seminar on Slavic History and Culture. We would also like to thank Barnard College and the Harriman Institute of Columbia University for their generous support.

J. Thomas Shaw's article "Pushkin on His African Heritage: Publications during His Lifetime" has been reprinted from the volume *Pushkin Today*, edited by David M. Bethea (1993), with the permission of Indiana University Press. Associated University Presses has granted us permission to publish a shorter version of a chapter from Catherine O'Neil's book *With Shakespeare's*

Acknowledgments

Eyes: Pushkin's Creative Appropriation of Shakespeare (University of Delaware Press, 2003). N. K. Teletova's article has been reprinted with permission of the author. The excerpt from Abram Tertz's *Strolls with Pushkin* (1993) has been republished here with the permission of Yale University Press.

Editors' Note

We are following a modified Library of Congress transliteration system in this volume. To make the text more readable to a general audience, first and last names ending in *-ii* have been changed to *-y*, such as Anatoly or Belinsky rather than Anatolii or Belinskii. We have also, for the sake of readability, collapsed *-iia* endings to *-ia*. For the same reason, names beginning with *-ia* or *-iu*, such as Iurii and Iazykov, have been changed to Yury and Yazykov. Names are given in their standard English form when one exists. Bibliographical references follow the standard Library of Congress transliteration system.

All of our references to Pushkin's work have been taken from the seventeen-volume *Polnoe sobranie sochinenii*, i.e., the "large Academy" edition (Moscow and Leningrad, 1937–59). References are cited by volume and page number and included in parentheses in the text, as for example (*PSS* 1:211).

Translations of the same Russian passages vary slightly from article to article due to the authors' translation preferences.

Under the Sky of My Africa

Catharine Theimer Nepomnyashchy and Ludmilla A. Trigos

Introduction: Was Pushkin Black and Does It Matter?

> Can the Ethiopian change his skin, or the leopard his spots? then may ye also do good, that are accustomed to do evil.
> —Jeremiah 13:23

> The native of Africa is a lazy, beast-like, dull-witted creature doomed to perpetual slavery and working under the threat of punishment and dire torment.
> —Vissarion Belinsky, *The Idea of Art*, 1841

> Pushkin was a Rastaman.
> —*Black Russians*

ROUGHLY IN THE YEAR 1705, a young African boy, acquired from the seraglio of the Turkish sultan by the Russian envoy in Constantinople (Istanbul), was transported to Russia as a gift to Tsar Peter the Great, who was known for his love of the exotic and the odd. As the vagaries of history would have it, this child, later known as Abram Petrovich Gannibal, was to become the godson of the ruler of the largest contiguous empire on earth, travel from one end of Europe to the other and across the huge expanses of Russia into Asia almost to the Chinese border, and survive six of Peter's successors to die at a ripe old age, having attained the rank of general and the status of Russian nobility. Most important, he was to become the great-grandfather of Russia's greatest national poet, Alexander Pushkin. It is the contention of the editors of this book, borne out, we believe, by the majority of essays included in this collection, that Pushkin's African ancestry has played the role of a "wild card" of sorts as a formative element in Russian cultural mythology. That is, not only has the fact of Gannibal's African origin functioned as an essential element in the "canonization" of his great-grandson as the exemplary Russian—heralded even in his lifetime by his fellow writer Nikolai Gogol as "the Russian as he will be in two hundred years"—but the ways in which Gannibal's legacy over the course of the past two centuries has been incorporated into or excluded from the cult of Pushkin's biography serve as shifting markers of Russia's self-definition.

Despite sparring over historical detail, it is safe to say that there is some consensus among biographers about the broad outlines of Gannibal's life, especially as concerns the better-documented period after he arrived in Russia.[1] Within months of his presentation to the tsar, he was baptized in Vilno (Vilnius) with Peter the Great standing as his godfather, and he appears to have traveled in Peter's entourage throughout the military campaigns of the next decade, eventually becoming Peter's amanuensis. In 1717 he went along on the tsar's second journey to western Europe and was left behind to study in France, in line with Peter's policy of sending youths abroad for education to stock the cadres he needed in his campaign to reform and westernize his empire. Gannibal spent five years in France, where he studied military engineering. He served in the French army from 1719 to 1721, apparently both to continue his training and to better the precarious financial position into which erratic deliveries of stipends from Russia and the French crisis in paper money had left those young Russians studying in France at the time. Gannibal apparently suffered a head wound in battle in 1719. From 1720 he studied mathematics, fortification, and artillery in a new school 100 miles outside of Paris. Despite the straitened financial circumstances of which Gannibal and his fellow students complained bitterly in periodic letters to Russia, and which one contemporary Russian observer lamented as bringing down "such shame on our fatherland," Gannibal managed to acquire a library of some 400 volumes on diverse subjects, which he took back with him to Russia.[2] After his somewhat reluctant return to Russia in 1722, Gannibal again appears to have served as Peter's personal secretary as well as to have put into practice the engineering training he had acquired in France. In February 1724 Peter awarded his protégé the rank of engineer-lieutenant in his own crack Preobrazhensky Regiment, where Gannibal taught fortification and mathematics to officer candidates. At the time of Peter's sudden death in 1725 Gannibal was in Riga, whither the tsar had sent him in the fall of 1724 to work on the strengthening of the city's fortress.

Since Peter had not designated a successor, his death plunged his court, including Gannibal and those vying for the throne, into intrigue. Gannibal was appointed tutor to the Tsarevich Peter Alekseevich (the future Peter II) and managed to maintain a position close to the court throughout the two-year reign of Peter the Great's wife, Catherine I, who had known him since his arrival in Russia. Deprived of Catherine's protection upon her death on May 6, 1727, however, Gannibal found himself at the mercy of the powerful Prince Menshikov against whom he had plotted, and was sent to Siberia, ostensibly to design and oversee the building of fortifications in the remote town of Selenginsk. (It is worthy of note that the first documented

Introduction

use of Gannibal's surname dates to this period.³ It would appear that Pushkin's forebear, hitherto referred to as Abram Petrov or Abram *arap* ("blackamoor"), adopted the name, and the putative genealogy back to the Carthaginian general Hannibal it implies, only after the deaths of Peter I and his wife, who might have challenged his genealogical pretensions.)⁴ Despite Menshikov's fall and attempted intercessions by his friends, Gannibal remained in Siberia—and was subjected to house searches and two months under arrest in Tobolsk as well as severe financial hardship—until 1730, when he was transferred to the Estonian town of Pernov (Pärnu), probably thanks to the influential Count B. Kh. Minikh, who was the head of military engineering for all of Russia at the time.

Gannibal's return from Siberia opened yet another dramatic, even melodramatic period in his life. After arriving in Petersburg in December 1730, he made the acquaintance of a Greek captain, one Andrei Dioper, and asked for the hand of his younger daughter, Evdokia, in marriage. Despite the disinclination of the woman herself, who was already engaged to another and who reportedly objected to Gannibal on the grounds that "he's an *arap* and not our breed," the couple was married in January 1731 and soon after left to take up residence in Pernov.⁵ Perhaps predictably, the marriage degenerated in short order, leading to the institution of divorce proceedings which dragged on for twenty-one years, the final divorce ruling coming only on September 9, 1753, and exonerating Gannibal of all guilt and consigning Evdokia to a nunnery for the rest of her life. Scholars' attempts to reconstruct the facts of the marriage and its prolonged aftermath have been hindered by the fact that the primary historical source remains the suits and countersuits in the court records.⁶ The legal documents include allegations that Gannibal set up a private torture chamber in his home to force his wife into testifying as he wished and that, for her part, Evdokia engaged in multiple infidelities and even plotted with one of her lovers to poison her husband.⁷ It is nonetheless evident that, quite apart from issues of blame, both parties were trapped by their willfulness in a legal morass. What was at stake for Gannibal, however, was the legitimacy of his children, for sometime no later than 1734 Gannibal met, took up residence with, and eventually succeeded in legally marrying Christina Regina von Schöberg, daughter of a Swedish captain who was of noble descent.⁸ Gannibal's second wife bore him seven children—four sons and three daughters—and the two lived together, apparently in harmony, for almost half a century, dying within months of one another.⁹

Whether because of personal or professional problems, Gannibal began requesting that he be allowed to retire from the military, and from his job teaching mathematics to junior officers in Pernov, in the autumn of 1731, and his request was finally granted on May 21, 1733. He bought the farmstead Kärikula outside of Revel (Tallinn) and remained there in retirement with his wife and growing family for seven years, apparently taking up the life of a gentleman farmer. Gannibal emerged from retirement in 1741, under the regency of Anna Leopoldovna, and served as an engineer in Revel with the rank of lieutenant colonel, probably owing this twist in his career again to Minikh. It was, however, only with the ascension to the throne of Peter's daughter, Empress Elizabeth I, in late 1741 that Gannibal's fortunes took a sharp turn for the better. In 1742 Gannibal was promoted to the rank of major general, was made chief commandant of Revel, and was granted land in the Pskov region, including the estate at Mikhailovskoe, which was to become so important to his great-grandson's life and work. In 1748 Gannibal was awarded the Order of Saint Andrew, and by 1752 he was finally reassigned to St. Petersburg, in the environs of which he was to live out his life. In 1759 he was promoted to full general and in 1760 received the Order of Saint Alexander Nevsky. In the same year, at the height of Gannibal's career, the Empress Elizabeth died, and at the age of 66, apparently under pressure from political enemies, Gannibal went into final retirement three weeks before the end of Peter III's brief and ill-starred reign brought Catherine II to the throne. In 1762 Gannibal moved to the estate at Suida, which he had bought along with other lands outside of the capital in the final years of his military engineering career, and there he lived the last nineteen years of his life, dying on April 20, 1781, in his mid-eighties.[10]

While wranglings among historians and Pushkin biographers over the course of Gannibal's life after he left Africa remain on the level of symbolically negligible detail, the question of his origins to this day constitutes a point of culturally loaded contention. Gannibal himself apparently left no written trace of the name of his country of birth. In his 1742 petition to the Empress Elizabeth requesting that he be granted a coat of arms based on purportedly noble African origins, Gannibal mentions only the name of a town, Logon, where he was born.[11] The first biography of Gannibal, the so-called German biography, names Abyssinia as Gannibal's country of origin, fueling the long-standing belief that Gannibal was Ethiopian.[12] As Vladimir Nabokov and others have pointed out, however, at the time the term "Abyssinia" was a catchall designation among Europeans for all of northern Africa and therefore tells us little in terms of hard geographical information.[13] Even if we were to accept incontestably the region historically occupied by Abyssinia as Gannibal's place of birth, it would tell us little, if anything, about Gannibal's ethnic derivation, given the diversity of Abyssinia's population—made up at the time of Gannibal's birth as today of Semitic or Hamitic and Negroid peoples. According to sources roughly contemporary with Pushkin, the country of Abyssinia, in eastern Africa, gained its name, "Habesh," from the appellation of its first explorers, the Arabs. It was inhabited by a people "who have a swarthy coloration to their skin [*smuglyi svet kozhi*] and are well-formed. The original Cushitic population . . . was edged out by Semitic newcomers who made themselves

Introduction

rulers of the country and the carriers of indigenous culture . . . In the 16th century, the Galla tribe penetrated into Abyssinia from the depths of Africa and gradually settled all over Abyssinia as the agricultural class of the population . . . The hot, low-lying regions of Abyssinia are occupied by half-wild Negro tribes."[14] The renowned compendium of Enlightenment knowledge compiled by the French philosophes, *Encylopédie ou dictionnaire raisonné des sciences, des arts, et des métiers* (1751–72), defines the African population thus: "Africa has no other inhabitants but the blacks. Not only the color, but also the facial traits distinguish them from other men: large and flat noses, thick lips, and wool instead of hair. They appear to constitute a new species of mankind. If one moves further away from the Equator toward the Antarctic, the black skin becomes lighter, but the ugliness remains: one finds here this same wicked people that inhabits the African Meridian."[15] A popular nineteenth-century Russian encyclopedia points out that "the scientific study of Negroes began in the 18th century, with the research of Zemmering, White, Campere and Blumenbach, who found that Negroes were closer to animals (monkeys) than the representatives of other races."[16]

As the foregoing citations should make clear, from the very beginning— or at least since the time of his great-grandson—hidden, and sometimes not so hidden, behind the sparring over geography in the reconstruction of Gannibal's biography, lies the deeper issue of race. Gannibal referred to himself as "black," for instance, in a petition to I. A. Cherkasov, secretary to the Empress Elizabeth:

> I would like everyone to be like me: dutiful and faithful to the limit of my ability (*except only for my blackness* [*chernoty*]). O, sovereign, do not be angry that I said so—it is truly out of sorrow and bitterness of my heart—either cast me away as a worthless monster and consign me to oblivion or complete the charity begun in me.[17]

By the same token, Gannibal's son Petr, in his brief autobiographical note, maintained: "My father was a Negro."[18] Moreover, as J. Thomas Shaw's article republished in this collection demonstrates, Pushkin did not hesitate to identify his forebear publicly as "Negro" or "black"—at least, as we shall see, until an 1830 attack on his genealogy rendered him more circumspect. Yet, as the following "exchange" makes clear, some Russian scholars have been reluctant to accept Pushkin's opinion on the matter. Thus, in his biography of Pushkin, Yury Lotman appends to the poet's assertion that his mother's grandfather "was a Negro" the following footnote:

> Pushkin's ancestor was not a Negro, but a Blackamoor [*arap*], i.e., an Ethiopian, an Abyssinian. His appearance at the court of Peter I was possibly

7

linked with deeper causes than the fashion, widespread in Europe at the beginning of the eighteenth century, for Blackamoor pages [*pazhei-arapchat*]; in plans for the destruction of the Turkish empire, which Peter I was plotting, ties with Abyssinia—a Christian country situated in a strategically important region, at the rear of the troubled Egyptian flank of Turkey—occupied a definite place. However, the prolonged Northern War did not allow these plans to develop.[19]

Lotman's note contains a number of salient features, the most important of which are the distinction he draws between "Negro" and "Abyssinian" or "Ethiopian" and his complicated political digression, which arguably serves to distract from the "racial" issue at hand. Tellingly, moreover, Lotman never mentions Gannibal by name in his biography of Pushkin. In this context, we would argue, Lotman stands in for generations of contributors to the construction of Pushkin's image who have, more or less subtly, "washed the Ethiope white," that is, downplayed, obscured, or left unspoken Pushkin's potentially unsettling racial ambiguity.

Was Pushkin black and does it matter? Of course, Pushkin's use of the Russian word for "black" or even "Negro" to describe himself or his forebear cannot be taken as unproblematically synonymous with the racially loaded discourse of American English, infected by centuries of slavery and segregation. As Lee D. Baker has observed:

> Although they often seem immutable, racial categories are always in flux; indeed, sometimes they change rapidly. Racial categories are produced and reproduced ideologically and culturally: they are constructed. In turn, these categories structure the access of specific groups to opportunities and resources. Complex political, economic, and cultural processes on a global scale produce various racial constructs that vary during particular periods in history from solid and generally accepted to tenuous and vigorously contested.[20]

Starkly put, the Russian aristocrat and serf owner Alexander Pushkin, acknowledged as Russia's national poet in his own lifetime, in the United States of his day would have been an octoroon potentially deprived by law not only of his freedom but even of basic literacy. In the words of the Slavophile Aleksei Khomiakov, Russians esteemed Pushkin, "the descendant of an Ethiopian . . . with pride and joy, whereas he would have been denied citizenship in the United States and would not have had the right to marry the daughter of a washerwoman in Germany or of a butcher in England."[21] Yet while it would be an egregious cultural anachronism to project our own country's ills onto the Russia of Pushkin's age, it would be equally misleading to assume—as so often has happened over the course of the almost two centuries

Introduction

since Pushkin "created the Russian literary language" and thereby "fathered" Russian literature (as the clichés of the Pushkin cult have it)—that Pushkin's ethnic heritage is irrelevant to understanding the poet's place in Russian culture. In this volume, therefore, we employ "blackness" as a marked term that invests superficially perceived physical characteristics with far-ranging symbolic significance. Henry Louis Gates Jr. has highlighted the rhetorical power of constructions of race: "When we speak of 'the white race' or 'the black race,' 'the Jewish race' or 'the Aryan race,' we speak in biological misnomers and, more generally, in metaphors"; that is, race is a "dangerous trope."[22] We are not then concerned in this volume with trying to define what race *is*, but with exploring the proposition that blackness has constituted an undeniably semiotically laden and potentially "dangerous trope" for Russians at least since Pushkin's day; and with examining the meaning with which that category has been charged.

What does matter, then, is that Pushkin himself and his contemporaries, living in an age in which race was becoming an increasingly important and virulent concept in the West and when the absorption of dark-skinned peoples into the empire was making the problem more immediate in Russia, appear to have taken Pushkin's "blackness" seriously as a marker of anxiety and ambiguity. It would seem, moreover, that as Pushkin has evolved in the course of the past two centuries into a complex metaphor for Russia, his black otherness has become an essential component of the Russianness he figures, perhaps at times all the more potent for being repressed, explained away, consigned to silence. In the remainder of this introductory essay, we will attempt to illustrate this contention.

GANNIBAL IN THE AGE OF PUSHKIN

In order to understand what the issue of Gannibal's origins meant to Pushkin, we must first ask what educated Russians of Pushkin's day could have known about Africa and Africans in order to determine how this information might have shaped their perceptions of Pushkin's origins. Unlike the countries of western Europe, which as early as the fifteenth century had both economic and expansionist interests overseas in Africa as a result of the trade in slaves and other commodities, the Russian Empire grew by incorporating contiguous lands and their inhabitants.[23] Therefore, without participation in the slave trade as impetus, Russia acquired a substantive interest in Africa relatively late in the game. Though attempts had been made by Peter the Great to encourage expeditions to Africa, Russian travel to that continent was not successfully undertaken before the late eighteenth century.[24] Until then, the primary sources on Africa available in Russia were foreign maps, geographies, and travelers' accounts. The British best sellers, James Bruce's and Mungo Park's journeys, had been translated into Russian by the beginning of the nineteenth century. The first Russian to visit Africa was the naval officer M. G. Kokovstov, who traveled twice to Tunisia and Algeria in the late 1770s; his notes were published in two volumes, *A Description of the Archipelago and the Barbary Coast* (St. Petersburg: F. Tumansky, 1786).[25] An even more up-to-date and accessible source on Africa for Pushkin was probably his friend, A. S. Norov, who undertook an expedition to Egypt and Nubia in 1834 to 1835.[26] It is hard to imagine, given Pushkin's interest in Africa as his forebear's land of origin, that he would not have spoken to Norov about his adventures on that continent. Pushkin also must have been familiar with the illustrated travel account of Pavel Svinin (1787–1839), whose *A Picturesque Voyage in the United States of America in 1811, 1812, 1813,* published in Russia in 1815, prominently features a number of images of the lives of free African Americans and provides the earliest account of America through a Russian's eyes.[27] Aside from travelers' accounts and what readings and lessons in geography he garnered during his studies at the Tsarskoe Selo Lycée, Pushkin was arguably au courant with the incipient racism pervasive in the works of Enlightenment philosophers and propounded by Johann Friedrich Blumenbach at the University of Göttingen, where Pushkin's mentors, Aleksandr and Nikolai Turgenev, had completed their education.[28] Moreover, educated Russians at least as early as the eighteenth-century political satirist Aleksandr Radishchev knew about the enslavement of Africans in the colonies of America and repeatedly exploited the analogy to excoriate Russian serfdom.

There were also a number of literary models accessible to the Russians of Pushkin's day which would have been formative in their conception of blackness. Pushkin himself was certainly familiar with such classic treatments as Daniel Defoe's *Robinson Crusoe* (1719), Samuel Johnson's *The History of Rasselas, Prince of Abyssinia* (1759), and Voltaire's *Candide* (1759).[29] Representations of Africans in literature drew attention not only to skin color but to a complex of associations of imagined and real physical and emotional traits. That most renowned representation of "African passion" and jealousy, Shakespeare's *Othello,* was well known to Pushkin and his social group.[30] Indeed, the fatal recasting of Pushkin's biography into the Othello plot occurred during his lifetime and served as a compelling narrative structure into which contemporaries projected the events leading to the poet's tragic death in 1837 in a duel with his wife's alleged lover, Georges d'Anthès. Leslie O'Bell remarks: "Perhaps society ladies liked to think that they were watching the plot to *Othello* unfold, with Pushkin as the jealous Moor."[31] Even the ambassador of the kingdom of Bavaria at the time, Maximilian von Lerchenfeld-Kofering, commented in a similar vein: "The details of this catastrophe, unfortunately provoked by the dead man himself with a blindness and a kind of frenetic

Introduction

hatred well worthy of his Moorish origins, have for days been the sole talk of the town here in the capital."[32] Even Pushkin's closest friends could not resist the sway of the literary paradigm, as implicitly evidenced by a letter written by P. A. Viazemsky while Pushkin lay at death's door: "His fiery and passionate soul and his African blood could not withstand the irritation produced by the doubts and suspicions of society."[33] The persistence of this explanation for the tragedy and its penetration to the highest levels of society is evidenced by the memoirs (1881–82) of the Grand Princess Olga Nikolaevna, Nicholas I's daughter, who ascribed the circumstances of the poet's death to the fact that "Pushkin's Negro [*negritianskaia*] blood boiled."[34] Thus we see that the mode of Pushkin's death only served to impress the comparison upon the public imagination.

Yet another significant literary paradigm that would have been familiar to educated Russians of Pushkin's day was that of the African prince sold into slavery. Aphra Behn's novel *Oroonoko, or The Royal Slave* (1688) provides an allegedly true account of an African prince who is captured and taken to Surinam as a slave. This story, in which social status transcends racial difference, became "the prototype for a vast literature depicting noble African slaves."[35] Oroonoko has been called the earliest example of the "noble primitive" who "stands as a complete, solitary, and alien *individual* against the values of the (colonial) society into which he is inserted."[36] Another international best seller, Claire de Duras's *Ourika* (1823), told the story of a young Senegalese slave girl taken in by an aristocratic French family during the Revolution.[37] They treat her like a member of the family and provide her with an education appropriate to their social position. She becomes aware of her racial difference and the prejudice it engenders only when the question of marriage arises. In 1824 an edition of *Ourika* was published in French in St. Petersburg, attesting to the accessibility of the novel to the Russian readership.[38]

A number of thematic permutations of the African slave transplanted into European society obtain in narratives that in many cases imitated or embroidered upon reality. In some versions, the slave is taken into service by a nobleman or ruler who undertakes an "educational experiment" in his training of the African; in others a virtuous, enslaved prince exposes in his narrative the bestiality of the condition of slavery and its allegedly "civilized" perpetrators, expounding upon the fleeting nature of innocent happiness and idealizing his former life. (In fact, a surprisingly large number of Africans brought to Europe in the eighteenth century claimed royal descent though in some cases, this lineage was later disputed).[39] Likely influences upon the aforementioned fictional works were accounts of famous Africans sold into slavery and later freed, many of whom took part in the abolitionist movement in Europe.[40] The most popular work of this genre was Olaudah Equiano's (1750–97) autobiography, *The Interesting Narrative of the Life of Olaudah*

Equiano or Gustavus Vassa, the African, Written by Himself (1789), which went through nine editions alone during Equiano's lifetime and was translated into Russian in 1794. (Like Gannibal, Equiano alleges that he was a kidnapped prince.) Ignatius Sancho (1729–80), Equiano's predecessor in the literary world, was an African who served the family of the Duke of Montagu. Sancho became famous after one of his letters to the author Lawrence Sterne was included in Sterne's posthumously published *Letters* (1775). Sancho, playing upon the fact that the figure of Othello was well known to his readership, characterized himself as a "sooty correspondent" who "though black as Othello has a heart as humanized as any of the fairest about St. James's."[41] Sancho's letters (published posthumously by subscription in 1782 and translated into French in 1788), Equiano's autobiography, and other works were seized upon by opponents of slavery as proof of black literary abilities and on the whole received extremely favorable reviews in the British press. Indeed, Sancho's name became so well known that by 1786 he could be mentioned without further biographical information, and at the end of the century he served as the model for positively depicted Africans in two anonymous novels.[42] These works represented Africans as men of feeling and intelligence and as examples of moral refinement, capacities that were denied to them by advocates of slavery.

Beyond whatever reading Pushkin and his contemporaries did, they might well have come upon Africans—called in Russian interchangeably *arapy, negry,* or *efiopy* (blackamoors, Negroes, or Ethiopians)—in their own social milieu.[43] We must recall that the Russian elite was already familiar with Africans as a result of the rage for black domestic servants that swept the Russian court during the seventeenth and eighteenth centuries in imitation of the courts of France, England, and Prussia. Peter the Great had several blackamoors in his court prior to and during Abram's residence (there is evidence that Pushkin's ancestor was accompanied in his journey to Russia by at least one other young African boy who was destined for the tsar's court), and other Russian noble families acquired black servants as a way of keeping up with the fashion for the exotic even a century after Peter's reign, as attested by the Muscovite noblewoman's frightening *arapka* servant in Aleksandr Griboedov's play *Woe from Wit* (*Gore ot uma*, 1824).[44] Though the practice was not so widespread that it reached the provinces, upon surveying Russian art of the eighteenth and nineteenth centuries, one can find many family portraits of members of the Russian nobility featuring a black male or female domestic servant as a sign of exalted social status.[45] In his notes and anecdotes Pushkin himself mentions a number of black servants. For example, among other anecdotes of questionable taste he cites in "Table-Talk" the scandalous tale of the *arap* belonging to Count S. who fathered a child on the count's daughter.[46] In addition to the small but growing number of *arapy* (acquired

Introduction

from both Africa and America) into the nineteenth century, it became increasingly common for African American sailors to travel to Russia as part of their service.[47] It is significant that these individuals all occupied the lower rungs of the social hierarchy, as servants or as seamen; the Gannibals, it seems, were the only Africans to make their way into the Russian upper crust.

Aside from questions of what Pushkin knew about Africa, Africans, or contemporary racial theories, there remains also the more particular issue of what Pushkin knew about the Gannibal family. After the scion of the family, the most famous Gannibal was Ivan Abramovich Gannibal, Abram Petrovich's eldest son, who received the Order of Saint George for his participation in the battle at Chesmensky (1770) and who, in Pushkin's words, belonged "unarguably among the ranks of the most distinguished people of Catherine's time" (*PSS* 6:655). Pushkin certainly knew of the monument erected in honor of that Russian victory in Tsarskoe Selo, which included a dedication to "the Victory of Gannibal." Pushkin began spending summers with his family at Mikhailovskoe in 1817; at that point, he began to meet the numerous Gannibal relatives—many of whom had made successful careers in the military or civil service—who had settled in the region.[48] Pushkin's primary sources on Gannibal were the biographical notes, written in German by A. K. Rotkirkh, that belonged to his great-uncle Petr Abramovich Gannibal, a retired major general. Pushkin most likely made a shortened translation of this biography in the autumn of 1824 during a visit to Petr Abramovich, who lived on the estate of Safont'evo about 40 miles from Mikhailovskoe where Pushkin was in exile. In an August 11, 1825, letter to his Trigorskoe neighbor Praskovia Osipova, Pushkin wrote: "*Je compte voir encore mon vieux nègre de Grand'Oncle qui, je suppose, va mourir un de ces quatre matins et il faut que j'aie de lui mémoires concernant mon aïeul*" (*PSS* 13:205). Whether he made the intended trip or not, Pushkin acquired either shortly before or after Petr Abramovich's death the copy of the full German biography. At some point his great-uncle's own fragmentary memoirs also came into Pushkin's possession.[49] And, of course, Pushkin learned of his great-grandfather from the "family legends" to which he refers in the extended biographical footnote he appended, in the first edition, to the line, "under the sky of my Africa" in stanza L of the first book of *Eugene Onegin* (*PSS* 6:654). Pushkin's many cousins and, especially, his Gannibal uncles, were among the few people with whom he spent any time during his Mikhailovskoe exile. Moreover, the residents of that province were well acquainted with the Gannibals as members of the local nobility.[50] Aside from his Gannibal relatives, Pushkin may well have heard about Gannibal from others who had known him, including his grandmother, Maria Alekseevna Gannibal (née Pushkina, who was married to Osip Abramovich Gannibal) and his nanny, Arina Rodionovna.[51]

What could Gannibal's blackness have meant to Pushkin? Pushkin's references to Gannibal and blackness in his published writings, private correspondence, and unpublished drafts make it clear that the fact of his African lineage was of the utmost importance to his own understanding of self and of his place in Russian society and letters. While other authors in this volume discuss these statements in detail, three references by Pushkin in particular beg our attention here. The first is Pushkin's earliest substantial, but uncompleted attempt at a novel, titled by the editors who published it shortly after the poet's death, *The Blackamoor of Peter the Great* (*Arap Petra Velikogo*). The extant chapters of the novel focus primarily on a young African named Ibragim, clearly based on Abram Gannibal. When the novel opens, Ibragim is in Paris, where he has been sent to study by Peter the Great. With entrée to the most select Paris salons, Ibragim becomes involved in a passionate affair with a married countess. When the countess gives birth to a black baby—spirited away at once and replaced by a white infant to hoodwink the cuckolded husband—Ibragim realizes that the affair must come to an end. He decides to return to Russia in response to a letter from his sponsor, the tsar, and remains unswerving in his intent despite an invitation from the Duke of Orleans to remain in his service in France. Peter the Great is waiting to greet him on the road when he returns and immediately welcomes Ibragim back into the intimacy of the imperial family and enlists him in the massive project of reforming Russia. The text of the novel as it comes down to us breaks off as Peter arranges a marriage between Ibragim and the reluctant daughter of one of the leading boyar families. While the novel romanticizes the events of Gannibal's life, it departs significantly from the German biography—which itself idealizes Gannibal's life perhaps in an attempt to advance his descendants' claim to enhanced noble status—only in the love intrigues.[52] Fabricating these episodes almost completely, Pushkin places his fictionalized forebear into situations fraught with sexual, social, and political complications. More to the point, Gannibal's status as a remarkably gifted alien in both of his adopted societies clearly served Pushkin as an opportunity to exercise in fiction issues that vexed his own life over a century later. The words of the foppish, Frenchified Russian Korsakov to Ibragim in the novel have a particularly ominous ring when we remember that Pushkin himself was seriously contemplating marriage at the time he took up writing the work: "With your fiery, pensive and suspicious character, with your flattened nose, bloated lips and woolly hair, how can you throw yourself into the dangers of marriage?" (*PSS* 8:30). Thus Gannibal's blackness became a touchstone for Pushkin's own anxieties regarding his life and work.[53]

In this context, scholars have long suggested that for Pushkin, Gannibal existed on the borders between fact and myth, and that Pushkin's depictions of his forebear's blackness are echoed in his descriptions of himself.[54] This brings us to our second and third focal texts by Pushkin on blackness, texts all too often cited only partially and out of context so that the full impact and sub-

Introduction

tle nuances of Pushkin's statements are dulled. The texts in question are two letters Pushkin wrote to his friend Prince Petr Viazemsky at two very different moments in his creative biography, demonstrating the poet's continued preoccupation with the meaning of blackness throughout his life. In the first letter, written from Odessa on June 24–25, 1824, Pushkin drew an analogy between the Greek struggle for independence and the plight of Negro slaves in the United States: "One can think of the fate of the Greeks in the same way as of the fate of my brother Negroes, and one can wish both of them liberation from unendurable slavery. But for all enlightened European peoples to rant about Greece is unforgivable childishness. The Jesuits harped away at us about Themistocles and Pericles so that we imagined that a mean people made up of bandits and shopkeepers is their legitimate descendant and the heir of their scholastic glory" (*PSS* 13:99). While scholars have rightly remarked upon Pushkin's identification with the plight of Negro slaves in the United States, they have passed over in silence the shadow of ambivalence that his negative appraisal of the modern Greeks casts over the equation he draws between the two groups. The second letter, written in late 1835 or 1836, deserves citation in full:

> *Arab* (does not have a feminine), a dweller or native of Arabia, an Arabian. *The caravan was plundered by the Arabs of the steppes.*
> *Arap* [blackamoor] feminine *arapka*; this is what Negroes and mulattoes are usually called. *Dvortsovye arapy,* Negroes serving in the palace. *He goes calling attended by three finely dressed blackamoors.*
> *Arapnik*, from the Polish *Herapnik* [whip] (de *harap*, cri de chasseur pour enlever aux chiens la proie. *Reiff*).[55] NB *harap* vient de ?*erab*.
> To tell the truth, it would not be a bad idea to embark on a dictionary, or at least a critique of dictionaries.[56] (*PSS* 16:208)

Most tantalizing about this letter is the fact that we can only speculate on the context that prompted Pushkin to address the issue of racial terminology in such punctilious detail in a private letter to a close friend.

As the poet's letter to Viazemsky indirectly attests, Pushkin's contemporaries also seem to have viewed him as black, which entailed, as we have seen, discernible racial stereotyping. From Pushkin's childhood on, people noticed and commented on his purportedly "African" appearance.[57] Viazemsky, for instance, testifies to the physical resemblance of Pushkin and his younger brother Lev: "Like his brother [Alexander], he [Lev] was somewhat swarthy, like an Arab [*smuglyi arab*], but looked like a white Negro . . . Their mother's African imprint left a visible impress on them both. They had no other resemblance to her."[58] Moreover, Pushkin's contemporaries were quick to ascribe Pushkin's temper and passionate nature to his African roots. Pushkin's

Lycée classmate S. D. Komovsky states, "In him was manifested all the ardor and sensuality of his African blood."[59] Komovsky associates Pushkin's African heritage with the formulaic hypersexuality long cited in European writings on race.[60] Another of Pushkin's schoolfellows, M. A. Korf, speaks similarly about Pushkin: "Flaring up into a fury, with unbridled African passions (such was his mother's ancestry), eternally absent-minded, eternally absorbed in his poetic dreams, from childhood on spoiled by praise and flatterers."[61] Many contemporaries, moreover, drew a connection between Pushkin's African nature and bestiality or wildness. For example, Dolly Fiquelmont's observation on Pushkin's appearance exploits his Lycée nickname: "It's impossible to be more ugly—it's a cross between the exterior of a monkey and tiger. He comes from an African race, and in the color of his face there remains an impress of something wild in his look."[62] F. F. Vigel' likewise mentions Pushkin's African origins in his description of Pushkin's mannerisms:

> On his mother's side he was descended from the Negro General Gannibal. In his bone structure and the rapidity of his movements he resembled somewhat the Negroes and the humanlike inhabitants [*chelovekopodobnykh zhitelei*] of Africa. He agilely jumped on the large and long table before the window, stretched out on it, seized a pen and began to write.[63]

In the same vein, another contemporary describes Pushkin's gestures as simian:

> Alexander Pushkin once arrived at the home of his acquaintance I. S. Timiriazev. The servant told him that the master and mistress had gone out for a walk but would soon return. In the hall at the Timiriazevs there was a large fireplace and on the table were some nuts. Before the Timiriazevs' return home, Pushkin took the nuts, climbed into the fireplace and making faces like a monkey, began to crack them.[64]

It is notable, however, that invocations of blackness in Russia never entailed slurs on Pushkin's intelligence. Indeed, Anna Khomutova, one of Pushkin's admirers, suggests a perceived link between his African lineage and his superior intellect:

> The ladies separated and counted on getting Pushkin's attention, so that when he entered, all of them headed towards him and surrounded him. Each one wished that he would say even one word to her. Being neither young nor good-looking and as usual possessing an unfortunate shyness, I didn't push myself forward and, imperceptible to the others, gazed from afar at that African face, on which was impressed his heritage, that face, which shone with intelligence.[65]

Introduction

Pushkin's African heritage nonetheless rendered him vulnerable to public embarrassment. In Pushkin's day there circulated an alternate version of how Gannibal made his way to Russia, namely, that he had been purchased in Europe by Peter the Great. In an August 7, 1830, article, "Second Letter from Karlov to Kammenyi Ostrov," published in the *Northern Bee*, the unsavory publisher Faddei Bulgarin insinuated that Pushkin's ancestor had been bought for a pittance:

> The anecdote is told that a certain Poet in Spanish America, . . . the offspring of a Mulatto man or woman, I don't remember which, began to contend that one of his ancestors was a Negro prince. In the town hall of the city it was discovered that in antiquity there was a lawsuit between a skipper of a ship and an assistant of his for this Negro, whom each of them wished to claim as his own, and that the skipper contended that he bought the Negro for a bottle of rum. Who would have thought then that a versifier would acknowledge connection with that Negro? Vanitas vanitatum![66]

This account could not have been anything other than repugnant to a person as sensitive to class status as Pushkin. Enraged by this imputation that Gannibal had been a slave, Pushkin responded with a note (*PSS* 11:153) and by circulating the poem "My Genealogy," in which he points out that the "skipper" in question was Peter the Great himself and that his ancestor was "the tsar's equal and not a slave" (*PSS* 3:263). In a letter to Count Benkendorf, the head of Nicholas's secret police, pleading his right to defend himself from the scurrilous attack, Pushkin made it clear that the none-too-veiled reference to him in the "letter" was easily decipherable:

> *Il y un an à peu près que dans l'un de nos journaux on imprima un article satyrique dans lequel on parlait d'un certain littérateur qui manifestait des prétentions à une origine noble, tandis qu'il n'était qu'un bourgeois-gentilhomme. On ajoutait que sa mere était une mulâtre dont le père, pauvre négrillon, avait été acheté par un matelot pour une bouteille de rhum. Quoique Pierre le Grand ne ressemblât guère à un matelot ivre, c'était me designer assez clairement, vu qu'il n'y a que moi de littérateur Russe qui comptasse un nègre parmi mes ancêtres.* (*PSS* 14:242)

Thus this incident indicates the complex intersection of race and class already evident in Pushkin's day. In this context, the timing of Bulgarin's attack is telling. As Susan Layton has suggested in her groundbreaking study on Russian literature and empire, Russian society became increasingly intolerant of dark-skinned people as a result of intensified warfare in the Caucasus in the 1830s.[67] We cannot help but speculate that this intolerance was a factor in the decline in Pushkin's public image in the later years of his life.

As a counterbalance to the Bulgarin attack, in January 1832, Pushkin's close friend Pavel Nashchokin sent him a New Year's gift which was to remain dear to the poet to the end of his life: an inkstand featuring a black man leaning against an anchor and standing in front of two bales of cotton (made to hold ink). Accompanying it was a note stating: "I am sending you your ancestor with inkwells that open and that reveal him to be a farsighted person [*à double vue*]" (PSS 14:250, translated by Shaw). Pushkin was extremely pleased with the gift, which he kept on his desk to the end of his days. As Shaw points out, there seems to be a great discrepancy between Pushkin's reactions to public and private references to his African origins. However, we must note not just the forum, but also the intention and, most important, the symbolism of those treatments here. Bulgarin obviously meant to denigrate Pushkin's ancestry, denying it any value whatsoever and slandering Pushkin's noble heredity, whereas Nashchokin positively validated it, underscoring Gannibal's destiny to have a great writer as a descendant. Nashchokin's gift gets to the heart of the issue: it holds the ink (*chernila*, literally, the "black stuff") for Pushkin to ply his trade and thus attests to the creativity of its owner. These two events, the Bulgarin attack and the Nashchokin gift, serve as defining moments for the future evolution of the semiotics of Pushkin's blackness, pitting black blood, with its potential for the pollution of the race, against black ink, as a mark of the poet's creative vigor.[68]

THE MAKING OF PUSHKIN AS A CULTURAL ICON

If Pushkin's African lineage was common knowledge among his contemporaries, it was consigned to silence by those writers and critics in the poet's own lifetime and in the succeeding years of the nineteenth century who were to become the canonical ideologists of Pushkin as Russia's national poet. They were interested in Pushkin's "Russianness" rather than in his exotic roots. In this context, two interrelated tendencies drove the mythogenesis which began upon Pushkin's death. While in the latter half of the nineteenth century fascination with and exploration of Pushkin's blackness was pursued for the most part by a small, select group of scholars engaged in producing erudite studies, the second and dominant mode, fed by the same German Romantic vision of history which created the imperative of national purity of blood and hence gave impetus to philosophical and political racism, prompted those who participated in the process of creating an "official" myth to view culture and therefore poetry and poets as the true gauge of national worth. A Russian national poet of the first order thus became necessary to prove the validity of

Introduction

Russia's imperial enterprise and to assert the health of its growing empire. This second tendency, most compellingly expressed by Gogol and Dostoevsky and arguably simply a particularly Russian variant of the pan-European trend, cast Pushkin as the paradigmatic Russian precisely because he was capable of assimilating other nationalities, much as the Russian Empire itself expanded by incorporating neighboring ethnic groups. In this way, largely through the figure of Pushkin, concerns largely confined earlier to the specialized realms of historiography and ethnography moved into the broader public literary arena: "to conflate—once and for all—the various independent components of Russian nationality."[69]

The image of Pushkin thus evolved in the latter half of the nineteenth century as two faces of the same coin: as an increasingly "official" myth suppressing Pushkin's exotic foreign origins developed through sanctioned commemorations, while fascination with and exploration of Pushkin's blackness was confined for the most part to a small, select group of scholars engaged in producing erudite studies.

Beginning with Gogol's famous comment that "Pushkin is an extraordinary and perhaps the singular expression of the Russian soul," public, official literary commentators played up the interpretation of Pushkin as the expression of the Russian national essence.[70] References to the African origins of the poet were disregarded in light of a larger, more urgent vision: to find a creditable exemplum of the national *Geist* so that Russia could be deemed worthy to join Western civilization on an equal footing with countries like England, Germany, and France.[71] Belinsky further propagated this notion with his statement that Pushkin expressed the Russian national spirit; Apollon Grigoriev followed with his own formulation that "Pushkin is the representative of all our spiritual singularity . . . He is still the single complete essay [*ocherk*] of our national personality. He is our distinctive type." Finally, in 1880, in his Pushkin speech, Dostoevsky proclaimed that Pushkin surpassed the great poets and writers of all other nations precisely because of his ability to embrace the foreign:

> No, I state categorically that there has never been a poet with such universal responsiveness as Pushkin. It is not only a matter of responsiveness but also of its amazing depth, the reincarnation in his spirit of the spirit of foreign peoples, a reincarnation that is almost total and is therefore miraculous . . . This we find in Pushkin alone, and in this sense, I repeat, he is a unique and unprecedented phenomenon, and as far as we are concerned, a prophetic one . . . for it is precisely in this that his national, Russian strength was most fully expressed, in the national spirit of his poetry, the national spirit in its future development, the national spirit of our future, which is already concealed in the present and is expressed prophetically. For what is the strength of the Russian

national spirit if not its striving, in its ultimate goals, for universality and common humanity?[72]

Dostoevsky does not speculate on the origin of Pushkin's unique capacities. What we witness here nonetheless is the culmination of the evolution of Pushkin as a metaphor for imperial hybridity, a trope of national quintessence which endorses assimilation as a higher form of national purity, a figure unquestionably appropriate to a multicultural empire seeking to absorb a variety of peoples from contiguous lands. Here then Dostoevsky makes an apologia for Russian imperialism in the broad sense, and, more specifically, for Russia's exalted role on the stage of international affairs.[73]

Pushkin biographers (including biographers of Gannibal) and scholars, on the other hand, throughout the nineteenth century and into the twentieth, remained fascinated with Pushkin's Africanness, if often less comfortable with his "blackness." Indeed, as indicated above, the ideologists and biographers engage in the same project of creating Pushkin as the national poet of Russia, but they approach it in different ways. From the middle of the nineteenth century on, the scholarly tradition fully acknowledged the fact of Pushkin's African roots in an attempt to account specifically for his singularity. Both P. A. Annenkov and P. I. Bartenev—considered to be the first biographers of Pushkin—recognized Pushkin's African roots and called Gannibal a "Negro," though they never went so far as to call Pushkin himself "black" or "mulatto." Annenkov dwells upon the recently discovered facts of the Gannibal story in his work *Pushkin in the Alexandrine Era* (*Pushkin v Aleksandrovskuiu epokhu*), drawing attention to the fact that aspects of Gannibal's biography as it had come down through family tradition were based more on fiction than on fact. In an attempt to correct the historical infidelity of Pushkin's portrayal of his ancestor in *The Blackamoor of Peter the Great*, Annenkov accounts for Gannibal's negative characteristics, which he enumerates, as part and parcel of his ethnic background: "his Abyssinian, soft, cowardly, and altogether hot-tempered nature."[74] Moreover, Annenkov attributes the contradictory components of Pushkin's personality specifically to his mixed origins: "which united in one person the African blood of the Gannibals with the pure Russian soul."[75]

P. I. Bartenev also features many references to Pushkin's blackness in the reminiscences he collected from Pushkin's contemporaries. Like Annenkov, he is interested specifically in Pushkin's hybrid genealogy, but, in Bartenev's case, Pushkin's mixed ancestry accounts, at least in part, for the uniqueness of his talent: "The ardor of Africa and the sobriety of the Great Russian—that is Pushkin's prose. His verse is fiery and at the same time measured. Feeling governed by reason."[76] Most important in this context, Bartenev first makes explicit what we believe to be the underlying, if often unstated, presence of Gannibal in Alexander Pushkin as a paradigm for the intersection of nationality, ethnicity, and empire. In Bartenev's words: "In the same way, the law noted by historians in modern times that great peoples arise from the mixture of different tribes, when applied to individuals is confirmed by our poet: besides Russian and African blood, in his veins flowed German blood as well."[77] Hence it is through Pushkin's very difference, his ethnic and racial hybridity, that the Russian people are elevated into one of the great nations of the world. Thus Bartenev comes to the same conclusion as Dostoevsky while making explicit what Dostoevsky leaves unspoken.

The 1899 celebration of the centennial of Pushkin's birth cast by the tsarist government as a blatant apologia for empire constituted a logical extrapolation of Dostoevsky's vision in the political sphere. Excerpts from an article published on the first page of the newspaper *Moscow News* (*Moskovskie vedomosti*) on May 26 (Pushkin's birthday) of that year convey the tenor of the commemorative discourse:

> Russia treasures Pushkin not only because he is the first of all Russian poets, but also because he stands in the ranks of the first poets of Europe, and consequently of all humanity. He is dear to Russia in that he first led her as a full member into the greater family of cultured peoples and gave her the opportunity to proclaim to them her own new *Russian* word . . .
>
> With his works, he showed that the Russian people are not one of those peoples of the East which strives only to adopt the latest fruits of European civilization . . . , but that the Russian people is capable of surpassing its teachers in many ways and in enriching the culture of mankind along with other creative peoples, new ideas and new ideals . . .
>
> Pushkin first sensed and understood the great *spiritual* superiority of the Russian people over the peoples of Europe and first expressed this consciousness not only in words which exuded profound, sincere conviction, but also in the living images of his artistic creations.[78]

If, as Marcus Levitt suggests, "The 1899 jubilee was broadly aimed at acculturating the Russian and non-Russian masses," then one begins to understand the delicate balance that needed to be established to propound Pushkin as the standard for official nationality.[79] On the eve of the twentieth century, with virulent racism running high in western Europe, Pushkin's importunate Gannibal lineage was broached—and creatively diffused—by the anthropologist Dmitry Anuchin in an extensive article, "A. S. Pushkin: An Anthropological Sketch," written in 1899 in honor of the centennial. Anuchin provides a purportedly scientific study of Pushkin's African heritage, basing his conclusions on the large body of Western racially charged ethnographic literature. The importance of Anuchin's work is that, through looking at European travelers' accounts and consulting with academics who had studied the region, he "establishes" the location of Gannibal's homeland in Abyssinia.[80] He then attempts to assess the effects of Pushkin's Gannibal origins on the poet's character and temperament. Though Anuchin acknowledged the fact of Pushkin's difference—"Pushkin was not a fully Russian man"—his agenda was to disarm the salient fact of Pushkin's blackness by staking the claim that Pushkin was Abyssinian—that is, not "black."[81] In this sense, he is the first in a long line of scholars who have denied Gannibal's and hence Pushkin's blackness per se in an attempt to circumvent Pushkin's inconvenient bloodline in light of his indisputable genius: "Actually, if Ibrahim Gannibal was a Negro, then his own far from ordinary personality, and in particular the brilliant personality of his great-grandson poet, must present itself as the notable exception in the history of Negro races."[82] As we can see from the beginning of this thread of Anuchin's argument, race does matter here.

Among other strategies, Anuchin deploys an analysis of an incorrectly documented portrait of Abram Gannibal[83] to justify his claim that Gannibal was not black: "The technique of the portrait is not very important, the painter was obviously not skillful . . . but in any case, before him was not a thick-lipped wide-nosed Negro, but a dark-skinned Hamite with facial features that resemble those of the white rather than the Negroid race."[84] By reducing a complex question to the issue of mere physical indicators, Anuchin simplifies his task greatly. He then attempts to prove that Pushkin was not perceived as dark-skinned by many of his contemporaries. He insists that those inhabitants of southern Russia who were surrounded by darker-skinned peoples—or those of Pushkin's acquaintances who were themselves dark-complected, like A. O. Smirnova—did not perceive Pushkin as swarthy, while the fair-skinned peoples in the capital cities may have viewed him as dark-skinned.[85]

In the final twist of Anuchin's argument, we witness the complete effacement of the significance of Pushkin's African heritage. This pièce de resistance consists of his analysis of the components of Pushkin's "African traits"—i.e., his thick lips, curly hair, and prominent brow—which Anuchin ultimately compares to the modern (nineteenth-century) physiognomy of the Jew, reflecting an admixture of Semitic blood, which can be accounted for as a result of Pushkin's "Abyssinian" origins.[86] In this last stroke of his pen, in the final installment of his serialized article, Anuchin has literally "washed the Ethiope white," while at the same time retaining Pushkin as the "other" present in Russian culture, the Jew.[87]

Introduction

PUSHKIN IN THE TWENTIETH CENTURY

In the twentieth century, invocations, interpretations, suppressions, and repressions of Pushkin's Gannibal ancestry became increasingly important as modes of appropriation by the Soviet cultural establishment of Pushkin's cultural legacy and the putative authority that came with it. This is perhaps not surprising given the fact that in the formation of their empire, the Soviets encountered many of the same challenges faced by their tsarist predecessors a century earlier; in their use of Pushkin as a culture myth Soviet ideologists responded similarly as well. Indeed, as Marcus Levitt has suggested, "The process of turning the literary holiday into an official instrument of political and cultural policy begun in 1899 reached its zenith under Stalin in the late 1930s."[88] We can, moreover, extrapolate this argument to apply to the construction of Pushkin in Soviet culture across the board, since the appropriation of his legacy became a cornerstone of Soviet cultural policy. While we find the same, often vexed, oscillation between denial and fascination with Pushkin's African origins in the twentieth century that we did in the nineteenth, we also find that the strategies for confronting and exploiting the issue became more complex and the spectrum of responses more politically charged.

At one extreme lay those who denied Gannibal's place in Pushkin's biography, including ultranationalists who even rejected Pushkin because of his African roots and certain Soviet Russophiles who "whited" Gannibal out of Pushkin's biography, suppressing references to Gannibal's origins or to Gannibal himself.[89] More insidious and deeply engrained in the very fabric of the Soviet appropriation of Pushkin, however, was the trend we have seen earlier to accept Gannibal's African roots, while denying his "blackness"; this was part and parcel of the official Soviet "line" which rendered Gannibal a canonic fact of Pushkin's biography, neutralized by rote memorization, while trotting Pushkin forth as Russia's great African poet when politically opportune, as when welcoming African students to Moscow. That all of these strategies existed to "whitewash" Gannibal testifies to the potency, even when latent, of Pushkin's African roots as a not insignificant constituent element of the cultural construct of Pushkin as Russia's great national poet.

While most Soviet scholars, like Soviet school texts, followed Anuchin in denying Pushkin's "blackness," the strategies employed to this end by two of the top Russian Pushkin scholars of the twentieth century—one Soviet and one émigré—are particularly revealing. We have already noted that Yury Lotman almost completely excluded Gannibal from his biography of Pushkin. It is even more significant that in his article on Pushkin's Lycée nickname, "a mixture of a monkey and a tiger," he spends much ink in an attempt to prove that the nickname is a marker of Pushkin's ties with French culture, never even mentioning Africa. Yet given the plethora of contemporary references associating Pushkin's African heritage with his "monkeylike" appearance, it is hard to imagine that Pushkin's nickname "monkey" came about as innocently as Lotman attempts to prove. Tellingly, in citing as evidence for his claim Fiquelmont's description of Pushkin cited earlier in this introduction, Lotman omits the words here given in italics: "It's impossible to be more ugly—it's a cross between the exterior of a monkey and tiger. *He comes from an African race, and in the color of his face there remains an impress of something wild in his look.*"[90]

If Lotman's silence is indicative of the prevailing strain in Soviet Pushkin scholarship, Vladimir Nabokov adopts a rather more complicated tactic in his extended essay on Pushkin's African forebear. Thus, Leona Toker describes and debunks Nabokov's own purported debunking of myth:

> The bulk of [Nabokov's] text is a critical scrutiny of these documents [presented by Nabokov's predecessors]. It dismantles their slapdash romanticized accounts of Gannibal's origins and early experience and cancels or subjects to doubt most of their so-called facts. In the end, however, Nabokov himself comes out with an avowedly unsanctioned yet breathtakingly beautiful theory of Gannibal's origins, a wild surmise to end all wild surmises.[91]

Thus, while Nabokov was perhaps the first twentieth-century scholar to entertain the possibility that Gannibal was "Negroid," he nonetheless does so, as Toker points out, only in the context of offering his reader a loaded choice: "It is upon nonbelievers in the Abyssinian theory that the burden of the proof rests; while . . . those who accept it must waver between seeing in Pushkin the great-great-grandson of one of those rude and free Negro nomads who haunted the Mareb region or a descendant of Solomon and the Queen of Sheba, from whom Abyssinian kings derived their dynasty."[92] Nabokov himself makes it clear that he favors the "breathtakingly beautiful" version tracing Gannibal's origins to biblical royalty of Hamitic descent. Moreover, the time and energy Nabokov expends in expounding his vision of Gannibal's origins is as eloquent as Lotman's silence on the subject as indications of the centrality of the issue to Pushkin as culture myth.

SOVIET PROPAGANDA AND PUSHKIN'S BLACKNESS

As the quotation from Marcus Levitt cited above indicates, celebrations of significant anniversaries in Pushkin's life served as nodal points for the elaboration of the Soviet Pushkin myth within an evolving political context. Certainly the 1937 commemoration of the centennial of the poet's death was particularly significant in this respect, for it marked as well the culmination of the process, begun even before the 1917 Revolution, first of repudiating, then of usurping the classical Russian literary canon into the ideological framework of Soviet culture. Hardly surprisingly then, some of the richest cultural texts—and precisely those with regard to the role of the Gannibal heritage in the construction of the Soviet Pushkin—were created at the time of preparations for the anniversary celebration.[93]

In this context the eminent Soviet director Grigory Aleksandrov's famous film-musical, *Circus*—made in 1936, a year before the monumental Stalinist celebration of the centennial of Pushkin's death—provides eloquent testimony to the resonance of Pushkin's racial ambiguity in Soviet mass culture, despite the fact that Pushkin is never directly mentioned in the film. *Circus* tells the story of an American circus performer, a white woman named Marion Dixon, who is driven out of her home country when she gives birth to a black baby. Brought to the Soviet Union to perform by an evil German impresario who blackmails her by threatening to reveal her secret, the American ultimately finds love and acceptance for both herself and her child and remains in the U.S.S.R. In the dramatic culminating scene of the movie, the villain, standing in the middle of the circus ring, displays the child to the audience and announces in outrage, "She was the lover of a Negro. She has a black child. A white woman has a black child . . . It's a racial crime. There's no place for her in civilized society. There's no place for her among white people." The audience merely laughs at him and grabs away the child. Resonating with Isaak Dunaevsky's mass song, "Wide Is My Motherland," which is reprised throughout the film, the ethnically diverse audience passes the child from one hand to another (from a Russian woman to a Ukrainian man to a sailor to a Jew—played by the famous Yiddish actor Solomon Mikhoels—and to a black man in military uniform), all the while singing a lullaby, figuring a myth of Communist inclusiveness. While Pushkin is never explicitly mentioned in the film, we would argue that the association is no less unmistakable for remaining unspoken, just as it always hovers beneath the surface of the Pushkin cult as a mainstay of Soviet imperial ideology.

Indeed, the Soviet authorities did utilize the convenient fact of Pushkin's African lineage in the development of relationships with both African nationals and African Americans, beginning in the 1920s. Though it was only during the Harlem Renaissance that Pushkin's name became widespread in the larger African American community, Soviet officialdom found that emphasizing the African origins of its national poet was extremely effective in propagandizing the lack of racism in Soviet society.[94] This acknowledgment of Pushkin's African roots on the part of the Soviet authorities greatly impressed many African Americans—including such distinguished figures as the poet Langston Hughes, the journalist Homer Smith, the activist

William L. Patterson, and the singer Paul Robeson, all of whom mention Pushkin's African origins in their reminiscences of time spent in Russia.[95] The promise of a life free of the humiliation of racial discrimination prompted a significant number of African American activists to take a sympathetic interest in the Soviet Communist experiment and even to spend time living in the U.S.S.R. Aside from segregation in the United States, the rising threat of Nazism in Germany was also a potent force impelling African Americans to seek a racially just society in the U.S.S.R. Thus, in 1937, in the *Negro Worker*, a journal devoted to spreading the word of Communism to African and African American communities, William L. Patterson exclaimed: "Its [the Soviet Union's] perpetuation of Pushkin's memory deals a smashing blow at the fascist myths of racial-national superiority. This is the great significance of Pushkin's centenary to the Negro people."[96] Paul Robeson's presence at the 1949 celebration of the sesquicentennial of Pushkin's birth in the U.S.S.R. is emblematic of the simultaneous Soviet exploitation and denial of the intersection of Pushkin's African blood and Soviet internationalism, an ambivalence apparently shared by Robeson himself, who made no mention of Pushkin's Gannibal ancestry in his jubilee speech on Russia's great national poet.[97]

As African countries sought greater independence, the Soviet Union endeavored to strengthen its ties with them and to Communism in the region. Beginning in the 1950s, increasing numbers of Africans were encouraged and invited to attend a variety of educational institutions in the U.S.S.R. In 1960 the Friendship University (renamed in 1961 in honor of the recently assassinated Patrice Lumumba of Congo) was established in Moscow specifically for the training of the inhabitants of the former colonies in Africa. This educational exchange increased knowledge of Pushkin's heritage among the inhabitants of different African countries. Despite the dominance of the Abyssinian or Ethiopian tradition concerning Gannibal's place of origin, a number of African countries—Guinea, Mali, Mauritius, and Senegal among them—have honored Pushkin in one way or another over the years.[98] In support of its claim to Gannibal and therefore Pushkin as a native son, Ethiopia holds vast materials on Pushkin and his great-grandfather.[99] As early as 1957, it dedicated an entire issue of the *Ethiopian Observer* to Alexander Pushkin. In tourist guides, Ethiopia even bills itself as the homeland of Pushkin's great-grandfather, though representatives from other African countries challenge this honor.[100] Indeed, as we shall see, in the late 1990s, the Ethiopian version of Pushkin's origins became hotly contested—by the countries of Benin, Chad, Sudan, Cameroon, and Nigeria—during the bicentennial of Pushkin's birth.

Introduction

THE ALTERNATIVE LITERARY TRADITION

Though official Soviet narratives and rituals for the most part suppressed or defused Gannibal's and thus Pushkin's blackness, some of Russia's most talented, formally innovative, and politically recalcitrant writers in the twentieth century subverted the party line by exposing its obverse side. They thus countered the official Pushkin and official Soviet culture by returning the repressed, by speaking that which has so often been left unspoken, thereby demonstrating the extent to which the status of Pushkin as the mythical figure of the national poet draws its power precisely from that which is consigned to silence.

In what is probably the first major text in this subversive countertradition, the prescient dystopian novel *We* (*My*, 1920–21), Evgeny Zamiatin was the first writer to expose the paradigm—and among the most effective. Placed in the twenty-sixth century, the novel describes what happens when a perfect society, exemplified by the OneState and populated by "numbers" rather than by individuals, is disrupted by the desire for personal freedom and the destabilizing forces of creativity and sexuality. In Zamiatin's novel, narrated by the engineer-turned-chronicler D-503, Pushkin's image appears twice. As an icon of official culture, he is represented directly—in bronzed form; his bust occupies a prominent place in the Ancient House, the repository of historical curiosities, things currently unknown, unnecessary, and unwanted: "On a little bracket on the wall was a bust of one of their ancient poets, Pushkin, I think. This asymmetrical snub-nosed face was looking straight at me with a barely detectable smile."[101] Zamiatin counters the official Pushkin by portraying a possible descendant of Pushkin in the character R-13, the state poet, whose most distinctive feature is his "Negroid lips." R-13 becomes a disruptive force in the novel; he challenges all the rules and destroys the easy symmetry and organizing principles of the OneState. In the course of the novel, he discovers that he is unable to continue churning out mathematical verses extolling the virtues of the OneState, and he allies himself with a conspiracy to bring it down.[102] In so doing, R-13 realizes the potential of the unofficial representation of Pushkin as a revolutionary, life-giving force.[103] Poetry and literature in Zamiatin's terms are the simultaneously creative and destructive forces ready to challenge the psychological entropy of the state and its submissive subjects figured in the bronze image of the "official" Pushkin. Thus in *We* Zamiatin, conflating Pushkin as unbound creative power with the noble savage, the Scythian, of his earlier essay "Scythians?" ("Skify li?" 1918), discloses the duality of Pushkin's image, which may be mustered to legitimate or to subvert authority. It is the "African" Pushkin, moreover, who eludes deadening convention and institutionalization and who becomes the lifeblood of poetry. Thus, beginning with the "Negroid lips" Zamiatin imputes to R-13, the state poet-turned-rebel, a counter, "black" Pushkin emerges as the poet's African blood becomes a complex metaphor for creativity, originality, independence, and vitality. In the same vein, Vladimir Mayakovsky (1893–1930), the futurist poet who became a Soviet state poet but ultimately committed suicide because he could not bow to the state's demands, rejects Pushkin transformed into the "dead matter" of the monument, while embracing the living, African Pushkin ("Afrikanets") in his 1924 lyric, "Jubilee" ("Iubileinoe"). He calls out to Pushkin: "I love you, but alive, not a mummy."[104]

The urge to reclaim Pushkin from the ossifying traditions of official culture manifested in the 1937 centennial of Pushkin's death recurs in works written for that occasion by the fiction writer and playwright Mikhail Bulgakov, the formalist critic and writer of historical fiction Yury Tynianov, the poet Marina Tsvetaeva, and the poet and critic Vladislav Khodasevich. The works all four of these authors composed at the time of the jubilee can be seen as reactions against the "sham Pushkin" created by official Soviet culture, and all four invoke, at least implicitly, the Gannibal legacy as a vibrant, creative force.[105] Bulgakov's play *The Last Days* (*Poslednie dni*), written in 1934 to 1935 for the centennial but not actually performed until 1943, appears at first glance to have little relevance to our topic, but upon closer consideration it actually presents the paradigm we are suggesting in rather direct form. In this play, which purports to document the final days of Pushkin's life, the poet never appears on stage at all, but remains beyond the range of the audience's vision as the unraveling of his fate is chronicled in conversations among members of his family, the court, literary society, and the secret police. Yet, as the second act of the play reveals, Pushkin's silence in the play is eloquent. The second act takes place at a ball at the palace of the Princess Vorontsova. The scene opens on a conversation in the garden between Nicholas I and Pushkin's wife. Most interesting, however, is the following line from the stage directions: "By the colonnade, immobile, is a Negro in a turban."[106] After Natalia Pushkina goes back inside, Zhukovsky comes out and the Tsar asks him, "Vasily Andreevich, I can't see very well from here. Who is that man in black [*chernyi*, literally "black man"] standing by the column?" (32). While Zhukovsky does not answer Nicholas directly, it becomes immediately clear that the "black man" is Pushkin, who appears in the place seemingly occupied at the opening of the act by the "Negro in a turban." The image is further complicated, however, by the fact that Nicholas is displeased that Pushkin is "in black," i.e., because he is in civilian clothes rather than in the uniform required by the humiliating rank of *Kammerjunker*, generally held by much younger and less distinguished men, which Pushkin was forced to accept so that his wife could attend court functions. Here, we would argue, Bulgakov gives us a potent image of the rebellious "black" poet, relegated to the margins by the intrigues of the philistines and bureaucrats who surround him and displace him from center stage.

Introduction

By the same token, the lyrical introduction to Tynianov's unfinished novel on Abram Gannibal provides a tantalizing window into the "silences" of accepted conventions about Pushkin: that he was proud of his mixed origins, and that a pure "Great Russian" nobility never existed in anything other than official mythology.[107] Tsvetaeva in "My Pushkin" also focuses in large part on Pushkin's blackness as a defining moment in Pushkin's creative persona. Tsvetaeva's idiosyncratic essay was written in emigration, as if to suggest that her claim on Pushkin and all of his unofficially acknowledged traits could not be made within the confines of official Soviet culture, thereby implicitly valorizing Pushkin's own "outsideness."[108] Khodasevich focused on Pushkin's Gannibal heritage in his unfinished biography of Pushkin, written in emigration during the mid-1930s, and excerpted in the émigré press during the centennial year.[109] Khodasevich, seeking an explanation for the extremes of Pushkin's personality, finds the source of his unruliness in his Gannibal ancestry and describes the clan as if it were an elemental force: "They began to take him calling to his relatives—that numerous Gannibal clan [*gannibalshchina*], that being fruitful and multiplying since the times of Abram Petrovich, settled all over Pskov *guberniia*. The *gannibalshchina* led a chaotic, rowdy, hospitable life. They would visit each other with their entire families for weeks on end. When the guests prepared to head home, their hosts would not let them go, ordering the horses unharnessed or hiding the trunks and suitcases. Uncles Petr and Pavel Isaakovich especially distinguished themselves in their drinking sprees and hospitality: African ardor was united in them with the breadth of Russian nature."[110]

The tradition of invoking Pushkin as African as a subversive, creative counterforce to the stagnating Soviet cultural bureaucracy flourished in the late Soviet years as well. In the late 1960s, the dissident Andrei Sinyavsky, writing under his pseudonym Abram Tertz, invoked Pushkin's African ancestry as a metaphor for free and subversive creativity in his *Strolls with Pushkin* (*Progulki s Pushkinym*), penned while its author was a prisoner in a Soviet labor camp during the Brezhnev regime. An irreverent deconstruction of the "wreaths and busts" of the official Pushkin, *Strolls with Pushkin* proved to be one of the most controversial works of the glasnost period. The publication of a small passage from the work in the Soviet Union in 1989 called forth a virulent outcry by Russian chauvinists who viewed the work as an attack on Russia's greatest poet.[111] It is certainly not irrelevant that in *Strolls with Pushkin* Sinyavsky-Tertz invokes the same opposition adumbrated by Zamiatin in *We* between the mummified Pushkin of academic convention and imperial mythogony, on the one hand, and the subversive, savage Pushkin, on the other, here performed in a series of scintillating metaphors, including Gannibal as biography turned trope, to reclaim Pushkin from canonicity. As in Tsvetaeva's *My Pushkin*, here Pushkin's blackness becomes an exaggerated figure, merging with writing itself, an emblem of the different, the uncontrollable, of rebellion against ossified authority.

Also in the latter years of the glasnost era, Tatiana Tolstaya, one of the most talented of Russia's younger writers, wrote a story entitled "Limpopo."[112] The title is drawn from the Soviet children's classic *Doctor Aibolit* (*Doctor Ouchithurts*) written by Kornei Chukovsky. Doctor Aibolit, who like his Western counterpart Dr. Doolittle can "talk to the animals," in Chukovsky's poem goes off to the mythical African country of Limpopo to serve as a veterinarian. Tolstaya, however, reverses Chukovsky. The central, though silent, figure in her long story is an African student called Judy who has come to the Soviet Union to become a veterinarian. She becomes involved with a poet named Lenechka, who envisages that their union will result in the birth of a new Pushkin: "if our luck holds we'll get a Pushkin right off; if not, we'll go at it again and again, or wait for our grandsons, great-grandsons" (144). As it turns out, their luck does not "hold," and Lenechka's hopes are dashed when Judy dies of a chill she contracts in the inclement Russian weather. Lenechka, bereft of Judy and therefore of his hopes for the regeneration of Russian poetry and culture, "lost his reason after Judy's death and ran into the forest on all fours—though they do say that he's alive and that some frightened children saw him lapping water at a stream, and there's a group of engineers, aficionados of the mysterious, who organized a society for the capture of 'the wild mid-Russian man,' as they refer to him scientifically" (189). While we cannot do justice here to the complexity of Tolstaya's narrative—or to the complicated cultural allegory it embodies in its extravagant digressiveness, allusiveness, and wordplay—let us suggest here that the incorporation of the alterity figured by Judy becomes necessary to the health of Russian culture. Without it, the Russian poet himself becomes a "wild man." Here Tolstaya invokes Pushkin's most famous statement of his poetic legacy, the 1836 lyric "I raised myself a monument not made by hands" ("Ia pamiatnik sebe vozdvig nerukotvornyi"), and suggests that cultural amnesia and xenophobia have impoverished Russian literature, transforming the Russian poet, that perennial gauge of the Russian national "self," into the very "wild Tungus" to whom Pushkin presages he will bring the music of his lyre. The African, in the person of the fictional Judy, then, becomes precisely that unruly otherness, perpetually suppressed by Soviet patriots and officials, which could, if embraced, reinvigorate Russian culture and community. Written on the eve of the collapse of the Soviet Union, Tolstaya's story presages the disintegration of empire, with the attendant exposure of its unsettling heterogeneity and the subsequent postcolonial revanche in the form of colonial subalterns claiming their voice—and the black Pushkin.

Introduction

THE POST-SOVIET PUSHKIN

In the decade following the collapse of the Soviet empire, which the Pushkin myth had so often been called on to validate, and as the 1999 bicentennial of Pushkin's birth approached, more attention was paid both in passing and in depth to Pushkin's African ancestry. Abram Petrovich Gannibal came to the forefront of Pushkin's biography in a multitude of ways in anticipation of the anniversary celebration. Dieudonné Gnammankou's work on Gannibal, culminating in the publication of *Abraham Hanibal: L'aieul noir de Pouchkine* (the Russian publication of which appears to have been timed to coincide with the 1999 Pushkin bicentennial), ushered in a new era in the study of Pushkin's African ancestry.[113] Gnammankou, a Beninese scholar who studied at Patrice Lumumba University in Moscow, has definitively established that Gannibal came from an area in central Africa bordering Lake Chad (currently a part of Cameroon) and not from Abyssinia or Ethiopia as scholars had earlier asserted. The interest (and in some cases scandal) that has ensued from this discovery is worthy of fiction. Rumors of a conflict between an Ethiopian "mafia" that has thrived for years off a generous fund devoted to Gannibal and Gnammankou as a result of his destruction of the Ethiopian version of Gannibal's origins circulated among Africans in Russia. There has been a flurry of new, largely academic works on Gannibal in the wake of Gnammankou's bombshell, and in 1996 scholars celebrated the tricentennial of Abram Gannibal's birth, which served as an occasion for a revisiting and revision of the previous research on Gannibal's life; most likely the tricentennial, nourished by the new information provided by Gnammankou, generated a new focus on Gannibal, which was further enhanced by the upcoming bicentennial of his great-grandson.[114]

And yet, as with so many of the most serious and hallowed figures in Russian and Soviet culture, perhaps the best gauge of the still-potent generative force of the figure of Gannibal has been his transformation into what in Russian is termed *anekdot,* which is only approximately and faintly rendered in English as "joke." V. Belobrov and O. Popov's novella *The Blackamoor of Peter the Great II* (*Arap Petra Velikogo II,* 1997) irreverently portrays Gannibal as a womanizer and a fop. Their whimsical, satirical narrative literally splits Gannibal into two: Gannibal Pushkin and his twin brother Zanzibal Pushkin, who were brought to the tsar as "souvenirs" from Africa. From beginning to end, the text satirizes the mythic status Gannibal attained in Pushkin's genealogy, and pokes fun at the other central figures who participated in that mythogenesis.[115] More to the point, its very existence points to the simultaneous tenacity and fragility of the traditional touchstones of Russian culture at a time when everything appears to be flying apart, up for grabs, and in flux.

The bicentennial of Pushkin's birth in 1999, the first major commemoration of Pushkin since the collapse of the Soviet Union and its cultural establishment, demonstrated the continued vitality of Pushkin's presence in Russian culture and the undaunted enthusiasm of Russian politicians for exploiting Pushkin as political capital. In the course of the festivities, the television station NTV broadcast a documentary, *Living Puskhin* (*Zhivoi Pushkin*), clearly invoking Pushkin as a vital cultural force, and providing a bizarre amalgamation of scholarly research, selective quotations from Pushkin's works, and pop anthropology. The program, narrated and coauthored by Leonid Parfenov of NTV fame, won a prestigious TEFI award. Its opening scene features an exotic African landscape with a dramatic, coursing waterfall, accompanied by the beat of tribal drums. Parfenov begins his story in northern Ethiopia, "the land of ancient Abyssinia and the homeland of Pushkin's great-grandfather, Abram Gannibal." The documentary narrator proclaims that in Ethiopia "they also celebrate June 6 [Pushkin's birthday by the Gregorian calendar]." As we can see, despite the compelling new research by Gnammankou and others, the film persists in underscoring Gannibal's "Ethiopian" origins. More striking, however, is the centrality of Africa to the documentary's depiction of Pushkin, and the remarkably muddled signs of race by which it is framed. From the opening, then, the scene shifts to images of young Ethiopian boys with deep chocolate-colored skin, then to a portrait of Pushkin in childhood, and then back to the African boys playing in the open air. The narrator comments: "It seems each young Ethiopian resembles young Pushkin, with his almost European facial features and [skin color] more dark brown than black," stating further that "the Ethiopians in general do not admit that they really derive from the Negroes of black Africa." The narrator then goes on to relate several familiar anecdotes from contemporaries about the physical appearances of Pushkin and his mother, Nadezhda Osipovna, to affirm their Ethiopian kinship before proceeding to the bulk of the story—a rather conventional rendering of the life, work, and legacy of Pushkin.

The documentary returns to Ethiopia at the end, segueing from a shot of Pushkin's death mask—the only "true image" of what Pushkin really looked like—to the northern Ethiopian city of Bahir Dar, which as part of its celebration of the Pushkin bicentennial screened the 1976 film *How Tsar Peter Married Off His Blackamoor* (*Skaz, pro to, kak tsar' Petr arapa zhenil*), starring a young Vladimir Vysotsky (1938–80), something of a Russian James Dean, popular as a movie star, but even more acclaimed as a bard poet and rebel among the intelligentsia and youth of his generation and even more so since his premature death. The film provides in its own right a uniquely revelatory text of the complexity of the conflation of race, national sentiment, nonconformism, and fetishism in casting the cult figure of Vysotsky—made up in heavy black greasepaint—as the upstanding and talented Gannibal. Certainly the original Soviet Russian audience could not have failed to catch the analogy between Pushkin and Gannibal, Gannibal and Vysotsky, virtue and alterity. The narrator's contention in the documentary that "the [Ethiopian] public claimed the made-up Vysotsky as its own," however, strains the imagination. The point here is not the Ethiopian audience, but the Russian audience and its perception of its greatest national poet among the ruins of empire. The documentary closes, against an African backdrop and to the beat of drums, with the line that "Abram Gannibal returned to the origins of the Nile."[116] Whether this odd homecoming signals nostalgia for a return to some primordial, natural source or merely a bid for sensation in a newly ratings-conscious television market, it appears evident that the same pattern of fascination and repudiation of the racial implications of Gannibal's origins persists close to the surface of post-Soviet anxieties over Russia's changed place in the world.

Tolstaya's "Limpopo" and the "high culture" tradition of troping on Pushkin's African descent that we have briefly surveyed here were strangely echoed in a post-Soviet "news" article on the fertility of hybridity. Using Pushkin as the "textbook example" of heterogenic people "who have exceptional health, sexuality and at the same time geniality" and, in the case of Pushkin, "left not only a rich literary legacy, but also, as the ranks of Pushkinists confirm, a multitude of children outside of marriage," the article described new research being done in Siberia to support the scientific claim of the greater fertility and good health of hybrids.[117] So Pushkin has become proof of the dangers of inbreeding, and a positive example for Russian science and the nation. If the Pushkin myth has in fact evolved and functioned as a complex metaphor for Russianness as a delicate amalgam of diverse peoples into a coherent whole under the umbrella of the Russian Empire and, later, the Soviet Union, then the foregrounding of the "black" Pushkin as an image of dissent, as an indication that the otherness residing within the nation would not peacefully assimilate itself to the reigning ideology and was, in fact, the driving creative if destabilizing force of the nation becomes understandable. Perhaps more disturbing in this context, however, was the resurgence of interest in Pushkin's blackness precisely at the moment when the empire had collapsed and when virulent racism had resurfaced toward dark-skinned people, especially in the context of the ongoing hostilities in the breakaway region of Chechnya. Tolstaya's story in particular may be read in this context as a meeting of reality and metaphor, an allegory of the collapse of empire which may be regenerated only by the appearance of a new hybrid, a new merging and assimilation.

What is clear is that the extraordinary journey across cultural and temporal boundaries that began with Abram Gannibal's birth in Africa some three centuries ago continues to generate richly multivocal interpretations that speak to us across time and space. At a time when Gannibal's adopted country—which has so long seen itself reflected in his remarkable great-grandson's image—is still in a process of redefining itself, it is telling that Pushkin has, so to speak, been returned to his origins. We hope that the essays in this volume are only the beginning of a dialogue aimed at reclaiming the full complexity of the intersection of discourse, power, and subversion that has allowed Pushkin to retain his preeminent position as Russia's metaphorical touchstone through history-shaking political upheavals.

Notes

The opening epigraph from Belinskii is cited in Kalpana Sahni, *Crucifying the Orient: Russian Orientalism and the Colonization of Caucasus and Central Asia* (Bangkok: White Orchid, 1997), 23.

The third epigraph is from an interview with Gera Leopoldovich Zacharin Morales in the documentary *Black Russians* (Strangefruit Productions), produced and directed by Kara Lynch. Prior to this statement, Morales explained, "Pushkin was an Ethiopian. I think Alexander Sergeevich was a Rasta . . . Because, I figure he was a genius and he felt his roots. He, thanks to his roots, his Ethiopianness, was a genius."

1. The primary sources on Abram Petrovich Gannibal's biography include Gannibal's own statements (letters and petitions, and an autobiography in a preface dedicating his book to Empress Catherine I, first published in N. K. Teletova, *Zabytye rodstvennye sviazi A. S. Pushkina* [Leningrad: Nauka, 1981], 141–44); a brief sketch by his son Petr Abramovich Gannibal (P. A. Gannibal, "Vospominaniia P. A. Gannibala," republished in full in Teletova, *Zabytye rodstvennye sviazi,* 171–72); the first, so-called German biography, apparently written by Gannibal's son-in-law A. K. Rotkirkh (A. S. Pushkin, "Biografiiia A. P. Gannibala," in his *Polnoe sobranie sochinenii,* 12:434 [shortened version of German biography]); *Rukoiu Pushkina,* ed. M. A. Tsiavlovskii, B. L. Modzalevskii, and T. G. Zenger (Moscow and Leningrad, 1935), 52 (German biography under title "Biografiia A. P. Gannibala," published by Zenger); [G. A. W. Helbig], *Russische Günstlinge* (1809); Pushkin's own writings on his great-grandfather; D. N. Bantysh-Kamenskii, *Slovar' dostopaniatnik liudei Russkoi zemli,* vol. 3 (Moscow, 1836); references in biographies of Pushkin; an article by his great-granddaughter, A. S. Gannibal, "Gannibaly, novye dannye dlia ikh biografii," in *Pushkin i ego sovremenniki,* vyp. 17–18 (St. Petersburg, 1913); D. N. Anuchin, "A. S. Pushkin: Antropologicheskii eskiz," *Russkie vedomosti,* nos. 99, 106, 114, 120, 127, 134, 143, 163, 172, 180, 193, and 209 (1899); B. L. Modzalevskii, "Rod Pushkina," in his *Pushkin: Vospominaniia, pis'ma, dnevniki . . .* (Moscow: Agraf, 1999), 13–50; M. O. Vegner, *Predki Pushkina* (Moscow, 1937); Vladimir Nabokov, "Abram Gannibal," in Aleksandr Pushkin, *Eugene Onegin,* trans. Vladimir Nabokov, 4 vols. (New York, 1964), 3:397–447; the first book-length biography of Gannibal by Georg Leets, *Abram Petrovich Gannibal: Biograficheskoe issledovanie*

Introduction

(Tallinn: Izdatel'stvo Eesti Raamat, 1980); I. L. Feinberg, *Abram Petrovich Gannibal praded Pushkina: Razyskaniia i materialy* (Moscow: Izdatel'stvo Nauka, 1983); N. K. Teletova, "Novoe o pradede Gannibale," in *Zabytye rodstvennye sviazi*, 115–58; N. Eidel'man, "Kolokol'chik Gannibala," in *Iz potaennoi istorii Rossii XVII–XIX vekov* (Moscow: Vysshaia shkola, 1993), 89–129; Dieudonné Gnammankou, *Abraham Hanibal: L'aieul noir de Pouchkine* (Paris and Dakar: Presence Africaine, 1998).

2. Lieutenant Captain Konon Zotov, charged by Peter with monitoring the students studying in France, to A. V. Makarov, 1717, cited in Leets, *Abram Petrovich Gannibal*, 37.

3. Leets, *Abram Petrovich Gannibal*, 61n10.

4. Teletova, *Zabytye rodstvennye sviazi*, 144.

5. "Ponezhe arap i ne nashei porody" (Leets, *Abram Petrovich Gannibal*, 74).

6. The court records were brought to public attention through the publication by S. I. Opatovich in 1877 of an article about Evdokiia Gannibal in the journal *Russkaia starina* based on his discovery of the divorce proceedings in an archive. However, to this day, it is Opatovich's interpretation of the records, rather than the records themselves, that remains generally available. See M. O. Vegner, "Predki Pushkina," in *Rod i predki A. S. Pushkina* (Moscow: Vasanta, 1995), 138.

7. On the "legend" that Evdokiia's infidelity was revealed when she gave birth to a white daughter, see Catharine Nepomnyashchy's article in this volume.

8. Anuchin speculates that von Schöberg's family had been taken prisoner by the Russians.

9. In fact, according to an apparently inaccurate family legend, Gannibal survived his wife by only one day.

10. For the various hypotheses on Gannibal's birth date, see Leets, *Abram Petrovich Gannibal*, 11–15.

11. The text of the petition is cited in Teletova, *Zabytye rodstvennye sviazi*, 170–71.

12. The biography was written in German shortly after Gannibal's death, in the 1780s, probably by the husband of Gannibal's youngest daughter Sophia, Adam Karpovich (Adolf-Reinhold) Rotkirkh. Rotkirkh served as the manager of Elitsy, the estate of Petr Abramovich Gannibal, Pushkin's great-uncle, and a copy of the biography remained among Petr Abramovich's papers.

13. For the most recent scholarly treatment of the controversy over Gannibal's birthplace, see N. K. Teletova's article in this volume.

14. Brokhaus and Efron, *Novyi entsiklopedicheskii slovar'* (1992 reprint), 1:55.

15. Entry written by M. le Romain, in Denis Diderot and Jean Le Rond d'Alembert, *Encyclopédie ou dictionnaire raisonné des sciences, des arts, et*

des métiers (1751–72), as excerpted in *Race and the Enlightenment: A Reader,* ed. Emmanuel Chukwudi Eze (Cambridge, Mass.: Blackwell, 1997), 91.

16. Brokhaus and Efron, *Novyi entsiklopedicheskii slovar'*, 40:820.

17. Cited in Eidel'man, "Kolokol'chik Gannibala," 125 (emphasis ours).

18. P. A. Gannibal, "Vospominaniia P. A. Gannibala," 171.

19. Iu. M. Lotman, *Pushkin* (St. Petersburg: Iskusstvo, 1995), 28.

20. Lee D. Baker, *From Savage to Negro: Anthropology and the Construction of Race, 1896–1941* (Berkeley: University of California Press, 2000), 1–2.

21. Aleksei Khomiakov, *Sobranie sochineniia* (Moscow, 1882), 3:107, as cited in Leon Poliakov, *The Aryan Myth: A History of Racist and Nationalist Ideas in Europe* (New York: Basic Books, 1974), 346n63. For a comprehensive analysis of the functional and contextual similarities and differences between slavery in the United States and serfdom in Russia, especially as concerns the complex interconnection between race and class and the ideologies that evolved to justify inequality, see Peter Kolchin, *Unfree Labor: American Slavery and Russian Serfdom* (Cambridge: Harvard University Press, 1987).

22. Henry Louis Gates Jr., "Introduction: Writing 'Race' and the Difference It Makes," in *"Race," Writing and Difference*, ed. Henry Louis Gates Jr. (Chicago: University of Chicago Press, 1985), 4, 5.

23. Marc Raeff points out that it was common practice to use education to co-opt local elites and thereby facilitate the absorption of new ethnic groups into the empire. See his "Patterns of Russian Imperial Policy toward the Nationalities," in *Soviet Nationality Problems* (New York: Columbia University Press, 1971), 22–42.

24. See Edward T. Wilson, *Russia and Black Africa before World War II* (New York: Holmes and Meier, 1974); and Allison Blakely, *Russia and the Negro: Blacks in Russian History and Thought* (Washington, D.C.: Howard University Press, 1986), for more complete coverage of the historical relationship between Russia and Africa. For a detailed discussion of Russian travelers to Africa, see M. Zabrodskaia's *Russkie puteshestvenniki po Afrike* (Moscow: Gosudarstvennoe izdatel'stvo geograficheskoi literatury, 1955).

25. In addition to foreign atlases and geography books, Pushkin's library featured Kokovstov's account. See B. L. Modzalevskii, "Biblioteka Pushkina," in *Pushkin i ego sovremenniki,* vyp. 9–10. Notable volumes in Pushkin's collection included, among others, *Souvenirs d'une expedition en Afrique, Encyclopedie des gens du monde, Nouveau dictionnaire geographique universel,* and *La physiognome ou l'art de connaitre les hommes d'apres les traits du visage.* Pushkin owned the three-volume universal geography published in Brussels by Malte-Brun in 1829–30; according to B. L. Modzalevskii, the pages devoted to Africa and Abyssinia were cut (cited in Aleksei Bukalov, "Pod nebom Afriki moei," *Aziia i Afrika segodnia,* no. 6 [1984]: 460n2).

26. The bulk of Russian exploration and involvement in Africa, however,

Introduction

took place after Pushkin's death. Increasing interest in the strategic placement of Ethiopia led Russia to strengthen its relationship with Ethiopian rulers at the end of the century in the hope of counteracting British influence in Africa.

27. Svinin, the secretary to the Russian consul in Philadelphia in 1811–13, was also a journalist, author, and painter. He had a twofold purpose for his volume: to provide a study of America and its mores, and to foster amicable relations between Russia and the United States. In addition to the travel account, he published a number of articles on American trade and transportation in the leading Russian journals of the day, *Son of the Fatherland* (*Syn otechestva*) and *Notes of the Fatherland* (*Otechestvennye zapiski*). For an overview of Pushkin's relationship with Svinin, see L. A. Chereiskii, *Pushkin i ego okruzhenie* (Leningrad: Nauka, 1989), 389–90.

28. See Chukwudi Eze, *Race and the Enlightenment*, as well as Catharine Nepomnyashchy's article in this volume.

29. On the two images of Ethiopia in the European imagination—one pastoral and idyllic, the other dark and savage—see Malvern van Wyk Smith, "'Waters Flowing from Darkness': The Two Ethiopias in the Early European Image of Africa," *Theoria* 68 (December 1986): 67–77.

30. See Catherine O'Neil's article in this volume for a detailed treatment of the Othello theme in Pushkin's oeuvre.

31. Leslie O'Bell, "Writing the Story of Pushkin's Death," *Slavic Review* 58, no. 2 (Summer 1999): 396. O'Bell's argument in general highlights the dependence of the Russian public on literature for their understanding of the duel, and discusses the story in terms of Pierre Choderlos de Laclos's epistolary novel *Les liaisons dangereuses* (1782). In this context, the detail—that Pushkin's close friends and confidants, including A. I. Turgenev, attended a performance of *Othello* (with the famed Karatygin in the leading role) on January 12, 1837, a mere two weeks before the fatal duel—seems particularly tantalizing. See P. E. Shchegelov, *Duel i smert' Pushkina: Issledovanie i materialy* (St. Petersburg, 1999), 267, for excerpts from Turgenev's diary.

32. Letter of January 29, 1837, cited in Serena Vitale, *Pushkin's Button* (Chicago: University of Chicago Press), 1. For similar remarks from foreign commentators, see Shchegolev, *Duel i smert' Pushkina*, 342–86.

33. V. V. Kunin, *Poslednii god zhizni Pushkina: Perepiska, vospominaniia, dnevniki* (Moscow: Pravda, 1988), 516.

34. Kunin, *Poslednii*, 604.

35. David Brion Davis, *The Problem of Slavery in Western Culture* (Ithaca, N.Y.: Cornell University Press, 1966), 473.

36. Peter J. Weston, "The Noble Primitive as Bourgeois Subject," *Literature and History* 10 (1984): 63.

37. The novel's second edition alone sold its entire print run of more than 3,000 copies; in addition, it went through a total of four new editions and

reprints in 1824, and a pirated edition sold out as well. A number of plays and poems based on the novel also emerged in 1824. See Joan DeJean and Margaret Waller's "Introduction" in Claire de Duras, *Ourika* (New York: MLA Texts and Translations, 1994), viii–xxi.

38. See DeJean and Waller, "Introduction," fn2.

39. See the story of Louis Anabia, an Assini hostage in the court of Louis XIV, in Hans Werner Debrunner, *Presence and Prestige: Africans in Europe: A History of Africans in Europe before 1918* (Basel: Basler Afrika Bibliographien, 1979), 70. Debrunner also provides a number of bio-bibliographies of other Africans, royal and otherwise, including Abram Gannibal.

40. Prince William Ansah Sessarakoo's story was published in the 1730s and 1740s. James Albert Ukawsaw Gronniosaw (c. 1717–72) claims noble descent in his *A Narrative of the Most Remarkable Particulars in the Life of James Albert Ukawsaw Gronniosaw, An African Prince, As Related by Himself* (Bath, 1772). Quobna Ottobah Cugoano (c. 1757–c. 1801), though he did not purport to be a prince like his friend Equiano, did live a life of privilege as the son of a companion to the chief of a region (Fantee) now in Ghana. Cugoano also published a treatise against slavery, *Thoughts and Sentiments on the Evil and Wicked Traffic of the Slavery and Commerce of the Human Species, Humbly Submitted to the Inhabitants of Great-Britain, by Ottobah Cugoano, a Native of Africa* (London, 1787). See *Unchained Voices: An Anthology of Black Authors in the English-Speaking World of the Eighteenth Century*, ed. Vincent Caretta (Lexington: University Press of Kentucky, 1996); and Brycchan Carey's website, at htpp://www.brycchan-carey.com, which has biographies and extensive bibliographies on Equiano, Cugoano, and Sancho. In addition, short biographical entries on many of these authors were first collected in Henri Gregoire's *De la literature des Negres* (1808); this volume also included brief biographical information on Abram Gannibal.

41. Ignatius Sancho, *Letters of the Late Ignatius Sancho, An African* (New York: Penguin, 1998), xv.

42. These novels were *Memoirs and Opinions of Mr. Blenfield* (1790) and *Berkeley Hall, or The Pupil of Experience* (1796).

43. Blakely, *Russia and the Negro*, 13.

44. Blakely puts the figure at less than ten *arapy* at the tsar's court during the eighteenth century and around twenty in the nineteenth century; apparently when one died a replacement was always found. Peter the Great had hired at least three black servants (one sailor, one artist, and one valet) when in Holland in 1697. In the nineteenth century, the court's blackamoor staff became populated not only by Africans but by African Americans. One such young African American woman, Nancy Prince, spent the years 1824–33 in the Russian court as a servant and left a valuable record of her time there. See

Introduction

A Narrative of the Life and Travels of Mrs. Nancy Prince Written by Herself (Boston: Nancy Prince, 1856). See also Blakely, *Russia and the Negro,* 13–16.

45. Blakely provides a brief discussion in his chapter "The Negro in Russian Art," in *Russia and the Negro,* 50–62. Pushkin's contemporary, the artist Karl Briullov, features a striking number of African male and female domestic servants in his high-society portraits.

46. A. S. Pushkin, *Dnevniki, zapiski* (St. Petersburg: Nauka, 1995), 108. We thank Clint Walker for bringing this text to our attention. For two other references to *arapy* in Pushkin's "Table-Talk," see 157, 177. The latter features a scurrilous anecdote involving Peter the Great and a young *arap*, a variant of which makes reference to Abram Gannibal.

47. Blakely, *Russia and the Negro,* 16–19.

48. For sources on the interactions between Pushkin and his Gannibal relatives, see the relevant entries in *Pushkin i ego okruzhenii* (Leningrad: Nauka, 1975).

49. Pushkin apparently first met Petr Abramovich Gannibal during his first trip to Mikhailovskoe; Pushkin last visited him in August 1825. See Pushkin's note from November 19, 1824, in which he refers to him as "starogo arapa"; in Pushkin, *PSS* 12:304. Hereafter page numbers from this edition of Pushkin's collected works will be given in parentheses in the text.

50. T. Iu. Mal'tseva, *Gannibaly i Pushkin na Pskovshchine* (Moscow: Russkii put', 1999), 19.

51. See N. Eidel'man, *Pushkin: Istoriia i sovremennost v khudozheskvennom soznanii poeta* (Moscow: Sovetskii pisatel', 1984), 35, for other people who may have supplied Pushkin with information about Gannibal.

52. Teletova, Eidel'man, and Leets have discussed how Pushkin's historical inaccuracies in his portrayal of Gannibal's life are dependent on the source materials available to him at the time. They debunk these inaccuracies by comparing Pushkin's text with recently discovered historical documents.

53. See, in this context, the articles by David Bethea and Richard Gustafson in this volume.

54. V. Listov, "Legenda o chernom predke," in *Legendy i mify o Pushkine* (St. Petersburg: Institut russkoi literatury RAN, 1995), 55–57. Listov notes the similarity between Gannibal's story and the biblical story of Joseph, and points out that Rotkirkh's biography of Gannibal makes these parallels clear.

55. As J. Thomas Shaw points out in notes to his edition of Pushkin's letters, "Pushkin is quoting from Philipp Reiff's *Russo-French Dictionary . . . or Etymological Dictionary of the Russian Language,* the first volume of which (A–O) appeared in Petersburg in 1835" (*The Letters of Alexander Pushkin,* trans. J. Thomas Shaw [Madison: University of Wisconsin Press, 1967], 799).

56. Shaw notes that "Pushkin has in mind a critique of the Russian Academy *Dictionary* and Plyushar's *Encyclopedic Lexicon*" (799). For more on the

lexicon project, see Shaw, trans., *Letters*, letters 479, 480, and 503 and corresponding notes 635, 656, and 678–79.

57. See Richard Borden's article in this volume.

58. P. S. Viazemskii in *A. S. Pushkin v vospominaniiakh sovremennikov* (Moscow: Khudozhestvennaia literatura, 1974), 1:156–57.

59. S. D. Komovskii, "Iz vospominanii o detstve Pushkina" (1851), cited in V. V. Kunin, *Zhizn' Pushkina raskazannaia im samim i ego sovremennikami* (Moscow: Pravda, 1988), 1:190–92. In another remark from Komovskii in a letter to the Pushkin monument commission, we see that Pushkin's African lineage was definitely not perceived as a positive aspect by many friends, let alone enemies: "In general, despite his fiery African nature, Pushkin managed to garner universal affection" (Kunin, *Zhizn' Pushkina*, 235–36).

60. For a survey of this topic, see David Brakke, "Ethiopian Demons: Male Sexuality, the Black-Skinned Other, and the Monastic Self," *Journal of the History of Sexuality* 10, nos. 3–4 (July–October 2001): 501–35.

61. From *Pushkin v vospominaniiakh*, 1:119, cited in Kunin, *Zhizn' Pushkina*, 1:193. Korf's memoirs, most likely written before the middle of 1852, were used by Annenkov for his biography of Pushkin; they were first published in *Russkaia starina* in August 1899, 304–11. Korf speaks about the eccentricity of Pushkin's entire family on both his father's and mother's sides (see *Pushkin v vospominaniiakh*, 1:459).

62. *Pushkin v vospominaniiakh*, 2:140; and T. G. Tsiavlovskaia, *Risunki Pushkina* (Moscow: Iskusstvo, 1987), 343. Lotman conveniently leaves out the last sentence of the above-cited quote in his essay.

63. From F. F. Vigel's *Vospominaniia* (1892), cited in *Pushkin v vospominaniiakh*, 1:220 (our emphasis).

64. P. I. Bartenev, *O Pushkine: Stranitsy zhizni poeta vospominaia sovremennikov* (Moscow, 1992), 300–301.

65. Bartenev, *O Pushkine,* no page number. The event Khomutova discusses took place on October 26, 1826.

66. Cited in J. Thomas Shaw, "Pushkin on His African Heritage: Publications during His Lifetime" (reprinted in this volume), 89–90.

67. Susan Layton, *Russian Literature and Empire: Conquest of the Caucasus from Pushkin to Tolstoy* (Cambridge: Cambridge University Press, 1994), 157.

68. After the Bulgarin incident, we witness an inward turn on Pushkin's part. The poet virtually ceased all public mention of his heritage after the early 1830s (with the exception of the republication of earlier poems). However, his unfinished autobiographical cum genealogical writings and his reading on a variety of topics concerning blackness, family history, and slavery in his last years suggest that Pushkin's interest in Gannibal and blackness actually increased in the last decade of his life. Thus, Pushkin's interest in these related

topics is reflected in his reading in the 1830s, notably John Tanner, *A Narrative of the Captivity and Adventures of John Tanner during Thirty Years Residence among the American Indians* (French translation, 1835); Alexis de Tocqueville, *De la démocratie en Amerique* (first two volumes, 1836); and Gustave de Beaumont, *Marie, ou l'esclavage aux Etats-Unis* (1836).

69. Yury Slezkine, "Naturalists versus Nations: Eighteenth-Century Russian Scholars Confront Ethnic Diversity," in *Russia's Orient: Imperial Borderlands and Peoples, 1700–1917*, ed. Daniel R. Brower and Edward J. Lazzerini (Bloomington: Indiana University Press, 1997), 49.

70. N. N. Gogol, "Neskol'ko slov o Pushkine," in his *Sobranie sochineniia v semi tomakh* (Moscow: Khudozhestvennaia literatura, 1967), 6:68.

71. See Dale Peterson, *Up from Bondage: The Literatures of Russian and African American Soul* (Durham, N.C.: Duke University Press, 2000). Interestingly, in his extensive analysis of the similarities between Russian and African American literatures, their nationalist discourses and their struggles to find their own voice within the European literary tradition, Peterson does not once mention the fact that Pushkin had African origins.

72. Fedor Dostoevskii, *Polnoe sobranie sochinenii v 30-ti tomakh*, 26:145.

73. Ludolf Müller, "Politicheskoe zaveshchanie Dostoevskogo. Dostoevskii o naznachenii Rossii. Po redu o Pushkine 8 iuniia 1880 goda," in *Poniat' Rossiiu: Istoriko-kul'turnye issledovaniia* (Moscow: Progress, 2000), 272–84.

74. P. A. Annenkov, *Pushkin v Aleksandrovskuiu epokhu* (1998), 19.

75. Annenkov as quoted in Anuchin, "A. S. Pushkin: Antropologicheskii eskiz," no page number given.

76. Bartenev, *O Pushkine*, 301. The Slavophile Ivan S. Aksakov made a statement similar to Bartenev's in his speech at the unveiling of the Pushkin monument in Moscow: "Pushkin represents in his person an astonishing, phenomenal, and deeply tragic combination of two of the most opposite types, as *man* and as *artist*: a fiery African temperament and pure Russian common sense, which is striking [even] in his earliest works and then becomes ever more developed; passionateness of *nature* and restraint of coloration in poetry; the self-possession of a master, an unwaveringly rigorous adherence to artistic measure; lightheartedness, frivolity, boiling blood, unfettered lust for life—and, at the same time, seriousness and the import of a priest of sacred works, the ability to ascend in spirit to the heights of chaste art" (V. Veresaev, "V dvukh planakh (o tvorchestve Pushkina)," in his *Zagadochnyi Pushkin* [Moscow: Respublika, 1996], 272).

77. Bartenev, *O Pushkine*, 49.

78. N. Znamenskii, "Pushkin," *Moskovskie vedemosti*, no. 143 (May 26, 1899): 1, 2.

79. Marcus Levitt, *Russian Literary Politics and the Pushkin Celebration of 1880* (Ithaca, N.Y.: Cornell University Press, 1989), 158–59. See also his article "Pushkin in 1899," in *Cultural Mythologies of Russian Modernism:*

From the Golden Age to the Silver Age, ed. Boris Gasparov, Robert P. Hughes, and Irina Paperno (Berkeley: University of California Press, 1992), 183–203.

80. The article was first serialized in *Russkie vedomosti* in 1899 and then republished as a separate pamphlet the same year.

81. D. N. Anuchin, "A. S. Pushkin: Antropologicheskii eskiz," *Russkie vedomosti,* no. 99 (1899).

82. Anuchin, "Antropologicheskii eskiz," *Russkie vedomosti,* no. 127.

83. For a long time scholars wondered whether the portrait, by an unknown artist, could be correctly said to portray Abram Gannibal, since the orders that the sitter wore did not correspond to the ones that he earned. N. Teletova has recently determined that the portrait in question represents General Meller-Zakomel'skii. See her article "O mnimon i podlinnom izobrazhenii A. P. Gannibala," in *Legendy i mify Pushkina,* 86–109.

84. Anuchin, "Antropologicheskii eskiz," no. 134.

85. On Pushkin's appearance, A. O. Smirnova-Rosset wrote in her diary: "There was nothing Negroid in him. One imagines that he must resemble a Negro because his ancestor Gannibal was a Negro. (I saw his portrait in Peterhof.) But Gannibal was not a Negro, he was Abyssinian; he had regular features, a long and dry face and a cruel but intelligent mien." See *Zapiski A. O. Smirnovoi (Iz zapisnykh knizhek 1826–1845 godov)* (St. Petersburg, 1895), 17, as cited in Teletova, "O mnimom i podlinnom izobrazhenii," 92.

86. Anuchin, "Antropologicheskii eskiz," no. 193.

87. In the twentieth century, the figure of the Jew was persistently evoked by dissonant Russian writers as a metaphor for the challenge the artist as outsider posed to official ideology. (On this, see Catharine Theimer Nepomnyashchy, *Abram Tertz and the Poetics of Crime* [New Haven: Yale University Press, 1995].) This trope tellingly resonates with the figure of the "African Pushkin" which recurs in twentieth-century Russian literature.

88. Levitt, *Russian Literary Politics,* 162.

89. See John Glad, *Russia Abroad: Writers, History, Politics* (Tenafly, NJ: Hermitage and Birchbark, 1999), 133; Kathleen Parthe, "Pure Pushkin: The Politics of Life and Death," unpublished manuscript.

90. *Pushkin v vospominaniiakh,* 2:140.

91. Leona Toker, "Fact and Fiction in Nabokov's Biography of Abram Gannibal," *Mosaic* 22, no. 3 (Summer 1989): 47.

92. Vladimir Nabokov, "Abram Gannibal," in his *Notes on Prosody and Abram Gannibal* (Princeton: Princeton University Press, 1964), 157.

93. Recently a number of studies have devoted much attention to the 1937 Pushkin celebration. For more detailed information, see David Brandenberger, "'The People's Poet': Russocentric Populism during the U.S.S.R.'s Official 1937

Introduction

Pushkin Commemoration," *Russian History/Histoire Russe* 26, no. 1 (Spring 1999): 65–73; Angela Brintlinger, *Writing a Usable Past: Russian Literary Culture, 1917–1937* (Evanston, Ill.: Northwestern University Press, 2000); Karen Petrone, *Life Has Become More Joyous, Comrades: Celebrations in the Time of Stalin* (Bloomington: Indiana University Press, 2000), especially 113–49; and Stephanie Sandler, *Commemorating Pushkin: Russia's Myth of a National Poet* (Stanford, Calif.: Stanford University Press, 2004), especially 85–136. Petrone specifically discusses the two films on Pushkin made by Lenfilm for the anniversary celebration: *Youth of the Poet* (*Iunost' poeta*) and *Journey to Erzerum* (*Puteshestvie v Arzrum*). Regarding the former film, she notes the critics' displeasure at its depiction of Pushkin: "Despite the official doctrine of racial equality, Soviet cultural authorities were not anxious to identify Pushkin as African. Pushkin represented the cultured, conscious, European New Soviet Man and not the spontaneous African with a 'stormy temperament'" (128).

94. See the articles by Olga Hasty and Anne Lounsbery in this volume.

95. In his memoir *I Wonder as I Wander* (New York: Hill and Wang, 1993), Langston Hughes comments: "Pushkin, a descendant of 'the Negro of Peter the Great,' is adored in Russia and his mulatto heritage was constantly played up in the press when I was there" (87). Homer Smith, an African American journalist who spent several years in Russia, had the opportunity to meet Pushkin's great-granddaughter during his stay in Moscow. At the end of their first meeting, Smith alleges that Catharine Pushkin told him: "Alexander Sergeevich was dark-complexioned, a few shades lighter than you. I am so sorry my color is so light. He would have been fond of you I am sure" (46). Smith's narrative includes a long digression on Pushkin's African ancestry, in which he remarks that had Pushkin lived in America, the U.S. Census Bureau would have classified him as a Negro. See Homer Smith, *Black Man in Red Russia* (Chicago: Johnston, 1964), 50–55. For a more detailed discussion of the cross-cultural forays of African Americans into the Soviet Union, see Kate A. Baldwin, *Beyond the Color Line and the Iron Curtain: Reading Encounters between Black and Red, 1922–1963* (Durham, N.C.: Duke University Press, 2002).

96. William L. Patterson, "The Negro and the Centenary of Alexander Pushkin," *The Negro Worker* 7, no. 4 (April 1937): 7. Patterson was one of the African American Communists sent to Moscow to study in 1927. He remained there until 1930, when he returned to the United States. For more information on Patterson, see Blakely, *Russia and the Negro*, 87–88.

97. For a detailed discussion of this issue, see Alexander Mihailovic's article in this volume.

98. For example, in Bamako, the capital of Mali, there is a Pushkin Institute (presumably dedicated to the study of Russian language and literature). On the island of Mauritius there is a monument dedicated to Pushkin (erected on June 6, 1986), with small oak trees brought from Mikhailovskoe

planted beside it. In Dakar, the capital of Senegal, they celebrate "Pushkin days" annually, and Guinea has issued a stamp with the image of Pushkin's monument on it.

99. The Ethiopian scholar Haile Gebré Johannes has written a biography of Pushkin in the Amharic language; another poet and playwright has penned a historical drama based on Pushkin's life.

100. We rely upon Aleksei Bukalov's "Bereg dal'nyi: Pamiati A. S. Pushkina, 1799–1837," *Aziia i Afrika segodnia*, no. 2 (1987): 38–41, for information on Pushkin's reception in Africa.

101. All references are taken from the Clarence Brown translation of Yevgeny Zamyatin, *We* (New York: Penguin Books, 1993).

102. In record 25's description of the Day of Unanimity, co-conspirators I-330 and R-13 sit shoulder to shoulder and raise their hands in opposition to the OneState: "R-13 had suddenly jumped up on a bench that was above me, to the left; he was red, spitting, in a rage. He was carrying I-330 in his arms . . . She had her arms round his neck and he was jumping from bench to bench in huge leaps, repulsive and agile as a gorilla, and carrying her toward the top" (133).

103. Only later, when D-503 records his conversation with I-330 on the necessity of contrast, fire, explosion, and revolution, do we understand the positive connotation of the alliance between I-330 and R-13. This exchange takes place, significantly, under the watchful gaze of the bust of Pushkin: "And all the while we were beneath the frozen marmoreal smile of the ancient flat-nosed poet" (167).

104. V. V. Maiakovskii, *Sochineniia v trekh tomakh* (Moscow: Khudozhestvennaia literatura, 1978), 1:381–82.

105. See Iurii Tynianov, "Mnimyi Pushkin," in *Poetika, istoriia literatury, kino* (Moscow: Nauka, 1977), 78–92; and Angela Brintlinger's discussion of the text in *Writing a Usable Past: Russian Literary Culture, 1917–1937*, 47–49.

106. Mikhail Bulgakov, *Poslednie dni (Pushkin)* (Letchworth: Prideaux, 1970), 30. Henceforth page numbers from this edition will be given in parentheses in the text.

107. Tynianov's introduction to "The Gannibals" is reproduced in translation in the appendix to this volume. See also Ludmilla A. Trigos's note accompanying the translation.

108. See Liza Knapp's article in this volume.

109. The émigré press published one of the earlier sections of Khodasevich's "The Beginning of Life" as an essay he retitled "Black Ancestors" ("Chernye predki"). Khodasevich also published an essay on the poet and his great-grandfather ("Great Grandfather and Great Grandson") in his book *About Pushkin* (*O Pushkine*, 1937). See Brintlinger, *Writing a Usable Past*,

Introduction

99–100, for a detailed discussion of the genesis of the biography and of differences between the newspaper articles and the biography.

110. V. F. Khodasevich, "Iz knigi Pushkina," in his *Sobranie sochineniia v 4-kh tomakh* (Moscow: Soglasie, 1977), 71.

111. On the controversy over the publication of *Strolls with Pushkin* both in emigration and in the Soviet Union, see Catharine Theimer Nepomnyashchy, *Abram Tertz and the Poetics of Crime.*

112. We are relying upon Jamey Gambrell's translation of "Limpopo" in Tatyana Tolstaya, *Sleepwalker in a Fog* (New York: Vintage Books, 1993). Henceforth page numbers from this edition will appear in parentheses in the text.

113. Dieudonné Gnammankou, *Abram Gannibal: Chernyi predok Pushkina* (Moscow, 1999).

114. Prior to 1995, a few scholarly works did mention the need for more attention to the Gannibal family tree, such as Teletova's *Zabytye rodstvennye sviazy A. S. Pushkina* and N. I. Granovskaia's *Rod Pushkinykh miatezhnyi: Iz istorii roda A. S. Pushkina* (St. Petersburg, 1992), but other than Feinberg's and Leets's works of the 1980s, no text focused primarily on the Gannibals. The studies published after Gnammankou's work include Mark Sergeev, *Zhizn' i zlokliucheniia Abrama Petrova, arap Petra Velikogo* (Moscow: Izograf, 1996); A. M. Bessonova, *Gannibaly v Rossii* (St. Petersburg: Izdatel'stvo St. Peterburgskogo Universiteta, 1999); T. Iu. Mal'tseva, *Gannibaly i Pushkin na Pskovshchine* (Moscow: Russkii put', 1999); and the aforementioned Russian translation of Gnammankou's book.

115. The epigraph to the novella's text is falsely attributed to Paul Robeson: "It's good for Negroes in America / But it's even better in Russia!"

116. In addition, the bicentennial celebration of Pushkin provided an unprecedented opportunity to Russian and foreign researchers; in a triumphant return to Gannibal's newly discovered homeland, two expeditions were undertaken to the shores of Lake Chad, to the town of Logon, where Gannibal's father had allegedly ruled in the seventeenth century. Igor Danilov, the editor of the Petersburg journal *Our Pioneer* (*Nash sledopyt*), put together a team of scholars, the historian and writer Felix Lurie, the Pushkinist Natalia Teletova, and the journalist Svetlana Lutova, to assist him in his endeavor. Their trip was filmed for posterity and should be released soon by Lenfilm. See "V Logon, na rodinu Arapa," *Novoe russkoe slovo*, October 22, 1999, 31.

117. Elena Lashko, "Tainu A. S. Pushkina i mulatok raskryli genetiki i perepelki," *Novaia Sibir'*, June 22, 1998.

N. K. Teletova

A. P. Gannibal: On the Occasion of the Three Hundredth Anniversary of the Birth of Alexander Pushkin's Great-Grandfather

ABRAM PETROVICH GANNIBAL died from a "cranial illness" on April 20, 1781, in the eighty-fifth year of his life.[1] The illness came about as the result of an injury to the head suffered long ago, when the young man, who was studying engineering in France, took part in a campaign and fought at the Spanish fortress of Fuenterrabia. That was in 1719.

The Spanish border. Paris. La Fère and its ancient fortress. Before that—the journey from Russia to France in Peter the Great's suite. Five and a half years of study—the French language and customs, and the sciences.

And even earlier, before Russia, a life out of an Arabian tale. The boy was born in the principality of Logon (or Lagon), south of Lake Chad, in the city of the same name as the small principality consisting of three cities. Both the principality and the city were named for the Logon River, a tributary of the lake. Today Logon is part of the territory of the state of Cameroon.

These were places settled by the African tribe Kotóko, to which the boy apparently belonged; he was the son of a local princeling who had been attacked by his more powerful neighbors. The father of Ibragim-Abram still professed the traditional animist religion of his tribe, while the neighboring principalities had already converted to Islam. This gave them grounds to view Logon as being at a lower stage of development, and to abduct their children and sell them into slavery. Most often the buyers proved to be the Ottoman Porte of Turkey.

Abram's father, as was the custom among African princes who practiced traditional religion, had many wives, and it was this and not Islam that was the reason for the abundance of these wives and the sons who aspired to power. Evidently the children were taken by force after a military defeat and sold or handed over to the Turks by the victors.

The boy was taken away, transported via the waterway to the caravan land route which ended in the port of Tripoli, and from there by sea he was delivered to Istanbul, or Constantinople, as it was then known by Christendom.[2] So began the boy's life in the seraglio of the Sultan Ahmed III, sovereign of the Turks. Yet another abduction from this second home and once again a journey north—to Muscovy, to Moscow itself.

If the boy had merely seen the Ottoman sultan from afar, then here in Russia he became the tsar's servant, his godson, the ward Abram Petrov. He accompanied the sovereign on all his campaigns, he was with him in decisive battles, and he later accompanied Peter I on his second—and last—European journey.

Naturally, it has been conjectured that the little blackamoor in the white turban on the canvas in the Hermitage by Pierre-Denis Martin the Younger (a copy) depicting the Battle of Lesnaia with the Swedes in 1708 is none other than Abram Petrov. Martin painted the work between 1717 and 1723 in Paris, and it is possible that in those years Abram Petrov, who had taken part in the battle and was then studying in France, may have given the artist some background for the painting. The artist probably portrayed the black adolescent in the picture with the features of Abram Petrov, the young engineer.

After France there were still several distant journeys, but they were all within the borders of Peter's realm, including the Baltic fortresses and cities; St. Petersburg; exile to Siberia and the Chinese border, thanks to the efforts of Menshikov. And again, Petersburg and the Baltics; and a tour of duty near Vyborg on the Swedish border. And in his advanced years, life in the capital and on the estates which he had acquired near Petersburg.

In the last of Abram's surviving letters, dated November 10, 1780, the venerable old man asks his son to buy him some white Siberian fur, because all other fur rots, but does not warm.[3] The old blackamoor was suffering from the cold in his country house Suida under the gray autumn sky of Ingermanland.

Africa. Turkey. Russia. France and the Spanish campaign. Once again Russia—and the Baltics, Siberia, and finally, Petersburg. South, north, west, east. Having experienced all four winds and having known both rise and fall, like Odysseus, made wise by experience, Gannibal wanted to leave behind some sort of memoir. However, as Pushkin informs us, having learned of this from family legend, this same life experience prompted Abram to burn his notes, when a courier from the city was espied on the road to his estate.

Naturally, Pushkin, who took pride in the Rzhevskys, his "Rurik" ancestors, and the 600-year-old nobility of the name he bore, particularly singled out the progenitor of the historically romantic origins of his family, Abram Petrovich Gannibal. The works Pushkin dedicated to this exotic great-grandfather are sufficiently well known.

We will note two of the distinguishing features of these works, the first of which comes as something of a surprise; namely, the surprising exactitude with which Pushkin reproduces the smallest details from the historical and biographical material at his disposal. Pushkin, the creator of rich plots constructed by means of artistic invention, upon becoming a statesman begins to regard documents with reverence when the subject turns to "matters of bygone days" and the actors of history, among whom he justifiably numbers his great-grandfather. He is proud of the "history of my family, that is, the history of the fatherland," which dictates to him the form of another sort of creative work.[4]

The second distinguishing feature is the scantiness of the materials he had at his disposal. And it was not only a case of lacking materials, but also that these materials often sacrificed the truth for colorful details. Elevating one's family, particularly when one's origins are in doubt, is a typical trait of all family genealogists. Pushkin encountered a typical specimen of this in the figure of his father's cousin Adam Rotkirkh, who in the late 1780s penned the so-called German biography of Gannibal. A Swede by birth, Rotkirkh excelled in the carelessness with dates for which the Russian nobility is noted, muddling almost all of them and leaving Pushkin with a series of unsolvable puzzles and riddles.

During the composition of the novel about his great-grandfather, *The Blackamoor of Peter the Great,* Pushkin made use of an abridged translation of the so-called German biography, copied out in his own hand. He painstakingly writes the dates mentioned in Rotkirkh's text in a column in the margins of his manuscript. He adds them up, and then subtracts—and nothing comes out right; for example, the fact that the blackamoor left behind in Paris to study was not twenty-one years (as he was in actual fact) but twenty-seven years old, and that he apparently returned to Russia only in the fourth decade of his life.

In the novel, Pushkin had "to squeeze" all the events into the first year of his great-grandfather's stay in France, whereas the episode with Countess D. could only have taken place during the final years of his stay when Abram (Ibragim in the novel), a captain in the French king's army, had broken free from poverty for a short period and was not isolated from society by his ignorance of the language.

We should note, however, the contamination of the plots here. The source of Ibragim's unlikely liaison with a French countess who gave birth to a black baby can be traced to a real-life biographical episode just as colorful: Gannibal's first wife, a dark-haired but fair-skinned Greek, presented him with a white baby girl, which according to the laws of genetics and Abram's understanding of the matter was an impossibility if the daughter was really his. The plot is turned inside out by Pushkin, in a variant that flatters his great-grandfather. Thus the lack of facts and, what's worse, their falsification greatly hindered the poet in his work on his novel, which was ultimately to be set aside unfinished.

All the works written about Abram Gannibal during the second half of the nineteenth century and into the twentieth century have been prompted by the need to fill in the gaps—belatedly—of this disappointing lack of materials. Gannibal's life is interesting, of course, not only as a subject in Pushkin's work, but also on the historical and genealogical levels. The author of this article was guided by all these concerns when embarking upon this study of the remarkable biography of Gannibal, which draws upon materials about the poet's great-grandfather that we now have at our disposal at the end of the twentieth century.

Let's begin with the fact that Gannibal did not know the date, month, and year of his birth. In his youth he took the day and month of his Christian baptism for his birthday. Abram (Avraam) was baptized in a Russian Orthodox church, which until recently was thought to be Paraskevy (or Paraskevy Piatnitsy, which was why the church was also called Piatnitskaia). Twenty-one years later he would write: "And His Majesty was my godfather at the sacred fount in Lithuania, in Vilno, in the year 1705." Unfortunately, there are no documents whatsoever about this, since the Vilno archive was removed beyond its borders and has still not been returned. However, in 1865, after the Paraskevy Church underwent major repairs, Governor M. N. Murav'ev ordered that a memorial plaque be affixed to the gate. The plaque survives to this day in the same place. The source of information was undoubtedly a document that has now been lost, but which must have belonged to the Vilno archive and which formed the basis for the following inscription:

> In this church
> Emperor Peter the Great
> In 1705 attended
> A service of Thanksgiving
> For the victory over the army of Charles XII,
> And presented a banner
> Taken in battle from the Swedes
> And had baptized here the African Gannibal,
> Grandfather of our renowned poet,
> A. S. Pushkin.

Abram then did not bear the surname Gannibal, but by the time of the appearance of this inscription the surname of the great-grandfather (here mistakenly called grandfather) was sufficiently well known from works about Pushkin. However, information about the christening in Vilno in 1705 had not yet appeared in studies about Pushkin and could only have been taken from the local archive. Thus we can assert that this inscription is based both on published information about the poet's descent from Gannibal as well as a Vilno document that has not yet surfaced about the christening of the blackamoor Abram by Peter I in 1705 in an Orthodox church. As scholars have pointed out, the Paraskevy Church from 1611 until the nineteenth century was Uniate, and the baptism of Abram that had taken place is arbitrarily ascribed to this church, which stands in the city center. However, there was an Orthodox monastery in Vilno where the baptism evidently took place, as recorded in the archive—but without specifying the place.[5]

In addition, the detail in the inscription that a service of thanksgiving was held for the victory over the Swedes helps to fix the time. The enemy's banner that had been seized and was presented to the church serves as material proof of the event. Although the exact date of the service is not indicated, it can be culled from the almost daily record of Peter I's life as presented in the historical works of I. I. Golikov and N. G. Ustrialov.[6] Peter I arrived in Vilno on July 8, 1705 (Old Style), and departed on either August 3 or 4. On July 11, victory over the Swedes at Mitava was won by Peter's forces under General Bour. News of this and the captured banner were probably brought back on the evening of July 12 or the following morning. The service of thanksgiving and the boy's baptism that followed took place on the same day, as recorded in the document whose contents were inscribed on the memorial plaque, but the place was arbitrarily ascribed to the Paraskevy Church.

The exact date of these events, July 13, is confirmed indirectly but tellingly: it was precisely on July 13, 1776, that the elderly Gannibal gathered together the members of his household, friends, and witnesses and drew up his last will and testament. This day marked his eightieth birthday. Not knowing the date or month of his birth, Gannibal, as I noted earlier, reckoned the date of his baptism as the date of his birth.

As far as the year of Abram's appearance in the world is concerned, we need to turn to the manuscript evidence Gannibal left on various occasions. Here we observe a certain peculiarity: the older this worthy of the eighteenth century becomes, the more years he adds to his age—either as a result of simple carelessness or, more likely, for the sake of self-importance, because he already possessed considerable rank. Abducted from his parents' home in his infancy, he evidently did not know the year of his birth—and that allowed him to adjust his age to his own advantage or to suit his whim.

However, when he was younger and had a lower rank he probably acted more responsibly. Thus, when presenting to Empress Catherine I on her name day (November 23, 1726) the two volumes of his works and copies made from French originals (on geometry and fortifications), he notes: "I had the honor of serving from my infancy, to wit, from the age of seven or eight."[7]

Passing over the calculations computed on the evidence of other documents left by Gannibal, we can state that in early 1705, when he entered imperial service, he reckoned that he was eight and one-half years old, and turned nine in the summer of 1705. Gannibal thus considered the date of his birth to be July 13, 1696 (Old Style).

Having established the putative date of his birth, let's now turn to the origins of Pushkin's great-grandfather and his arrival in Russia.

Among the small number of relevant documents first comes the German biography, already mentioned, written by A. K. Rotkirkh (1746–97), who was from 1782 the husband of Abram's daughter Sofia Abramovna (1759–1802).[8]

The existence of the second document about Abram's delivery to Russia was completely unknown to Pushkin and entered Pushkin studies quite recently.[9] I refer to the letter by the translator of the ambassadorial chancellery in Moscow to the chancellery's director, Count Fedor Alekseevich Golovin, about the delivery of three little blackamoors from Constantinople. This letter has allowed us to clarify the muddle and inaccuracy of the German biography in regard to Abram's age, the time of his arrival in Russia, and the date of his entry into service for Peter I. I will return to this letter later.

For all practical purposes, with the exception of short indirect references, these two documents represent all the material we have about Gannibal during the year following his arrival in Russia.

The blackamoor's origins remained a murky and seemingly insoluble issue. Only the German biography gives an account of Gannibal's native land and infancy. This story is followed by Pushkin, and then later by a great number of biographers, scholars, and even writers (for example, Yury Tynianov). Rotkirkh maintains that the poet's great-grandfather was of princely descent. He echoes Gannibal himself, who declared in 1742, in a petition to the Empress Elizabeth: "I, your humble subject, am an African by birth, born into the high nobility there. I was born in the domain of my father, in the town of Logon; in addition, my father ruled two other towns."[10]

The ethnographer D. N. Anuchin[11] and the Soviet political figure N. P. Khokhlov[12] have devoted special studies to hunting down the native land of Gannibal and his forebears, but they did not succeed in establishing his family or the exact place of his birth. However, in Vladimir Nabokov's meticulous study devoted to this subject, "Pushkin and Gannibal," we find a fleeting remark of some significance:

> It would be a waste of time to conjecture that Abram was not born in Abyssinia at all; that he had been captured by slave traders in a totally different place— say, the Lagona region of equatorial Africa, south of Lake Chad, inhabited by Mussulman Negroes.[13]

Dieudonné Gnammankou writes that he was not familiar with Nabokov's article, and that working independently he came to the conclusion that the principality Gannibal mentions, comprised of Logon and two other towns, was in fact the town of Logon, in present-day Cameroon. Nabokov's hypothesis has become a proven fact. Moreover, it became clear that Abyssinia, named by Rotkirkh as his father-in-law's native land, was taken by him from Samuel Johnson's novel *The History of Rasselas, Prince of Abyssinia* (1759). The novel enjoyed great popularity, and in 1785 Friedrich Schiller translated it into German, Rotkirkh's native language, and thus it became the source of the diligent biographer's inspired fantasy.

Nabokov draws direct parallels between events in this novel and Rotkirkh's account of Abram's childhood at his father's court. But Nabokov did not dare propose that not only the details but Abyssinia itself came to Rotkirkh from Johnson's work, while Logon, which enjoyed neither fame nor repute, was expunged from Gannibal's biography.

Two proper nouns mentioned in the story of Abram's childhood have caused some confusion due to their similarity. His native town is Logon; his sister, who supposedly swam after the vessel on which Abram was being carried away by the Turks, is named Lagan. However, it is impossible to check the source of Rotkirkh's account, which was either a story told by the old blackamoor or the latter's notes, the whereabouts of which were unknown already by Pushkin's time. In Rotkirkh's account, the boy is not abducted by slave traders from a neighboring tribe, but rather is taken hostage by the Turks.

The ancestral origins that Rotkirkh traces to Hannibal, the ancient Carthaginian commander, are of course purely his own invention.

Abram's long and difficult journey to Constantinople was completed by the summer of 1703, when the boy would have turned seven. He apparently was placed along with other young blackamoors in the palace—the sultan's spacious residence, which was divided into two halves, where on one side the harem was located, with the seraglio on the other side, separated by a corridor with the men's quarters. There the masters and guests of the house played chess, ate, amused themselves, and slept. The blackamoors were housed in the seraglio, where they were learning the customs of the place and beginning to understand the foreign language.

Istanbul is much farther north than Logon but is much farther south than Moscow. One could say that half of the journey to which fate had destined Abram had already been accomplished, and that Constantinople was merely a stopping-place on this enormous and unknown sojourn into the future. The boy of course did not guess then or later that he was journeying to his immortalization through the works of his great-grandson.

The first representatives from faraway Muscovy to appear before the boy were apparently two distinguished gentlemen. The first was Petr Andreevich Tolstoi, who had not yet been granted the title of count, the cunning Russian ambassador to Constantinople (from 1701 to 1714). He will facilitate the child's abduction to Russia, but the entire operation will be executed by an even more cunning agent of Peter I who hides behind the mask of a merchant, Savva Lukich Vladislavich. He is a Bosnian of the Orthodox faith who fled from his native land, the Ragusan Republic, in order to escape persecution by the Turks. Later, in 1711, his native land will bestow upon him the title of count, and in Russia he will be known by the hyphenated surname Vladislavich-Raguzinsky. For now, in the year 1704, he is simply called Savva Vladislavich, so that later his surname will be mistaken for his patronymic.[14]

The cruelty of the Muslim Turks drove him away from Ragusa, present-day Dubrovnik on the coast of the Mediterranean Sea, lands inhabited by southern Slavs since ancient times. Savva Lukich first came to Russia in 1702 under the guise of a merchant with "olive oil, red calico and cotton." Here, having made the acquaintance of a translator and prominent figure of those days, Spafarius, and evidently not without his assistance, as he was a person with exactly the same fate, Savva Lukich became a trusted agent of Peter I and already in 1703 was sent to Constantinople with expensive Russian furs, which he supposedly was to sell, but to all appearances the furs were used to bribe important Turks.[15] He had journeyed to assist P. A. Tolstoi and even substituted for him temporarily as acting ambassador in 1704 (before June), when Tolstoi traveled home.

We should note that on August 22, 1703, Sultan Mustafa II, after a military coup, was overthrown by his younger brother, who now occupied his place as Ahmed III. Shortly afterward a new grand vizier, Hasan, came to take the place of the old one, and he held his post during the period we are interested in: from November 16, 1703, to September 28, 1704. He was the new sultan's son-in-law and, as Nabokov writes, "he was a very honest and comparatively humane pasha of Greek origin and cannot be suspected of selling the sultan's pages to a foreigner."[16]

However, it was precisely during Hasan's reign that Savva Lukich received three blackamoor boys in the summer of 1704, during the period when he was acting ambassador for P. A. Tolstoi in the Turkish capital. Then he sends them to Moscow with a trustworthy person—a certain Vasil'ev. So as to avoid capture they travel north through the territories of Bulgaria and Muntenia (the eastern part of Walachia, from whence hailed Spafarius, who probably had prudently furnished Savva with letters of introduction to his friends and relatives).

Thus, having spent about a year in Constantinople, Abram once again finds himself on a journey. He would later say that he had set out for Russia from Turkey on his own initiative.

We will cite almost in its entirety a very important letter written by Spafarius in Moscow to Count F. A. Golovin, who may have been with Peter I on the campaign that ended with victory over the Swedes at Narva in August. The letter, dated November 15, 1704, says that the "convoy" from Savva had arrived two days earlier, that is, on November 13. Allow me to say in advance that the date of the arrival of Pushkin's great-grandfather in Moscow and the recording of this event is not the work simply of a bureaucrat but of a contemporary writer, and therefore is a remarkable circumstance.

> My dear sir, Fedor Alekseevich. Before my journey from Constantinople on June 21, Mr. Savva Raguzinsky wrote me that in accordance with the order of Your Grace he had come by at great risk and danger to his life from the Turks *two little blackamoors, and a third* for Ambassador Petr Andreevich, and that he had sent these blackamoors with a man of his over dry land[17] through the Multianian[18] and Volosk lands for reasons of safety. And today, Sir, on the 13th of November, this man of Savva's arrived safely with these blackamoors, and of the three I have selected the two who are better and more clever, and who are *brothers,* and I have delivered them to your most excellent house, the house of your most excellent lady wife, and your most noble children, while the *third one,* who is unfit, I have left for Petr Andreevich, because those were my instructions from Mr. Savva, and his man also said that this one is not suitable.
>
> The younger one was christened Abram, after the nephew of the Multianian ruler, but the older one is still a Moslem . . .
>
> All of Savva's wares arrived safely in Azov with *his young nephew,*[19] and as soon as they arrive here, that which is required by Your Excellency will be taken and delivered.[20]

This letter precisely establishes that three blackamoors were transported and delivered to Moscow, but that the third one was "unfit," that is, sick and weak; and that the other two, who were brothers, were earmarked for Golovin. However, the director of the ambassadorial chancellery undoubtedly intended to make a gift of these two blackamoors to Peter I—and that is why Savva Lukich took such pains "at such great risk and danger to his life."

From Spafarius's letter we learn that the younger of the two brothers, Avraam, was baptized during the journey. This is a completely unexpected piece of information. It has not been possible to establish the identity of the first godfather. However, a few other things can be said in this regard. From June 15, 1704, until 1707 the ruler of Muntenia and Walachia (this was one land which was called by one or the other of its parts) was Constantin Brancoveanu, who at the beginning of his rule was a secret ally of Peter I.[21] Evidently, Spafarius is speaking of Brancoveanu's nephew when he says that "The younger one was christened Abram, after the nephew of the Multianian ruler." Walachia and neighboring Moldavia and Bulgaria on its southern border were Orthodox, which guaranteed sympathy for Savva's envoy while he was traveling through lands subjugated by the Turks.

"Avraam" was a name that had been given to a blackamoor more than once in the early eighteenth century. In addition, we should point out that the feast day of Saint Avraam is celebrated on October 9 (Old Style). Most likely, this first baptism of Abram came about in connection with a stopover on the journey, probably in Iasi. They endeavored to have the baptism coincide with the day of the saint, whose name the child bore. Thus we can surmise that this took place on October 9 (20, New Style), 1704. Undoubtedly, the child understood almost nothing; he may even have subsequently forgotten that he had been baptized, since he would not have understood either the ritual or the language. But he would remember his name—Abram (Avraam).

Savva, fearing for the safety of the blackamoors as well as the fate of important papers he was secretly carrying to be delivered to Peter I, dispatched these blackamoors with an agent, and then departed for Azov, from whence he arrived in Moscow significantly later than the land convoy. Spafarius's letter also tells us that at the same time, perhaps as a blind, Savva sent his regular goods with his nephew by another route from Constantinople to Azov. The boy waited for Savva in Azov, and they then continued the journey together.

Remarkably, documents about Russia's foreign relations preserve the date and list the people who arrived with Savva—there were no blackamoors traveling with him: "January 30, 1705, Savva Raguzinsky returned to Moscow with confidential letters from Ambassador Tolstoi. Traveling with him were the clerk Petr Lukin and his nephew Efim Ivanov Raguzinsky."[22]

Finally, in the same letter Spafarius mentions Abram's older brother. A quarter of a century ago this brother became known from another account as well. In the second and last document concerning the arrival of Pushkin's great-grandfather in Russia, A. K. Rotkirkh writes: "He [Peter I] hit upon the idea of writing to his ambassador who was then in Constantinople,[23] requesting him to secure and send several young African blackamoors [*Mohrenknaben*] of excellent abilities." Later comes the story that after bribing the grand vizier, "he received *three boys*, smart and capable."[24] Raguzinsky—we know from Spafarius's letter that it was he—was

> happy to carry out the will of his sovereign, and dispatched to Moscow *Ibragim Gannibal*[25] *and one other black boy* of noble birth, his countryman, who died on the journey from smallpox, and *one Ragusan, almost the same age, all were younger than nine years of age.*
> The Sovereign, saddened by the loss of the third boy, was pleased to receive these two boys who had arrived and took upon himself the care of bringing them up . . . The Emperor . . . quickly sized up the inclinations of his newly arrived charges and earmarked *his Gannibal*, a lively, smart and hot-tempered

boy, *for military service*, while the Ragusan, later known in Russia as Count Raguzinsky, a quieter and more pensive boy, should go into the civil service [italics mine].[26]

This document corroborates Spafarius's letter, but differs from it in certain details.

Gannibal's children and Rotkirkh had probably heard a number of times that three blackamoors had been abducted from the seraglio. This agrees with Spafarius's communication. But by the end of the eighteenth century the fate of the three boys was murky, and everything had been muddled.

Thus, Rotkirkh reckoned the third boy to be the Ragusan, who could not have been raised in the seraglio, if for no reason other than that he was white and was not suited to be one of the sultan's future pages, all of whom were black. Therefore, Savva Lukich's nephew, a Ragusan, who moreover arrived later and by another route, could not have been one of the three boys. Rotkirkh "kills" one of the young blackamoors on the journey, supposedly from smallpox. This could not have happened on the journey, as becomes clear from Spafarius's letter, but the weak and perhaps youngest one of them evidently did die soon after coming to P. A. Tolstoi's house. The two other boys, who were brothers, found themselves in the care of Peter I.

The elder of these Peter I had baptized in the Preobrazhensky Chancellery, named him Aleksei, and his patronymic (which was also his surname) became the same as his younger brother Abram's—Petrov. In spring 1716 Aleksei set off north to his wife, a serf belonging to the exiled Golitsyn princes. He traveled "by the petition of his, Aleksei's, brother, valet to the sovereign, Abram Petrov." This same document from 1716, housed in the TsGADA archive, makes mention of the fact that Aleksei "has served in the Preobrazhensky Regiment as an oboist from the age of eight."[27]

Such is the fate of the elder brother until the year 1716. However, an obvious lack of special abilities resulted in his rising no higher than regimental musician. His name does not appear again—either he died while his younger brother was studying in France, or he left Russia. Gannibal's children and Rotkirkh knew nothing about him.

Pushkin knew that his great-grandfather did not travel to Moscow with Raguzinsky. He notes that the latter "sent him [Abram] to Peter I, along with two other blackamoor boys."[28]

In Rotkirkh's account the Ragusan whom Peter I had "earmarked . . . for the civil service" grew up to be a count. Evidently the author of the biography has confused the uncle (Savva Lukich) with his nephew Efim Ivanovich, who was a soldier, earned the rank of lieutenant general, was awarded the Order of Alexander Nevsky, and was five years older than Abram. The dates of his life are known: 1691–1749.

However, in his novel Pushkin succeeds in distinguishing the two and in hunting down some materials on the younger one: in *The Blackamoor of Peter the Great,* he notes that upon his return from Paris, Ibragim sees "the young Raguzinsky, his former comrade," in the company of Peter I.[29]

It has been established that this Efim, like Abram, studied abroad, where he ended up in debtors' prison on account of his poverty, and was redeemed from there through the efforts of Konon Zotov, who on March 16, 1716, communicated his pupil's pitiful fate.[30] Thus Pushkin most probably had in mind the friendship between his great-grandfather and the younger Raguzinsky during these student years.

Let us now return to Abram and his older brother, who find themselves in the house of Count Golovin. On December 19, 1704, Tsar Peter returns from the Narva campaign victorious over the Swedes; it's possible that Golovin returned home then as well. Both boys were made a present by him to Peter. The date of this gift cannot be determined, because Peter took up residence in the count's home, and the brothers, it goes without saying, were transferred to his authority. He was able to observe them there, where they had lived for some time before his arrival. Then the older brother was baptized and named Aleksei, and was later appointed regimental musician; Peter drew the younger one closer to himself.

In documents Abram places the beginning of his service to the tsar in the year 1705, that is, he apparently reckons it from the start of the new year. The first surviving evidence of the tsar's favor to him is a note in Peter's ledger of accounts: "February 18, 1705, Abram the blackamoor has been given 15 rubles, 45 kopecks for a service full uniform with trimmings."[31]

Two drawings depicting events from the spring of 1705 have survived. The first is a view of Golovin's residence (by the artist Adrian Schoonebeck) in which Peter held a reception for the Turkish embassy; the departure of the embassy is depicted. The second is a portrait of Peter I with scepter and orb; Swedish ships are exploding in the background (behind his left hand), and the figure of a blackamoor appears to rest his chin on the tsar's right hand. This double portrait, painted from life, was executed by the same Schoonebeck several months before his death in September 1705. Apparently this is the first likeness made of Abram.

Peter continued living in Golovin's house in the German *sloboda* (settlement) until his birthday, May 30 (Old Style). On the following day he set out for Polotsk and Vilno.

Peter set out on the "campaign" (before the eighteenth century any journey, including a pilgrimage, was called a campaign), taking the blackamoor with him.

We have already spoken of their arrival in Vilno and the boy's baptism on July 13, but we should add one remarkable detail. Since Abram had already been baptized, this second baptism was perhaps performed merely to change his name. Peter had decided to call the boy Peter, after himself. The second baptism was performed, but the new name became identified with the boy only formally, which clears up the story about this in the German biography of Gannibal.

Following Rotkirkh, Petr Abramovich Gannibal and Pushkin both repeat what seems to be an odd story. A. K. Rotkirkh: "He was named Peter after his exalted godfather . . . But the general practice of calling him Avraam continued, so that until his death he was called not by his new name, but by the old one . . . and he was called Peter only in clerical records."[32]

P. A. Gannibal in his "Memoirs": "He was given the name Peter, but he was so young and would cry so when he was called by that name, that the Sovereign ordered that he be called by his former name, Avram, the name he bore before his baptism."[33]

A. S. Pushkin's account, based on the preceding sources: "At the baptism he was christened Peter, but he cried so because he did not want to bear the new name that he was called Abram to the day he died."[34]

Thus, this was not a baptism but a rechristening, for which Peter I was present as godfather. Abram's godmother is not mentioned, but Rotkirkh gives his father-in-law a Polish queen to play the role of godmother. This was Christina Eberhardine, the wife of August II. But neither August nor his wife were in Vilno at the time, so this story must remain on Rotkirkh's conscience, or perhaps that of Petr Abramovich, who also presents this version in his "Memoirs." It is difficult to say who took this episode from whom, but Abram himself is innocent.

In the initial period of his service, Abram's duties included giving the tsar slate and chalk when he would wake up during the night. All the biographies of Abram note this fact and treat it as a quirk of Peter's. But only D. N. Bantysh-Kamensky has explained this odd behavior, perhaps basing himself on Pushkin's own account of the matter.[35] The boy did not yet know the language of his new country and did not understand his godfather's speech and, therefore, could only hand him the slate on which Peter would write his notes.

Abram took part in Peter I's military campaigns by the tsar's side in the battle at Lesnaia, and Poltava and in the Prut campaign (1711) and in Gangut (1714). They parted only in June 1717, when the ward was left in Paris to study military science.

What should Abram's duties be called? Pushkin justifiably would become angry when they would call his great-grandfather a valet or lackey. These were duties of a different order. In a document from those years he is rightly called a sentry. The ever-present boy, counted among the trusted and intimate, upon becoming an adult shares both the fate and plans of his godfather.

The conclusion of the triumphant Peace of Nystad (1721) and the end of the long Northern War evoked an ardent response in Abram, who was living in France at the time. He recalled this time five years later when writing the dedication to his manuscripts on geometry and fortifications to Empress Catherine I: "I had the satisfaction of hearing Fame proclaim the glory of the works of our most radiant Russian Mars."[36]

Perhaps the allegorical canvas from the eighteenth century (in the Russian Museum) that depicts Peter I victorious over the Swedes represents the second portrayal of his godson. A dark-skinned youth wearing the uniform of a Preobrazhensky soldier holds the reins of the horse next to the figure of Peter, who has triumphantly placed his foot on the chest of the prostrate Charles XII.[37] We have already spoken about the likelihood of the depiction of a "more youthful" Abram on Pierre-Denis Martin's canvas, which portrays the battle near the village of Lesnaia.

The next stage in the life of Abram Petrov is his residence in France for a period of some five years.

Pushkin did not know how his great-grandfather came to be in Paris. He writes: "Until 1716 Gannibal was inseparable from the sovereign, he slept in his workshop, accompanied him on all his campaigns, and later he was sent to Paris."[38]

However, Abram was not "sent," but rather, he was left there by the tsar whom he had accompanied on his European journey. Among the papers in Peter's archive, approximately ten entries have survived that record gifts made to "Abram the blackamoor" during the course of the journey. Here we find new clothes, boots, stockings, fringe, a special hat, broadcloth, brocade, and finally, just before their parting, when Peter set out for Spa to take the waters before returning to Russia, leaving his godson in Paris, on June 8, 1717: "Avram the blackamoor was given the remainder of his salary for the present year of 1717, 15 *chervontsy,* for which he signed a receipt."[39]

Peter I left Paris on the afternoon of June 9. At first, Abram was very much in want in Paris. He was living with Aleksei Yurov, who, it has come to light, was studying methods for cleaning cockleshells and other things from the bottoms of ships that caused the planks to rot. In other words, he was to some extent connected with engineering and naval matters.

First of all, they had to master the French language. If we bear in mind that the Petersburg Colleges routinely delayed stipends for the students, then it will become clear why Abram in late 1718 wrote to A. V. Makarov, the cabinet secretary: "I have practically neither caftan nor shirt to my name, the masters are teaching us on credit."[40]

In the 1726 dedication of his manuscripts to Catherine I, Abram writes that Peter I entrusted him in Paris to the care of three French grandees. And he names them: the Duke of Maine and his son the Prince of Dombes, that is, the natural son and grandson of Louis XIV; and the chief of the French artillery forces, de Valiere. Abram confused the latter with the Duke of Maine and called him "the natural son of the glorious French king, Louis the Great." The story about the attentions of these grandees was clearly an exaggeration on the part of Abram after he had returned from France, although two of the three names do figure in documents concerning military schools that did indeed open their doors during Abram's tenure.

Worn out by poverty and half-starving for a period of one and a half years, Abram decided to join the king's army as a volunteer when a vacancy presented itself, that is, with the beginning of the war with Spain. This war lasted from January 9, 1719, to February 17, 1720. When the French took the fortress of Fuenterrabia in northern Spain (1719), a skirmish took place in an underground passage and Abram suffered an injury to the head.

In the last days of the war new "centers of instruction" were opened for officer training, by decree of the ten-year-old Louis XV and his regent, Philippe, Duke of Orleans. Abram does not name the location of the school he immediately entered as a captain in the king's army. But in his letters he mentions that it was 100 miles from Paris, which indicates it may have been the fortress and center of instruction in La Fère, located northwest of Paris.[41]

A few letters from Abram and other persons requesting permission to stay on in France have survived. Thus Abram writes to Makarov in the same letter: "If His Imperial Majesty should order me to reside here for the present year so that I might see at least a little practice, because in that school of engineering they have caused to be built an earthen city, which this year we will commence to build, lay out entrenchments, dig trenches, and so forth, which one should know in practice."[42] On March 9, 1722, V. L. Dolgoruky writes in support of this request: "as Abram told me that he needs to live here another year in order to see a great deal more practice."[43]

Poverty once again pursued Abram, because his few *efimiki,* which he had exchanged for the paper currency introduced by the speculator John Law, left him at the mercy of strangers. Thus in a letter to Makarov dated March 5, 1722, he refers to the kindness of Count P. I. Musin-Pushkin who had been in Paris: "We are all in debt here, not because of extravagance but on account of the paper currency about which you, I believe, have heard from Count Musin-Pushkin. What a life it has been here with the local money, if Platon Ivanovich had not been here I would have starved to death: in his mercy he did not abandon me, I lunched and dined with him every day."[44] One must suppose that with the end of the war with Spain, Abram Petrov was no longer paid his officer's salary, so that he now had to pay tuition for his studies.

Only in 1721 did life for the young captain become more attractive, and then only for a short period. If the story of his romance is not to be taken as artistic invention, then the events it presents can only be attributed to these months.

We should say a few words here about the military training in France during this period, training that was completely unknown in Russia, but with which Abram became so familiar. The first French artillery school, which taught both tunneling and the "science" of land fortifications as well as many other things, was opened in Douai in 1679. In addition, training was conducted for regiments of musketeers and bombardiers who were joined together in the artillery regiment by royal decree, dated February 5, 1720. The regiment then began to take up positions in four locations where the "centers of instruction" were situated, the larger of which were called schools. These were located in Douai, Metz, Strasbourg, and La Fère. These schools were in the charge of that same Duke of Maine, to whom, in Abram's words, Peter I had entrusted his fate.

The question of where Abram studied has provoked controversy. In one of the first biographies of him, written by Anna Semenovna Gannibal, Abram's great-granddaughter, the city and school in Metz are named. But this is contradicted by several circumstances, of which we will note two. First, it was precisely La Fère that was situated 100 miles from Paris, while Metz was further away. Second, Abram's teacher, according to the German biography, was the well-known engineer Belidor, who taught in the school at La Fère. However, nobody has considered that the young man may have been in the Metz school before enlisting in the army and the commencement of military action in 1719, and then later found himself in La Fère after the opening of the "center of instruction." The poverty and neglect of Russian students were so great that they were drawn to Paris, where some assistance could be had from the Russian ambassador, Prince V. L. Dolgoruky, and the commercial attaché, Count Musin-Pushkin (in the 1730s he was president of the Commercial College).

Having finished his practical studies in La Fère, Abram embarked on his return journey to Russia in the late fall of 1722. He and several other youths traveled in the suite of the Russian ambassador Dolgoruky, who was returning home after several years of service.

"The latter, upon receiving leave in Rheims on October 17, arrived in Moscow on January 27, 1723, and while presenting himself to the sovereign in the village of Preobrazhensky, he delivered from the King and Regent the re-creditations [dated October 15, 1722] with assurances of loyalty and zeal of that same Dolgoruky in the execution of his commands and the manner of his conduct." This same document concerning Dolgoruky's arrival in Moscow, published by N. N. Bantysh-Kamensky, discloses that "on October 17, the students who were studying in Paris were summoned—Abram the blackamoor, Rezanov, and Korovin—and their accumulated debts were paid in full."[45]

There is an entry in the *Iurnal* for January 27, 1723:

This morning Privy Councillor Vasily Dolgoruky, who had been minister in Paris and who was ordered to return from there, presented himself to His

Majesty; and later, after mass, he, Dolgoruky, was given an audience by Her Majesty the Empress Ekaterina Alekseevna. Today there was a very great snowstorm and it was wet.[46]

Abram later reminded Catherine I of this arrival in the following manner:

> I had the honor upon my return to Russia in 1723 to embrace the feet of Your Majesty, and His Imperial Highness was pleased with his usual mercy towards orphans to appoint me lieutenant in his bombardier company, and by verbal order commanded me to teach military architecture to the young noncommissioned officers and soldiers in the Life Guards.[47]

Peter I met both Dolgoruky and his trusty blackamoor in the village of Preobrazhensky. Rotkirkh did not know about this, and he therefore moved the meeting between godfather and godson to Krasnoe Selo, another small town outside of St. Petersburg. Not only did he muddle the place of this meeting, but he also maintained for the purposes of greater effect that the tsar himself and the tsarina set out to meet the young engineer. Once again Pushkin has no choice but to rely on this family document, and he repeats Rotkirkh's information in his novel.

For an entire year Peter I put his godson to the test. Once again Abram served as secretary and custodian of blueprints. In the summer of 1723 he took part in the grandiose land works in Kronstadt, when they were digging foundation pits for the docks. In a love note to a certain Asechka Ivanovna, Abram complains that every day he is "up to his knees in mud . . . already for a week now . . . there hasn't been a single day that it didn't rain."[48]

On February 4, 1724, a year after his return from France, Peter I made the well-tried Abram "a lieutenant in the bombardier company [to teach] the engineers, from whom it is necessary to select junior officers to be conductors."[49] A "conductor" here means a transmitter, a bearer: a transmitter of knowledge from the "center of instruction"—as the Preobrazhensky Regiment had become—to other officers and other regiments.

According to the stories of his godson, Peter had decided to introduce to Russia the same system of military training as the French one. The twenty-eight-year-old engineer alternated his instruction with trips, most often to the Baltics, to inspect and work on the restoration of the fortresses, which entailed their reorientation toward the sea, against the Swedes. Before the Northern War the fortresses had been intended to provide defense from land routes to the south.

Abram Petrov appears on the rolls of the Preobrazhensky Regiment as Number 1540 during the course of four years, 1724–28. He is named Petrov, Arab [the blackamoor] Abram. The column "Arrival" reads: "1724, lieutenant," and in the column "Departure" the notation reads: "1728, major, transferred to Siberia, to the garrison in Tobolsk."[50] But before these sad and anxious years in Abram's life began, he may be truly considered a "fledgling in Peter's nest."

From late 1724 he was busy with the fortress works in Riga, where the news of Peter's death reached him. The Empress Catherine entrusted the educated blackamoor with the instruction of the heir to the throne, Petr Alekseevich, in the exact sciences. This is when Abram's two-volume work consisting of "Geometrie practique" and "Fortification" comes into being and is presented to the empress. The work includes texts and plans with elements of constructions by Vauban himself. Evidently the notebooks that Abram had brought back with him from France laid the foundation for this work. Both volumes are furnished with the same dedication, copied twice.

Half a year passed, and an adolescent, Abram's pupil, ascended the Russian throne, which, however, would not prove to be beneficial to the teacher. Abram found himself dependent on the favorites, first Menshikov and then the Dolgorukys, who viewed the learned blackamoor with suspicion and hatred, both because he was a foreigner by birth and because he possessed an education. Moreover, Abram had known Aleksasha, the young tsar, from an intimate vantage point; Abram was fully aware of his corruption and thievery.

Abram was exiled to Siberia for his ties with a circle of Menshikov's enemies, Princess Agrafena Volkonskaia and her brother Aleksei Bestuzhev. His journey was anticipated by a letter written by Menshikov: "Due to the fact that he is a foreigner and that it would be dangerous if he were to go abroad, it is ordered that he be kept under strict surveillance."[51]

Abram first traveled to Kazan, then to Tobolsk and Irkutsk, and then to Selenginsk. He was also in Troitskosavsk, named in honor of Savva Raguzinsky, who was Russia's envoy to China during these years. Then Abram returned to Tobolsk and once again set out for Selenginsk.

On July 17, 1728, the Senate issued a decree "on the construction of a fortress on the Chinese border and commissioning Lieutenant Abram Petrov for this task."[52] Abram was to wait for the arrival of the plans from St. Petersburg. From the Senate's summary of Gannibal's report, one can learn how Savva Lukich tried to deliver him from the intrigues of his enemies. He was "dispatched at the request of the ambassador, Savva Raguzinsky, to make a copy of the place he had selected for the relocation of Selenginsk."[53] Selenginsk suffered from floods. Some of Abram's topographical work later became the stuff of family legends, for example, that one of the young engineer's tasks was to measure the Great Wall of China (Rotkirkh and Pushkin).

However, the persecution continued and even intensified. Thus, on December 22, 1729, Abram was searched, dismissed from service, and allotted a ration of ten rubles a month. Later he was transferred to Tomsk, where his ordeals resulting from intrigues, now on the part of the Dolgoruky favorites, came to an end. It was only now that he received the "protocol of the Supreme Privy Council on making Lieutenant-Bombardier Avraam Petrov a major in the Tobolsk garrison."[54] The apparent promotion in fact was a transfer from the Preobrazhensky Life Guards, where he still was formally on the rolls, to the Siberian army regiment, with a recalculation of rank, as stipulated by the law.[55]

In 1729 reconstruction of the Kronstadt fortress commenced, and the Ladoga Canal, which would open in 1731, was being brought to completion, all of which created an acute need for engineers. In 1730, by special decree, foreigners were invited to enter the service, but meanwhile, in September 1730, Count B. Kh. Minikh, making use of the new political situation, secured Abram the blackamoor's transfer to the Estonian town of Pernov (Pärnu).

In Siberia, apparently in an attempt to defend himself from being treated as an exile, Abram Petrov had turned the second part of his name into a patronymic and added on the fine-sounding surname "Gannibal," which he had never used before. In March 1731 he made his way to Pernov, where this surname acquired legal status.

On his journey there he spent some time in St. Petersburg, where on January 17, 1731, Petrov was married to the younger daughter of Andrei Dioper, a Greek captain in the Russian service. This forced marriage was to bring the young couple nothing but sorrow. For Evdokia it was a complete disaster, because their divorce proceedings lasted more than twenty years (1732–53). At their conclusion the unfortunate woman was installed in the Uspensky Staroladozhsky Convent and later the Vvedensky Convent in Tikhvin. Here she was registered as a "novice," that is, she did not take the veil, and here, it seems, she died. By an interesting coincidence, Evdokia Lopukhina, wife of Peter I, languished in the Uspensky Staroladozhsky Convent for six years (1718–24). She had been transferred there from Suzdal for violating her enforced seclusion and for having a liaison with a man. Evidently the court regarded Evdokia Gannibal's offense to be of the same order.

In 1732 Gannibal bought the country house Kärikula, situated 18 miles south of Revel (Tallinn), and he lived there upon his retirement in 1733. There were probably several reasons for his retirement, which lasted about seven years. First, the scandal in the Pernov garrison resulting from the divorce, when he accused Evdokia of adultery and attempting to poison him. It is impossible today to verify the truth of these accusations. Second, the circumstance that in the autumn of 1731 his wife presented him with a little white baby girl, after which the thirst for revenge perhaps led Abram to undertake certain "extreme" measures against his wife.

Ugly rumors about the family of the blackamoor engineer and his reputation as a cuckold probably tormented him, and he tried to escape everything by retiring. It is worth noting that his first petition to retire dates from October 11, 1731, that is, it was submitted soon after the child's birth. The second petition dates from June 7, 1732, but it was not until May 21, 1733, that his petition was granted.

Gannibal's life in the country was filled with fear. Pushkin believed that this fear was the result of his great-grandfather's illegal return from Siberia. However, this was not the case. The fear resulted from an entirely different circumstance: Gannibal had become intimate with the daughter of a retired Swedish army captain, Matthias von Schöberg. Christina Regina von Schöberg was the daughter of an impoverished family. Her mother, born into the distinguished Albedelia family in Riga, found herself in Riga with her eldest son when the city was taken by Peter's army (June 1, 1710). Christina's father was in Sweden, where he had conveyed a group of Russian prisoners. Making use of the cordial invitation of the local nobility to join the Russian army, Matthias returned to his family, but then resigned and moved from Riga to Pernov. It was evidently in Pernov that his eldest daughter Christina came out in 1717 or 1718, followed later by her sisters Juliana and Anna.

According to Evdokia Andreevna's testimony, Gannibal became intimate with Captain von Schöberg's daughter in Pernov as early as 1732, but this is unlikely. There are no grounds to believe that the marriage of Christina and Gannibal was prompted solely by a difficult financial situation, but this factor should be considered as well. While Matthias's landholdings are not documented, the prominent Albedelias, Christina's mother's family, had a number of estates, which surely must have helped to ease the life of Captain von Schöberg's family.

It was most likely in Kärikula on June 5, 1735, that Christina gave birth to her firstborn, Ivan, who was sufficiently dark-complexioned and who bore the typical facial structure (three portraits of him as an adult have survived) to finally calm Abram's jealous heart, and he decided to remarry.[56] Gannibal procured a counterfeit marriage certificate stating that he was a bachelor, and he was married in one of the Revel churches. This took place in 1736, and from that moment his unlawful cohabitation with Christina became even less lawful, since this second marriage was subject to severe punishment by the Christian church, given the existence of a wife whom he had not divorced and whom he had accused of adultery.

Thus began a period in Gannibal's life full of apprehension. With the exception of Count Minikh he had no highly placed patrons. In order to strengthen his position he submitted a petition for an engineer's license, which he received signed by Empress Anna and General Field Marshal Minikh (dated February 7, 1737): "Retired Avraam Petrov Gannibal, formerly Captain in the Engineers, is hereby promoted to the rank of major."[57] Having waited for a vacancy in Revel, Abram terminated his retirement upon his promotion. This took place during the nominal reign of Ivan VI, the regency of his mother Anna Leopoldovna, and Minikh's near sovereignty.

On January 26, 1741, it was recorded that "for his lengthy and impeccable service, Major Avram Petrov Ganibal [sic] is awarded the rank of lieutenant colonel in the Revel artillery garrison."[58] Gannibal's tenure of duty there the first year was marked by innumerable and lengthy messages of complaint he sent to Petersburg about Governor Levendal, the chief commandant of Revel, Major General de Brini, and the major's subordinate Gol'mer. Gannibal was an interloper with a Russian orientation amidst this group of Swedes, and his contentions bear the marks of a troublemaker and at times appear to be motivated by pettiness.

On November 25, 1741, a coup took place in St. Petersburg and Peter the Great's daughter, Elizabeth, became empress. Minikh was arrested and exiled to Pelym. However, his protégé Abram not only did not suffer but was promoted from lieutenant colonel to major general; moreover, he was appointed chief commandant of Revel. At the same time he was granted enormous estates in the Mikhailovskoe district of Pskov with several dozen villages and 569 souls (women and children did not figure in this total), so that more than a thousand peasants lived there. All this was granted on January 12, 1742. The documents, however, were executed only later: the promotion by a license in December 1743, by which Abram Petrovich "formerly lieutenant-colonel in the artillery is today, January 12, 1742, granted the rank of major general."[59] The landholdings were legally assigned by a document executed only on February 6, 1746, which was countersigned by both Elizabeth herself and Abram's old friend, Count Aleksei Bestuzhev-Riumin, now chancellor.

The family legend that was passed down to Pushkin held that after learning about the change in regime in the capital, Abram organized fireworks in Revel and sent a message of congratulation to the new tsarina with a line from the Gospels, namely, the words of the robber who had come to believe in Christ: "Remember me when you enter your kingdom." In addition, in September 1743 Gannibal received the country house Rakhula, which exceeded three times over the acreage of his village and its lands, after which he promptly sold Kärikula.

From the moment Elizabeth came to power Gannibal's interests and plans became more and more tied to St. Petersburg. She had known the loyal blackamoor since childhood, for he was thirteen years older and had probably entertained her more than once during his period of attendance on Peter I.

The war with Sweden (1741–42), which commenced before Elizabeth's reign and was concluded during her rule, and the conditions of the Abo Peace after the war (conclusively settled on August 7, 1743) functioned as a supplementary subject in Abram's intercourse with Petersburg, since Revel had belonged to the Swedes until 1710 and, naturally, there was much there to alarm "Peter's fledgling." In June and July 1742 he bombarded Petersburg with reports that the merchant Witte was a spy; that military proceedings were in progress in Revel; that the Swedes in Courland were buying up grain; that he had seen from a distance Swedish ships on the sea; and that from a tower he had espied fifteen Swedish ships sailing in the direction of Petersburg.[60] He requested that he be made a member of the staff of the provincial office in order to be on the lookout for treachery. However, the empress denied this request, apparently regarding his vigilance as unnecessary fuss and a means to remind her of his person yet once again.[61]

By the summer of 1742 the major general and chief commander of Revel and his wife "Krestina" Matveevna already had several children. Apparently his eldest daughter lived with her nominal father—documents refer to her both as Evdokia and Poliksena (1731–May 11, 1754)[62]—as well as his son Ivan, daughters Elizabeth (b. 1737) and Anna (1741–88), and the newborn Petr (June 21, 1742–June 8, 1826). While Ivan, Elizabeth, and Anna came into this world in Kärikula, Peter (as he would later write) was born in the chief commandant's house in Revel, where Pushkin's grandfather Osip was later born on December 20, 1744.

Allow me to jump ahead of the story somewhat and fill in the other children. Agrippina, who died before 1749, was born in Revel, or possibly in Rakhula or Mikhailovskoe, where Gannibal's wife was living with the children at about this time. Isaak, originally named Savva in honor of Raguzinsky, was born in 1747; and in 1749 Yakov, who died in adolescence some time before 1762, was born. The youngest and last child, Sofia Abramovna, was born after a long interval, on January 24, 1759, apparently in Petersburg, when her mother was about forty-one and her father was in his sixty-third year.

Returning now to Gannibal's military career, we should note that his reminders about himself did not go for naught—he was charged with an important commission: he and the field office, comprised of several men, were to meet in the fall of 1745 with Swedish delegates for the long and exacting work of establishing precisely where the Russian-Swedish borderline ran beyond Vyborg. Initially, the chief person in this matter was his direct superior, General Johann-Ludwig Luberas.

A Scotsman by nationality and a Swede by birth, upbringing, and education, Luberas had become an engineer under Peter in 1709, possibly after the Battle of Poltava, and after transferring to the Russian military, he supervised (from 1722 on) the construction of the port in Paldiski to the west of Revel. From 1741 he was the chief of all engineering and fortification matters in Russia, precisely the post Gannibal would occupy immediately upon Luberas's death in August 1752.

Now, however, in 1745 Luberas was detailed to serve as special ambassador to Sweden. Old age, illness, and most important, his Swedish sympathies rendered his ambassadorship ineffective. Throughout all of autumn 1745, despite the irate rescripts he received from Elizabeth, he delayed concluding the treaty on drawing the borders, whereupon he was removed from his post on December 12, 1745, and was replaced by Baron Korf. However, even then he did not step down and hand over the necessary documents. It was not until mid-November 1746 that he set sail on a yacht for Abo and arrived at the boundary site.

Chancellor M. Vorontsov, in the name of the empress, wrote him that the matter "of such import entrusted to his care, the drawing of the borders, should be concluded with speed."[63] But there was no progress. The arrival of Luberas to the site where he was supposed to put his engineering knowledge to use finally came about after yet more pressure from above, in response to a letter of petition from Gannibal.

While living in various small towns in Finland, Abram had waited for months on end for the arrival of his superior from Stockholm to commence the work of demarcating the border. Gannibal's letter (sent from Stakfors, dated October 12, 1746) to the empress's cabinet secretary, I. A. Cherkasov, can be understood when the preceding delays are taken into consideration. The letter reflects both Gannibal's businesslike nature and his impatience. He asked to be granted leave to travel to his Pskov estates, because "my work here on the border commission, by what misfortune I do not know, has yet to bear fruit."[64] Luberas set out from Sweden a month after this reminder, and Gannibal was not granted leave that autumn of 1746.

In July 1752, six years later, the matter still showed no progress and Luberas was sent inquiries, in particular about why he and his men had dragged their feet back in 1746 and then met with the person "who had drawn the border incorrectly," that is, with Baron Sternstet, "and then later, without the slightest cause, *after the departure of Major General Gannibal,* continued to stay for so long in the same place [italics mine]."[65]

In his replies Luberas wrote about that autumn of 1746: "When I arrived at the border in order to conduct the border commission with Major General Gannibal and the Swedish commissioner, a usable Swedish map had still not been presented."[66] Luberas also referred to a witness of his illness, the same major general, and that together they had made progress with the matter, "to which Major General Gannibal who has been ordered to work with me on the border commission must agree."[67]

Did Gannibal visit in 1746–47 the villages bestowed upon him? It is impossible to reach a conclusive judgment, although we see from the above that he did travel from his station on the border. We know that in 1746 his children (neither he nor his wife are mentioned) lived in the village of Petrovskoe in the parish of the Voronichshkaia Voskresenskaia Church, which is recorded in the church records.

It is firmly established that he was granted leave while in St. Petersburg and from there he set out to "the village indicated" on September 20, 1749. Moreover, the report concerning his return, dated October 30, has been discovered.[68] Not long before his leave he was awarded his first medal, the Order of Saint Anna, which gave him the right to sign himself "Cavalier Abram."

The time from Luberas's death to the end of 1752 remains an obscure period in Gannibal's life. Evidently, the commission continued drawing the border and the process of designating every convenient hill or expanse of water to mark the boundary. Luberas left Finland and saw to completion the Kronstadt Canal, which opened on July 30, 1752. He died two weeks later and his offices were assumed by Gannibal. But the first order of business was once again the demarcation of the border.

On December 17, 1752, A. P. Bestuzhev wrote to M. I. Vorontsov that the empress "has commanded me to notify you that Major General Gannibal should be dispatched as before for the task of the demarcation of the border with Sweden."[69] But this business could only move forward come summer, when the earth was free of snow, which is why it was postponed until May 7, 1753, when the empress "was presented for Her signature an order from the Office of State Affairs regarding a leave of absence for Major General Ganibal from the College of Foreign Affairs, where he is commissioned with the task of demarcating the border with Sweden, to travel to his country house, and is granted a sum of 1,000 rubles to cover his ration allowance and official expenses."[70]

Elizabeth signed the order on July 9, 1753. On April 25, 1752, Abram had already been officially transferred from Revel to St. Petersburg. In 1755 a Senate decree designated Gannibal "the chief commander of fortifications," and on December 25 of that year he was promoted to the rank of lieutenant general (or engineer-general). It was also in 1755 that he was to be appointed governor of Vyborg, closer to his commission and the border, but he flatly refused the appointment—his interests were tied to the capital, as his acquisitions of property there attest. On May 31, 1745, Gannibal had bought for 500 rubles a house and the adjacent buildings, garden, and courtyard "on Vasilevsky Island on the second line on Malyi Prospekt." On June 30, 1750, he bought the adjacent courtyard and buildings in his son Ivan's name. These significant holdings today correspond to the address Malyi Prospekt, Nos. 11 and 13.

Not long before his 1745 acquisition of the buildings, Gannibal was for all practical purposes living in St. Petersburg on a permanent basis, which necessitated, among other things, looking for a student to tutor his children and teach them French. Christina Matveevna asked her confessor, the pastor of the Lutheran church in the Cadet Corps, Hillarius Hartman Henning, to find one for her. On February 21, 1750, Henning wrote to some worthy in Germany about this commission, in the process imparting information about the Gannibal couple. Henning writes: "This gentleman is himself an African and by birth a Moor, he possesses, however, great abilities in the fields of knowledge that he has chosen" (*dieser Herr ist eigentlich ein Afrikaner und ein gebohrener Mohr besetz aber Sonst eine grosse Geschicktlichkeit in denen jenigen Wissenschaftern die zu seinen Foro gehoren*). Henning adds that the general has a good command of French. He speaks with even greater respect of Christina: "The general's wife, moreover, is a very dear lady of good heart and she now is in her full bloom" (*Die Frau Generalin ist sonst eine gai feine Dame von guten Gemüth und stehet an jetzo in einer guten Erweckung*).[71] We should note that it was to Henning that the whole of Gannibal's property was later sold on May 15, 1757, when the general apparently moved to his house outside the city.

In that same year of 1757 Gannibal was listed as a member of the commission charged with the inspection of Russian fortresses. Two years later, as recorded by decree, dated November 1, 1760, he was made a full general: "On October 23, 1759, General Engineer Gannibal is promoted to the rank of full general in conjunction with his appointment to the Ladoga Canal and to the commission on the Kronstadt and Rogervik construction works."[72] And so Gannibal was made a full general and was awarded his second and last Order of Alexander Nevsky (August 30, 1760), which was presented by the empress in person. This was the pinnacle of his career.

In January 1759 the last child of the honorable general was born, his daughter Sofia, through whom the Gannibal family would subsequently form ties with many prominent German-Swedish families, including the Vrangels. Direct descendants of this youngest daughter would include the poet L. D. Zinov'eva-Annibal, the art historian N. N. Vrangel, and his brother, the White general P. N. Vrangel.

Gannibal was not obliged to make regular appearances at the Engineer Corps, and in the period 1756–57, apparently carried away by the acquisition of properties near Petersburg, he "reported sick for eighteen months, was present 17 days, and for the remainder performed his duties as commander for 23 days."[73]

It is possible that he spent some time on his Mikhailovskoe estate, most likely after the sale of his Petersburg property in May 1757. We do not know when he purchased his first property near the capital, that is, the country house Suida and the villages. However, this can be easily calculated by events in the life of the family from which he made this first purchase.

Peter I had made presents of the lands in Ingermanland, liberated from the Swedes during the course of the Northern War, to members of his closest circle. The first Russian owner of Suida and its villages in 1716 was the eldest of the three Apraksin brothers, Petr Matveevich (1659–1728). These lands then were inherited by his son Aleksei, who died in 1735. The owner then became his widow Elena Mikhailovna, née Princess Golitsyna (1712–47). She left behind two young sons, both officers in the Semenovsky Regiment. The elder, Prince Petr Alekseevich (1728–57), married Princess Anna Borisovna Golitsyna (1730–1811), but scandalous divorce proceedings were soon begun (the second such in the eighteenth century!). She had powerful connections and in an attempt to give her less of his grandfather's patrimony, Petr came to an agreement with Gannibal regarding the swift conversion of his immovable property into cash. The matter, however, had not been concluded when the offended husband passed away. His brother, Prince Fedor Alekseevich (1733–89) came into possession, but this legal transfer required time. The church records of the Voskresenskaia Church name Fedor the owner of Suida in 1758. Fearful of his brother's widow's claims, he was also interested in converting as much of his property as possible into cash. The purchase and sale evidently took place in late 1758, when Lieutenant Captain Fedor, aged twenty-five, resigned his commission and left the estates that had once belonged to his grandfather. In any event, in the spring of 1759 the name Gannibal replaces the name Apraksin in those same church records of the Voskresenskaia Church near Suida. Thus Gannibal's long absence from duty can also be explained by the upheavals concerning his property holdings that continued for two years.

In addition to the country estate of Suida and the village of Voskresensky, Abram also received the villages of Melnitsa and Kobrino. Two or three years later he also purchased the adjoining land. This land purchase included the country house Elitsa and the villages Kuznetsovo, Pogost, and Malaia Vopsha. Soon afterward the third and last purchase of land was made from General A. I. Golovin, the brother of Pushkin's great-grandmother Evdokia. This time Gannibal bought estates that did not border on his own land, though they were not far away: Malye Taitsy and the villages Imochala, Staritsy, Ivanovskaia, Tikhvino, Istiny, Pegelevo, and Malaia i Bol'shaia Orovka.

In the will made on his eightieth birthday Abram divided the ownership among his four sons. (The daughters received, upon their marriage, a cash dowry.) The eldest, Ivan, was given all of the Pskov lands granted Gannibal, as well as Suida and the villages (with the exception of Kobrino); Petr got Elitsa and its villages; Osip was given Kobrino and the country house Runovo that had been built nearby. The striking unfairness to Osip was brought about by his father's displeasure at his son's sensational divorce from Maria Alekseevna, née Pushkina—Pushkin's maternal grandmother—which had taken place the same year. Isaak and his innumerable descendants were given all of the Taitsy property. The house in St. Petersburg is not mentioned in the will; its construction was begun later, in 1779–80 (it has been rebuilt and today bears the address 29 Chaikovsky Street). Petr Abramovich would sell this house in the early nineteenth century.

From the late 1750s Gannibal's businesslike nature and conscientious performance of his duties somewhat gave way to his efforts on behalf of his estates. The information regarding his absences, the 2,755 protocols and 189 orders that went unsigned by him, may not be completely accurate: the general was at odds with his direct superior, Count P. I. Shuvalov.

In late 1761 Empress Elizabeth died, and Shuvalov died in January 1762. Field Marshal A. N. Vil'boa assumed his position. During the reign of Peter III, several days before Catherine's coup, Gannibal was retired "on account of his advanced age" (June 9, 1762). But no reward was forthcoming—they were clearly dissatisfied with him.

Upon his return from twenty years of exile, which he had spent in seclusion in the city of Pelym, Minikh was appointed to Gannibal's position, even though he was considerably older than his one-time protégé.

A month later, when Catherine II had already assumed the throne, Gannibal petitioned that he be granted, in recognition of his fifty-seven years of service, property that bordered his to the south—Kurovitsy and others. But no reply was ever made to this petition.

Deeply offended, Gannibal parted with the world of St. Petersburg for good, lived in Suida, and probably occasionally visited his Pskov estates. It should be noted that he spoke of his resentment to his intimates and that the legend of the ingratitude shown him by Russia's rulers lived on in his family. This legend was repeated to his great-grandson who, combining the lime-tree avenues of Suida and Petrovskoe in his imagination, writes about the "forgotten one who had lived in the same house" as tsars and tsaritsas, "who concealed himself under the shade of linden lanes," who in his old age would recall his "far-off Africa."

The aged Gannibal's reminiscences would be recorded five or six years later by Sofia's fiancé Adam (or Adolf) Karpovich Rotkirkh, who adorned them with colorful details of his own. The last twenty or so years of Abram's life belonged to Suida, as they had once been claimed by Kärikula, and "he began a second time, like a wise man, country life in peace and quiet." That is how Rotkirkh phrases it in the German biography.[74] In his paraphrase of these words, Pushkin notes that his great-grandfather "died a philosopher."[75]

Rotkirkh composed the German biography on Petr Abramovich's estate, where he was the steward. At first Petr lived in Kherson, then in Petersburg, and from 1786 on he lived in Petrovskoe in Pskov. Apparently Petr's sister Sofia and her husband Adolf-Adam brought their children into the world while living on this estate. Upon becoming a judge in the city of Sofia (today part of the city of Pushkin) after Petr Abramovich's sale of Elitsy in 1792, Adam Karpovich, several months before his death, was granted extensive properties by Paul I. His eldest daughter inherited the country house of Kaibola and his son Ivan received Novopiatnitskoe, on the outskirts of the city of Iamburg.

A. P. Gannibal

The German biography apparently was kept in Kaibola, where Nadezhda Osipovna Pushkina and her daughter Olga paid a visit from Revel in 1827.[76] Very probably, a local German clerk made a copy of the German biography there and it is this copy (the paper of which was manufactured in 1826) that they brought to Pushkin.[77] The reasons for Pushkin suspending work on *The Blackamoor of Peter the Great* may be attributed to several causes, one of which was the lack of concrete historical information about his great-grandfather, material that was to be found only in Rotkirkh's complete text. The full copy of the German biography was acquired by Pushkin no earlier than the beginning of October 1827, that is, *after* he had set aside the novel that he was never to take up again. There is no doubt, however, that he had at his disposal his own abridged translation of the German biography when he had begun work on the novel in late July 1827.[78]

The hypothesis that the copy of the German biography was in the possession of Petr Abramovich and came to Pushkin after the old man's death (June 8, 1826), as proposed by N. G. Zenger in the commentary to the publication of the German biography and then seconded by myself, is groundless.[79] However, Petr Abramovich must have had some variant of the German biography, because the abridged translation was in Pushkin's possession as early as fall 1824, when he wrote the commentary to the first chapter of *Eugene Onegin* about his great-grandfather, as well as in the summer of 1827, when he was writing *The Blackamoor of Peter the Great*.

The source of this abridged translation can *only* be the text that was in P. A. Gannibal's possession. Otherwise, we must suppose that Pushkin at some point before 1820 visited his relatives who lived near Iamburg, read the German biography and made an extract of it for himself, and then kept it safe for a period of approximately five years during his southern exile.

The original of the German biography traveled to Novopiatnitskoe, where it became the property of Vladimir Rotkirkh, Adam Karpovich's grandson. In the late nineteenth century it was discovered by the Lelong family, which inherited the Novopiatnitskoe estate from Vladimir Rotkirkh. In 1900 the original became the property of B. L. Modzalevsky and was then given to Pushkin House. The copy of the German biography remained in Pushkin's possession until his death and later ended up in that same Pushkin House among other documents that had belonged to the poet.

As we conclude this sketch of the "life and works" of Abram Petrovich Gannibal, we should say a few words about the personality and temperament of this Russian African. His character was marked by resourcefulness and complaisance, tempered by tenacity, and a flexibility that was mixed with stubbornness. As a result of the difficulties he experienced as a child, Gannibal became a fawner who knew how to humble himself (in the tradition of the eighteenth century), but he could also be obstinate and fairly provoking. He distinguished himself by his devotion not only to his godfather Peter I but also to Peter's daughter Elizabeth, and consequently he sided with the "Russian" party of Princess Agrafena Volkonskaia and her brother Count Bestuzhev-Riumin. His thirst to fit in with his new country was great and understandable, for his African appearance, French training, and unknown origins made for a very uneasy position. This made for trouble with his Swedish-German colleagues during his years of duty in the Baltic region, and later by his almost scandalous unwillingness to compromise that prolonged the conclusion of the border settlement with Sweden. The victory of the "German" faction under Peter III brought about his downfall and he retired. Cruel to his first wife, whom he used to beat "unmercifully," according to Evdokia Andreevna's own testimony, he was capable of gratitude and thoughtfulness for his faithful Christina. We should note that in his will he asks that his sons not divide the property among themselves until after the death of their mother. A zealous landlord, who in old age enjoyed the same sense of freedom and an equal footing with the Petersburg grandees—rank, honors, and wealth gave him the right to do so—he gained respect in society, acquired a sense of self-respect hitherto suppressed and a stately demeanor. His difficult and colorful life was crowned by a noble end in deep old age with the knowledge that he had brought up four fighting sons for Russia, of whom the eldest, the hero of Navarino, who was treated with such affection by Catherine II, brought particular joy to the father.

The age of excess and good living would frustrate Gannibal's dream of securing for his descendants a place among the aristocracy. The Petersburg properties would eventually be sold and the dwindling family would remain firmly established only on the distant Pskov estates.

Nobody would remember the innumerable provincial gentryfolk, whose most remarkable feature was their legendary forebear (whom they found an embarrassment), if it were not for the trick of fate that sent this "blackamoor of Peter the Great" a great-grandson who would be born years after the blackamoor's death and who would be the grandson of Abram's dissipated son Osip and his abandoned wife, whose maiden name he would immortalize, as well as all his family and everybody who even from afar touched upon his life or its origins.

Notes

This article has been translated by Ronald Meyer. The original publication, "P. A. Gannibal (k trekhsotletiiu pradeda A. Pushkina," which appeared in *Russian Studies* (St. Petersburg) 12, no. 3 (1996): 58–93, has been slightly abridged.

1. The date of Abram's death is given by his son Petr. See N. K. Teletova, "K nemetskoi biografii Gannibala," in *Pushkin: Issledovaniia i materialy*, vol. 10 (Leningrad, 1982).

2. For this new information, see Dieudonné Gnammankou's *Abraham Hanibal: L'aieul noir de Pouchkine* (Paris, 1996).

3. A. Gannibal, "Pis'mo ot 10 noiabria 1780," Vserossiiskii muzei Pushkina, f. 3, d. 3.

4. A. S. Pushkin, *Polnoe sobranie sochinenii*, 17 vols. (Moscow and Leningrad, 1937–59), 11:162.

5. L. Skiliavichius, "Istochniki tain," *Vechernie novosti* (Vilnius), February 26, 1985.

6. I. I. Golikov, *Deianiia Petra Velikogo* (Moscow, 1788), 2:175, 179; N. G. Ustrialov, *Istoriia tsarstvovaniia Petra Velikogo* (St. Petersburg, 1863), 4:374.

7. N. K. Teletova, "Vospominaniia P. A. Gannibala," in *Zabytye rodstvennye sviazi A. S. Pushkina* (Leningrad, 1981), 142.

8. The German biography and a translation into Russian with commentary were published by N. G. Zenger in *Rukoiu Pushkina* (Moscow and Leningrad, 1935), 43–56. See also Teletova, "K nemetskoi biografii Gannibala."

9. Teletova, "Vospominaniia P. A. Gannibala," 123.

10. Ibid., 170.

11. D. N. Anuchin, *A. S. Pushkin: Antropologicheskii eskiz* (Moscow, 1899).

12. N. P. Khokhlov, *Prisiaga prostoram* (Moscow, 1973).

13. Vladimir Nabokov, "Abram Gannibal," in Aleksandr Pushkin, *Eugene Onegin*, trans. Vladimir Nabokov, 4 vols. (New York, 1964), 3:436.

14. In his *History of Peter I*, Pushkin pays particular attention to Savva Vladislavich, since he is aware of his role in the fate of his great-grandfather. (See, for example, *Polnoe sobranie sochinenii*, 10:158.)

15. Nikolai Gavrilovich Milescu Spafarius (1636–1708), a scholar and writer, fled to Russia to escape the persecution of the Turks, who had tortured him and cut off his nose. "Spafarius," a high rank in Walachia, became his sobriquet in Russia. Later, like Raguzinskii, he traveled to China on an important ambassadorial mission.

16. Nabokov, "Abram Gannibal," 418.

17. The usual route from Constantinople to Moscow passed through Azov, that is, it began via the sea.

18. The eastern mountainous part of Walachia.

19. That is, Efim Ivanovich Vladislavich (Raguzinskii).

20. "Pis'mo Spafariia k boiarinu Golovinu," *Russkii arkhiv* (Moscow, 1867), 308–9 (emphasis mine).

21. A. Kochubinskii, "Snosheniia Rossii pri Pertre Velikom s iuzhnymi

slavianami i rumynami," *Chteniia v. imp. obshchestve istorii i drevnastei Rossiiskikh pri Moskovskom universitete* no. 2 (1872).

22. D. N. Bantysh-Kamenskii, *Slovar' dostopamiatnykh liudei russkoi zemli*, 5 vols. (Moscow, 1836), 2:243.

23. That is, Raguzinskii, acting ambassador, who "was *then* in Constantinople."

24. Zenger, *Rukoiu Pushkina*, 51.

25. He adopts this surname only much later.

26. Zenger, *Rukoiu Pushkina*, 51.

27. V. Kozlov, "Kogda rodilsia praded Pushkina Gannibal?" *Nedelia*, no. 44 (1969): 14.

28. Pushkin, *Polnoe sobranie sochinenii*, 12:312.

29. Ibid., 8:11.

30. P. P. Pekarskii, *Vvedenie v istoriiu prosveshcheniia v Rossii XVIII stoletiia* (St. Petersburg, 1862), 1:158.

31. N. A. Malevanov, "Petra pitomets A. P. Gannibal," *Neva*, no. 2 (1972): 192.

32. Zenger, *Rukoiu Pushkina*, 52.

33. Teletova, "Vospominaniia P. A. Gannibala," 172.

34. Pushkin, *Polnoe sobranie sochinenii*, 12:312.

35. Bantysh-Kamenskii, *Slovar' dostopamiatnykh liudei russkoi zemli*, 2:12.

36. Teletova, "Vospominaniia P. A. Gannibala," p. 143.

37. For more information on the iconography of A. P. Gannibal, see my articles "Gannibaly—predki Pushkina," in *Belye nochi* (Leningrad, 1978); and "O mnimom i podlinnom izobrazhenii A. P. Gannibala," in *Legendy i mify o Pushkine* (St. Petersburg, 1994).

38. Pushkin, *Polnoe sobranie sochinenii*, 12:312.

39. E. I. Ukraintsev, *Sbornik vypisok iz arkhivnykh bumag o Petre Velikom* (Moscow, 1872), 2:68.

40. M. Vegner, *Predki Pushkina* (Moscow, 1937), 146.

41. M. A. Tsiavlovskii was the first to put forward La Fère as the place where Gannibal studied.

42. A. S. Gannibal, "Gannibaly, novye dannye dlia ikh biografii," in *Pushkin i ego sovremenniki*, vyp. 17–18 (St. Petersburg, 1913), 208–9.

43. A. S. Gannibal, "Gannibaly," 212.

44. Ibid., 211.

45. N. N. Bantysh-Kamenskii, *Obzor vneshnikh snoshenii Rossii: (po 1800 g)*, pt. 1 (Moscow, 1894), 93–94.

46. *Iurnal 1723* (St. Petersburg, 1855), 6.

47. Teletova, "Vospominaniia P. A. Gannibala," 143.

48. S. N. Shubinskii, "Kn. A. P. Volkonskaia i ee druz'ia," *Istoricheskii vestnik*, no. 12 (1904): 931.

49. Vegner, *Predki Pushkina*, 33.

50. *Istoriia Leib-gvardii Preobrazhenskogo polka: 1663–1883* (St. Petersburg, 1883), 4:169.

51. Vegner, *Predki Pushkina*, 45.

52. P. I. Baranov, *Opis' vysochaishim ukazam za XVIII vek (1725–1740)* (St. Petersburg, 1875), 2:157, no. 3116.

53. *Senatskii arkhiv* (St. Petersburg, 1901), 9:532.

54. Baranov, *Opis' vysochaishim ukazam*, 2:215, no. 3725.

55. A number of works have been written about Gannibal's Siberian exile. See, for example, N. Pavlenko, "Gannibal v Sibiri," *Neva*, no. 8 (1983).

56. According to A. K. Rotkirkh's account, Ivan was born in 1735, but on February 13. See A. K. Rotkirkh, "Nemetskaia biografiia A. P. Gannibala. Podlinnik 1786/87 g.," Pushkinskii dom, f. 244, op. 24, ed. khr. 19.

57. "Patent. O dvorianstve Gannibalov, 1842–1843," RGIA, f. 1343, op. 19, ed. khr. 617.

58. *Senatskii arkhiv* (St. Petersburg, 1889), 2:455.

59. "O dvorianstve Gannibalov, 1842–1843," RGIA, f. 1343, op. 19, ed. khr. 617.

60. *Senatskii arkhiv*, vol. 5 (St. Petersburg, 1892).

61. Ibid.

62. The date of her death and the place of burial at the Church of the Annunciation on Vasil'evskii Island were established by L. I. Broitman on the basis of an archival document. See her "Belaia noch' Gannibala," *Vechernii Leningrad*, April 14, 1988.

63. *Arkhiv gr. M. Il. Vorontsova* (Moscow, 1887), 33:436.

64. A. S. Gannibal, "Gannibaly," 244.

65. *Arkhiv gr. M. Il. Vorontsova* (Moscow, 1887), 33:436 (emphasis mine).

66. Ibid., 440.

67. Ibid., 444.

68. A. i Ia. Gordiny, "Gannibal, Mikhailovskoe, Pushkin," *Neva*, no. 6 (1988): 195.

69. *Arkhiv gr. M. Il Vorontsova* (Moscow, 1871), 2:169.

70. *Arkhiv gr. M. Il. Vorontsova* (Moscow, 1875), 7:322.

71. We should note that a woman's full bloom, her acme, came at the age of thirty-three. Christina Matveevna was thirty-three years old in 1750. See E. A. Prianishnikov, "Novyi dokument ob Abrame Petroviche Gannibale i ego sem'e," in *Iz kollektsii redkikh knig i rukopisei nauchnoi biblioteki Moskovskogo universiteta* (Moscow, 1981), 76–77.

72. P. I. Baranov, *Opis' vysochaishim ukazam za XVIII vek* (St. Petersburg, 1878), 3:447, no. 11717.

73. D. Blagoi, "A. P. Gannibal—arap Petra Velikogo," *Molodaia gvardiia*, no. 3 (1937): 85.

74. Zenger, *Rukoiu Pushkina*, 56.

75. Pushkin, *Polnoe sobranie sochinenii*, 12:313.

76. *Pis'ma S. L. i N. O Pushkinykh k ikh docheri O. S. Pavlishchevoi* (St. Petersburg, 1993), 206.

77. It is worth noting that two miles from Kaibola (known as Kaibolovo today) lay the village of Udosol (now Udosolovo), the entailed estate of the Bloks, which was given by Paul I to the physician Ivan Leont'evich Blok, great-great-grandfather of another great poet.

78. In the Academy edition of Pushkin's complete works, the abridged translation is designated as "Biografiia Gannibala" (12:434).

79. Teletova, "K nemetskoi biografii Gannibala," 10:272.

J. Thomas Shaw

Pushkin on His African Heritage: Publications during His Lifetime

PUSHKIN WAS PROUD of both sides of his family genealogy. At the same time, he was sensitive about each of them. Any consideration of his African heritage and his attitude toward it must be undertaken in the context of his Russian heritage and his attitude toward it. This essay will focus on the direct reflection of Pushkin's African ancestry in works published during his lifetime, particularly those he himself completed and published (or wished to publish). It would require an extensive monograph to examine with any adequacy all aspects of the relationship of Pushkin to his African heritage—how that ancestry affected him as man and writer. That would have to include not only his public life as writer and man of society, but his private life as well; it would need to include consideration of works he began but did not complete, the indirect effects of that heritage on his work and personality, and the testimony of contemporaries to these points in such things as letters and memoir literature. Here we shall concentrate on what Pushkin said about his African ancestry for the perusal of the reading public of his day and the effects of these publications on his own career. I have found no previous study that has approached the question from this angle.

There has been much study of Pushkin's ancestry on both sides of his family, and recently there has been great interest in his African great-grandfather and his descendants in Russia.[1] Pushkin was particularly proud of Abram Petrovich Gannibal, as he came to be known, and one of his sons, Ivan Gannibal. Abram Gannibal was obtained for Peter the Great in Constantinople; he became the godson, ward, and favorite of Peter, who took Gannibal on expeditions with him and sent him to France for a time. However, Peter the Great died suddenly in 1725, not long after Gannibal's return from France. After that, Gannibal was out of favor until Peter's daughter Elizabeth came to the throne in 1741. He was recalled to active duty in the army and promoted to the rank of general. Under the system set up by Peter the Great, his rank gave him and his family the status of members of the hereditary Russian nobility. However, Gannibal's appeal for the recognition of noble status was made on the basis of his father's being a local ruler in Africa. No action was ever taken on this petition. Abram's son Ivan also eventually became a full general in the army, and served with distinction, especially during the Greek archipelago campaign of 1770, when, as the commander of a landing party, he defeated Turkish forces on the Greek mainland at Navarino; he was in charge of fire control in the naval Battle of Chesma Bay in the same year. Ivan Gannibal acted as sponsor of Pushkin's mother at her social debut, which led to her marriage to Pushkin's father.

Any treatment of Pushkin's African heritage with regard to both his published works and his life must concern itself also with terminology and the overtones of words used in Russia at the time. The relevant terms are "Negro" (Russian *negr,* French *nègre*), "blackamoor" (Russian *arap*), and mulatto (Russian *mulat, mulatka*). Pushkin himself, in a letter written during the last year or so of his life, clearly presented his view of the difference between the homonyms *arap* and *arab,* emphasizing an orthographic distinction that is not always observed in memoirs about him:

> *Arab* (does not have a feminine), a dweller or native of Arabia, an Arabian. *Karavan byl razgrablen stepnymi arabami* [The caravan was plundered by the Arabs of the steppes].
>
> *Arap* [blackamoor], feminine *arapka*; this is what Negroes and mulattoes are usually called. *Dvortsovye arapy,* Negroes serving in the palace. *On vyezzhaet s tremia nariadnymi arapami* [He is leaving with three finely dressed blackamoors]. (Letter to P. A. Viazemsky, second half of 1835 or in 1836; *PSS* 16:208[2])

Neither Pushkin (as the above passage shows) nor other Russians of his time made any distinction between *negr* and *arap,* that is, between blacks from different parts of Africa. Later on, ethnographers classified northern Africans as "Hamitic" and "Caucasoid," and Africans south of the Sahara as "Negroid." This distinction has usually been made in studies of Pushkin since D. I. Anuchin's "anthropological study" (1899)—both in Russia and abroad.[3] By *arap* or *negr* or *mulat(ka)* Pushkin included all black Africans. When he spoke of "my brothers the Negroes,"[4] he included not only blacks from Egypt or Tunis but also the black slaves then in the New World (that is, blacks from south of the Sahara, now classified as Negroid, as well as the blacks now considered Caucasoid).

It should be emphasized that there is nothing to indicate that Pushkin's having a black ancestor hindered his acceptance as a Russian man of letters. On the contrary, when his first Romantic verse tale, *The Prisoner of the Caucasus,* appeared in 1822, his publisher, N. I. Gnedich, obviously thought it would help sales to have a frontispiece emphasizing Pushkin's black heritage; Gnedich provided such a lithograph without consulting the author.[5] Furthermore, there is no evidence that Pushkin's African ancestry hindered his acceptance in Russian society, though neither his father's nor his mother's heritage gave him immediate entry to the highest circles of it. Curiously enough, it was not the Pushkin (or the Gannibal) family connections, or Pushkin's genius as a writer that, after his marriage, resulted in his having access to the "great world around the throne," but rather his wife's beauty and her family connections.

No work of Pushkin's deals exclusively with his African ancestry. His mentions of, or allusions to, that ancestry always occur in a larger context; they form only *passages* or *parts* of longer works, even when the entire work is only a short lyric. These mentions are listed in table 1, along with the date of composition, publication, and republication, if any, during his lifetime. There are ten of them, five in verse and five in prose. The first was published in 1825, and between 1828 and 1831, *all* that were published or widely circulated during his lifetime either appeared for the first time or were republished. This time of concentrated publication includes Pushkin's most productive literary period, and it coincides with his period of courtship with a view to marriage and the first year of his married life.

Table 1

	Written	Published	Republished
1. "To Yur'ev"	v 1820	1829	
2. *EO* 1.50 verse	v 1823	1825	1829, 1833, 1837
3. *EO* 1.50 note	p 1824	1825	1829; rev. 1833; 2nd rev., 1837
4. "To Yazykov"	v 1824	1830	1832
5. "To Dawe, Esq."	v 1828	1828	1829
6. "Chapter IV"	p 1827	1828	1834
7. "Assembly"	p 1827	1830	1834
8. Note on *Poltava*	p 1830	1831	
9. "My Genealogy"	v 1830		
10. "Table-Talk"	p 1835–36		

Note: v = in verse; p = in prose

The first two that Pushkin published appeared in the first chapter of his novel in verse, *Eugene Onegin*: he mentions his African ancestry specifically both in the verse and in a rather lengthy note in prose. Pushkin also wrote four individual lyrics that allude to his African ancestry.[6] He published separately two individual chapters ("Chapter IV" and "Assembly") of his uncompleted

J. Thomas Shaw

novel *The Blackamoor of Peter the Great* about his black great-grandfather (though he is not explicitly named in the part Pushkin himself published). Pushkin's African heritage may also be considered to be implied in two notes in which he mentions Othello, the most famous Moor in literature: one of them was in the Note on *Poltava*, the other in his "Table-Talk"; the second of these was written during the last year or so of his life, and he did not live to see it in print. *Both* sides of Pushkin's ancestry are dealt with in a lyric, "My Genealogy," which was not printed but was widely circulated in handwritten copies.[7]

Thus the publication and/or republication of all of Pushkin's works that deal with his African heritage and appeared in print during his lifetime was concentrated in the years 1828–31: every one of them was published or republished during these years. And the wide circulation of "My Genealogy" constituted an obviously deliberate kind of publication.

EUGENE ONEGIN, CHAPTER 1, STANZA 50, AND NOTE

The most important of Pushkin's publications on the subject of his African heritage during his lifetime is part of a "flight of the imagination" at the end of the first chapter of *Eugene Onegin*. This chapter appeared as a separate publication early in 1825. At the time of its writing (1823), Pushkin was in exile in Kishinev and then Odessa, under the guise of a transfer in government service, because of "liberal" (Russians say "revolutionary") poems. When he published it, he had been dismissed from the service and was in open exile and disgrace (*v opale*) on his mother's estate of Mikhailovskoe. Under the censorship of the time, direct mention of his exile was impossible in print, and the notion of his actually "fleeing" from Russia could not have been published. One could, however, present a poetic flight of the imagination. In the *Onegin* passage, the first such "poetic flight" is to Italy (*EO* 1.49). The second, in the following stanza, is to "my Africa." This second "flight of the imagination" is so important and relevant that it should be quoted, and the note he appended to it as well:

Придет ли час моей свободы?
Пора, пора! — взываю к ней;
Брожу над морем жду погоду,
Маню ветрила кораблей.
Под ризой бурь с волнами споря,
По вольному распутью моря
Когда ж начну я вольный бег?
Пора покинуть скучный брег

> Мне неприязненной стихии,
> И средь полуденных зыбей,
> Под небом Африки моей,
> Вздыхать о сумрачной России,
> Где я страдал, где я любил,
> Где сердце я похоронил. (*EO* 1.50)

> Will the time of my freedom come? It's time, it's time! I call to her; I wander along the shore, I await good weather, I beckon the sails of ships. When shall I begin my free flight under the canopy of storms, contesting with the waves, over the free crossroads of the sea? It is time to abandon the boring shore of the element hostile to me, and amid southern billows under the skies of my Africa, to sigh for gloomy Russia, where I have suffered, where I have loved, where I have buried my heart.

The point of view expressed here is paradoxically and typically Pushkinian: he will take a "free flight" from the Russian shore where the sea is "hostile to me," to the friendly southern billows under the skies of "my Africa." However, once there, he will sigh for Russia. The important themes include "poetic flight" (for one whose actual fleeing would have constituted a crime), travel to the south, memory of Russia from afar (from south to north), and "my Africa."

In a long footnote Pushkin explained the term "my Africa" and gave information about his great-grandfather. During his lifetime, he published the stanza four times, with no changes in the verse. In the 1829 reprint of the first chapter, the appended note remained almost identical in form to that published in 1825. However, in the last two reprintings of the first chapter (when all the chapters of the novel were published together, in 1833 and 1837), the note was sharply cut. Here we shall focus on the long form of it.

Here follows my translation of the note as it originally appeared (the only changes in 1829 are the transposition of the last two paragraphs and the incorporation of the square-bracketed note into the text). It is curious that he here cites his great-grandfather's surname as "Annibal," instead of the form "Gannibal," which he uses later.

> The author, on his mother's side, is of African extraction. His ancestor Abram Petrovich Annibal in his 8th year was abducted from the shores of Africa and taken to Constantinople. The Russian ambassador, after rescuing him, sent him as a present to Peter the Great, who had him christened at Vilno. A brother of his came to get him, first to Constantinople, and then to Petersburg, proposing a ransom for him; but Peter I did not agree to return his godson. Until deep old age Annibal still remembered Africa, his father's luxurious life, 19 brothers, of whom he was the youngest; he remembered how they would

be led to their father with hands bound behind their backs, while he alone was free and would go swimming under the fountains at his father's house; he also remembered his favorite sister, Lagan', who swam from a distance after the ship on which he was departing.

At 18 years from his birth, Annibal was sent by the Tsar to France, where he began his service in the army of the Regent; he returned to Russia with a broken head and the rank of a French lieutenant. From that time, he was constantly in attendance upon the Emperor. During the reign of Anna, Annibal . . . was sent to Siberia under a plausible pretext. Bored with the absence of human life and the severity of the climate, he returned to Petersburg without authorization. . . . Annibal departed to his own estates, where he lived during all Anna's reign, while being considered as being in the service and in Siberia. Elizabeth, upon ascending the throne, showered him with favors. A. P. Annibal died only in the reign of Catherine, freed from the important occupations of the service, with the rank of full general [*general-anshef*], in the 92nd year from his birth. [We hope, in time, to publish his full biography. *Pushkin's note.*]

In Russia, where the memory of noteworthy people soon disappears for reason of lack of historical memoirs, the strange life of Annibal is known only from family traditions.

His son Lieutenant General I. A. Annibal belongs indubitably among the most outstanding people of the age of Catherine (he died in 1800). (*PSS* 6:654–55)

Pushkin had written stanza 50 in Odessa in fall 1823. The note was written in fall 1824 in Mikhailovskoe, the estate his mother had inherited from his great-grandfather's property, where his great-grandfather had lived in "deep old age," still remembering his childhood in Africa.

Other points in the note which seem not to have been sufficiently emphasized hitherto are the themes (1) of exile under the guise of transfer in the service, and (2) of Gannibal's voluntarily breaking his exile to return to Russia proper. In the *Onegin* passage in verse, Pushkin, utilizing a "poetic flight" of the imagination, is hinting at voluntarily breaking that kind of exile in order to flee to "my Africa."

It is worth emphasizing that Pushkin's biographical note including information about his great-grandfather's return without permission from Siberia to St. Petersburg was not only published in late March 1825, six months before the Decembrist Uprising, but also reprinted in 1829, four years after it.

"TO YAZYKOV"

Pushkin's friendly poetic epistle "To Yazykov" ("Yazykovu"), a fellow poet, was written in September 1824, some months after the *Onegin* passage, and a month or so before he wrote the accompanying prose note. Part of the poem was published in 1830 as "To Yazykov (Fragment of a Poem)," ending with Pushkin's invitation to his fellow poet to visit him at Mikhailovskoe, which the poem alludes to directly as having formerly been part of the estates of his great-grandfather Abram Gannibal. The poem's location and year of composition were both stated explicitly: Mikhailovskoe, 1824. Here follows the relevant part of the poem in the form in which Pushkin published it twice.

В деревне, где Петра питомец,
Царей, цариц, любимый раб
И их забытый однодомец,
Скрывался прадед мой Арап,
Где, позабыв Елизаветы
И двор и пышные обеты,
Под сенью липовых аллей
Он думал в охлажденны леты
Об дальней Африки своей,
Я жду тебя. (S 11.218.25–34)

In the village where Peter's ward, the servant (*rab*) beloved of tsars and tsaritsas and the forgotten one who had lived in the same house with them, my ancestor the Blackamoor concealed himself, where, having forgotten the court and the splendid solemn promises of (Tsaritsa) Elizabeth, under the shade of linden lanes he thought in cool summers of his far-off Africa—I await you.

In the verse passage in *Eugene Onegin,* Pushkin imagined himself in "my Africa" remembering Russia—in memories going from south to north. In "To Yazykov," he imagines his great-grandfather in Russia, remembering "*his* Africa," with memories going from north to south.[8]

In the passage, Pushkin uses the specific term *rab,* literally "slave," in speaking of his great-grandfather. Under the autocracy in Russia, particularly under Peter the Great, anyone could be treated as a "slave." One of the burning questions in Pushkin's time was that of serfdom: the word "slave" could not then be applied in print to a serf except by the serf himself; Pushkin's reference in print to his great-grandfather as *rab* meant that he was not really a slave. One way of alluding to serfdom as slavery was to speak of the condition of blacks elsewhere, as Pushkin himself did in 1836 (in a review of the autobiography of an American, John Tanner).[9] One may compare this use of *rab* as servant to the tsar with the term *xolop/xolopii,* which is used in the meaning "vassal/vassal's," as a boyar applies it to himself with regard to Peter the Great in *The Blackamoor of Peter the Great* (*PSS* 8:26; in chapter 5, which Pushkin did not publish): in modern Russian, the word *xolop* is pejorative and means something like "flunky." As we shall see, Pushkin's speaking of his great-grandfather's coming from Africa, and his term *rab* (slave) provided the journalist Bulgarin with a bludgeon with which to beat him.

CHAPTERS FROM *THE BLACKAMOOR OF PETER THE GREAT*

All posthumous editions of Pushkin's works include in his prose fiction his uncompleted historical novel, called by editors *The Blackamoor of Peter the Great*, a fictional story based on the life of Abram Gannibal. Pushkin wrote six chapters in 1827 and the beginning of a seventh in early 1828 before dropping it. He himself published only parts of two chapters of this work, one in 1828 and the other in 1830, and republished both in 1834. In the part Pushkin chose to publish, little is explicitly about his great-grandfather, though more is implied.

The first of these chapters to be published came out under the title "Chapter IV from a Historical Novel." Gavrila Afanas'evich (his surname is not given in the passage), the head of the "old Russian" family, compares someone named K—— unfavorably with the "Tsar's blackamoor": "of all the young people educated abroad (God forgive me), the Tsar's blackamoor is the one that most resembles a man" (Debreczeny 29; *PSS* 8:22). To anyone who had read the note to the first chapter of *Onegin*, the term "Tsar's blackamoor" might have revealed that the character named G—— (as he is called in "Chapter IV" as it was published and republished during Pushkin's lifetime [see *PSS* 8:533]) was Gannibal—though in the *Onegin* note he was called "Annibal."

The other passage Pushkin published, actually part of the preceding chapter 3 in the manuscript, was called "An Assembly at the Time of Peter I." Here the Frenchified K—— is punished for unknowingly breaking the "rule" at Peter's "Assembly" that the lady ask the gentleman to dance the minuet, and he is made to suffer the punishment allotted for it. Then the young lady, at her father's behest, asks G—— to dance.

The focus of the parts of the novel Pushkin published is not at all on G—— (Gannibal), but on the manners and mores of the time, including Peter the Great's personal manners and his method of operating in the state, his construction of St. Petersburg, and G——'s setting to work to help Peter in the undertaking.

"TO DAWE, ESQ."

In the late 1820s two more Pushkin lyrics were published that directly concern his African ancestry, though they do not specifically mention his great-grandfather. The first was a little poem addressed to a portrait painter, with its title in English: "To Dawe, Esq." The portrait (if one was made) has not survived. The poem was written and published in 1828 (and republished in 1829, in the first volume of Pushkin's collected poetry [*Stikhotvoreniia*]). The first stanza reads as follows:

Зачем твой дивный карандаш
Рисует мой арапский профиль?
Хоть ты векам его предашь,
Его освищет Мефистофиль. (*S* 111.59.1–4)

Why is your marvelous pencil sketching my blackamoor profile? Though you entrust it to the centuries, Mephistopheles will hiss it off the stage.

The remainder of the poem suggests that the artist should, instead, dedicate his talents to painting a beautiful woman such as O—— (identified after Pushkin's death as Anna Olenina, whom Pushkin was courting at the time; his suit was rejected). The contrast of the poem is between O——'s beauty and the implied lack of beauty of his own "blackamoor profile."[10] The poet-persona suggests himself as having no possibility of being converted into a handsome Faust, so that Mephistopheles would "hiss him off the stage."

"TO YUR'EV"

In 1829 another poem including the theme of Pushkin's African ancestry appeared in print—this one without his approval and against his wishes. It includes specific mention of his black ancestry, and "ugliness" is an explicit theme. This poem was written in 1820 in a friendly poetic epistle ("To Yur'ev"). It describes a handsome man and his exploits with the ladies, and ends with comment in the first person about the poet-persona himself.

А я, повеса вечно-праздный,
Потомок негров безобразный,
Взрощенный в дикой простоте,
Любви не ведая страданий,
Я нравлюсь юной красоте
Бесстыдным бешенством желаний;
С невольным пламенем ланит
Украдкой нимфа молодая,
Сама себя не понимая,
На фавна иногда глядит. (*S* 11.94.21–32)

But I, an eternally idle rake, ugly descendant of Negroes, brought up in wild simplicity, not knowing the sufferings of love, I please young beauty with the shameless frenzy of desires; [thus] sometimes, with an involuntary flame on her cheeks, a young nymph, not understanding herself, looks stealthily at a faun.

The relevant themes here are, in my literal translation, "ugly descendant of Negroes," and how young beautiful women are pleased "with the shameless frenzy of [his] desires" like a nymph involuntarily aroused by watching a faun while remaining unseen. We now consider the poem a delightfully sensuous and sensual "imitation of the ancients" embodying the theme of the nymph and the faun. Indeed, upon reading it shortly after it was written, Pushkin's older contemporary Batiushkov—the poet whose sensuous poems "From the Greek Anthology" (published earlier in the same year, 1820) led immediately to the popularity of that genre in Russia—is said to have remarked: "How that young devil has learned to write."

We have noted that Pushkin objected to the publication of this poem; he never published it himself. This is in sharp contrast to another lyric written in the same year, "The Nereid." The essential difference between the poems "To Yur'ev" and "The Nereid"—another "imitation of the ancients" that Pushkin published and republished—is the conspicuous presence in the "Yur'ev" epistle of the poet-persona directly identifiable as the author himself. One of the most complex problems with regard to Pushkin has to do with the type and amount of self-revelation, or apparent self-revelation, he might allow to be reflected in a poem he would publish.[11]

THE THEME OF OTHELLO

It is not surprising that the theme of Othello the Moor would be in Pushkin's consciousness. His friend F. F. Vigel' in his *Memoirs* says that while in Odessa (sometime in 1823–24) he "once told Pushkin jokingly that by his African extraction I would like to compare him with Othello, and [Alexander N.] Raevsky with Othello's unfaithful friend Iago." He added that Pushkin "only laughed."[12] Thus, at least from 1823–24 on, Pushkin was aware of the literary theme of jealousy in relation to the love of a blackamoor and a white.

However, Pushkin mentioned Othello only once—briefly—in the publications that appeared during his lifetime; this mention is contained in "Fragment from a Manuscript of Pushkin's (*Poltava*)," a prose note written in 1830 and published in 1831 in such a manner as to suggest that the publication was not by him or at his wish. In response to those who objected that it was "unreasonable" for young Maria to fall in love with old Mazepa in *Poltava*,

Pushkin lists a number of myths and stories not "devoid of poetry," and specifically includes the love of Desdemona for Othello, "that old Negro who captivated her with stories of his wanderings and battles" (*PSS* 11:164).[13]

The theme of Othello and jealousy is explicit in one of his pieces of "Table-Talk" (title in English) which he wrote in 1835–36, the last year or so of his life, and planned to publish: "Othello is not by nature jealous—on the contrary, he is trusting. Voltaire understood that, and developing Shakespeare's creation in his imitation, he placed in Orosmane's mouth the following verse: 'I am not at all jealous . . . If ever I were! . . . '" (*PSS* 12:157). The man who wrote this obviously did not think of himself as having a jealous disposition, though he might be capable of becoming jealous with cause; in that event, "African passion" might be manifested.

"MY GENEALOGY"

The next important published document with regard to Pushkin's African heritage was neither written nor published by him; it was an attack on Pushkin in the form of a transparent "foreign anecdote" published by Faddei Bulgarin, a Pole who fought with the French against the Russians in 1812 and then went over to the side of the Russians. Pushkin made a rejoinder to this attack in his poem "My Genealogy."

Bulgarin is the most unsavory figure in Russian nineteenth-century literary life, and publishing this anecdote was perhaps the most unsavory deed of all.[14] According to his partner Nikolai Grech, in memoirs written many years later, Bulgarin arbitrarily discharged an assistant, Orest Somov, and then when Somov began to work on Baron Del'vig's publications, the almanac *Northern Flowers* and the *Literary Gazette,* Bulgarin launched attacks on authors whose works appeared in them as the "literary aristocracy." Bulgarin's technique was to attack, often utilizing a pseudonym, in crude, coarse, but indirect fashion, in such manner that an effective answer would be difficult or impossible, but so as to get around the law against publishing a "personality" without that "personality's" consent. In 1830 Bulgarin attacked Pushkin twice in "foreign anecdotes." The second of these refers transparently to Pushkin's African ancestry. Here follows Bulgarin's anecdote (published in August 1830).[15]

> The anecdote is told that a certain Poet in Spanish America, . . . the offspring of a Mulatto man or woman, I don't remember which, began to contend that one of his ancestors was a Negro Prince. In the town hall of the city it was discovered that in antiquity there was a lawsuit between a skipper of a ship and an assistant of his for this Negro, whom each of them wished to claim as his own, and that the skipper contended that he bought the Negro for a bottle of

rum. Who would have thought then that a versifier would acknowledge connection with that Negro? Vanitas vanitatum!

We have seen that Pushkin "acknowledged connection" with his "Negro" maternal great-grandfather in several works. Although Bulgarin does not use the word "slave," the mention of purchase and possession of the "ancestor" clearly implies slavery, and alludes to Pushkin's use of the word *rab* (literally "slave") in the poetic epistle "To Yazykov." The anecdote stops with the supposed initial status of the "Poet's" original black ancestor—nothing is said of his later career or accomplishments. What to Pushkin was worse was bringing his mother into the affair; the mention in the anecdote of a Poet in Spanish America, an "offspring of a Mulatto man or woman," was an obvious allusion to his mother's being known as the "beautiful Creole."

Pushkin was stung to the quick by Bulgarin's anecdote. The question was how to respond. Pushkin's public rejoinder[16] was a two-part poem, "My Genealogy," which he at first proposed to publish but instead allowed to circulate in manuscript—so widely that, like some of his early poems, this amounted to a kind of *"public-ation"* (see *PSS* 3:1225–30, where sixty-four such surviving manuscript copies are described). The first part of the poem was a response to Bulgarin's previous attacks on "aristocratic authors": it compares the Pushkin family genealogy with that of "new" families that became prominent in the eighteenth century. The part of the poem that is directly relevant to this essay—that dealing with Pushkin's heritage on his mother's side—is called in it a "postscript":

Решил Фиглярин, сидя дома,
Что черный дед мой Ганнибал
Был куплен за бутылку рома
И в руки шкиперу попал.

Сей шкипер был тот шкипер славный,
Кем наша двинулась земля,
Кто придал мощно бег державный
Рулю родного корабля.

Сей шкипер деду был доступен,
И сходно купленный арап
Возрос усерден, неподкуплен,
Царю наперсник, а не раб.

И был отец он Ганнибала,
Пред кем средь чесменских пучин

Громада кораблей вспылала,
И пал впервые Наварин. (*S* 111.187.65–80)

> Figliarin decided, sitting at home, that my black granddad Gannibal was bought for a bottle of rum and fell into a skipper's hands. // That skipper was the glorious skipper by whom our land was set in motion, who in mighty fashion set the course of state to the rudder of his native ship. // That skipper was accessible to [my] granddad, and the blackamoor purchased cheaply grew up diligent, unpurchasable, a confidant to the tsar, and not a slave. // And he was the father of the Gannibal before whom amid the Chesma billows the armada of ships flamed up, and Navarino first fell.

The poem does not respond to the supposition that Gannibal was "bought" but has a pointed rejoinder with regard to the themes of "skipper" (Peter the Great), "purchase" (and "purchasable"), and "slave." The poet-persona proudly responds that "that skipper was accessible to [my] granddad, and the blackamoor purchased cheaply grew up diligent, unpurchasable, a confidant to the tsar, and not a slave." Then, with regard to Abram Gannibal's son Ivan, it speaks of two feats in 1770: his being in charge of fire control in the Russian fleet that destroyed the Turkish fleet in Chesma Bay off the coast of Turkey, and his commanding Russian troops that landed and captured the important Turkish fortress on the Greek mainland at Navarino, *for the first time* (three years before the poem was written, Navarino had been conquered again by Allied forces in the Greek War for Independence).

In November 1831, Pushkin sent a copy of the poem, and an explanation of its being circulated, to Count Benkendorf, to be shown to Nicholas I. The result is a rare example of a poet's explanation and a sovereign's response. Both deserve quoting. They are as follows:

> About a year ago in one of our journals was printed a satirical article in which a certain man of letters was spoken of, who manifested pretensions of having a noble origin, whereas he was only a bourgeois-gentleman. It was added that his mother was a mulatto whose father, a poor pickaninny, had been bought by a sailor for a bottle of rum. Although Peter the Great little resembled a drunken sailor, I was the one referred to clearly enough, since no Russian man of letters except me can count a Negro among his ancestors. Since the article in question was printed in an official gazette, since indecency has been pushed to the point of speaking of my mother in a feuilleton which ought to be only literary, and since our gazetteers do not fight in duels, I believed it my duty to answer the *anonymous* satirist, which I did in verse, and very sharply. I sent my answer to the late Del'vig, asking him to insert it in his journal. Del'vig advised me to suppress it, calling to my attention that it would be ridiculous to defend

oneself, pen in hand, against attacks of this nature and to flaunt aristocratic feelings, when everything considered, one is only a gentleman-bourgeois, if not a bourgeois-gentleman. I yielded to his opinion, and the affair rested there; however, several copies of this response circulated, at which I am not displeased, considering that there is nothing in it which I wished to disavow. I confess that I pride myself on what are called prejudices: I pride myself on being as good a gentleman as anybody whoever, though it profits me little; lastly, I greatly pride myself on my ancestors' name, since it is the only legacy that they have left me.

But inasmuch as my verses might be taken as an indirect satire on the origin of certain prominent families, if one did not know that they are a very moderate response to a very reprehensible provocation, I have considered it my duty to give you this frank explanation, and to enclose the piece in question. (*PSS* 14:242; Shaw 1967, 536)

Here follows the response (the original is in French) in Nicholas I's hand:

You can tell Pushkin from me that I am completely of the opinion of his late friend Del'vig; abuse so low, so vile as that with which he has been regaled dishonors the one who utters it rather than the one at whom it is directed; the only weapon against it is *contempt,* which is what I would have shown in his place. As for the verses, I find wit in them, but still more bile than in the other piece. It would do more honor to his pen and especially to his *reason* not to have them circulate. (*PSS* 14:377)

Nicholas did not consider Pushkin's response "moderate," whatever the provocation, and he was completely right about how others would look at the poem.

Thus Pushkin reacted sharply to "Figliarin's" alluding to the initial status in Russia of his black ancestor rather than his accomplishments for the Russian state. In his letter to Benkendorf, Pushkin shows how offensive it was to him that that his mother (a "mulatto woman") was brought into literary polemics (a feuilleton). The nature of Pushkin's relationships with both his parents, and especially his mother, was such that he would have objected at any time if an allusion to her were brought into a literary struggle; irrespective of Pushkin's own relationship to his parents or his mother, strife in the presence of, or involving, a lady was unconscionable to him. The letter to Benkendorf clearly implies that Pushkin would have challenged Bulgarin to a duel (in spite of the illegality of dueling at the time) if Bulgarin had belonged to Pushkin's social class. However, Pushkin was trapped: the "nobility around the throne" never forgave him for the first part of the poem, in which he ironically calls himself, a descendant of boyars, a "bourgeois," in contrast to the "new high nobility"—descendants of cooks, flunkies, foreign renegades, and adventurers. Much of the pain and difficulty of Pushkin's final years can be attributed to this poem—to what provoked it and to Pushkin's response.

Thus Pushkin's black ancestry was directly involved in the personal-literary-social struggle with which he began the final stage of his life. Pushkin did not cease to be proud of his black great-grandfather and great-uncle. His early comments about them are linked with feelings of exoticism, as well as with pride in their accomplishments in Russia. He reprinted the statements calling attention to exoticism; the comments written later emphasize his pride in their feats in their adopted land.

After 1831, Pushkin published no new works dealing directly with his African heritage, though he continued to be interested in using the theme in biographical or fictional works. He republished all the items we have dealt with that he was clearly responsible for publishing in the first place—that is, all those we have discussed except the poem "To Yur'ev" and the Note on *Poltava*. The only changes in these republications were in the long prose note about his great-grandfather in chapter 1 of *Onegin*. When all the chapters of the novel in verse were combined in one book in 1833, the long note was replaced by the terse comment "The author, on his mother's side, is of African descent." When the entire novel was republished in early 1837, the note was changed again, to read: "See the first edition of *Eugene Onegin*." The "first edition" of *Onegin* was the individual chapters published as separate books; chapter 1 was so published in 1825.

Pushkin's war with Bulgarin ended with a cease-fire—though not as a consequence of "My Genealogy." What proved effective was the tactic Bulgarin himself had employed—the use of a pseudonymous "author." Pushkin succeeded in reducing Bulgarin to silence by publishing two articles signed "Feofilakt Kosichkin"—a persona with character, views, and style all quite different from Pushkin's. The second "Kosichkin" article in devastating fashion "revealed" detailed information about the heredity and career of "Figliarin," beginning with his birth in a "kennel."

Perhaps nothing so clearly shows the paradoxical relationship between the *public* and the *private* question of Pushkin and his African heritage as Pushkin's diametrically opposed reactions to the *public* treatment of that heredity by Bulgarin, which resulted in "My Genealogy," and to a *private* or *personal* treatment of that heritage only a month after he wrote the above-cited letter to Benkendorf. The *personal* story has to do with a New Year's gift and accompanying greeting sent to Pushkin by Pavel Nashchokin, perhaps Pushkin's dearest friend in his final years. Nashchokin, a man of the ancient high Russian nobility, was well acquainted with Pushkin's difficulties with Bulgarin; indeed, he was the one who directly provided Pushkin with the biographical materials that effectively silenced Bulgarin in the second of the "Feofilakt Kosichkin" articles.[17] Nashchokin's gift was a bronze inkstand with a statuette of a black man leaning on an anchor and standing in front of two bales of cotton—two inkwells. In the letter accompanying the gift, Nashchokin said: "I am sending you your ancestor with inkwells that open, and that reveal him to be a farsighted person [*à double vue*]" (*PSS* 14:250).

Pushkin was obviously delighted with the gift, with its suggestion that his "farsighted" black ancestor had anticipated (by the inkwells) that a descendant of his would be a writer: so that not only did Pushkin look backward with pride at his black great-grandfather, but that person looked forward to him. The answer to Bulgarin's rhetorical question—who could have predicted in the time of Peter the Great's blackamoor that a descendant of his would be a writer?—was Gannibal himself. Upon receiving the gift, Pushkin wrote to thank Nashchokin "for the blackamoor," and he kept it on his working desk for the rest of his life.

The lineage of most of the important nineteenth-century Russian authors includes a mixture of non-Russian and Russian blood—not only Pushkin but Zhukovsky, Lermontov, Turgenev, Dostoevsky, Tolstoy, and others. However, Pushkin is the only important Russian author known to have an African heritage. Whatever his ancestry, there has never really been any question to the Russians that Pushkin is their own most important author and cultural figure. To us, Pushkin is the most European and cosmopolitan of Russian authors. To Russians, he is, paradoxically, the most "Russian" of authors, but at the same time not only one who had an African heritage and temperament, but also one whose African temperament is reflected in his literary works and contributes to their nature. This essay has focused on the theme of Pushkin and his African heritage in works published during his lifetime. How his "African temperament" affected his literary works beyond the explicit use of the theme is a subject for further investigation—and speculation.

Notes

J. Thomas Shaw's article "Pushkin on His African Heritage: Publications during his Lifetime" was originally printed in *Pushkin Today*, ed. David M. Bethea (Bloomington: Indiana University Press, 1993), and then reprinted in a longer version as "Pushkin and Africa" in J. Thomas Shaw, *Pushkin Poems and Other Studies, Part II* (Los Angeles: C. Schlacks Jr., 1996). This article appears with the permission of Indiana University Press. Any inconsistencies in styling between this article and the rest of the volume are due to a different format in the article as originally published.

1. The most extensive treatment of the question of the precise homeland of Abram Gannibal is that of Vladimir Nabokov in Aleksandr Pushkin, *Eugene*

Onegin, trans. and ed. Vladimir Nabokov, 4 vols., 2nd ed. (Princeton: Princeton University Press, 1975). S. S. Geichenko gives an interesting account of a Russian journalist visiting in 1960 what he takes to be Pushkin's ancestral home in Ethiopia. See his *U lukomor'ia* (Leningrad: Lenizdat, 1977), 332–34. Interest in Pushkin's black ancestry has been shown by biographers and scholars since 1855, when Annenkov's biography first appeared (P. V. Annenkov, *Materialy dlia biografii A. S. Pushkina,* ed. A. A. Karpov [Moscow: Sovremennik, 1984]). The most thorough recent studies are those of N. K. Teletova, *Zabytye rodstvennye sviazi A. S. Pushkina* (Leningrad: Nauka, 1981); I. L. Feinberg, *Abram Petrovich Gannibal, praded Pushkina: Razyskaniia i materialy* (Moscow: Nauka, 1983); and George Leets, *Abram Petrovich Gannibal: Biograficheskoe issledovanie,* 2nd ed. (Tallinn: Eèsti Raamat, 1984). Among the important earlier studies, one should mention Sergei Auslender's "Arap Petra Velikogo," in *Pushkin,* 6 vols., ed. S. A. Vengerov (St. Petersburg: Brokhaus-Efron, 1910), 4:104–12; B. L. Modzalevskii, "Rod Pushkina," in *Pushkin* (Leningrad: Priboi, 1929), 19–63; M. Vegner, *Predok Pushkina* (Moscow: Sovetskii pisatel', 1937); and E. S. Paina, "Ob obstoiatel'stva otstavki A. P. Gannibala," in *Pushkin: Issledovaniia i materialy,* vol. 4 (1962), 413–48.

2. In this essay, citations directly from Pushkin's text are from the "large Academy" edition (1937–59) of his collected works and are indicated by *PSS* plus volume and page, except that poems are cited by volume and number according to the system in *Slovar' iazyka Pushkina,* ed. V. V. Vinogradov (Moscow: Gosudarstvennoe izdatel'stvo inostrannykh i natsionalnykh slovarei, 1956–61). Factual information regarding dating, titles, and publication is drawn from the notes to that edition. For precise timing of publications, *PSS* has been supplemented by N. Siniavskii and M. Tsiavlovskii, ed., *Pushkin v pechati: 1814–1837* (Moscow: GSEI, 1938). Reliance for biographical information has been placed mainly on M.A. Tsiavlovskii, ed., *Poet: Aleksandr Pushkin and the Creative Process* (Ann Arbor: University Microfilms International, 1951); and L. A. Chereiskii, *Pushkin i ego okruzhenie* (Leningrad: Nauka, 1975). Translations from the letters are from *The Letters of Alexander Pushkin,* trans. and ed. J. Thomas Shaw (Madison: University of Wisconsin Press, 1st ed., 1963; 2nd ed., 1967). Translations from Pushkin's prose fiction are from *Alexander Pushkin: Complete Prose Fiction,* ed. and trans. Paul Debreczeny (Stanford: Stanford University Press, 1983); plain translations of the verse and other translations from the prose are mine. The translation of this letter is from Shaw, *The Letters,* 783.

3. For example, see E. J. Simmons, *Pushkin,* 2nd ed. (Gloucester, Eng.: Peter Smith, 1971); Iu. M. Lotman, *Roman A. S. Pushkina "Evgenii Onegin" kommentarii* (Leningrad: Prosveshchenie, 1983); and Feinberg, *Abram Petrovich Gannibal.*

4. The specific reference here is to Negro slaves in the Americas; those

slaves were from south of the Sahara. Pushkin uses the term in a letter in which he is less than enthusiastic about the modern Greeks he had seen during the early part of the effort at independence from Turkey: "About the fate of the Greeks, one is permitted to reason, just as of the fate of my brothers the Negroes—one may wish both groups freedom from unendurable slavery" (letter to P. A. Viazemskii of June 24–25, 1824; *PSS* 12:99; Shaw, *The Letters*, 161). It should be noted that the kind of "brotherhood" Pushkin speaks of here did not preclude the possibility of social distinctions. Russian peasant serfs, like all other Russians, were also his "brothers," but that hardly made them his social equals, however much he may have favored the liberation of the serfs. In Odessa, according to I. P. Liprandi, Pushkin thought of Morali (the "Moor Ali"), a ship captain originally from Tunis, as possibly a descendant of a close relative of his own great-grandfather—so that the Moor very well might be a relative. See V. E. Vatsuro, *A. S. Pushkin v vospominaniiakh sovremennikov* (Moscow: Khudozhestvennaia literatura, 1974), 1:338.

5. The lithograph was of Pushkin as a blackamoor boy, some thirteen to fifteen years old. Pushkin was obviously unenthusiastic at the publication of this lithograph; he commented as follows: "Alexander Pushkin is masterfully lithographed, but I do not know whether it resembles him" (letter to N. I. Gnedich of September 27, 1822; Shaw, *The Letters*, 102; *PSS* 13:48).

6. In 1824, in addition to the prose note to *Eugene Onegin* 1.50 and the verse epistle to his friend Yazykov, Pushkin also wrote of his "blackamoor" great-grandfather in an uncompleted poem which exists only in rough draft and which was first published sixty years later. It is one of Pushkin's earliest experiments in imitating Russian folk poetics and diction: "When the Tsar's Blackamoor Took a Notion to Get Married" ("Kak zhenit'sia zadumal tsarskii arap"). It ends, in plain translation, as follows: "The blackamoor has chosen a lady [*sudarushku*] for himself; the black raven, a white swan, but he is a black blackamoor [*arap chereshenek*], and she is a white darling [*dusha beleshenka*]."

7. Pushkin's surviving papers show that he retained his interest in biographical information about his ancestors and apparently thought of publishing a biography or autobiography including information about them (see *PSS* 11:310–14). The closest he comes to dealing with the question of his black ancestry in works he completed after 1830–31 and himself wished to publish is in a number of individual items (mainly anecdotes) in his "Table-Talk" (title in English, written 1835–36); there are mentions of *arapy* in Russia, and one of the items, as noted above, is about Othello. If Pushkin had lived longer, apparently he would have published them; they appeared only after his death, like the uncompleted *Blackamoor of Peter the Great*, except for the two chapters he published and which are treated here.

8. The south-north, north-south theme here may be compared with his

poem "To Ovid," in which the poet-persona, in exile from St. Petersburg at a place close to where Ovid had been exiled so many years ago, identifies himself with Ovid and at the same time—as both being poets in exile in the same general place, Ovid from south to north (like the enforced movement of old Gannibal from Africa), and Pushkin from north to south (St. Petersburg to the Black Sea area). The contrast of north and south—and of thinking of or remembering one from the other—recurs in Pushkin's verse, particularly in "The Bad Day Has Ended . . ." ("Nenastnyi den' potukh . . ."; Odessa and Mikhailovskoe), and, curiously enough, in *The Stone Guest* (Paris and Madrid).

9. See J. Thomas Shaw, "Pushkin on America: His 'John Tanner,'" in *Orbis Scriptus: Dmitrij Tschizewcskij zum 70 Geburtstag*, ed. Dietrich Gerhardt et al. (Munich: Wilhelm Fink, 1966), 739–56.

10. In reading memoirs about Pushkin, one can never be sure whether he might not have suggested both the term and the perception. Contemporaries, in memoirs written after Pushkin's death, spoke of his "blackamoor profile." An example is the novelist I. I. Lazhechnikov, who uses the term in his account of meeting Pushkin in 1819 or 1820, some eight or nine years before the composition of "To Dawe, Esq." (See Vatsuro, *A. S. Pushkin v vospominaniiakh,* 1:178; and V. Veresaev, ed., *Pushkin v zhizni,* 6th ed. [Moscow: Sovetskii pisatel', 1936], 1:119.) In this essay, citations from the memoir literature of Pushkin's contemporaries are, for convenience, from these two compilations: Vatsuro has particularly useful notes and introductions evaluating the accuracy and importance of the materials included.

11. There is a curious history of the printing of this poem. Yur'ev himself privately printed the poem when it was first written, in a very limited number of copies. Obviously Pushkin considered the first *publication* to be the unauthorized one of 1829. See Annenkov, *Materialy dlia biografii A. S. Pushkina,* 55n.

12. Vatsuro, *Pushkin v vospominaniiakh,* 1:226.

13. Debreczeny interestingly compares Pushkin's characterizations of Ibragim and Mazepa as "explorations of how disadvantaged men might fare in love—one disadvantaged by the color of his skin, the other by his age." See his *The Other Pushkin: A Study of Alexander Pushkin's Prose Fiction* (Stanford: Stanford University Press, 1983), 34. One major contrast might, however, be mentioned. In the full form, as we now have it, of *The Blackamoor of Peter the Great*, there is no hint that Gannibal thinks it will be possible for him to inspire a real love that will be faithful—*respect* is the most he can hope for. However, Mazepa, like Othello, inspires a young woman's intense and faithful love. The irrationality of Desdemona's love for Othello is specifically mentioned in the lack of "laws" for the wind, the eagle, a maid's heart, and the poet in Pushkin's unfinished *Ezerskii* (1833–36; *Ez* 168–82), and the passage from it inserted in the unfinished *Egyptian Nights* (1835?; *PSS* 8:269).

14. But only barely so. Pushkin and his friends were convinced that Bulgarin read *Boris Godunov* for Count Benkendorf, head of the secret police, through whom Pushkin had to communicate with Nicholas I, supposedly his "only censor." Before Nicholas I allowed *Boris Godunov* to be published, Bulgarin's historical novel *Dmitry the Pretender* (*Dmitrii Samozvanets*, 1829) appeared, containing some of Pushkin's own fictional inventions. However, when Pushkin's play was finally published, Bulgarin accused Pushkin of plagiarizing from him, citing points in common between the two works. For details, see Shaw, *The Letters,* and references there.

15. The anecdote appeared in Bulgarin's article "Vtoroe pis'mo iz Karlova na Kamennyi Ostrov" in *The Northern Bee* (*Sevemaia pchela*), no. 104 (1830). For a detailed study of Pushkin's use of a fictional journalistic persona, Feofilakt Kosichkin, so as to succeed in publishing an unanswerable response, see Shaw, *The Letters*. The second of the two articles, "Feofilakt Kosichkin," gives details of Bulgarin's life, beginning with his birth in a kennel (making clear *his* maternity). According to Grech, Bulgarin heard the "Spanish Poet" anecdote told by Count S. S. Uvarov in the home of A. O. Olenin (Veresaev, *Pushkin v zhizni*, 11:121). Olenin was the father of the O[lenina] whose beauty is contrasted to Pushkin's "blackamoor profile" in "To Dawe, Esq.," treated above.

16. Before writing "My Genealogy," Pushkin wrote of Bulgarin's attacks in one of his notes which he never published; these notes were combined as "Rebuttal to Criticisms" and published after his death (*PSS* 11:152). In the note, as in the poem, Pushkin does not deny the possibility that his great-grandfather was "purchased"; in both places he insists that people should be remembered for what they do, specifically their important service to the nation.

17. For Nashchokin's sources, see P. I. Bartenev, *Rasskazy o Pushkine zapisannye so slov ego druzei P. I. Bartenevym v 1851–1860 goda,* ed. M. Tsiavlovskii (Moscow: Sabashnikovy, 1925), 35.

Richard F. Gustafson

Ruslan and Ludmila:
Pushkin's Anxiety of Blackness

PUSHKIN WAS BORN DIFFERENT. On the genealogical surface he was the descendant on both sides of a distinguished Russian boyar family. He had, it would seem, every right to the privilege of his heritage. At the same time, however, Pushkin was inordinately obsessed with his lineage, even as he was "proud to the point of hypersensitivity of his aristocratic pedigree."[1] The source of this obsession and hypersensitivity has generally been found in the social and economic conditions of his life: the decline of the old boyar aristocracy with the concomitant rise of the new *dvorianstvo* (nobility) and the economic impoverishment of the Pushkin family. While there is much evidence in Pushkin's own writings that these conditions played an important role in his conscious awareness of his social status, I believe the *emotional* obsessiveness and hypersensitivity of Pushkin's concern can be traced back to a less than conscious reaction to the "dark" side of his lineage.

Pushkin's maternal great-grandfather, as we all know, was black. From his early years Pushkin knew the family legend telling the story of Abram Gannibal, and shortly after leaving the Lycée he began to inquire further about his black ancestor.[2] As the poet matured, the story of his great-grandfather and his relationship to Peter the Great became a central and conscious concern that surfaced first in a direct and honest footnote to the first edition (1825) of chapter 1 of *Eugene Onegin* and then appeared in fictional disguise in the poet's first attempt in prose, the unfinished historical novel we refer to as *The Blackamoor of Peter the Great* (*Arap Petra Velikogo,* 1827). It is significant, however, that after meeting his future wife Natalia Goncharova in 1828, Pushkin removed the telling footnote from the second (1829) and all subsequent editions of *Eugene Onegin.* Nevertheless, to judge from the famous engraving by E. Geitman (see figure 1) which was used, against Pushkin's wishes, as the frontispiece to the first published edition (1822) of *The Prisoner of the Caucasus* (*Kavkazsky plennik*), the traces of this African lineage could not be deleted or fictionalized, because they were inscribed on

Pushkin's body. This essay is an attempt to uncover in the body of his early texts the traces of the young Pushkin's anxiety over his blackness, the sign of his difference that he carried with him into the Lycée at Tsarskoe Selo and later into St. Petersburg society. This anxiety, as we shall see, culminates in his first major narrative poem, *Ruslan and Ludmila* (*Ruslan i Ludmila,* 1818–20), which Pushkin claimed he began while still at the Lycée but actually wrote later, during his sojourn in St. Petersburg before his exile to the Caucasus.

What must it have been like to get away from a home where you were never really happy or loved and to find yourself among a select group of young men by whom you had every right except one to be accepted? For at some level of your consciousness, however hidden from your awareness, every time you looked into a mirror you knew that you were different from those fellow students whose friendship you desired almost as a substitute for the parental love you, unlike your brothers and sisters, were never given. And those students knew too that you were different, calling you by that nickname that cut you to the quick, *frantsuz* (Frenchie), which they understood, as you did too, according to Voltaire's characterization of the French as a "mixture of monkey and tiger."[3] In the poem "My Portrait" ("Mon portrait," 1814) which you wrote while at the Lycée but of course never published, you even agreed with them, describing yourself in their terms: "By looks a real monkey"(*Vraie singe par sa mine*). Since acceptance by your fellow students and hence the attractiveness to the girls that would earn you the desired homosocial association[4] were excessively important to you, how did you cope with being seen by both the boys and the girls as that "mixture of monkey and tiger"? As might be expected, you began to deal with your obviously embodied blackness by attempting to deny it.

Pushkin's first extant Russian lyric, written when he was fourteen years old, is an erotic piece entitled "To Natalia" ("K Natal'e," 1813). It is addressed to a young peasant girl who was an actress in Count V. V. Tolstoi's theater in Tsarskoe Selo. We may see this first lyric, however, as the first example in Pushkin's work of what David Bethea calls "realizing metaphors."[5] That Pushkin some eighteen years later sensed the fated connection between this first lyric and first "love" on the one hand and his hoped-for future wife also named Natalia on the other, can be seen in the famous Don Juan list of 1830, which begins with Natalia I and concludes the first, more serious half with a Natalia not yet identified as II.[6] While the surface resistance to the famous poet suitor of Natalia II seemed to revolve around economic concerns, the issue for the suitor of Natalia I was, at least in part, his blackness.

Pushkin's procedure in the poem is first to announce his love for Natalia: *priznaius'—i ia vliublën* ("I declare that I also am in love"; *PSS* 1:5); *priznaiusia, / Ia toboiu polonën* ("I declare / That I am captivated by you"). He then attempts to demonstrate to the addressee that he is *Lish' toboiu zaniat* ("interested only in you"; *PSS* 1:6) by retelling an erotic dream in which he is in ecstasy over the *Beloi grudi kolebanie* ("heaving of her white breast") and the vision of this *devstvennu lileiu* ("virginal lily"). Alone with her in this dream he is all aroused: *Trepeshchu, tomlius', nemeiu . . . / I prosnulsia . . .* ("I thrill, I languish, I grow numb . . . / And I awakened . . ."). Thus the first preserved Russian poem by Pushkin has at its center an erotic dream that ends with the interruption of the erotic moment just before its consummation and the discovery of himself in bed alone: *vizhu mrak / Vkrug posteli odinokoi* ("I see the darkness all round my lonely bed"). At this point the poem turns away from the erotic to an explanation of what *nikto iz nas / Damam vslukh togo ne skazhet* ("none of us would say aloud to the ladies"). What would not be said aloud is that Pushkin's lyrical "I" wants to be like all those other lovers who can pronounce with confidence the key words of possession so often repeated in Pushkin's later poetry, *ona moia* ("She's mine"; *PSS* 1:7). But he cannot do this because he is different. In fact, Natalia does not know who her *nezhnyi Seladon* ("tender Seladon") really is. Pushkin then proceeds to define himself as neither some *Ne vladetel' ia Seralia* ("sovereign of a seraglio") *ne arap, ne turok ia* ("nor an alien blackamoor or Turk") nor one of his presumed rivals, the beer-drinking, cigar-smoking, war-loving horse guardsmen by whom all the girls seemingly desire to be possessed. Thus, in 1813, Pushkin seems to know the family legend which associated his black ancestor with seraglios and Turks. But he denies any relation to this black ancestor as strongly as he dissociates himself from the stereotypes of his rivals. It is significant that Pushkin's first reference to his blackness is an avowed denial of it in an erotic context. Being an *arap* is a disadvantage on the battlefield of love. The poem then concludes with the poet's self-definition: *Znai, Natal'ia!—ia . . . monakh!* ("Know, Natalia! I am a monk"; *PSS* 1:8). Of the three poems that have survived from the pen of the fourteen-year-old Pushkin, the longest and most successful explores the significance of this self-definition, even as it is entitled *The Monk* (*Monakh*, 1813).

"Monk" is not an inappropriate nickname for Pushkin in his days at the Lycée. The boys naturally tended to gather in various groups, and Pushkin tried to belong to several of them, but was mostly on the periphery of them all. He was to a considerable extent an outsider. He did have several friends—Kiukhel'beker, Malinovsky, Pushchin, and especially Del'vig—but the cult of friendship at the Lycée, so needed psychologically as a replacement for the family he never had, was a retrospective creation.[7] Even among the budding poets Pushkin stood somewhat alone, not completely following them in style or manner. True, the poems he published at the time did more or less conform to the taste of the young Lycée poets for madrigals, songs, and the like; such conformity would have been necessary for publication.[8] Therefore, those poems that awaited posthumous publication, not surprisingly, tend to be the more self-revealing texts, like "To Natalia," "My Portrait," and *The Monk*. In these poems we see that the nickname "monk" suggests someone who is rather isolated or alone, a poet who is seeking his own style, and someone who for whatever reason cannot pronounce the words of sexual possession, "She's mine."

Traditionally, and especially in the Soviet period, the unfinished narrative poem *The Monk* has been read as an "anti-monastic satire,"[9] in the vein of the anticlerical poetry of the French Enlightenment, especially of Voltaire, whom Pushkin evokes early in the poem. The plot of Pushkin's poem is borrowed from an incident in the vita (*zhitie*) of Saint John of Novgorod, designated as a reading for September 7 in the *Chet'ii Minei* of Dmitry Rostovsky. But Pushkin not only renames the monk "Pankraty" (in Greek, "all-powerful" or "all-mighty") and uses just the one incident of erotic temptation which he develops at length, but he in fact creates an original work with such signature features as erotic dreams, authorial intrusions, and metapoetic digressions. Rejecting both the models of Voltaire and Barkov, the narrator-poet proclaims himself an improviser: *Ia stanu pet', chto v golovu pridëtsia / Pust' kak-nibud' stikh za stikhom pol'ëtsia* ("I'll sing what comes into my head / Just let verse somehow flow after verse"; *PSS* 1:9). I shall read the poem, then, not as Pushkin's satire on religion, but as an expression of his more or less unconscious anxiety of identity. What does it mean that I am a monk?

The narrative poem *The Monk*, even in its unfinished state, combines to create for the first time what I consider a central thematic triangle of Pushkin's poetry: sexual attraction, a struggle with a friend, rival, or enemy often related to this sexual attraction, and the issue of art, in short *eros, eris, poesis*. The opposition of love and strife, of course, has an ancient lineage in the Western tradition, going back to the fundamental opposition of the Homeric universe, to the metaphysical vision of the pre-Socratic philosopher Empedocles who saw all reality resulting from the two forces of *filia* (love) and *neikos* (strife), and to the domesticated variation on this theme by Euripides in whose plays we see the inevitable conflict of what he calls *eros* and *eris*. I borrow his terms. *Eros* we all at least think we understand. *Eris,* however, is a complex concept, a notion of strife that at its most abstract suggests discord, but that in general branches in one direction toward quarrel and debate and in another direction toward rivalry, contention, and jealousy. It is this broad sense of *eris* that I believe operates in the Pushkinian universe where it is linked to *eros* and the issue of poetic creation, *poesis*. We see this triangle in some of Pushkin's most accomplished works, *Eugene Onegin, The Stone Guest,* and *The Bronze Horseman.*

In *The Monk* Pushkin's hero *zhil schastliv v uedinenie* ("lived happy in his isolation"; *PSS* 1:10) until *chërnyi satana* ("black Satan"; *PSS* 1:11), named Molok in the poem, decides to tempt Pankraty, whose first response is to *pod chërnoi riaskoi skrylsia* ("hide under his black cassock") and *molilsia uzh, molilsia* ("pray and pray"). But to no avail, for the devil tires him out and soon he falls asleep. Then suddenly Pankraty seems to awaken ("or is it just a dream?") only to see *Chto-to v uglu kak budto zabeleno* ("over in the corner something that seemed to turn white"; *PSS* 1:12). This something he discovers is a skirt. *Kak vkopannyi, pred beloi iubkoi stal, / Molchal, krasnel, smushchalsia, trepetal* ("As though rooted to the ground, he stood before the white skirt, / He was silent, he blushed, he was troubled, he trembled"). This first textual encounter with the object of erotic desire is then immediately interrupted. As we shall see, this trope of what I call *textus interruptus*, which appeared in "To Natalia" as well, will resurface in *Ruslan and Ludmila,* where its iconic function becomes quite evident.

What replaces the consummation of the erotic urge at this point in *The Monk* is an authorial intrusion that marks the relationship of *eros* to *poesis*. This is most significant, for here, as well as in much of Pushkin's life and work, the erotic event serves as the stimulus for the poem: *O iubka! Rech' k tebe ia obrashchaiu, / Stroki sii tebe ia posviashchaiu, / Odushevi pero moë, liubov'* ("O skirt! I turn my speech to you, / These lines I dedicate to you, / Animate my pen, O love"). This telling apostrophe, the trope of presence, is then followed by two erotic fantasies made present: the narratorial "I" here recalls a moment when Natalia was awaiting his arrival and then transposes this erotic event into a pastoral scene with Filon and Chloe, who are just about to embrace when the text is again interrupted, now by the narrator's need to tell of his own passion aroused by the telling: *I on ... no net; ne smeiu prodolzhat'. / Ia trepeshchu, i serdtse sil'no b'ëtsia, / I, mozhet byt', chitateli, kak znat'? / I vasha krov's stremlen'em strasti l'ëtsia* ("And he ... but no, I dare not continue, / I am trembling, and my heart is beating quickly / And, perhaps, readers, how can I know? / Even your blood is flowing with the desire of passion"; *PSS* 1:13). Thus the first of the three completed cantos of the poem *The Monk* ends with a contrast between the passionate "I" and the monk who is *ne byl rad, chto iubku uvidal* ("not happy that he has seen the skirt") and realizes that *v kogti on nechistogo popalsia* ("he has fallen into the clutches of the unclean spirit"). In this way the first canto establishes a complex relationship between the monk and the teller of the tale. The poet, whose relationship to Pushkin himself is marked by the reference to Natalia, is aroused by the "black Satan's" erotic temptation, which the monk attempts to withstand. The monk and the poet-narrator represent the two different responses to *eros* that function in Pushkin's psychic universe: the unfulfilled temptation of his "loves" (I do not speak of the more sordid adventures of the young Pushkin) and the passionate lyrical response to the experience of attraction.

In the second canto the devil again tempts the monk, this time with a "wondrous dream" (*chudnyj son; PSS* 1:14). The first half of the dream consists of a description of a typical pleasure garden scene characteristic of the poetry of Ariosto or Spenser, ending with erotic suggestion: *Sred' radostei sladostnykh prokhlad, / Obniavshiesia liubovniki lezhat* ("Midst joys and sweet breezes / The embracing lovers lie"; *PSS* 1:15). In the second half of the dream the monk looks directly at the maidens. It is significant that at precisely this voyeuristic moment of yielding to the temptation, the word for "monk" switches for the first time from *monakh* to another word with the same meaning and metrical structure, *chernets* (literally, the "black one"). Now the "black Satan" seems to have overpowered the monk and overwhelmed his identity. The black monk and the black Satan are versions of each other, doubles of the passionate poet-narrator. *I vdrug, v dushe pochuvstvovav kurazh / I na bekren' vz"iarias'* ("And suddenly, taking courage in his heart / And in a frenzy tilting his monkish headgear") the monk, with a sense of dissatisfaction, disappointment, and vexation (*dosada* means all three), *za devkoiu pognalsia* ("takes off after the girl"). But why he does so is not clear. Is he vexed and attempting to confront the black devil disguised as a white skirt (is this *eris*?) or is he dissatisfied and in a frenzy of black passion trying to catch up with the enticing maiden (is this *eros*?)? At any rate he keeps on chasing her until "suddenly" the devil flings the skirt in his face. *I vdrug ischez priiatnyi vid lesochka* ("And suddenly the pleasant wood disappeared") and *i net sleda krasotochki prelestnoi* ("there was no trace of the enticing beauty"; *PSS* 1:16). Finding himself once again all alone, the monk is struck by the sound of roaring thunder and *vdrug prosnulsia on* ("suddenly wakes up"). Frightened, the monk prays for strength to resist temptation and comes up with a plan to win the *grozny ada bitvy* ("terrible battles of hell"; *PSS* 1:17) by throwing water on the devil. He fills a jug in readiness, but *Mogushchii Rok, vselennoi Gospodin, / Pankratiem, kak kukloi, zabavlialsia* ("Powerful Fate, the Master of the universe / Was amusing itself with Pankraty, as with a doll"). In this second canto the monk, now equated with blackness, pursues a girl/skirt (*eros*) and/or enters into a struggle with his enemy, the "black Satan" (*eris*). It is precisely the ambiguity of this pursuit that marks the poet's own anxiety over his blackness. The opening of the third canto brings this anxiety to the fore in a most extraordinary way.

The third canto begins with a long authorial digression which is metapoetic in nature. It is unusual in Pushkin's ouevre because it is built around an opposition of poetry to painting, a subject he rarely touched upon. Apparently inspired by the study of art required at the Lycée and referring to painters attractive to the taste of the time—Correggio, Poussin, Titian, and Rubens, among others—this digression takes the form of a lament.[10] The poet would rather be a painter who could really do justice to describing *vse prelesti Natal'i* ("all the charms of Natalia") or the beautiful colors of nature. And then there would be an added benefit too, for *Chernilami ia ne maral by pal'tsy* ("I would not have to stain my fingers with ink"). Now this is rather a curious statement, for surely painters have at least as messy a job as writers using quill pens. But the latent issue in this authorial digression is hidden in the word for ink, *chernilo,* which could be translated literally as "black stuff." If I were somebody else, I wouldn't be tainted with blackness. But I am not, so the long digression ends: *Opiat' beru chernil'nitsu s bumagoi / I stanu vnov' ia pesni prodolzhat'* ("Again I take my paper and inkwell / And once more continue my song"; *PSS* 1:18). In 1821, it should be recalled, Pushkin wrote a poem "To My Inkwell" ("K moei chernil'nitse"; *PSS* 2:182–85) in which he referred to himself as an *otshel'nik* (monk), treated the inkwell as the source of his poetry, and addressed it as his *napersnitsa* (confidante). In 1830, furthermore, this metaphoric inkwell was realized in the form of a gift from his friend Nashchokin—an inkwell with the figure of a black sailor on it (see figure 2). The digression on the inkwell, therefore, marks the deep-seated relationship between Pushkin's sense of difference because of his blackness and his need to "continue my song." This continuation returns in *The Monk* to the struggle between Pankraty and his *kosmatyi* ("shaggy") enemy.

This battle is represented first as a repeated temptation. Following immediately upon the authorial reference to *chernilo,* the monk is for the second and last time referred to as a *chernets.* This black monk is praying before the icons, when *I vdrug bela, kak vnov' napavshii sneg / Moskvy reki na kamenistyi breg, / Kak lëgka ten', v glazakh iavilas' iubka . . .* ("suddenly, white as the newly fallen snow / On the stony shore of the Moscow River / The skirt appeared before his eyes like a light shadow"). The monk, now referred to as *monakh,* resists this temptation and throws water all over the skirt, which both disappears and is transformed into Molok, *I vot pred nim s rogami i s khvostom, / Kak seryj volk, shchetinoi ves' pokrytyi* ("with horns and a tail / Like a gray wolf all covered with stubble"). Thus black satan is transformed from the "white skirt" into horns (*rog,* the sign of the cuckold and the effective homonym of fate, *rok*) and a tail/beard (*shchetina* refers both to the rough fur of an animal and the stubble of a beard). Furthermore with his water Pankraty actually catches his fateful "shaggy" enemy-tempter Molok, and the two then enter into a conversation. In brief, this conversation consists of Molok's attempts to keep Pankraty from imprisoning him in a bottle by offering him money, status in society, association with poets, and *zhën i krasnykh dev* ("women and pretty maidens"; *PSS* 1:20). In short, Molok offers Pankraty everything Pushkin himself desired. In the poem, Pankraty finally succumbs, however, when Molok offers to fly him to Jerusalem (*Erusalim*), a situation to be reversed in *Ruslan and Ludmila,* Pushkin's major reworking of this unfinished poem. *The Monk,* at least in the form we have it, represents the tale of a black monk who conquers his enemy and double, the black Satan, who figures the monk's erotic desire and the narrator's poetic urge. That this image of the monk tempted by a horned and hairy devil is an important figure in Pushkin's psychic universe is evidenced by Pushkin's self-portrait as a monk sketched in 1829 (see figure 3).

Pushkin's self-identification as a monk and the accompanying story of erotic temptation and poetic passion was so important to his psychological makeup that five years later, now in St. Petersburg, he wrote a short ballad, entitled "Rusalka" (1819), which serves as a reprise of the earlier narrative poem *The Monk*. Tomashevsky considered this ballad but "the temptations of Pankraty transposed into a sentimental atmosphere."[11] But it is much more than that. While repeating the theme of the monk tempted by a woman, the poem transforms the image of the skirt into the folkloric "rusalka" who serves as the temptress and completely replaces the demonic figure. The monk is moved from the monastery into the forest, and he is pictured looking out over a lake, while praying to save his soul. What is striking, however, is that at the first moment of temptation *Dubravy delalis'chernei* ("the forest grew blacker"; *PSS* 2:96), and then the text repeats words and images from the temptation of the *chernets* in the third canto of *The Monk* quoted above. In "Rusalka" we read: *I vdrug . . . legka, kak ten' nochnaia, / Bela, kak pannii sneg kholmov, / Vykhodit zhenshchina nagaia / I molcha sela u bregov* ("And suddenly . . . light as a nocturnal shadow, / White like the early snow on the hills / A naked woman came forth / And sat silently on the shore"). The monk in this poem also attempts to resist. However, the rusalka's call as she disappears into the water, *Monakh, monakh! Ko mne, ko mne*! ("O monk, O monk, come to me, come to me"; *PSS* 2:97) is very enticing. The *otshel'nik strastnyi* ("passionate hermit") sits for three days awaiting the return of the rusalka. Then night descends, and when dawn appears, *Monakha ne nashli nigde* ("The monk is nowhere to be found"). All that remains is his *borodu seduiu* ("gray beard") floating in the water. We do not know what has happened. Did the monk commit suicide to thwart the temptation or in despair over the failure of the rusalka to return, or did she return and he yield, only to fall into despair over the loss of his identity as a monk for the sake of an erotic experience? What is important to note is that the monk is conquered or overcome by water, as was the figure of the black Satan in the earlier narrative poem. Furthermore we once again find a confusion of identities or the effect of doubling at the erotic moment. This confusion of identities at the erotic moment reappears, incidentally, in *The Stone Guest* (*Kamennyi gost'*) when Don Juan, who is represented as a poetic figure, disguises himself as a monk in an attempt to seduce Donna Anna, the sole instance of such a representation and such a disguise in the literary renditions of the Don Juan legend. In "Rusalka" this confusion of identities is further enhanced by the transformation of the monk into his beard, as in the earlier poem Molok was transformed into a figure with horns and a tail, all covered with stubble. These images, of course, surface once again in *Ruslan and Ludmila*,

Ruslan and Ludmila

even as the object of the final journey in *The Monk,* Jerusalem (Erusalim), and the eponymous object of erotic desire in "Rusalka" evoke the name of the monk's replacement, Ruslan. To this major work we now turn.

The dedication to *Ruslan and Ludmila* is addressed to the "Tsaritsas of my soul," the beautiful maidens the poet imagines trembling with love while reading "my sinful songs." I doubt the maidens Pushkin had in mind were the denizens of the brothels and back alleys who were the real objects of his "affection" during the years of debauch in Petersburg when Pushkin wrote *Ruslan and Ludmila,* often in the rest periods when he was recuperating from venereal disease.[12] Such a dedication, however, does reveal the complex and unconscious motivation of the aesthetic urge. The readers of the young poet's verses were not the maidens to whom he refers, but most often his male friends and critics in St. Petersburg. Indeed, it has been convincingly argued that this poem is the final realization of the aesthetic ideals of many of Pushkin's contemporaries, written in response to them and for them, all men.[13] In reality Pushkin here, as he will often do later as well, traffics in women in order to gain respect from men. Thus the dedication announces the underlying anxiety of identity and belonging the poet is seeking to hide. *Eros* fosters the *poesis* which serves to eliminate *eris* and ensure homosocial association.

It is important at the outset to remind ourselves that Pushkin's first major narrative poem, *Ruslan and Ludmila,* is a highly original and strange work. It is in part an attempt to suggest the world of Russian folklore and its literary variants, from which a number of the names are borrowed.[14] Pushkin's poem, however, in fact includes only a very few of the characteristic topoi of the *skazka* (fairy tale) or the *bylina* (folk epic)—for example, the magical water, the disembodied head, and the unexpected triumphant battle scene at the end. There is at the same time an accompanying attempt to suggest the historicity of the poetic representation: the names of two of the major characters, Rogdai and Farlaf, are culled from Karamzin's *History of the Russian State,* as is the description of Vladimir and the association of the Finnish people with wizardry. The enemies of the Kievan people are represented correctly as Pechenegs and not as Tatars, as in many of the epic forms. Of course, the general story follows the chronotope of romance, with its plot made of hindrances to the union of the lovers. While many details of the poem can also be traced to contemporary literary works, in the main *Ruslan and Ludmila* is a true Pushkin creation, not just in the beauty of its language, but in the peculiarities of the plotting and the imagery.[15] It is by these peculiarities that I will attempt to demonstrate the relationship to the earlier poems I have discussed here and to uncover the latent anxiety of blackness around which this first masterly work, I believe, is built.

The first canto of the poem, minus the famous introduction which was written five years later at Mikhailovskoe, tells the story of a marriage interrupted at the moment of consummation by the magical abduction of the bride. The wedding feast preceding the attempted consummation is attended by the groom's three rivals who, after the abduction, are reinstated as possible suitors. The four men are then sent on a journey to find the lost Ludmila, with the understanding that the finder is the keeper. The canto ends with Ruslan's encounter with the strange figure Finn who announces to Ruslan his fate, even as he tells of his own.

The first canto thus focuses on the themes of *eros* and *eris*. Although Ruslan is the chosen groom and apparently husband of the bride, both before and after the "wedding" he is surrounded by the rivals who threaten to steal his prize. The insecurity amidst all the official ceremony is signaled by the change Pushkin made in the historical name used for one of these rivals: Karamzin's Rakhdai is transformed into Rogdai.[16] The text of the whole poem then resounds with the sounds of the ominous homonyms, *rog/rok* (cuckold/fate) which mark this anxiety. What makes this insecurity so palpable, however, is the magical abduction of the bride. As in *The Monk*, the text approaches the moment of sexual union only to interrupt it, but here the coitus interruptus destabilizes the status of the lovers. The source of this destabilization is not yet clear, for at this point the abductor is identified only as *I kto-to v dymnoi glubine / Vsvilsia chernee mgly tumannoi* ("someone" who "soared in the hazy depths, blacker than the foggy darkness"; *PSS* 4:9). Furthermore, this destabilization is clearly marked throughout the text of the whole poem where Ludmila is inconsistently referred to as a *deva* (maiden) and unmarried *kiazhna* (princess), as well as a *nevesta* (bride) and even a *supruga* (spouse). The anxiety of this moment is made further manifest, however, by the authorial intrusion that follows immediately after the abduction: *I vdrug minutnuiu suprugu / Navek utratit'... o druz'ia / Konechno, luchshe b umer ia!* ("To lose suddenly forever one's momentary spouse ... O friends / Of course, I would rather die"; *PSS* 4:10). Needless to say, the psychological implications of this moment for the unfolding events in Pushkin's own marriage some ten years later (the "realizing metaphor") are as significant as they are obvious.

The rest of the first canto and by far its longest part is devoted to the encounter between Ruslan and the "elder" (*starets* and *starik* both occur in the text), named Finn. What most immediately strikes the reader is that this providential relationship between the hero and the voice of his fate is cast as a relationship between father and son. From this father Ruslan learns the name of his chief rival, the abductor, and his fated task, which is to gain entrance to the abductor's chambers (*obitel'* refers literally to a "cloister") and slay his rival. *Sud'ba tvoikh griadushchikh dnei, / Moi syn, v tboei otnyne vole* ("The fate of your days to come, / My son, is henceforth in your command"; *PSS* 4:13). This declaration of Ruslan's purpose and fate is then immediately followed by Finn's long tale of his own life story.

This story, however, is limited to one central event, Finn's love for Naina. She keeps on rejecting him, no matter what identity he shapes for himself, a shepherd or a hero. Frustrated, he resorts to magic, thinking the fateful words of erotic possession *Teper', Naina, ty moia!* ("Now, Naina, you are mine"; *PSS* 4:18). What he learns is that as in the case of Pankraty in *The Monk*, it is not he, but *rok* (fate) itself that controls his life. The magic does work and Naina falls in love with him, but Naina, he now discovers, is not the Naina he thought she was. His subsequent rejection of her love distorts Naina's own love and casts its shadow on Ruslan's fate. *Eshchë starushka ne zabyla / I plamia pozdnoe liubvi / S dosady v zlobu prevratila, / dushoiu chërnoi zlo liubia, / Koldun'ia staraia konechno / Voznenavidit i tebia* ("The old lady has not yet forgotten / And the late flame of love / She has transformed from vexation into spite / Loving evil with her black soul / The old sorceress, of course, / Will come to hate even you"; *PSS* 4:20). Naina's function in the rest of the work will be to use her "black soul" with its "vexation" and "spite" to create the obstacles on Ruslan's journey to regain Ludmila. Finn, however, assures Ruslan that this wicked mother-figure with the "black soul" will not conquer in the end: *No gore na zemle ne vechno* ("Grief on earth is not eternal"). Finn's story thus functions as both an anxiety vision and a wish fulfillment. The latent anxiety is that the wicked mother-figure with the black soul is the source of all rejection. The wish is that the good father-figure *Otets moi, ne ostav' menia* ("not abandon me"; *PSS* 4:21) and thus guarantee Ruslan's success in overcoming his rival (*eris*) and regaining his love (*eros*). The poem functions as a fantasy resolution of the anxiety and fulfillment of the wish.

The second canto is devoted to this *eris* and *eros*. It opens significantly, however, with a narratorial intrusion on the theme of rivalry. Just as the story has three named *soperniki* (rivals), so this digression refers to three types of rivals, also referred to as *soperniki*. The narrator begins this canto with the observation that there are rivals in *bran'* (battle), in *rytsari parnasskikh gor* (poetry), and in love, that is *eris*, *poesis*, and *eros*. But at this point it is the rivals in love who command his attention and give cause to his advice: *Zhivite druzhno, esli mozhno!* ("Live in friendship if you can"; *PSS* 4:22), because *sud'boiu nepremennoi / Devich'e serdtse suzhdeno* ("by fate absolute / Is a maiden's heart destined"). This narratorial intrusion is then followed immediately by Naina's machinations to help several of Ruslan's rivals in love. This short sequence is brought to a close when Ruslan, "faithful sword" in hand, actually encounters one of these rivals and is about to do battle with him. The text, however, is again interrupted, now by the central sequence of this second canto, which is devoted to the fate of Ludmila.

Only at the end of the canto does the text return to this interrupted battle between Ruslan and the *Rusi drevnii udalets* ("ancient warrior of Rus'"; *PSS* 4:36), Rogdai. This battle scene between these two rivals is significant for two reasons. First, Rogdai, the rival whose historical name Rakhdai, we recall, Pushkin transformed into an image of cuckoldry and *rog/rok* (fate), is the only rival whom Ruslan actually kills. Second, the representation of the battle (*eris*) is cast in erotic imagery. While the *borzy koni* ("swift steeds"; PSS 4:35) raise *chërnyi prakh* ("black dust") to the heavens, *Bortsy, nedvizhno spleteny* ("the warriors are immobily intertwined") and *Drug druga stisnuv* ("squeezing each other"), so that *Ikh chleny zloboi svedeny* ("their limbs are united by spite"; the word *chlen* also means "penis") and *Po zhilam bystryi ogon' bezhit* ("a quick fire rushes through their veins"). With *Na vrazhd'ei grudi grud' drozhit* ("breast trembling against hostile breast"), Ruslan suddenly *sryvaet* ("tears") his opponent from his saddle *zheleznoiu rukoiu* ("with his iron hand") and tosses him from the shore into the water. The second canto ends with the rumor that a rusalka caught Rogdai in her embrace and that henceforth the ghost of the former rival has haunted the shores, an ending that recalls the ballad "Rusalka." Thus the encounter with Rogdai, a character and episode Glinka eliminated in the operatic version of the work, serves to reveal both Ruslan's sexual anxiety and his wish-fulfilling encounter with his erotic double, spurred on by the characteristic *zloba* (spite). The textual interruption of the battle reiterates iconically the trope of *textus interruptus* that we saw also in the two Lycée poems. At the same time, however, the "black dust" of the sexual anxiety does not settle onto his fate, and he conquers his feared rival. Thus this first encounter with a rival prefigures the whole poem, for this is a tale in which the hero indeed overcomes all obstacles and attains his most cherished wish. *Ruslan and Ludmila* is truly the stuff which dreams are made of.

The central episode in the second canto shifts the focus from the rivals to the fate of Ludmila after her abductor *sorvav* ("had torn") Ludmila from her marital bed *rukoiu moshchnoiu svoei* ("with his mighty hand"; PSS 4:27). The parallel action and wording between Ruslan's moment of overcoming his double-rival Rogdai "with an iron hand" represented at the end of this canto and the "scoundrel's" moment of abduction described at the beginning of the central episode of the canto mark the latent connection between Ruslan and the abductor. This connection is underlined by the narratorial intrusion which follows in the text and takes the form of a simile: one male bird, a cock, has just embraced his "girl friend" (*podruga* is also used to refer to Ludmila at the moment of her abduction in the first canto), when another male bird, a kite, swoops down and carries her away, thus again interrupting the erotic moment. The simile marks the latent connection, but the difference between the two rival birds is that only one can fly. In this simile, as in the later cantos of this poem and of *The Monk*, we might recall Freud's well-known association of the image of flying with sexual intercourse. At any rate, this simile is then followed by a long description of Ludmila in captivity.

Ludmila is represented as unwavering in her love despite all the temptations of opulence and luxury. It is striking that in captivity Ludmila is accompanied by three surrogate rivals to Ruslan, the three maidens who assist her in her toilette and adorn her for the erotic encounter with her abductor that is to ensue. These three figures thus parallel the three rivals who set out with Ruslan to find the abducted Ludmila in the first canto, but their function is different: they are not out to get Ludmila away from her abductor and for themselves, but to abet the abductor in his erotic quest. However, neither the elegant attire provided by the three maidens, nor even the erotic atmosphere created by the *vesëlye pesni* ("gladsome songs"; *PSS* 4:29) of a *nezrimaia pevitsa* ("invisible singer") and the Tasso-like pleasure garden described now at length can sway Ludmila from her love for Ruslan. Ludmila is the first archetypal *vernaia zhena* ("faithful wife") in Pushkin's poetic universe. But then while walking in the pleasure garden she is overcome by sleep and *I vdrug nevedomaia sila* ("suddenly an unknown force"; *PSS* 4:33) whisks her through the air into the palace. The three maidens now undress her, the door to her room is opened, and her abductor enters for his awaited erotic conquest. To this abductor, the double of the narrator's hero Ruslan, I now turn.

His name is Chernomor, a name found in no Russian folklore, but probably known to Pushkin from Karamzin's folkloric poem "Il'ia Muromets."[17] The first half of the name is the Slavic root for *chern* (blackness), which we saw in various guises in *The Monk*. At first glance the abductor's name recalls the Russian word for the Chërnoe More (Black Sea). However, the second root component (*mor*) has two other meanings, "massive deaths," as in an epidemic, and "silk brocade." Thus the abductor's name encodes not only the connected themes of blackness and death-dealing water, themes we saw in *The Monk* and "Rusalka," but now more explicitly, if still latently, the underlying anxiety of a deadly threat from a coating of blackness. Furthermore, the extended description of Chernomor's entry into Ludmila's chamber reveals the layers of anxiety he represents, and therefore I shall cite in full this most significant passage:

Bezmolvno, gordo vystupaia,
Nagimi sabliami sverkaia
Arapov dlinnyi riad idët
Poparno, chinno, skol' vozmozhno,
I na podushkakh ostorozhno
Seduiu borodu nesët;
I vkhodit s vazhnost'iu za neiu,
Pod"iav velichestvenno sheiu,
Gorbatyi karlik iz dverei. (PSS 4:34)

Silently, stepping with pride,
Their naked sabers flashing,

> A long line of blackamoors enters
> In pairs, as properly as possible,
> And carefully on pillows
> They bear a gray beard;
> And behind it in dignity through the doors,
> With his neck raised up majestically,
> There enters a hunchbacked dwarf.

The *arap* (blackamoor), any identification with which Pushkin denied in his very first lyric, here returns in multiple form as the bearer of Chernomor's most significant marker, his long beard. The gray beard, of course, had already been associated with the monk, the assumed identity of the poet-narrator in Pushkin's first lyric and the central character in his first narrative poem; later in the ballad "Rusalka" this beard resurfaced precisely after what was either the death of the monk or his erotic encounter with the rusalka. Now the beard clearly functions as a phallic symbol, a gigantic penis on pillows handled with care. We need not draw upon Freud for such a symbolic reading, for certainly Pushkin would have known the infamous poem by Lomonosov, "A Hymn to the Beard" ("Gimn borode," 1756–57), which has a refrain repeated ten times that draws a parallel between a beard and one's *sramnaia chast'* ("private parts").[18] Furthermore, Pushkin himself seems to have been obsessed with the male private parts, particularly with the length of the penis, as can be seen in his epigram of 1817 (*PSS* 2:37) about General Orlov, whose lover needs a "microscope," and with his own genitals which in the poem "A Comparison" ("Sravnenie," *PSS* 1:296) he compares favorably to Boileau's.

In *Ruslan and Ludmila* the beard/penis has a particular psychological resonance. It is attended by what is referred to as *arapov chërnyi roi* ("a black swarm of blackamoors"; *PSS* 4:34) and is attached not to a monk as in the lyrics discussed above, but to another persona for the five-foot-six Pushkin, a dwarf. In "My Portrait," we should recall, Pushkin confessed that *Ma taille à celles des plus longs / Ne peut etre égalée* ("In height I cannot be compared to the tallest ones"; *PSS* 1:90). Chernomor, the would-be suitor, spouse, or just seducer, is thus not only the dark double of Pushkin's hero Ruslan, but of Pushkin himself. At the sight of him Ludmila jumps from her bed, grabs his cap, threatens him with her fist, screams in terror, and tries to run away. She is saved by the blackamoors' panic, for they rush Chernomor out the door, leaving behind the magical cap of invisibility which Ludmila will eventually put to good use. This interrupted erotic encounter is followed by a characteristic iconic, textual interruption of the narrative; what follows in its stead is the passage I discussed earlier, the erotically charged struggle between Ruslan and Rogdai, ending with latter's death apparently in the arms of a rusalka.

Ruslan and Ludmila

Thus Ruslan's victory over his *rog/rok* (fate), which closes the second canto, is only apparent; the dreadful Chernomor is still on the loose.

The third canto tells the story of Chernomor and his beard. It is a tale of rivalry (*eris*) between brothers, between Chernomor's brains and his big brother's brawn. But the canto opens with a most curious authorial digression addressed to his "verses" and "my kind reader." The narrator, in ironic tones, speaks of the "fateful question" raised by a critic of his poem: *Zachem Ruslanovu podrugu, / Kak by na smekh eë soprugu / Zovu i devoi i kniazhnoi?* ("Why as if to laugh at her spouse / Do I call Ruslan's girlfriend / Both a maiden and an unmarried princess?"; *PSS* 4:37). The ambiguity of Ruslan and Ludmila's sexual congress and hence marital status, which was hinted at in the narrative of the coitus interruptus and expressed iconically in the poetic structure of *textus interruptus*, is now directly thematized. Thus the story of Chernomor is immediately and intimately related to the central sexual anxiety of the whole poem. This anxiety itself is *zloby chërnuiu pechat'* ("the black imprint of spite").

This spite materializes in the person of the wicked mother-figure Naina, who in the form of a winged dragon flies into Chernomor's room while his "servants" (*raby* may be taken to suggest *arapy*) are combing out his curly beard. She announces to the dwarf that *No tainyi rok soediniaet / Teper' nas obshcheiu vrazhdoi* ("Mysterious fate has united / Us now in a common enmity"; *PSS* 4:38). To Naina Chernomor now reveals his *chudesnyi zhrebii* ("wondrous lot"; *PSS* 4:39), which will reduce Finn's prophetic words to naught. None of the three rivals can keep Ludmila from him, because he is protected by his beard. His sole undoing would be castration, the beard cut off by a *vrazhdebnyi mech* ("hostile sword"). Encouraged with this news, the *chërnyi zmii* ("black dragon"; *PSS* 4:39) Naina flies off. Terrified by the beard, Ludmila, off in her own room, picks up the cap of invisibility and disappears into safety. The elaboration of Chernomor's "wondrous lot" is then given by his rival brother whom Ruslan encounters on the field of death. This tale comprises the bulk of the third canto.

Chernomor's brother is modeled on the folkloric trope of the disembodied head, although his biography and fate are Pushkin's invention. Ruslan encounters him after his battle with Rogdai, while he is in search of a new sword. What Ruslan first sees is a *Vdali cherneet kholm ogromyi* ("huge black hill in the distance"; *PSS* 4:43) which seems to cough and breathe. His response is heroic: he attacks and overcomes the head, gaining his sword in the process. Helpless, the head explains to Ruslan how his "younger brother" and *sopernik* (rival), the *Kovarnyi, zlobnyi Chernomor* ("crafty, spiteful Chernomor"; *PSS* 4:47), tricked him with the story of a hidden sword. This sword, Chernomor claimed to have learned in *chërnye knigi* ("black books"; *PSS* 4:47), had the power to do them both in, by severing the older brother's head and the younger one's beard. The crafty dwarf, who like his counterpart Naina is continuously characterized in the text by the key emotions of *dosada, zloba* (frustration/vexation and spite), got his older brother to find the sword, tricked him into gaining its possession, then chopped off his bigger brother's head and set him in place to guard the dangerously powerful sword. The third canto ends with Ruslan, the powerful sword in hand, off on a mission of revenge against Chernomor, the ultimate rival of the betrayed brother and the apparently cuckolded hero. Thus at the end of the first half of the work, we see that the whole poem revolves around the two key emotions of *dosada, zloba* (frustration/vexation and spite) and two central images of power, the beard and the sword, symbols of the penis and the phallus, private sexual power (*eros*) and public power over sex (*eris*). *Poesis* is made by the pen dripping black ink, which is mightier than the penis (*eros*) or the sword (*eris*). Only in his poem does Pushkin, through his hero Ruslan, conquer the frustration over his uncertain public status and attain the love he could not find in the brothels of St. Petersburg.

The fourth canto switches to a new key. It begins once again with an authorial intrusion, this time returning to the themes of *eros* and *poesis*. Pushkin cites Zhukovsky's "Twelve Sleeping Maidens," only to transform the intertext into an erotic and poetic romp by telling of the adventures of Ratmir and the maidens who attend him. The inevitable erotic encounter is told with the marked voice of the voyeuristic narratorial "I" and, in opposition to the earlier scene with Chernomor and Ludmila, entails the seduction of the man by the maiden. This seduction ends, as do all others, with the iconic *textus interruptus*. The canto ends by returning to Ludmila and Chernomor. *Dosadoi, zloboi obmrachënnyi* ("Darkened by frustration and spite"; *PSS* 4:58), Chernomor resolves to make his conquest. He tricks Ludmila, ever hidden under her cap of invisibility, into thinking she sees Ruslan. In her excitement Ludmila lets the cap fall off her head, only to hear Chernomor's proclamation of possession, "She's mine!" But just at the moment of seduction, the dwarf hears the call of a *rog* (horn), and the canto ends yet again with the interruption of the sexual act. Chernomor flies off to meet the call, *Zakinuv borodu za plechi* ("his beard tossed onto his shoulders"; *PSS* 4:59).

The fifth canto gathers together the three central themes of *eros, eris,* and *poesis,* thus preparing for the conclusion of the work. It opens once again with a narratorial intrusion, this time about the virtues of "My Ludmila." This intrusion, however, segues directly into the culminating encounter of Chernomor and Ruslan. Flashing the sword, Ruslan gets Chernomor to fly him to Ludmila, as Pankraty was about to let the "black Satan" fly him off to Jerusalem. Once inside the castle, however, Ruslan cuts off the dwarf's beard. *Gde tvoia krasa? / Gde sila?* ("Where is your beauty? / Where is your power?"; *PSS* 4:63) he asks, as he weaves the strands of the beard onto his own helmet. With this symbolic castration and incorporation of his black double's erotic power, Ruslan emerges as the almighty hero before whom the *arapov chudnyi roi* ("wondrous swarm of blackamoors") takes fright and flees. In search of Ludmila with sword still in hand, Ruslan destroys Chernomor's pleasure garden and finds his beloved spouse, who has been cast into a deep sleep. Finn reappears to tell Ruslan to return to Vladimir's court in Kiev where all will be resolved. The anxiety of blackness seems to have been overcome, and the tale about to end. The key emotions, *dosada* and *zloba*, never again recur as markers of the poet's underlying psychological state, figured in Chernomor (the black self) and Naina (the black mother).

The representation of the journey to Kiev begins with a most curious authorial intrusion. The narrator begins to wonder: Could the young knight, *Bezplodnym plamenem tomias'* ("languishing with the fruitless flame"; *PSS* 4:65) of love, really have *Smiriv neskromnoe zhelanie / Svoe blazhenstvo nakhodil* ("found his bliss, while having restrained his immodest desire")? The answer the narrator gives to his enigmatic question reveals another layer of the latent erotic anxiety expressed in this text.

Monakh, kotoryi sokhranil
Potomstvu vernoe predan'e,
O slavnom vitiaze moëm,
Nas uveriaet smelo v tom:
I veriu ia! Bez rasdelen'ia
Unyly, gruby naslazhden'ia:
My priamo schastlivy vdvoëm.

The monk, who preserved
For posterity this true legend
About my renowned knight,
Boldly assures us he did:
And I believe him! Not shared,
Pleasures are depressing and crude:
We are only happy two together.

For the first and only time we are now told that the narrator has learned of this "true legend" from a monk. Now the narrator may be suggesting that he has read this story in some chronicle. But at the same time we know that "monk" is the adopted identity of Pushkin himself in his earlier poems. The not-so-hidden reference to masturbation, then, seems to elucidate those voyeuristic passages of erotic pleasure that surface in this text and in a number of the early works. The "monk" may be the one for whom sex with a woman of his fancy is denied, but who indulges himself with the idea of it, and not only in the body of his texts. If Byron thought that poetry was a kind of mental masturbation, for Pushkin masturbatory fantasy, *eros*, may be the muse that inspires his verse, *poesis*. At any rate, in real life Pushkin had a preference for prostitutes and loose women of the lower classes, for sex with them, as he wrote, was *Vivent les grisettes. C'est bien plus court et bien plus commode* ("shorter and more convenient"; 1828, *PSS* 14:32). In this regard the well-known Don Juan list is perhaps best read not as the more or less accurate record of Pushkin's consummated "loves," as some seem to imagine, but as a record of the "pleasures" aroused by the infatuation and often shared only in their transformation into poetry, as was the case with Natalia I. We may even well wonder whether Pushkin wrote poems about and to his "loves" because he "loved" them or whether he "loved" them in order to write the poems.

The fifth canto then continues the journey home, even as it returns to Ruslan's two other rivals for Ludmila, Ratmir and Farlaf. The main focus is on Ratmir, now a fisherman happily in love, ever singing the praises of his beloved. Ratmir has abandoned the life of the sword and erotic indulgence for the poetry of love. For him both *eris* and *eros* have become *poesis*. Ruslan and Ratmir sit in the midst of nature, as Ratmir waxes lyrical in the manner of Lensky a few years later:

Ona mne zhizn', ona mne radost'!
Ona mne vozvratila vnov'
Moiu utrachennuiu mladost',
I mir, i chistuiu liubov'. (*PSS* 4:70)

She is my life, she is my joy!
To me she has returned anew
My youth once lost,
And peace, and pure love.

But this idyll is quickly interrupted by the reappearance of Farlaf, who is now under the sway of the ever-threatening, black-souled, wicked mother figure Naina. With her help, Farlaf manages to steal Ludmila and the powerful sword. He then wounds Ruslan, who at the very end of the canto lies *nedvizhnyi, besdykhannyi* ("immobile and lifeless"; *PSS* 4:74). With his hero dead, the narrator will need a miracle to end his poem. The sixth canto is that miracle of transformation, the triumph of *eros, eris,* and *poesis* and the poetic conquest of the anxiety of blackness.

The last canto opens with an extended metapoetic digression (ll. 1–33) in which the narrator speaks of the relationship between *eros* and *poesis*. It is addressed to *milaia podruga* ("my dear friend"; *PSS* 4:75) and speaks of the narrator's indulgence in love at the expense of the *zvuki liry dorogoi* ("sounds of his dear lyre"). He confesses that *Liubov' i zhazhda naslazhdenii / Odni presleduiut moi um* ("Love and the desire for pleasures / Alone pursue my mind"). But then he notes that his dear friend *inogda svoi nezhnyi vzor / Nezhnee na pevtsa brosala* ("sometimes casts her tender gaze / More tenderly at the singer"; *PSS* 4:76) and decides *Sazhus' u nog tvoikh i snova / Brenchu pro vitiazia mladogo* ("once again to sit at your feet and strum about the young knight"). Not only does *eros* foster *poesis,* but *poesis* fosters *eros.* In either case the desired result is the transformation of *eris* into homosocial association. The address is to an imagined female admirer, but the tale is told to and for his male friends in order to gain their admiration.

The concluding canto quite rightly then continues the story by turning to an expansion of the theme of *eris.* Ruslan is magically brought back to life in order to reveal himself in all his heroic glory. Kiev is under attack by the Pechenegs, and Ruslan leads the battle and becomes the savior of Rus'. *S karloi za sedlom* (with the "dwarf on the back of his saddle"; *PSS* 4:83), the *V desnitse derzhit mech pobednyi* ("victorious sword in his right hand"; *PSS* 4:84), and the *Na shleme v'ëtsia boroda* ("beard wound round his helmet"), the heroic Ruslan arrives at court. He then enters Vladimir's chambers and magically awakens the sleeping Ludmila. All embrace, as even the two most feared rivals, Farlaf and the dwarf, are forgiven. To a number of critics this final forgiveness is the key to the meaning of the whole poem.[19] Like Glinka in his opera, they prefer to glide over the all-important battle unto death with the rival Rogdai, Ruslan's erotically charged conquest of the obstacle (*rog/rok*) to his love. And they fail to note that Naina is absent from the triumphant feast. The theme, I therefore believe, is not forgiveness, but fulfillment. It is significant that the poem ends with Vladimir presiding over a feast for all the family in the grand hall of his palace, for *Ruslan and Ludmila* concludes with what for Pushkin would be the ultimate fantasy wish: the victim-double of the black dwarf has been transformed into a hero, accepted into a noble family, rewarded with a bride both ever loyal and of ancient Russian heritage, and reconciled with his rivals. What is important to remember, of course, is that all live in harmonious association because Ruslan has disempowered Chernomor and Naina, the signs of his own anxiety of blackness.

Both *The Monk* and *Ruslan and Ludmila* end with reference to the main character riding (flying) off on his horse in a moment of apparent triumph. The image of the hero as horseman is significant not only because of the later poem *The Bronze Horseman* (*Mednii vsadnik*), but also because the horseman surfaces in several of Pushkin's self-portraits penned during the 1820s.[20] But in the self-portraits of this period there also occurs a glide from the man to the horse itself: one of the self-portraits represents Pushkin in what appears to be a likeness of a horse (see figure 4, 1825), and this is further complicated by his horselike self-portrait as an *arap*, drawn in the manuscripts of a draft of *The Blackamoor of Peter the Great* (see figure 5). Now in Pushkin's drawings horses are usually associated with sexuality—mounting a woman, with phallus erect, or copulating.[21] Thus the ending to these two works seems to reflect Pushkin's unconscious identification of his erotic fate with his less than noble ancestry, figured in his self-portraits as a horselike black man. The association of blackness and animality, of course, can be traced back to the "mixture of monkey and tiger" that troubled his youth. But in *Ruslan and Ludmila* the horse is associated with a triumph over the anxiety provoked by that "mixture." In *The Bronze Horseman,* however, where Pushkin's black ancestor putatively attains his highest power through the association with his godfather, Peter the Great, an association to which Pushkin devoted a great deal of psychic and literary time, the anxiety surfaces again. The great contradiction of this poem, the introductory praise of Peter the Great and his city built on the Neva versus the story of Evgeny's undoing by the very forces unleashed by Peter's accomplishments, is the sign of this anxiety. After all, once again we have a figure undone by water, a poet-lover who like the monk dies awaiting the love he cannot attain. Read thus, Pushkin's famous poem suggests that despite all the conscious effort, the anxiety of blackness never was resolved.

Ruslan and Ludmila, therefore, functions as a poetic wish fulfillment which serves as a denial of Pushkin's underlying anxiety of identity. His later obsessive fears of betrayal, rivalry, and cuckoldry can be seen beneath the manifest meaning of this work. These fears seem to be grounded mainly in an anxiety about sexual attractiveness, which erupts as frustration, anger, and spite that is somehow connected to the black ancestry so visible in his features which appear to him as animal-like. That this poem did not resolve this anxiety is directly evident from the lyric Pushkin wrote shortly after finishing the long narrative poem. In "To Yur'ev" ("Yur'evu") Pushkin opposes the handsome "Adonis," to whom all the young ladies are drawn but who happily has no need of their kisses, to the lyrical "I." The self-description of this lyrical "I" (quoted earlier in this essay) both deprecates and compliments the self: he is a *Potomok negrov bezobraznyi* ("ugly descendant of Negroes") who finds *Ia nravlius' iunoi krasote* ("favor with young beauties"), who *Na favna inogda gliadit* ("Once in a while take a glance at the faun"). What is striking for our purposes is that in this poem, written apparently just before leaving for his exile in the South, Pushkin not only refers disparagingly to his black ancestry, but replaces the image of the monk with the image of a faun, the mythic god, half-human and half-goat, whose animal features are horns, short legs, and a tail.

Like the monk, this image of the self as faun was shaped in Pushkin's Lycée years, in a poem entitled "The Faun and the Shepherdess" ("Favn i pastushka") which was published without the poet's permission in 1827. The poem, which consists of eight "scenes" (*kartiny*), is an idyll that tells of the love of Lila and Filon, whose first erotic moment is interrupted by a voyeuristic faun who stares at the lovers with the signature emotion of *dosada* (frustration and vexation; *PSS* 1:275). This faun is a *sopernik* ("rival") with *dva roga* ("two horns") who jealously weeps as he stares at the lovers. The centrality of this moment for Pushkin is marked by another realizing metaphor. In 1836 at the height of the drama of rivalry and cuckoldry in his life, Pushkin penned as a kind of image of this poetic metaphor an ambiguous portrait of himself which can be read as a sketch of Dante, his imagined poetic forefather crowned with laurel (the sketch is entitled "il gran Padre"), and a faun with two horns (see figure 6).

In "The Faun and the Shepherdess" the faun does not forget this erotic moment he sees but cannot share. Then one day, when he happens upon Lila, he gives her the chase. But to no avail, for she saves herself by jumping into a river from which she is soon miraculously transported back into the arms of her beloved Filon. Once again water dampens the hero's erotic temptation. The faun can only wander along the shore in despair: *Prosti, liubov' i radost'!— / So vzdokhom molvil on:— / V pechali tratit' mladost'. Ia rokom osuzhdën!* ("Farewell, O love and joy! / Said he with a sigh. / To lose my youth in sadness / Have I been destined by fate"; *PSS* 12:278). Thus the faun, like the monk, is an image of sexual desire frustrated by *rok* (fate).

Furthermore, the faun in the lyric "To Yur'ev," with his assumed horns, tail, and short legs as well as his declared black ancestry, also recalls Ruslan's doubles, the transformed Molok in *The Monk* and Chernomor. This faun is *bezobraznyi* ("ugly") and hence but an intruder on the erotic scene. The ugliness stems from the animal-like features which the lyrical "I" seems to read as the embodied traces of his black ancestry. And furthermore, this black ugliness is associated with the lyrical "I's" failure to know love, even as he seems to associate his own erotic impulse, the *Besstydnym beshenstvom zhelanii* ("shameless frenzy of desires"), with this black heritage and *v dikoi prostote* ("savage simplicity"). The poem undercuts this psychological honesty and stereotyped assumption, however, in its culminating assertion. The lyrical structure of opposition between the addressee and the lyrical "I" turns out to be a form of argument in which the poet tries to convince both the addressee and himself that his ugliness and shameless desires are the source of a kind of attractiveness that wins him a glance if not a kiss, let alone the *liubvi ne vedaia stradanii* ("sufferings of love"). Apparently Pushkin was not convinced enough by the argument to publish the poem for others to see. That was done by Yur'ev himself in 1829, just at the time when Petersburg was abuzz with the rumors of Pushkin's impending betrothal to the court beauty, Natalia Goncharova. That the latent fears hidden in his early verse became manifest in the marriage that was to follow, we all know. What is important to remember, however, is that Pushkin's fundamental anxiety of blackness, which seems to have caused him much psychological distress, was one of the major factors in creating the monk and faun who became the poet of Russia.

Notes

1. Catharine Theimer Nepomnyashchy, introduction to Abram Tertz, *Strolls with Pushkin* (New Haven: Yale University Press, 1995), 7.

2. M. N. Virolainan, ed., *Legendy i mify o Pushkine* (St. Petersburg: Gumanitarnoe agentsvo, 1995), 55.

3. Iu. M. Lotman, "Smes' obez'iany s tigrom," *Vremennik Pushkinskoi komissii*, no. 14 (1974): 110–12. Although Lotman admits that this phrase was used to refer to Pushkin's "physiognomy," he then wields his erudition to write/white out the reference to Pushkin's black African heritage. The obvious association of monkeys and tigers with Africa is not explored. Furthermore, Lotman fails to deal with Pushkin's references to his own ancestry (or this phrase) in such works as "To Natalia," "My Portrait," or "To Yur'ev." This ambivalence on the part of Russian scholars to the issue of Pushkin's blackness is by now widespread. The best treatment of this subject is in the seminal work by the American Pushkinist, J. Thomas Shaw, "Pushkin on His African Heritage," which is reprinted in this volume. My article is meant as a friendly rejoinder to Shaw's quite correct contention that "Pushkin was proud of both sides of his family genealogy." I am interested in the unconscious sources for this extraordinary pride.

4. Eve Kosofsky Sedgwick, *Between Men: English Literature and Male Homosocial Desire* (New York, Columbia University Press, 1985). This book explores among other things the way in which heterosexual men use their relationships with women, real or imagined, in order to foster their association with other men (homosocial desire). This notion is grounded in the work of Levi-Strauss on "trafficking with women" in *The Elementary Structures of Kinship,* especially in its reworking by Gayle Rubin, "The Traffic in Women: Notes toward a Political Economy of Sex," in *Toward an Anthropology of Women,* ed. Rayna Reiter (New York: Monthly Review, 1975), 157–210.

5. David M. Bethea, *Realizing Metaphors: Alexander Pushkin and the Life of the Poet* (Madison: University of Wisconsin Press, 1998).

6. P. K. Guber, *Don-zhuanskii spisok A. S. Pushkina* (Petrograd, 1923), 43–44.

7. Iu. M. Lotman, *Aleksandr Sergeevich Pushkin: Biografiia pisatelia*, 2nd ed. (Leningrad: Prosveshchenie, 1983), 19–21.

8. B. Tomashevskii, *Pushkin* (Moscow and Leningrad: Akademiia nauk, 1956), 1:40–41.

9. Tomashevskii, *Pushkin*, 1:41.

10. Ibid., 1:44.

11. Ibid., 1:544.

12. Guber, *Don-zhuanskii*, 48–51.

13. V. A. Koshelev, *Pervaia kniga Pushkina* (Tomsk: Volovei, 1997), 26–44.

14. Koshelev, *Pervaia kniga*, 53–60.

15. Tomashevskii, *Pushkin,* 1:339. But see Koshelev, *Pervaia kniga,* passim, for many precedents in the poetry of the period.

16. The form "Rogdai" can also be found in earlier works by Narezhnyi and Zhukovskii, which may have served as Pushkin's immediate source. See Koshelev, *Pervaia kniga,* 56.

17. Koshelev, *Pervaia kniga,* 58.

18. M. V. Lomonosov, *Izbrannye proizvedeniia* (Moscow and Leningrad: Sovetskii pisatel', 1965), 279–82. I am thankful to the anonymous reader who reminded me of this poem.

19. Koshelev, *Pervaia kniga,* 120.

20. R. G. Zhuikova, *Portretnye risunki Pushkina: Katalog atributsii* (St. Petersburg, 1996), figures 64, 74, 79.

21. Sergei Denisenko, *Eroticheskie risunki Pushkina* (Moscow, 1997), 129, 133, 135, respectively. For a discussion of this theme in relation to Pushkin's verse, see pp. 59–63.

David M. Bethea

How Black Was Pushkin? Otherness and Self-Creation

ALEXANDER PUSHKIN is Russia's national poet, with all that means in the larger and smaller senses. One thing this means is that the difference we identify as *Russian* culture, whether viewed from the outside in or from the inside out, is simply not there without Pushkin. Make Dostoevsky or Tolstoy or Chekhov the central figure in that culture, its "origin without origins," and that margin of difference looks very different, and considerably less Russian, indeed. But Pushkin also had a black great-grandfather, Abram Petrovich Gannibal, who according to family history was the son of an Abyssinian prince as well as (but this "as well as" counts for a great deal) the ward and godson (hence the patronymic) of the most illustrious of all Russian tsars. Somewhere between these terms—between how Pushkin *became* the poet who best or most fully exemplified the Russians' views of their culture as forever both/and (both "European" *and* something else) and how the *given* of his racial inheritance entered into his psychic makeup—lies our quarry. The extent of Pushkin's "blackness" is not, as I hope to demonstrate, exclusively or even primarily a question of "blood." In this respect, what one contemporary writer (Itabari Njeri) terms ironically the "little-dab'll-do-you" rule would be a clear impoverishing of the Pushkin phenomenon.[1] At the same time, how the poet saw himself on the surface (his "Negroid" features) certainly played a prominent role in his self-fashioning, from the adolescent "mirror phase" of "My Portrait" (1814) on.

Blackness was for Pushkin both something real, given (he cared about surfaces), *and* something styled, something to be worked with. Yes, race counts for Pushkin, but it does not necessarily count more than other gifts/curses of "fate," especially that of class. That his genealogy on his father's side could be traced back some six centuries to the "old" Russian nobility (*stolbovoe dvorianstvo*), with numerous ancestors playing visible, often obstreperous roles in his country's history, was a fact of immense significance and pride to him. By the same token, Gannibal himself was not just any African but the *son of a prince* whose own name was reputed to have ties to the famous Carthaginian general.[2] What Pushkin wrote about Byron near the end of his life could have been said (and considering the exclamation, *was* being said) with equal validity about himself: "The Byron family is one of the most ancient in the English aristocracy . . . [its] name is mentioned with honor in the English chronicles. The title of lord was bestowed on the family in 1643. It has been said that Byron held his genealogy dearer than his artistic creations. A feeling very understandable!"[3] The idea here is that the Byrons (and, by implication, the Pushkins) had a history and *belonged* to history, a fact that no one in the present, despite scandal and obloquy, could take away from them. Thus, when the democratic journalist Faddei Bulgarin (who strictly speaking had roots in the lower-level Polish gentry/*szlachta*) made fun of Pushkin's aristocratic pretensions by calling his mother (known in her youth as the "beautiful Creole") a *mulatka* (mulatto woman), the jibe, however underhanded, was not racial *tout court*. Rather, it was racial *and* political (not only the Russian/Polish fault line, but the fact that Bulgarin was a spy for the tsarist police) *and* social (the "aristocrats" and the "democrats" vying for primacy in the new no-holds-barred literary marketplace) all at the same time. Race is such an elusive category to get at in Pushkin precisely because he rarely presents himself or his characters/poetic speakers as being defined wholly by this given (there are exceptions). But before venturing further, I would like to propose why, from within our space-time, it is so difficult for us to construct a conceptual bridge back to Pushkin in his.

PUSHKIN AND BLACKNESS: HOW TO APPROACH IT

We have heard it more than once, but it bears repeating: rape is a crime not only of the body, but of the mind, and not only of the mind (intellect, cognition), but of the "soul" (the place, mythical or no, where one's private emotions and personhood reside). Beneath the sexual violation lies another violation, more horrifically magnetized still. Rape cannot be spoken of to the victim in cool forensic terms because that is itself a repetition—describing rationally the savaging of a part of you that was more than rational—of the rape. A white woman (or a white man, i.e., the inmate as potential victim) can, with a small leap of imaginative empathy, not only understand what happens during a rape, but *feel* it, begin to internalize its pathology of humiliation and power. Yet what happens when it is a people who experience their past as a rape, a violation both figuratively and (as was too often the case) literally *of one race by another*? Here we have entered the haunted realm of collective trauma, of pan-psychic violation, so that no amount of "explaining" and "rationalizing" and even-tempered "denial" can get to and extinguish the flames of this molten core of what Dostoevsky so aptly termed *obida* (hurt, insult). How does one give back what was not one's to take in the first place (in this case, not only the tabooed territory of reproductive access, but *personhood* itself)?

As I have already suggested, given his family history, Pushkin clearly did not feel violated by the past. To be sure, he was deeply dismayed in the 1830s by the decline of his class, but that decline was never imagined as a dark and malevolent assault on one's personhood, as a deliberately cruel insistence that one's people had never existed as human beings. On those occasions in his life when Pushkin felt most deeply offended and came closest to expressing something akin to Dostoevskian *obida,* such as the rumor spread in his youth that he had been whipped by the authorities (an aristocrat's person was always supposed to be respected) or the instances after his marriage when the police opened and perused his letters to his wife (this was his private space), we are again faced with the category of class—the nobleman's amour propre. Therefore, despite his keen awareness of racial prejudice (about which I will speak more in due course), Pushkin would not have shared the "voice zone" of someone like Frantz Fanon when the latter seethes,

> What! When it was I who had every reason to hate, to despise, I was rejected? When I should have been begged, implored, I was denied the slightest recognition? I resolved, since it was impossible for me to get away from an *inborn complex,* to assert myself as a BLACK MAN. Since the other hesitated to recognize me, there remained only one solution: to make myself known.[4]

Pushkin is pre-Dostoevskian both in terms of his understanding of genre (the rules of a particular discourse formation can be bent or played with but they cannot be broken or dismissed altogether) and in terms of the consciousness (poetic, prosaic, historiographic, epistolary, etc.) that can be given speech within that genre. Fanon, on the other hand, is clearly post-Dostoevskian, post-Nietzschean, post-Freudian. His writing is a cri de coeur that attempts to break down, through its "unlawful" blend of psychoanalysis, personal interview and anecdote, and literary criticism, the walls of polite academic discourse because there is no place for him in that discourse. In order to "make himself known" to the other (France, Europe) that has overdefined him (the Antillean), he opts out. He becomes THE BLACK MAN. For what is it the white man can say, what is it any person can say, to this Underground Man who is hurt to the core precisely because he senses that you don't *see* him? Fanon's language here is the verbal equivalent of the scene in Dostoevsky's novel when the hero/antihero decides to "play chicken" with his arrogant adversary on the sidewalk. The rage of the victim has put an end to dialogue because the terms of that "dialogue" are deemed inherently unjust.

Still—and here is where I believe we can begin to build our conceptual bridge back to the poet—Pushkin understood well and wrote powerfully about the dangerous dynamics of group violation (in this instance, the Russian peasantry) in such later works as *The History of Pugachev* (*Istoriia Pugacheva,* 1834) and *The Captain's Daughter* (*Kapitanskaia dochka,* 1836). One of my framing assumptions in the discussion to follow is that the poet, while never a psychological realist in the post-Romantic sense, would be in essential agreement with James Baldwin in "Here Be Monsters": "Each of us, helplessly and forever, contains the other—male in female, female in male, white in black, and black in white. We are part of each other. Many of my countrymen appear to find this fact exceedingly inconvenient and even unfair, and so, very often, do I. But none of us can do anything about it."[5] Pushkin would not have expressed it this way—again, how he did express it will be our primary topic—but that he understood implicitly, and long before Bakhtin, that each of us, whatever our *givens,* is defined *through the other* is absolutely certain. Proof of this assertion is found virtually everywhere in Pushkin, beginning with his favorite heroine, Tatiana in *Eugene Onegin,* who, observed more closely, is a charmingly novelistic version of the Jungian anima, a distillation of all those traits (isolated and unappreciated in her family, raised by a beloved nanny from the common people, at home more in nature than in society, deeply superstitious, an impressionable devourer of books, etc.) that the poet held sacred but could not speak about "sincerely" in his own male person. Hence when Henry Louis Gates writes, "Coming from a tiny segregated black community in a white village, I knew both that 'black culture' had a texture, a logic, of its own *and* that it was inextricable from 'white' culture,"[6] the psychological vector here could belong to Pushkin, only it was the "texture" of *Russian* culture, its uniqueness and consciousness of its own worth and dignity, he was protecting against an "inextricable" relation to Europe (mainly France) that threatened to make what was his either invisible or, the same thing, too much the creation of that other. We as contemporary readers will never understand Pushkin until we acknowledge the force field, the competing vectors, of his core loyalties. When addressing "Europe" (Shakespeare, Byron, Voltaire, Ovid, Goethe, Scott, etc.), as he often did in his creative work, he was first and foremost *Russian* (European + something "other"); when addressing his countrymen, especially those who did not necessarily respect him or his métier, he could be Russian (one of "us") + *other* (impoverished nobleman among the wealthy and influential, unreliable political subject among the obsequiously loyal, a fuming Othello among the young courtiers and tsar who had their eye on his beautiful Desdemona—in short, one of "them"). The point, one that resonates with much contemporary African American thinking, is that, regardless of the situation, Pushkin wrote and lived in such a way that he refused, as a matter of honor, to be defined by a majority alterity that denied his uniqueness and creative potential *as a human being.*

David M. Bethea

What does this (the refusal to be overdefined by the other) mean, how does this work, in concrete terms? To begin with, Pushkin was utterly unsentimental about human nature. Yet he gave all people, without regard for the givens, credit for having their own tangible desires. This is what is liberating about reading Pushkin: no one in his world exists as an abstraction, finished off, which is another way of saying that everyone exists in the fullness of his or her own potentiality. Similarly, there are no discounts for the accidents of "fate," since that very *sud'ba* or *rok* could be arbitrary, cruel or beneficent without reason, to anyone. While he went on record several times with statements bemoaning the general fact of slavery in the United States, Pushkin did not feel the emotional need to idealize out of that suffering (he also had the good sense not to say too much about that of which he had only limited knowledge). If the pangs of personal remorse were well known to him, he seemed to have no sense of corporate guilt.[7] Here, for example, he writes to his good friend Prince Viazemsky on the theme of Greek independence in connection with Byron's death at Missolonghi in April 1824:

> Your idea of glorifying his [Byron's] death in a fifth canto of his Hero [i.e., *Childe Harold*] is charming. But it is not in my power—Greece defiled this idea for me. About the fate of the Greeks one is permitted to reason, just as of the fate of my brothers the Negroes—one may wish both groups freedom from unendurable slavery. But it is unforgivable puerility that all enlightened European peoples should be raving about Greece. The Jesuits have talked our heads off about Themistocles and Pericles, and we have come to imagine that a nasty people, made up of bandits and shopkeepers, are the legitimate descendants and heirs of their school-fame. You will say that I have changed my opinion. If you would come to us in Odessa to look at the fellow countrymen of Miltiades, you would agree with me.[8]

It is the unvarnished quality of these statements—the sarcastic refusal to inflate or deflate artificially the situation of the Greeks—that is refreshing to the modern (or postmodern) psyche. Direct contact with the foreign/other (the melting pot of 1824 Odessa) may be interesting, stimulating (mainly aesthetic categories), indeed it may be the only way one learns anything, but it does not by itself confer moral grandeur. People in Pushkin's eyes are always escaping out from under the literary clichés we apply to them, and that itself is *good*. However, they don't escape *to someplace better,* only back into their own distinctive humanity. The butt of Pushkin's sarcasm is not aimed at the "bandits and shopkeepers" (after all, they are doing what bandits and shopkeepers usually do, if only we would see them as people and not types), but at the notion, somehow too full of Byron's own hubris, that European Romanticism can or should come to the aid of a far-flung freedom movement in the name of a now-abstract classical heritage (Themistocles, Pericles, Miltiades). Pushkin is saying, Don't dragoon me into your Manfredian passion play—I have my own life to live and my own literary culture (ultimately un-Byronic) to create. I will make up my own mind. Respect for the other cannot be prior to respect for oneself.

Before turning directly to Pushkin's poetic "episteme" and to the theme of blackness in his work, I should also mention how this Russian writer forces us, as Americans, to question our own indwelling ways of knowing. For if he is aristocratic or noble (in both the class and the spiritual senses), Pushkin is likewise intensely *undemocratic,* and this orientation too has serious implications for how the category of race is presented in his writings. He begins, for example, his 1836 essay on the "notes" of John Tanner with the following:[9]

> For some time now the North American States have been attracting the attention of the most thoughtful people in Europe. The reason for this has nothing to do with political events—America has been calmly carrying out its way of life [*poprishche*], a way of life thus far flourishing and free of danger, one strong in a peace made secure by its geographical position, and one become proud through its institutions. But several profound minds have recently taken up the study of American manners and decrees, and their observations have again raised questions once thought long resolved. Respect for this new people and for their [legal] code [*ulozhenie*], the fruit of the latest enlightenment, has been seriously shaken. With amazement one has seen democracy in its repugnant cynicism, cruel prejudices, and intolerable tyranny. Everything noble, disinterested, everything that elevates the human soul, has been suppressed by implacable egoism and passion for comfort: a majority brazenly oppressing society; the slavery of Negroes amid a high level of education [*obrazovannost'*] and freedom; the persecution of those with family trees [*rodoslovnye goneniia*] in a people not having a nobility; on the part of the voters, greed and envy; on the part of those governing, timidity and servility; talent that through respect for equality is forced to accept voluntary ostracism; a rich man who dons a tattered blouse [*kaftan*] in order not to offend the haughty poor he sees on the street yet secretly despises. Such is the picture of the American States recently presented to us.[10]

I cite this passage at some length because it again gives us a rich context in which to place any statements Pushkin might make about "my brothers the Negroes." What Pushkin objects to, through the lens of Tocqueville's "profound mind" in *De la démocratie en Amérique,* is the potential absence of the spiritually beautiful (the notion of *blagorodnoe* as something done not out of personal gain) in this new world.[11] Yes, an aristocracy can be smug and blind to the other (Pushkin knew his share of such people, beginning with the Count Vorontsov who was responsible for having him sent into internal exile to Mikhailovskoe), but if the very form of government, in its "leveling" fervor, makes an aristocracy of the spirit unlikely or impossible as well, then Pushkin has serious doubts about its future trajectory. He fears, as do Tocqueville and Talleyrand, throwing the baby (the "poetic" impulse to the *blagorodnoe*, "leav[ing] the hero his heart,"[12] as he wrote elsewhere in a famous poem) out with the bath water (the aristocracy as historical class that had outlived its time). To give the poet his due, he is certainly not arguing as an insider in these lines: he understands all too well that his own class is in eclipse, having been supplanted by Peter's "meritorious" or service aristocracy, and he knows that he and his "loyal opposition" colleagues have been relegated to the margins by history, forced to eke out an existence as writers in this new "third estate." In short, his position, whether we agree or disagree with it, is not *from power*. All the fears that Pushkin expresses in this opening passage—the envy and pettiness that are indistinguishable as voice zone from legitimate criticism, the talent that must cloak itself in egalitarian disguise, the sacrificing of principle on the altar of majority whim, the "passion for comfort" that can be spiritually deadening, etc.—are with us today. And it is into this litany of doubt that Pushkin inserts his own condemnation of slavery: America—as opposed to Russia, with its huge population of serfs/indentured "souls"—is wealthy, free, and educated enough to afford (in every sense) to treat its people, including the Negroes still waiting to be citizens, equally. This is the post-Karamzinian Pushkin speaking, the "conservative liberal" who feared a too-conscious emulating of either Europe (the French Revolution) or America (the American Revolution).[13]

VOLIA/DOLIA, OR FATE AND THE FREE MAN

The gifted critic and writer Andrei Sinyavsky (who wrote his creative work under the pseudonym Abram Tertz) was the first to point out the important rhyme pair *volia/dolia* ("freedom," "will"/"lot," "fate") in Pushkin's poetry and thinking in general: "Despite dissensions and preventative measures Pushkin had a sense of fellowship with fate, which liberated him from fear, suffering, and vanity. *Volia* (freedom) and *dolia* (fate) are synonymous rhymes in his works. The more we trust in Providence, the more freely we live, and complete submission is as happy as a lark."[14] Here the otherwise fine English translation cannot fully convey the lightness and insouciance of Tertz's prose, a prose consciously staged to challenge the heaviness and seriousness of the "philological" tradition in Russian and Soviet Pushkin studies. But with his typical brilliance the critic-interlocutor overstates the case: *volia* and *dolia* are not "synonymous" rhymes in Pushkin. Rather, they are words with identical endings but different beginnings. It is the sameness within the difference that is the miracle of poetic speech. The poet is not interested in superimposing *volia* on *dolia,* in carving out an exact fit where the one becomes the other. There is not enough plot potential for the poetically lived life in this. Instead, he takes the givenness which it is the "fate" of every human being to have—one's gender, class, race, national history, etc.—and he asks for the rhyme partner that can, potentially, emerge from that fate—the "freedom" we all must seek, *given the givens.* Something is allotted (as a poet is vouchsafed "out of nowhere" the first partner in a rhyme pair), something is striven for (the second partner that one has to believe *will* come if one is willing to live in a condition of risk, openness to chance and change, "trust in Providence"). All rhyme schemes (as games and social codes in life) are arbitrary by definition—that in and of itself is literally *not worth questioning.* Character is formed and beauty is created in life and in words, which for Pushkin are clearly alchemical extensions of one another, when the arbitrary is not transcended (movement beyond, outside of) but struggled with (as a sculptor labors with stone)[15] in such a way that energy and movement and the thrill of unexpectedness arise out of the inert material itself. The dazzling arabesques of the ballerina Istomina's dance within the tightly corseted structure (a modified sonnet) of the Onegin stanza is a prime example of this.[16] Tertz's formulation is perhaps as close as we can come as moderns to a "philosophy" on Pushkin's part, since the poet had a kind of congenital allergy to describing his way of knowing in abstract or philosophical terms.

At the same time, Tertz is quite skeletal and elliptic—in a way as revealing of himself as of his subject. Under the circumstances, it might help to show the reader how the *volia/dolia* rhyme pair operates in different concrete situations:

1. From *The Fountain of Bakhchisarai*:
    The old man's law was
    Her youthful *whim.*
    He knew only one care:
    That his beloved daughter's *lot*
    Would be, like a spring day, clear . . .[17]

2. From *The Gypsies*:
    Be one of us—grow accustomed to our *lot,*
    That of vagrant poverty and *freedom*—
    You are not born for our wild *lot,*
    You only wish *freedom* for yourself . . .[18]

3. From *Eugene Onegin*:
    Now I know you are *free* [lit. "it is in your will/power"]
    To punish me with your scorn.

> But if you possess even a drop of pity
> Toward my unhappy *lot*,
> You will not abandon me.[19]

4. From the poem "It's time, my friend, it's time":
   > There is no happiness on earth, but there are peace and *freedom*.
   > For a long time now I have been dreaming of an enviable *lot*—
   > For a long time, I, a weary slave, have contemplated flight
   > To a distant abode of labor and pure pleasure.[20]

Each of these examples, except perhaps for the last, which is a special case, explores the relation of self to other in a quintessentially Pushkinian way. The first describes how the parent, in this instance the father of Maria, tries to do everything in his power so that this spiritually luminous child can experience a perfect seamlessness between "lot" and "freedom." He wants the givens of her background/upbringing to mimic as closely as possible the phrase "your wish [pleasure principle] is my command [reality principle]." Unfortunately, this sort of cloudless happiness is not sustainable in the sublunar world, and it is not long before the girl falls into captivity in Khan Girei's seraglio. It is also true that this deployment of the *volia/dolia* pairing is the least interesting in terms of plot creation—a kind of prelapsarian "before." After all, life is struggle, and character is formed and spiritual beauty created only when one's personal will/freedom and one's lot are not in perfect harmony.

The second example shows Pushkin, as speaking intelligence behind the plot as well as veiled autobiographical presence ("*Aleko*" vs. "*Alek*sandr") in it, living down the self-indulgent excesses of the Byronic type. Now the self-other contrast is between the old gypsy, with his wisdom and life experience, and Aleko, who is fleeing a dark past of crime and passion and who chooses to try to fit in to the *dolia* of his new gypsy "family." The first quote, spoken in the voice of the old man, welcomes Aleko into the group, provided he accept the notion that the freedom of the gypsy life comes at a cost: nothing in this world, neither people nor things, can be owned or fixed in place. Like the carts at the center of this chronotope, everything is in motion. This *dolia* is precisely the opposite of the one Maria's father wishes for her. And Aleko, a child of civilization whether he likes it or not, cannot genuinely internalize his new lot. As fast as he in his alienation runs from the society and its codes he would spurn, he runs to them, especially the one that dictates the free-spirited Zemfira must be "his." In other words, Aleko, and the self-absorbed type Pushkin is trying to exorcise through his characterization, refuses to live by the rules of the game he has asked to join. That is what the old man means in the second use of the rhyme pair, at the poem's tragic climax, when he says "you are not born for our lot"— i.e., you do not *have it in you*—precisely because you want freedom/whim only for yourself. To play the *volia/dolia* game, to have the pleasure of being Zemfira's lover, one has to be willing to live with the condition that she can, and probably will, leave for another at any moment. Every expression of *volia* is tethered to its corresponding *dolia*: we experience ourselves through the other. What makes the use of the rhyme pair more damning (and potentially self-critical) in *The Gypsies* than in *The Fountain of Bakchisarai* is that Aleko appears to agree to the terms of his adoptive fate; nothing is forced upon him as an accident of birth. Therefore, when he traduces the spirit of the old man's original invitation and murders Zemfira and her young gypsy, he commits an act not only criminal and "Byronic," but also, and more importantly, ignoble. In effect, he *cheats*.

Our third example comes from Tatiana's famous letter to Onegin, which happens to have been written very near the time (fall 1824) that Pushkin was completing *The Gypsies*. In this instance the *volia/dolia* tension is presented from the point of view of Pushkin's favorite (and, as mentioned above, personally most revealing) heroine. Although Pushkin can be very critical of the feminine other in letters and notes, especially when that other provokes jealousy and appears to manipulate the poet's hot feelings with a cool reserve he cannot reach, in the more disinterested truth of his creative laboratory he understood with great sensitivity and insight the different "givens" of the female world. He understood, for example, that desire is particular and more often than not unreasonable (here Tatiana has fallen in love with the new neighbor Onegin not because of any inherent merit on his part, but because the season and sensibility happen to be right for this *baryshnia*/"village maiden"), but he also understood that *acting on that desire* was considerably more risk-laden for a young woman of the heroine's class and background than for her male counterpart. In other words, when Tatiana says that Onegin has the will/power/freedom to scorn or dismiss her, she is really saying that she is herself going against the rules of polite discourse by initiating the epistolary exchange, stepping out of her assigned role, so to speak. This is something that makes her potentially "unbecoming" (at least with respect to current societal norms) and ridiculous. Yet it is Pushkin's great gift to make this shy forwardness both charming and poignant. We as readers allow Tatiana her verbal indiscretion because, as opposed to Aleko's rule-breaking, she is making herself more rather than less vulnerable. She is not cheating, not using her situation, but is in fact acting honestly and honorably by not playing the flirt. By thus putting her fate in Onegin's hands in a gamble that could cost her everything, she creates poetic expectation and heightened interest in her as a personality and sensibility. At the same time, we do not as it were "make allowances" (disregard the givens) for her because she is a woman, for the very reason that she makes no such allowances for herself. Instead, we are persuaded by the power of her portrait, its seeming spontaneity and non-self-consciousness that are also real and highly conventional, to enter into its world and recognize its desires as legitimate. That those desires are not ultimately acted upon is not a reflection on Tatiana (she was ready to give herself) but on a world, so presciently captured in the novel-in-verse genre, that needs her poetry (the imaginative potential in all of us) yet cannot ignore its own prose. It is hard to imagine a self-other, in this instance male-female, dialogue richer and more exquisitely intertwined than this.

Our final example of the *volia/dolia* rhyme is, if possible, even more telling. It is written in the voice of Pushkin's own late lyric speaker, a voice that, while arguably not coterminous with the words and thoughts of the historical person, is much closer to that person than any of the previous examples. That may be one reason why Pushkin never published this uncompleted fragment: perhaps it sounded too personal, too private, for the universalizing tendency (the overcoming of the particular) inherent in his understanding of the lyric impulse. In any event, the poet included on the surviving manuscript copy an outline for the poem's continuation: "Youth has no need for the 'at home,' [while] maturity is horrified at *its own* isolation [*uedinenie*]. Happy is he who finds a spouse [*podruga;* lit. 'female friend']—then he should withdraw *home*. O, shall it be soon that I carry my Penates to the country—the fields, garden, peasants, books; poetic labors—the family, love, etc.—religion, death."[21] Not only does this outline reproduce accurately the poeticized values of Tatiana's youth (the *derevnia*/"countryside") that she is forced, through her own contract with fate, to forgo in her move to the capital and marriage, but it also shows how her own plot is worked out in maturity, only in reverse, from the city *back to the country*. "There is no happiness on earth, but there are peace and freedom": this could be spoken by the elegant society princess who, unhappy in love yet secure in her lot, keeps a place in her heart for the girl she once was. It is not the good-natured general's fault, something Tatiana understands implicitly, that he does not correspond to the "secret guest" of her girlhood dreams. *Pokoi* (peace—"inner tranquility") and *volia* (freedom), recalled against the Mikhailovskoe-inspired backdrop of those qualities of "home"—fields, garden, peasants (Tatiana's and Pushkin's nanny), books, family, love, religion, death—shared by the heroine and her creator, are the most a poetic nature can ask for. Happiness has no ontological rhyme partner. But of course Pushkin, when he utters these words, is not looking back (Tatiana's youth), but forward (his longed-for flight out of St. Petersburg, debt, jealousy, and the demeaning role of aging *Kammerjunker*). The *ustalyi rab* (weary slave), a concept that leads us directly into Pushkin's treatment of the theme of blackness, *mechtaetsia* (dreams) of giving up the game, but knows in his heart that he can't. One's lot (the rules of the game) is fixed by fate; one's freedom (how one exercises choice within the rules) is fixed by the nature of the game. Pushkin's way out was in the end not voluntary flight but involuntary (because left to chance) liberation—a duel.

Finally, the expression of what might be termed Pushkin's philosophy of life through the *volia/dolia* rhyme pair could be relegated to a footnote in any study of "Pushkin and blackness" except for one important reason: it is, as I understand it, almost identical to the philosophy of certain influential "conservative liberals" among contemporary black thinkers, writers, and academics. As the economist Glenn C. Loury eloquently confronts both the importance and nonimportance of racial difference in his life:

> Who am I, then? Foremost, I am a child of God, created in his image, imbued with his spirit, endowed with his gifts, set free by his grace. The most important challenges and opportunities that confront me derive not from my racial condition, but rather from my human condition. I am a husband, a father, a son, a teacher, an intellectual, a Christian, a citizen. In none of these roles is my race irrelevant, but neither can racial identity alone provide much guidance for my quest to adequately discharge these responsibilities. The particular features of my social condition, the external givens, merely set the stage of my life; they do not provide the script. That script must be internally generated, it must be a product of a reflective deliberation about the meaning of existence for which no political or ethnic program could ever substitute.
>
> Or, to shift the metaphor slightly, the socially contingent features of my situation—my racial heritage and family background, the prevailing attitudes about race and class of those with whom I share this society—these are the building blocks, the raw materials, out of which I must construct the edifice of my life. The expression of my individual personality is to be found in the blueprint that I employ to guide this project of construction. The problem of devising such a plan for one's life is a universal problem, which confronts all people, whatever their race, class, or ethnicity.[22]

Although the genre here is prose essay, and the context a much different century and culture, Pushkin would certainly have understood these sentiments and embraced their liberating power and dignity. It is not the "external givens," the *dolia,* that determines character, creates beauty and poetry (broadly defined), inspires others; it is the "internally generated script," the "blueprint that I employ to guide this project of [life] construction," the *volia* that doesn't opt out of the "raw materials" and "building blocks" but works with them and through them, that is all.

BLACKNESS IN PUSHKIN: THE RECORD OF THE POET'S AND OTHERS' WORDS

J. Thomas Shaw has done scholars interested in the question of Pushkin and blackness a service by identifying and commenting on those instances in the poet's *published* work where the theme arises. I would now like to expand on Shaw's findings by focusing the remaining discussion on a subset of illustrative citations taken both from the poet's published and unpublished writings, as well as from the observations of others. While not exhaustive, this list gives the reader a good overall sense of the *context* of Pushkin's musings on blackness.

1. "To Yur'ev":
   But I, [. . .] / an ugly descendant of Negroes (*PSS* 2:139)

2. Chapter 1, stanza 50 of *Eugene Onegin*:
   under the sky of my Africa (*PSS* 6:26)

3. Pushkin's note to the above stanza:
   The author is, on his mother's side, of African descent. His great-grandfather Abram Petrovich Annibal was, at eight years of age, kidnapped from the shores of Africa and taken to Constantinople. The Russian ambassador rescued him and sent him as a present to Peter the Great, who christened him [i.e., took him as a godson] in Vilno. Annibal's brother came in search of him first to Constantinople and then to St. Petersburg, and offered to buy him back. But Peter I would not assent to return his godson. Until very old age Annibal still remembered Africa, the luxuriant life of his father, his nineteen brothers, of which he was the youngest. He remembered how these brothers had been taken before their father with their hands bound behind their backs, while he alone had been free and had swum in the fountains of his father's home. And he remembered his favorite sister Lagan', who swam in the distance after his departing boat. (*PSS* 6:654)

4. From *The Blackamoor of Peter the Great*:
   All the ladies, wanting to see "le Nègre du czar" in their drawing rooms, vied with each other in trying to captivate him . . .
   He felt that in their [i.e., society women's] eyes he was a kind of rare animal, a peculiar and alien creature who had been accidentally brought into a world that had nothing in common with it . . .
   Little by little she [Countess D.] grew accustomed to the young black's appearance and even began finding something attractive in that curly head, standing out with its blackness among the powdered wigs in her drawing room . . .
   Why struggle [as stated in Ibragim's departing letter to Countess D.] to unite the fate of such a tender and graceful creature with the unlucky lot of the Negro, a pitiful being, scarcely granted the title of man? . . .
   The thought [Ibragim's about Peter the Great] of being closely associated

with a great man and of shaping, together with him, the destiny of a great nation awoke in his heart, for the first time in his life, a noble sentiment of ambition.

[Peter's words to Ibragim] "Your appearance! What nonsense! You're a fine young man in every way. A young girl must obey the wishes of her parents, and we'll see what old Gavrila Rzhevsky says when I come as your matchmaker."

[Ibragim thinking to himself] The Emperor is right: I must ensure my future. Marriage with the young Rzhevskaia will affiliate me with the proud Russian gentry, and I will no longer be a newcomer in my adopted fatherland. (*PSS* 8:4–27)

5. Pushkin's answer, in the poem "My Genealogy," to the democratic critic Bulgarin's scurrilous anecdote that the poet's great-grandfather had been bought for a bottle of rum by a sea captain (skipper, i.e., Peter the Great):
My grandfather had entrée to that skipper,
and the blackamoor thusly bought
grew up zealous, incorruptible,
the tsar's confidant, and not a slave. (*PSS* 3:263)[23]

6. Pushkin's letter to his wife of May 14–16, 1836:
Here [in Moscow] they want a bust of me to be sculpted. But I don't want it. Then my Negro ugliness [*arapskoe moe bezobrazie*] would be committed to immortality in all its dead immobility. (Shaw 767; *PSS* 16:116)[24]

7. M. N. Makarov, "A. S. Pushkin in Childhood":
In his childhood years Pushkin was not well-proportioned and possessed the same African facial features he would have as an adult. But his hair in these early years was so curly and so elegantly waved according to its African nature that once I. I. Dmitriev said, "Look, this is a real little blackamoor [*arabchik*]."[25] The child laughed and, turning to us, pronounced quickly and boldly, "At least I'll be distinguished by the fact that I won't be [as was Dmitriev] full of pockmarks [*ne budu riabchik*]."[26]

These excerpts, both in their sheer number and in their wealth of detail, prove one thing beyond a doubt: race *was* a serious category in Pushkin's and others' minds. What I would like to offer now is a way of reading these statements that, on the face of it, is both paradoxical and, to many, unthinkable: the "blackness" that Pushkin perceived in his ancestry and in himself became a sharp edge—and perhaps even *the* sharp edge—he needed both in his self-creation and, what for us amounts to the same thing, the creation of a modern Russian literary consciousness. Pushkin understood the other and gave that other speech as no Russian before him because that other was, in some significant and not wholly imaginary sense, he. Speaking symbolically, the outsiderly brinkmanship that Pushkin learned through the example of his great-grandfather, an example, as I will show, he duly embellished, became the same strategy he used in making Russian culture fully aware and fully "European." It was a way of seeing, this "hump" that so often accompanies the psychology of creativity, that allowed Pushkin, in the alchemy of his poetry, to turn the curse of biology into the blessing of culture. Not only was Pushkin Russia's Shakespeare, he was, inasmuch as race played a role in his thinking, Russia's W. E. B. DuBois. But, as I intimated in my opening comments, such sweeping generalizations cannot be made out of context, nor can they be made to refer to someone's skin color or facial features alone (as distinct from one's psychology), nor can they be cited independently of other implied categories, such as class and gender. The *vsemirnaia otzyvchivost'* (universal responsiveness) that Dostoevsky so perceptively (and, in his way, ethnocentrically) associated with Pushkin's Russian genius was, I would submit, precisely this ability to define a potentially "minority" (in all senses of the word) self through and against a potentially majority other in such a way that both sides became more self-aware, yet more disinterested, less parochial, in the process.

Let us now return to our examples to make some concrete formulations. First, Africa ("my Africa") was for Pushkin a mythologically magnetized topos that bore little relation to his "lot" (*dolia*) as a Russian: it was warm and southern (as opposed to the cold, northern place of his birth); it represented a state of maximal freedom where the boy Ibragim is singled out from all his siblings as the one allowed to gambol unsupervised in his father's fountains (here, of course, the opposition is to the heavily monitored and scrutinized adult Pushkin); it is surrounded by images of tropical opulence (as compared to Pushkin's relative poverty and ongoing financial concerns); and it was a setting rich in family love and loyalty (the trusting father and the brave, self-sacrificing sister rather than the tangled, unhappy relations with the poet's own biological parents). In other words, this Africa is the partially real, partially constructed myth that Pushkin needed to define a part of himself, that part that was "hot-blooded," "free-spirited," and "loved for who he was" (no *other* is implied here as part of this ideal), against his Russian inheritance. All of Nabokov's brilliant efforts to track down the discrepancies in the German biography of Gannibal and to strip away the myth from the reality are, while interesting as "scholarly" excursus run wild, totally beside the point. The great-grandfather *became* Russian—he adopted his new homeland, with all the good and the bad that that involved; Pushkin *was* Russian, and he knew it—in him the act of adoption (Peter of Ibragim in the first instance, but also Ibragim of Peter, to be discussed in a moment) was raised to the level of full self-consciousness, made an act of language and culture.

How Black Was Pushkin?

We can sense how consciously Pushkin wrote aspects of himself into Gannibal's biography by the way the footnote to *Eugene Onegin* is creatively transmogrified in the plot of the unfinished *Blackamoor of Peter the Great*. To begin with, the dark, brutal side of Gannibal's personality is only vaguely hinted at in the novel's largely positive portrait.[27] This is because Pushkin wants "to leave his hero [especially this hero!] his heart" and to place him in situations that reveal him to be much more than the role ascribed to him as *le Nègre du czar*. Given his meager allowance while in France, for example, it is highly unlikely that Gannibal "threw himself into the whirl of social life with all the ardor of his youth and race." This social whirl probably has more in common with the post-Lycée Pushkin's sowing of wild oats in St. Petersburg than with the real opportunities for meeting and interacting with others afforded the penurious young black man in Paris. In fact, as Nabokov seems to imply, the very *le Nègre du czar* epithet, with its appeal to power, prestige, and the foreign/exotic, may have been Pushkin's Trojan horse strategy for smuggling his ancestor into a setting (the highest circles of Parisian society) where the seams of class, race, and gender could be maximally exposed and played off one another. Is it not more probable that, without thinking, French aristocrats would assign Ibragim to the role of "footman" than to that of royal helper and confidant? Likewise, the fascination that the African's skin color and implied "satyr-like" sexuality held for these bored, lascivious French ladies sounds, when viewed through the subject's eyes (compare "To Yur'ev"), very close to the sentiments that Pushkin himself voiced, both in his correspondence (more guardedly) and especially through various of his literary characters (more openly): why can't I be desired and loved for who I am, for my inherent worth as a person, not for some "idea" of me that others have formed independently and that I experience as "external" and not necessarily essential? When, to cite an obvious example, a character such as the Pretender in *Boris Godunov* says to the woman (Marina Mniszek) he is trying to woo, "Don't torture me, my lovely Marina, / Don't say that it is my office [his role as tsarevich], and not me / That you have chosen,"[28] he is speaking out of his creator's own experiences as a perceived romantic "type." For Pushkin's blackness had not only to do with his racial inheritance, that which was most obvious to him and closest to the surface, it also had to do with his "chosen" status as poet. Thus, the women's not-so-innocent "curiosity" as well as their eagerness to see Gannibal as a "rare animal, a peculiar and alien creature" hurts his pride because such reactions do not see the man, the human being, behind the mask. What should have been "sweet attention" becomes instead a source of pain because it is misdirected from the start. This black man, like his great-grandson the poet, does not want "to be destined [the idea of *dolia*/lot] to spend [his] life in solitude, never experiencing the greatest joys and most sacred obligations of a man just because [he] was born below the fifteenth parallel" (*PSS* 8:27). Here "below the fifteenth parallel" is not simply the mythical other place that is "my Africa," it is also the source of the blessing and curse that make Pushkin himself different—poetry, poetic inspiration, the "flame" of his words.

Enter Countess Léonore D. As Tatiana Tsiavlovskaia was the first to argue in a brilliant but controversial article, Countess D.'s portrait in *The Blackamoor* bears a striking resemblance to that of Countess Elizaveta Ksar'evna Vorontsova ("Elise"), perhaps the most significant and most indelible of the poet's "southern loves."[29] Elizaveta Vorontsova was, according to such memorists as F. F. Vigel', extremely charming and youthfully attractive (though at the time of her acquaintance with the poet in fall 1823 she was already past thirty and no longer "in her first bloom"),[30] warm and unaffected in her manners, and above all possessed of the capacity *to please*—all qualities describing the Countess D. in the novel.[31] Indeed, referred to as "Tatiana" in the encoded language of the poet and his Iago-like rival-friend Aleksandr Raevsky, no one among Pushkin's romantic attachments either before or after was apparently more capable of inspiring his passion and trust than this utterly comme il faut[32] society lady: "Her glance conveyed such a good nature, her conduct with him was so simple and unaffected, that it was impossible to suspect her even of a shade of coquetry or mockery." Moreover, as Tsiavlovskaia presents the case further, the fact that the poet became in a short period of time obsessed with the wife of his superior in Odessa, the governor-general of Bessarabia, Count M. S. Vorontsov, is testified by the large number of sketches he did of her (mostly in profile) from memory and placed throughout his manuscripts. But the crux of Tsiavlovskaia's argument rests on *the transposition of race (the black man as outsider) and class (the poet as outsider);* through an elaborate series of close readings and datings, the scholar shows, with great insight into the poet's psychology, that in all probability Pushkin came to believe that Vorontsova had become pregnant with his child after he was forced to quit Odessa and retire into northern exile at Mikhailovskoe as a result of his increasingly strained relations with her husband. And while one can dispute the fact that a "swarthy" child (a daughter Sophia) born to the Vorontsovs in April 1825 was actually Pushkin's (I. A. Novikov's theory, developed by Tsiavlovskaia), what cannot be denied is that in several poems and fragments written by Pushkin that fall and winter in Mikhailovskoe the theme of a "natural child" comes to the fore. Among these works are the lyric "To an Infant Child" ("Mladentsu"), where the speaker does not dare give the child his paternal blessing (*PSS* 2:351), and, most convincingly, Aleko's song over the cradle of his child with Zemfira, which Pushkin composed three months *after* completing *The Gypsies* and decided for good reason *not* to include in the poem's final version.[33] It is, then, this latter *ditia liubvi, ditia prirody* ("child of love, child of nature"; *PSS* 4:447) that makes its way two years later into *The Blackamoor* as the *black* baby of Ibragim and Countess D., a detail which, as already discussed, was not present in the German biography of Gannibal available to Pushkin, *except* in reverse form (the rumor that the African's first wife had betrayed him by giving birth to a white baby). Given this background, it is hard not to agree with Tsiavlovskaia's reading of Gannibal's "blackness" in *The Blackamoor*:

> These last words fix our notice: "He [Gannibal] even envied people who attracted no one's attention, regarding their insignificance as a happy state." These words so suddenly interrupt the evolving theme (what's the point of the "insignificance"?) that an impression is created that one is speaking here not of a Negro among whites but of a poet among ordinary people. It seems that the author has forgotten himself and blurted out something by mistake [*progovorilsia*], given away his real thoughts and feelings. We can reread this paragraph and hear alongside the word "Negro" another word, "poet," which resonates here as a subtext [*zvuchashchee obertonom*]. Then this last phrase [i.e., about the happiness of those who are "insignificant"] will flow completely naturally from what preceded it.[34]

There is a strong tendency among some of the "patriarchs" of Russian/Soviet Pushkin studies not to indulge in fantasies about the poet's erotic life, including the biographical truth or falsehood of his relations with women on his famous "Don Juan list." Such conjecture appears unseemly, "gossipy," while what is really important are the texts themselves. Let us, goes this logic, stick to the "facts." The rest is not our business. But to dispute Tsiavlovskaia's findings seems both wrong on the face of it (her case *is* persuasive) and wrongheaded in terms of Pushkin's psychology of creation. It is, again, an instance both literally and figuratively of throwing the baby out with the bath water. For it does not matter in the end whether Pushkin was in fact the father of Sophia Vorontsova; what matters is that this notion of paternity, which is there in the texts, became intertwined in his mind with issues of race and class (acceptance in "society") in such a way that he clearly seems to have imagined his own fate as implicated in his great-grandfather's story: "Who was the father of Sophia Vorontsova is for us a matter of no significance," concludes Tsiavlovskaia. "What is important to us is Pushkin's psychology."[35] Not to speak about how words and deeds came together in Pushkin's mind around the theme of "love" is to avoid contact with a—perhaps the—crucial aspect of his creative personality. Yet the poet's creativity did not stop with his separation from Vorontsova and his departure from Odessa. His turn *back* to Russia (i.e., his stay in the countryside of Mikhailovskoe, his rejection of the high Romanticism of Napoleon, Byron, and the sea, his newfound interest in Karamzin and native history) is also hinted at in the story line of *The Black-*

amoor, whose hero leaves behind his dreams of high-society eros and Parisian drawing rooms and decides to rejoin his godfather in his adoptive homeland. And it is here, in the return of the (erotically) prodigal godson who is also the forefather, that we can find a continuation of Tsiavlovskaia's argument and a way of reading "blackness" into some of Pushkin's most mature and far-reaching creations.

In a poem of 1825 written in the aftermath of the Vorontsova affair, the speaker explains the secret of his newfound passion for fame: "I desire glory so that it is my name / with which your hearing will be struck hourly."[36] Fame is necessary wholly to impress her, to remind her of his existence. Something happens, however, during the poet's "imprisonment" in Mikhailovskoe that shifts the need for fame away from the all-consuming selfhood of eros. In *The Blackamoor of Peter the Great*, begun two years later, Ibragim is rescued from his destined-to-be-unhappy affair with the Countess D. not by an abstract wish for glory on his part (something that *he* initiates) but by the direct intercession of none other than Peter the Great.

> He was in Petersburg; he had once again met the great man [Peter] in whose company, not yet comprehending his worth, he had spent his childhood. He had to confess to himself, almost with a sense of guilt, that for the first time since their separation the Countess D. had not been the sole preoccupation of his day. He could see that the new way of life that was awaiting him—the work and constant activity—would be able to revive his soul, fatigued by passions, idleness, and an unacknowledged despondency. The thought of being closely associated with a great man and of shaping, together with him, the destiny of a great nation awoke in his heart, for the first time in his life, a noble sentiment of ambition. (*PSS* 8:12; *Complete Prose Fiction* 19–20)

The message here, one that was apparently not lost on the post-Odessa Pushkin, is that a love, no matter how passionate and seemingly genuine, that grows out of "French" salon intrigue and that has infidelity as its basis cannot be sustained and is "fated" to fade. But in Pushkin's rewriting of the meager facts of the German biography, it is *through Peter* that Gannibal receives all his lessons about self-esteem, *Russian style*: he sees that Peter cares for him as a father and treats him as someone *inherently* worthy even when *it was he* who did not first see the worth of the emperor and who now appears to want to linger in France; Peter meets him at the post station as soon as he returns home and invites him to his table as "one of us"; Peter agrees to serve as his matchmaker and sees no obstacle to amorous advancement in his "African" appearance. In a word, Peter is both tsar and fairy godfather, the all-powerful one who can confer goodness and even "attractiveness" *from the outside in*. How different appear the customs of the Russian court and nobility—crude but also honest and not dissembling—from those that had caused Ibragim such pain in Paris and are still epitomized in the, to Russians, ridiculous behavior of the Francophile Korsakov.

But the Peter of *The Blackamoor* is even more than this. It is, in Pushkin's rendering, because of him, because of his faith in his *rab* (servant/"slave"), that Ibragim can become a free man who *chooses* to return to Russia even when it may be in his interest to remain in France. Peter, as it were, seems to allow his godson *to adopt him* (what the French of *The Blackamoor* care nothing about), just as he gives Ibragim a reason for living that in time comes to counterbalance the pain of his failed affair with Countess D.: the "noble ambition" to work side by side with this monarch-titan in order to "shap[e] . . . the destiny of a great nation." This of course is Pushkin's, now the born Russian's, ambition as well; only where his ancestors were more apt, as warriors, to win their historical spurs through martial deeds, the descendant must do so through words, through the consciousness of being a poet. Most important of all, Peter, in what is perhaps Pushkin's sharpest departure from the historical record (recall Gannibal's first marriage to the daughter of a Greek sea captain), grants his outsider godson entry into "the proud Russian gentry" through an arranged marriage.[37] It is through the mingling of bloodlines that the black man's place will be guaranteed in the future history of his new homeland. "Having given up sweet libertinage forever, I have succumbed to other allurements, more significant ones. . . . I will no longer be a newcomer in my adopted fatherland." It does not matter that the relatives with whom Peter comes to arrange the match are horrified, referring to Gannibal as a *chernyi diavol* ("black devil") and a *kuplennyi arap* ("bought Negro"); nor does it matter that the appointed bride (Natalia) swoons in terror at the sight of her "monstrous" groom (*PSS* 8:25–26). For not only is this sort of prejudice as "honest" (as opposed to hiding behind salon-style amiability) as it is comically outrageous, given the blackamoor's spreading reputation as a decent and intelligent man, it is—and here is the trump card—*out of royal favor.* "'Gavrila Afanas'evich, dear brother . . . Tell us what you answered to the Emperor's proposal.' 'I said that he ruled over us, and it was our duty as his vassals to obey in all things'" (PSS 8:25–26; *Complete Prose Fiction* 32). The Russian for "our duty as his vassals," *nashe kholop'e delo*, says a great deal about Pushkin's own psychology as he masterminds this very fictional reversal of fortune: in this instance, *kholop'e*, the adjective formed from behavior fitting for a "bond slave" (literal) or a "lackey" (figurative), signifies that, when it comes to the *volia* of this high-born family, it is their *dolia* to obey their tsar as though they are his bondsmen or his "lackeys." But they do so with the knowledge that their family is being joined by one who, socially, despite his connections to African royalty, is beneath them. In this patriarchal world that is both old-fashioned and somehow new/"enlightened," Peter has the power to make the bondsman a master. As Pushkin once wrote in his diary, upon learning that his correspondence with his wife was being opened and inspected by tsarist censors, "I can be a subject [*poddannyi*], even a slave [*rab*], but a lackey [*kholop*] and jester [*shut*] I will not be even at the feet of the King of Heaven"; *PSS* 12:329).[38] By making Ibragim the gift of this essential distinction—he can from this moment forth be a *rab* (physical servitude) but he will never be a *kholop* (the spiritual attribute)—Peter displays the very essence of nobility. At the same time, the tsar can preside over a marriage for his godson which, as unappealing as it may sound to modern ears, is based first and foremost on mutual respect and trust (not eros), yet out of which "love" and "desire" might, with luck, grow (certainly Pushkin's own fondest wish for his conjugal life together with Natalia Goncharova). All this then, taken together, is why Pushkin reacted so hotly when Bulgarin, in his unseemly anecdote, suggested that the poet's great-grandfather grew up something less than "zealous, incorruptible, / the tsar's confidant, and not a slave." Gannibal, in Pushkin's version, was a loyal servant, but he was never a *lackey*. Bulgarin had not left this, for Pushkin, originary hero his heart. Instead both the literal (the biological bloodline) and the figurative (the *gift* of magic entry) meanings of "noble" had been publicly calumniated.

In conclusion, I would like to make three related points about Pushkin's blackness and about how others have viewed it. First, Pushkin's feelings about *arapskoe moe bezobrazie* ("my Negro ugliness"): the truth is, they were with him to the end, as this phrase from his May 14–16, 1836, letter to his wife indicates. For someone as sensitive to issues of "form" and "beauty" as this poet, it is clear why he did not want others, in this case a sculptor, to fix his features in "dead immobility," when it was the fire and quicksilver motion and captivating energy behind the mask that was the real him. As Countess Dolly Fiquelmont wrote in her diary, "The writer Pushkin conducts a conversation in a charming fashion, without pretense, [but] with animation and fire. It is impossible to be more ugly: he is a mix of the exterior of a monkey and a tiger. He is descended from African ancestors and he has retained a certain blackness [*chernota*] in his complexion and something wild in his glance."[39] It is my argument, however, that the purely personal insecurities and feelings of injustice at being judged for what he had been born with rather than for who he had become (and was still becoming) were *worked through* thanks to the creative rewriting of Gannibal's life in *The Blackamoor*. Never again would Pushkin's fate (the biography going on behind/beyond the poems, prose, and history) be tied to the *merely erotic*. But the mechanism for that transformation would remain at some deeply alchemical level *language*, the same language that allowed the child Pushkin to turn to the esteemed adult (the writer I. I. Dmitriev, in the above-cited anecdote) and transform, with instantaneous wit, the fixed category ("a real little blackamoor" [*arábchik*]) into energy-in-motion, a joke with fangs slightly bared ("At least . . . I won't be full of pockmarks" [*ne budu riábchik*]). The poetic principle (the rhyme that turns *arábchik* into *riábchik*), which as we saw in *The Blackamoor* was embedded in and finally coterminous with the "hump" of color, would be his savior. Blackness would be for Pushkin not something to hold him down, but something to propel him, the slingshot underlying his creativity and indistinguishable from it.

My second concluding point has to do with how others have perceived the issue of Pushkin's blackness. Here of course we find significant variation, from those who note the "African" exterior without psychologizing further (I. I. Panaev, V. P. Burnashev),[40] to those who attempt to read the exterior into temperament (Fiquelmont), to those who deny any trace at all of the African in Pushkin (A. O. Rosset-Smirnova, or more probably, her daughter),[41] to those who undertake a full "scientific" investigation of the extent and composition of Pushkin's "Negroid" racial inheritance (D. N. Anuchin).[42] While all of these sources are not without value as ways of "vectoring in" on Pushkin's complex personhood from the outside, they can be rendered problematic by the memorist's or scholar's preconceived notions about this greatest and, as the tradition has asserted, most *Russian* of poets. Why, for example, is Smirnova (it does not really matter which one) so insistent that "There is nothing in him that is Negroid" (*V nem net nichego negritianskogo*)? It may be that that is what she really thinks, or it may be that these *Notes*, published in the years before the first bicentenary (1899), reveal a tendency to "touch up" the words of the mother-contemporary in order to make her Pushkin more "ours" and less "theirs." But as I have tried to demonstrate throughout this study, the "Russianness" that Pushkin embodied was a way of seeing the world that defined, in an ongoing and never static process, the self *through the other*, and one of those others that Pushkin experienced as absolutely inseparable from his self was "blackness." Russia's greatest poet was indeed black. Or, to invoke once again the magic economy linking tsar and godson in *The Blackamoor*, to the extent that he was black, he *became* Russian (in a broader sense), and to the extent that he became Russian (more Catholic than the Pope, so to speak), he *was* black.

Last but not least, what happened to Pushkin's blackness, where did it go, in the 1830s, once he stopped writing *The Blackamoor*, got even with Bulgarin/Figliarin in "My Genealogy," and married the woman who he hoped against hope would be more than Desdemona to his Othello? It spread out into his last and most far-reaching works, becoming that which defined the Russian-as-everyman in *The Bronze Horseman, The History of Pugachev*, and *The Captain's Daughter*. Now Peter, the "wonder-working" creator of the city and a new Western-style state, is not the little-man hero's matchmaker, but his life-wrecker, the author (through his hubris) of the flood that carries away his betrothed and plans for domestic happiness. The role of matchmaker or *posazhennyi otets* (proxy father) falls instead to the novelistic Pugachev, that "dark" force of Russian history who personifies the terrible violence resulting from group brutalization at the hands of the powers that be. The "blacks" of these last years are, one might say then, more and more the Russian peasantry. And if it was Peter who was given a noble countenance in *The Blackamoor*, it is the fictional (as opposed to historiographic) Pugachev who is "left his heart" in *The Captain's Daughter.* By the mid-1830s, having grown weary of his humiliating treatment by Nicholas, Pushkin was considerably less sanguine about his, the verbal "wonder-worker's," ability to stand shoulder to shoulder with the tsar to "shape[e] the destiny of a great nation." That noble gesture from above was nowhere to be found. Thus, the darkness of these last works, a darkness Pushkin would do anything in his power to avert, is that of open rebellion, of breaking out of "dialogue" because one side brazenly refuses to listen.[43] Where has the "blackness" gone that fixes Ibragim in place in Parisian salons and doesn't allow him to be a man? It has dissolved into the tragedy of Russian history proper, into the mad Evgeny's clenched fist raised in protest at Peter's statue and into Grinev's carnage-filled dream of an ax-wielding muzhik. *Volia/dolia* works as an ontological rhyme, one with at least a minimal spark of "poetry" in it, only when the "fate" involved allows for something resembling *human* dignity and freedom. Anything less is, in Pushkin's book, no rhyme at all.

Notes

1. Itabari Njeri, "Sushi and Grits: Ethnic Identity and Conflict in a Newly Multicultural America," in *Lure and Loathing: Essays on Race, Identity, and the Ambivalence of Assimilation,* ed. Gerald Early (New York: Penguin, 1993), 24.

2. In point of fact, how and when Pushkin's great-grandfather took the name Gannibal (Hannibal) has never been reliably established. Pushkin himself wrote, in the unfinished draft of an autobiography he had begun to compose in the 1830s, that Peter gave Ibragim (Abram) this surname (*familiia*) when he christened him in 1707 (*PSS* 12:312). However, Modzalevskii, one of the finest Pushkin scholars, established that in official documents and correspondence Gannibal normally signed his name "Abram Petrov" and that the African "sobriquet" (*prozvishche*) was added only after Peter's death, "not earlier than 1733 and not later than 1737" (B. L. Modzalevskii, *Pushkin* [Leningrad: Priboi, 1929], 48). On the other hand, Nabokov writes that "The surname Gannibal was applied to Abram in official documents as early as 1723, upon his return from France," but on what basis he makes this state-

ment is never made clear (Aleksandr Pushkin, *Eugene Onegin,* trans. Vladimir Nabokov, 4 vols., rev. ed. [Princeton: Princeton University Press, 1975], 3:432).

3. Pushkin, *PSS* 11:275. The essay was probably written in 1835 and was a draft of a short biography of Byron, based in part on the French version of Thomas Moore's memoirs/life of his friend (Paris, 1830), that Pushkin was intending to write.

4. Frantz Fanon, *Black Skin, White Masks,* trans. Charles Lam Markmann (New York: Grove, 1967), 115. The original French title is *Peau Noire, Masques Blancs* (Paris, 1952).

5. "Here Be Monsters" is the essay with which Baldwin concluded *The Price of the Ticket* (1985). This passage is cited from Henry Louis Gates Jr., "The Welcome Table," in Early, ed., *Lure and Loathing,* 162.

6. Gates, "Welcome Table," 148.

7. Why is an interesting question. Perhaps because the notion of a guilt "for all mankind" was more the province of the Catholic/Protestant West, or because, given his more brutal epoch, he simply could not afford (did not see the reason for) such abstract emotions?

8. Alexander Pushkin, *The Letters of Alexander Pushkin,* trans. J. Thomas Shaw (Madison: University of Wisconsin Press, 1967), 161. The letter to Viazemskii was dated June 24 or 25, 1824 (Old Style). This edition of the letters is referred to subsequently in the text and notes as "Shaw."

9. John Tanner's "narrative" about his thirty years in the wilds of North America, dictated by the author to Edwin James, was first published in New York in 1830. In his essay, which contains substantial excerpts from Tanner in Russian, Pushkin is working from the French edition which appeared in Paris, in two volumes, in 1835. The "other" in Tanner's narrative is primarily the American Indian, but the observations that Pushkin draws from the American's story could easily be applied to black-white race relations as well. In fact, Pushkin ends his elaborate retelling with reference to the fact that recently Tanner has been in a legal dispute with his stepmother over several Negro slaves left to him in a legacy (*PSS* 12:132).

10. Pushkin, *PSS* 12:104.

11. Alexis de Tocqueville, *De la démocratie en Amérique,* 4th ed. (Paris, 1836), which Pushkin also had in his library. As Tatiana Wolff points out, "In the first issue of the *Sovremennik* [*The Contemporary*: Pushkin's journal, where the Tanner essay appeared], [the poet's older friend] A. I. Turgenev mentions in his Paris diary that he spent an evening reading Tocqueville's book on democracy in America and continues:

> Talleyrand calls it the wisest and most remarkable book of our time; and he knows America, and is himself an Aristocrat, as is Tocqueville, all of whose con-

nections are with the Faubourg of St. Germain. You will agree with the author's conclusion: 'On remarque aujourd'hui moins de différence entre les Européens et leurs descendants du Nouveau-Monde, malgré l'Océan que les devise, qu'entre certaines villes du treizième siècle qui n'étaient séparées que par une rivière. Si ce mouvement d'assimilation rapproche des peuples étrangers il s'oppose à plus forte raison à ce que les rejetons du même peuple deviennent étrangers les uns aux autres,' etc." (*Pushkin on Literature*, ed. and trans. Tatiana Wolff, rev. ed. [Stanford: Stanford University Press, 1986], 447–48n1)

12. A. S. Pushkin, "Geroi" ("The Hero," 1830), in *PSS* 3:253.

13. If Pushkin in his maturity could be called a "conservative liberal," then Karamzin, the great historian whose *History of the Russian State* (*Istoriia gosudarstva Rossiiskogo*) had a profound impact on the younger man's thinking and whose moderate Enlightenment values he largely shared, could be called a "liberal conservative"—i.e., he was slightly "to the right" of the poet. Neither Karamzin nor Pushkin felt Russia was ready for an American-style democracy; she had to go her own way.

14. Abram Tertz (Andrei Sinyavsky), *Strolls with Pushkin*, trans. Catharine Theimer Nepomnyashchy and Slava I. Yastremski (New Haven: Yale University Press, 1993), 72–73; the original is found in *Progulki s Pushkinym* (London: Overseas Publications Interchange/Collins, 1975), 48.

15. My metaphor here is borrowed from the great Pushkinist and semiotician Iurii Lotman, who uses the image of the sculptor working with stone—he even uses the concrete image of Michelangelo—in an October 1986 letter to his friend Boris Egorov explaining the central idea behind his Pushkin biography: everything the poet touched in life he, like King Midas, turned with fabulous alchemical efficiency into the gold of art. But King Midas's story ends sadly, as did Pushkin's, because he turned his food to gold as well, and by so doing starved. Lotman is in this letter quite passionate in defense of his idea: the fact that Pushkin worked with, struggled with, codes did not seem to him a matter of facile or cold-blooded "manipulation." I might add that this, significantly, is not the only time Lotman resorts to the King Midas metaphor for creative behavior: in his preface to *Universe of the Mind*, he writes of the semiotic researcher (including of course himself) that the latter "has the habit of transforming the world around him/her so as to show up the semiotic structures. Everything that King Midas touched with his golden hand turned to gold. In the same way, everything which the semiotic researcher turns his/her attention to becomes semioticized in his hands" (*Universe of the Mind*, trans. Ann Shukman [Bloomington: Indiana University Press, 1990], 5). My thanks to Mikhail Lotman and Boris Egorov for providing me with a copy of the October 1986 letter.

16. See stanza 20 in chapter 1 of *Evgenii Onegin*, in *PSS* 6:13.

17. A. S. Pushkin, *Bakhchisaraiskii fontan* (1824), in *PSS* 4:160: Для

старика была закон / Ее младенческая воля. / Одну заботу ведал он: / Чтоб дочери любимой доля / Была, как вешний день, ясна.

18. Pushkin, *Tsygany* (written 1824, published 1827), in *PSS* 4:180: Будь наш—привыкни к нашей доле, Бродящей бедности и воле; *PSS* 4:201: Ты не рожден для доли, / Ты для себя лишь хочешь воли.

19. Pushkin, *Evgenii Onegin* (written 1823–31, published 1833), in *PSS* 6:65: Теперь, я знаю, в вашей воле, / Меня презреньем наказать. / Но вы, к моей несчастной доле / Хоть каплю жалости храня, / вы не оставите меня.

20. Pushkin, "Pora, moi drug, pora" (written 1834), in *PSS* 3:330: На свете счастья нет, но есть покой и воля / Давно завидная мечтается мне доля—/ Давно, усталый раб, замыслил я побег / В обитель дальнюю трудов и чистых нег.

21. Pushkin, *PSS* 3:941.

22. Glenn C. Loury, "Free at Last? A Personal Perspective on Race and Identity in America," in Early, ed., *Lure and Loathing*, 8–9.

23. Сей шкипер деду был доступен, / И сходно купленный арап / Возрос усерден, неподкуплен, / Царю наперсник, а не раб. Written in December 1830, "My Genealogy" ("Moia Rodoslovnaia") was not published in the poet's lifetime, although it circulated widely in manuscript copy. Its contents were too personal and ad hominem to pass the censorship, and the tsar himself urged Pushkin not to settle such scores through publication. This poem cost Pushkin dearly in high society, since in the previous stanzas (not excerpted here) he "took on" in the most sarcastic and disparaging terms the wealthy and influential scions of the "new" (service) as opposed to the "old" nobility. Pushkin was naturally sensitive to the difference between willing service (as in serving a monarch) and slavery/forced servitude. One of the examples from his work not commented on by Shaw involves the "little tragedy" *Feast in Time of Plague* (*Pir vo vremia chumy*, 1830), where we find the stage direction "A cart passes by, filled with dead bodies. A Negro drives it" (*PSS* 7:178). Here the reader senses a dovetailing of two concepts: the black man both symbolizes "death" and is assigned a task (carting off the contaminated bodies) that borders on the inhuman/subhuman. In this respect, the Negro is, without being designated as such, a "slave" because he does what no other human is willing to do.

24. The sentiments here correspond virtually exactly to those expressed in the poem "To Dawe, Esq.": "Why is your wondrous pencil / sketching my blackamoor profile? / While you may entrust it to the ages, / Mephistopheles will hiss it off stage" (Зачем твой дивный карандаш / Рисует мой арапский профиль? / Хоть ты векам его предашь, / Его освищет Мефестофиль; *PSS* 3:101). Once again the contrast is between beauty and the beast, between the blackamoor profile of the first stanza and the lovely

contours of a woman's face (that of Anna Olenina, Pushkin's current object of affection) of the second stanza. See as well in this context the comparison, based on the illogicality of love, between the young Maria and the old hetman Mazepa in *Poltava,* on the one hand, and "Othello, the old moor, who captivated Desdemona with stories of his wanderings and battles," in the uncompleted "Rebuttal to Criticisms" ("Oproverzhenie na kritiki"), on the other (*PSS* 11:158). This particular section of "Rebuttal to Criticisms" was, as Shaw points out, published as a Note in 1831 in M. Maksimovich's almanac *The Morning Star* (*Dennitsa*).

25. *Arap* (with a "p" at the end) means "blackamoor" in Russian, while *arab* (with a devoiced "b" at the end that sounds like a "p" when undeclined) means "Arab." However, given the context, I have translated *arab* here as *arap.*

26. M. N. Makarov, "A. S. Pushkin v detstve," *Sovremennik,* no. 29 (1843): 377–83; cited in V. Veresaev, *Pushkin v zhizni* (Moscow: Sovetskii pisatel', 1936), 54–55.

27. Though this was presumably unknown to Pushkin, since details of it began to emerge only much later (1877), Gannibal apparently abducted and variously tortured his first wife, Evdokiia Andreevna Dioper, the daughter of a Greek sea captain, when she became unfaithful to him and would not enter a female monastery and grant him a divorce. See Modzalevskii, *Pushkin,* 52, who bases his findings on an article ("E. A. Gannibal") published by S. I. Opatovich in the January 1877 issue of *Russian Antiquity* (*Russkaia starina*). Opatovich also concludes that there is no basis for the legend (a reversal of the *Blackamoor* plot) that Evdokiia gave birth to a white baby, thereby proving her infidelity to Gannibal. Nabokov, for his part, does not mince words, summing up Gannibal's character as "sour, groveling, crotchety, timid, ambitious, and cruel" (*Eugene Onegin,* 3:438).

28. Pushkin, *PSS* 7:61: Не мучь меня, прелестная Марина, / Не говори, что сан, а не меня / Избрала ты.

29. Tsiavlovskaia's article was originally published as "Khrani menia, moi talisman" in *Prometei* 10 (1974): 12–84. I am using the version reissued in *Utaennaia liubov' Pushkina,* ed. R. V. Iezuitova and Ia. L. Levkovich (St. Petersburg: Akademicheskii proekt, 1997), 295–380.

30. Alexander Pushkin, *Complete Prose Fiction,* trans. Paul Debreczeny (Stanford: Stanford University Press, 1983), 12; Pushkin, *PSS* 8:4. Debreczeny's translation is hereafter referred to in text and notes as *Complete Prose Fiction.*

31. "With her inbred Polish levity and coquetry she desired to please [*zhelala ona nravit'sia*], and no one was better at this than she" (F. F. Vigel', *Zapiski* [Moscow, 1892], pt. 4, 84–85; cited in Tsiavlovskaia, "Khrani menia," 297).

32. See, for example, the description of the magically transformed and utterly comme il faut Tatiana in chapter 8 of *Evgenii Onegin* (*PSS* 5:171, stanza 14).

33. See the discussion in Tsiavlovskaia, "Khrani menia," 333–37 and 348–50.

34. Ibid., 358.

35. Ibid., 376–77.

36. A. S. Pushkin, "Zhelanie slavy" ("Desire for Fame"), in *PSS* 2:392–93: Желаю славы я, чтоб именем моим / Твой слух был поражен всечасно.

37. Recall that, chronologically, Peter the Great had already died (1725) by the time of Gannibal's first marriage to Evdokiia Dioper (1731). Hence Peter's fear in the novel that "If I should die today, what would become of you tomorrow, my poor blackamoor?"

38. Pushkin is rephrasing here a famous passage from a letter (January 19, 1761) that M. V. Lomonosov wrote to I. I. Shuvalov.

39. N. B. Izmailov, "Pushkin v dnevnike gr. D. F. Fikel'mon," *Vremennik pushkinskoi komissii*, no. 1 (1962): 33.

40. See *Pushkin i ego vremia: 1799–1837* (Moscow: Terra, 1997), 318 and 358.

41. Pushkin's good friend A. O. Rosset-Smirnova is a potentially interesting contemporary source because she provides a description—"There is nothing in him that is Negroid" [*V nem net nichego negritianskogo*]—that quite contradicts other accounts (*Zapiski, 1826–1845*; cited in *Pushkin i ego vremia*, 254). However, these *Notes*, edited by Rosset-Smirnova's daughter O. N. Smirnova and published in *The Northern Herald* (*Severnyi vestnik*) in 1895–97, are considered today to be a skillful (if often factually based) forgery.

42. D. N. Anuchin, *A. S. Pushkin: Antropologicheskii eskiz* (Moscow, 1899); cited in Veresaev, *Pushkin v zhizni*, 26. Anuchin's study was published in the newspaper *The Russian Gazette* (*Russkie vedomosti*) from April 10 to July 31, 1899. Nabokov, with his typical tetchiness, calls Anuchin's work one "that in its historical, ethnical, and geo-nomenclatorial portions is below criticism" (*Eugene Onegin* 3:399), but then of course he goes on to use Anuchin where it suits him.

43. One of Pushkin's most famous lines, taken from a draft chapter he did not include in the final version of *The Captain's Daughter,* reads, "May the Lord save us from another such senseless and ruthless Russian rebellion" (*PSS* 8:383; *Complete Prose Fiction,* 450).

Catharine Theimer Nepomnyashchy

The Telltale Black Baby, or Why Pushkin Began *The Blackamoor of Peter the Great* but Didn't Finish It

> Recently Zhukovsky read us Pushkin's wonderful novel, *Ibragim, the Tsar's Blackamoor.* This Negro is so charming that you are not at all surprised that he could inspire passion in a lady of the court of the Regent. Many traits of his character and even his appearance would seem to have been copied from Pushkin himself. The writer's pen stopped at the most interesting place. My God, what a misfortune, what a loss, how one can not cease to regret this . . .
> —Sof'ia Nikolaevna Karamzina, 1837

> Their round eyes, squat noses, and invariable thick lips, the different configuration of their ears, their woolly heads, and the measure of their intellects, make a prodigious difference between them and other species of men; and what demonstrates, that they are not indebted for this difference to their climates, is that Negro men and women, being transported into the coldest countries, constantly produce animals of their own species; and that mulattoes are only a bastard race of black men and white women, or white men and black women, as asses, specifically different from horses, produce mules by copulating with mares.
> —Voltaire, *Philosophy of History*

PUSHKIN BEGAN WRITING his first major attempt at a prose novel at the end of July 1827 at Mikhailovskoe, the estate granted to his great-grandfather Abram Gannibal by the Empress Elizabeth.[1] By the end of August he appears to have finished six chapters of the novel. On September 15

The Telltale Black Baby

of that year, Pushkin related to Aleksei Vul'f an outline of the projected further development of his prose work in progress. Pushkin gave readings of the completed chapters of the novel in December 1827 and March 1828, but by the spring of 1828 work on the novel appeared to have progressed little, if at all, further than it had during Pushkin's first spurt of creativity the preceding year. By the end of 1828, the budding novelist had apparently given up the idea of finishing his first assay in the genre and decided to publish two excerpts from it independently.[2] Pushkin himself never titled his unfinished novel. The highly suggestive title under which the six more or less completed chapters and the seventh fragmentary chapter have come down to us, *The Blackamoor of Peter the Great* (*Arap Petra Velikogo*), was conceived by the editors who published the novel shortly after Pushkin's death.[3] As S. L. Abramovich has observed, scholars have been fascinated by the question of why Pushkin left the work unfinished: "There exist as many as ten versions of why *The Blackamoor of Peter the Great* remained unfinished. The very number of versions serves as an indication that each researcher considered the explanations of his predecessors unconvincing."[4] Scholars have also speculated on the equally compelling and certainly related questions of why Pushkin began the work at all and which of his major characters—Peter the Great or the fictionalized version of the poet's forebear Ibragim or even Valerian, the *strelets*'s son—was to be the focus of the novel. In this article I will explore these questions in relation to the assumptions previously made about them by earlier commentators. I will suggest that the subject of Pushkin's African ancestor provided the incipient novelist with evocative analogies to his own situation at the time of writing, but that the implications of seeing the projected plot through to the end and making it public were too disturbing to allow Pushkin to finish what he had begun with such apparent élan.

Let me begin by outlining the context, broadly defined, in which Pushkin conceived and abandoned the novel. That context, as it relates to my argument, is determined by three questions. Where does *The Blackamoor* fit in Pushkin's prose? Where does *The Blackamoor* fit in Russian letters? Where does *The Blackamoor* fit in Pushkin's life? Arguably, the novel is interesting precisely because it represents a point of intersection for the three contexts defined by these questions: the dynamics of Pushkin's life and works in relation to the evolving state of Russian literature. *The Blackamoor* becomes something of a laboratory in which Pushkin works out his anxieties over the changing shape of his life and art, so that, in the end, both the fact that he set out to write the work and the fact that he left it unfinished appear to be "overdetermined" in particularly revelatory ways which take us beyond the simple fact of Pushkin's tendency to leave prose works unfinished as he struggled to find his footing as a prose writer.

Clearly, *The Blackamoor* holds a special place in Pushkin's prose, as in his oeuvre as a whole, for the simple reason that it is first. While Pushkin did begin experimenting with prose as early as the Lycée, *The Blackamoor* remains his first sustained effort at a novel and is considerably longer than any of his other abandoned prose works, with the exception of the significantly later *Dubrovsky,* written after he had already successfully completed the *Belkin Tales.*[5] Thus, precisely by virtue of being first *The Blackamoor* acquires a privileged status as an indicator of Pushkin's understanding of the significance of prose as a literary medium in contradistinction to poetry, specifically with regard to issues of appropriate content, function, audience, the structure of cultural institutions, and the semiotics of genre hierarchies.

In addressing the issue of why Pushkin turned to his great-grandfather as the subject of his first novel, critics have tended to focus on Pushkin's famous statements on Sir Walter Scott's novels as exemplars of historical fiction. If the essence of what Pushkin admired in Scott's fictions lay in the Scottish novelist's portrayal of the historical through the domestic, then it is hardly surprising that Pushkin chose a point at which his own genealogy intersected with a tumultuous moment in Russian history, just as he had interpolated his Pushkin ancestors—albeit in passing—into the plot of *Boris Godunov.* Pushkin had, after all, called public attention to Gannibal's ambiguous relationship to Russia's nascent history in his longest public statement about his Gannibal ancestry made shortly before he began writing *The Blackamoor,* in the footnote appended to line 11 of stanza 50 of the first chapter of *Eugene Onegin* ("under the sky of my Africa") in the first edition of the work published in 1825. The note concludes: "The strange life of Annibal is known only from family legends—in Russia, where the memory of remarkable people vanishes because of the lack of historical notes. In time we hope to publish his full biography."[6] Scholars have, moreover, emphasized the fact that Gannibal, as Peter the Great's godson, provided Pushkin with a family tie with the reformer tsar in whom he was evincing increasing interest in the mid-1820s. It has been argued that Pushkin abandoned *The Blackamoor* for *Poltava* because the *poema* better suited his stately image of the tsar and even that Peter the Great, rather than Ibragim, is the true "hero" of *The Blackamoor.* Pushkin's own words cited above testify to his belief that Gannibal's life posed especially vividly the problem of the individual's relation to history—and particularly to the developing understanding of Russia as a historical nation in the western European sense of the time. Moreover, arguments linking Pushkin's interest in his ancestor with his interest in Peter the Great, both of which appear to have intensified at roughly the same time, and drawing attention to the consanguinuity of *The Blackamoor* and *Poltava,* unquestionably have merit. Yet neither appeals to Walter Scott's example, nor does emphasis on Peter the Great exhaust the question of why Pushkin chose to show Peter's age through the eyes of his exotic forebear, nor why he chose prose as his medium.

As we move on to our second context, that of the evolution of Russian letters in the 1820s, we must recognize that in turning to prose, Pushkin was confronting point-blank the problem of the evolution of Russian letters away from the intimate and exclusive domain of poetry toward the broader, less discerning audience for prose, away from the realm of formal virtuosity and play to that of plot and "thought."[7] The growing commercialism even of poetry was both Pushkin's boon and bane, as evidenced by the poet's ambivalent treatment of the subject in the 1824 poem "Conversation between the Bookseller and the Poet" ("Razgovor knigoprodavtsa s poetom"), in which the poet, resorting to prose in the final line of the poem, agrees to sell his manuscripts, if not his inspiration. (Pushkin would return to this topic in the unfinished *Egyptian Nights,* which, as I will argue later, tellingly breaks off on the issue of the "salability" of an African queen.) Yet the connection between writing and money was unquestionably more direct when it came to prose, so that certainly, even if Pushkin turned to the historical novel in part to counter on a higher plane the patent commercialization of prose promoted by Bulgarin and his journalistic cronies, it is unlikely he could be completely comfortable at this "selling out" of poetry.

It is, however, the third context of the writing of *The Blackamoor,* its place in Pushkin's life, that, closely interconnected as it is with the preceding two, is perhaps the most complex and interesting. Soviet scholars understandably tended to privilege the watershed moments of the Decembrist revolt and Pushkin's subsequent reconciliation with Nicholas I as the immediate context of the writing of *The Blackamoor.* This version runs that in his initial optimism about his rapprochement with the tsar, Pushkin turned to his great-grandfather's relationship with Peter the Great as an analogy for his own situation. As a corollary to this argument, Pushkin reputedly abandoned *The Blackamoor* when his relations with Nicholas soured. While Pushkin unquestionably saw an analogy to his own situation in his great-grandfather's life, I will argue that this analogy is far more complex and multifaceted than the reductive Soviet reading allows. For the time being I will confine myself to suggesting several other biographical "moments" I believe to be relevant. For one thing, Pushkin appears to have begun seriously to gather information about his great-grandfather's biography while in exile at Mikhailovskoe, the estate granted to Gannibal by the Empress Elizabeth after he had returned from his own exile from the centers of power. Pushkin's stay at Mikhailovskoe, moreover, afforded him a number of opportunities to learn about his great-grandfather's life. He apparently visited his "Negro" great-uncle, Gannibal's last remaining son, during this period, and he came into possession of the "German biography" of Gannibal. Perhaps most interesting, and hitherto largely overlooked by scholars, was another source of information on Pushkin's ancestor—his nanny, who may have taken the opportunity to tell him more than folk tales. While Arina Rodionovna herself was too young to have known Gannibal well (although interestingly enough she was christened in the same church in which his funeral was held), her brother was a house servant in the Gannibal menage at Kobrino and was certainly privy to the intimate life of its owner. It is not much of a stretch to imagine that his sister also heard the stories of the place where she grew up and later passed them on to the poet to while away the lonely time they spent together at Mikhailovskoe.

On an even more personal note, in the period following his return from exile, which coincided with his writing of *The Blackamoor*, Pushkin was clearly contemplating marriage. In this context, T. G. Tsiavlovskaia has argued, linking her argument specifically to *The Blackamoor*, that soon after Pushkin left Odessa, the Countess Vorontsova gave birth to a dark-haired baby daughter, and Pushkin, at least partly on the basis of the child's coloring, considered the baby his.[8] This biographical "fact" dovetails tellingly both with the plot of *The Blackamoor* and with Gannibal's biography. Gannibal's first wife, Evdokia Dioper, the daughter of a ship's captain, cuckolded him and gave birth to a white baby. As Pushkin tells the story of his great-grandfather's private life in "Beginning of an Autobiography" ("Nachalo avtobografii"):

> My Gannibal forebear was just as unlucky in his family life as was my Pushkin forebear. His first wife, a beauty, of Greek origin, bore him a white daughter. He divorced her and forced her to take vows in the Tikhvinsky Convent, and kept her daughter Poliksena with him, gave her a rigorous education, a rich dowry, but never allowed her into his presence. His second wife, Christina Regina von Schöberg, married him when he was stationed in Revel and bore him many black babies of both genders.[9]

Shortly thereafter in the same narrative, Pushkin underscores the family motif of the telltale baby in an aside on his great-grandmother's difficulties in pronouncing Russian:

> My grandfather, Osip Abramovich (his real name was Yanuary, but my great-grandmother would not agree to call him by that name, difficult for her German pronunciation: the black devil, she would say, makes me black kids and gives them devilish names [*shorn short, govorila ona, delat mne shorny repiat i daet im shertovsk imia*]).[10]

Thus, as Aleksei Vul'f reports in the same diary entry from September 16, 1827, mentioned above, family tradition resonates with the typically Pushkinian symmetrical plot in which, echoing Gannibal's own life, the black baby to which the Countess Leonora gives birth in the opening, Parisian chapters of *The Blackamoor* was to be "answered" at the end of the novel: "The main denouement of this novel will be—as Pushkin says—the infidelity of the blackamoor's wife, who bore him a white child and for that was imprisoned in a convent."[11] This recurring motif of the telltale baby, I will argue, surfacing

The Telltale Black Baby

in Pushkin's writing at precisely the moment when he was thinking about marriage, becomes an expression of Pushkin's anxieties about his place in Russian life and letters, eerily echoing the "Othello" plot which so poetically and tragically dogged Pushkin's fate.[12] More disturbingly, *The Blackamoor of Peter the Great* seems to invoke a lesser known but even bloodier Shakespeare tragedy, *Titus Andronicus*. In that play the black baby bred, like the evil events of the plot itself, out of intercourse between the villainous Moor Aaron and the queen of the Goths turned Roman empress Tamora becomes damning evidence and a disturbing remnant that survives beyond the boundaries of the play of horrors unleashed by contact with the foreign. Anthony Gerard Barthelemy reads "the valiant Moor Othello" in the light of his predecessor Aaron's "display of real sexual power" in cuckolding the emperor of Rome:

> Of course, Othello's sexual anxiety is an intrinsic component of his larger fear of being a stereotypical stage Moor . . . Othello seeks no such [sexual] power over his masters . . . Othello . . . attempts to diminish whatever threat he may pose to the state. But his marriage itself compromises the state's security . . . And although Othello intensely wishes not to be a typical stage Moor, he finds himself in exactly that position. He is the black man who provokes a crisis by his sexual relationship with a white woman.[13]

Othello, Barthelemy concludes, "struggles to destroy evil as he struggles to escape the identity of a Moor. But he escapes neither and becomes both."[14] I would suggest that a similar shadow dogs Ibragim's footsteps in Pushkin's novel.

At this point I would put forward the proposition that to understand fully the impact on Pushkin's writing of the three contexts outlined above, *The Blackamoor* must be examined with regard to a fourth context, hitherto largely ignored by scholars. This context is the contemporary (to Pushkin) debate in Western intellectual centers over the nature and origins of differences among the diverse peoples of the earth. Arguably the debate, which had been brewing since humans with strikingly different physical attributes had been brought into increasing contact by European exploration and commerce with foreign lands, and which had been simultaneously charged with very real practical and ethical implications by the slave trade, reached a critical point shortly before and during Pushkin's lifetime. This was the point at which the attribution of physical and psychological variety in human beings to climate and levels of civilization, causes that could be meliorated and therefore overcome, gave way to "racial" thinking, the conviction that the "races" of humankind were the result of permanent, irremediable genetic differences—including intelligence, aptitude, and moral worth—and the corollary belief that some races were superior to others in a clearly defined hierarchy. Thus, George Stocking, examining the origins of French anthropology in the early nineteenth century, maintains:

In the largest sense, the change we are discussing was an aspect of that intellectual reorientation which we call the Romantic reaction to the eighteenth-century Enlightenment. On the level of the logic of ideas, the characteristically "diversitarian" impulse of Romanticism had, as A. O. Lovejoy has pointed out, an important racial potential. Despite his broadly humanistic view of man's cultural development, Johann Gottfried von Herder's picture of the Negro was not without racial implications. On a general political level, the change may perhaps be viewed as part of the conservative reaction against the egalitarian optimism of the French Revolution. On a broader social level it has been suggestively discussed as a defensive reaction against the idea of equality on the part of groups whose traditionally unquestioned class superiority was being undercut by the social changes of the nineteenth century. More specifically, some writers have suggested that the idea of race arose as a defensive ideology when slavery and the slave trade came under serious attack in the late eighteenth century.[15]

By the same token, Martin Bernal, in his controversial book *Black Athena: The Afroasiatic Roots of Classical Civilization*, also views the late eighteenth and early nineteenth centuries as a key moment in the development of racism, pointing out that "the first 'academic' work on human racial classification—which first put whites, or to use his new term, 'Caucasians,' at the head of the hierarchy—was written in the 1770s by Johann Friedrich Blumenbach, a professor at Göttingen."[16] Bernal moreover contends that as "the world began to be viewed through time rather than across space . . . [r]eal communication . . . was now seen as flowing through feeling, which could touch only those tied to each other by kinship or 'blood' and sharing a common 'heritage.'"[17] Hence, "the tidal wave of ethnicity and racialism, linked to cults of Christian Europe and the North, that engulfed Northern Europe with the Romantic movement at the end of the 18th century."[18] Examining the evolution of racism in philosophy, Richard Popkin, while tracing the appearance of racism to the Inquisition, nonetheless concurs in viewing the late eighteenth century as a watershed moment, preparing the way for the more virulent racism of the nineteenth century: "During the 18th century . . . there was a vast amount of literature on why blacks are black."[19]

By the mid-eighteenth century, as all of the commentators cited above concur, there were two theories in competition to explain racial difference: the degeneracy theory and the polygenetic theory. The former, accepting a common origin for all human beings, viewed the cause of the purported superiority of Europeans to lie in differences of geography, climate, and customs. Hence, this theory left open the possibility that all people, given access to the riches of European civilization, could achieve the same attainments and, assumedly, even the same physical attributes. The polygenetic theory answered this "nurture" argument with "nature," with the contention that different races had different biological origins and therefore differences that were permanent and irremediable.

Given the high empirical stakes involved in this philosophical debate, it is hardly surprising that proponents on both sides sought evidence to further their causes. Those on the abolitionist side found support for their case in the examples of Africans who attained European education and made their mark in publishing toward the end of the eighteenth century, notably Phyllis Wheatley, whose *Poems on Various Subjects* was published in London in 1775; Ignatius Sancho, whose letters were published posthumously in 1782; Ottobah Cugoano, whose *Thoughts and Sentiments on the Evil and Wicked Traffic of Slavery* appeared in 1787; and Olaudah Equiano, whose *The Interesting Narrative of the Life of Olaudah Equiano or Gustavus Vassa, the African, Written by Himself* appeared in 1789.[20] Keith A. Sandiford has placed these relatively well-known Africans in a tradition of African learning in Europe, including the achievements of two African scholars "more nearly coeval to Sancho, Cugoano and Equiano"—and, I would add, to Abram Gannibal—Anthony William Amo and Jacobus Capitein.[21] In this context, the case of a third black scholar, Francis Williams, who was born in Jamaica in 1702 and went on to study at Cambridge, is particularly interesting: "Francis Williams became the protégé of the Duke of Montagu (also Sancho's patron). The Duke arranged for his education out of curiosity 'to see whether a black boy taken and trained at an English school and then at a university, could not equal in intellectual attainments a white youth similarly educated.'"[22] The case holds obvious resonance with that of Peter and Gannibal.

On the other hand, those who believed that the differences among the races were ineradicable predictably feared mixing, and here we find the motif of the telltale black baby emerging persistently. Karen Newman, in her discussion of the threat posed by miscegenation in *Othello,* traces to the publication in 1589 of Richard Hakluyt's compendium of geography and travel accounts, *Principal Navigations,* a new version of the origin of blackness adduced to counter the ancients' belief that dark skin pigmentation was caused by proximity to the sun:

> In his *Discourse* (1578, repr. in Hakluyt, 1600), George Best, an English traveler, gives an early account of miscegenation and the causes of blackness: "I my selfe have seene an Ethiopian as blacke as a cole brought into England, who taking a faire English woman to wife, begat a sonne in all respooects as blacke as the father was, although England were his native countrey, and an Eenglish woman his mother: whereby it seemeth this blacknes proceedeth rather of some natural infection of that man, which was so strong, that neither the nature of the Clime, neither the good complexion of the mother concurring, coulde any thing alter."

Newman then goes on to cite Best's identification of the original source of this "infection" in the biblical story of Noah and his sons:

> Who all three being white, and their wives also, by course of nature should have begotten and brought foorth white children. But the envie of our great and continuall enemie the wicked Spirite is such, that as hee coulde not suffer our olde father Adam to live in the felicitie and Angelike state wherein hee was first created, but tempting him, sought and procured his ruine and fall: so againe, finding at this flood none but a father and three sonnes living, hee so caused one of them to transgresse and disobey his father's commaundement, that after him all his posteritie shoulde bee accursed. The fact of disobedience was this: When Noe at the commandement of God had made the Arke and entered therein . . . hee straitely commaunded his sonnes and their wives, that they . . . should use continencie, and abstaine from carnall copulation with their wives. . . . Which good instructions and exhortations notwithstanding his wicked sonne Cham disobeyed, and being perswaded that the first childe borne after the flood (by right and Lawe of nature) should inherit and possesse all the dominions of the earth, hee contrary to his fathers commandement while they were yet in the Arke, used company with his wife, and craftily went about thereby to dis-inherit the off-spring of his other two brethren: for the which wicked and detestable fact, as an example for contempt of Almightie God, and disobedience of parents, God would a sonne should bee borne whose name was Chus, who not only it selfe, but all his posteritie after him should bee so blacke and lothsome, that it might remaine a spectacle of disobedience to all the worlde. And of this blacke and curses Chus came all these blacke Moores which are in Africa.[23]

By the time of the Enlightenment, this scriptural explanation had been displaced, as we have seen, by the polygenetic theory, reflected in the passage from Voltaire's *Philosophy of History* cited in the second epigraph to this article. The association of racial exogamy with monstrous births, destabilizing to the community, had been placed on a putative "scientific" basis.[24]

It is generally assumed that Russia, which did not participate in the triangular trade in slaves, and therefore Russia's native son Pushkin as well, remained outside these debates and the racial attitudes and policies they symbiotically served. I would contend, however, that not only did Russians—relegated by these trends in racial classification to the undesirable, peripheral status of what Martin Bernal terms "fringe Europeans"—have a stake in this philosophical trend, but that Pushkin's African ancestry placed him in a particularly vexed position in this regard. While it goes beyond the scope of this article to try to trace all of Pushkin's reading and exposure to contemporary racial theories, it is probable—given his extensive reading of the eighteenth-

The Telltale Black Baby

century philosophes and his wide acquaintance with well-educated and traveled Russians of his generation, not to mention his own "exotic" background—that he was acquainted with the general outlines of the debate over race. I will also attempt to demonstrate that the fact that he wrote *The Blackamoor*—and especially that he abandoned it before completion—and the text of the novel itself expose his familiarity with the issues of the day with regard to human classification and his realization of their implications for himself personally.

As a preface to my own reading of *The Blackamoor* through the prism of the contexts outlined above, I would like to summarize a related, but significantly different reading, of the unfinished novel by the Soviet scholar D. I. Belkin. Belkin, who argues that Ibragim "occupies a visible space in the gallery of *oriental* images created by Pushkin"[25] in his article "O rossiiskikh istochnikakh 'Arapa Petra Velikogo,'" does indeed place Pushkin's unfinished novel in relation to the debate outlined above. He contends that Pushkin's conception of *The Blackamoor* was informed by his reading at Mikhailovskoe of Batiushkov's *Assays* (*Opyty*):

> This work had a large impact "on the refining of judgments of Montesquieu by Russian progressive writers and thinkers of the first quarter of the XIX century." Montesquieu's name enjoyed in Russia "great popularity at the time." "An Evening at Kantemir's" was popular and loved for a long time, particularly in the Decembrist circle.[26]

In Batiushkov's work, his "positive hero," the poet Antioch Kantemir, at the time Russian emissary to the court of Louis XV and a believer in the great potential of Petrine Russia, participates in a discussion in Paris with Montesquieu and the Abbot V. In Belkin's words: "Through the reasoning of his hero K. N. Batiushkov argued with Montesquieu's theory about the determining influence of climate as the 'first power' over human character, habits and customs, finally, on the forms of government organization."[27] As Belkin sees this reflected in *The Blackamoor*:

> From the episodes of the novel the reader understands that the severe climate did not hinder Ibragim from manifesting great abilities, which in Petrine Russia were revealed more fully than at the court of the Duke of Orleans. It is interesting that the latter, in trying to persuade the "young African" to remain in Paris, has recourse to Montesquieu's theory: "Your long stay in France has made you equally *alien* [*chuzhdym*] *to the climate and way of life of half savage* Russia" . . . The bankruptcy of the reasoning of both the philosopher and the duke on the impossibility of Enlightenment in Russia was refuted by the circumstances of Gannibal's fate, the profundity of his spiritual inquiries, the tableaux of the life of the young Russian capital.[28]

While I agree with Belkin that, as I suggested earlier, the text of *The Blackamoor* asks to be read within the context of the debates on the formative elements of nationality, ethnicity, and race, I would draw attention at this point to the way that Africa "gets lost" in Belkin's argument. While on the most superficial level this silence would seem to be elicited by a corresponding silence in the text of Pushkin's novel, I would now like to turn to a reading of Pushkin's text to show that this apparent silence is eloquent—and evocative—indeed.

Silence, absence, blankness, after all, characterize the imaginative geography of *The Blackamoor* from its very opening pages. I have in mind, of course, the deafening silence about Ibragim's past which, with only a few rare and telling exceptions, reigns throughout the text. This silence is particularly apparent in the opening sentence of the first chapter: "Among the young men sent by Peter the Great to alien [*chuzhie*] lands to acquire the knowledge necessary to a transformed state was his godson, the blackamoor Ibragim."[29] This apparently straightforward, one might even be tempted to say innocuous, sentence is in fact rather slippery. The dense factual information offered up in this in medias res beginning is skewed by the particularly loaded word *chuzhie*. *Chuzhie* in relation to whom, we must ask, and we immediately sense a problem where the "blackamoor Ibragim" is concerned. The only reference to the actual events of Ibragim's African childhood, and those primarily concerned with how he left Africa, are placed in the mouth of his putative future father-in-law toward the end of the completed section of the novel.[30] I will quote the exchange between Rzhevsky, his father, and sister almost in full:

> "What," exclaimed the old prince, whose drowsiness had completely passed, "Give my granddaughter Natasha to a *bought* [*kuplennogo*] blackamoor!"
>
> "He's not of simple birth [*on rodu ne prostogo*]," said Gavrila Afanas'evich, "He's the son of a blackamoor sultan. The infidels took him prisoner and sold him in Tsargrad, and our emissary rescued him and gave him to the Tsar. The blackamoor's older brother traveled to Russia with a noble ransom and . . ."
>
> "My dear fellow, Gavrila Afanas'evich," interrupted the old woman, "We've all heard the fairy tale of Bova Korolevich and Eruslan Lazarevich." (49, my emphasis)

Ibragim's story, relegated to the realm of the adventure tale by the old woman, tells us little about his African past, but significantly focuses on his "lineage" (*rod*), privileging genealogy (class) and family ties in defining identity.[31] For the time being, I will ask you merely to bear in mind the "commercial" aspects ascribed to Ibragim's life here, in such close proximity to mention of the imported popular prose tale as well. The only other references to Africa in the novel are to climate. Here, for example, is a fuller version of the Duke of Or-

The Telltale Black Baby

leans's appeal to Ibragim to remain in France, including his reference to Africa, which Belkin tellingly omits:

> "Russia is not your fatherland; I do not think that you will ever see your *torrid* [*znoinuiu*] homeland again; but your long stay in France has made you equally alien to the climate and way of life of half savage Russia." (19, my emphasis)

Here the Regent reminds Ibragim that he is a man without a country, clearly casting climate as an issue of that to which one is accustomed. Ibragim himself, however, is not so sure. Faced with Peter the Great's offer to serve as his matchmaker with Natalia Rzhevskaia, Ibragim asks himself:

> "Get married!" thought the African, "why not?[32] Am I really fated to spend my life alone and not know the superior delights and sacred responsibilities of man because I was born in a *(torrid) clime* [*pod (znoinym) gradusom*]?" (52, my emphasis)

I contend that Ibragim's question underscores the power that Africa, and what it means to be African, exerts in the text, a power that is intensified precisely because of the silence that enshrouds the geographical place itself in the novel.

Of course, the silence about Africa facilitates Ibragim's function as a tabula rasa, the perfect test case for the Petrine reform of Russian society, which pits education and natural ability against genealogy. Svetlana Evdokimova, who underscores Ibragim's role as an observer who is simultaneously an insider and outsider, points out in her *Pushkin's Historical Imagination*:

> Incorporating both perspectives, being both foreign and Russian, Ibragim emerges as the very image of the epoch—as an emblem of the syncretism of Russian culture during the reign of Peter the Great. Ibragim is emblematic of the intersecting of boundaries of race, social status, citizenship, conventions, traditions—all social institutions Peter was trying to reshape. Thus, the very choice of the character—whose personal merits, education, and devotion are opposed to tradition, race, and social origins—is already a historically accurate characterization of the epoch. The character here represents a historical milieu and becomes translucent to allow the historical process to penetrate through him.[33]

Certainly, Ibragim's "homelessness" and effective lack of genealogy do particularly suit him to stand as an emblem of Peter's age, just as his choice of "newborn" (*novorozhdennyi*, 53) Petersburg over aging, decadent Paris passes judgment on the comparative worth of the two civilizations. Evdokimova even suggests, in the spirit of the Belkin argument cited above: "In a sense, Gannibal with his African origin and European education could be viewed as symbol of Petrine Russia with its 'dark' and unknown past and forced europeanization."[34] I would counter by maintaining that beneath the idealized plot surface of Peter's apparent indifference to race, there remains the persistent subtext, reiterated by Ibragim himself and figured by the motif of the telltale baby, that "race" is not irrelevant to Peter's experiment—or, at least, to Pushkin's. Ibragim remains the perfect gauge of the success of Peter's reforms precisely because he is a "curiosity,"[35] because if he can be transformed, anyone can be.[36] (Here we recall the Duke of Montagu and other European aristocrats who indulged in similar social experimentation with Africans in the eighteenth century.) We must also remember that all of the French intellects—Voltaire, Montesquieu, and Fontenelle—who, we learn from the text of the novel, frequent the same Parisian salons as Ibragim, participated in the contemporary discussions on race and history.[37] In the case of Ibragim, as in the case of St. Petersburg (as Pushkin would so dramatically illustrate some years later in *The Bronze Horseman*), Peter's will is pitted against nature. In both cases, in Pushkin's rendering, the results remain inconclusive, but nature appears far from completely vanquished.

Ibragim himself appears painfully aware of what is at stake from the beginning. To understand this, we need to interrogate what Ibragim's blackness means to him. Neither the "young African's" intellectual capacity nor his moral worth is ever cast in doubt.[38] This makes Gannibal's own low opinion of himself all the more striking. Most obviously, Gannibal's blackness, in his own eyes, marks him as ugly and unlovable, a perpetual outsider. His most negative assessment, heartrendingly so, appears in his farewell letter to the countess: "Why try to join the fate of such a gentle, such a beautiful being with the calamitous fate of a Negro, a pitiful creature barely worthy to be called human?" (21). The most virulent racist of the age could hardly have expressed it in less flattering terms. While back in Russia, basking in the fatherly attention of Peter, Ibragim seems to gain confidence, even Peter understands that only a biological tie, so to speak, will ensure Ibragim's acceptance into Russian society: "Listen, Ibragim, you are a man alone, without family or tribe, alien to all except me. If I were to die today or tomorrow, what would happen to you, my poor blackamoor? You must get settled while there's still time, find support in new connections, enter into an alliance with the Russian boyars" (52). Just as Peter seeks to bend Rzhevsky to his will by forcing him to give his daughter to Ibragim, so he seeks to bend biological difference to his will as well. Just as, in *The Bronze Horseman,* the flood will belie Peter's subjugation of nature in the building of St. Petersburg, so the telltale white baby looming at the end of Pushkin's plan for *The Blackamoor of Peter the Great* suggests that Peter cannot so lightly ignore difference in his building of the Russian nation. Ibragim may act more "Russian" than the pedigreed Russian Korsakov, but even with Peter as his godfather, he cannot remake his genealogy. He can-

The Telltale Black Baby

not be Russian. The blackamoor will inevitably introduce alien blood into the "race."

It has been suggested that Pushkin finally abandoned his writing of *The Blackamoor of Peter the Great* only after Faddei Bulgarin's scurrilous attack on the poet's own African origin. The commentary which accompanied the publication of the novel in the 1937 jubilee edition of Pushkin's works, under the editorship of M. A. Tsiavlovsky, propounds this theory. Arguing that Pushkin was originally distracted from the novel by *Poltava,* the completion of the seventh chapter of *Eugene Onegin,* and *Journey to Arzrum (Puteshestvie v Arzrum),* among other works, and that the appearance of Zagoskin's *Yury Miloslavsky* and Bulgarin's *Dmitry the Pretender (Dmitry samozvanets)* attenuated the issue of creating a Russian historical novel à la Walter Scott which had originally motivated Pushkin to take up *The Blackamoor,* the commentator contends that Pushkin nonetheless planned to return to the novel until Bulgarin's attack adminstered the final blow:

> For a time *The Blackamoor of Peter the Great* was once again put to the side, but, evidently, Pushkin had not renounced completion of the novel. This is evidenced by the fact that he continued to rework the manuscript even after the very plot of his unfinished novel had been compromised by Bulgarin. We have in mind the latter's notorious feuilleton in *The Northern Bee* of 7 August 1830, no. 94 ("Second Letter from Karlov to Kamennyi Ostrov" ["Vtoroe pis'mo iz Karlova na Karmennyi Ostrov"), in which the following lines were directed against Pushkin: "There is in circulation an anecdote that a Poet in Spanish America, also an imitator of Byron, descended from a Mulatto or a Mulatta, I don't remember, tried to prove that one of his ancestors was a Negro prince. In the town hall it was discovered that in olden days there was a legal dispute between a skipper and his assistant over this Negro . . . between the skipper and what the skipper was trying to prove, that he had bought the Negro for a bottle of rum . . . ," etcetera.

Pushkin had a very painful reaction to Bulgarin's anecdote, which he answered, also in 1830, in the concluding stanzas of "My Genealogy" ("Moia rodoslovnaia"): "Sitting at home, Figliarin decided, / That my black great-grandfather Gannibal / Was purchased for a bottle of rum / And fell into the hands of a skipper . . ." etcetera (*Reshil Figliarin, sidia doma, / Chto chernyi ded moi Gannibal / Byl kuplen za butylku roma / I v ruki shkiperu popal . . .*); and in the pages of "Attempts to Reflect Several Nonliterary Accusations" ("Opyty otrazheniia nekotorykh neliteraturnykh obvinenii"): "In one (almost official) newspaper it was said that my forebear Abram Petrovich Gannibal, godson and ward of Peter the Great, his confidant, etcetera—was purchased for a bottle of rum. My forebear, if he was purchased, then probably it was cheaply, but he was acquired by a skipper whose name every Russian utters with respect and does not take in vain . . ." etcetera. There could be no ques-

163

tion of finishing *The Blackamoor of Peter the Great* after Bulgarin's foray (it is characteristic of Pushkin that after the article in *The Northern Bee* he even removed the note about Gannibal from new editions of *Eugene Onegin*).[39]

While I do not entirely accept this view, I do find the incident telling from a symptomatic, if not from a causal point of view. The weaknesses of the argument here are obvious, beginning with the contention that Pushkin continued to work on *The Blackamoor* after Bulgarin's attack, which is countervened by the argument that the novel was unfinishable after Bulgarin's attack. More to the point, there is no reason given for why Pushkin would have been distracted from *The Blackamoor* into other projects in the first place. However, it is equally clear that Bulgarin's attack brought into the public sphere in a particularly ugly form issues imminent in the novel itself.

To clarify my point here, and before concluding my argument, I would like to look at one more unfinished Pushkin work, tellingly a mixture of poetry, begun at roughly the same time Pushkin began to show interest in Gannibal, and prose written later. I have in mind *Egyptian Nights* (*Egipetskie nochi*). I will try to show that, like *The Blackamoor of Peter the Great*, *Egyptian Nights* breaks off in a particularly significant place, illuminating the vexed issues both texts raised for their author. At the core of *Egyptian Nights* stands the relationship between poetry, sex, and commerce; specifically, what it means to turn something into a salable commodity. The gentleman poet Charsky, who tries to place himself above the market and to assert the freedom of his poetry from the demands of social intercourse, is pitted against the impecunious, swarthy, black-clad, foreign *improvizatore,* who willingly composes verses on topics proposed by others for money. Most significant, in the context of my argument, are suggestive resonances between the verses the improvisor composes to order and issues I have tried to demonstrate are key to Pushkin's motivations in writing and abandoning *The Blackamoor of Peter the Great.* First, there is the curious reference to *Othello* in the verses the Italian produces in response to Charsky's paradoxical request for an improvisation on the topic of the poet's freedom to choose his themes:

> Such is the poet: like Akvilon,
> He does what he wants,
> He soars down like an eagle
> And, asking no one,
> Like Desdemona selects
> An idol for his heart.

> Таков поэт: как Аквилон,
> Что хочет, то и носит он,

The Telltale Black Baby

Орлу подобно он слетает
И, не спросясь ни у кого,
Как Дездемона набирает
Кумир для сердца своего.⁴⁰

The imputation of freedom of agency to the white maiden Desdemona is "answered" at the end of the text of *Egyptian Nights* in the improvisor's unfinished verses, putatively dictated to him again by Charsky, on the subject of Cleopatra's loves. In this poetic rendering of Cleopatra's offer to spend the night with—and grant her sexual favors to—any man willing to pay with his life, the *improvizatore* underscores the mercenary aspect of the transaction:

Who will enter into passionate trade?
I'm placing my love up for sale;
Tell me: who among you will buy
A night with me at the price of your life? (8:274)

Кто к торгу страстному приступит?
Свою любовь я продаю;
Скажите: кто меж вами купит
Ценою жизни ночь мою?

Just as in *The Blackamoor* one telltale baby entails another, so here one act of female will (Desdemona's) is countered by another (Cleopatra's), and the free flight of inspiration is checked by commerce, by Cleopatra's placing of a price on what is most precious. The analogy between the *improvizatore*'s virtuoso trade in poetry and the African queen's trade in "love" is clear. The text of *Egyptian Nights* breaks off in the middle of the *improvizatore*'s verses, tellingly before the consummation of either love or death.

At this point let us return to *The Blackamoor of Peter the Great* and remember that the very adjective, *kuplennyi*, that so angered Pushkin in Bulgarin's slur on Gannibal had earlier been placed by the poet himself in the words of the old count cited above. Seen in the context of the cluster of associations in which it appears, the reference to slavery, the dehumanizing commerce in human beings, resonates with commerce in poetry and commerce in sex, with anxieties about "selling out" to prose or to tsars and, finally, with fear that, in the final analysis, one cannot escape one's birth. We recall here yet another Shakespeare text implicated in the proto-racial ideology of the Bard's age, *The Tempest*, specifically the description of that eminently "marketable" monster, Caliban:

Ste. This is some monster of the isle, with four legs: who hath got, as I take it, an ague: I will give him some relief, if it be but for that: If I can recover him,

165

and keep him tame, and get to Naples with him, he's a present for any emperor that ever trod on neat's leather.

 Cal. Do not torment me, pr'ythee;
 I'll bring my wood home faster.

 Ste. He's in his fit now; and does not talk after the wisest. He shall taste of my bottle: If he have never drunk wine afore, it will go near to remove his fit. If I can recover him, and keep him tame, I will not take too much for him: he shall pay for him that hath him, and that soundly.[41]

The same monstrousness that makes Caliban a fit gift for an emperor makes him "no doubt marketable" [Antonio, act 5, scene 1].[42] May the same, perhaps, be said of Ibragim? And, if so, what peril for the author lies hidden in this public demonstration of his origin?

Here let us consider the suggestive resonance between the lines from Pushkin's "Conversation between the Bookseller and the Poet" and "My Genealogy":

Inspiration cannot be sold,
But manuscripts can.

Не продаётся вдохновенье,
Но можно рукопись продать. (2:330)

This skipper was accessible to my grandfather,
And the blackamoor bought for a fair price
Grew up diligent, incorruptible,
The Tsar's equal and not a slave.

Сей шкипер деду был доступен,
И сходно купленный арап
Возрос усерден, неподкуплен
Царю наперсник, а не раб. (3[1]: 263)

Pushkin draws attention to the issue of what can and cannot be bought and sold by the echo of the root of *kuplennyi* in *nepodkuplen*. Yet the riskiness of the contrast, the fine line separating the two, also resonates here. Does not the danger to the poet himself—selling his own life in the prose of *The Blackamoor*—lurk not far beneath the surface here?

So let me conclude by returning to the title of my article. I invoke there, if you will remember, not the telltale *white* baby which was purportedly to appear as a sign of Natasha Rzhevskaia's fidelity, and therefore serve as an indication of Ibragim's failure to achieve belonging in the Russian boyar class, but the telltale *black* baby sired by Ibragim at the beginning, and spirited away to be raised in the distant provinces before the infant can serve as irrefutable evidence of transgression. For it is indeed the black baby, mark of the intractability of nature, that entails the inevitable white baby at the end, the mark of Ibragim's perpetual status as an alien, his seed a potential pollutant of the nation's blood. The plot, after all, is not exactly symmetrical, since in both cases Ibragim remains an outsider to a community that rejects exogamy. Pushkin, as he contemplated his own imminent marriage, could not help but fear that blood would out, metaphorically if not literally. Nor was the commercial aspect, the specter of buying himself a bride, absent from this social transaction.[43] And was Pushkin not selling out poetic inspiration and selling himself into bondage to the market and the "crowd" by putting his private ancestral history out for sale in the bazaar of "lowly prose"? Perhaps in the end, *The Blackamoor of Peter the Great*—or at least the chapters in which Abram figures and which were not published in Pushkin's lifetime—became something of a telltale black baby that Pushkin himself consigned to silence or at least indefinitely deferred.

Notes

The first epigraph for this chapter is a quotation of Sof'ia Nikolaevna Karamzina in a letter of April 9, 1837, cited in I. L. Andronikov, *Rasskazy literaturoveda* (Moscow, 1973), 277–79.

1. For a bibliography of critical works on *The Blackamoor of Peter the Great,* see G. A. Lapkina, "K istorii sozdanii 'Arapa Petra Velikogo,'" in *Pushkin: Issledovaniia i materialy,* vol. 2 (1958), 293–94.

2. Pushkin published significant parts of the fourth and third chapters of *The Blackamoor* respectively as "IV Glava iz istoricheskogo romana" in *Severnye Tsvety na 1829* (St. Petersburg, 1828), 111–24; and "Asambleia pri Petre 1-m" in *Literaturnaia gazeta* 1, no. 13 (March 1, 1830): 99–100. These two excerpts were republished in sequential order as "Dve glavy iz istoricheskogo romana" in *Povesti, izdannye Aleksandrom Pushkinyn* (St. Petersburg, 1834), 161–85.

3. A. S. Pushkin, "Arap Petra Velikogo," *Sovremennik* 6 (1837): 97–145.

4. S. L. Abramovich, "K voprosu o stanovlenii povestvovatel'noi prozy Pushkina (Pochemu ostalsia nezavershennym 'Arap Petra Velikogo')," *Russkaia literatura* 17, no. 2 (1974): 56.

5. On Pushkin's early attempts at prose, see Paul Debreczeny, *The Other Pushkin: A Study of Alexander Pushkin's Prose Fiction* (Stanford, Calif.: Stanford University Press, 1983), 14–20.

6. A. S. Pushkin, *Polnoe sobranie sochinenii,* 17 vols. (Moscow and

Leningrad, 1937–59), 6:655. In the first full edition of *Eugene Onegin,* published in 1833, Pushkin cut all but the first line of the footnote ("The author, on his mother's side, is of African origin"), omitting Gannibal's biography in its entirety. Here we should draw attention to the close connection Pushkin clearly made between prose and history, which was unquestionably related to the blurred line between prose and nonfiction in Russian letters of the time and in Pushkin's own conception. In this context, Pushkin's tendency to "double" historical fictions with historical nonfictions—*The Blackamoor* and *The History of Peter the Great* (*Istoriia Petra Velikogo*), *The Captain's Daugher* (*Kapitanskaia dochka*) and *The History of Pugachev* (*Istoriia Pugacheva*)—may be seen as testifying to his attempts to delineate and differentiate the two.

7. See Waclaw Lednicki, "The Prose of Pushkin, Part I," *Slavonic and East European Review* 28, no. 70 (1949): 109.

8. T. G. Tsiavlovskaia, "Khrani menia, moi talisman," in *Utaennaia liubov' Pushkina,* ed. D. M. Klimova (St. Petersburg, 1997), 295–380. I am grateful to David Bethea for having brought this article to my attention.

9. A. S. Pushkin, "Nachalo avtobiografii," in *Zhizn' Pushkina rasskazannaia im samim i ego sovremennikami,* ed. V. V. Kunin (Moscow: Pravda, 1988), 1:71–72. Perhaps it is not amiss to suggest that Pushkin's account evinces a note of fatalism here, as if he is doomed to replay the same "unhappiness" as his ancestors, especially given the fact that this was probably written in 1834, when his marriage was already strained by his wife's social success.

10. Pushkin, "Nachalo," 72 (italics in the original). Pushkin's German great-grandmother's ineptness in Russian forms an implicit contrast with his African great-grandfather's linguistic prowess. The motif of Gannibal's high level of education, especially underscored by the family "legend" that he became almost immediately and at a very young age Peter the Great's amanuensis, contrasts interestingly with the motif of "the talking book" that Henry Louis Gates Jr., in *The Signifying Monkey,* isolates in African American writing on the "Middle Passage" from Africa to American slavery.

11. M. G. Kharlap, "O zamysle 'Arapa Petra Velikogo,'" *Izvestiia Akademii Nauk SSSR: Seriia literatury i iazyka* 48, no. 3 (May-June 1989): 270.

12. V. D. Rak argues that Pushkin first read *Othello* in French translation either toward the end of his Odessa exile or when already in Mikhailovskoe. He further proposes as the earliest trace of Shakespeare's tragedy in Pushkin's works the fragment "How the Tsar's Blackamoor Thought to Marry" ("Kak zhenit'sia zadumal tsarskii arap"), "written in the last days of October and beginning of November 1824 in the atmosphere of heightened interest in his exotic ancestor manifested by the poet almost from the first days of his forced residence in the family nest" (V. D. Rak, "Pushkin i frantsuzskii perevod

Otello," *Pushkin Journal* 1, no. 1 [1993], 36–44). He contends that the fragment was inspired by Iago's words (which arguably set Shakespeare's tragedy in motion), "Even now, very now, an old black ram / Is tupping your white ewe." Even more interestingly from the point of my argument here, Rak suggests that a variant of these words appears in *Poltava* with respect to the relationship between Mazepa and Maria. I would point out that this underscores the extent to which *Poltava,* the work to which Pushkin turned from *The Blackamoor,* reconfigures the same issues raised in the unfinished novel. While underscoring the complex interconnections and disjunctions between history and personal life, *Poltava* replays an Othello and Desdemona-like relationship, which has been deracialized and desexed, thereby removing the explosive elements which may have made Gannibal such a disturbing figure for Pushkin. For more on Pushkin and *Othello,* see Catherine O'Neil's article in this volume.

13. Anthony Gerard Barthelemy, "Ethiops Washed White: Moors of the Nonvillainous Type," in *Critical Essays on Shakespeare's Othello,* ed. Barthelemy (New York: G. K. Hall, 1995), 95.

14. Barthelemy, "Ethiops," 99.

15. George Stocking, "French Anthropology in 1800," in his *Race, Culture and Evolution* (Chicago: University of Chicago Press, 1982), 36.

16. Martin Bernal, *Black Athena: The Afroasiatic Roots of Classical Civilization,* vol. 1, *The Fabrication of Ancient Greece 1785–1985* (New Brunswick, N.J.: Rutgers University Press, 1987), 27–28. For the purposes of this article, it should be noted that while Bernal has been vigorously attacked for his central thesis, that ancient Greek civilization is heavily indebted to ancient African civilization, a debt that has been erased from history because of racism, the controversial nature of his theory does nothing to detract from his impressive research in the area I am discussing. In this context it is worth remembering that Pushkin's friends, the Turgenev brothers, studied at Göttingen.

17. Bernal, *Black Athena,* 28.

18. Ibid., 29.

19. Richard H. Popkin, "The Philosophical Bases of Modern Racism," in *Philosophy and the Civilizing Arts: Essays Presented to Herbert W. Schneider,* ed. Craig Walton and John P. Anton (Athens: Ohio University Press, 1974), 134. For an excellent anthology, enriched by commentary, of Enlightenment writings about race, see Emmanuel Chukwudi Eze, ed., *Race and the Enlightenment: A Reader* (Cambridge, Mass.: Blackwell, 1997).

20. For more on Ignatius Sancho, see "Ignatius Sancho (1729–1780), The White-Masked African," in *The History and Historiography of Commonwealth Literature,* ed. Dieter Riemenschneider (Tübingen: Narr, 1983), 189–97.

21. Keith A. Sandiford, "Early Traditions of African Learning in Europe: Renaissance to Enlightenment," in *Images de l'africain de l'antiquité au xxe siècle*, ed. Daniel Droixhe and Klaus H. Kiefer (Frankfurt: Peter Lang, 1987), 75 (my emphasis).

22. Sandiford, "Early Traditions," 77.

23. Karen Newman, "'And Wash the Ethiop White': Femininity and the Monstrous in Othello," in Barthelemy, ed., *Critical Essays*, 127–28.

24. On the specter of monstrous birth in *Othello*, see Michael Neill, "Unproper Beds: Race, Adultery, and the Hideous in *Othello*," in Barthelemy, ed., *Critical Essays*, 187–215. See particularly Neill's discussion of the link between the "hidden" and the "hideous" and between "the exotic obscurity of Othello's origins" (203), Africa, adultery, and monstrousness.

25. D. I. Belkin, "Zametki o pushkinskoi traktovke natsional'nogo i obshchechelevecheskogo v obraze afrikantsa Ibragima Gannibala," *Literaturnye sviazi i traditsii*, no. 3 (1972): 53. Here, as in the article I will discuss above, Belkin casts racial and national differences in terms of the paradigm of East vs. West, in a highly unsophisticated form anticipating Edward Said's argument in *Orientalism*. Again as I will suggest above, this has to do with the terms—and something of a confusion of terms when Africa is thrown into the mix—in which Russian intellectual thought has for two centuries tried to make sense of Russia's place in the world, above all in relation to the West. This bipolar view, as we shall see, leaves no room for "third parties."

26. D. I. Belkin, "O rossiiskikh istochnikakh 'Arapa Petra Velikogo,'" in *Boldinskie cheteniia* (Gor'kii: Volgo-Viatskoe knizhnoe izdatel'stvo, 1987), 230–31. Here Belkin is citing from V. B. Sandomirskaia, "K voprosu o datirovke Pushkina vo vtoroi chasti 'Opytov' Batiushkova," *Vremennik Pushkinskoi komissii* (1972): 30; and M. P. Alekseev, "Montesk'e i Kantemir," *Vestnik LGU seriia obshchestvennykh nauk*, no. 6 (1965): 56–57. Compare with the transformation of Othello into an "Oriental" Moor.

27. Belkin, "O rossiiskikh," 231.

28. Ibid., 231–32 (emphasis in the original).

29. Pushkin, *PSS* 8:9. Page numbers of *The Blackamoor* will hereafter be cited parenthetically in text.

30. We should note here that the only remembrances of Ibragim's youth are those associated with Peter the Great and Russia. Over dinner with the imperial family after Ibragim's return to Russia, Peter "remembered several features of Ibragim's adolescence and related them with such good humor and cheer that no one would have discerned in the affectionate and hospitable host the hero of Poltava, the powerful and awesome transformer of Russia" (24). This passage is particularly interesting given the fact that Pushkin went on to write—and some scholars have even claimed abandoned *The Black-

amoor of Peter the Great—for *Poltava*, in which Peter is indeed portrayed as the hero of Poltava as described here.

31. Compare Newman, "'And Wash the Ethiop White': 'Othello' doesn't lose 'his own origins'; his only access to those origins are [*sic*] the exotic ascriptions of European colonial discourse. Othello's stories of slavery and adventure are *precisely* a rehearsal of his origins, from his exotic tales of monstrous races to the story of the handkerchief's genealogy in witchcraft and Sibylline prophecy" (131, emphasis in original).

32. It is worth noting that in *The Bronze Horseman*, Evgenii will repeat the same words in contemplating marriage.

33. Svetlana Evdokimova, *Pushkin's Historical Imagination* (New Haven: Yale University Press, 1999), 151.

34. Evdokimova, *Historical Imagination*, 152.

35. For more on the leitmotif of "curiosity" in *The Blackamoor of Peter the Great*, see my article, "A Note on Curiosity in Pushkin's *The Blackamoor of Peter the Great*," *Pushkin Review/Pushkinskii vestnik* 4 (2001): 37–50.

36. In fact, as the example of the hopelessly foppish Korsakov demonstrates, Ibragim's rootlessness is an advantage in his reeducation. He ends up becoming a better "Russian" than a Russian nobleman, showing us that what in fact is being redefined is the very nature of "Russianness."

37. On Fontenelle, see Bernal, *Black Athena*, 181.

38. Pushkin's portrayal of Ibragim as an exemplar of reason, duty, dignity, and honor is particularly striking given some of the less palatable aspects of Gannibal's life, particularly his treatment of his first wife.

39. A. S. Pushkin, *Polnoe sobranie sochinenii v deviati tomakh pod obshchii redaktsii M. A. Tsiavlovskogo* (Moscow: Khudozhestvennaia literatura, 1938), 7:805–6.

40. Pushkin, *Polnoe sobranie sochinenii v deviati tomakh*, vol. 7. The commentary points out that these verses are a reworking of the draft of *Ezerskii*: "Why does the Young Desdemona / Love her Blackamoor / As the moon loves the darkness?"

41. William Shakespeare, *The Tempest*, in *The Complete Works of William Shakespeare* (New York: Avenel Books, 1975), 11 (act 2, scene 2).

42. On the link between marketability, monstrosity, and race in *Othello*, see James R. Aubrey, "Race and the Spectacle of the Monstrous in *Othello*," *Journal of Literature, History, and the Philosophy of History* 22, no. 3 (Spring 1993): 221–38.

43. On this, see Roman Jakobson, *Pushkin and His Sculptural Myth*, trans. and ed. John Burbank (The Hague and Paris, 1975).

Richard C. Borden

Making a True Image:
Blackness and Pushkin Portraits

FEW POETS, few dictators even, have had their physiognomies more ubiquitously represented in their native land than has Alexander Pushkin. Given the vitality of the Pushkin cult in Russia, and especially due to the state promotion of the cult during the Soviet era, it is not surprising to find Pushkin's features gracing everything from candy wrappers and coffee cups to carafes, cafeterias, and classrooms.[1] Many a famous artist of Pushkin's day painted the poet's portrait, and in the century and a half that followed the list of painters who have done a "Pushkin" reads like a Who's Who of Russian art.[2] His face is truly a national icon, perhaps *the* national icon today, now that Lenin's and Stalin's prominence has severely declined. But despite the fact that he possesses one of the most recognizable faces in his nation's history, it remains unclear just how "familiar" Pushkin's features really are. In fact, few public personae have had the essential components of their physiognomies represented so variously, even contradictorily, as has Pushkin.

In one portrait we find a Pushkin with a dark complexion, but in another he is fair-complected. Here he has piles of frizzy hair, but over there it is gently waved. His nose in this portrait is long and pointed, and in that one it is flat and broad. His outsized side-whiskers are mounds of fuzz in one painting, but neat ringlets in another. His forehead here is square and strong, while there it is round and sloping. His lips are full and sensual, his mouth large and fleshy, or his lips are thin and tight, and his mouth hard and sculpted. Most of the time all of these representations, no matter the constituent combinations, are immediately identifiable as "Pushkin" nonetheless. But not always (see figures 7 and 71). Is this any way for an icon to behave? Where does the true image lie, and why is it so elusive?

This study first examines the historic foundations upon which the physical representations of Pushkin familiar to every Russian were based. These include the portraits of the poet executed during his lifetime, those done after his death by artists who had actually seen the poet alive, the poet's death masks and the portraits of him in his coffin, and the words of contemporaries who had seen Pushkin in the flesh. Second, I will suggest what I consider to have been the primary impulses involved in the evolutionary shaping of those few "Pushkin" models that have attained a certain iconicity over the past 175 years.

It is apparently a fact that Pushkin's "true" image was more than a little protean in real life. His portraitists and other eyewitnesses have left testimonials to the changeability of the poet's appearance, to its capacity to refigure itself abruptly depending on mood or the state of his health.[3] The journalist N. A. Polevoi, reviewing V. A. Tropinin's famous portrait in the *Moscow Telegraph,* observed that "Pushkin's physiognomy is so defined, so expressive, that any artist can capture it, at the same time it is so changeable, so unsteady, that it is difficult to assume that one Pushkin portrait could give a true understanding of it."[4] It is also true that the elusiveness of Pushkin's representational image may be ascribed to the uneven skills of the artists involved. No matter how often one sees the portrait attributed to I. Linev (1836–37?; figure 8), for example—likely the last portrait completed during the poet's lifetime—one is shocked by how *un*Pushkin-like it seems, how startlingly it contradicts the more iconic "Pushkins."[5] It is, for one thing, highly unflattering: this Pushkin appears to be spiritually and physically crushed, not at all the bold and lively Pushkin of lore, or the "heroic" Pushkin model championed by nationalists.[6]

Before one takes consolation from the notion that this, after all, is one of the more amateurish "Pushkins" done in the poet's lifetime, and thus dismissable as a representational failure, one should examine the Pushkin death masks, taken but a few months after Linev contrived his likeness (figure 9).[7] Here we might find something like a *physically* "true" image. The death masks, it turns out, actually support Linev's figuration of the poet as being, at the end, a physically unappealing man who had aged dramatically in the decade since his best-known portraits were completed. Several of the paintings of Pushkin in his coffin also confirm this impression. Even in the case of the coffin paintings, however, Pushkin's image remains elusive. For while three of them (figures 10, 11, and 12) confirm Linev's reading of the poet's visage, they in many ways *resemble one another not at all,* while a fourth (figure 13) makes the dead poet look positively youthful, with delicate, pretty features.

So what did Pushkin actually look like? More important, what has become, or is becoming, the poet's "true image"?

This latter question, of course, obtains in Russian culture far more significantly than we are accustomed to in the West, given the centrality of icon veneration in the Russian Orthodox Church and, more importantly, in the popular and historical consciousness of the Russian people. In the Eastern tradition—and in the popular imagination—the portrayals of saints in icons constitute no mere plastic representation of the sanctified. They embody, rather, a "true image"—one made (metaphorically) "not by human hands," but immediately, that is, from the living image of the sanctified, whose representation remains iconically fixed for all time—à la Veronica's Cloth or the Shroud of Turin—and comprise nothing less than an incarnation of spiritual essence.[8]

In some ways, it may be said that Russians have made of Pushkin as well a deeply venerated, only quasi-secular saint (martyrdom and all), and that his representations have attained a nearly iconic status, much as during Soviet times the Party leadership—notably Lenin, Stalin, and Brezhnev—were ubiquitously represented in iconically fixed, government-prescribed images and venerated (often as actual, physical replacements for the religious icons of the vanquished culture, removed from the traditional "beautiful"—*krasnyi*—corners of Russian homes).[9] And as with those dictators and those true saints, certain nearly fixed iconic models for representing Pushkin may be discerned, even if their subject itself remains (paradoxically) elusive.

Abram Tertz has evoked the notion of an omnipresent, but somehow elusive, iconic "Pushkin" occupying the Russian national consciousness when he describes the poet as "one big familiar blur with sidewhiskers."[10] At the same time, Russians from childhood nurse a personal, familiar "Pushkin" within their souls—a sort of magical spirit, the concertmaster of the Russian tongue and genie of its fables, and they demand an equally familiar icon, a true and pure image to represent that spirit.

Andrei Bitov captures the urgency of this national thirst satirically in the story "Pushkin's Photograph (1799–2099)," in which a Pushkinist of the distant future, regretting the lack of any verifiably true image of the bard, directs one of the first time-travel expeditions back to Pushkin's time to photograph the poet.[11] The mission fails, for the wily Pushkin remains elusive, his image uncaptured even as the man from the future tracks him doggedly, camera in hand, back through the years.[12]

Russian fascination with the true image of their secular icon also informs Bitov's *Pushkin House*. There, in the actual (and also metaphorical) Pushkin House (all of Russian culture, after all, is Pushkin's "house")—the Leningrad literary institute—it suddenly intrudes upon the scene of a fight between two highly metaphorical characters, analogues, as it were, to opposing positions in debates over matters of Russian cultural heritage, tradition, and legitimacy. As the brawl rages out of control, the most unspeakable crime is committed: Pushkin's death mask—the dead poet's "true image"—is removed from its display cabinet, dropped, and shattered. As an alternative to this mock-tragic ending, however, the narrator allows for the possibility that the mask was just a copy, of which there lie stacks in a storeroom. One might ask, then, whether even in "Pushkin House" itself there exists no one true, irreplaceable, iconic image of the poet, but merely stacks of interchangeable masks?

1. E. I. Geitman, *Pushkin*, 1822

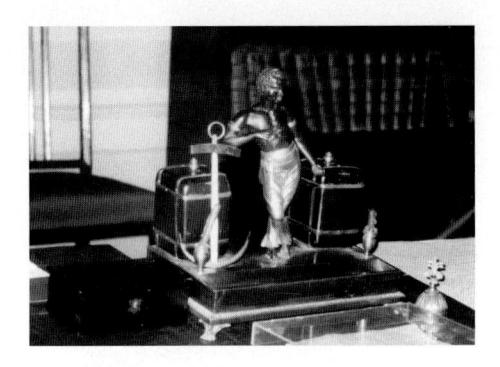

2. Pushkin's inkwell

3. A. S. Pushkin, self-portrait from Elizaveta Ushakov's album,
September or October 1829

4. A. S. Pushkin, self-portrait as a horse, among drawings of horses' heads; on the manuscript of the poem "André Chenier," 1825

5. A. S. Pushkin, self-portrait as a blackamoor (*arap*), in a manuscript of the novel *The Blackamoor of Peter the Great* (chapter 3), 1827

6. A. S. Pushkin, self-portrait as Dante,
with the inscription in Italian "il gran Padre AP," 1835–36

7. Artist unknown, *A. S. Pushkin* (no date)

8. I. Linev, *Pushkin*, 1836–37?

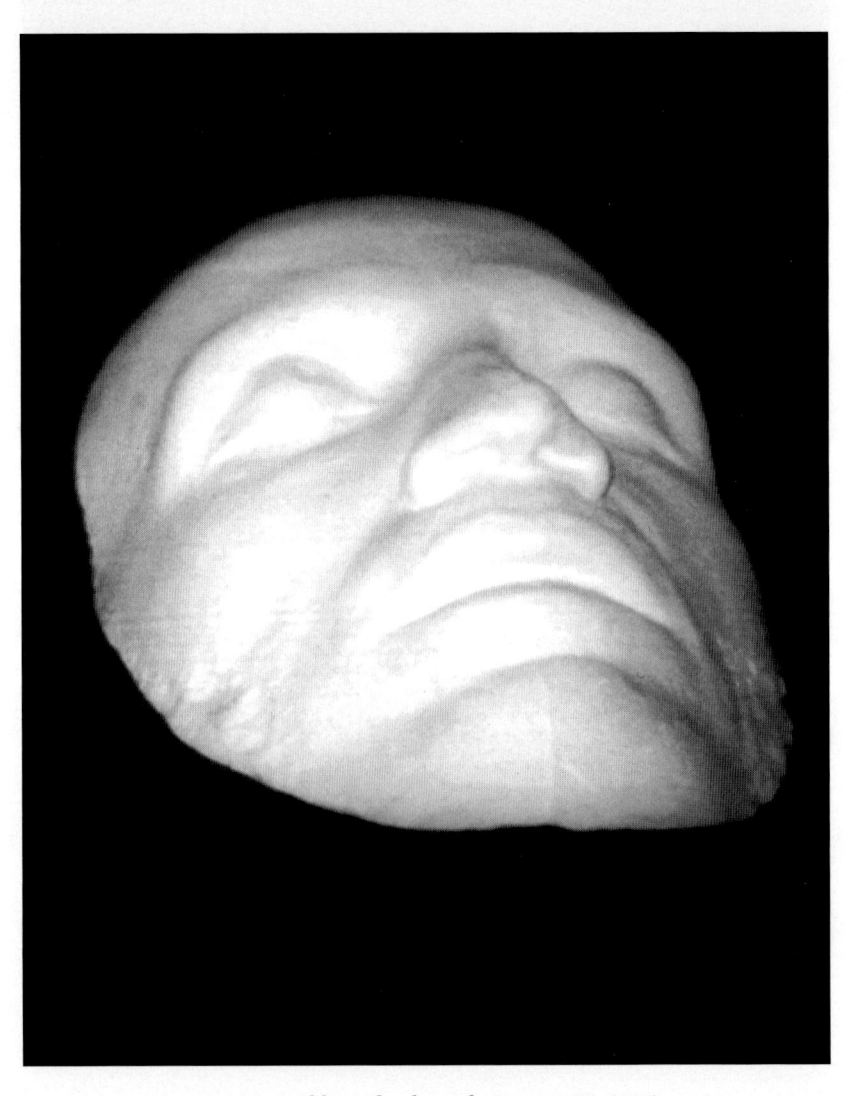

9. A. S. Pushkin's death mask, January 29, 1837

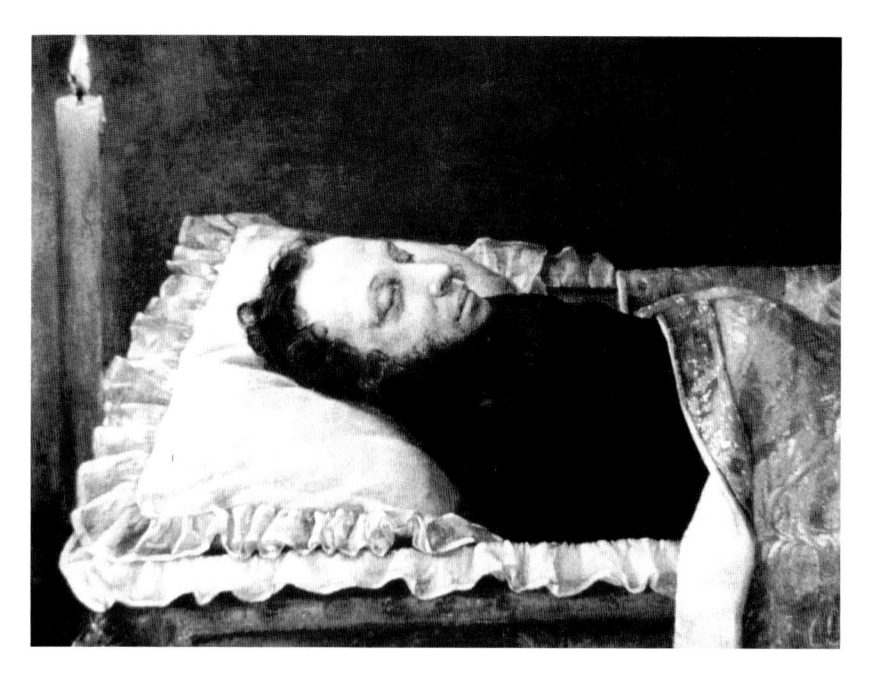

10. A. A. Kozlov, *Pushkin in His Coffin*, 1837

11. F. A. Bruni, *Pushkin in His Coffin*, 1837

12. A. N. Mokritsky, *Pushkin on His Deathbed,* January 29, 1837

13. V. A. Zhukovsky, *Pushkin in His Coffin,* January 30, 1837

14. Artist unknown (S. G. Chirikov?), *A. S. Pushkin*, c. 1810s

15. K. Somov, *Pushkin at Work*, 1899

16. I. Repin, I. Aivazovsky, *Farewell, Free Elements!* 1887

17. I. Repin, *Pushkin at the Lycée Examination*, 1911

18. A. M. Opekushin, model of Pushkin's head for the Pushkin monument, 1880

19. N. P. Ul'ianov,
Pushkin and His Wife before the Mirror at a Court Ball, 1936

20a. G. Chernetsov, detail from *Pushkin, Krylov, Zhukovsky, and Gnedich in the Summer Garden*, 1832

20b. G. Chernetsov, *Pushkin, Krylov, Zhukovsky, and Gnedich in the Summer Garden*, 1832

21. S. Gal'berg, *Pushkin*, 1837

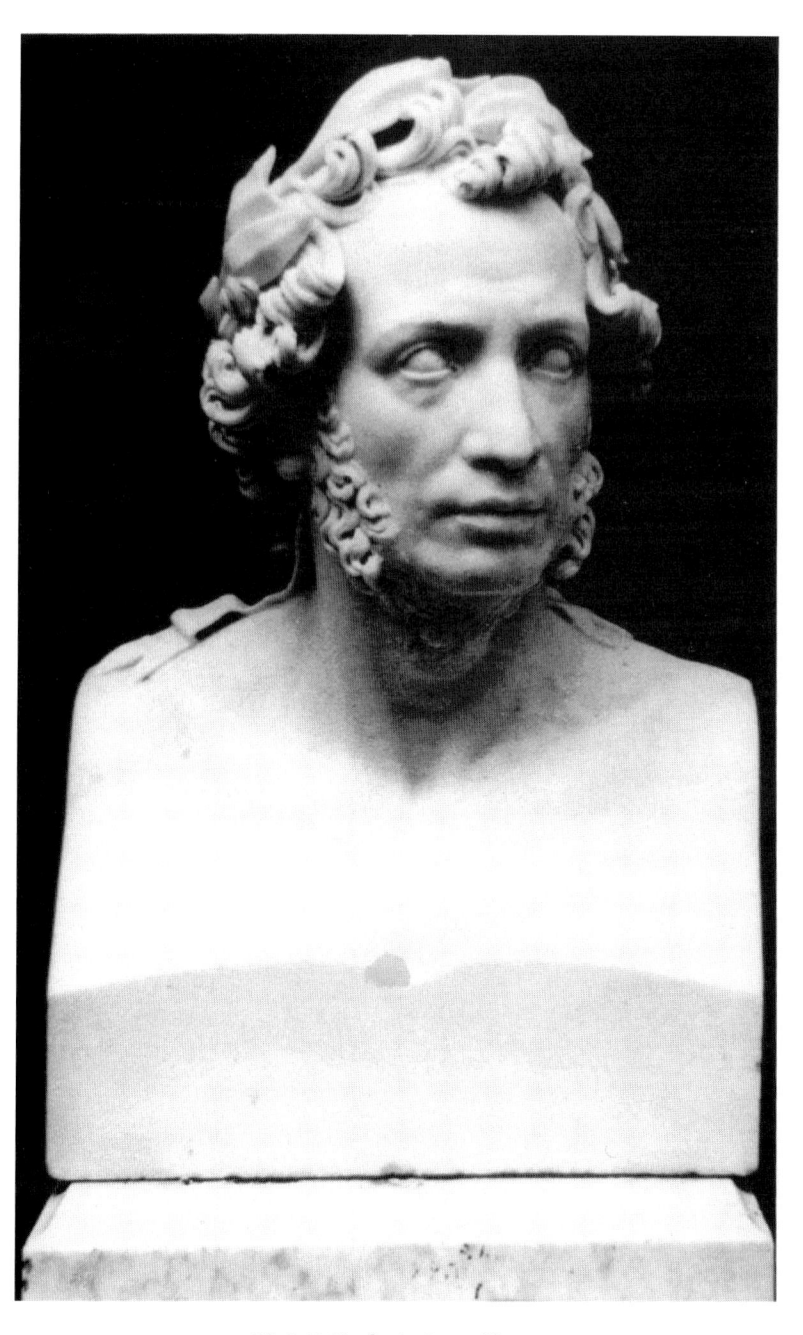

22. I. P. Vitali, *A. S. Pushkin*, 1837

23. P. F. Sokolov, *A. S. Pushkin*, 1836

24. T. Wright, *A. S. Pushkin*, 1836–37

25. P. Chelishchev, *Pushkin Taking a Stroll*, 1830

26a. Artist of the Venetsianov school, detail from
A Saturday Gathering at Zhukovsky's, 1837–39

26b. Artist of the Venetsianov school, detail from
A Saturday Gathering at Zhukovsky's, 1837–39

27. Unknown artist, *A. S. Pushkin*, 1831

28. J. de Vivien, *A. S. Pushkin*, 1826–27

29. G. A. Gippius, *A. S. Pushkin*, 1827

30. Xavier de Maistre(?), *Pushkin as a Child*, 1800–2

31. V. A. Tropinin, *A. S. Pushkin*, 1827

32. V. A. Tropinin, sketch, 1827

33. V. A. Tropinin, study, 1827

34a. A. P. Elagina, *Portrait of Alexander Pushkin*, copy from the original by V. A. Tropinin, 1827

34b. A. P. Elagina, detail from *Portrait of Alexander Pushkin*, 1827

35. I. Repin, *A. S. Pushkin,* copy from the original by V. A. Tropinin, 1913

36. O. A. Kiprensky, *A. S. Pushkin,* 1827

37. N. I. Utkin, gravure from the original by O. A. Kiprensky, 1827

38. V. V. Mathé, *Pushkin*, 1899

39. A. Bezliudnyi, lithograph from the original by O. A. Kiprensky, 1830

40. A. I. Kravchenko, *Pushkin*, 1936

41. K. F. Iuon, *Pushkin*, 1950

42. A. P. Briullov, *Pushkin at the Housewarming Party at Smirdin's Bookshop*, 1832

43. S. F. Galaktionov, *Pushkin at the Housewarming Party at Smirdin's Bookshop*, engraving after A. Briullov's drawing, 1833

44. A. M. Opekushin, Pushkin monument in Moscow, 1875

45. M. K. Anikushin, model of the Pushkin monument in St. Petersburg, 1950

46. V. V. Kozlov, model of the Pushkin monument in St. Petersburg, 1936

47. I. D. Shadr, model of the Pushkin monument in St. Petersburg, 1940

48. B. Z. Zelensky, poster, 1949

49. V. I. Shukhaev, *A. S. Pushkin,* 1960

50. R. R. Bakh, *Pushkin*, 1886

51. N. Gogol, *Pushkin*, 1837

52. V. A. Favorsky, *Pushkin as a Boy at the Lycée*, 1935

53. V. A. Serov, *Pushkin in the Park*, 1899

54. V. F. Shtein, *Pushkin as a Boy*, 1910

55. N. P. Ul'ianov, *Pushkin in the Lyceum Gardens*, 1935

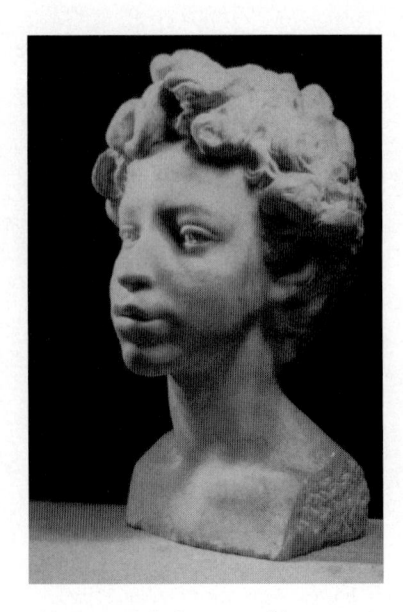

56. E. F. Belashova, *Pushkin as a Boy*, 1959

57. A. Z. Itkin, *Pushkin-Lycéeist*, 1968

58. A. Z. Itkin, *Pushkin-Lycéeist*, 1968

59. A. M. Nenasheva, *Pushkin-Lycéeist*, 1961

60. G. B. Dodonova, *Pushkin-Lycéeist*, 1969

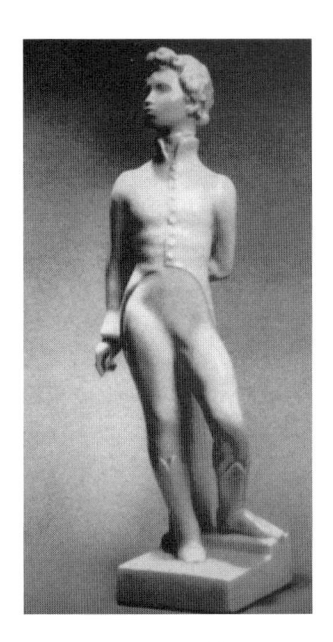

61. E. A. Gendel'man, *Pushkin-Lycéeist*, 1962

62. G. S. Stolbov, *Africa*, 1961

63. I. Aivazovsky, *Pushkin on the Black Sea Coast*, 1868

64. I Aivazovsky, detail from *Pushkin on the Black Sea Coast*, 1868

65. M. Dobuzhinsky, *Pushkin and the Decembrists*, 1924

66. J. de Vivien(?), detail from miniature portrait of Pushkin, 1826

67. V. Taburin, cover design for the book *Pushkin for Children*, 1899

68. M. Skudnov, medal, *Pushkin*, 1899

69. P. P. Trubetskoi, *Pushkin*, 1899

70. N. V. Kuz'min, *Pushkin and Kaverin*, illustration to *Eugene Onegin*, 1928–33

71. N. V. Kuz'min, *Pushkin*, illustration for the poem "To Chaadaev," 1959

72. V. N. Masiutin, *Pushkin*, 1918

73. Iu. L. Obolenskaia, *Pushkin*, 1925

74. P. Ia. Pavlinov, *Pushkin*, 1924

75. A. A. Naumov, *Pushkin's Duel with d'Anthès*, 1884

Memoirists and diarists have left no dearth of Pushkin descriptions. Of physical characteristics, the most universally noted are his fiery eyes.[13] Liveliness, agility, short stature, fingernails like claws, eccentric dress, an iron walking stick, and, of course, the huge side-whiskers, are also cited. Of particular interest in this regard is the frequency with which animals are evoked: he is a "fiery steed," a "wild beast," a "little tiger," a "cricket," a "cross between a tiger and a monkey." The monkey half of this last moniker is often linked with the many eyewitness testimonies to the poet's "African," "blackamoor," or "Negroid" features. It is, I believe, this particular trait—the poet's ostensibly Negroid facial characteristics—that has determined the history of inconsistency in plastic representations of Pushkin's physiognomy. Pushkin's portraits differ one from the other, throughout his lifetime and since, mostly in the degree to which portraitists have perceived, or not perceived, highlighted, downplayed, or effaced entirely the outward features Pushkin supposedly inherited from his African great-grandfather, Abram Gannibal, known to history as the "blackamoor" or "Negro" of Peter the Great. Evidence suggests that the chief determinant in portraitists' "takes" on Pushkin's physiognomy is the question of whether the poet did or did not have "Negroid" physical characteristics, and whether those features were an essential component of his overall countenance, or, if those "Negroid" traits were not physically significant, whether they were metaphorically significant as an expression of character.[14]

Did Pushkin in fact have Negroid features? It would seem an easy matter to resolve. But as Bitov's futuristic Pushkinist rightly complains, "What do we actually know *objectively* about the external appearance of the great poet? The iconography is extraordinarily meagre and, perhaps, tells us more about the personalities of the portraitists than of the model." This is quite true.

Despite some slight variance in scientific descriptions of "Negroid"—in contradistinction to "Caucasoid" and "Mongoloid"—facial traits, to the layman's understanding—both in Pushkin's time and today—"Negroid" features primarily comprise a darker skin pigmentation, full lips, a broad and flattish nose, and spiral-tuft hair.[15] Did Pushkin in fact noticeably display such features? The party line seems to be "Yes!" One of the foremost specialists in the field of Pushkin iconography asserts that

> This unusually strong African blood, admixed to Russian blood, told in Pushkin's impulsive-passionate temperament, just as it did in his exterior—in the fine, drawn-out nose with the strong relief of the nostrils, in the large lips, in the gleaming grin of white teeth, in the elongated form of the eyes, in the skin's dark complexion and in the rare beauty of the small hands with long fine fingers.[16]

Did Pushkin himself believe he possessed Negroid attributes? Again, apparently he did. The Pushkinist T. G. Tsiavlovskaia, for example, notes that

Pushkin was so sure of the strong resemblance with his African great-grandfather that, when drawing his imaginary portrait, he gave him his own profile.[17]

Pushkin famously described himself in one poem as "An ugly descendant of Negroes," and once referred in a letter to his "Negroid [*arapskii*] profile."[18] In an 1836 letter from Moscow to his wife Pushkin writes that "They want to model a bust of me here. But I don't want to. Then my ugly Negroid [*arapskoe*] face would be handed over to immortality."[19] Countess D. F. Fiquelmont concurred about this particular "ugliness," trotting out the "monkey" metaphor in her diary: "It's impossible to be more ugly—it's a mixture of the exterior of a monkey and a tiger. He comes from an African race, and in the color of his face there remains an impress and something wild in his look."[20] The dramatist and diplomat Aleksandr Griboedov once called the poet a "marmoset."[21] Pushkin himself, at the age of fifteen, characterized himself as "A true ape by his face."[22]

The gypsy Tania, describing her first impression of the adolescent poet, called him "a perfect monkey!"[23] Anna Olenina, whom Pushkin contemplated marrying, noted in her diary that "Having given him a singular genius, God did not reward him with an attractive exterior ... The Negro profile he inherited from his mother's line did not enhance his face. And add to that his terrible side whiskers, his disheveled hair, his nails long as claws, his short stature, his mincing manners."[24] M. N. Makarov tells of an incident from the poet's childhood:

> In his childhood years Pushkin was not tall and had all the African features of physiognomy that he was to have as an adult; but his hair as a boy was so curly and so elegantly waved by his African nature that one day I. I. Dmitriev said to me, "Look, it's a real little blackamoor."[25]

I. S. Turgenev referred to Pushkin's "African lips."[26]

On the other hand, Pushkin's Lycée classmate Ivan Pushchin makes no mention of any Negroid characteristics in his description of first seeing the future poet,[27] and neither do the poet's brother, Lev, his friend Zhukovsky, and numerous others. M. F. Yuzefovich remembered Pushkin as

> not at all swarthy, nor black-haired, as some assure, but ... fully fair-skinned, and with curly, chestnut-colored hair ... In his appearance there was something familiar to the African type; but it wasn't of the sort that would justify his verse about himself: "A descendant of ugly Negroes."[28]

The writer Lazhechnikov, however, describes his first impression of Pushkin as "a very young man, thin, short, curly-haired and with an Arabian [*arabskii*—as opposed to *arapskii*—Negroid] profile."[29] Countess Rostopchin also described the poet's profile as "Arabian," not "Negroid."[30] But another contemporary said of the poet's brother, Lev, that, "like his brother, he was a somewhat dark-complected Arab, but looked like a white Negro."[31] "Arab" or "Arabian" actually makes more anthropological sense than "Negroid," given the likelihood that Pushkin's African ancestor was, technically, not a Negro at all, but an Abyssinian, or Ethiopian, and thus, in theory, belonged to a branch of the Caucasian race.[32] Why then should his descendant display Negroid features?

D. S. Mirsky, while noting that Pushkin seems to have inherited a certain thickness of lip and curliness of hair from the "black ancestor" of whom he was "so romantically proud," nevertheless cautions that

> Gannibal was not a Negro in the technical, anthropological sense of the word—he was an Abyssinian. He belonged to the race which Deniker calls Ethiopian, and which is distinguished by the curliness rather than the fuzziness of its hair. Though often jet-black their features are rather like those of the Arabs. But on the other hand, the practice of slave hunting may have infused into them a certain proportion of purely Negro blood.[33]

Vladimir Nabokov muddies matters further:

> Abyssinians (or Ethiopians, in the strict sense) have a skin color varying from dusky to black. Their type represents a Hamito-Semitic component of the Caucasian race; and a Negro strain may so strongly predominate in some tribes that the term "Negro" is in such cases applicable in the general sense; but apart from these considerations . . . the European layman of the time—and, in fact, Abram Gannibal himself—would classify colloquially as a "Negro" or "black-amoor" (in Russian *negr* or *arap*—note the ultima) any more or less dark skinned African who was not an Egyptian and not an Arab (in Russian, *arab*).[34]

Nabokov further comments that

> According to Barsukov (1891), who had it from Elizaveta Pushkin, widow of our poet's brother Lev, the hands of Nadezhda Gannibal, Pushkin's mother, had yellowish palms; and according to another source, quoted by V. Vinogradov (1930), all the daughters of Isaak Gannibal, Pushkin's grand-uncle, son of Abram, spoke with a peculiar singsong intonation—"an African accent," quaintly says an old-timer, who remarks that they "cooed like Egyptian pigeons." There exists no authentic portrait of Abram Gannibal. A late eighteenth-century oil, which some suppose represents him, wearing a decoration he never received, is, anyway, hopelessly stylized by the dauber. Nor can we draw any conclusion from the portraits of his progeny as to what blood

dominated in Abram, Negro or Caucasian. In Pushkin, admixtures of Slavic and German strains must have completely obscured whatever definite racial characteristics his ancestors may have possessed, while the fact that certain portraits of Pushkin by good artists, and his death masks, do bear a remarkable resemblance to modern photographs of typical Abyssinians is exactly what one might expect in the descendant of a Negro married to a Caucasian. It should be repeated that "Abyssinian" implies a very complicated blend of the Hamitic and the Semitic and that, moreover, distinct Negroid types commingle with Caucasian ones in the northern plateau [of Ethiopia] and among ruling families almost as much as they do among the nomadic heathens of the lowland bush. The Galla tribes (the Ormota), for example, who overran the country simultaneously with the Turkish invasion in the sixteenth century, are Hamites with a strong Negro strain. Abram may have had the characteristics that Bent found in the Tigré and Hamasen tribes: "skin . . . of a rich chocolate color, the hair curly, the nose straight with a tendency toward the aquiline, the lips thickish," or—while still technically an Abyssinian—he might have possessed the traits that Pushkin, a conventionalist in these matters, gives Ibrahim in his novel: "a black skin, a flat nose, inverted lips, and rough woolly hair" (ch. 5) [*sic?* ch. 6??]. The taxonomic problem remains unsettled and will probably remain so.[35]

Bitov's Pushkinist, thus, is probably correct when noting how little objective information we have about the poet's external appearance. Perhaps the best measure of the unreliability of Pushkin's physiognomic iconography is the apparently inconclusive debate among Pushkinists, extending over nearly a century, on the question of whether the poet had blond or dark hair as a child.[36]

Another ground for caution in trying to establish a physically "true image" of the poet (as opposed to a mythic one) is the enthusiasm with which Pushkin himself, people in his life, and some biographers have cultivated the "African blood" motif. The poet liked to think that his passionate nature originated with his African blood. J. Thomas Shaw has observed that, contrary to the notion that Pushkin's having a black ancestor might have "hindered his acceptance as a Russian man of letters," "when his first Romantic verse tale, *The Prisoner of the Caucasus,* appeared in 1822, his publisher, N. I. Gnedich, obviously thought that it would help sales to have a frontispiece emphasizing Pushkin's black heritage; Gnedich provided such a lithograph without consulting the author."[37] This lithograph is one of the most famous of all Pushkin portraits, and indeed has attained iconic status as a representation of the poet as an adolescent. Based on a watercolor uncertainly attributed to Pushkin's Lycée drawing teacher, S. G. Chirikov (figure 14), this lithograph (figure 1), by one of the leading artists of the day, E. I. Geitman, alters the original exclusively by enhancing the "Negroid" features. It is true that the Chirikov original itself is one of the more "Negroid" of Pushkin portraits, but Geitman adds a touch of thickness to the lips, a pinch of wildness to the hair, a slightly broadened nose, and a darker complexion. Pushkin apparently admired this portrait, writing to Gnedich: "Alexander Pushkin masterfully lithographed, but I don't know if it resembles [him]."[38]

The tradition of the young Pushkin displaying pronounced "Negroid" features has prevailed. Today pictures of a "Negroid" Pushkin as a child and adolescent overwhelmingly predominate, while portraits of Pushkin as an adult, as we shall see, are predominantly less Negroid in their physiognomic orientation.[39] Perhaps the most unequivocally "Negroid" Pushkin is that by Konstantin Somov (1899; figure 15), called *Pushkin at Work,* which shows a rather bizarre adolescent, almost a caricature, baring his teeth to the viewer.

Some accounts of Pushkin's features do, however, recall only his ostensibly Negroid features—the actor Karatygin, for example, describes Pushkin as he first saw him as but "a stranger with a flattened nose, thick lips, and the dark skin of a mulatto."[40] Other exuberant celebrants of the notion that the great national poet came from African stock are biographers who play on their subject's "exoticism." Henri Troyat in his biography *Pushkin* is particularly licentious. His youthful Pushkin "looked like an ill-bleached blackamoor" (21). He later refers to the adolescent Pushkin's "cannibal lips" (50), and to the adult Pushkin as "this swarthy seducer with the devil's eyes" (256) and "strong white cannibal teeth" (82). Such rhetorical exaggeration suggests that the reporters are pursuing private agendas.

While it is true that Pushkin did refer to himself as looking like a monkey, the frequency with which others cited his simian appearance may be based on a misunderstanding. Yury Lotman has explored the question of the description *smes' obez'iany s tigrom* ("mixture of monkey and tiger") which is so frequently evoked. In fact, this was one of the nicknames the Lycéeists bestowed upon Pushkin. But, rather than a description of the poet's habits of mimicry and certain characteristic dispositions, taken together with his physiognomy, Lotman suggests that this phrase was also a synonym for Pushkin's other Lycée moniker, *frantsuz* ("the Frenchman"), which he received because of his passion for the French language. A "mixture of monkey and tiger" is a term that originates in Voltaire's metaphor for the moral cast of the French mind as half dandy and half tyrant, which term later became a common synonym for "Frenchman." Lotman assures us that Pushkin and his classmates understood it to mean precisely that. Lotman argues that the nickname later became known outside the poet's Lycée circle, where it became currency exchanged within a court society that was in his later years unfavorably disposed to the poet. There it came to define only Pushkin's physical appearance. The term thus in and of itself may have influenced the comparisons that memoirists and diarists came to employ when describing the poet. Lotman, for instance, cites Fiquelmont's "misuse" of the term when describing the poet's ostensible ugliness.[41]

A final point in favor of caution when seeking a "true image" of the poet is one Mirsky makes over and over again when he warns against using Pushkin's art to determine the facts of his life. Like many artists, Pushkin was more than willing to twist and color the "facts" of his experience in the creation of artistic effect. Pushkin was proud of his African heritage, and was not shy about exploiting it, even exaggerating it. It is possible that it was in part his own efforts at creating a mythic persona that influenced the perceptions of artists, memoirists, and diarists.

There are many representations of Pushkin that are so well known that they have acquired a certain iconicity. One particular category are the innumerable paintings that construct some sort of Pushkin narrative involving a well-known moment in the poet's actual life, but more often representing some key motif from the constructed, mythic narratives of the poet's "life." These range from Derzhavin's benediction, to Mikhailovskoe evenings with Nanny, Pushchin's visit to the exile, strolls with Onegin, encountering Griboedov's corpse, the poet declaiming verse to future Decembrists, and the final duel. In most such cases, artists have selected those iconographic features they require to evoke their required tenor, and for the rest they have employed the features and gestures of convention. Among the most famous of this genre is the collaborative effort by Ilia Repin and Il'ia Aivazovsky entitled *Farewell, Free Elements!* (1887; figure 16), in which the poet is cast as a stereotypical Romantic figure—a generic Byron—standing above the storm-tossed sea, gazing into raging chaos.[42] Context, I would suggest, is the only means of identifying this figure as "Pushkin."

Much the same may be said of Repin's *Pushkin at the Lycée Examination* (1911; figure 17). Here a slight adolescent, elegantly striking a "declamation" pose, recites his verse to the amazement of the examiners. Again, without knowing the scene's familiar iconography, it would not be likely that one would recognize the figure as Pushkin. The iconography of this painting has itself become a revered model, frequently recast for both *Lycée Examination* and *Pushkin Declaiming to the Decembrists* paintings.[43]

Most "narrative" portrayals of Pushkin follow this trend, especially in the Soviet era, when the adult Pushkin generally was outfitted as a rugged "democrat," a fiery revolutionary, following the heroic tradition of A. M. Opekushin's 1880 monument in Moscow (figure 18) or Repin's generic "Byron" at the shore, with few traces of the African, of the dandy, or the little monkey. A notable exception is N. P. Ul'ianov's 1936 painting of *Pushkin and His Wife before the Mirror at a Court Ball* (figure 19). The artist here pursues an ironic "beauty and the beast" theme, with the lovely Goncharova admiring herself in the mirror, which also reflects members of the court staring down their noses at the short, dark, thick-lipped poet with the burning eyes and broad nose, who scornfully returns their gaze.[44]

As a rule, however, Pushkin portraits select their model from one of the fifteen or so works that were done during the poet's life, or shortly after his death, and which thereby lay some claim to being a "true image." These include the "classics"—Tropinin's and, especially, O. A. Kiprensky's portraits of 1827, the S. G. Chirikov and E. I. Geitman portraits of the adolescent Pushkin, G. G. Chernetsov's 1832 group portrait of Pushkin strolling in the Summer Garden with Krylov, Zhukovsky, and Gnedich (figures 20a and b), Linev's oil, described above, Gal'berg's and Palazzi's death masks, Gal'berg's and I. P. Vitali's busts (figures 21 and 22), and group pictures by A. P. Briullov and S. F. Galaktionov (see figures 42 and 43). Chernetsov depicts a Pushkin bereft of Negroid characteristics except, perhaps, for a nose somewhat more flattened at its tip than those of his companions. A watercolor of 1836 by P. F. Sokolov (figure 23) is generally deemed not to have been painted from life, but based on Kiprensky. The pose of the poet in both works is identical, but the Sokolov version has a less "Negroid" orientation: hair less curly, a longer, thinner nose, a smaller mouth with thinner lips, and a longer and narrower face. The poet's uncle supposedly considered Sokolov's work a poor resemblance, but others who knew the poet said it was entirely reasonable.[45] In fact, this likely represents the first of the innumerable incidences in which artists have worked with the Kiprensky model only to diminish or efface its "Negroid" features, a tendency which, as we shall see, constitutes the principal dynamic in the creation of an iconic Pushkin physiognomy over the ensuing 160 years. An engraving by Thomas Wright (figure 24) also belongs to the poet's lifetime (though it appeared for sale only in the spring of 1837). It is slightly less "de-Africanized" than Sokolov's portrait and, while an original sketch (not preserved) was made from life, the engraving seems to have been modeled after Kiprensky.

A caricaturish sketch of Pushkin and Count Khvostov by P. Chelishchev (*Pushkin Taking a Stroll*, 1830; figure 25), made during the poet's lifetime, seems to play lightly on the "monkey" theme. The busts by Vitali (1837; figure 22) and Gal'berg (1837; figure 21) were created by sculptors who had had direct personal impressions of the poet, and were done soon after the poet's death, and thus also may make some claim for being "true."[46] Gal'berg's, based on the mask he took, offers an apparently Caucasian man who nevertheless possesses thick lips, a large and fleshy mouth, very curly hair, and a broad and slightly flattened nose which concludes in a sharpish point. Vitali's bust is similar, with a touch more emphasis on the flatness of the nose, but with somewhat thinner lips and a smaller and less fleshy mouth.

A rather primitive painting (1837–39; figures 26a and b) attributed to the school of A. G. Venetsianov portrays an evening at Zhukovsky's and shows at some distance a rather old Pushkin, with hair thinning severely at the forehead(!), thick lips, and a flat, broad nose.[47] An unknown artist's peculiar painting (June 13, 1831; figure 27) of the poet wearing a broad-brimmed hat displays a certain thickness of lip and broadness of nose, but hardly suggests an "African" theme. A pencil drawing by Jean de Vivien (1826–27; figure 28) is decidedly more "African," the effect deriving largely from its prognathism.[48] The broad mouth, high, roundish forehead, open expression, and frame of black curls also contribute to the effect. Pushkin liked this portrait, just as he liked the Geitman picture of him as a youth, also perhaps due to its emphasis on features traceable to his African heritage.[49]

The Gustav A. Gippius lithograph (figure 29), also dating from 1827, effaces all "Negroid" traits, as well as any nuances of personality. This "Pushkin" looks more likely to be a warrior than a poet, and in fact anticipates in a secular sense the sentimental, quasi-religious portraits of the poet that appeared in the early years of the twentieth century, such as the 1909 lithograph representing Pushkin "with a halo around his head and angels over each shoulder (all traces of an African physiognomy having been laundered out)."[50]

Geitman's engraving, as mentioned, has become the definitive adolescent Pushkin, the icon of his youth. An unattributed picture (possibly by de Maistre, or, as family tradition has it, a serf; figure 30)[51] of a slightly swarthy, chubby-cheeked child is often trotted out as "Pushkin." Pavlova observes, perhaps tendentiously, that "already in this child portrait of Pushkin in both composition and facial expression, the features inherited by him from his great-grandfather show through."[52]

Among adult portraits, a distant second in terms of iconic influence is the Tropinin (figure 31), done at the beginning of 1827 at the poet's behest. It has had more than its share of copyists, and of artists who have used it as a model for their own interpretations. This portrait, of which preliminary sketches and a study in oil also exist (figures 32 and 33), portrays a rather unattractive man with a long, fleshy nose. N. A. Pogodin wrote approvingly of this portrait and its "striking resemblance to the original."[53] The general tendency among epigones of this painting, however, is to efface its possibly "Negroid" features. Thus, in Avdotia Elagina's portrait (1827; figures 34a and b), made "from the original of V. A. Tropinin," we find a thinning of the poet's lips, a diminution of fleshiness about the mouth, and an overall reduction of that extraordinary nose. Later artists went even further in this "cleansing" tendency (figure 35).

The story of what comes closest to being *the* iconic Pushkin, however, lies in the long tradition of adapting Kiprensky's portrait to suit individual tastes and purposes. It is also in the history of painters working from the Kiprensky original that the evolution of Pushkin iconography most resembles

Making a True Image

the traditions of church iconography, wherein the fixed iconic image, taken from the actual subject by eyewitness or "not by human hands," recurs through the ages, with only more or less subtle remodelings to fit individual and epochal tastes and spiritual, political, or aesthetic requirements. There have been thousands of Pushkin portraits based on Kiprensky's painting, or on N. I. Utkin's engraving of same (figures 36 and 37).[54] Kiprensky's portrait was one of the poet's personal favorites. It had been commissioned by his friend A. A. Del'vig, and Pushkin eventually acquired the work himself and hung it in his living room.[55] Since the time of his death, at least every second edition of his works has had a Kiprensky or Kiprensky clone gracing its frontispiece. And it is here that the issue of whether or not Pushkin had strongly expressed "Negroid" features—or whether artists wish to highlight this notion or efface its impression—is most demonstrably manifest. Here we find a marked tendency on the part of copyists or epigones to "de-Africanize" the original—to refigure slightly the icon, touch up the "true image." These adaptations begin with the wholesale "de-negrification" by Utkin and reach their nadir in the turn-of-the-century sentimental angels, the heroic casts of late nineteenth-century Russian nationalists and of the Stalin era, and insipid book illustrations in both the East and the West.[56]

While Pushkin liked the Kiprensky portrait greatly, he wrote the painter a little verse which observed that

> I see myself as in a mirror,
> But this mirror flatters me.[57]

The poet's acquaintances, however, were struck by the similarity of the Kiprensky portrait and its model."[58]

Utkin, who was in his day the master of the engraved portrait, turned when commissioned to do Pushkin in 1827 to Kiprensky for his model, but significantly departed from the original. His alterations come almost entirely in the realm of the poet's "Negroid" features, which he largely eliminates. Utkin also gives the poet a more cheerful mien, eyes that are less deep, a slightly rakish smile, and leaves out the poet's right hand, with its dandyish long nails. This latter omission is a feature shared by virtually all portraits based on the Kiprensky iconography, one apparently intended to sanitize the poet's less "heroic" characteristics. In any case, it transpired that Utkin's lithograph became one of the most popular of its day. Pushkin's brother and some of his closest friends found it to bear the closest resemblance to the poet of all his portraits. Pushkin himself also favored it, requesting Utkin to make a new plate when the original had become worn.[59]

Innumerable other representations made after the poet's death pursue a similar "de-negrification." The portrait by V. V. Mathé (1899; figure 38), for instance, retains the Kiprensky iconography to the smallest details. But again, tiny alterations reduce the hints of a Negroid physiognomy. At first glance, the viewer might easily think Mathé's work a mere copy, and yet the effect of the changes is an image that more closely conforms to Caucasian conventions of attractiveness. Even more subtle are similar alterations in the portrait by A. Bezliudnyi (1830; figure 39).

A more original creation which follows this trend is A. I. Kravchenko's woodblock portrait of 1936 (figure 40). Kravchenko, unlike Bezliudnyi or even Mathé, is obviously creating his own picture, which is much more stylized in a Romantic vein than the Kiprensky (it has as background not just the standard muse statuary, but also a moonlit night). But he also follows Kiprensky's iconography almost slavishly, except in those slight changes that amount to a Caucasian prettification.[60] An appealing exception to this tendency among Kiprensky progeny is K. F. Iuon's 1950 portrait (figure 41), which evokes the Kiprensky iconography but with an original reading of the poet's physiognomy and psychology, retaining immediately identifiable "Negroid" features.

Another telling episode in the battle over Pushkin's "true image" involves how sketches by one artist are transformed by an engraver when creating a lithographic plate. Briullov in 1832 made a sketch (figure 42) of a housewarming party for Smirdin, the book dealer, for the title page of the almanac *Novosel'e (The Housewarming)*. His work shows a clearly "Negroid" Pushkin sitting amidst his colleagues, but a man apart, and not just because he is the only one who is obviously listening to the speaker. S. F. Galaktionov's engraving (figure 43), the actual title page based directly on Briullov's sketch, completely "de-Africanizes" the poet's physiognomy, as well as removing his aura of *différence*. Now Pushkin is just one of a group. Comparable changes in the others in the group, aside from features attributable to the artists' distinct styles, are absent.

Another sharp discrepancy arises in two of the portraits made while Pushkin lay in state. A. N. Mokritsky's work (January 29, 1837; figure 12) shows a nearly elderly man with receding hairline, thin or tightly compressed lips and a slightly curved nose, flattened at the tip. The next day, F. A. Bruni did Pushkin's portrait in the coffin (figure 11). This figure looks less like any familiar "Pushkin" than one of Gogol's provincial scoundrels with its smirk of self-satisfaction, thick lips, fleshy mouth, and a fleshy nose that is not merely not flattened at the tip, but slightly upraised—a "reading" of physiognomy which distinctly contradicts the nose the poet consistently rendered himself in his self-portraits. He also appears to be about twenty years younger than he had appeared to Mokritsky the day before. The full lips in Bruni's portrait preclude any definitive judgment about how "blackness" informs such a discrepancy, for in every other way the Mokritsky Pushkin is more the man with a

Making a True Image

"Negroid" physiognomy. Two additional portraits of the poet in state do nothing to resolve this conflict. V. A. Zhukovsky's sketch (figure 13) portrays a sharp-featured Caucasian prince without a trace of "Negroid" influence (and featuring sweeping waves of straight hair!). A. A. Kozlov's remarkable Pushkin (figure 10), on the other hand, is quite "Negroid," and closely resembles the death masks.

An especially telling example of how protean remains the iconic Pushkin(s) (within a certain circumscription) arises in the highly regarded series of sketches made by N. V. Kuz'min for book illustrations (figures 70 and 71).[61] While, for example, five of the drawings in one volume offer nearly identical profiles, which are similar to those that recur in Pushkin's self-portraits—strong brow, sharply pursed lips, elongated and somewhat flattened nose with pronounced, "flared" nostrils and receding jaw—a sixth drawing bears little resemblance. This Pushkin has rounded features, most notably a large, thick-lipped mouth.

Works of art that were produced long after the poet's death but which make some claim to iconicity due to their prominence include Opekushin's statue on Moscow's Pushkin Square (figure 44) and the St. Petersburg Art Square monument by M. K. Anikushin (1950; figure 45). These portrayals are based on the Kiprensky model, but have been heroicized almost out of recognition. Opekushin's statue, for example, does not greatly efface the poet's "Negroid" features as much as exaggerate other features to the point where the thickish lips and broad nose are secondary traits. Opekushin thus lends the poet a heroic stature by packing his brow, nose, and jaw with rocklike strength and endowing the poet with a powerful chest and shoulders. This Pushkin could never be confused with a cricket or little monkey. Opekushin established a trend that would reach its grotesque apotheosis in Stalin's day, with powerful Pushkin gods such as V. V. Kozlov's mighty Pushkin-cum-Lenin in St. Petersburg (1936; figure 46); I. D. Shadr's heroic rebel (1940; figure 47), with the gigantic worker's hands, casting off his overcoat; and B. A. Zelensky's revolutionary warrior (1949; figure 48), boldly striding the Russian soil on his way to the Radiant Future.[62] At the other extreme, there is B. M. Kustodiev's delightful sketch of *Pushkin in Petersburg* (1915), which more resembles a monkey in a top hat than a dandy about town.

Within a certain range, Pushkin's fifty-some self-portraits remain markedly similar over an eighteen-year span.[63] The thick lips we see in the death masks are one feature they almost all lack. On the other hand, the self-portraits' most striking feature—and the one most frequently caricatured by the poet himself—is the nose, which Pushkin sharpens and flattens, highlighting in many the elongated, "flared" nostrils to a degree no portraitist ever essayed. Given that these were among Pushkin's most conspicuously "Negroid" features, at least as cited by eyewitnesses, what does it tell us that he highlights one and downplays the other? Can we attribute his highlighting of the nose to a celebration of his African heritage? But then can we attribute his downplaying of the lips to a discomfort with what he felt to be an unattractive mien?[64] Must we not ask the same questions of portraitists? Do not some highlight the "African" attributes to honor the poet's self-identity and spirit, his passion, his sensuality, his vigor, or to make of him a more exotic figure, while others downplay those same features to free the Russian national poet of his foreign blood, or simply to prettify him for a broader popular consumption in accordance with European tastes?

Just as the Russian people may have seized on the notion of Pushkin as a martyr, a sacrificial lamb, a passive adherent of fate in his duel with d'Anthès, in order to make of him a truly national poet, one who conforms in irreducible essentials to national myth, so have painters and sculptors perhaps treated his ostensibly Negroid features less with any objective perception of his physiognomy than with ideological (or financial or psychological) agendas of their own. Certainly this was true in the Romantic "negrification" of an adolescent Pushkin by Geitman in 1822, and certainly it is true of all the epigones of Kiprensky who turn the poet into a European-standard fairy-tale prince or warrior-hero. Many Pushkin portraits, then, may indeed tell us more about the portraitists than about their subject.[65]

Of recent Pushkin portraits, perhaps the most remarkable is that painted by V. I. Shukhaev in 1960 (figure 49). It is noteworthy not only for its artistry, but for its originality. It is unmistakably Pushkin, but it belongs to no iconographic line. This is an indisputably "African" Pushkin, though not in any stereotypical fashion, as Geitman's and Somov's were. There is nothing "romantic," nothing savage or bestial in the poet's mien. His dark brown skin is set off dramatically against his elegant white suit. His eyes are intense, but distant, reflecting something like a blend of self-containment, satisfaction, and calm. His fine hands, crossed daintily on his knees, have long, sharp nails, but they are not the nails of a tiger or a monkey, but of a dandy, and the hands rest at peace. Like the poet himself, this "Pushkin" is unique. It reaches beyond convention and tradition, creating its own image. In this, perhaps, it makes its image true.

Notes

1. E. V. Pavlova, *A. S. Pushkin v portretakh,* 2 vols. (Moscow: Sovetskii khudozhnik, 1983), 1:78, tells of Pushkin's image, in primitive representations and often wearing laurels, appearing for the 1899 jubilee on stationery, candy bars, candy wrappers, matchboxes, kerchiefs, cups, pencil holders—there was even a "Pushkin" vodka bottle in the form of a bust of the poet. Antique stores in

Making a True Image

Moscow still offer a variety of "Pushkin" porcelains, of both pre- and post-Soviet manufacture.

2. Well-known artists who have painted well-known "Pushkins" include Vrubel', Aivazovsky, Gay (Ge), Kramskoi, Briullov, Repin, Leonid Pasternak, Klodt, Serov, Konchalovskii, A. M. and V. M. Vasnetsov, K. A. and S. A. Korovin, Surikov, Somov, Miasoedov, Kustodiev, Favorskii, Ul'ianov, Dobuzhinskii, Benois, Tishler, Petrov-Vodkin, Iuon, Kravchenko, Al'tman, Sar'ian, Shukhaev, Gerasimov, and many more.

A random September 1997 inspection of the commercial galleries housed in the Central House of Artists in Moscow turned up eighteen Pushkin representations painted or sculpted within the previous year by some fifteen different artists.

3. See T. G. Tsiavlovskaia, *Risunki Pushkina* (Moscow: Iskusstvo, 1987), 343; G. P. Balog and A. M. Mukhina's introductory article in their *A. S. Pushkin i ego vremia v izobrazitel'nom iskusstve pervoi poloviny 19-ogo veka* (Leningrad: Iskusstvo RSFSR, 1987), n.p.; and Pavlova, *Pushkin v portretakh,* 1:11.

4. Quoted in Pavlova, *Pushkin v portretakh,* 1:31 (my translation). Pavlova (1:47) cites several additional testimonies to the unusual changeability of Pushkin's face and mood.

5. The frequency with which Linev's rather mediocre painting is reprinted is perhaps explained by Paul Debreczeny's thesis (advanced in *"Zhitie Aleksandra Boldinskogo*: Pushkin's Elevation to Sainthood in Soviet Culture," in *Late Soviet Culture: From Perestroika to Novostroika,* ed. Thomas Lahusen [London: Duke University Press, 1993], 47–68; and "The Elevation of Pushkin to Sainthood," in *Social Functions in Literature: Alexander Pushkin and Russian Culture* [Stanford, Calif.: Stanford University Press, 1997], 223–30) that Pushkin was elected the Russian national poet, the embodiment of Russian national spirit, because of his ostensibly voluntary submission to martyrdom, because he was cast as a saintly sufferer, like Russia's first native saints, Boris and Gleb, who displayed *smirenie* (noble resignation) in the face of death ("The poet as sacrificial lamb had become the nation's patron saint"). Certainly Pushkin in Linev's portrait looks very much like a sacrificial lamb, mournfully and humbly awaiting slaughter. Balog and Mukhina, while noting the "amateurishness" of Linev's portrait, laud it as standing apart for its insight into the "deep spiritual drama" Pushkin was experiencing on the eve of the "fatal events."

6. Another reason the Linev portrait stands apart so dramatically, its subject appearing so surprisingly old, is that, as Pavlova (1:37) notes, not a single portrait of the poet was made (except as a figure in groups) between Hippius's lithograph of 1827 and Linev's painting of nearly a decade later. Pushkin's self-portraits from 1830 on reveal that the poet himself recognized that he was aging noticeably.

Richard C. Borden

7. For comparison of the two death masks, see V. Veresaev, *Pushkin v zhizni*, 6th ed. (1936; reprint, Chicago: Russian Language Specialities, 1970), vol. 2, illustrations to pp. 432 and 440. Pavlova (1:57) finds the similarity between Linev's idiosyncratic representation of the poet and portraits of him lying in his coffin so remarkable that she offers the hypothesis that Linev's model was, in fact, the poet's corpse.

8. For an interesting exploration of this tradition in Christian iconology, see Eva Kuryluk, *Veronica and Her Cloth: History, Symbolism, and Structure of a "True" Image* (Oxford: Basil Blackwell, 1991).

9. In *Echos of a Native Land: Two Centuries of a Russian Village* (London: Abacus, 1997), Serge Schmemann talks of his meeting with one of the leading iconographers of Lenin, Stalin, and other Soviet leaders, who complains that since the collapse of the Soviet Union "the demand for his Soviet icons had all but vanished": "'Not even the French buy them any more,' he groused . . . The floor of the studio was lined with studies for paintings of Lenin and Stalin (there were strict iconographic rules for portraits of the leaders, and every project required approval from a special committee)" (290).

10. Abram Tertz (Andrei Sinyavsky), *Strolls with Pushkin*, trans. Catharine Theimer Nepomnyashchy and Slava I. Yastremski (New Haven: Yale University Press, 1993), 49. A curious echo of Tertz's metaphor comes from the Soviet critic Pavlova (1:86), who, speaking of the numberless sculptures and paintings devoted to the subject of Pushkin between 1880 and the 1917 Revolution, notes that with few exceptions they were rarely more than "variations on the theme of a curly-headed person with side-whiskers" (my translation). An illustration of Pavlova's faceless crowd is R. R. Bakh's bust of 1886 (figure 50).

The notion that Pushkin has become a sort of secular saint in the Russian national consciousness is indicated by the violent outpourings of righteous wrath that greeted Tertz's light-hearted, brilliant, but iconoclastic portrayal of the national poet in *Strolls with Pushkin*. See Catharine Nepomnyashchy, "Andrei Sinyavsky's 'Return' to the Soviet Union," *Formations* 6, no. 1 (Spring 1991): 24–44; and Stephanie Sandler, "Sex, Death and Nation in the *Strolls with Pushkin* Controversy," *Slavic Review* 51, no. 22 (Summer 1992): 294–308.

11. A translation of "Pushkin's Photograph (1799–2099)" by Priscilla Meyer appears in *The New Soviet Fiction: Sixteen Short Stories*, comp. Sergei Zalygin (New York: Abbeville, 1989), 15–59.

12. Bitov's Pushkinist also takes shocked notice of the changes Pushkin's face underwent in the last years of his life. After failing to wheedle his way into Pushkin's world near the conclusion of the poet's life, the Pushkinist retreats some three years to the second Boldino autumn where he discovers writing *The Bronze Horseman* a bearded "child." Bitov footnotes his story here to comment: "There exists no representation of Pushkin with a beard. However,

there is an account that, returning from Boldino in 1833, Pushkin rode through Moscow incognito so that his wife could be the first to see him in a beard" (Bitov, "Pushkin's Photograph," 45).

13. Eyewitnesses often note that his eyes were the most expressive and lively they had ever seen, and rue portraitists' general failure to capture those eyes. See, for example, V. A. Nashchokina's assertions, as quoted in Balog and Mukhina, *Pushkin i ego vremia*.

14. In none of the studies of Pushkin portraits cited in this essay, nor, for that matter, in any study I have located, is the question of the poet's Negroid traits advanced as a defining issue in deciding the iconography of the poet's appearance, except in discussion of the Geitman portrait of the adolescent Pushkin.

15. Anthropologists define Negroid traits somewhat variously and with qualifications, but these definitions have remained largely unchanged since Pushkin's time. *The Great Soviet Encyclopedia* (translation of the third edition [New York: Macmillan, 1973], 2:49), for example, describes "the Negro people" as "characterized by dark skin color, strongly expressed curliness of hair, thick lips, broad nose, appreciable prognathism, and tallness," but then goes on to note many variations. *The New Encyclopaedia Britannica* ([Chicago: Encyclopaedia Britannica, 1990], 8:584) states that "Characteristic of the Negroid race are medium to heavy skin pigmentation, curly to extreme spiral-tuft hair forms, linear (slim, angular) body build, broad lips, minimal body hair and little pattern balding, broad nose, some evidence of fatty deposits in the buttocks" (etc.). *Collier's Encyclopedia* [(1972), 17:276) states that "Negroes are usually regarded as quite dark in color, with large flat noses and broad lips," but then cautions:

> Actually, there is a great variation in their physical appearance, from reddish brown to very dark brown in color, from tightly curled to almost straight hair, from short and stocky to tall and slender in physique, and from large lips and broad noses to thin lips and narrow noses.

In the context of defining "Negroid" traits as they did or did not apply to Pushkin's physiognomy, it may be argued that more important than scientific characterizations of "Negroid" appearance in Pushkin's time were the popular notions of such held by Pushkin and his contemporaries. Caricatures aside, there existed in the museums and private collections of Pushkin's Russia numerous plastic representations of Negroes that fully conform to anthropological definition and natural fact, and which would have been familiar to Pushkin and anyone in the upper levels of society. Gerbrand Van Den Eeckhout's 1658 oil painting of *The Levite and His Concubine Invited to Lodge at Gibeah*, which today hangs in the Pushkin Museum of Fine Arts in Moscow, for example, features a strikingly handsome servant boy—or young man—with unmistakably Negroid traits: a broad mouth with very full lips, a very broad nose flattened at its tip, and a dark, olive-brown complexion. He wears a jaunty cap and poses leaning against his donkey's saddle. Close examination reveals him to have long, sharply pointed, glossy fingernails on his left hand, which hangs languidly on the saddle, much as Pushkin's glossily long-nailed left hand rests languorously on his right arm in Kiprenskii's portrait. One is tempted to speculate that Pushkin admired precisely this figuration of a native African in this well-known work of art, and strove to emulate its subject's flamboyant beauty.

A second Eeckhout painting in the Pushkin Museum collection, the highly regarded *Adoration of the Magi* of 1665, features one very dark-complected Magus, clearly a Negro, with two handsome young Negro attendants (his sons?). They share almost identical features—skin that is nearly black, extraordinarily thick lips, and broad, flat noses with prominent, flaring nostrils. Taken as a group, with their earrings and exotic raiments, they offer a sort of typology for the European imagination of negritude.

16. Tsiavlovskaia, *Risunki Pushkina*, 341.

17. Ibid.

18. "To Yur'ev" (1820). The letter was addressed to the English painter, Dawe, who once sketched the poet.

19. As quoted in Balog and Mukhina, *Pushkin i ego vremia*. The authors cite this letter as possible explanation for there having been no sculptures featuring the poet during his lifetime.

20. As quoted in Iurii Lotman, "Smes' obeziany s tigrom," in *Pushkin: Biografiia pisatelia; stat'i i zametki, 1960–90; Evgenii Onegin. Kommentarii* (St. Petersburg: Iskusstvo-SPB, 1997), 329–331; and Tsiavlovskaia, *Risunki Pushkina*, 343.

21. "*Un sapajou.*" Pavlova (1:18) has "*un sapajon.*" Bitov, in "Pushkin's Photograph (1799–2099)," plays with this Pushkin/Negro/monkey motif when his time traveler witnesses the poet eating fruit: "'No, he doesn't look like a monkey . . .' Igor thought stupidly." Later, involved in an awkward conversation with the poet, "Igor opened his eyes and saw Alexander Sergeyevich unexpectedly close—face to face. A Negro was looking at him."

Nikolai Gogol's curious sketches of Pushkin (figure 51) are surprisingly Negroid in most respects. As Pavlova observes (1:109), however, they also resemble Gogol himself more than his putative model.

22. "My Portrait," a poem written in French.

23. Pavlova, *Pushkin v portetakh*, 1:28. Henri Troyat (*Pushkin*, trans. Nancy Amphoux [New York: Doubleday, 1970], 53) reports that the young Pushkin, in his first days at the Lycée, feared his classmates would make fun of him and call him a monkey: "He looked like a little monkey, and he knew it." Troyat does not provide a source for his assertion.

24. Quoted in Tertz, *Strolls with Pushkin*, introduction, 17.

25. Quoted in Veresaev, *Pushkin v zhizni*, 1:54.

26. Pavlova, *Pushkin v portretakh*, 1:53. Il'ia Repin, who made more than a hundred Pushkin representations over a period of twenty years while working on his *Pushkin on the Banks of the Neva*, referred to his subject as, among other things, a "monkey" and a "pure-blooded Arab" (Pavlova, 1:83).

27. Ibid., 1:55–56.

28. Ibid., 1:37.

29. Ibid., 1:21. It is worth noting that Troyat (110) fiddles with facts, perhaps to heighten his subject's exoticism (not unlike Geitman's highlighting the "African" features in his portrait of Pushkin as an adolescent), by changing "Arabian" (*arabskii*) to "Negroid" (*arapskii, negrskii,* or *negritanskii*), using "*profil negroïde*" in the French original.

30. Ariadna Tyrkova, *Zhizn' Pushkina* (Paris: YMCA, 1948), vol. 2 (1824–37), 141.

31. Pavlova, *Pushkin v portretakh*, 1:16.

32. Dieudonné Gnammankou has recently challenged this conventional understanding of the origins of Pushkin's African ancestors. See the discussion by Catharine Nepomnyashchy and Ludmilla Trigos in the introductory essay to this volume.

33. D. S. Mirsky, *Pushkin* (New York: Dutton, 1963), 4–5.

34. Vladimir Nabokov, "Abram Gannibal," appendix 1 in vol. 4 of Aleksandr Pushkin, *Eugene Onegin*, trans. Vladimir Nabokov (Princeton: Princeton University Press, 1975), 396.

35. Nabokov, "Abram Gannibal," 437–38.

36. Veresaev, *Pushkin v zhizni*, 1:55–56.

37. J. Thomas Shaw, "Pushkin on His African Heritage: Publications during His Lifetime," in *Pushkin Today*, ed. David Bethea (Bloomington: Indiana University Press, 1993), 122. Shaw's article is reprinted in this volume.

38. As quoted in Pavlova, *Pushkin v portretakh*, 1:10. Pavlova notes the absurdity of this representation of the twenty-three-year-old, already-famous poet as an adolescent with the "exotic appearance of a little Negro" (*s ekzoticheskoi naruzhnost'iu arapchonka*).

39. Examples of this tradition of portraying the child or adolescent Pushkin with strongly "Negroid" features may be seen in such works as Vladimir Favorskii's 1935 woodcut, *Pushkin as a Boy at the Lycée* (figure 52), which Pavlova (93) considers, together with V. A. Serov's *Pushkin in the Park* (1899; figure 53), to be one of the two most "inspired" retrospective portrayals of the poet; V. F. Shtein's sculpture, *Pushkin as a Boy* (1910; figure 54), which appears to be but a three-dimensional realization of the Geitman model; N. P. Ul'ianov's *Pushkin in the Lyceum Gardens* (1935; figure 55); E. F. Belashova's sculpture of *Pushkin as a Boy* (1959; figure 56); A. Z. Itkin's

Pushkin-Lycéeist (1968; figures 57 and 58); A. M. Nenasheva's figurine of *Pushkin-Lycéeist* (1961; figure 59); G. B. Dodonova's *Pushkin-Lycéeist* (1969; figure 60); and the porcelain figure *Pushkin-Lycéeist* (1962) by E. A. Gendel'man (figure 61). Note the remarkable coincidence of physiognomies between this porcelain figure of Pushkin and the porcelain figure of an African adolescent, entitled *Africa* (figure 62), done a year earlier (1961) by a different sculptor at the same factory. One of the exceptions that proves the rule is Mstislav Dobuzhinskii's adolescent Pushkin in his *Pushkin and the Decembrists* (figure 65) in which the younger poet has a button nose and seemingly straight hair.

40. As quoted in Troyat, *Pushkin,* 117. The parenthetical page numbers that follow in text refer to this book.

41. On the other hand, Lotman's handling of the available evidence in this matter appears to be selective and perhaps unobjective. See Catharine Nepomnyashchy's and Ludmilla Trigos's discussion in the introductory essay to this volume.

42. Pavlova notes that Aivazovskii devoted at least ten paintings to the *Pushkin on the Shores* of *the Black Sea* theme over the course of ten years. She observes, however, that Pushkin's figure always occupies an insignificant, static, and inexpressive position in them, especially in comparison with the dynamic, emotionally charged seascapes, and that the painter apparently recognized this failing, which is why he invited Repin to do the Pushkin figure in their 1887 collaboration. In fact, the *Pushkin on the Black Sea Coast* that Aivazovskii did in 1868 (figures 63 and 64) pictures a sweet-faced, mildly smiling Pushkin, perched rather primly before the raging sea, looking entirely out of place. His face features large round eyes, a largish but not appreciably flattened or thick nose, and a very ordinary mouth. The masses of hair encircling his face lend him a sort of monkeyish mien, but one could never call him "Negroid" in appearance. In fact, Repin's generically Byronic Pushkin in the collaboration with Aivazovskii displays considerably more "African" attributes.

43. See, for example, D. N. Kardovskii's picture *Pushkin amidst the Decembrists in Kamenka* (1934) in E. Iu. Gal'perina, *A. S. Pushkin v izobrazitel'nom iskusstve* (Moscow: Izogiz, 1961; figure 28), where a nearly identically declaiming Pushkin loses even more resemblance to an African. Dobuzhinskii (figure 65) once again provides the iconoclastic exception, depicting a shy, shocked Pushkin among the Decembrists, seemingly staggered at his comrades' revolutionary words or intentions.

44. An earlier version of the work (*Pushkin and His Wife before the Mirror at a Court Ball,* 1927) underscores the thematic tenor, with a frankly shrewish Goncharova and the weary sneer of a much uglier poet (*La Galérie Tretiakov, Moscou* [Leningrad: Editions d'art Aurora], figure 229).

45. Gal'perina, *Pushkin v izobrazitel'nom,* n.p.

Making a True Image

46. Balog and Mukhina, *Pushkin i ego vremia*, n.p.

47. Pavlova (1:62–63), however, makes a strong case for this painting having been made after the poet's death, perhaps in 1839–40.

48. Pavlova (1:23) describes Vivien as "a modest French artist . . . about whom almost nothing is known."

49. Legend has it that Pushkin mounted copies of this portrait himself and gave them to friends (Balog and Mukhina, *Pushkin i ego vremia*, n.p). There is a similar portrait, a miniature (figure 66), possibly also attributable to Vivien, which features similar characteristics, but offers a less determinedly "Negroid" reading of the poet's features.

50. Debreczeny, "*Zhitie Aleksandra Boldinskogo*," 53. Such sentimental, quasi-religious apotheoses of great Russian writers seem to have been a common phenomenon of that time. The narrator of Leonid Dobychin's comic novel *The Town of N*, for example, describes a postcard which appears soon after the death of Tolstoy: "Tolstoy comes flying to heaven and Christ embraces and kisses him" (*The Town of N*, trans. Richard C. Borden with Natalia Belova [Evanston, Ill.: Northwestern University Press, 1998], 95).

51. Pavlova, *Pushkin v portretakh*, 1:7.

52. Ibid., 1:7–8.

53. Ibid., 1:31.

54. Pavlova (1:61) observes that until the 1880s, nine of every ten representations of Pushkin reproduced the Kiprenskii/Utkin model, and only one the Tropinin, such that Kiprenskii became the sacred, canonical image for the generation of Russians which had known the poet and remembered his living image. A third, rather idiosyncratic tradition may also be discerned. In this iconographic line it is Linev's late portrait, and perhaps the death masks as well, which serve as the model Pushkin. The popularity of this model in the post-Stalin years may indicate a deliberate iconoclasm by Soviet artists, a desire to wrestle the poet's image from the stale, heroic clichés of the Russian nationalist and Stalinist Soviet traditions. Or perhaps it could reveal a desire to invest more heavily than has been traditional in the notion of Pushkin as martyr, and could support Debreczeny's thesis about the canonization of Pushkin as national poet by underscoring his humility and self-sacrifice. See note 5.

55. Kiprenskii's portrait of Pushkin was done in June and July of 1827. Pushkin acquired it following Del'vig's death in 1831.

56. One example of the first category is figure 67, which, typically for Kiprenskii knockoffs for the 1899 jubilee, offers a sort of insipidly pretty, fairy-tale prince Pushkin, not a "Negroid beast," as an illustration for a children's book. Likewise, compare Somov's highly stylized, "Negroid" Pushkin (figure 15) with the centennial medal, produced the same year (1899) by M. A. Skudnov (figure 68), in which no one without prior knowledge could identify any

of the poet's features as "Negroid." In the second category one could cite P. P. Trubetskoi's bust (1899; figure 69), which is mightily heroicized, with a muscular steely forehead, a handsomely bumped nose, a large, sculpted mouth, but nothing recalling "African" traits.

57. Pavlova, *Pushkin v portretakh*, 1:35.

58. Ibid. One Mukhanova wrote that it was "unusually like," Bulgarin said that it was the "living Pushkin," and Lazhechnikov described it as "irreproachably like."

59. Pavlova, *Pushkin v portretakh*, 1:37. Pavlova also reports (1:41) that I. A. Goncharov, the writer, having seen Pushkin at a lecture in 1832, observed that the poet most resembled the Utkin lithograph, just as the poet's close friend, Pushchin, wrote that when he made his famous visit to the exile in Mikhailovskoe, he was struck by how much Pushkin then resembled the Utkin engraving (69).

60. Western representations of Pushkin are, on the whole, worse than their Russian counterparts, but then most Western book illustrators are surely less (if at all) motivated by any one version of the Pushkin myth. See, for example, the very different, but equally appalling Pushkins by Paul Davis on the paperback cover of Walter Arndt's *Pushkin Threefold* (New York: Dutton, 1972) and by Isadore Seltzer on the paperback cover of D. S. Mirsky's *Pushkin* (New York: Dutton, 1963), the latter being unrecognizable as Pushkin, but certainly possessing no "Negroid" traits.

61. The particular illustrations cited here may be found in Iakov Smolenskii, *V soiuze zvukov, chuvstv i dum* (Moscow: Sovetskaia Rossiia, 1976), 3, 9, 37, 40, 52, 128. Compare figures 70 and 71 for a similar discrepancy in Pushkin iconography by Kuz'min.

62. It is dangerous to generalize too much in terms of the sociological, political, or historical biases at play in determining the trends in Pushkin iconography, for the exceptions to all hypothetical rules are legion. Thus, in contrast to the "heroic" Pushkin that flourished in the hearts (or nerves) of artists during the 1937 centennial—at the height of Stalinism—there are also from the same period contemplative, even melancholy Pushkins, Pushkins with distinctly simian features, distinctly Negroid Pushkins, old and weary Pushkins, which seem to have been modeled on Linev's portrait or the death masks, glum and ugly Pushkins, and idealized and distinctly Caucasoid Pushkins.

Pavlova in *Pushkin v portretakh* does not completely resist the temptation to generalize. She describes Pushkin's Soviet incarnation as a "second birth" (1:87) and talks of the paths of the "revolutionary transfiguration" of Pushkin iconography (1:89), one example being V. N. Masiutin's 1918 *Pushkin* (figure 72), a heroicized Soviet man of the future, with a cherubic if pursed mouth, an almost straight nose, and a long, narrow face with a large strong jaw. Another example, however, is Iu. L. Obolenskaia's 1925 *Pushkin* (figure 73),

Making a True Image

in which the poet retains his "Negroid" nose and full lips but also acquires a heroic jaw, a powerful brow, long, streaming hair, and a steely gaze: he resembles a cross between a Byron caricature and a Soviet propaganda poster. In fact, one somewhat surprising feature in early Soviet representations of Pushkin (if one allows some generalization) is an affinity for highlighting the poet's "African" traits. In what, for example, Pavlova calls a "classic of Soviet decorative Pushkiniana"—P. Ia. Pavlinov's *Pushkin* of 1924 (figure 74)—we find a highly "Africanized" poet, with a dark complexion, full lips, fleshy mouth, kinky hair, and a broad and flattened nose with flared nostrils. It is, in fact, perhaps the most "Negroid" of all adult portrayals of Pushkin that I have located (it also features what looks like a nimbus about the poet's head). Several of the earliest Soviet Pushkins invest quite heavily in the "African" iconography, even as they create an idealized figure—a warrior-hero, implicitly Bolshevik, gazing determinedly into a Radiant Future he will help build. See, for example, Pavlova's figures 174, 176–77, and 178. Of figures 176–77, V. N. Domogatskii's sculpture portrait of 1925, Pavlova observes that the artist has followed the Tropinin model, "somewhat exaggerating the 'African traits'" (1:91; she also calls this one of the best and most profound of Pushkin sculptures). It might be hypothesized that this trend in the first Soviet decade—which was largely displaced by a tendency to efface the "Negroid" aspect of the Pushkin-Bolshevik hero's face in the Stalin years—is a function of the romanticization of the poet-hero into an elemental force, like the Revolution itself: a vital, animal, passionate being. It also might reflect some of the romantic internationalization of the revolutionary ideology of these early Soviet years, when people of all nations and bloods were seen to be on the verge of wresting power from their class enemies—and the Russians were glad to lend their national poet to other nations as a model of inspiration.

63. An exception is a sketch of 1823, in which Pushkin caricatures himself as an old man.

64. Tsiavlovskaia, *Risunki Pushkina*, 341: "Suffering from his outward appearance, Pushkin talked about it—in verse and in prose, drew himself, leaving his self-portraits to friends. Might there not be a certain challenge, a bravado in all this?" (my translation).

65. Pavlova, writing in 1983 (1:116), describes "today's" generation of artists "more than ever endowing their model [Pushkin] with feelings characteristic of their own time, with their own individual, even national traits." If this is true, and it does appear to be so, Tertz's notion of Pushkin as a "blur with sidewhiskers" is more true than ever. Pushkin has become a sort of national tabula rasa upon which any group (or individual) may inscribe its own values and aspirations.

Catherine O'Neil

Pushkin and *Othello*

DESPITE THE NUMEROUS STUDIES on the influence of Shakespeare on Pushkin's work, the subject of the significance of *Othello* to the Russian poet has not been treated separately.[1] Yet Pushkin's response to this particular play deserves special attention because of the pointed nature of his interest in and interpretation of Shakespeare's tragedy. For example, the features Pushkin singles out as central to Othello's character are his skin color and, rather unusually, his age, which Pushkin posits as quite advanced (he refers to Othello as an "old Negro," *staryi negr* [*PSS* 11:164]). Equally striking are his comments on Desdemona, whose "capricious" and "willful" passion Pushkin likens to the arbitrary nature of poetic inspiration. When Pushkin's views are compared to those of his contemporaries and predecessors, one major point of departure becomes apparent: Pushkin does not associate the hero of *Othello* with jealousy, nor indeed does Othello's jealousy constitute the play's primary interest for him. Instead, Pushkin was drawn to Shakespeare's hero because of the color of his skin, a feature that allowed the Russian poet to identify with Othello as a man with the same "African blood" that ran through Pushkin's veins from his great-grandfather on his mother's side, Abram Petrovich Gannibal (c. 1698–1781). In fact, Pushkin's earliest references to *Othello* are combined with allusions to his own African ancestry, which indicates his consistent association of Shakespeare's hero with his great-grandfather. As his interest in his family history grew, Shakespeare's play provided a literary model on which he could base his own fictionalized renderings of his African heritage.

In this article I explore the traces of *Othello* in Pushkin's work, following up on suggestive hints in the poet's own works, especially the traces of Shakespeare's play in his writings from 1827 and 1828. Of particular interest are the unfinished historical novel *The Blackamoor of Peter the Great* (*Arap Petra Velikogo*) and the narrative poem *Poltava,* two pieces closely linked by their date of composition (1828), their setting (the era of Peter the Great), and their explicit connection to *Othello*. In order to determine the place of *Othello* in Pushkin's art, I have set myself two basic tasks: an examination of the reception of *Othello* in Russia from 1825 on (that is, the reception and interpretation at that time of the play's main themes: jealousy, race, and misalliance in marriage), and an exploration of the specific way these themes are worked out in Pushkin. *Othello* is a play that was read against a heritage of received ideas about jealousy and blackness. Its treatment of a love relationship between a black man and white woman makes it particularly subject to changing interpretations in different periods. In Pushkin's day Africa was seen as a wild and uncivilized place, and as we shall see, analyses of *Othello* and his passion bear the stamp of these ideas.

In Pushkin's reading, Othello's origins had an additional interest; one of the few black people seen in Russia was his own ancestor, the "tsar's blackamoor" (*tsarskii arap*), Abram Gannibal.[2] To be sure, Russians (including Pushkin) were not immune to stereotypes about Africa and black men as wild, fiery and sensual, threatening, and at the same time fascinating in their sexual prowess. Yet these themes assume a particular form in Pushkin's work; it is clear from his comments on his own appearance that he thought he was unattractive and that he more than partly blames his "Negroid" features—his famous "blackamoor profile" (*arapskii profil'*)—for this.[3] At the same time, he claimed an exotic attractiveness which he also seemed to base on his ancestry, a paradox that is articulated in the 1820 poem "To Yur'ev" ("Yur'evu").[4] In this poem Pushkin implies a correlation between his "ugliness," which he ascribes to his African heritage ("ugly descendant of Negroes"), and his claim to a certain sexual fascination ("faun," "shameless desires"). This coupling of blackness with sexual power of an unnatural (here "involuntary") sort occurs elsewhere in Pushkin's work; for example, the blackamoors and the magician Chernomor in *Ruslan and Ludmila* (1820), or the love affair between a French countess and Ibragim, the hero of *The Blackamoor of Peter the Great*. These examples suggest that Pushkin not only blamed his African heritage for his unprepossessing appearance, but regarded it as well as the source of his virility and passion. These same motifs are expressed and confronted in *Othello*, a play which presents an exalted, heroic black man, in love with and loved by a beautiful white woman, who is nonetheless unable to battle the prejudice that does not acknowledge a black man's right to a white woman's heart. Although it would be absurd to claim that Pushkin's interest in *Othello* was exclusively or even primarily on the level of "identification" with an African literary hero, it is nonetheless clear that as he approached the task of presenting the blackamoor Ibragim in his historical novel *The Blackamoor of Peter the Great* and his other works of the period, he drew on Shakespeare's hero as a literary model.[5]

The period of Pushkin's work in which the influence of Shakespeare's play is most apparent is 1827–28, when he started *The Blackamoor of Peter the Great* and then later turned to *Poltava*. The figure of Ibragim in *The Blackamoor of Peter the Great* bears some resemblance to Othello, as an "exotic" blackamoor of noble background who is making his way in a foreign society. Mazepa in *Poltava* also resembles Othello, as Pushkin points out in his response to the poem's critics, in the "unnatural" love he feels for and arouses in a much younger woman.[6] According to the Russian scholar M. P. Alekseev, during this period Pushkin started reading Shakespeare with renewed interest, and he began reading him seriously in English around 1828, the year of *Poltava*'s composition.[7] It is also worth noting that there were three performances of the standard Russian version of *Othello,* translated by I. A. Veliaminov, in the winter season of 1827–28 in St. Petersburg, and six in Moscow, one of which Pushkin may well have attended.[8]

Perhaps the most important journalistic piece on *Othello* to be published in Russian in 1828 was the "literal" prose translation of act 3, scene 3 of *Othello* in the Moscow literary journal *The Moscow Herald* (*Moskovskii vestnik*), introduced by a lengthy article on *Othello* by S. P. Shevyrev. The episode in question is the pivotal scene in which Iago first plants the seed of jealousy which takes root and grows so quickly in the course of just a few lines. It is a tour de force of insinuation and manipulation on Iago's part, and the choice of this scene for publication reflects the attempt in the Romantic era to reinstate Shakespeare's Iago as a supremely subtle villain in his own right; in eighteenth-century stage adaptations he had been reduced by and large to a stock melodramatic villain, a superficial foil to the hero. Alekseev notes that Pushkin spent a good deal of time with Shevyrev in the autumn of 1826. It is possible therefore that Pushkin was discussing Shakespeare with the leading Russian Romantic Shakespeare critic a year before beginning his work on *The Blackamoor of Peter the Great*.[9]

In order to get a better sense of how *Othello* is reflected in Pushkin's work, it would be useful to examine the play's impact on the Romantic period in general. *Othello* is a provocative play, with its tense sexuality, the introduction of a black hero, and the final death scene, in which Desdemona is smothered in her own bridal sheets. It seems to have been more acceptable to address the question of Othello's blackness more directly in critical and theoretical discussions than it was to portray it on stage, and so the French productions of the period, and hence the Russian ones, tended to lighten the hero's skin.[10] The most popular stage adaptations in France in the late eighteenth century were by Jean-François Ducis, whose versions can only be loosely termed translations, as the example of *Othello* poignantly illustrates. In addition to keeping the entire action of the play in Venice and renaming all the characters but Othello himself, Ducis softened some of the more disturbing aspects of Shakespeare's play to make it more acceptable for the French stage, including the color of the hero's skin. Ducis writes on this theme: "I thought that a yellow, copper-like complexion, which is, in fact, suitable also for an African, would have the advantage of not revolting the public, and especially the female eye."[11] Another extreme alteration to Shakespeare's play was

Ducis's ending. He could not allow Othello to smother Desdemona with her bridal sheets as Shakespeare does, presumably because this was too intimate a slaying for genteel sensibilities, but had him stab her instead. Even this ending proved too much for his spectators, who rose to their feet in horror at the sight, compelling Ducis to rewrite the final act so that Pézare's (that is, Iago's) villainy is discovered in time and the couple lives happily ever after.[12]

Ducis's *Othello* is very important for the Russian stage history of the play, because the first translation of *Othello* into Russian, by I. A. Veliaminov, was based on this version.[13] Like Ducis, Veliaminov did not know English, but he was perspicacious enough to compare Ducis's version with Le Tourneur's more or less conscientious prose translation from 1776, and managed to put some Shakespeare back into the play. First, he gave Iago back some of his centrality to the story (although he retained the name Pezarro, which itself attests to the popularity of Ducis's play). More important, he preserved the final scene in which Othello strangles Desdemona. This version was performed in Russia to thunderous applause throughout the 1820s, mainly thanks to the acclaimed Muscovite actor Pavel Mochalov, who played the title role.[14]

In the context of the eighteenth and early nineteenth centuries, the character of Othello is imbued with qualities of the "noble savage," "son of nature" (*syn prirody*), as he is called in Ducis's and Veliaminov's translations. Sergei Aksakov in his review of a Moscow performance from 1828—a key year in Pushkin's immersion in *Othello*—quotes the following lines from one of Othello's speeches:

> But I, son of the scorching steppe, son of nature, I am beholden for everything to myself alone and not at all to vile deceit, I walk through the world without fear, without any pangs of conscience, in all my strength, in all my freedom.[15]

From this perspective, Desdemona's "aberration" was read as the sensitive response of a sensitive soul. The couple was generally viewed sympathetically as a "beauty and the beast" pair, an aspect of their love that may have particularly appealed to Pushkin.[16]

In scholarly editions and journals, a good deal of Shakespeare criticism at this time focuses on details of Othello's race and possible origin. Although in Elizabethan England the term "Moor" was applied indiscriminately to people of African and Arabian origin,[17] the distinction between Arabian "Moors" and African "Negroes" became a pressing issue in late eighteenth- and early nineteenth-century discussions of the play and the treatment its hero received and deserved. Samuel Taylor Coleridge in his lectures "ridiculed the idea of making Othello a negro, he was a gallant Moor, of royal blood, combining a high sense of Spanish and Italian feeling," and he is very disturbed by Roderigo's reference in the play to Othello as a "thick-lips," since this would make Othello a Negro, not a Moor.[18] He attributes this insult to Roderigo's rivalry with and spite for Othello:

> No doubt Desdemona saw Othello's visage in his [Othello's] mind; yet, as we are constituted, and most surely as an English audience was disposed in the beginning of the seventeenth century, it would be something monstrous to conceive this beautiful Venetian girl falling in love with a veritable negro.[19]

August-Wilhelm Schlegel, like Coleridge, focuses on Othello's African origins in his lectures on Shakespeare, and distinguishes between Negro and Moor:

> What a fortunate mistake that the Moor (under which name in the original novel, a baptized Saracen of the Northern coast of Africa was unquestionably meant), has been made by Shakespeare in every respect a negro! We recognize in Othello the wild nature of that glowing zone which generates the most ravenous beasts of prey and the most deadly poisons, tamed only in appearance by the desire of fame, by foreign laws of honour, and by nobler and milder manners.[20]

As to how this problem was treated in Russia, a revealing illumination can be found in a Russian review of an opera version of *Othello* staged at the German theater in St. Petersburg. The reviewer notes, among his other objections, the following observation about how the singer playing Othello handled Othello's blackness:

> While playing Othello, M. Keler adorned his face entirely with black paint: he was like coal. To this face he added extraordinarily colorful clothing, so that he bore a greater resemblance to a harlequin than to Othello. Until this time all artists have given Othello a face of an olive complexion, and so it should be; a completely black face is both ludicrous and ugly.[21]

The racial aspect of *Othello* has always been central to staging and criticism of the play. Like the character of Shylock in *The Merchant of Venice*, the complexity of Othello's character offers a way of expressing issues of prejudice and race in general. As far as Coleridge, Schlegel, and other Romantic theorists go, it seems that it was essential to them to distinguish between the "noble savages" who dwell between some primordial "golden age" and the Christian "civilized" epoch of modern Europe (that is, "Moors"), and the primitive peoples sold as slaves ("Negroes"). Othello's conflict was seen as one between the elemental passions of his original "natural" state and the controlling force of the enlightened world. "He suffers as a double man," writes Schlegel, "at once in the higher and lower sphere into which his being was divided."[22]

Russian Shakespeare criticism follows German and French criticism quite closely.[23] The distinction between "Moor" and "Negro" had less significance in Russia primarily because Russia was not involved in the African slave trade and so, consequently, Russians had less personal contact with actual blacks.[24] Nor, for that matter, did they need to justify dehumanizing blacks. Nonetheless, to Russians as to western Europeans, Africa—as opposed to Moorish Spain—was considered a land inhabited by passionate and uncivilized peoples. In an 1827 issue of the *Moscow Herald,* Mikhail Pogodin translated into Russian a German ethnographic description of the world, which the author divides into four spheres: Europe, Asia, America, and Africa. He writes of the hot climate in Africa which creates a reign of "fiery sensuality" and causes the human soul to revert to the animal:

> Thus a fiery sensuality, it seems to me, is the reigning queen of Africa. Surrounded by a drowsy nature, all the noble forces of the soul weaken in Africa; Science disappears completely, Art almost completely. Man's spiritual formation reverts again to the animal.[25]

The author then proceeds to describe the dilemma for Africans living in Europe: "And we observe in Europeans with Negroid faces a natural good-nature and openness [*dobrodushie i otkrovennost'*]" at odds with the fury and cruelty aroused by their "tortuous enslavement."[26]

These ideas, informed by those of Herder and Rousseau, clearly resemble Schlegel's statements on *Othello.* Likewise François Guizot, in his preface to his updated translation of *Othello* (the edition Pushkin had in his library), describes the play's hero as a product of the sun-scorched realm where he was born: "the Moor, burned by the sun, [is] hot-blooded, with a lively and brutal imagination, credulous in the violence of his temperament as much as of his person."[27] Shevyrev, himself highly influenced by Schlegel, similarly cites Othello's African origin as determining his character:

> From what stormy elements was this child of the south created! Fiery as his scorching sun; powerful, noble, but also irritable as the African Lion; open as the broad steppe; . . . quick and stormy as the steppe whirlwind; innocent, virginal and coarse [*nevinnii, devstvennyi i grubyi*] as that wild nature which has never been touched by human hand.[28]

Underlying all these passages are the formative myths of the black man as sensual, savage, repellent but fascinating, which have dogged criticism of *Othello* over the years. Although Pushkin's reading of Othello and his blackness contains elements of these myths, the fact that they are equally attached to the poet's view of his own black heritage allows him to associate the best-known Moor in literature with his fictional version of his own ancestor and, by extension, with himself. For, as has been noticed many times before, there is a high degree of identification on Pushkin's part with Gannibal in all his literary evocations of his ancestor: the footnote to chapter 1 of *Eugene Onegin*, the poem "To Yazykov" ("Yazykovu," 1824), *The Blackamoor of Peter the Great*, and "Beginning of an Autobiography" ("Nachalo avtobiografii," 1834). The common elements he feels he shares with his ancestor's life include the problem with royal patronage and life in exile.[29] His accounts of Gannibal's search for a bride likewise resonate with his own fears as he contemplated marriage. His interest in his ancestor's matrimonial plans appears even before this, in 1824, when he wrote the verse fragment "When the Tsar's Moor Thought of Getting Married" ("Kak zhenit'sia zadumal tsarskii arap").[30] Just as the personal (psychological) model for Gannibal is provided by the poet himself, so the literary model is provided by Shakespeare's Othello.

Pushkin's earliest references to *Othello* coincide with his increasing interest in Gannibal. For example, the reference to Morali in *Eugene Onegin* ("*Korsar v otstavke Morali*"; *PSS* 6:201]) has as a variant "Othello-Morali" (*PSS* 6:465). The manuscript of "Onegin's Journey" was written in 1829, but the events described in it date from 1823–24, when Pushkin livened his days in Odessa in the company of this flamboyant character. In his memoirs I. P. Liprandi recalls Pushkin saying of Morali: "My soul is drawn to him; who knows, perhaps my grandfather was a close relation of his ancestor."[31] Liprandi's memoirs were published in the almanac *Russian Archive* (*Russkii arkhiv*) in 1866, long after Pushkin's death, yet if the sense of Pushkin's words is accurately conveyed, then Pushkin early on associates a black man with his own maternal grandfather on the one hand ("who knows, perhaps my grandfather . . .") and also links him with Othello on the other ("Othello-Morali"). Subsequent references occur during Pushkin's stay at Mikhailovskoe (1824–26), where he visited his maternal great-uncle, the last surviving Gannibal to have known Abram Petrovich. He refers to him in French as "my great-uncle the old Negro" (*mon vieux nègre de Grand Oncle*, letter to P. A. Osipova, August 11, 1825 [*PSS* 13:205]), a phrase which he later uses in Russian when speaking of Othello (*staryi negr*), significantly the only time he refers to Shakespeare's hero as *negr* instead of *arap*.[32] Thus it is possible that in applying the Russian phrase *staryi negr* to Othello, Pushkin has at least one Gannibal (*mon vieux nègre de Grand Oncle*) in the back of his mind.

A third connection between Othello and Gannibal can be found in *Poltava*. Pushkin connects *Poltava* with *Othello* directly in "Objections to the Critics of *Poltava*," and although there are neither Moors nor Negroes in this particular poem, it too does not lack associations for him with his African ancestry. For example, K. F. Ryleev's poem on the same historical theme, *Voinarovsky* (1825), was one of the inspirations for Pushkin's poem, and

Pushkin and *Othello*

Pushkin writes to his brother in 1825 (again, from Mikhailovskoe) the following message to Ryleev regarding his poem: "Tell Ryleev that he should include our granddad in Peter I's suite in [*Voinarovsky*]. His Blackamoor mug [*arapskaia rozha*] will produce a strange effect on the entire canvas of the battle of Poltava" (January or February 1825 [*PSS* 13:143]).[33] Thus in one of the earliest records of Pushkin's imagining of the Battle of Poltava he associates that historical era with his own black ancestor, just as in one of his later references to it ("Objections to the Critics") he associates these events with *Othello*.

In order to explore the thematic dynamic between *The Blackamoor of Peter the Great, Poltava,* and *Othello* it is worth juxtaposing Pushkin's description of Othello in "Objections to the Critics" with Othello's own words in Shakespeare's play. In "Objections to the Critics" the poet speaks of Desdemona's love for the "old Negro" (*staryi negr*) Othello as an analogy for his story of a young girl's love for a much older man in the narrative poem *Poltava*:

> [Our critics] . . . have announced to me that no one has ever seen a woman fall in love with an old man, and that therefore Maria's love for the old Hetman (NB: historically proven) could not exist . . . I cannot agree with this explanation: love is the most capricious of passions. I don't even mention the ugliness and stupidity preferred on a daily basis to youth, intelligence and beauty. Recall the legends from Ovid's Metamorphoses—Leda, Philyra, Pasiphae, Pygmalion—and admit that all these fictions are not foreign to poetry. And what about Othello, the old Negro who captivated Desdemona with his tales of his travels and battles? Or Mirra, who inspired the Italian poet [Alfieri] with one of his best tragedies? (*PSS* 11:164)

These lines resonate well with a central passage from *Othello*. Left alone soon after Iago has roused an initial suspicion in him of Desdemona's infidelity, Othello, in despair, tries to understand why, as he thinks, her feelings for him should have changed so quickly:

> Haply, for I am black,
> And have not those soft parts of conversation
> That Chamberers have, or for I am declin'd
> Into the vale of years (yet that's not much),
> She's gone. (*Othello* 3.3.263–67)

The points Othello enumerates in this muted outburst of distress are what Pushkin captures in his understanding of the play: Othello is black ("Haply for I am black"), Othello is old ("I am declin'd / Into the vale of years"), women's hearts are incomprehensible ("(yet that's not much), / She's gone"). Compare this to Pushkin's "Objections": Desdemona loved Othello who was black and

203

old ("the old Negro"), but, still, this love is incomprehensible ("love is the most capricious of passions," "I don't even mention the ugliness and stupidity preferred on a daily basis to youth, intelligence and beauty"). The most striking thing about Pushkin's reading of Othello is that he does not merely perceive Shakespeare's hero through the eyes of Venetian society or Iago or Desdemona, as do most Romantic-era readers of the play, but he uses Othello's own self-characterization and applies it to his own hero, Ibragim, in *The Blackamoor of Peter the Great*. We see this particularly in the Paris episode (chapter 1) of the unfinished novel, the completely fictional account of Ibragim's romance with a French countess. When Pushkin turns to *Poltava* in 1828 he also uses *Othello* as a model for his unequal love relationship, this time a misalliance of age, but he puts much less of Othello into the characterization of Mazepa. Instead, as I will argue below, he draws on Desdemona in his characterization of Maria and his explanation of her love for the much older Hetman.

In *The Blackamoor of Peter the Great* Pushkin makes the sexual issues in *Othello* explicit, particularly when contrasting Ibragim's amorous conquest in Paris with his suitability for marriage in Russia. On the one hand, Ibragim's Parisian mistress's choice is seen as quite "natural" by part of society (*PSS* 8:6)—that is, it is natural she should pick an exotic lover—yet his very blackness is given as a reason not to marry by his friend Korsakov once they are in Russia (*PSS* 8:30). In France, women are expected to have lovers, that is, to pursue and explore their desires, even aberrant ones, with the understanding that the bond is not lasting. In Russia, such mores are not accepted in the period of the novel's setting, and the supposedly permanent (dynastic) bond of marriage is thus precluded for a black man who by definition can only arouse unnatural and impermanent desire in a woman, if that. Korsakov assures Ibragim that his "ugliness" will ensure his wife's infidelity. Peter, on the other hand, wants Ibragim to marry to protect him in the future—through alliance to the Russian nobility and, presumably, the production of Russian children.

The characters surrounding Ibragim in both Paris and Russia react to his skin color in much the same way as do the minor characters in Shakespeare's play to Othello. For example, the aunt of the young heroine Natasha responds to the shock of finding out about the proposed marriage between Natasha and Ibragim with demonizing rhetoric similar to that of Iago in *Othello*. She implores Natasha's father: "My brother . . . don't destroy your own dear child, don't surrender Natashenka to the talons of a black devil [*v kogti chernomu diavolu*]" (*PSS* 8:25). This phrase is very close to Iago's line addressed to Brabantio, Desdemona's father, in which he reports that Desdemona has been "transported . . . to the gross clasps of a lascivious Moor" (1.1.125ff).[34] Although Iago's words are understood by the audience to be manipulative and unjust, there is an extent to which, as has been observed more than once, the audience is implicated in and responsive to his language as much as is Brabantio.[35]

The demonizing rhetoric does not end here, however. Ibragim's friend Korsakov tries to dissuade Ibragim from marrying, arguing that even were he handsome, women are never faithful anyway. Korsakov is a basically comic character, but his language at this point resembles that of Iago in *Othello*: given Ibragim's added disadvantage of his "monstrous" appearance, Korsakov argues, he cannot even hope for a successful marriage:

> You can't rely on a woman's faithfulness. Happy is he who looks upon this indifferently! But you! With your fiery, brooding, and suspicious character, with your flat nose, thick [blown-out] lips, with that rough woolly hair, to throw yourself into all the dangers of marriage? (*PSS* 8:30)

Korsakov uses the same racially charged language as does Iago, and claims superior knowledge of the ways of European women because Russia is his native land. This recalls Iago's statement to Othello that Desdemona will inevitably deceive him, since that is the way all Venetian women are:

> I know our country disposition well;
> In Venice they do let God see the pranks
> They dare not show their husbands; their best conscience
> Is not to leav't undone, but to keep't unknown. (3.3.205–8)

Directly following this generalization about women, Iago proceeds to point out that it is doubly deceitful for Desdemona to choose Othello against the claims of "nature," or race:

> Ay, there's the point: As—to be bold with you—
> Not to affect many proposed matches
> Of her own clime, complexion, and degree,
> Whereto we see in all things nature tends—
> Foh! One may smell in this a will most rank,
> Foul disproportion, thoughts unnatural. (3.3.235–40)

Korsakov's "privileged" understanding of European mores is meant to be judged skeptically, of course, for the conflicting worlds in Pushkin's novel are not Africa and Russia, but rather France and Russia. For that matter, the slurs of Iago and Roderigo against Othello are obviously not to be taken as the correct assessments of Shakespeare's hero. Nonetheless, there is an extent to which the audience and reader are ensnared by Iago's language, listening in fascination to his spiteful monologues, and this is why so many of the critics in Pushkin's day (notably Coleridge, but also Schlegel) draw on Iago's own language when they explain what is "wrong" with Othello (how black is he, exactly, ethnically, how Desdemona could love him, and so on). It is more difficult to dismiss the attitude of Desdemona's father Brabantio, who at first admires Othello but later turns against him. Indeed, even the Venetian duke, who likes and needs Othello and wishes to placate the offended father, uses language that does little to undermine the prejudice at the heart of objections to Othello's suitability as a match for Desdemona: "If virtue no delighted beauty lack / Your son-in-law is far more fair than black" (1.2.100).

Pushkin was sensitive to the way even sympathetic characters in *Othello* react to the hero's blackness. This sensitivity is suggested by Ibragim's awareness of the interest he arouses in Parisian society because of his appearance:

> He sensed that for them he was a kind of wild beast, a particular, foreign creature that was brought to the world by accident, having nothing in common with them. He even envied people who remained unnoticed by anyone and considered their insignificance the greatest blessing. (*PSS* 8:5)

Although Ibragim overestimates his ugliness, as he later finds out, there is a degree to which other characters and the author himself share this assessment. Korsakov's views may not be shared by creator or reader, but he is not an altogether negative character and he is expressing what everyone else in the novel is feeling. Although Peter and the boyars agree in ridiculing Korsakov and admiring Ibragim, the compliment the boyar Lykov pays the young man is revealing: "Of all our young men raised in foreign countries (God forgive me) the tsar's blackamoor most resembles a human being" (*PSS* 8:22). And we may well ask what our poet thought of Natalia Gavrilovna's aversion to Ibragim; he explains it as her love for someone else, yet there is every indication that he (as well as his readers) considered it perfectly natural just on its own. Her terror, after all, is expressed before the reader finds out about her love for the young tutor Valerian, and there is no reason to suppose it stems from anything but revulsion for Ibragim himself. Lastochka confirms this reading when she tells Natasha: "That's just it, my lady, if you had thought less about the Strel'tsev's orphan [Valerian] you wouldn't have spoken about him in your fever . . . Now, if you ask [your father] not to marry you to the blackamoor he will think Valerian is the reason" (*PSS* 8:32). The understanding is that, were it not for Valerian, she would have every "natural" reason to object to the match.

Yet the account of Ibragim's affair with the Countess D. in Paris is the episode in *The Blackamoor of Peter the Great* that most resembles Shakespeare's depiction of Othello and Desdemona. Pushkin takes pains in the first chapter of his unfinished novel to evoke sympathy for Ibragim and to establish his attractiveness, despite the fact that Ibragim considers himself ugly. The complete ahistoricity of this episode strengthens the argument that Pushkin was drawing on *Othello* as he imagined a love relation between a black man and a white woman, for the very changes Pushkin makes in his ancestor's biography render him more like Shakespeare's hero. For example, Pushkin makes much of a wound Gannibal historically received after the events described—in the War of the Spanish Succession—after which he appears in Paris society with a bandage on his head instead of a wig, "his curly black head standing out among the powdered wigs of the Countess's salon" (*PSS* 8:5). This wound serves to emphasize Ibragim's blackness (because of it his black head stands out among white wigs) and his prowess as a soldier; Pushkin writes that he "distinguished himself" in battle and was "seriously wounded" (*PSS* 8:3). Othello is likewise a distinguished warrior and the greatest general in Venice, and although Pushkin never makes quite such extravagant claims for Ibragim, the apparent exaggeration of Ibragim's wounds and of his patronage by the highest members of Paris society render his ancestor a noble and well-protected blackamoor indeed.[36] Furthermore, Pushkin emphasizes Ibragim's physical attractiveness, a service none of his contemporaries could render Othello, whose worthiness they saw in his "greatness of heart" and "simplicity of manner," rather than in any possible appeal in his appearance. Pushkin imagines a handsome black man in Ibragim: "He was twenty-seven years old; he was tall and slim and more than one beauty glanced at him in a more flattering way than mere curiosity" (*PSS* 8:5). This both legitimizes the Countess's love for him and fulfills the novelistic need for a handsome hero.

Yet Ibragim's blackness renders him uncommonly modest in Parisian society, and in this as well he resembles Othello. Neither Ibragim nor Othello imagines that a white woman could love him, and so in both cases the woman's love must be pointed out by someone else. In *The Blackamoor of Peter the Great* we are told "the Countess guessed at his feelings before he did," and that "Merville was the first to notice their mutual attraction and congratulated Ibragim" (*PSS* 8:5). Othello as well would never have suspected Desdemona's love had she not hinted it to him herself:

> She thank'd me,
> And bade me, if I had a friend that lov'd her,
> I should but teach him how to tell my story,
> And that would woo her. Upon this hint I spake. (1.3.159–60)

The very simplicity of Othello's speech which wins him Desdemona's heart is borrowed by Pushkin when he creates his sympathetic Ibragim: "The thought that nature had not created him for mutual passion freed him of ambition and the dangers of self-love, and this lent a rare charm to his conversation with women. His speech was simple and serious; he attracted the Countess D., who had become thoroughly sick of the endless jokes and subtle allusions of French wit" (*PSS* 8:5). We know this aspect of Othello and Desdemona's courtship appealed to Pushkin because he recalls Othello's "wooing" in his "Objections to the Critics of *Poltava*": "And what of Othello, the old Negro who captivated Desdemona with the tales of his travels and battles?"

Ibragim's character to a certain degree represents for Pushkin a personal fantasy—that is, of how he thinks it would feel to be a black man in the court of Peter the Great—for which he draws on Othello's character rather than that of his great-grandfather. That Pushkin's strategy was effective can be seen from the Russian critic L. I. Vol'pert's account of Gannibal: "It is as though Shakespeare, in creating the character of Othello, guessed at the historical double in far-off Russia . . . Othello, like Gannibal, is black, a Blackamoor; he, just like the other, is of royal descent, a field marshal in the service of a foreign and distant country, he has experienced ferocious attacks of jealousy."[37] Although it is true that the reason for the impenetrability of Ibragim's character may be accounted for by his status as a historical "emblem" of Peter the Great's Russia, the personal empathy felt for him by his creator cannot be discounted completely.[38] Vol'pert correctly points out that it is the feeling of love between Othello and Desdemona—and the fragility of this bond—that Pushkin sifted from Shakespeare's play in turning to his own work.[39]

In addition to drawing on Othello in his description of a black man in a white society, Pushkin evidently used details from his own experience in his fictional portrait of his ancestor, and it is possible that this is what led him to abandon the project. The fact that Ibragim's projected marriage is to a young Russian girl from an ancient boyar family and not, as Gannibal's biography has it, to the daughter of a Greek sea captain, makes the story more closely resemble Pushkin's own search for a bride in this period. Indeed, Ibragim's curt reply to Korsakov in a manuscript variant of the novel—"I am marrying of course not for passion, but in consideration, and then only if she does not feel complete revulsion" (*PSS* 8:518)—anticipates Pushkin's own disclaimers to his friends when he was preparing to marry Natalia Nikolaevna Goncharova in 1831: "I am marrying without hope, without childish enchantment. The future appears to me not in roses but in all its nakedness" (letter to Krivtsov, February 10, 1831 [*PSS* 14:151]). Ibragim's return to Russia and the patronage of Peter that wins him access into the best houses of Russian society also recall Pushkin's return from exile to Moscow in 1826 and his unexpected promotion to favorite of the new tsar, Nicholas I.[40]

For whatever reason, as Pushkin abandons *The Blackamoor of Peter the Great* and turns to *Poltava* he detaches himself personally from his new hero (or antihero) Mazepa but preserves his Shakespearean inspiration, Othello. For Mazepa can be equated with the other feature of the *staryi negr* Othello that Pushkin singles out in his "Objections to the Critics": his age. Othello, like

Mazepa, is considerably older than Desdemona, although his age is not emphasized in the play as much as is his blackness.[41] However, at the beginning of the play it is conveyed in Iago's spiteful lines aimed at provoking Brabantio, Desdemona's father: "Even now, now, very now, an old black ram is tupping your white ewe" (1.1.89–90). Othello himself admits the "young affects in him defunct" when he asks the Duke to allow Desdemona to accompany him on the campaign to Cyprus:

> I therefore beg it not
> To please the palate of my appetite,
> Nor to comply with heat—the young affects
> In me defunct—and proper satisfaction,
> But to be free and bounteous to her mind. (1.1.264–68)

But even though the theme of age in *Othello* is not as pronounced as it is in *Poltava*, the fact that Pushkin characterizes Othello as a *staryi negr* when comparing him to Mazepa shows that for him Othello's age is part of the drama of the play and an explanation of its hero's psychological makeup.

Yet it is Maria, the heroine of *Poltava*, who provides the strongest link with *Othello*, both because her elopement with Mazepa recalls that of Othello and Desdemona and because her "rebellious" will resembles Desdemona's. The courtship of Mazepa and Maria recalls Shakespeare's *Othello* in several ways. After Maria "elopes" with Mazepa, her astonished parents recall her behavior in his presence:

> Only then did it become clear . . . Why so quietly at table she listened to the hetman alone when the talk got lively and the cup overflowed with wine; Why she would always sing those songs that he composed when he was young and poor, when public opinion did not yet know him; (*PSS* 5:22)

> Тогда лишь только стало явно . . .
> Зачем так тихо за столом
> Она лишь гетману внимала,
> Когда беседа ликовала
> И чаша пенилась вином;
> Зачем она всегда певала
> Те песни, кои он слагал,
> Когда он беден был и мал,
> Когда молва его не знала;

Compare this to Othello's account of his courtship of Desdemona before the Venetian Senate:

> Her father lov'd me, oft invited me;
> Still question'd me the story of my life,
> From year to year—the battles, sieges, fortunes,
> That I have pass'd.
> I ran it through, even from my boyish days
> To th' very moment that he bade me tell it . . .
>   This to hear
> Would Desdemona seriously incline; . . .
>   and with a greedy ear
> Devour up my discourse. (1.3.130ff)

Not only do the two heroines share the experience of falling in love through hearing tales, but their recalled demeanors appear similar in their combination of passivity and aggression. Maria passively hears Mazepa's tales (*vnimala*), and actively sings the songs he wrote (*pevala*), just as Desdemona's passive act of hearing is extremely aggressive ("seriously incline," "with a greedy ear / Devour up my discourse"). There is a play on military imagery in accounts of Desdemona's character: Othello calls her "my fair warrior" (2.11.180), and Cassio refers to her as "our great captain's captain" (2.1.75). Desdemona herself confesses a violence of passion for Othello: "That I did love the Moor to live with him, / My downright violence and storm of fortunes / May trumpet to the world" (1.3.250–52). Similarly, Maria's parents mark an "unwomanly" (*nezhenskaia*) spirit in their daughter's love of martial displays:

> Only then did it become clear . . . Why with unwomanly soul she loved the horse formations, and the brave ring of the kettledrums and the cries before the staff and mace of the Little Russian ruler. (*PSS* 5:22)

> Тогда лишь только стало явно . . .
> Зачем с неженскою душой
> Она любила конный строй,
> И бранный звон литавр и клики
> Пред бунчиком и булавой
> Малороссийского владыки . . .

The military imagery signals the rebellious streak in both women, and it is to this that their parents are reacting: they feel their daughters have deceived them by disguising their aggressive and disobedient natures under a mask of modesty and timidity. Both Desdemona and Maria choose these "unnatural" suitors in preference to the more respectable matches they were expected to make. In *Othello* Brabantio describes his daughter as he understood her: "a maid so tender, fair and happy, / So opposite to marriage that she shunn'd / The wealthy curled darlings of our nation" (1.2.67–69). He attributes this lack of interest in marriage on Desdemona's part to her self-containment, not to any potential aberration in her taste, as his next lines attest:

> A maiden never bold;
> Of spirit so still and quiet that her motion
> Blush'd at herself; and she, in spite of nature,
> Of years, of country, credit, everything,
> To fall in love with what she fear'd to look on! (1.3.96–100)

He is shattered by the incongruity between his idea of her and her behavior.

Pushkin's characterization of Maria is similar to this account of Desdemona by her father:

> But not for beauty alone (momentary bloom!) did noisy opinion revere young Maria; she was renowned everywhere as a modest and intelligent maid. For this reason enviable suitors are sent to her from Ukraine and Russia; but from the bridal wreath, as from chains, timid Maria runs away. (*PSS* 5:20)

> Но не единная краса
> (мгновенный цвет!) молвою шумной
> В младой Марии почтена:
> Везде прославилась она
> Девицей скромной и разумной.
> Зато завидных женихов
> Ей шлет Украйна и Россия;
> Но от венца, как от оков,
> Бежит пугливая Мария.

Both women are described in terms of timidity and modesty that are completely at odds with the "unwomanly" assertiveness which manifests itself later, even though arguably both sets of parents should have been prepared by the decidedly aggressive avoidance of marriage "bonds" their daughters have always exhibited. In *Othello* this assertiveness gives Iago ammunition for awaking jealousy in Othello, for he is able to characterize Desdemona's love in terms of willfulness and deceit:

> She did deceive her father marrying you;
> And when she seem'd to shake and fear your looks,
> She lov'd them most. (3.3.212–14)

Compare this account of a seemingly fearful Desdemona with Maria's behavior when Mazepa is suing for her hand. She is described as a timid mountain goat fleeing the eagle's approach:

> That is not a chamois running under the cliff at the sound of the eagle's heavy flight; the young girl wanders alone in the garden, she trembles and waits for a decision. (PSS 5:20)

> Не серна под утес уходит,
> Орла послыша тяжкий лет;
> Одна в сенях невеста бродит,
> Трепещет и решенья ждет.

When her indignant mother informs her of the "impertinent" request of the "shameless old man" Mazepa, Maria faints and falls ill for several days, to all appearances as horrified as her parents:

> Maria started. A grave-like pallor covered her face and, having gone all cold, like a dead woman, the young maid fell upon the steps. (PSS 5:21)

> Мария вздрогнула. Лицо
> Покрыла бледность гробовая,
> И, охладев, как неживая,
> Упала дева на крыльцо.

Because of Maria's behavior, typical of a modest virgin, her parents are completely unprepared for her elopement with Mazepa.[42]

Both Maria and Desdemona are aware of what they lose by the choice they make in love. In one of the few moments in which she is given direct speech, Maria tells Mazepa:

> Listen, hetman. For your sake have I forgot everything in the world. Once in love in love forever, I have always held one thing in my heart: your love. For that have I destroyed my own happiness. But I have no regrets . . . (PSS 5:34)

> Послушай, гетман, для тебя
> Я позабыла все на свете.
> Навек однажды полюбя,
> Одно имела я в предмете:
> Твою любовь. Я для нее
> Сгубила счастие мое,
> Но ни о чем я не жалею . . .

Pushkin and *Othello*

That Maria's assessment of her situation is correct can be seen from the narrator's comment: "And merciless opinion struck her down with its mockery" (*I besposhchadnaia molva / Ee so smekhom porazila; PSS* 5:28). She shows the same defiance of social opinion that Desdemona exhibits in the "trumpet to the world" passage cited above. Her defiance here suggests she shares her father's conviction that her marriage to Othello will "incur a general mock" (1.2.70), and that her love must be "in spite of country, credit, everything." In act 4 Emilia's admonition to Iago also reveals how much Desdemona has given up for Othello's sake: "Hath she forsook so many noble matches, / Her father and her country and her friends, / To be call'd whore?" (4.2.127–29). Despite Desdemona's seeming passivity and resigned submission to Othello's murderous delusions, she is also a brave and reckless woman, especially in the first two acts of the play, and it is to this part of her that Pushkin clearly responds.[43]

The rebellious and brave aspect of Desdemona's character, so effectively captured by Pushkin in his creation of Maria, is one that is rarely addressed in the criticism of *Othello* of his day, other than that in his own remarks in *Ezersky* and *Egyptian Nights*. We see in these poems that Desdemona is a model of freedom of spirit for Pushkin. Her love for Othello is an expression of caprice and rebellion, as is at times the poet's choice of subject. In these passages he repeats the same lines comparing the poet's choice of his subject to the "lawless" and natural flight of an eagle and the love of a young girl. In answer to the anticipated question from his readers and the "mob" respectively (the passage is ironic in *Ezersky*, yet completely serious in *Egyptian Nights*), the poet responds that you may as well ask what causes the wind to blow, or the eagle to fly:

> Why does the wind twist in the ravine, lift the leaves and raise the dust, while a ship greedily awaits its breath in still water? Why does the eagle fly, heavy and dreadful, from the mountain and past the tower into the black sea-foam? Ask him. Why does young Desdemona love her Moor, as the moon loves the night's gloom? Because wind and eagle and young girl's heart know no law. (*Ezersky*, 1830; *PSS* 5:102])

Зачем крутится ветр в овраге,
Подъемлет лист и пыль несет,
Когда корабль в недвижной влаге
Его дыханья жадно ждет?
Зачем от гор и мимо башен
Летит орел, тяжел и страшен,
На черный пень? Спроси его.
Зачем арапа своего
Младая любит Дездемона,

> Как месяц любит ночи мглу?
> Затем, что ветру и орлу
> И сердцу девы нет закона.

These lines are repeated in *Egyptian Nights* (c. 1835)—with the alteration of "sickly [*chakhlyi*] foam" for "black foam"—and then followed by another reference to Desdemona:

> Such is the poet: like Aquilo, he carries off what he wants—like an eagle he flies, and, not asking permission of anyone, like Desdemona, he chooses the idol of his heart.[44] (*PSS* 8:229)

> Таков поэт: как Аквилон,
> Что хочет, то и носит он —
> Орлу подобно он летает,
> И, не спрося ни у кого,
> Как Дездемона избирает
> Кумир для сердца своего.

This attitude toward Desdemona seems unique to Pushkin. Romantic interpreters of Shakespeare either overlook Desdemona entirely (as does Guizot in his introduction to *Othello*) or stress her virtue, naïveté, and passivity. Shevyrev writes of her as a "faithful wife" given Othello by fate, "who combines innocence with the sort of light-hearted good-nature characteristic of women":

> With what sweeping, bright and graceful features is her charming character drawn! . . . She falls victim to her own simple-heartedness, with which she innocently facilitated the deceit of her husband [by Iago].[45]

Shevyrev objects to Veliaminov's translation in which "the faithful, good-natured, simple-hearted Desdemona is converted into the weepy, simple-minded Edel'mona."[46] In an article translated from the French and published in the *Moscow Telegraph* (*Moskovskii telegraf*) in response to Shevyrev's article in the *Moscow Herald,* a similar complaint is made by the critic about Ducis's Hédelmone (the prototype for Veliaminov's Edel'mona) in comparison to Desdemona. But in this case Ducis's heroine is seen as flawed for having too much intelligence and reasoning power: "Desdemona, so tenderly created by the English poet, simple, meek, touching, so simple that she has almost no mind or character [*prostaia do togo, chto v nei net pochti uma i kharaktera*], in Ducis appears as a reasoning little girl [*devochka rassuzhdaiushchaia*], and is as extravagant of speech [in Ducis] as she is scant of words in the original."[47]

Schlegel feels Desdemona is "calculated" by Shakespeare "to make the most yielding and tenderest of wives," and is deliberately abstracted and idealized to become Othello's "good angel" in opposition to his "evil genius," Iago.[48] He has an extraordinary account of her "rebellious" elopement with Othello, which he describes as the "only fault of her life": "The female propensity wholly to resign itself to a foreign destiny has led her into the only fault of her life, that of marrying without her father's consent."[49]

There is an obvious longing on the part of these writers to see Desdemona as a "good girl," a meek and innocent heroine. The Russian poet Nikolai Karamzin is true to this tradition in his sentimental epistle to his fellow poet I. I. Dmitriev (*Poslanie k Dmitrievu*, 1794)—a poem with which Pushkin was certainly familiar. In this epistle Karamzin includes an account of Desdemona's love for Othello. He admits her bravery ("she ran headlong into danger with him"), but emphasizes her gentleness and tenderness when speaking of her passion by referring to a "shining tear in her eye" and the "tender flame" of her love:

> Othello in his old age captivated the young Desdemona . . . She listened, was astonished, she took part in everything, ran headlong into danger with him, and with her tender flame, with shining tears in her eyes, she said: "I love you!"[50]

> Отелло в старости своей
> Пленил младую Дездемону . . .
> Она внимала, удивилась;
> Брала участие во всем:
> В опасность вместе с ним вдавалась
> И в нежном пламени своем,
> С блестящею в очах слезою,
> Сказала: я люблю тебя!

Karamzin follows these lines with an expression of his hope that he and the poem's addressee will also find a "young friend," like Desdemona, to brighten their declining years: "You and I, dear friend, will also find a friend for ourselves . . . She will adorn the sunset of our days with her sweetness" (*I my, liubeznyi drug, s toboiu / Naidem podrugu dlia sebia . . . / Ona priiatnost'iu svoei / Ukrasit zapad nashikh dnei*). This Desdemona is of quite a different temperament from the "downright violence and storm of fortunes" of Shakespeare's heroine.[51]

In short, the interpretive stance toward Desdemona tended either to admire her fidelity, passivity, and naïveté or to criticize those very qualities as indicative of her stupidity and lack of balance. Critics still to a large extent take either Cassio's attitude—"a maid / That paragons description and wild fame" (2.1.61–63), "the divine Desdemona" (2.1.74)—or Iago's: "Bless'd fig's end. / The wine she drinks is made of grapes" (2.1.251).[52]

215

In *Ezersky* and *Egyptian Nights* Pushkin compares Desdemona's love for Othello to the poet's arbitrary choice of inspiration: "Why does young Desdemona love her Moor, as the moon loves night's gloom?" (*Zachem arapa svoego / mladaia liubit Dezdemona, / Kak mesiats liubit nochi mglu?; PSS* 5:102). In his equation of Desdemona's heart with the poet's inspiration, Pushkin enacts a curious reversal: it is not Othello with whom he identifies, but rather Desdemona, the poet figure in the passage. This reversal is indicative of the other aspect of Shakespeare's play that appealed to Pushkin and which constitutes a departure from other readings of its protagonists: a baffled interpretation of Desdemona's passion which at the same time glorifies her (in equating her love with poetic inspiration and the forces of nature) and dismisses her as chaotic and arbitrary. This question of Desdemona's love is a key to the idea of monstrosity that runs throughout *Othello* and the works by Pushkin that draw on it. Is it the choice of love object—Ibragim in *The Blackamoor of Peter the Great,* Mazepa in *Poltava,* Othello himself—that is monstrous, or rather the woman herself, who in her desire defies expectations and "nature" in choosing him? The disparate pairs that Pushkin cites in Maria and Desdemona's "defense" in "Objection to the Critics" all represent a variation on the "beauty and the beast" love relationship, which held particular interest for Pushkin in 1827–30 as he searched for a bride in Moscow and St. Petersburg; hoping to arouse love himself in one of a series of beautiful and much younger women, Pushkin perhaps strove to imagine an unequal love in which he could believe. The equation of Desdemona's love with the creatures in Ovid's *Metamorphoses,* with Mirra, who harbored an incestuous love for her own father (also taken from Ovid, although Pushkin here refers to Alfieri's treatment of the story in his tragedy), combined here with the idea of poetry ("all these fictions are not foreign to poetry"), reveals a decided ambivalence and incomprehension on Pushkin's part toward the idea of a woman's love. Indeed, in placing Othello and Desdemona next to this group of truly monstrous Ovidian couplings to explain an unequal love relationship in which he wants very much to believe, as he writes parenthetically: "NB: historically proven," Pushkin betrays a distinct incomprehension of the basic attraction between the lovers, and we must question how "natural" he found their love to be. He desires it to be plausible, but still cannot place it outside the realm of fiction and poetry.[53]

In Pushkin's final critical comments on *Othello,* in "Table-Talk" (mid-1830s), he indicates that he did not consider jealousy to be the defining feature of this tragedy. He compares Shakespeare's hero to Orosman, the hero of Voltaire's tragedy *Zaire* (1735)—itself, as Pushkin notes, loosely based on *Othello*:

> Othello is not jealous by nature. On the contrary, he is trusting. Voltaire understood this and, developing Shakespeare's creation in his imitation, places in

Orosman's mouth the following line: "I am not jealous at all . . . If I ever were!"(*PSS* 12:157)

Pushkin speaks of Othello's character as not inherently jealous; rather, it is the manipulation of his fundamentally trusting nature that provokes jealousy in the Moor. We may say that in both "Objections to the Critics of *Poltava*" and "Table-Talk," Pushkin's sympathy for Othello contains an element of consolation for him: in "Objections" Othello and Desdemona are, perhaps, the only human examples he can offer as models for his heroes in *Poltava,* and in "Table-Talk" (written after his marriage and when signs of jealousy were beginning to be noticed in him) he describes Othello as one who was not born to jealousy, but who had jealousy thrust upon him. We note that Pushkin does not mention Shakespeare's villain, Iago, as the cause of Othello's jealousy; rather, he deliberately leaves the forces at work against Othello unnamed.

In fact, the poet's "real-life" jealousy was often compared to that of Othello both in his lifetime and by subsequent critics and biographers, so that the distinction between Pushkin's image as poet and his biography—murky enough to begin with—becomes more complicated still by the equation of him with a fictional character who has become over the years an emblem of the passion of jealousy. If the memoirs of F. F. Vigel' are accurate (they were published in 1891, long after the events described), the equation of Pushkin with Othello occurred as early as 1823 or 1824 in Odessa, where Vigel' told the poet to his face that the intrigues being conducted by his friend Alexander Raevsky were like the workings of Iago on Othello.[54]

We should note, moreover, that any story of murderous jealousy was associated at the time with *Othello.* There were two plays in the early 1840s entitled *A New Othello,* whose plots centered around the unfounded jealousy of the heroes.[55] Also, Mikhail Lermontov's play *Masquerade* (1835–36) is considered to be the quintessential "Russian *Othello*" since it concerns a man who murders his wife after mistakenly assuming her to have been unfaithful to him. All these "Othellos," great and small, fictionalized and historical, are so named because they share one feature: jealousy. Yet Pushkin does not admit this to be the most important characteristic of Shakespeare's hero. He was certainly aware of the poetic potential of jealousy—as treated, for example, in *The Gypsies* (1824)—as well as his own propensity to jealousy. It is clear from Pushkin's 1834 "Beginning of an Autobiography," as well as his account of his ancestor in *The Blackamoor of Peter the Great*, that he felt Gannibal, like Othello, was not jealous by nature. After all, Gannibal only divorced his first wife after she gave birth to a white daughter—that is, after clear evidence of her infidelity. He describes Gannibal as stern, but clearly feels sympathy for him:

> In his family life my great-grandfather Gannibal was just as unhappy as my grandfather Pushkin had been. His first wife, a great beauty, by birth a Greek woman, bore him a white daughter. He divorced her and forced her into the Tikhvin convent. He kept her daughter Polyksena in his home, gave her a good education and a generous dowry, but never allowed her into his sight. (*PSS* 12:313)

Compare this with his account of his paternal grandfather, Lev A. Pushkin (1723–90):

> My grandfather was a hot-tempered and cruel man. His first wife, née Voeikova, died on a bed of straw, kept prisoner in her own house for an imagined or actual liaison with a Frenchman, the former tutor of his sons, who in turn was hung in the back courtyard in the feudal manner. (*PSS* 12:311)

The characteristic laconism with which Pushkin writes about Gannibal ("He divorced her and forced her into the Tikhvin convent") differs from the direct condemnation in his account of his grandfather Pushkin ("hot-tempered and cruel"). Although Pushkin uses the same word for "hot-tempered" (*pylkii*) for both his grandfathers, in the case of L. A. Pushkin it is combined with "cruel" (*zhestokii*), whereas in that of Gannibal it is combined with "foolhardiness" (*legkomyslie*). Also, Pushkin emphasizes that Gannibal was not jealous and did not punish his wife until her infidelity was proven (she "bore him a white daughter"), whereas the guilt of L. A. Pushkin's wife is unclear and, it seems, unimportant ("an imagined or actual liaison"). Gannibal, in Pushkin's thinking, was merely an unfortunate cuckold, whereas L. A. Pushkin was jealous by nature, like all the "Othellos" at large in his grandson's day. Pushkin's "jealousy gene," it seems, originated in his mind on the white side of his family tree. His African side he rather associated with passion and caprice, or excessive emotionality, which he was careful to separate from the mad tyranny he saw in his paternal grandfather. We see this identification of African origins with excessive passion in his account of Gannibal's son, O. A. Gannibal, our poet's maternal grandfather, who himself was unfaithful to Pushkin's grandmother and caused her a great deal of misery: "The African character of my grandfather, his hot-tempered passions combined with a terrible foolhardiness, led him into astonishing error."

It is a quirk of Pushkin's metapoetic fate that although he refused to associate either Gannibal or Othello with jealousy, his own jealousy as his wife was being courted, first by the tsar and then by d'Anthès, was attributed by contemporaries to his African heritage and consequent "passionate" nature, if not with Othello himself.[56] Although Othello provided an initial model for Pushkin to portray his African ancestor, he was never by himself the only aspect of the tragedy to occupy Pushkin's mind. Indeed, Pushkin's interest in the character of Othello diminished after *Poltava*. Instead, it is Desdemona who was invoked in the later poetic passages from *Ezersky* and *Egyptian Nights;* it is the heroine of Shakespeare's tragedy that continued to interest our poet. As we have seen, in Pushkin's troubled but exalting evocation of Shakespeare's heroine in the 1830s we find echoes of the idea that women's love is inherently arbitrary. There was no Othello without Desdemona for Pushkin, and the story of their love provided a constant reminder of both the miraculous in and the fragility of human love.

Notes

1. Many Pushkin scholars mention *Othello,* certainly, but only in passing; by and large Pushkin's interest in this play has not been pursued beyond the level of speculation because of the apparent dearth of direct references to the play on Pushkin's part. For example, M. P. Alekseev writes in his comprehensive essay on Pushkin and Shakespeare: "There can be no doubt that the whole story of Desdemona and Othello's love, as it is depicted by Shakespeare, in all its subtlest nuances, served as the source of diverse thoughts and perceptions for the author of *The Blackamoor of Peter the Great* (1827–1828)" ("Pushkin i Shekspir," in *Pushkin: Sravnitel'no-istoricheskie issledovaniia* [Leningrad: Nauka, 1972], 269). John Bayley cautiously refers to *Othello* in his discussion of *Poltava*: "It is only a guess, certainly, but the heroic atmosphere of [*Othello*], and the dramatic contrast between its two great protagonists, might have entered Pushkin's mind" when he developed the relationship between Mazepa and Kochubei in *Poltava* (*Pushkin: A Comparative Commentary* [Cambridge: Cambridge University Press, 1971], 120). Paul Debreczeny, equally cautiously, draws parallels between Ibragim in *The Blackamoor of Peter the Great* and Mazepa as "explorations of how disadvantaged men might fare in love," like Othello (*The Other Pushkin* [Stanford: Stanford University Press, 1983], 34). L. I. Vol'pert describes the influence of *Othello* on Pushkin's first prose work, *The Blackamoor of Peter the Great,* and observes that "the image of Othello attracted the creative fantasy of Pushkin throughout the course of his entire life" ("Pushkin i Stendal'," in *Pushkin: Issledovaniia i materialy,* vol. 12 (1986), 213; see also her "Shekspirizm Pushkina i Stendalia," in *Pushkin v roli Pushkina* [Moscow: Iazyki russkoi kul'tury, 1998], 231–36). J. Thomas Shaw has included Pushkin's critical comments on *Othello* in his overview of Pushkin's attitude toward his African ancestry, reprinted in this volume: "Pushkin's African heritage may be considered to be implied in two notes in which he mentions *Othello,* the most famous Moor in literature." N. V. Izmailov connects Maria from *Poltava* and

Shakespeare's Desdemona in a footnote to his article "Pushkin v rabote nad Poltavoi" (*Ocherki tvorchestva Pushkina* [Leningrad: Nauka, 1975], 65–66), but does not develop this intriguing link any further. Finally, the most recent treatment of the *Othello* theme in Pushkin is an article by V. D. Rak in which concrete textual evidence is used to prove Pushkin's familiarity with the 1821 French translation of *Othello* ("Pushkin i frantsuzskii perevod Otello," *Pushkin Journal* 1, no. 1 [1993]: 36–45). Gradually scholarship is casting a broader glance at the study of Pushkin's understanding of Shakespeare's play.

2. There were, however, other blacks in Russia both at court and in the larger society, many moving to Russia to offer a life of service in exchange for their freedom. See Allison Blakely, *Russia and the Negro: Blacks in Russian History and Thought* (Washington, D.C.: Howard University Press, 1986), 14–16. Although many blacks prospered in Russia and there was a "black aristocrat" noticed at the Russian court as late as 1916, "Hannibal and his family were the only Negroes to have lasting significance in tsarist Russian history" (19).

3. See, for example, Pushkin's letter to his wife concerning plans to make a bust of him in Moscow: "Here my blackamoor ugliness [*arapskoe moe bezobrazie*] will be conveyed to eternity in all its lifeless immobility" (May 14, 1836 [*PSS* 16:116]). On the other hand, Pushkin's mother, Nadezhda Osipovna, was considered a great beauty in her day exactly because of her black heritage; she was known to contemporaries as "the beautiful creole," *prekrasnaia kreolka* (see, for example, V. V. Veresaev, *Pushkin v zhizni* [Moscow, 1927], 1:16).

4. "To Yur'ev" is reprinted in J. Thomas Shaw's article in this volume.

5. Pushkin had read *Othello* by 1825, when he mentions the play in an unfinished essay, "On Nationalism in Literature" ("O narodnosti v literature," 1825). In this fragment he lists *Othello* along with *Hamlet* and *Measure for Measure*(!) as Shakespeare's greatest achievements (*PSS* 11:40). This statement reflects a broad examination of Shakespeare by Pushkin that took place in Mikhailovskoe in 1824–25 while the poet was working on *Boris Godunov*. An earlier acquaintance with the play is of course possible, but certainly by this point he knew it well, if only in the French translation by Pierre Le Tourneur, edited by Amadée Pichot and François Guizot (1821). It is possible, moreover, that Pushkin saw a Russian adaptation performed in 1819–20, but this is by no means certain (see note 13 below).

6. "Objections to the Critics of *Poltava*" ("Vozrazheniia kritikam *Poltavy*," 1831). I discuss this passage in detail on page 203.

7. Alekseev, "Pushkin i Shekspir," 243.

8. *Istoriia russkogo dramaticheskogo teatra v semi tomakh* (Moscow: Iskusstvo, 1978), 3:290.

9. Alekseev, "Pushkin i Shekspir," 243.

10. In recent years the stage history of *Othello* has been treated with

growing scholarly interest and insight, particularly regarding this question of lightening Othello's skin color. For a good overview of the acting tradition in England, see Michael Neill, "Unproper Beds: Race, Adultery, and the Hideous in Othello," in *Critical Essays on Shakespeare's Othello* (New York: G. K. Hall, 1994), 187–215. For a full discussion of the acting of *Othello* over the years, see Julie Hankey, ed., *Othello: Plays in Performances Series* (Bristol: Classical Press, 1987).

11. Quoted in J. J. Jusserand, *Shakespeare in France: Under the Ancien Régime* (New York: American Scholar Publications, 1966), 434.

12. J.-F. Ducis, *Oeuvres de J.-F. Ducis*, vol. 2 (Paris: 1819). For accounts of Ducis's version, see Margaret Gilman, *Othello in France* (Paris: Librairie Ancienne Honoré Champion, 1925), especially 63–70; and Jusserand, *Shakespeare in France*, 433–34.

13. *Otello, ili venetsiianskii mavr: Tragediia v piati deistviiakh* (St. Petersburg, 1808). B. V. Tomashevskii cites Veliaminov's *Othello* as one of the plays in which Pushkin may have seen the famous actress Ekaterina Semenova in St. Petersburg in 1819–20 (*Pushkin* [Moscow and Leningrad: Akademiia nauk, 1957], 1:239, fn).

14. For accounts of Veliaminov's version, see A. S. Bulgakov, "Rannee znakomstvo s Shekspirom v Rossii," *Teatral'noe nasledie* 1 (1934): 66–70. For accounts of Mochalov's acting, see B. Alpers, *Teatr Mochalova i Shchepkina* (Moscow: Muzgiz, 1949).

15. S. T. Aksakov, *Sobranie sochinenii v 4-x tomakh* (Moscow, 1896), 4:393. The lines occur in Veliaminov's play at a point at which Othello compares his humble birth to that of the Venetian noblemen (*Otello*, 36). This emphasis on Othello's low origins, so common in eighteenth-century versions of the play, is a serious departure from Shakespeare's play, in which Othello speaks on the contrary of his noble origin: "I fetch my life and being / From men of royal siege" (1.2.21–22).

16. Belinskii shares this assessment of the pair in his article on Mochalov in the role of Hamlet: "[Desdemona] knew how to love the great-hearted Othello in an old and ugly Moor" (*Polnoe sobranie sochinenii* [Moscow: Akademiia nauk, 1953], 2:294). This sympathetic assessment marks a change in attitude, judging by an interesting example of unacknowledged *Othello* criticism from eighteenth-century Russia, in Vasilii Trediakovskii's "New and Short Method for Composing Verse" (1735). Trediakovskii writes of "le mariage des vers": "Such a combination of verses would be with us just as loathsome and disgusting as it would be if one should see the most attractive, tender, European beauty, aglow in the full flower of her youth, coupled with a decrepit ninety-year-old blackamoor!" (quoted in and translated by W. E. Brown, *A History of 18th Century Russian Literature* [Ann Arbor: Ardis, 1980], 62).

17. David Bevington, introduction to *Othello*, in *Complete Works of Shakespeare* (Glenview, Ill.: Scott, Foresman, 1980), 1121.

18. Quoted in Jonathan Bate, ed., *The Romantics on Shakespeare* (London: Penguin Books, 1992), 38. The lines to which Coleridge is referring are in act 1, scene 1: "What a full fortune does the thick-lips owe / If he can carry it thus" (ll. 66–67).

19. Bate, ed., *Romantics on Shakespeare*, 483.

20. August Wilhelm Schlegel, *Lectures on Dramatic Art and Literature*, trans. John Black (London: George Bell, 1889), 401–2.

21. V.V.V., "Nemetskii teatr g Kelera," *Severnaia pchela*, no. 163 (July 21, 1834): 651. An important case study of black acting in *Othello* is the fate of the black American actor Ira Aldridge (1807–67). He stands out not only because he was a black man playing Othello as early as 1825, but because he performed in the play in the United States, England, and continental Europe (Germany, Switzerland, and Poland), including Russia. He did not come to Russia until 1858, well after Pushkin's death, and so I have not included him in this study. When he first arrived in London in 1825 an announcement was published in *Severnaia pchela*: "A Negro [*negr*] has appeared on one of London's stages: a North American actor in the role of Othello (the Moor of Venice) in Shakespeare's tragedy" (M. P. Alekseev, ed., *Shekspir: Bibliographiia russkikh perevodov i kriticheskoi literatury na russkom iazyke, 1748–1964* [Moscow: Kniga, 1964], 108). His reviews, it seems, were middling to bad in the United States and in Britain, yet he was more successful in Russia and Poland (indeed, he died in Poland and is buried in Łódz). See, for example, Joyce Green MacDonald, "Acting Black: *Othello, Othello* Burlesques, and the Performance of Blackness," *Theatre Journal* 46, no. 2 (May 1994): 231–49; and Herbert Marshall and Mildred Stock, *Ira Aldridge—The Negro Tragedian* (Carbondale: Southern Illinois University Press, 1958). For accounts of Aldridge in Russia, see I. M. Levidov in Alekseev, ed., *Shekspir: Bibliographiia*, 582–89; and M. P. Alekseev, ed., *Shekspir i russkaia kul'tura* (Moscow and Leningrad: Nauka, 1965), 541–43.

22. Schlegel, *Lectures*, 402.

23. Few Russian writers were aware of English Romantic criticism directly with the exception of P. A. Pletnev, who introduced the writings of Hazlitt to the Russian critical public (see Iu. D. Levin, *Shekspir i russkaia literatura XIX veka* [Leningrad: Nauka, Leningradskoe otdelenie, 1988], 93).

24. See J. Thomas Shaw's article in this volume for a discussion of the use of the Russian words for "blackamoor" (*arap*) and "Negro" (*negr*) in Pushkin's day.

25. *Moskovskii vestnik* 24, no. 39 (1827): 419.

26. Ibid., 421.

27. François Guizot, "Notice sur *Othello*," in *Oeuvres complètes de Shakespeare* (Paris, 1821), 5:12.

28. S. P. Shevyrev, "Otello, Mavr Venetsianskii: Tragediia Shekspira, peredelannaia na Russkii iazyk," *Moskovskii vestnik,* no. 12 (1828): 429.

29. For a discussion of Pushkin's ascription of aspects of his own experience to that of his great-grandfather, see N. Eidel'man, "Kolokol'chik Gannibala," in *Iz potaennoi istorii Rossii: XVII–XIX vekov* (Moscow: Vysshaia Shkola, 1993), 89–129.

30. V. D. Rak uses this fragment as evidence to argue an early familiarity on Pushkin's part with the 1821 French translation of *Othello* because in it there is bird imagery similar to that which appears in the Guizot/Le Tourneur version. Pushkin refers to Gannibal as a raven (*voron*), and to his bride as a swan (*lebedushka*) ("Pushkin i frantsuzskii perevod," 38). However, Pushkin did not need to borrow this image of swan and raven from the French version of *Othello* for his poem, since the exact image of swan and raven appears in the German biography of Gannibal, Pushkin's main source of information about his ancestor used for his footnote to *Eugene Onegin* (Eidel'man, "Kolokol'chik Gannibala," 94). The image in the French *Othello,* that of a vulture (*vauture*) and a dove (*colombe*), is in any case substantially different from that in the lyric fragment about Gannibal.

31. Quoted in V. V. Veresaev, *Sputniki Pushkina v 2-kh tomakh* (Moscow: Sovetskii sport, 1993), 1:403.

32. The Russian editors of Pushkin's letters translate the French phrase *vieux nègre* as "old blackamoor," *staryi arap.*

33. Pushkin's inclusion of the figure of Voinarovskii in *Poltava* (it is he who kills the young Cossack) can be seen as his tribute to Ryleev (see Paul Debreczeny, "Narrative Voices in *Poltava,*" *Russian Literature* 24 [1988]: 333), just as the fate of the Decembrists is an evident subtext to the poem as a whole.

34. This observation was made by Paul Debreczeny in *The Other Pushkin,* 34.

35. For example, Michael Neill writes about the way the audience is implicated in Iago's racism in *Othello*: "The play thinks abomination into being and then taunts the audience with the knowledge that it can never be unthought: 'What you know, you know' . . . it would be almost as difficult to say whether its racial anxieties are ones that the play discovers or implants in an audience as to say whether jealousy is something that Iago discovers or implants in Othello" ("Unproper Beds," 193).

36. On Pushkin's "idealization" of Gannibal in his portrait of Ibragim, see, for example, Vladimir Nabokov, *Prosody and Abram Gannibal* (Princeton: Princeton University Press, 1964).

37. Vol'pert, "Pushkin i Stendal'," 214.

38. Svetlana Evdokimova, *Petra Scandali: History, Fiction and Myth in Pushkin's Narratives of Peter the Great* (New Haven: Yale University Press, 1991), 151.

39. Vol'pert, "Pushkin i Stendal'," 215.

40. See, for example, A. A. Olenina's account of Pushkin's return to Moscow after his six-year exile and his triumphant reception in Russian society; he was invited and flattered for any number of reasons but, Olenina relates, "the majority did this because he was in favor with the Tsar Nikolai Pavlovich, who was his censor" (quoted in V. E. Vatsuro, ed., *A. S. Pushkin v vospominaniakh sovremennikov: V dvukh tomakh* [Moscow: Khudozhestvennaia literatura, 1985], 2:83).

41. See, for example, Janet C. Stavropoulos, "Love and Age in *Othello*," *Shakespeare Studies* 19 (1987): 125–41.

42. This behavior, from her trembling to her "death-like" pallor and swoon, all correspond to "appropriate" maidenly behavior when confronted with extreme emotional agitation. The "young maid pacing" strongly recalls the agitated Tatiana from *Eugene Onegin* as she awaits Onegin's "verdict" on her declaration of love. Maria's agitation likewise recalls Natasha Rzhevskaia's terrified reaction to the news of the proposed marriage between herself and Ibragim in *The Blackamoor of Peter the Great*: "And when she heard her father's final words, the poor girl lost her senses and, falling, bruised her head on the hammered chest in which her dowry was kept" (*PSS* 8:26).

43. Many scholars have noted the discrepancy between the brave and defiant Desdemona of acts 1 and 2 and the submissive wife she becomes thereafter (for an overview of this criticism, see Janet Adelman, *Suffocating Mothers: Fantasies of Maternal Origin in Shakespeare's Plays, Hamlet to The Tempest* [New York: Routledge, 1992], 279–80, fn67). It is interesting in this connection that an analogous deterioration can be seen in Maria in *Poltava*, a deterioration that for some readers undermines the coherence of the poem (for example, Bayley, *Pushkin*, 118–19). This inability on the part of both Pushkin and Shakespeare to dispose of their female characters once they are possessed (that is, after marriage) is another affinity between them.

44. Aquilo is another name for Boreas, the north wind.

45. Shevyrev, "Otello," 432.

46. Ibid., 437.

47. [F. Ekshtein], "'Otello' Shekspira i 'Otello' Diusisa," *Moskovskii telegraf* 22, no. 13 (July 1828): 77.

48. Bate, ed., *Romantics on Shakespeare*, 480.

49. Ibid., 480–81.

50. N. M. Karamzin, *Polnoe sobranie stikhotvorenii* (Moscow and Leningrad, 1966), 138–39.

51. It is interesting that in this passage Karamzin does not mention Othello's blackness at all, but instead, like Pushkin, emphasizes his advanced age ("Othello in his old age"). However, unlike Karamzin, Pushkin does not see that "old age" as indicative of a decline in powers: Mazepa, like Othello,

is still very much a leader, whereas Karamzin is articulating a sort of retirement fantasy. It is tempting in the spirit of Pushkin studies to juxtapose Karamzin's ideas in this poem and his fate in marriage with Pushkin's. The "fantasy" of Karamzin's epistle is not very secure: quite apart from the humorous effect produced by the plural subject of the two men ("you and I, dear friend") desiring a single girl ("friend," "she"), Karamzin presumably knew that Othello and Desdemona's marriage does not exactly offer a comfortable image of conjugal bliss. Pushkin's own "retirement fantasies" are similarly troubled, as Roman Jakobson suggests in his essay "The Statue in Pushkin's Poetic Mythology" (*Pushkin and His Sculptural Myth*, trans. and ed. John Burbank [The Hague: Mouton, 1975], 22–26).

52. For an account of the critical tradition of applying to Desdemona the very saint-whore dichotomy to which she is subjected by the male characters in the play, see S. N. Garner, "Shakespeare's Desdemona," *Shakespeare Studies* 9 (1976): 233–52, especially 234–36.

53. Pushkin's comparison of Desdemona to the moon in *Ezerskii* and *Egyptian Nights* evokes another Pushkinian moon—one associated with female love and desire: the moon in *The Gypsies* (*Tsygany*, 1824), which represents female inconstancy. Although the moon in the Desdemona passages, unlike in *The Gypsies,* does not suggest inconstancy, it expresses an "aberrant" passion, as the love of the bright (white) moon for the dark (black) night parallels the white Desdemona's choice of the black Othello. Thus the two greatest dangers in female desire presented in Pushkin's poetry—"natural" infidelity and "unnatural" attraction—are united in this image of the moon. A third moon—the romantic, dreamy moon associated with Tatiana in *Eugene Onegin*—is likewise evoked in the Desdemona passages, since the element of night (compared to Othello's blackness) is so heavily emphasized.

54. "Already in the winter [of 1823–24] I heard a rumor of danger to Pushkin and once said to him that because of his African origin I am tempted to compare him to Othello and Raevskii to his treacherous friend Iago. He merely laughed" (quoted in Veresaev, *Pushkin v zhizni*, 1:144).

55. *Novyi Otello, ili bez diadi ne oboidetsia. Komediia v odnom deistvii Ia. Ia. Feigina* (manuscript: St. Petersburg Theater Library [1841]; and *Novyi Otello, ili Poslednee prosti. Tragediia v 2-kh deistviiakh, soch. Tika* (manuscript: St. Petersburg Theater Library [1839]).

56. P. Guber in his sensationalist account of Pushkin's love life makes the link between jealousy and Othello explicit, as he cautions the reader: "we must not juxtapose Pushkin's jealousy with that of Othello, as has been done often enough in the past. The Moor of Venice was trusting and blind ... Pushkin, on the other hand, [was of] an uncommonly jealous disposition and extremely suspicious" (*Don-zhuanskii spisok A. S. Pushkina* [Petrograd, 1923], 236).

Olga P. Hasty

The Pushkin of *Opportunity* in the Harlem Renaissance

THE SECOND AND THIRD DECADES of the twentieth century, when "white writers ignored the race question more than at any other time in American history," marked a vibrant blossoming of African American literature as writers of African descent countered racism with concerted efforts to establish a distinct cultural identity.[1] On the basis of his African blood, Pushkin was drawn into the struggle to overturn prevalent notions about race and to raise African American consciousness. A century after his death, the greatest poet of the Golden Age of Russian literature became part of the cultural ferment of the heady American movement that came to be known as the Harlem Renaissance.

My purpose in this essay is not to rehearse Pushkin's genealogy, which has already attracted considerable scholarly attention. I will consider instead the significance that this genealogy assumed first for Pushkin himself and subsequently for African Americans during the Harlem Renaissance, when he was introduced to a wide African American reading public, held up as a model for aspiring writers, and invoked to challenge Eurocentric notions of African cultural inferiority. Of interest to us here are the points of similarity that African American writers discerned between their own project and Pushkin's achievements as we consider what the Russian poet came to signify in the context of the cultural agenda promoted by leading figures of the movement. Naturally, I cannot presume to exhaust the rich topic I introduce here of Pushkin's role in the Harlem Renaissance. I will therefore base my discussion primarily on Pushkin's introduction into this fertile cultural terrain as it was accomplished in the pages of *Opportunity: A Journal of Negro Life,* a publication that more than any other of its time was dedicated to promoting African American letters.

Because "the Renaissance largely accepted that poetic form was inherently linked to social identity," it was not Pushkin's verse, but the fact of Pushkin himself that was of greatest relevance to the movement.[2] Although there was naturally an interest in his writings, the potential for African American enablement was seen primarily in Pushkin's own biography and in the stories that he recorded of his African ancestors. Crucial too was Pushkin's stature—the fact that a writer of African blood wrote poetry of genius and was hailed as the progenitor of the great tradition of Russian letters.

It is important to understand that Pushkin became an appealing model for African Americans not simply because he had African blood in his veins, but, more important, on the strength of how he himself related to this fact of his genealogy, and the possibilities for self-affirmation he derived from it. The connections that the African American intelligentsia of the Harlem Renaissance established with Pushkin went beyond race and extended, significantly, to the social and political climate in which the Russian poet wrote. Pushkin's attachment to the program of the Harlem Renaissance in general and to *Opportunity* in particular was thus doubly motivated: the poet's own highly positive attitude to his African heritage combined productively with what African Americans perceived as significant parallels between his circumstances and their own.

Because our grasp of how Pushkin was regarded by African Americans depends on understanding how he himself related to his ancestry, I will begin by looking at the cultural and historical context in which Pushkin himself shaped the African image that was carried forward into the Harlem Renaissance. This material permits us to recognize those points of similarity that were perceived and elaborated by intellectuals of the Harlem Renaissance between their own situation and Pushkin's. It shows us, too, incidentally, the extent to which assumptions about African character traits held in Pushkin's time were still intact a full century later in the United States. Pushkin's invocations of his African heritage in literary affirmations of his own individual creative freedom help us to appreciate the profound appropriateness of the seemingly improbable coalition of the Russian Golden Age poet and aspiring African American writers of the Harlem Renaissance. As we study the meaning Pushkin assigned his African blood, we are alerted to the remarkable continuity in the spirit in which he invoked his African forebears and the spirit in which he was in turn invoked by African American writers. Here we observe the integrity of creative discourse that points beyond questions of race and nationality to the essential question of what the creative individual can do to oppose large-scale oppression.

In an article which is reprinted in this volume, J. Thomas Shaw observes that Pushkin does not devote any single work exclusively to his African ancestry, and that he inevitably embeds his references to Africa in broader contexts.[3] We can deduce from this fact that of paramount concern to Pushkin is not his lineage in and of itself, but rather what this lineage can be made to signify in the broader cultural, social, and political milieu in which he writes. Of primary significance, in other words, is not what Pushkin tells us about his African ancestry, but what he needs to say about himself when he invokes it. Along the same lines, of particular interest is not what African American writers tell us about Pushkin, but what the image they create of the Russian poet reflects of their own agenda.

We can begin by recalling that Pushkin's stance toward his African forebears developed in a sociopolitical setting that was sensitized to the plight of Africans enslaved in the United States. Pushkin's liberal contemporaries took considerable interest in the question of slavery. Indeed, the topic of *Negr v nevole* ("the Negro in bondage") attracted the attention of Russian writers of the 1820s and 1830s and became a popular theme in the press. The Russian image of the American slave was colored by Shakespeare's *Othello,* which highlighted the intrinsic merits of the Moor, but also his ungoverned passions. It derived primarily, however, from French sources that bore the distinct mark of Rousseau's ideas about the "noble savage." French accounts generally emphasized the exotic nature of the race and described the idyllic setting from which it sprang. At the same time they focused on the harsh oppression of sensitive, freedom-loving Africans by narrow, greedy whites who were for the most part inferior by nature to those unfortunates they enslaved. Uncorrupted by Western civilization, free from its prejudices and narrow social strictures was a being more honest, more loyal, and more passionate than the civilized European.[4] Pushkin's descriptions of his African ancestry, like his African self-representations, are based on precisely such representations. At the same time they engage the politicized image of the American slave that was important to liberals of his time.

As a relative newcomer to the European cultural scene, Russia was naturally inclined to see a kindred spirit in the even newer United States of America. The marginal place accorded the two nations in a Eurocentric world presupposed a certain similarity of outlook and suggested a broad variety of social and cultural parallels between them. Russian liberals who chafed under autocratic rule were especially enthusiastic about the Constitution of the United States, which, although forbidden by the tsarist censorship, was widely circulated. At the same time, these liberals directed intense opprobrium at the institution of slavery, which betrayed those democratic ideals the Constitution espoused. On the strength of the readily drawn parallel between slavery in the United States and serfdom in Russia, American slavery entered the Russian Aesopic vocabulary, providing a convenient vehicle for slipping criticism of serfdom into the press.

Like his liberal contemporaries, Pushkin too took considerable interest in America and the question of slavery. Familiar with accounts that appeared regularly in the Russian press of the time, Pushkin was also personally acquainted with P. I. Poletika, secretary of the Russian mission in Philadelphia from 1809 until 1811, ambassador from 1817 to 1822, and author of "The State of the Society in the United American States" ("Sostoianie obshchestva v soedinennykh amerikanskikh oblastiakh"), which appeared in the *Literary Gazette* (*Literaturnaia gazeta*) in 1830.[5] Pushkin spoke highly of Chateaubriand's writings on America, read James Fenimore Cooper avidly, and was especially enthusiastic about de Tocqueville's *Democracy in America*, the first two volumes of which appeared in Pushkin's lifetime. Pushkin seems to have been especially interested in the question of slavery, for he cut only the opening forty-five pages of the first volume of de Tocqueville's study in which the structure of the government is described, but all of the pages of the second volume, which is devoted to the institution of slavery.[6] Pushkin also appears to have read the now-forgotten, but then-popular *Marie, or l'Esclavage aux Étas-Unis, tableau de moeurs Américaines*, which was written by de Tocqueville's traveling companion Gustave de Beaumont. *Marie, or Slavery in the United States, a Novel of Jacksonian America*, as the English version was entitled, is a fictional work augmented with an appendix of the author's sociological observations. Both parts of the work focus almost exclusively on the plight of the African in American society. Examples of deep-seated racial intolerance abound in the appendix, while the recurring motif in the novel itself is the African blood that at significant junctures of Marie's life stands tragically in the way of her self-fulfillment. Central to the novel are the adamant refusals of Marie and her brother to disclaim their African heritage, although neither looks African and could easily pass for white. This loyalty to their bloodline invests Marie and her brother with personal dignity. It serves as a sign of an innate nobility which Beaumont's characters are not prepared to surrender for personal gain. Their staunch loyalty to their own selves stands in sharp contrast to the mercantilism of the surrounding world. Pushkin, as we will see, draws on just such an opposition between innate nobility and a willingness to sell out in order to reorient the concept of slavery from its literal sense to a metaphoric one. His own pride in his African ancestry and his public avowals of his African blood became exemplary for aspiring African American writers. We have only to recall Athol Fugard's play *The Blood-Knot* to appreciate the crucial role a minority individual's racial self-affirmation plays in the resistance to pressures from a dominant culture and to realize the extent to which this theme, in endless variations, remains relevant in our own times.

Pushkin absorbed representations of the African that were current in his day into the images he shaped of his maternal great-grandfather Abram Gannibal and into what he construed to be his own inherited African characteristics. Popular conceptions abundantly perpetuated by the current press fleshed out the material he gleaned from family archives and figured also in the poet's creation of a self-image. Thus, for example, in his 1820 poem "To Yur'ev" ("Yur'evu"), Pushkin speaks of his physical unattractiveness and passionate sensuality, while in "To Dawe, Esq." (1828) he insists that his *arapskii* ("Negro") profile makes him unsuitable for sketching.

Pushkin was fully aware that the situation of the American slave was in many ways comparable to that of the Russian serf, and M. Eremin's contention that the criticism of America in the opening of Pushkin's essay "John Tanner" ("Dzhon Tenner") implicitly extended to Russia is certainly plausible.[7] For Pushkin, however, this sociopolitical issue took on an additional, intensely experienced personal dimension. The poet was quick to recognize that the questions of liberty and bondage that centered on the oppressed Russian serf and the abject American slave applied with compelling immediacy to the frustrating, arbitrary, and demeaning restrictions to which he himself was subjected. He saw too the analogical possibilities that the theme of slavery afforded him for registering protest against his own situation. Thus, for example, in a letter he wrote to his friend and fellow poet Petr Viazemsky from Odessa in June 1824, Pushkin hinted darkly at his own situation when he compared the plight of the Greeks with the oppression of "my Negro brothers" (*moia brat'ia negrov*) in America and added, "we can wish both sides liberation from insufferable slavery" (*mozhno i tem i drugim zhelat' osvobozhdeniia ot rabstva nesterpimogo*; PSS 12:157).

If for his liberal contemporaries the institution of slavery furnished an Aesopic vocabulary to criticize Russian serfdom, for Pushkin it became an Aesopic language for protesting his own treatment by the tsarist regime. Combined, the two conventional aspects of the American slave—the noble savage of Rousseau's philosophy and the political emblem of Russian liberals—provided him with the means to register his own defiance of the limitations placed on his personal liberty. "His" Africa, as he refers to it in canto 50 of the first chapter of *Eugene Onegin*, became a hospitable destination for voyages of the imagination, a genealogically motivated escape route from the cold, hostile climate of Russia beyond whose borders he was never granted permission to travel. A subversive analogy suggested an underlying similarity between the unjust treatment to which Africans were subjected in America and those barbarous limitations to personal liberty Pushkin himself endured in what he increasingly felt to be his Russian captivity. The Africa of his ancestor emerged as a complex metaphor that conveyed Pushkin's own sense of bondage and alienation, offered him the chance to criticize his oppressors, and embodied the intense longing for escape that fueled much of his creativity.

When the opening chapter of *Eugene Onegin* came out in separate publication in 1825, Pushkin supplied the mention of "his" African skies in canto 50 with an extensive explanatory note that chronicled his maternal great-grandfather's extraordinary life from the time of his abduction from the shores of his native land at the age of eight to his death in his mid-eighties in Russia in the year 1781. Pushkin wrote the stanza in question in the autumn of 1823,

The Pushkin of *Opportunity* in the Harlem Renaissance

when he was in exile in Odessa, and penned the note to it the following year at his Mikhailovskoe estate to which he was banished in 1824, having been dismissed from the service.[8] The ostensible function of the note is to supply concrete historical data from sources unavailable to the general public. Yet the note does considerably more, for with his thumbnail sketch of his maternal great-grandfather Abram Gannibal, Pushkin smuggles subversive criticism of the ruling tsar past his censors.

It is appropriate that Pushkin should recollect his African ancestor during his own exile at Mikhailovskoe. The estate had belonged to his African forebear, and descendants of his who could provide Pushkin with invaluable source material still lived in the area.[9] The information Pushkin supplies in his note to *Onegin* about his great-grandfather is highly suggestive when considered in the specific context of his own uncomfortable political situation. By juxtaposing the era of Peter the Great with his own times, Pushkin creates a highly advantageous parallel between himself and Gannibal and at the same time presents Alexander I—who could not but fare poorly in juxtaposition with his august predecessor—in a particularly bad light. Peter the Great is shown to appreciate, cultivate, reward, honor, and befriend his African subject, in implicit contradistinction to the sovereign of Pushkin's own time, who suspiciously regards the descendant of the illustrious African as an insidious, unruly subject in need of restraint.[10]

Shaw remarks on the parallel that Pushkin suggests between his own creative activity and his great-grandfather's unauthorized return from Siberian exile: "In the *Onegin* passage in verse, Pushkin, utilizing a 'poetic flight' of the imagination, is hinting at voluntarily breaking that kind of exile in order to flee to 'my Africa.'"[11] This is a daring gesture, to be sure, but Pushkin does more here than hint at breaking his exile. He indicates the essential unlawfulness of the restraint imposed on him and asserts that the loyalty of a subject must be earned and not simply commanded. On the strength of his own creative integrity—an analogue of his great-grandfather's personal integrity—Pushkin eludes the confinement imposed on him by what he implies to be an unlawful political order and suggests a longing not only for Africa but also for a monarch who could value him, who could win his loyalty, and against whom there would be no cause to rebel.

In "To Yazykov"("Yazykovu"), another poem written during his Mikhailovskoe exile, Pushkin similarly invokes his great-grandfather in protest at his own situation. The message he addresses to his fellow poet delineates the fundamentals of unfreedom and suggests that it is the monarch who makes the slave. Thus Pushkin's African great-grandfather who is a *pitomets* (foster child) to Peter the Great is regarded as but a *rab liubimyi* (favored slave) by the unnamed monarchs who follow Peter. In the period after Peter's reign—a debilitating period of problematic successions—the famous ward of the great tsar is exiled, rendered useless, and forgotten. Like his gifted African ancestor in post-Petrine times, so too Pushkin in the time of Alexander I finds himself at the mercy of autocratic whim which transforms potentially loyal and worthy subjects into threatening slaves. By means of the connection he establishes between himself and his great-grandfather, Pushkin condemns the arbitrary rule that debases both those who wield it and those who are subject to it. At the same time, the ties Pushkin establishes with Gannibal enable him to proclaim his freedom from the here and now and to shake off the restrictions imposed on him by the authorities as the Africa of his ancestor is once again aligned with the creative imagination—the warmer, more hospitable elsewhere well beyond the reach of tsarist police that is the poet's rightful home. "His" African homeland hearkens back to an ideal state that antedates enslavement and which, although no longer accessible literally, becomes the destination of metaphysical poetic flight. Realized in Pushkin's African references is the liberating force of individual creativity—both as it is enacted in the process of writing and as it remains encoded in his verse.

Pushkin repeatedly engages his African forebears in self-presentations that challenge the authorities and assert his personal and creative independence, as he draws on Gannibal to generate statements that throw his own political difficulties into relief and point more broadly to the larger problem of asserting personal liberty within an inimical setting. Yet even as Pushkin synchronizes Gannibal's past with his own present to generate his self-assertive statements, he opens himself to scurrilous attack. Neither the sympathy that the plight of the American slave aroused among liberal nobles nor the nobility acceded the "savage" in accord with Rousseau could eradicate completely the contempt aroused by the demeaning social status of slave. Pushkin was referred to as "*afrikanets*" by friends and enemies alike, but the latter gave a pejorative twist to this distinctive feature of his genealogy, using it to barb epigrams and satires directed against him. Pushkin, who, as we have seen, had recourse to metaphorical manifestations of freedom, responded with a redefinition of enslavement, one that moved the concept from the concrete world into the ethical. From this perspective he maintained that literal bondage denigrated the enslaver, not the enslaved, and that it was the slave mentality that was despicable and not the state of being held captive against one's will. In a five-stanza "Post Scriptum" appended to "My Genealogy" ("Moia rodoslovnaia"), Pushkin replies to a scurrilous squib in which Faddei Bulgarin—in transparent reference to Pushkin's ancestry—writes of a slave purchased for a bottle of rum. Turning the tables on his would-be detractor, Pushkin asserts that although his African forebear was indeed *kuplennyi* ("purchased"), he proved to be *nepodkupen* ("incorruptible"). It is one thing to be sold, but another to sell out.

Pushkin composed *The Blackamoor of Peter the Great* (*Arap Petra Ve-

The Pushkin of *Opportunity* in the Harlem Renaissance

likogo), a fictional tale based on his maternal great-grandfather, in 1827. It is no coincidence that he wrote "The Poet and the Mob" ("Poet i tolpa") in the same year, for this lyric emphatically connects slavery not with imposed bondage, but with a state of mind. The definition of slavery that emerges in this poem hinges on a complacent, narrow-minded rootedness in the here and now, opposed to which is the genuine freedom of poetic inspiration that we have seen Pushkin align repeatedly with his African ancestry. Enslaved by exclusively pragmatic concerns (*rab nuzhdy, zabot*—"slave to need and cares"), the *chern'* ("mob") remains insensible to the poet's creative flights of imagination and demands that he use his lyre for concrete ends. The mob that the poet confronts here remains complacent in its mercantilism and pragmatism, forms of slavery that Pushkin attributes directly to the absence of imaginative faculties. Pushkin's conviction that the creative imagination remains the most powerful manifestation of genuine freedom was reaffirmed in "The Poet and the Mob" and continued to inform his writings as ever more constraints closed in around him.

Lest Pushkin's interjection of a personal, poetic dimension into the large and troubling issue of human bondage seem self-centered or frivolous, we must remember that Pushkin's public insistence on his African blood specifically in connection with his assertions of individual creative freedom became a compelling source of enablement—one on which African Americans drew during the Harlem Renaissance and in which they continue to engage to the present day.[12] A century after Pushkin referred to "my Negro brothers" in his letter to Viazemsky, his fraternity with disenfranchised African Americans was fully realized when, on the strength of his distinctive genealogy, the Russian poet became a participant in the Harlem Renaissance, a heady cultural movement that, in the words of one historian, "succeeded in laying the foundation for all subsequent depictions in poetry, fiction, and drama of the modern African American experience."[13] What I have said thus far of the meaning Pushkin himself attached to his African heritage has prepared us to recognize the profound appropriateness of this seemingly improbable coalition. In the struggle that the African American intelligentsia launched in the face of ignominious constraints, we find an alignment of the creative imagination with the exercise of individual freedom and the assertion of personal dignity that is fully in keeping with Pushkin's philosophy. In the literary endeavors of African American writers of this period we find a complex interrelation of culture, politics, and racial identity that accords well with the dynamics of Pushkin's projections of an African self-image.

Like any significant cultural phenomenon, the Harlem Renaissance was too complex and diverse to lend itself to strict, exhaustive definition. Cary Wintz describes it as "basically a psychology—a state of mind or an attitude—shared by a number of black writers and intellectuals who centered their activities around Harlem in the late 1920s and early 1930s." "There was no common bond," he explains, "of political or racial ideology, personal experience, background, or literary philosophy that united the various elements in the Renaissance. What they held in common was a sense of community, a feeling that they were all part of the same endeavor."[14] The cultural—rather than sociological or political—bias of the movement privileged individual self-expression over adherence to a particular ideology. The fruits of this self-expressivity were folded into a two-pronged plan designed to bolster confidence in and respect for the creative capacities of the African American individual and to create an overarching sense of cultural unity among the distinctive voices it encouraged.

It was not until the Harlem Renaissance that African American readers gained familiarity with Pushkin's life and work, but the poet had already been invoked in African American circles well before that movement.[15] Already in 1849, the anthology *Wheatley, Banneker, Horton,* which, in the words of Henry Louis Gates Jr., "sought to refute intellectual racism by the act of canon formation," noted Pushkin's achievements—together with those of Placido and Augustine—as part of an African tradition and thus also of the African American heritage.[16] Such multiculturalism became an important facet of the African American identity that was developed over the course of the Harlem Renaissance. Torn forcibly from their roots, African Americans needed to establish themselves in their present surroundings and yet also to connect with their origins and the African diaspora. At the same time, they sought not simply passive acceptance in a rapidly changing American culture, but an active role in its development. To this end, much attention was devoted to the language of African American self-expression and to the evolving cultural identity of the United States in general and of the African American writer in particular. It was thus highly relevant to the African American cause that Pushkin was credited with developing both a literary language and a cultural identity for Russia. Indeed, the fact that a writer of African descent had played a crucial role in establishing a Russian literary tradition provided an example of the fruitful assimilation of African roots into national identity. It is scarcely surprising in our increasingly multicultural world that the question of such assimilation remains central and that Pushkin continues to be of interest to African scholars in precisely this regard. Thus, for example, Molefi Kete Asante, writing on the bicentennial of Pushkin's birth, explains:

> I am interested in him as a Russian of mixed heritage, African and European, who activated an entire nation with the eloquence of his poetry as in *Eugene Onegin* and other lyrical works. This is not merely a biological interest, but a cultural one inasmuch as Pushkin was evidently visibly of African descent. Nevertheless, he captured Russian sentiments and myths and created the most fundamental literature of his age.[17]

Although shared African blood was the point of origin for African American interest in Pushkin, this interest soon led beyond questions of racial origin to the broader social, cultural, and political contexts in which African American identity was to be defined. It was not only because Pushkin had African blood, but because he championed individual freedom in a socially and politically inimical climate that he became important. I have noted already that within a Eurocentric context Russia and the United States saw their marginal status as a common bond. For the African American, the affinity with Russia was clearly focused: "The tsarist Russian and American black intelligentsia have also shared an intense sense of alienation, because they compare their respective societies to others considered more advanced and free."[18] The similarities between American slavery and Russian serfdom were obvious, but for the Harlem Renaissance, a movement spearheaded by a group of intellectuals, another resemblance suggested itself: "Black American intellectuals can instinctively relate to the plight of the Russian intelligentsia in so many of its facets. There is a direct parallel in DuBois's notion of the 'talented tenth,' and in the need to speak for and raise up a largely rural, uneducated mass population."[19] The responsibility that the elite ought rightly to assume for the less fortunate was projected onto Pushkin, making him a champion of the oppressed masses. The poet's well-documented calls for personal freedom were seen to apply, by extension, to disenfranchised social orders. In the 1920s and 1930s, this image—and I will have more to say on this subject—was actively promoted by Soviet propaganda targeted specifically at African Americans.

In the early stages of the Harlem Renaissance, Pushkin was still relatively little known in the United States, and the African American community was in the vanguard of his discoverers. The review of Ernest J. Simmons's biography of the Russian poet in the April edition of the *Journal of Negro History* in 1937, the centennial of Pushkin's death, noted the paucity both of works about Pushkin and of translations of his poetry then available to the English-speaking public. By this time, however, the Russian poet figured importantly in the pages of *Opportunity*. In the remainder of this essay I will consider specific representations of Pushkin that appeared in this important journal, in order to provide concrete examples of his engagement in the broad areas I have delineated thus far.

Opportunity: A Journal of Negro Life, as it was titled in full, was published continuously from January 1923 through the winter of 1949. It was the official organ of the National Urban League, an interracial organization devoted to improving the condition of urban African Americans. The two closely interrelated meanings carried by the motto of *Opportunity*, which read "not alms but opportunity," captured the spirit of the Harlem Renaissance. To begin with, it indicated that African Americans were to take an active role in creating their own opportunities and making responsible use of them. Second, it suggested that members of this sector of American society had something of value to contribute to the culture by which they had been marginalized. The journal was thus to be seen as offering opportunity not only for developing African American writers, but also for the developing culture of the United States. The point was to draw on individual creativity in order to raise African American consciousness—individual and collective—and in so doing to challenge prevalent notions about race that upheld the segregation of Americans of African descent.

The editor of *Opportunity* for the crucial five and a half years of its Harlem Renaissance period was the World War I veteran Charles S. Johnson, the chief promoter of the Renaissance who is credited by Langston Hughes with having done "more to encourage and develop Negro writers during the 1920s than anyone else in America."[20] There had been but little African American fiction and poetry in print before the Harlem Renaissance, and Johnson made it his mission to rectify this situation. The significance of literature to the African American cause was widely recognized by prominent figures who came to be associated with the Renaissance. Like James Weldon Johnson, who maintained that "no race can ever become great that has not produced a literature,"[21] so too, Charles S. Johnson insisted that a flourishing African American cultural movement was "an effective means of combating racism and advancing the political objectives of the black race."[22] Nor did the importance of the material side of the enterprise escape him. As the poet Arna Bontemps summarizes, Johnson "promptly detected a relationship between artistic labors and the doctrine of useful, gainful employment as built into the aims of the Urban League."[23] Accordingly, Johnson devoted considerable energy to stimulating a much-needed market for the new literature and to serving as a liaison between African American writers and white publishers. It was to this end that Johnson instituted a series of literary contests and banquets that became a moving force on the Harlem literary scene, launching the careers of young writers and drawing the high quality of their achievements to the attention of the public. His purpose in establishing the contests was not to stimulate propaganda or protest, but to foster serious literature that would develop increased awareness of African American life and the creative potential of African Americans.

At the same time, Johnson sought "to bring these writers into contact with the general world of letters to which they have been for the most part timid and inarticulate strangers."[24] It is specifically in this vital area that Pushkin was invoked. The Russian poet was a highly appropriate model in two ways. To begin with, as a writer of African descent who was credited with shaping Russian cultural identity, Pushkin demonstrated the feasibility of the larger cultural agenda of the Harlem Renaissance. At the same time, the fact that his

The Pushkin of *Opportunity* in the Harlem Renaissance

personal biography included public avowals of African blood and a struggle for personal freedom made him an ideal model for individual writers. It was thus fitting that Pushkin's name should be invoked both to stimulate African American creativity and to bring it to the attention of a wide reading public.

In 1925 *Opportunity* sponsored a round of literary contests with precisely these ends in mind. The enterprise was hailed as a tremendous success: "It marked, rather dramatically, the awakening of artistic effort among the newer Negroes," announced *Opportunity,* adding, "The world is hearing more of this sector of American life than it ever thought existed."[25] One of the judges of the 1925 contests was the white novelist Edna Worthley Underwood, a prolific translator who was instrumental in bringing a sizable body of world literature to an English-speaking public and who did much to introduce Pushkin to the readers of *Opportunity.* Her enthusiastic assessment of the entries she judged led her to speak of "the entrance into the domain of art of a new race, differently dowered, but with something we can not well do without. In the future we must learn to look—more and more—to the black races for art, because joy—its mainspring—is dying so rapidly now in the Great Caucasian Race."[26] Though it was not without its problems, the idea that an anemic American culture could be revitalized by an infusion of African blood suggested new possibilities to many cultural leaders.

In light of the success of the contests—for *Opportunity* received no fewer than 800 entries "from nearly every state in the union"[27]—Casper Holstein, resident of New York and president of the Virgin Islands Congressional Council, pledged funds to expand and continue such literary competitions. The announcement of his pledge underscored the twofold mission of the journal to encourage individual writers and to make a cultural statement to the surrounding world:

> Encouraged by the remarkable record of these young writers in their first impassioned effort at self expression, Mr. Casper Holstein . . . has exactly doubled his original gift, making possible an increase in the awards and further funds for reaching an even greater number of writers. This is a faith and service deserving of more than casual appreciation. A Negro who is by no means a millionaire has faith enough in the future of his own developing race to give of his means to encourage it.[28]

Among the additional categories Holstein's largesse made possible was the Alexander Pushkin Poetry Prize. The terms in which this category is announced leave no doubt as to the high esteem in which the Russian poet was held: "This section is expected to call forth the most ambitious and most mature work of the Negro poet, and it is requested that to this section only the best work be sent."[29]

It was perhaps no coincidence that the October 1925 issue of *Opportunity* that announced the Pushkin Poetry Prize also carried "The light of day grew pale and paler—died," Edna Worthley Underwood's excellent translation of Pushkin's lyric "Pogaslo dnevnoe svetilo." Thematically this lyric was very much in harmony with the journal's efforts to encourage aspiring African American writers. The romantic elsewhere of poetic inspiration for which the persona of the poem longs is closely identified with the distant shores of what might easily be read as Pushkin's African homeland. Implicit in this identification is that rather than impede his self-expression, Pushkin's African blood enables it. Indeed, as was repeatedly suggested, Pushkin was a genius of universal stature not in spite of his African lineage, but because of it. It was the breadth he gained from the conjunction of African blood and Russian nationality that made Pushkin truly great. Thus, by implication, African Americans similarly stood to gain much from the confluence of their African heritage and their American nationality.

When the Pushkin Prize was first announced in October 1925, the Russian poet's name was already familiar to readers of *Opportunity*. The February 1924 issue had carried a biographical sketch of the poet Alexis Sergiewitch Pushkin (sic) written by Edna Worthley Underwood, whose translation of *Arap Petra Velikogo*, "The Negro of Peter the Great," was published serially in the February, March, and April issues of that year. Underwood records Pushkin's genealogy at the opening of her biographical sketch without placing particular emphasis on it. The portrait of Pushkin that was published next to Underwood's biographical sketch is one in which Pushkin looks far less "African" than those we are accustomed to seeing. This rather low-key treatment of Pushkin's racial profile was in keeping with the overall program of the Harlem Renaissance, which sought to achieve what George E. Kent describes as "a dissociation of sensibility from that enforced by American culture and its institutions," but to do so without lapsing into the propaganda and self-isolationism against which Charles S. Johnson repeatedly cautioned.[30] The Pushkin that Underwood presented to readers of *Opportunity* was a genius who could not be contained by racial or national boundaries. This was a writer who asserted himself as an individual in an inimical political environment and amongst what Underwood describes as the "dissipated and frivolous courtiers, who looked down with something of contempt upon his poet's calling and who were unable rightly to estimate his intellectual worth."[31] In the context of the Harlem Renaissance, this vivid example of a gifted individual faring badly at the hands of a distinctly inferior group urged aspiring African American writers to look beyond their immediate detractors with self-assurance as they worked to realize their own potential. Such agency is further promoted in the suggestion that Pushkin was largely self-taught. Underwood devotes considerable attention to the remarkable breadth of

The Pushkin of *Opportunity* in the Harlem Renaissance

influences that Pushkin absorbed: his famous Russian nanny, Voltaire, Rousseau, the French Encyclopedists he "devoured" at the age of nine in his grandfather's library, Byron, Goethe, and Shakespeare.

Although Underwood notes Pushkin's difficulties with the authorities, she chooses to focus on the benefits that he was able to derive from his enforced banishment to Mikhailovskoe. "The two years of enforced solitude spent here," she writes, "had a salutary influence upon his excitable and stormy nature, taught him in some measure, self-control, which he greatly needed, and helped to ripen and perfect his genius."[32] In the detail of the poet's "excitable and stormy nature" we recognize an "African" trait that was first broadcast in Shakespeare's *Othello* and that subsequently remained a constant of African stereotypes.[33] The Pushkin who emerges from Underwood's account is a Russian writer of world stature who has African blood, who freely assimilates a broad variety of national cultures, and who, far from succumbing to harsh treatment, turns to good stead the regrettable limitations imposed on him by the tsarist government. And this portrait is in full harmony with the cultural program of the Harlem Renaissance that neither segregates aspiring African American writers from world literature by focusing exclusively on race nor limits the form of their self-expression to tirades against the limitations imposed on them by American society.

Underwood's biographical sketch introduces Pushkin's own account of his African ancestry in the prose piece Underwood translates as "The Negro of Peter the Great." In this historical romance, Underwood explains, "it was Pushkin's intention to tell the true life story of his great-grandfather, the Abyssinian Negro who, by his bravery and fine intelligence, won the favor of Russia's cruel and capricious ruler."[34] The October 1923 issue of the *Journal of Negro History* had already carried Albert Parry's article "Abram Hannibal, the Favorite of Peter the Great," which, as its title suggests, was devoted to Pushkin's remarkable ancestor.[35] Chronicled in this essay is the life of a man who began, as Parry summarizes, "under yoke in Africa but died a general and wealthy landlord of the frozen North, leaving his children and grandchildren to be prominent in the politics and literature of Russia."[36] Like Parry's essay on Gannibal, so too, Underwood's biographical sketch of Pushkin urges not the overthrow of a sociopolitical system, but rather the individual creative self-affirmation that can overcome the limitations imposed by that system. It insists too on the self-mastery and self-fulfillment that are necessary to such an enterprise.

Underwood's translation of "The Negro of Peter the Great" brought to the readership of *Opportunity* the text that Parry recommended as the best source available on Gannibal. That this text was a fictionalized account of Gannibal's life mattered less than the fact that it presented a rags-to-riches story of a historical figure who had much to offer African American readers.

The "Ibragim" of Pushkin's narrative exemplifies native intelligence, integrity, and diligence—qualities that win him a place of honor in the Russian court and in the heart of Russia's formidable ruler. His deep-seated sense of honor and duty and his loyalty to the tsar are seen in everything he does. For his part, the "cruel and capricious" autocrat rightly earns this loyalty precisely because he denies Ibragim neither the freedom nor the opportunity to develop his innate capacities. With this model of mutual respect between the Caucasian ruler and his African subject, Pushkin, as we have seen, projected his own ideal of individual liberty and the ideal state. In Pushkin's representation, the sterling qualities of his ancestor are only one half of the equation. The responsibility for supplying the second half falls squarely on others who must prove capable of perceiving his gifts. (We have seen already that Pushkin applies this equation also to the poet and the milieu in which his work is received.) In *The Blackamoor of Peter the Great* only Peter—and this is what makes him truly great—is capable of appreciating Ibragim fully. Ibragim, for all his innate gifts and unprecedented rise to glory, experiences also the alienation of an African in a white society, for there are few like Peter the Great who rise above prejudice to recognize his exceptional personal qualities.

Ibragim's story, like Pushkin's own identification with his African forebear, carried, as we have seen, considerable political significance in the Russia of Nicholas I. In the context of a segregated American society, the life of Gannibal resonated once again and with particular urgency. Both the larger cultural context of the Harlem Renaissance and the more immediate context created by Underwood's introductory biographical sketch suggested a reading that brought Pushkin's text close to home. Considered within the framework of the Renaissance, the unfinished tale Pushkin based on his African ancestor offered an entire series of axioms that were central to Pushkin himself and that were now cogent to his "Negro brothers," who could recognize in Gannibal's story a concrete realization of the enabling strategies promoted by leaders of the Harlem Renaissance. Individual strength and personal integrity make it possible to overcome externally imposed restrictions, while a sense of personal dignity can offset the sense of alienation. An individual or a society that allows perceived difference to interfere with the appreciation of a person's merit demonstrates only its own uncontestable inferiority. The creative imagination provides the surest path to self-affirmation and the attainment of inner freedom under even the harshest of circumstances.

Warrington Hudlin states that the philosophy of the Harlem Renaissance "in essence rested on a single axiom: It will be necessary for blacks to change their perspective of their selves before whites will change their image of them."[37] Through the agency of *Opportunity*, Pushkin and his great-grandfather were engaged to change the perspective of both sides. Gannibal and especially the great-grandson who recorded his life emerged as models that remain vital to this day.

Thus, almost two centuries after Pushkin's death and seventy years after the Harlem Renaissance, John Oliver Killens's *Great Black Russian: A Novel on the Life and Times of Alexander Pushkin* shows us how closely this major African American novelist identifies with the Russian poet, while the prominent Afrocentric scholar Molefi Kete Asante lauds Pushkin for what he continues to teach marginalized groups:

> If there is one lesson to be learned from the centeredness and agency of Pushkin it must be that regardless of the environmental and social conditions of our lives we can always rise to the challenge of transforming ourselves and the world in which we live. Even in this lesson we see the energizing and flourishing of the most African of all attributes, the creative science of effective human relationships.[38]

While we cannot objectively evaluate the inspiration young African American writers might have drawn from Underwood's biographical sketch and her translations of Pushkin's works, the poetry prize established in his name inspired the composition of many hundreds of lyrics by aspiring African American poets who entered the contest. The winner of the first round in 1926 was Arna Bontemps, whose "Golgotha Is a Mountain" was selected by a panel of judges that included William Rose Benet, William Stanley Braithwaite, Witter Bynner, Robert Frost, James Weldon Johnson, Alain Locke, Vachel Lindsay, and Clement Wood. Bontemps, whose poem "The Return" won him the Pushkin Prize for a second time the following year (1927), described his decision to enter the competition in terms that clearly reflect its significance for beginning writers: "I took my courage in my hands, and my life has never been the same since."[39] Although there is no evidence in Bontemps's writings that his knowledge of Pushkin extended beyond what might have been gleaned from the pages of *Opportunity,* the career of this major African American writer who became a leading figure in the Renaissance was successfully launched by the prize he was awarded in the Russian poet's name.

Precisely when the Harlem Renaissance came to an end remains in dispute among scholars. Some designate the stock market crash of 1929 as its terminus, others cite the Harlem race riots of 1935 as signaling its end, while others still insist that it persisted, albeit with some breaks, into the 1960s.[40] In any event *Opportunity* continued its publication through the winter of 1949, and although a decade had passed since the last Pushkin Prize was awarded, the February 1937 issue marked the 100th anniversary of Pushkin's death with Guichard Parris's tribute "In Honor of Alexander Pushkin: 1799–1837."[41]

The essay opens with an impressive list of festivities planned in both the United States and the Soviet Union to mark the centenary of Pushkin's death. Parris's note that he "is indebted to Soviet government reports for this information,"[42] reminds us that even as African Americans were deriving creative support from their distant but sympathetic Russian model, the government of his native land was promoting him for its own political ends. The U.S.S.R. Society for Cultural Relations (Vsesoiuznoe obshchestvo kul'turnoi sviazi s zagranitsei; VOKS), which came into being in April 1925, had its own agenda as it readily supplied materials intended to familiarize African Americans with Pushkin, who was revered as the greatest of all Russian poets and who was of African descent. Here was a golden opportunity to claim that the racial prejudice, discrimination, and cultural marginalization to which African Americans were subjected in the United States were not to be found in enlightened Soviet society. The flow of African Americans from the rural South into urban centers in the North and the riots that shook major cities in the early twentieth century were powerful manifestations of a newly emerging working class that seemed rife for indoctrination into the Marxist cause. In this context, Pushkin suggested a possible link between Soviet Russia and urban African Americans. The Russian futurist poet Vladimir Mayakovsky, one of several writers who represented VOKS during his journeys abroad, drew attention to this possibility in "My Discovery of America" ("Moe otkrytie Ameriki"), his travel account of a visit to the United States in 1926:

> Recently the Negro publisher Caspar Holstein announced a one-hundred-dollar prize in the name of the greatest Negro poet, A. S. Pushkin, for the best Negro poem.
> The prize will be awarded 1 May 1926.
> Why shouldn't the Negroes consider Pushkin one of their own writers? After all even now Pushkin would not be admitted into a single "decent" hotel or living room in New York. After all Pushkin had kinky hair and a Negro bluishness under his nails.
> When the so-called scales of history dip, a lot will depend on which side the 12 million Negroes put their 24 million weighty hands. The Negroes heated over Texas bonfires provide gun powder that is dry enough for explosions of revolution.[43]

Even a hundred years after Pushkin's death, the political authorities of his homeland still had their eye on him and still sought to bend him to their own purposes.

Parris's assertion that "for Pushkin political liberty was intimately bound up with the freedom of the peasant, and the desire of a general amelioration of social conditions required a union of all classes against social injustices" must surely have come from a "Soviet government report."[44] Yet it is clear from Parris's conclusion that Pushkin's works take him beyond the narrow confines of Soviet politics. Modestly noting his own lack of expertise in Russian literature, Parris, who obviously did a good bit of research in preparing his essay, perceptively observes that, "as one reads the criticisms on Pushkin's works, one becomes a bit puzzled at the divergent and sometimes totally opposite views that are expressed regarding his social philosophy." "But," he continues, "anyone with a not too biased mind who is at all familiar with Pushkin's own writings will not do him the injustice of putting a special party label upon him. His many-sidedness is the one certain indication of his universal genius."[45] In this regard Parris shows himself to be a model reader of Pushkin's poetry. Apparently the Soviets were mistaken in their decision to incorporate Pushkin into their propaganda machine, for his poetry opened minds where they sought to close them. A brief digression from the pages of *Opportunity* provides another telling example in this vein.

The African American journalist Homer Smith conducted extensive research on Pushkin and interviewed the poet's surviving descendants during his sojourn in Russia in the 1930s and 1940s. (Among other things, Smith researched Pushkin's ancestry in an attempt to disprove assertions by scholars such as E. J. Simmons that Pushkin was Abyssinian and therefore not black.) Receiving no answer to his question of how Pushkin would have reacted to the Soviet regime, he arrived at his own conclusion that the poet "would have been too much of a freedom lover to like it."[46] Yet this is not to say that the great Soviet socialist experiment failed to attract significant attention from African Americans. In the 1930s, the revolutionary social and political goals of African Americans "were associated almost exclusively with communism."[47]

Like Underwood's biographical sketch, Parris's essay on Pushkin highlights the poet's broad cultural background, his commitment to individual liberty, and his pride in his African ancestors. Parris, however, places far greater emphasis on Pushkin's African lineage and focuses particular attention on its relevance to the African American cause:

> The nation-wide observance of this centenary should be of particular interest to the American Negro and it may very appropriately serve to direct his attention to some of the intellectual and literary contributions of the *Occidentalized* African or his descendants to the common fund of human progress and culture. Pushkin was a Negro.[48]

Both Pushkin and his illustrious African forebear are now drawn not into African American consciousness-raising, but into a direct struggle against racism, a circumstance that reflects the growing frustration of the African American intelligentsia and the increasing politicization of the cultural agenda of the Harlem Renaissance. What was implicit in earlier descriptions of Pushkin is now made explicit in forceful terms:

The amazing intellectual development of Hannibal in Paris, his brilliant career at the court of Peter and later the distinguished contribution of his great grandson to the world of letters should eradicate from the prejudiced mind the thought that the African and his descendants are, by nature, incapable of the highest mental exercise."[49]

Parris's tribute to Pushkin was preceded on the pages of the February 1927 issue of *Opportunity* by two reviews that similarly emphasized the Russian poet's race. The first of these was Elbert Aidline-Trommer's "'Alexander Pushkin' and Alexander Pushkin," a review of Maurice Schwartz's Yiddish Art Theater production of Valentine Carrera's play *Alexander Pushkin*. Writing the play off as a "silly, ridiculous pseudo-Pushkin melodrama," Aidline-Trommer devotes the bulk of his review to Pushkin's life and African ancestry in terms suggestive of the changing mood of the Harlem Renaissance.[50] Hailing the poet as a "sweet singer and martyr of Freedom," Aidline-Trommer credits him with bringing "the fire of his Negro ancestry" to the "altar of Russian letters."[51] Visible here is a shift from the earlier emphasis on the poet's universal, many-faceted genius to what were regarded as his expressly African traits. The second review was devoted to Natalie Duddington's translation of *The Captain's Daughter*. The reviewer, Alice Dunbar Nelson, demonstrates an impressive command of Russian literature and provides a superb account of Pushkin's text and its place in the Russian tradition. She too focuses above all on the significance of the Russian poet to her own people. Her treatment of this aspect is far more direct and politicized than what we have seen in earlier representations of the poet.

The importance Pushkin's African blood had come to carry by 1937 is perhaps most forcefully expressed in the epigraph with which Parris opens his homage to the African Russian poet on the 100th anniversary of his death:

> To some it will be a surprise to learn that one of the great figures in world literature and the greatest of all the Russian poets had Negro blood and, according to American theories of race, was a Negro. What will be more surprising still to others is that he was proud of it.[52]

It must give us pause to realize that had Pushkin, a century after his death, appeared in the United States not on the pages of *Opportunity* but in the flesh, he would have been barred from all areas designated "for whites only" and subjected to incalculable indignities because of that African ancestor in whom he took such pride and whom he engaged in his own assertions of liberty. Yet it was also on the strength of that ancestor that Pushkin inspired in his African American brethren the very creativity that had been his own way to freedom. And it was on the strength of that ancestor that Alice Dunbar Nelson could proclaim:

> To the Americans of darker skin, Pushkin's name connotes more than a Russian poet and novelist. Pushkin is one of the gates of liberation of the race from the fetters which bind it earthward.[53]

Notes

1. Cary D. Wintz, *Black Culture and the Harlem Renaissance* (Houston: Rice University Press, 1988), 2.

2. Steven Nardi, "Expanding Cultural Spaces: James Weldon Johnson and Poetry as Palimpsest," in "Inciting Meter: Race, Music, and the Re-Invention of Aesthetics in the Harlem Renaissance" (Ph.D. diss., Princeton University), available at www.princeton.edu/~snardi/pdf/weldon.pdf (accessed October 2, 2001).

3. J. Thomas Shaw, "Pushkin on His African Heritage: Publications during His Lifetime," is reprinted in this volume.

4. For a study of representations of America in general and the issue of slavery in particular in the Russian press of the time, see Dieter Boden, *Das Amerikabild im russischen Schriftum bis zum Ende des 19. Jahrhunderts* (Hamburg: Cram, De Gruyter, 1968).

5. Boden, *Amerikabild*, 75.

6. See B. L. Modzalevskii, *Pushkin i ego sovremenniki: Biblioteka A. S. Pushkina* (Moscow: Izdatel'stvo Kniga, 1988).

7. M. Eremin, *Pushkin publitsist* (Moscow: Gosudarstvennoe izdatel'stvo khudozhestvennoi literatury, 1963), especially 278–80. For an extensive discussion of "John Tanner" and Pushkin's attitude toward America, see J. Thomas Shaw, "Pushkin on America: His 'John Tanner,'" in *Orbis Scriptus: Dmitrij Tschizewcskij zum 70 Geburtstag*, ed. Dietrich Gerhardt et al. (Munich: Wilhelm Fink, 1966), 739–56. Shaw provides a list of Pushkin's references to America and considers what sources might have been available to the poet.

8. Pushkin wrote the first chapter of *Eugene Onegin* in 1823, and the note to it in 1824. A summary of its publication history can be found in Shaw's essay, which is reprinted in this volume. For additional discussion of Pushkin's references to his African ancestors, see N. Teletova, "Afrikanskaia prarodina v tvorcheskom osoznanii Pushkina," in *Alexandre S. Pouchkine et le monde noir*, ed. Dieudonné Gnammankou (Paris: Présence Africaine, 1999), 53–62.

9. On this, see Teletova, "Afrikanskaia prarodina," 57–58.

10. Pushkin again compared Peter the Great and Alexander I, much to the latter's detriment, in his long poem *The Bronze Horseman*.

Olga P. Hasty

11. See Shaw's essay, reprinted in this volume.

12. Thus, for example, the contemporary scholar of African history Allison Blakely cites the passage from Pushkin's letter to Viazemskii in his discussion of Pushkin's significance to African American writers and artists. See his essay "John Oliver Killens's *Great Black Russian*: Afro-American Writers and Artists and the Pushkin Mystique," in Gnammankou, ed., *Alexandre S. Pouchkine,* 159–60.

13. Arnold Rampersad, introduction to *The New Negro: Voices of the Harlem Renaissance,* ed. Alain Locke (New York: Atheneum, 1992), xxii–xxiii.

14. Wintz, *Black Culture,* 2.

15. See Anne Lounsbery's essay in this volume.

16. Henry Louis Gates Jr., "Canon-Formation, Literary History, and the Afro-American Tradition: From the Seen to the Told," in *Afro-American Literary Study in the 1990s,* ed. Houston A. Baker Jr. and Patricia Redmond (Chicago: University of Chicago Press, 1989), 32.

17. Molefi Kete Asante, "The Cultural Location of Alexander S. Pushkin," in Gnammankou, ed., *Alexandre S. Pouchkine,* 64.

18. Blakely, "Killens's *Great Black Russian,*" 164.

19. Ibid., 163–64.

20. Langston Hughes, *The Big Sun: An Autobiography* (New York: Knopf, 1940), 218.

21. "The Opportunity Dinner," *Opportunity,* June 1925, 177.

22. Cited in Wintz, *Black Culture,* 123.

23. Arna Bontemps, "The Awakening: A Memoir," in *The Harlem Renaissance Remembered,* ed. Arna Bontemps (New York: Dodd, Mead, 1972), 9.

24. "An Opportunity for Negro Writers," *Opportunity,* September 1924, 258.

25. *Opportunity,* October 1925, 291.

26. *Opportunity,* May 1925, 130. For a cogent discussion of Worthley's assessment, see Nardi, "Expanding Cultural Spaces."

27. Ibid., October 1925, 291.

28. Ibid., 292.

29. Ibid., 309. The same wording announced the Pushkin Prize, which was offered the following year as well.

30. George E. Kent, "Patterns of the Harlem Renaissance," in Bontemps, ed., *Harlem Renaissance Remembered,* 9.

31. Edna Worthley Underwood, "Alexis Sergiewitch Pushkin," *Opportunity,* February 1924, 54.

32. Underwood, "Alexis Pushkin," 54.

33. The tenacity of this detail is well illustrated by the fact that it is still in place in John Oliver Killens's novel *Great Black Russian: A Novel on the Life*

and Times of Alexander Pushkin (Detroit: Wayne State University Press, 1989).

34. Underwood, "Alexis Pushkin," 54.

35. Albert Parry, "Abram Hannibal, the Favorite of Peter the Great," *Journal of Negro History,* October 1923, 350–66.

36. Parry, "Hannibal," 359.

37. Warrington Hudlin, "The Renaissance Re-Examined," in Bontemps, ed., *Harlem Renaissance Remembered,* 276.

38. Asante, "Cultural Location," 68.

39. Bontemps, "Awakening," 20.

40. Wintz, *Black Culture,* 1.

41. Guichard Parris, "In Honor of Alexander Pushkin: 1799–1837," *Opportunity,* February 1937, 48.

42. Parris, "In Honor of Pushkin," 48.

43. Vladimir Maiakovskii, "My Discovery of America," in *America through Russian Eyes,* ed. O. Hasty and S. Fusso (New Haven: Yale University Press, 1988), 194–95 (with slight adjustments to the translation).

44. Parris, "In Honor of Pushkin," 50.

45. Ibid.

46. This information on Homer Smith is drawn from Blakely, "Killens's *Great Black Russian,*" 161.

47. Arnold Rampersad, "Introduction to the 1992 Edition," in Arna Bontemps, *Black Thunder* (Boston: Beacon, 1992), xii.

48. Parris, "In Honor of Pushkin," 50.

49. Ibid., 49.

50. Elbert Aidline-Trommer, "'Alexander Pushkin' and Alexander Pushkin," *Opportunity,* August 1928, 241.

51. Aidline-Trommer, "'Alexander Pushkin' and Alexander Pushkin," 241.

52. Parris, "In Honor of Pushkin," 48.

53. Alice Dunbar Nelson, "*The Captain's Daughter* by Alexander Pushkin," *Opportunity,* January 1930, 25.

Anne Lounsbery

"Bound by Blood to the Race": Pushkin in African American Context

> Pushkin is a prophecy and a revelation.
> —Fyodor Dostoevsky, 1880
>
> Here we have Negro youth, with arresting visions and prophecies; forecasting in the mirror of art what we must see and recognize in the streets of reality tomorrow, foretelling in new notes and accents the maturing speech of full racial utterance.
> —Alain Locke, 1925
>
> Our literature will give us our very selves.
> —Nikolai Gogol, 1835
>
> My art will aid in giving the Negro to himself.
> —Jean Toomer, 1922

UNDER THE HEADING "Pushkin," the *Dictionary Catalog of the Schomburg Collection of Negro Literature and History* at the New York Public Library contains 118 entries. Some of these entries note that "The author was a Russian with Negro blood," while many state merely "Negro author."[1] The Schomburg Collection's impressive array of Pushkiniana—which includes everything from critical studies in Latvian to newspaper clippings and postage stamps commemorating various Pushkin jubilees—is only one testament to Pushkin's enduring presence in black American culture. Other examples abound. As early as 1899, in Charles Chesnutt's landmark collection of short stories, one snobbish character's mark of refinement is his ability to "give the pedigree of Alexander Pushkin."[2] By the 1920s, Pushkin had become more than a "pedigree" to be cited in defense of Negro intellect, as both his works and his biography were gradually incorporated into African American literary discourse. In 1925, *Opportunity* magazine, which was among the most important publications of the Harlem Renaissance of the 1920s and

"Bound by Blood to the Race"

1930s, instituted an annual Pushkin Prize to recognize outstanding poetry written by Negroes. In 1926 the first book-length study of Pushkin in English (published by the émigré Russian scholar Prince D. S. Mirsky) was reviewed in the black press in places both culturally and geographically remote from traditional centers of Russian literary study: in Muskogee, Oklahoma, for example, the African American newspaper *Weekly Progress* lauded Mirsky's work alongside news items of decidedly local interest.[3]

In the late 1930s the 100th anniversary of Pushkin's death consolidated his position in black American culture, helped along (though not totally propelled) by Soviet propaganda and news dispatches from black American journalists who had traveled to the U.S.S.R.[4] In February 1937, the 136th Street Library in Harlem exhibited works by and about Pushkin, as well as mementos recently acquired by Langston Hughes in the Soviet Union. That same month at the Harlem People's Bookshop, Pushkin's centennial was marked in conjunction with Frederick Douglass's birthday, in a celebration that included an "impressive window display" on the Russian poet and a "Pushkin-Douglass tea."[5] Pushkin remains a presence in black American culture today: what is probably the only standing exhibit on the Russian poet in the United States is located at the African-American Museum in Cleveland; the course catalog of Lincoln University, a historically black college in Pennsylvania, lists two classes devoted largely to Pushkin and the black experience; and discussions of Pushkin as a black writer occur regularly on the Internet. Perhaps most strikingly, the Russian national poet, in a 1983 comic book called *The Life of Alexander Pushkin*, merits inclusion in a series of comics devoted to black heroes.[6]

These examples should mitigate the surprise of the average Slavist upon learning that Pushkin is today, for many Americans, a black man. Just as these examples attest to Pushkin's long-standing prominence in black American culture, so the deceptively straightforward label that recurs in the Schomburg catalog ("Negro author") evokes the complexities of race and nationality that both African Americans and whites have confronted in writing about the national poet of Russia. This article will treat American texts that focus on Pushkin as a "Race writer," on the Pushkin who was, in the words of a black intellectual in 1904, "bound by blood to the race."[7] Most, though not all, of these writings were published by black Americans in the black press, and most were intended for a popular rather than a scholarly audience. By examining these texts' main themes, I hope to reveal how the figure of Pushkin was relevant to African American culture for reasons *including but not limited to* his race. My analysis will emphasize earlier writings (that is, those dating from approximately 1847 to 1946), both because these are generally less accessible than later works and because it is during this historical period that the figure of a multiracial genius was fraught with especially perilous significance in the American context. In the wry words that introduced the first English translation of Pushkin's brief biography of his African great-grandfather (published in a 1937 issue of W. E. B. DuBois's journal *The Crisis*), "An utterly fascinating topic to white Americans—indeed, to white people everywhere—is mixture of the races."[8]

While Russian culture allowed Pushkin to play with the idea of being African (and through such play to turn his heritage to his own advantage, aesthetic and psychological), it is abundantly clear that for Americans who write about Pushkin, race is no game. In fact, in two American novels based on Pushkin's life, racial identity has the power to write the scripts of characters' lives even as "race" as a category eludes (or actively confounds) clear definition. One of these novels was published in 1922 by a white woman, Edna Worthley Underwood; the other was published in 1989 by a black man, John Killens. Underwood's and Killens's agendas could hardly be more different, but both writers represent race as the key to both Pushkin's identity and his genius. As a result their work illuminates important ways in which Pushkin has long been used to focus an American discourse about race, a discourse which began in the black and abolitionist press in the mid-nineteenth century and continues to develop today. While my primary focus will be the recurrent themes of these journalistic writings, I will conclude with a look at Killens's and Underwood's versions of Pushkin's life, the distortions of which reveal the persistent power of racial categories to shape Americans' understanding of a Russian poet.

While this paper treats African American ideas about Pushkin, it is not concerned to trace the sources of these ideas (sources which will often be clear to any Slavist, particularly those familiar with Soviet literary propaganda), nor to indict American texts which at times rehearse clichés of Pushkin criticism or embroider upon the facts of Pushkin's life. I am interested, rather, in the Pushkin who emerges from African American writings. For example, a black journalist writing in 1932 gleefully imagines that the racist southerner Edgar Allan Poe (who in fact never went to Russia) traveled to St. Petersburg to pay tribute to Pushkin, only to be shocked to find that the Russian poet was black. Pushkin would have challenged the lowly foreigner to a duel, the story goes, but Russian aristocrats did not duel with their social inferiors.[9] What are we to make of such inventions? Similarly, what does it mean to celebrate Alexander Pushkin alongside Frederick Douglass in 1937, or to write about Prince Mirsky in Muskogee, Oklahoma, in 1926? Clearly, such pairings imply a Pushkin who is new to many readers, and it is this Pushkin I hope to illuminate.

Pushkin's place in African American culture cannot be understood without first understanding the role played by writing and high culture in nineteenth-century efforts to defend the basic humanity of black people. In 1848 the black intellectual Wilson Armistead published a book with a formidable title that reveals the burden that accomplished individuals of African descent were made to bear in arguments for abolition: *A Tribute for the Negro. Being a Vindication of the Moral, Intellectual and Religious Capabilities of the Coloured Portion of Mankind with Particular Reference to the African Race, Illustrated by Numerous Biographical Sketches, Facts, Anecdotes, etc. and Many Superior Portraits and Engravings.*[10] Books like Armistead's aimed—in the words of William Wells Brown, who wrote one of the genre's influential examples—to marshal evidence of the "genius, capacity, and intellectual development" of black people so as to refute "calumniators and traducers of the Negro."[11] Pushkin's great-grandfather, Abram Gannibal, was a staple of such texts. His name appeared in the African American press as early as 1828, when the first black newspaper in the United States, *Freedom's Journal,* published a brief account of his achievements, a paragraph which was republished in *The Anti-Slavery Record* in 1837 and again in *The Colored American* in 1839. (*Freedom's Journal* identifies this passage as an extract from an influential antislavery treatise of the eighteenth century written by the French cleric Henri Gregoire, a treatise which appeared in America first in 1810 and later in various other translations. Most early American texts that describe Gannibal probably used Gregoire as their source.)[12]

The story of Gannibal, a brilliant military tactician and engineer who was free to rise in a society unburdened by "color prejudice," clearly served to bolster abolitionist arguments for blacks' innate ability. A literary genius, however, was far more useful to the cause of abolition—and, after emancipation, to the struggle for equality—than the most brilliant general or courtier. The very act of writing, and especially the writing of literature, had come to play a peculiarly significant role in Western ideas of race and "civilization." As Henry Louis Gates Jr. has chronicled, since the Renaissance "the act of writing has been considered the visible sign of reason," the primary means of demonstrating both the selfhood of an individual and the history of a collective.[13] Africans and black slaves, the story went, had not written because they were not fully human: "Without writing, there could exist no *repeatable* sign of the workings of reason, of mind; without memory or mind, there could exist no history; without history, there could exist no 'humanity,' as was defined consistently from Vico to Hegel."[14]

Gates insists on the strangeness of the belief that literacy is a necessary sign of humanity, but he also points out that blacks themselves long accepted this idea.[15] A great many African Americans, beginning with the scores of escaped slaves whose life narratives provided one key foundation for the black literary tradition, wrote with the urgency of people who were being required to demonstrate their own humanity to whites through the creation of literary art. Thus in the words of the black intellectual Daniel Murray, writing in 1904, we hear an echo of German historicism, with its emphasis on a collective cultural memory essential to civilization and achievable only through writing: "Every nation is estimated largely by its literature, and justly so, since it is the only means by which distant people can properly judge. Have they produced anything in the literary line worthy of recognition and preservation? That is the test. If they have, . . . we may justly assign them to their proper place in the ranks of civilization." "Semi-barbarous and semi-savage people," on the other hand, "may be unerringly identified by the little progress exhibited in the formation of a literature."[16] Compare Katherine Tillman (another American intellectual of African descent), writing in 1898: "Let no man who loves the Negro race then decry poetry, for it is by this and other proofs of genius that our race will take its place among the nations of the earth."[17]

Both Murray and Tillman point to Pushkin as evidence of blacks' capacity for literary creation, and their statements help explain why Pushkin's name began to appear in the American press as soon as he became known to blacks and abolitionists.[18] The most notable piece of antebellum writing on Pushkin was published in 1847 by John Greenleaf Whittier, a white abolitionist. Whittier's essay, which appeared in the abolitionist newspaper *The National Era*, seems to have been the first information about Pushkin to reach a substantial audience in the United States.[19] Whittier acknowledges as his source the British periodical *Blackwoods Magazine*, which had published two articles on Pushkin's life in 1846. Whittier's essay focuses less on Pushkin's literary achievements (which are the main focus of the *Blackwoods* pieces) than on his impressive standing in Russian society and that society's willingness to honor a man who "bore, in his personal appearance and mental characteristics, the most unequivocal marks" of his African origins. Both the poet's accomplishments and his high social status are adduced to "[expose] the utter folly and injustice of the common prejudice against color in this country" and to demonstrate "the intellectual capacity of the colored man." Pushkin is represented as "the favorite alike of Emperor and people," "so honored, so lamented" by "the wealthy, the titled, [and] the gifted of St. Petersburg," all of whom gather to pay tribute to the poet on his deathbed.

Whittier's chief observations were to recur for years in the black press's treatment of Pushkin; the poet's own pride in his African descent, the respect he enjoyed at all levels of Russian society, and his achievement, in *Eugene Onegin*, of "the fullest and most complete embodiment of the nationality of the country" all became staples of African American writings on Pushkin. Interestingly, however, the mainstream (white, nonabolitionist) press emphasized different facets of the poet's life and attributed his distinctive personality and achievements to an entirely different set of influences. Besides Whittier's article, I have found two others on Pushkin in the American antebellum press, both of them reprinted from British publications in the 1850s. In these texts, both of which appeared in nonabolitionist publications, the poet's race is not emphasized. While one notes in Pushkin "a certain smack of rough, genuine, healthy savagery," the author attributes this "savagery" not to Pushkin's African blood (the "unmistakable impress" of which is nevertheless acknowledged) but rather to his "boyar" origins. Similarly, Pushkin's inability to control his "fiery passions" is ascribed to the "semi-barbarism" of the *Russian* nation, the nation whose "awakening song" he was destined to bring forth. The other article describes Pushkin in similar terms, calling him "the most universal and at the same time the most national of [Russia's] writers," and again attributing his combination of brilliance and carelessness to "the national [i.e., the Russian] character."[20]

Until the turn of the twentieth century when translations and critical studies of Russian works began to reach more American readers, most references to Pushkin remained unsupported by significant knowledge of his works. The Russian poet long remained, as the critic and historian Benjamin Brawley has written, "merely a name" for black intellectuals—but an important name nonetheless.[21] Pushkin's name and biography were important not simply because he was "black," but because at the time when most of the texts that are the focus of this study were being written, America was a culture obsessed with racial classification, a culture capable of producing legally binding mathematical formulae for determining a person's race and thus his or her social fate. White American institutions (legal, educational, medical, "scientific") were obsessively focused on defining and quantifying race with the clear purpose of segregating "coloreds" from "whites" and maintaining the subordination of people of African descent. American racial laws, notoriously complex and contradictory, would have classified Pushkin variously as mulatto, octoroon, or simply Negro or white.[22] But as African American writers pointed out even before 1900, these legal niceties meant little compared to the basic fact of appearance, which in Pushkin's case would very likely have required him to live as a "black" person. As Katherine Tillman wrote in 1909, "in our country [Pushkin] would be classed a Negro."[23] In 1929 the *Amsterdam News* (a black newspaper in New York) noted that "in America Pushkin would have to ride in dirty Jim Crow cars, would have been refused service in restaurants, libraries and theaters. For Pushkin was a Negro."[24]

Black Americans who have claimed for "the Race" a poet said to embody the Russian soul have not failed to recognize a certain paradox inherent in such claims. These writers have generally recognized Pushkin not simply as a Negro but also as fully, even supremely, Russian. Thus they have not left unexplored the relationship between "Negroness" and "Russianness," nor have they drawn the same sort of impermeable line between the categories of Negro and Russian as were often drawn between those of Negro and American. This nuanced view is not surprising, since black writers had long remarked on the folly of American efforts to quantify race in a society where people of various races have for centuries intermarried. In the words of one writer in 1913, "In the U.S. and the U.S. alone does a Negro 'race' exist."[25] Thus even as black Americans claimed Pushkin as a Race writer, they often did so with the implicit understanding that the categories of race that operate in American society are, as George Schuyler put it in 1940, "not . . . 'racial' but primarily social."[26] But at a historical moment when the very existence of a mixed-race person testified to possibilities both criminal and seductive, it was arguably more honest to write about Pushkin as a Negro than to ignore his race or to write about him as a "white" man—as white scholars regularly did.

In fact, in the first half of the twentieth century the white Americans (mostly professional Slavists) who discussed Pushkin's African heritage were often deeply entangled in racialist thinking.[27] On occasion Slavists who treated Pushkin's race revealed considerable anxiety about the issue. In 1934 Boris Brasol remarks on Pushkin's apparently surprising lack of shame in his ancestry: "Poushkin himself did not try to conceal or deny the fact that one of his ancestors was a descendant of the black race. In his talks and correspondence he frequently brought up this delicate subject with naive candor." Brasol then denies that Pushkin attached any significance to this "admixture of African blood," and again lauds the poet for "wisely [accepting] this genetic flaw, if it was a flaw at all, as a *fait accompli.*"[28] E. J. Simmons—who rejects what he calls the oft-expressed idea that Pushkin's "hot African blood" predisposed him to insane jealousy, "garish clothes," and "[swift] changes in mood"—offers a generally even-handed treatment of Pushkin's background, but he nonetheless wishes that the uncomfortable question could be ignored ("it would be profitable to dismiss here and now the whole muddled question of negro blood"). Simmons acknowledges, however, that "Pushkin himself prevents this," because of the significance the poet clearly attached to his own heritage.

Simmons therefore goes on to examine this heritage, and to put forth the common (and incorrect) argument that Pushkin's ancestor was not technically Negro but rather "Abyssinian."[29] The latter term, he explains, means "mixed," and was originally a derisive label used by Arabs to denote the "polyglot nature" of the population of Ethiopia, a region inhabited by a great mixture of peoples, including "Beja, Somalis, Arabs, Turks, Hebrews, Portuguese, Negroes, and other peoples." However, Simmons asserts, "the population of Abyssinia is . . . largely of Hamitic and Semitic base, with a negro admixture"—and therefore, he concludes, "the Abyssinians belong fundamentally to the Caucasian division of races." Simmons thus shifts from a geographical definition of the label applied to Pushkin to a racial one, once he is able to claim that the "Abyssinians" from whom Pushkin is descended are "fundamentally" Caucasians.[30] This line of reasoning was common in early twentieth-century ethnography, and was often used to deny the "blackness" of accomplished Africans. In Pushkin's case, the notion that the poet's origins were "Abyssinian" in the sense of "not really Negro" gained currency thanks in large part to the Russian academician D. N. Anuchin, who was active around the turn of the century. In his tendentious glossing of Pushkin's origins, Anuchin stated his motives quite clearly: one must question, he writes, "whether a pure *Negro* . . .

could give proof of a talent such as seen in Ibragim Hannibal . . . and that, finally, the great-grandson of this Negro, A. S. Pushkin, marked by his person a new era in the literary and artistic development of a European nation."[31]

Black writers challenged such interpretations of Pushkin's background, just as they had long contested various "racial" distinctions intended to support arguments that were either overtly or covertly racist. The journalist and historian J. A. Rogers wrote in the 1940s, "from time to time there are writers who will say that [Pushkin's] ancestor Hannibal was 'an Abyssinian and not a Negro'—for example, Professor E. J. Simmons of Harvard University. But this contention is not worth taking seriously. Not only are some of the most pronounced Negroid types . . . to be found in Ethiopia, but it would be extraordinarily difficult to find a native Ethiopian . . . who would be able to pass for other than a Negro in America."[32] Rogers's last sentence makes clear that he is writing about Pushkin in the context of American racial thought and practice, that in this context Pushkin is Negro, and that American writers who strain to make fine racial distinctions with the goal of minimizing Pushkin's blackness would be unlikely to make such taxonomic efforts on behalf of any dark-skinned American who was trying to get on a bus.

When Mirsky described Pushkin's Negro appearance but then immediately stated that Gannibal was Abyssinian rather than "Negro in the technical, anthropological sense of the word," a reviewer in *Opportunity* took note of this contradiction (while otherwise appreciating the absence of "contempt or patronage" in Mirsky's work).[33] Almost all black writers noted Pushkin's Negro features, his "broad nose, thick lips, and curly hair,"[34] and they often linked such physical facts to personality traits that they assumed to be the product of race: as one writer put it, "[Pushkin's] racial features are as powerfully evident in his original as in some of his writings."[35] As this last quote suggests, while writings by African Americans do not associate "Negro blood" with negative traits, they do on occasion reveal assumptions about the influence of race on character and intellect that are similar to those expressed by whites. Blacks as well as whites write of Pushkin's "hot blood" and "primitiveness,"[36] and of the contribution that this "African blood flowing in his veins gave to the cold sluggish Russian temperament."[37]

Arguments like Simmons's and Mirsky's, combined with the occasional vulgarly racist account of Pushkin's background,[38] probably led black Americans to believe that his African heritage explained his neglect in English-speaking lands (a neglect often noted by both black and white writers on Pushkin). Alice Dunbar-Nelson asked whether it might not be "the innate prejudice of the English-speaking world because of his Negroid extraction" that had made Pushkin "the least known of ranking Russian writers."[39] Eric Walrond noted in a 1922 issue of the *Negro World,* "I have talked to no fewer than half a dozen white persons who, I was made to understand, knew something about the origin of books and their makers, and I was astounded to discover that not one of them knew, or was willing to acknowledge, that Pushkin was a Negro. 'Yes, I've read Pushkin, but I didn't know that he was a Negro.'"[40] There are more convincing explanations for Pushkin's years of relative neglect in this country (most notably a paucity of good translations), but the white press's failure to provide a fair account of the poet's race must have reinforced blacks' suspicions that a writer of Negro descent was not likely to be fairly assessed in America, and that the Negro heritage of a genius was liable to be suppressed.[41] Thus African Americans insisted on the relevance of this heritage to an understanding of Pushkin's life and work, naming him "the celebrated Negro poet of Russia,"[42] "the great Negro-blooded poet,"[43] or simply, as many texts put it, "a Negro."

Black Americans who have seen Pushkin as black have on occasion attributed racist motives not only to white American readers but to the poet's Russian contemporaries as well. According to such accounts, Pushkin was persecuted by racists who finally drove him to his death. Sometimes this argument is made explicitly. In a text for children published in 1921, Elizabeth Ross Haynes writes that people stared and whispered as Pushkin walked by, remarking on his strange appearance and calling him homely because he was a Negro.[44] Elsewhere, a white writer claims (in the black press) that Pushkin's African appearance explains his mother's failure to love him.[45] In Rogers's description of Pushkin's life and trials, the poet's contemporaries subject him to the sort of racist invective that was common in the United States: "all that was left to [Pushkin's rivals] was to mock him about his Negro ancestry. They would point to the crisp, curly hair of his head and whiskers, his dark skin, and his full lips, crying, 'There is the Negro.' . . . Because he was lively in his movement, they would declare that he inherited that trait from the apes of Central Africa."[46]

Similar interpretations of the role played by race in Pushkin's fate have continued to find voice in our time. A 1989 article by Dorothy Trench-Bonett in *Black Scholar* compares Pushkin's plight with that of American slaves ("Although fortunate compared with enslaved Afro-Americans, the poet was a victim of oppression"), thus implying that it was the poet's race—not his class affiliation, his politics, his problematic status as both nobleman and writer in a society that provided literary artists with neither respect nor money—that determined the shape of his life. The same article, in a brief consideration of *The Blackamoor of Peter the Great*, takes Pushkin's description of Gannibal's alienation in Parisian society ("generally the young Negro was regarded in the light of a curiosity . . . He felt that he was for them a kind of rare beast, a peculiar alien creature") as a direct representation of Pushkin's own feelings of specifically racial apartness.[47]

Other texts simply represent the oppressed Pushkin as "the sweet singer and martyr of Freedom," "unshackled" only in death,[48] and leave it up to the reader to make the obvious parallel with the black American experience, particularly the experience of the artist denied full expression because of his race.

"The boy was a caged bird with free flight proscribed. Yet the creative faculty within him, struggling for utterance and opportunity, found both," according to W. S. Scarborough in 1904.[49] Even when other explanations for Pushkin's persecution were advanced (most notably explanations that echoed official Soviet criticism in their emphasis on class), race remained the inescapable subtext, as the following quote suggests: "The Soviet proletariat remembers, it recalls that the same parasitic and feudal class which hounded to death Alexander Pushkin, 'dark and curly-headed,' also oppressed, exploited and *enslaved* millions of their ancestors until it went to its inevitable doom . . . in 1917" (italics here are mine).[50] Virtually all African American accounts of Pushkin cite his famous "Ode to Freedom" and stress his sympathy with serfs, democrats, and the "common people"; some cite Pushkin's own acknowledgment of solidarity with "brother Negroes" held in slavery.[51] According to such accounts, Pushkin's "democratic ideas made him an exile";[52] he "wrote of liberty and freedom";[53] he "protested against bondage and serfdom . . . [and] made known his sympathy for the poor and oppressed."[54] This last quote follows a passage drawing a parallel between serfdom and slavery, thus making Pushkin's opposition to serfdom speak directly to the plight of American slaves.

Such parallels (as well as important differences) between Russian serfdom and American slavery had been noted in the black press as early as the 1820s, and these parallels are put to use in many African American texts about Pushkin.[55] As Rogers put it, "'Serfdom' was the name of this system, but it was slavery at its worst."[56] In Rogers's two accounts of Pushkin's life (published in 1929 and 1947), the point is driven home in the charged rhetoric of the American South: Pushkin, Rogers writes, learned the Russian language "from his niania or white 'mammy,' and the slaves on his father's plantation." "Thirty millions of his fellow-Russians, all white, were held in the grip of a hard, cruel slavery," and Pushkin, knowing their plight, was loyal to the rebels who had "pledged themselves to the overthrow of autocracy and the liberation of the slaves."[57] Insisting on Pushkin's profound sympathy for the slaves and on their reciprocal love for him, Rogers claims that Pushkin sought refuge from both political oppression and social pettiness by "[going] off to live among the slaves and peasants on a distant estate." Thus Pushkin's poetry, as Rogers writes in what must certainly be his most fantastic flourish, became "the delight of millions of illiterate peasant women and slaves."[58]

In Rogers's writings, the miseries of Russian serfdom are made to mirror the primal and wrenching scenes of American slavery: "These unfortunates were branded, whipped, and sold like cattle. They were sold from estate to estate and whole families were torn apart in the process."[59] Similarly, in Trench-Bonett's 1989 article in *Black Scholar*, Gannibal learns to read by using his master's discarded slates, a scene that clearly recalls a transformative moment in the narratives of many escaped slaves, for whom the surreptitious acquisition of literacy marked an essential entry into consciousness.[60] Trench-Bonett, citing but in fact elaborating freely upon Nabokov and Troyat, also recounts how Pushkin fathered a child with the serf Olga Kalashnikov.[61] According to Trench-Bonett, this child—"visibly black"—had to be, "for fear of scandal, sent away."[62] The story of a rejected black baby fathered by a master and born of a slave recurs, of course, over and over in American stories of plantation life, and was offered by abolitionists as a prime example of the moral degradations (miscegenation, corruption of female virtue, child abandonment) that slavery inevitably engendered.

These affirmations of Pushkin's commonality with black Americans and with slaves, however, do not preclude an equally emphatic affirmation of the poet's Russianness. In fact, Pushkin's absolute centrality to Russian culture is a principal theme of African American texts, which often call attention to his quintessential Russianness even as they insist upon his racial identity as a Negro. As I noted above, Whittier called Pushkin the "embodiment" of Russian nationality as early as 1847, and in subsequent texts, black writers have often quoted Russian and Soviet critics waxing mystical about Pushkin's ability to incarnate the Russian national essence. Pushkin is said to have "lived at the very core of Russian life"[63] and produced work that is Russian in its very "fibre."[64] Thanks to an ineffable intimacy with the Russian people, he is the one poet "without whose companionship it would be impossible [for Russians] to breathe, to live."[65] Aubrey Bowser draws on Soviet critical axioms to assert that Pushkin is "the highest expression of the national genius," "the culmination of all the Russian poetry that went before him and the radiating center of all that has come after him."[66] Such quotes could be multiplied many times over. J. A. Rogers cites an unnamed Soviet critic to drive the point home: "'Pushkin's works represented the epitome of all the preceding development of Russian poetic thought. Pushkin was and is an inexhaustible source of its further development . . . For the greatest writers of the country, Pushkin was the starting-point and it was to him they constantly reverted.'" In fact, Rogers quotes a whole series of rapturous Soviet testimonies not just to Pushkin's greatness, but to his absolute centrality to the Russian tradition, a tradition which, it seems, would simply not exist were it not for him: "one of the most remarkable geniuses of the world," a poet who "embraces all, sees, and hears everything," "our Voltaire, our Shakespeare, our Goethe."[67]

As early as 1904, Scarborough wrote that Pushkin "had taken into his being the spirit of his country; he had demonstrated in his work the Russian quality of mind and heart, and Russia did not hesitate to recognize it."[68] In these lines describing the Russian national poet, we can begin to discern a cautious hope for the place of the Negro artist in America. Scarborough's analysis of Pushkin suggests that a black American writer, too, might one day become not merely a recognized literary talent (and thus a "credit to his race"), but also a vehicle for the *national* genius, the creator of a truly national literature. This is a vision of a writer who is both a "Race writer" and a representative American, one who stands not on the culture's periphery but at its "core." (Significantly, in Scarborough's vision, the poet's ability to become a central cultural figure depends on his being acknowledged *by* the center: "Russia did not hesitate to recognize" Pushkin's embodiment of the national spirit. This implies that the Negro genius, too, would need the recognition of the dominant white culture in order to become its representative.) Like Pushkin, who performs a service for the Negro race as he embodies the Russian national essence, this writer would remain authentically Negro even as he became representatively American. Similarly, as Rogers insists tirelessly on Pushkin's blackness, he also implies that Pushkin performs an essential service for the entire Russian nation by doing cultural work that reveals the dignity inherent in a previously despised vernacular tradition. "In the dawn of our literature," according to a Russian critic whom Rogers quotes, "[Pushkin] taught us this human pride, this knowledge of one's own dignity."[69]

Pushkin, that is, did for Russians what many thought had to be done for African Americans. This fact helps explain why a Russian nobleman—black perhaps, but nonetheless a figure profoundly alien to the culture of nineteenth- and early twentieth-century America—was the subject of such sustained interest among black Americans. Black writers repeatedly emphasized Pushkin's glorious redemption of a lowly and despised tradition. Before Pushkin, according to a biographical note on the poet published in 1921, "There was no Russian literature. The nobles were ashamed of their language and their civilization."[70] Pushkin was the first to recognize the aesthetic power of the Russian vernacular, formerly "used only in intercourse with domestics and serfs," and thereby "[raise] it from a subservient position to its present-day dignity."[71] Rogers again quotes an unnamed Russian critic to make the point: "With one cut of the sword Pushkin had freed Russian literature from the ties that were keeping it enslaved."[72]

Thus the Russian language itself, province of "domestics and serfs," is described in vocabulary that evokes the plight of Negro culture in America, with the result that Pushkin's courageous embrace of the "neglected Russian language"[73] is made to speak directly to educated black Americans' efforts to make use of a rich oral tradition which had long been ignored or even reviled. Black intellectuals in the early decades of the twentieth century, as Dale Peterson has pointed out, were engaged in a project similar to that undertaken by Russians in the previous century: both turned to a "denigrated ancestral subculture" in search of inspiration for art that would be both a genuine expression of the people's culture and highly sophisticated in its own right.[74] Alain Locke, in the famous aesthetic manifesto *The New Negro* (1925), described the contemporary black artist's need to "evolve from the racial substance [i.e., folk culture] something technically distinctive, something that as an idiom of style may become a contribution to the general resources of art."[75] Pushkin could be seen to have done precisely that.

Articles in the black press, again drawing on an axiom of Russian and Soviet criticism, argued that Pushkin's nanny, Arina Rodionovna, opened the young poet to a culture more authentic, more truly "national" than that of the deracinated upper classes. "It was Arina," wrote one journalist in 1928, "who taught him Russian, the language of the common people, the tongue of the soil . . . The primitive, yet unconsciously poetic mind of Arina Rodionovna, who was a veritable treasure chest of fairy tales, legends, songs and myths of Russia's folk lore, found a responsive chord in the young 'Barin' (gentleman)," and her influence "remained with Pushkin for life, often breaking through the veneer of pseudo-civilization in torrents of inspired, invincible, undying melody."[76] It was she who, in Scarborough's words twenty-four years earlier, "[permeated] him with national fervor—the 'uncompleted national spirit,' the undiluted richness, raciness, and grace of his native language."[77] Compare the Harlem Renaissance writer Jean Toomer writing on the imperative to mine traditional black culture for its equally "racy" riches: "Georgia opened me . . . There one finds soil, soil in the sense that the Russians knew it,—the soil every art and literature that is to live must be imbued in."[78]

An enserfed peasant woman, the mirror image of the black female slave, is credited with the salvation of Russian literature. "Every writer on Pushkin," according to Scarborough, "attributes most largely to this Russian peasant woman the saving of the greatest Russian poet for Russia."[79] The young aristocrat (male), in danger of succumbing to a derivative and superficially sophisticated high culture (Aidline-Trommer's "pseudo-civilization"), is saved by the "primitive, yet unconsciously poetic mind" (female) of the common people, which he effectively channels into the creation of an art that is both incontestably high and authentically national. By passing down to her aristocratic charge the riches of the lower orders' traditions, the female serf provides the soil in which the flower of high art will blossom. Presumably Pushkin was not the only young and talented *barin* to be nurtured by a peasant woman, but he alone proved capable of laying claim, through a bond with his serf-nanny, to the cultural and linguistic heritage of the common people.

In certain African American accounts, it is Pushkin's blackness that makes possible his deep bond with Arina Rodionovna. Nanny and charge are linked by shared feelings of exclusion and apartness: he was her favorite, according to one text, "possibly because he suffered humiliation from his family [presumably due to his race], just as Arina suffered from the Russian social system."[80] Thus did the black nobleman become uniquely receptive to the folk legacy of the female serf. Other black writers, too, implied that it was precisely Pushkin's *race* (Negro) that enabled him to discern and express the "soul" of his *people* (Russian): Pushkin becomes the embodiment of the Russian national essence not *despite* being a Negro, but *because* of it. Thomas Oxley, for example, implies that it was Pushkin's "racial features" that allowed him to become "the first writer to express the inner soul of his [the Russian] people. He felt their heartbeat."[81]

Rogers's insistence on the black Pushkin's identification with Russian "slaves" implies, too, a solidarity rooted in race consciousness—but it is a solidarity that seems, strangely, to be intensified rather than diminished by the fact that these slaves were white. That is, even as Rogers writes about Russian serfs in the racially charged language that American history dictates, he deliberately underlines the fact, unavoidably and fruitfully paradoxical for Americans, that these slaves, "thirty millions of them," were "all white."[82] They were all white, but they seem inevitably to become all black as soon as they are translated into an American context. The act of cultural translation, serf to slave, leads without fail to such inversions. For example, in the story of Pushkin's affair (if it can be called that) with a woman who was his family's property, American terms are transposed: Pushkin is a black master exercising his power over a white slave (a painful fact which explains why no African American writer besides Trench-Bonett repeats this story).

None of these transformations, however, is more striking or more significant than Arina Rodionovna's. In American terms, the figure of Pushkin's nanny becomes, one might say, structurally black: as Rogers makes explicit, she is in effect a "mammy."[83] Arina Rodionovna's figurative blackness, her ability to stand in for the rural, poor, maternal black woman who is the repository of a powerful oral tradition, may well have heightened the significance that her relationship with Pushkin held for black intellectuals in the early decades of the twentieth century. In their descriptions, the culture transmitted to Pushkin by a female slave is the authenticating and maternal culture of the common people—authenticating in that it ensures the art he creates will avoid derivativeness, maternal in that it nurtures and shapes a young artist who aspires to something notably higher. It is the same sort of folk culture that black American artists sought both to mine and to transcend in order to give voice to what the Harlem Renaissance writer Alain Locke called "the maturing speech of full racial utterance."[84] Thus in African American accounts of Pushkin's life, Arina Rodionovna plays a role similar to the one she plays in so many Soviet hagiographies: she links the great poet to "the people." Indeed, in such writings it seems at times that Pushkin is the child of two "black" parents: Arina Rodionovna, the serf who links him to the (Russian) common people, and Abram Gannibal, the African who renders him legitimately noble.

In a great many African American interpretations, the Russian national poet draws on a folk culture that is represented as implicitly female, but he does so in order to become the Father of Russian Literature, the emphatically male progenitor of an artistic line. Over and over he is assigned this name;

over and over it is asserted that without Pushkin the Father, Russian literature would not have been conceived. As one headline tells us, "Pushkin 'Made' Russian Literature."[85] It was this "minstrel of Negro blood" who "gave a vast empire its tongue of today, whose pioneer work paved the way for Gogol, Tolstoy, Turgenev, Goncharov, Chekhov, Gorky and many other knights of the glorious galaxy of his successors!"[86] "But for him," Rogers writes, "Tolstoi, Dostoevsky, Gogol, Gorky, Lenin, and other famous Russian writers might have written in French instead of in Russian. Pushkin, in the fullest sense, is 'The Father of Russian Literature.'"[87]

These words recall the ecstatic commonplaces of Soviet (and some earlier Russian) criticism, but such claims may well have carried particular significance in the American context. As both Henry Louis Gates Jr. and Deborah E. McDowell have pointed out, the search for a patrilineal and thus, it seems, dignifying line of artistic descent has played a significant role in shaping and misshaping the African American canon. In McDowell's argument, the black literary genealogy has too often been represented as a line of "sons descending from stalwart fathers in a kind of typological unfolding," a line beginning with Frederick Douglass, "the founding father" who "produced a kind of Ur-text of slavery and freedom" that gave shape to all that followed.[88] If this argument is correct (and the evidence is convincing), the African American emphasis on Pushkin as father figure is anything but surprising. Pushkin is in effect made to assume the same position in the literary history of Russia that Douglass is made to occupy in that of black America.

According to this version of Russian literary history, Pushkin, the Negro genius, creates the Russian language and becomes the father of all great Russian artists, artists who seem thus to have been white only by chance (though male perhaps by necessity). Furthermore, a "vast *empire*" of letters (to adopt Rogers's formulation) implies a literature with boundaries defined not by race but by language, an idea that in the American context may again hint at the possibility of blacks' role in an expanded canon of American literature. In the end, such ideas derive their power from the implication that it was precisely Pushkin's race (Negro) that enabled him to discern and express the "soul" of his people (Russian): Pushkin is a Race Man for the Russian people. As a result, Pushkin the Founding Father becomes not only a way of focusing an American discourse about race, but also a way of revealing how and where certain lines blur (be they racial, ethnic, or national), and how they might be redrawn—because the Pushkin of African American journalistic writing may be black, but he is Russian and universal as well, a man who, in Rogers's words, was "one of the completest human beings who ever lived."[89]

It is therefore particularly striking that the two American novels which take Pushkin as their main subject—novels which could not be more divergent in their assumptions and biases—seem inclined to reinstate boundaries that other texts have sought to erase. Edna Underwood's *The Penitent* (1922) was the first book of a projected trilogy set in the time of Pushkin and Alexander I. Underwood's dedicatory preface describes her novel's theme as "the crumbling of the great civilization of the past," a dissolution that is figured as both racial and political (1789 prefigures 1917, and Underwood is on the side of the ancien régime).[90] *The Penitent* is clearly the work of an American shaken by the Bolshevik Revolution, but more significantly, it is a text written by a representative of a "master race" that fears itself to be in eclipse. Thus the book's obsessions are those of reactionary American political discourse in the late nineteenth- and early twentieth-century immigration debates.

John Oliver Killens's *Great Black Russian* (1989)[91] grew out of the novelist's years of study of Pushkin's life, as well as Killens's lifelong commitment to creating literature intended to advance the cause of social justice (as a result of which he has been called to task at least once for his "rather inflexible theory of socialist realism").[92] Born in 1916, Killens was a founder of the Harlem Writers' Guild and a contributor to Paul Robeson's *Freedom* newspaper. His work gives voice to a defiant racial pride and to the black left-wing activism of midcentury, an activism that aimed to address economic injustice without allowing issues of race to be subsumed by those of class.[93] Ultimately in *Great Black Russian*, for Killens's characters no less than for Underwood's, there is no ignoring the imperatives of race, as a reading of these two novels will reveal.

Underwood repeatedly alerts us to the reason behind her interest in both Pushkin and Russia: "He who is nearest to the primitive past . . . is still a hybrid. That is what Petersburg society was. And that is what its leader, [Tsar] Alexander, was too, an exquisite, political hybrid, not reducible to exact cataloguing anywhere" (129). In Underwood's book, Pushkin the mulatto and, to some degree, Russian society as a whole are images for *hybridity* itself.[94] Pushkin stands for a sort of creeping mongrelism that is said to characterize Russia's population ("an ethnological mosaic"), as well as for the "unaccountable but inevitable intermingling of blood" that threatens to overtake the population of the entire globe (128, 344). In this world, race is the script to which every individual and every "civilization" must inevitably adhere. And while the quote that opens this paragraph implies that Pushkin (along with other hybrids like the gypsy, who is said to represent "some wild, uncatalogued mixing of races") resists classification, in fact this novel seems to set itself precisely the task of "cataloguing" racial differences (92).

Perhaps, however, one might more accurately argue that *The Penitent*'s task is to *appear* to classify, catalogue, and define the various "races" it treats, while in fact permanently deferring the very question of what race itself might be. At times in *The Penitent*, race is skin color: "[Pushkin] had . . . the lack of dependable persistency which characterizes the black people . . . He lacked, too, the moral energy, the purpose of direction, of the white races" (145). At times, race is nationality (Polish, Greek, Russian, English). At other times, race is simply class, as in the "celebrated *boyar* race," or the race of aristocrats in general ("A race of specially trained men and women, delicately tempered, witty, brilliant, and some of them noble . . . freed from work, freed from forced effort, from base emotions such as envy, poverty [sic], greed, and busied with cultivation of the things of the mind" [120, 207]). Race can also be a mark of place, a sign left behind by geographic or climatological difference ("desert races"; "that negro race . . . burned, tempered, by the rays of the deadly sun" [131, 133]). Race can be time, a synchronic representation of the diachronic process of human progress over the ages, with "lower" races making visible the temporal stages through which "higher" ones have already passed: "Governments, peoples, races, pass through cycles of existence just like flowers, just like fruit trees; bud, flower, fruit, decay." (Hence the contemporaneous existence of "youthful, honest, unsophisticated races" and "antique races" [208, 11, 197]).

Perhaps most important, as the quotation about fruit trees demonstrates, race in *The Penitent* can be a classificatory tool of the allegedly dispassionate scientific observer: "Count Woronzow was interested in horticulture . . . He had made independent scientific observations of his own. He was coming to believe in certain peculiar but interesting affiliations between men and plants . . . The same laws were applicable, largely, to both. Both were *life, only in different stages of progression.*" These laws—ostensibly unbiased, because scientific—absolve Pushkin of responsibility for his lamentable shortcomings. Woronzow (the author's mouthpiece) declares, "Not so long ago some of [Pushkin's] progenitors were *savages—of the jungle.* He is not to be blamed because *he is as he is* . . . One should not be angry because the jungle flowers more profusely than the plain. That view would be unintelligent—*unscientific*" (119). Strangely, however, although Woronzow speaks as a scientist, the "laws" he expounds seem to gain rather than lose authority by what is in the end their inexplicability, their transcendence of the merely empirical. Woronzow acknowledges that in order to "explain" Pushkin to himself, "he would have to fall back upon unexplored, unexplained ethnic laws, profound, organic" (145). Race explains everything, but race itself is something too "profound" to be adequately explained, something that can be defined perhaps only by saying what it is *not*—hence the "un-European" face of Pushkin, the "un-Russian" expression of his mixed-race mother and her hair "of a color no one could name," or the "ungypsy eyes" of a gypsy girl (14, 69, 92).

In the end, Underwood leaves the category of race quite spectacularly overdetermined in order that it might be called upon to answer almost every question, from the sweepingly general to the comically specific. Race can explain why "desert peoples" are sly, and it can explain why a particular character sleeps late. (After a chapter or two, no reader would be surprised to come across such a claim as, say, "He had that love of backgammon [or puppies or erotica or pleasure boating] so deeply characteristic of his race.") In Underwood's view, one need look no further than race to explain the complexities of individual character: "all individuals, in their petty discontents, hatreds, their personal preferences, give expression again to the old primitive impulses of races" (128–29). Thus we are told that Pushkin (whom we might have mistaken, were it not for Underwood, for a highly complicated man) was merely the pawn of "atavistic flesh-memories, which he did not understand . . . forgotten cell-memories of the colors of Africa" (148).

Underwood's is clearly not the only text I have considered in which the Russian national poet serves as a vehicle for certain ideas about race, but in this novel, Pushkin is absolutely nothing more than such a vehicle. *The Penitent* is uninterested in the artist who is its ostensible subject, because all questions about him have been answered in advance. Pushkin is merely an emblem of race itself.[95] Killens's *Great Black Russian,* in strong contrast to Underwood's work, is intensely interested in Pushkin as a distinct individual. But *Great Black Russian* is no less concerned with race than is *The Penitent.* For Killens the figure of Pushkin stands not for the fact of racial difference, but rather for the experience of the oppressed black man who must struggle heroically against racism in order to nurture his own, specifically black, genius.

In *Great Black Russian,* as in Frederick Douglass's autobiography (the paradigmatic slave narrative), a sensitive boy enters into moral and political consciousness by witnessing the flogging of a slave. In Douglass's famous account, that slave is his Aunt Hester. In Killens's novel, the young witness is Pushkin, and the serf is an unnamed sufferer who stands in for all bondsmen. But strikingly, incredibly, Killens's serf is *black*. First introduced as a "male serf . . . dark of skin, almost black," he soon becomes simply "this little black man," with "ebon shoulders," black hair, and eyes "entirely black."[96] In this crucial moment of awakening, the sympathy of young Pushkin, whom Killens always represents as African, is elicited not merely by the suffering of a slave, but by the suffering of a slave who is black. It is as much the color of this serf's skin as his silent courage under the knout that seems to call forth the poet's emotional identification. Thus even as *Great Black Russian* insists tirelessly on the equivalence of Russia's white serfs and America's black slaves ("A serf was chattel, owned every limb, tooth and genital by his ennobled master. Like slavery in the 'New World,' he could be sold at any moment to satisfy the slightest whim, away from his wife, mother, father, son, or daughter" [29]), the novel implies that Pushkin's moral sensibility developed in response to the sufferings of dark-skinned people.

Interestingly, Killens's vocabulary here suggests that the slave whose experience this passage represents as universal is in fact male, a slave who can be sold "away from his wife, mother, father, son, or daughter," but not apparently from her husband. Indeed, it is clear that the focus of *Great Black Russian* is always the plight of the *male* serf/slave. For example, in the book's powerful whipping scene, the black sufferer is repeatedly called "the male serf" (even after his exposed genitals have been described, thereby making entirely clear his gender), because part of what this passage aims to establish is the fact that one of slavery's chief horrors is the slave's loss of "manhood." (This emphasis on the stolen manhood of the slave—a manhood that is often equated with humanity itself—was long a cornerstone of descriptions of slavery, and in recent years feminists have analyzed the ways in which it has distorted representations of female slaves' experiences.) However, Killens comes closer than other American writers to acknowledging the difficult contradictions (in American racial terms) implicit in the fact of Pushkin's affair with an enserfed woman. Killens's Pushkin is tormented by the knowledge that his ownership of Olga Kalashnikov is what has enabled him to exploit her sexually. Though Pushkin's guilt is mitigated in the novel by the fact that the young woman loves him, Killens has a jealous male serf ("the blonde-haired Igor") accuse Pushkin of hypocrisy: "The master is upset because I gave his personal whore a well deserved whipping . . . [what] he writes about the rights of serfs is so much horseshit!" (230). In this passage a white slave both challenges his black master and reclaims his "manhood" by establishing his rights over "his" female.

Killens's Pushkin does, however, identify with the white serfs whose fate he protests. In fact, Pushkin constructs for himself an alternative genealogy based on identification with both his African great-grandfather (who appears to him in visions, and for whom he writes) and with the various white serfs who nurture him. He claims peasant culture as his own, believing it to be "at the very core of the Russian language and its soul" and therefore using it to create a "national literature . . . a narodnost" (240, 79). Indeed, Pushkin's link to the culture of the common people is represented almost as one of blood: an enserfed family on his parents' estate "in many ways . . . [*is*] his family" (50). Rather than the racist noblewoman who rejects him in favor of his blonde siblings, it is Arina Rodionovna—who "sometimes imagined that she had actually birthed him"—who is represented as his true mother. As an adult Pushkin even calls his serf valet his "father" (26, 18).

Ultimately, though, it is race that shapes both Pushkin's character and others' responses to him. For example, color terms that have their origins not in racial distinctions but in twentieth-century political designations are racialized. When the poet's friend Pushchin declares, "We're white Russians," Pushkin retorts, "Obviously, *I* am not a White Russian . . . I'm an African-Russian" (79).[97] In *Great Black Russian* neither the reader nor Pushkin himself, who is repeatedly subjected to prejudice and crude racial insults by members of the gentry, is ever allowed to forget that the poet is black. Certain villains, moreover, are markedly white. When Pushkin goes to labor alongside the serfs (in order to "know their tiredness in his own bones") and is mistaken for a malingering worker, it is not merely an overseer who attempts to beat him, but a "blonde-haired, blue-eyed overseer" (72–73). The crude and vicious peasant who batters Pushkin's serf-lover Olga Kalashnikov is likewise "the blonde-haired Igor" (230). There is no escaping such black/white divisions, even among peoples whose ethnicity would seem to confound them. Killens's Pushkin "[feels] a kinship" with gypsies, for example, "these almost-brown complexioned people reminding him of his African ancestry" (153).

Pushkin's identification with his black ancestor is represented as an act of choice. "I'm an African because I choose to identify with my great-grandfather," the poet asserts (167). Little in Killens's novel, however, supports the idea that racial affiliation is a matter of personal preference. Pushkin has a black ancestor; he looks black; he is treated and mistreated like a black man; this experience allows him to see truths to which white people are blind. There appears to be very little room for choice in facts as hard as these, facts which inscribe themselves indelibly into the lives of the novel's hero and all its other characters.

For the historical Pushkin, to a degree virtually incomprehensible to Americans both white and black, race truly was a matter of choice. Pushkin could and did assume the identity of *boyar*, for example, as well as that of *afrikanets*, and while his most contemptible rival (Faddei Bulgarin) targeted his African ancestry in a notorious newspaper squib, the poet's enemies targeted many other facets of his identity and past as well.[98] Furthermore, it was very likely Pushkin's own interest in his African ancestry—his fruitful intellectual and aesthetic *play* with the complexities of his own origins—that drew his rivals' attention to these origins in the first place. The historical Pushkin, famously and painfully constrained in so many ways, was not denied the freedom to turn questions of race to the advantage of his own supple intellect. In the two novels I have considered, however, the Pushkin of the American imagination must live with race as a form of compulsion, a set of inescapable imperatives and imposed loyalties which often operate, it seems, at the expense of a larger humanity.

Yet the apparent strangeness of these African American versions of Pushkin can only be understood in reference to Russia's own tradition of writing about the national poet—writings that constitute a tradition no less strange, and a "Pushkin" no less invented. According to Dostoevsky, Pushkin, by the grace of God, "appeared precisely at the very inception of [Russians'] true self-consciousness," and he alone embodies the "all-humanitarian and all-unifying Russian soul."[99] Writers in the final years of the nineteenth century drew on such comments to produce rapturous affirmations of Pushkin's genius and his miraculous incarnation of the nation's spirit. The poet Dmitry Merezhkovsky called him "both the primordial unitary source and the final synthesis of the Russian spirit," "a knight of eternal spiritual aristocracy."[100] In depicting Pushkin as a sort of Russian *Übermensch*, the originator of a radically new kind of human being, Merezhkovsky and other modernists drew on

Dostoevsky's ecstatic assertion that Pushkin was the only "universal man" to have appeared in the history of the world.[101]

Dostoevsky's Pushkin was universal, but he was also destined to usher Russia into a specifically European version of history and culture. "Had there been no Pushkin," Dostoevsky declared, "perhaps our faith in our Russian individuality, in our national strength, and our belief in our future independent mission in the family of the European nations, would not have manifested itself."[102] As I noted above, for racist ethnographers (Russian as well as Western), Pushkin's Africannness had to be explained away before the poet might be seen to have accomplished this task: witness one Russian's doubt, expressed in 1899, that the descendant of a Negro could have "marked by his person a new era in the literary and artistic development of a *European nation.*"[103]

Pushkin did indeed "mark by his person a new era in the literary and artistic development of a European nation"—or at least, a nation whose literature is part of the European tradition. And even as Russians insisted on Pushkin's *narodnost'* (his perfectly native quality, literally his "peopleness"), they also recognized him as the most cosmopolitan and the most European of writers. As Dostoevsky asserted, Pushkin stood as incontrovertible proof that Russians had before them an "independent mission in the family of the European nations." By expressing their national particularity, Russians would finally be able to unite themselves with the "universal" humanity represented by Europe. They were to become Europeans—which might be taken to mean that they were finally to become *humans*—by giving voice to their Russianness. But the Russian national essence was to be expressed in high art addressed not only to Russians: Europeans would at last be forced to take notice as well. Thus in Russians' understanding of their national poet, Russianness, Europeanness, and "universal humanity" have been inextricably linked, if not strategically confused.

The epigraphs that precede this article begin to suggest why the Russian national poet—nobleman, aesthete, rake, a figure seemingly alien to the culture of nineteenth- and twentieth-century America—has been the subject of such sustained interest among black Americans. While his great-grandfather's origins can account for the poet's having entered African American cultural discourse, Pushkin's abiding prominence in this discourse must be explained not only by his "Africanness," but also by his place in the tradition of his own country. Pushkin is indisputably of Negro "blood," but he is deemed the perfect representative of the Russian "race"—and it is this combination that has rendered him a singularly powerful figure for many Americans.

Notes

1. New York Public Library, *Dictionary Catalog of the Schomburg Collection of Negro Literature and History*, vol. 7 (Boston: G. K. Hall, 1962). See also volume 2 of the first supplement to the catalog, published in 1967. Helpful electronic references for information on the African American reception of Pushkin include the full-text database *The African-American Newspapers: The Nineteenth Century* (Pennsylvania: Accessible Archives CD-ROM Edition, 1998 [version 2]); and Henry Louis Gates Jr., *The Black Literature Index on CD-ROM* (Alexandria, Va.: Chadwyck-Healey, 1994–97) and accompanying microfiches. Other essential sources include Randall K. Burkett, Nancy Hall Burkett, and Henry Louis Gates Jr., eds., *Black Biography 1790–1950: A Cumulative Index*, 3 vols. (Alexandria, Va.: Chadwyck-Healey, 1991) and accompanying microfiches; Allison Blakely, *Russia and the Negro: Blacks in Russian History and Thought* (Washington, D.C.: Howard University Press, 1986); Donald M. Jacobs, *Antebellum Black Newspapers: Indices to New York Freedom's Journal (1827–1829), The Rights of All (1829), The Weekly Advocate (1837), and The Colored American (1837–1841)* (Westport, Conn.: Greenwood, c. 1976); Howard University Libraries, *The Dictionary Catalog of the Jesse E. Moorland Collection of Negro Life and History of the Howard University Library* (Boston: G. K. Hall, 1970); Werner Sollors, *Neither Black nor White yet Both* (New York: Oxford University Press, 1997); Rose Bibliography [Project], *Analytical Guide and Indexes to the Voice of the Negro, 1904–1907* (Westport, Conn.: Greenwood, [1974]); *Opportunity: A Journal of Negro Life. Cumulative Index, Volumes 1–27, 1923–1949* (New York: Kraus Reprint, 1971).

2. Charles Chesnutt, "A Matter of Principle," in his *The Wife of His Youth and Other Stories of the Color Line* (1899; Ridgewood, N.J.: Gregg, 1967), 109.

3. "Memories of Alexander Pushkin," *Weekly Progress* 23, no. 21 (June 10, 1926): 3.

4. See, for example, Chatwood Hall, "*Defender*'s Moscow Correspondent Gets Interview with Pushkin's Descendant," *The Chicago Defender* 32, no. 1 (May 2, 1936): 24. Hall's interview with Ekaterina Alexandrovna Pushkin quotes her assertion that Pushkin "would be whole-heartedly in favor of the Soviets." For many more articles on the Soviets' celebration of the 1937 jubilee, see *The Amsterdam News* for 1936–38.

5. "Famous Russian Author Honored by Celebration," *Amsterdam News* 28, no. 10 (February 13, 1937): 1.

6. *The Life of Alexander Pushkin* (Seattle: Baylor, 1983). The comic book series is called Golden Legacy.

7. W. S. Scarborough, "Alexander Sergeivitch Pushkin" (part 1 of a two-

part article), *Southern Workman* 33, no. 3 (March 1904): 162. For part 2, see vol. 33, no. 3 (March 1904): 234–36.

8. Headline to Anna Heifetz, "Pushkin in Self-Portrayal," *The Crisis* 44, no. 5 (May 1937): 144. (Heifetz was a white woman who published translations of Chekhov and Lermontov.) The note reproduced in *The Crisis* was the one Pushkin appended to chapter 1 of *Eugene Onegin.* A comment by Hazel V. Carby is telling in this context: "It is no historical accident that the mulatto figure occurs most frequently in African-American fiction at a time when the separation of the races was being institutionalized throughout the South" (and, one might add, in the North as well, if by custom more than by statute). See Hazel V. Carby, introduction to Frances W. Harper, *Iola Leroy, or Shadows Uplifted* (1892; Boston: Beacon, 1987), xxi–xxii.

9. Laren Miller, "Poe Tried to Snub Pushkin, Russia's Greatest Poet," *Norfolk Journal and Guide* 32, no. 41 (October 8, 1932): 7. For a discussion of Poe's racist views, see Stephen D. Dougherty, "Poe and the Sacred Nation: Race, Imperialism and Enlightenment in Antebellum America" (Ph.D. diss., Indiana University, 1999).

10. Armistead's book was originally published in Manchester, England, in 1848; it was reprinted in the United States in 1970 (Westport, Conn.: Negro Universities Press).

11. William Wells Brown, *The Black Man: His Antecedents, His Genius, and His Achievements*, 2nd ed. (New York: Thomas Hamilton, 1863), 1. See also, for example, Henry Highland Garnet, *God's Image in Ebony: Being a Series of Biographical Sketches, Facts, Anecdotes, etc., Demonstrative of the Mental Powers and Intellectual Capacities of the Negro Race* (London: Partridge and Oakey, 1854), or for a later example, Beatrice J. Fleming and Marion J. Pryde, *Distinguished Negroes Abroad* (Washington, D.C.: Associated Publishers, 1946). For an index of both Pushkin's and his great-grandfather's appearance in such volumes from the eighteenth century through the twentieth, see *Black Biography 1790–1950* and corresponding microfiches.

12. The earliest American edition of Gregoire's text was translated by D. B. Warden and published as *Enquiry concerning the Intellectual and Moral Faculties and Literature of Negroes; Followed with an Account of the Life and Works of Fifteen Negroes and Mulattoes Distinguished in Science, Literature, and the Arts* (Brooklyn: Thomas Kirk, 1810). For more references to Gannibal in the black press, see *The African-American Newspapers: The Nineteenth Century* (CD-ROM).

13. Henry Louis Gates Jr., "The Language of Slavery," introduction to *The Slave's Narrative*, ed. Gates and Charles T. Davis (Oxford and New York: Oxford University Press, 1985), xxiii. Gates's introduction to this volume provides a concise and powerful overview of this phenomenon, tracing the ideas of such thinkers as Bacon, Heylyn, Hume, Kant, Hegel, and Jefferson, among others.

14. Gates, "Language of Slavery," xxviii.

15. "Where," asks Gates, "in the history of narration does there exist a literature that was propelled by the Enlightenment demand that a 'race' place itself on the Great Chain of Being primarily through the exigencies of print?" Gates, "Language of Slavery," v. The answer is, in Russia: as Dale Peterson has pointed out, Slavs, like Africans, were "made painfully aware of their expulsion from modern Europe's philosophy of history" (as anyone who has read Chaadaev will realize). "Russians," Peterson writes, "fared only slightly better [than Africans] in nineteenth century German historicism's evolution of the human scale," and their literature, like that of African Americans, bears the marks of this attempted exclusion (Dale Peterson, "Justifying the Margin: The Construction of 'Soul' in Russian and African-American Texts," *Slavic Review* 51, no. 4 [Winter 1992]: 751, 752).

16. Daniel Murray, "Bibliographica-Africania," *The Voice of the Negro* 1, no. 5 (May 1904): 191, 187.

17. Katherine Davis Chapman Tillman, "Afro-American Poets and Their Verse," in *The Works of Katherine Davis Chapman Tillman*, ed. Claudia Tate (New York: Oxford University Press, 1991), 94.

18. Murray makes a brief reference to Pushkin, while Tillman devotes an entire essay to Pushkin's life, to which I will refer below. Murray, "Bibliographica-Africania," 187.

19. John Greenleaf Whittier, "Alexander Pushkin," *The National Era* 1, no. 6 (February 11, 1847): 2. In the black and abolitionist press I have found only one other antebellum reference to Pushkin, a one-line note ("Pushkin, one of the most distinguished men of Russia . . . a mulatto"), also in *The National Era*, vol. 2, no. 79 (July 6, 1848): 105. There may have been other references as well, though it is unlikely that they had substantive content. In the mainstream white press, Pushkin's name came before the American public at an even earlier date, but his African descent was not mentioned: in May 1832, the highbrow *Foreign Quarterly Review*, an English journal published in London and New York and enjoying a moderate circulation in the United States, printed a long and intelligent essay entitled "Pushkin and Rilaeev." (Despite the title, nearly the entire text is devoted to Pushkin.) This article, though it reached American readers, was almost certainly written by an Englishman (no author is listed), and was clearly intended for an English audience. The author gives no biographical details for either poet, concentrating instead on comparing Pushkin's style with Byron's and critiquing the "fragmentary" nature of Pushkin's works. It is doubtful that an essay on such an obscure foreign poet, whose works were being assessed in relation to the British and French poetic traditions, attracted much attention from American readers. See "[Pushkin and Rilaeev.] Art. VI.—*Poltava: Poema* Aleksandra Pushkina. St Petersburg. 1929," *Foreign Quarterly Review* 9 (May 1832): 398–418.

(Apparently only in some editions of the journal did the article bear the complete title listed above. It is not clear how the author knew Russian.)

20. For the first reference, see "Russian Literature and Alexander Pushkin," *National Review* (London), vol. 7 (October 1858): 361–82. (This article was reprinted in *The Eclectic Magazine* [New York], vol. 46 [January 1859]: 123–26.) For the second reference, see "Alexander Pouchkine," *Living Age* 33 (June 1852): 454–57. (A note at the end of the article indicates it was reprinted from *Chambers' Journal.*)

21. Benjamin Brawley, *The Negro Genius: A New Appraisal of the Achievement of the American Negro in Literature and the Fine Arts* (New York: Dodd, Mead, 1937). For passing references to Pushkin in African American writing of this period, see, for example, the Chesnutt story cited above, as well as Harper, *Iola Leroy,* 84 (a character mentions "Alexander Sergevitch, a Russian poet, who was spoken of as the Byron of Russian literature"); Victoria Earle Matthews, "The Value of Race Literature," reprinted in *The Massachusetts Review* (Summer 1986; originally an oration delivered in 1895), 177 (Matthews says that Pushkin is "well known and appreciated by the cultured minds"); and Edward Elmore Brock, "Literary Thoughts," *The Freeman* 11, no. 51 (December 24, 1898): 3 (Brock cites Pushkin as one promise of "the future possibilities of the Negro as a poet").

22. For an overview of America's contradictory racial laws, see George S. Schuyler, "Who Is 'Negro?' Who Is 'White?'" *Common Ground* 1, no. 1 (Autumn 1940): 55. For an earlier discussion of similar issues in the black press, see Carter G. Woodson, "The Beginnings of the Miscegenation between the Whites and Blacks," *Journal of Negro History* 3, no. 4 (October 1918): 335–53. Woodson attributes whites' reluctance to call North Africans "Negroes" to the fact that these dark-skinned people have "achieved more than investigators have been willing to consider the civilization of the Negro" (335).

23. Katherine Davis Chapman Tillman, "Alexander Sergeivich Pushkin," in *Works of Katherine Davis Chapman Tillman,* 123. Tillman's article was originally published in the *A. M. E. Church Review* 25 (July 1909): 27–32.

24. Aubrey Bowser, "Russia's Black Genius: 'The Captain's Daughter,'" *Amsterdam News* 20, no. 30 (June 26, 1929): 20.

25. [J. R. Clark], *A Memento of the Emancipation Proclamation of the State of New York. October 22–31, 1913* (souvenir pamphlet), 22.

26. Schuyler, "Who Is 'Negro?'" 55.

27. For example, in 1902, one white southerner mentions Pushkin briefly as part of a blandly cautious defense of black intellect and morals, but he treats the question of the poet's race so elliptically that the reader is left mystified by the delicate implication that a mulatto person *somehow* came into being in Russia. Just how did there come to be a black Russian, if the subject of inter-

"Bound by Blood to the Race"

racial marriage is, as this text's silence implies, too awful to contemplate? (J. J. Pipkin, *Story of a Rising Race* [Texas?: N. D. Thompson, 1902], 116).

28. Boris Brasol, *The Mighty Three: Poushkin, Gogol, Dostoievsky* (New York: William Farquhar Payson, 1934), 14, 15.

29. Recent scholarship has determined that Gannibal was not from northern Africa, but rather from what is now Cameroon, just south of Lake Chad. See Dieudonné Gnammankou, "New Research on Pushkin's Africa: Hanibal's Homeland," *Research in African Literatures* 28, no. 4 (Winter 1997): 220–23. Furthermore, as Gnammankou notes, according to the *General History of Africa* published by UNESCO, through the eighteenth century the geographical label "Abyssinia" indicated "all the territories south of Egypt to the Island of Zanzibar or Mozambique in eastern Africa" (Gnammankou 221). For more information on Pushkin's African roots, see a special number of the journal *Presence Africaine* entitled *Pouchkine et le monde noir,* ed. Dieudonné Gnammankou (Paris and Dakar: Presence Africaine Editions, 1999).

30. Ernest J. Simmons, *Pushkin* (Cambridge: Harvard University Press, 1937), 11–12.

31. Cited in Gnammankou, "New Research on Pushkin's Africa," 221.

32. J. A. Rogers, *World's Great Men of Color,* ed. John Henrik Clark (New York: Collier Books, 1972), 2:87.

33. Brenda Ray Moryck, review of *Pushkin,* by Prince D. S. Mirsky, *Opportunity* 6, no. 4 (April 1928): 121. Moryck refers to a passage in D. S. Mirsky, *Pushkin* (New York: E. P. Dutton, 1926), 3.

34. Tillman, "Alexander Sergeivich Pushkin," 125. Such observations recur in nearly all the writings about Pushkin that I am describing here.

35. Thomas L. G. Oxley, "The Negro in the World's Literature: Alexander S. Pushkin," *Amsterdam News* 18, no. 29 (June 15, 1927): 14.

36. These particular remarks were made by a white author but were published in the black press. Elbert Aidline-Trommer, "'Alexander Pushkin' and Alexander Pushkin," *Opportunity* 6, no. 8 (August 1928): 241. "Elbert Aidline-Trommer" was a pseudonym used by Lazarus Trommer, a Russian immigrant who worked on various Jewish newspapers in New York. Although Trommer was white, the fact that this article appeared in a prominent black journal meant that it entered the African American discourse about Pushkin, and I will be considering it in this context.

37. Tillman, "Alexander Sergeivich Pushkin," 123.

38. Rosa Newmarch, for example, writes that "On the maternal side Poushkin's descent was less impeccable [than on the paternal], though he did his best to set his maternal grandfather [sic] in a picturesque and romantic light." Gannibal, she claims, "retained a good deal of the savage in his nature," and Pushkin's own physiognomy suggested "an admixture of pure *negro,* rather than of *Arab* blood." Newmarch is unaware of the distinction in

Pushkin's Russian between the words *arap* (Negro) and *arab* (Arab), and thus charges Pushkin with "euphemistically" describing his ancestor as "Peter the Great's Arab." She further claims that Pushkin himself acknowledged, "in moments of cynical frankness . . . 'the inherited taint of negro concupiscence'" (Rosa Newmarch, *Poetry and Progress in Russia* [New York: John Lane, 1907], 32). Scarborough refers to another critic of Pushkin, a "Madame Ragozin" who wrote around the time of the 1899 jubilee, as a racist as well (he quotes her claim that Pushkin had a "savage spirit due to his fierce African blood"; Scarborough, "Alexander Sergeivitch Pushkin," pt. 2, 235).

39. Alice Dunbar-Nelson, review of *The Captain's Daughter,* by Alexander Pushkin, trans. Natalie Duddington, *Opportunity* 8, no. 1 (January 1930): 24.

40. Eric D. Walrond, "'The Penitent' Shows Alexander Pushkin, Russia's Great Poet, Was Influenced by Shelley," *Negro World* 13, no. 10 (October 21, 1922): 3.

41. A certain number—though far from all—of the early texts that introduced Americans to Pushkin simply ignored the issue. See, for example, S. P. B. Mais, *Why We Should Read* (New York: Dodd, Mead, 1921), 226–40. This enthusiastic and intelligent "appreciation" of Pushkin says nothing about his race. In 1937 the *New York Times,* in its listings of the various celebrations in the city marking Pushkin's jubilee, failed to take note of those undertaken by Negro organizations. Such distortions persist in our own time: as Werner Sollors has pointed out, Pushkin's African heritage is often ignored in the white press today, and Robert W. Wallace's scholarly article "Afrocentricity, Multiculturalism, and *Black Athena,*" *Caribana* 3 (1992–93): 45–53, "even lists Pushkin in a lineup of great figures from Jesus to Beethoven who have been falsely claimed as blacks" (Sollors, *Neither Black nor White,* 428n29).

42. Walrond, "'The Penitent,'" 3.

43. Chatwood Hall, "Entire Soviet Union Turns Out for Poet Pushkin: Rename Streets and Buildings for Great Russian Writer," *Amsterdam News* 28, no. 11 (February 20, 1937): 4.

44. Elizabeth Ross Haynes, *Unsung Heroes* (New York: Dubois and Dill, 1921), 105.

45. Aidline-Trommer, "'Alexander Pushkin' and Alexander Pushkin," 241.

46. J. A. Rogers, "Pushkin 'Made' Russian Literature," *The Advocate* (Oregon), vol. 25, no. 39 (May 25, 1929): 3, 9. Rogers's language is echoed in Fleming and Pryde, *Distinguished Negroes Abroad,* 171.

47. Dorothy Trench-Bonett, "Alexander Pushkin—Black Russian Poet," *Black Scholar* 20, no. 2 (April 1989): 4, 5. Trench-Bonett cites "The Negro of Peter the Great" in translation by Thomas Keane in Alexander Pushkin, *The Works of Alexander Pushkin,* ed. Avrahm Yarmolinsky (Random House, 1936), 305.

48. Aidline-Trommer, "'Alexander Pushkin' and Alexander Pushkin," 242.

49. Scarborough, "Alexander Sergeivitch Pushkin," pt. 1, 163.

50. Chatwood Hall, "Was Pushkin's Duel a Frame-up?" *Crisis* 43, no. 12 (December 1936): 370. Hall (whose real name was Homer Smith) was a Minnesotan who, like considerable numbers of black Americans, went to the Soviet Union in search of opportunity in the 1930s. Clearly the articles he sent home to the black press reflect the impact of Soviet propaganda, although he was not a Communist.

51. For Pushkin's comments on his "brother Negroes," see his letter to P. A. Viazemskii, June 24–25, 1824 (A. S. Pushkin, *Polnoe sobranie sochinenii*, 17 vols. [Moscow and Leningrad, 1937–59], 12:99).

52. Clement Richardson, ed., *The National Cyclopedia of the Colored Race* (Montgomery, Ala.: National Publishing, 1919), 11.

53. Anon., "Guiding Lights," *Amsterdam News* 30, no. 29 (July 1, 1939): 10.

54. Fleming and Pryde, *Distinguished Negroes Abroad*, 176.

55. See, for example, an anonymous article in *Freedom's Journal* (August 24, 1827), 93, comparing the costs of slave vs. free labor in Russia, as well as another anonymous article entitled "Russian Serfs" in *The Colored American and Advocate* (October 20, 1838), 4. The latter article opens with a key distinction that later writers were often to ignore: "The serfs of Russia differ from slaves with us in the important particular that they belong to the soil, and cannot be sold except with the estate; they may change masters, but cannot be torn from their connections or their birthplace." Nonetheless, it continues, serfs who are owned by nobles (as opposed to state peasants) "are the absolute property and subject to the absolute control of their masters, as much as the cattle on their estates."

56. Rogers, *World's Great Men of Color*, 2:81.

57. Rogers refers here to Pushkin's sympathies with the Decembrists, the small group of Russian noblemen who in 1825 led a failed attempt at a revolution that aimed at instituting a constitutional monarchy.

58. Rogers, "Pushkin 'Made' Russian Literature," 3, 9.

59. Rogers, *World's Great Men of Color*, 2:81.

60. Trench-Bonett, "Alexander Pushkin—Black Russian Poet," 2. Trench-Bonett cites Nabokov's commentary on *Eugene Onegin* as the source of this anecdote. Aleksandr Pushkin, *Eugene Onegin*, trans. Vladimir Nabokov, 4 vols., rev. ed. (Princeton: Princeton University Press, 1975), 4:425.

61. Henri Troyat (b. 1911) was a French scholar who published a biography of Pushkin in 1946. Vladimir Nabokov (1899–1977), Russian-American novelist, memoirist, and translator, published a copiously annotated translation of Pushkin's novel in verse, *Eugene Onegin*, in 1964.

62. Trench-Bonett, "Alexander Pushkin—Black Russian Poet," 6. The idea that the child was "visibly black" and therefore had to be disposed of is Trench-Bonett's invention. Nabokov writes that "We know nothing of his fate"

(and presumably nothing of his appearance). Troyat merely speculates that while no one knows what happened to Pushkin's son, he was "[a] little muzhik, probably, with dark skin and thick lips," and that "some people claim he was still alive at the turn of the century." Neither Nabokov nor Troyat suggests that the child's color was the reason for his being sent away. See Pushkin, *Eugene Onegin,* trans. Nabokov, 2:462; Henri Troyat, *Pushkin* (Garden City, N.Y.: Doubleday, 1970), 302.

63. Scarborough, "Alexander Sergeivitch Pushkin," pt. 2, 235.

64. Oxley, "Negro in the World's Literature," 14; Scarborough, "Alexander Sergeivitch Pushkin," pt. 1, 235.

65. Aidline-Trommer, "'Alexander Pushkin' and Alexander Pushkin," 242. Aidline-Trommer is quoting an unnamed Russian critic.

66. Bowser, "Russia's Black Genius," 20. Occasionally the echo of Dostoevsky's 1880 speech on Pushkin is heard even more clearly: "although essentially *the* Russian national poet, [Pushkin] possessed the remarkable faculty of interpreting the spirit of every other nation" (Guichard Parris, "In Honor of Alexander Pushkin: 1799–1837," *Opportunity* 15, no. 2 [February 1937]: 36).

67. Rogers, *World's Great Men of Color,* 2:85–86.

68. Scarborough, "Alexander Sergeivitch Pushkin," pt. 2, 235.

69. Rogers, *World's Great Men of Color,* 2:85–86. An earlier black writer concurs: Pushkin "gave dignity to Russian poetry" (Anon., "Celebrated Negroes," *The Freeman* 24, no. 38 [September 30, 1911]: 2).

70. Catharine Deaver Lealtad, "A Black Russian: A True Story," *The Brownies' Book* 2, no. 6 (June 1921): 182.

71. Aidline-Trommer, "'Alexander Pushkin' and Alexander Pushkin," 241, 242. Rogers, too, writes that Russian in Pushkin's day was "used chiefly by the enslaved serfs and the masses" (Rogers, *World's Great Men of Color,* 2:79).

72. Rogers, *World's Great Men of Color,* 2:80.

73. Fleming and Pryde, *Distinguished Negroes Abroad,* 171.

74. Peterson, "Justifying the Margin," 749.

75. Alain Locke, ed., *The New Negro* (1925; New York: Atheneum, 1975), 51.

76. Aidline-Trommer, "'Alexander Pushkin' and Alexander Pushkin," 241.

77. Scarborough, "Alexander Sergeivitch Pushkin," pt. 1, 163, 165.

78. Quoted in Peterson, "Justifying the Margin," 749. Toomer's original quote may be found in Locke, ed., *The New Negro,* 51.

79. Scarborough, "Alexander Sergeivitch Pushkin," pt. 1, 163, 165.

80. Fleming and Pryde, *Distinguished Negroes Abroad,* 174. Such African American accounts refer to the fact that Pushkin's mother, who seems to have neglected him, reputedly thought he looked more "black" than her other children.

81. Oxley, "Negro in the World's Literature," 14.

82. Rogers, "Pushkin 'Made' Russian Literature," 9.
83. Ibid., 3.
84. Locke, ed., *The New Negro,* 47.
85. Rogers, "Pushkin 'Made' Russian Literature," 3.
86. Aidline-Trommer, "'Alexander Pushkin' and Alexander Pushkin," 242.
87. Rogers, *World's Great Men of Color,* 2:79.
88. Deborah E. McDowell, "In the First Place: Making Frederick Douglass and the Afro-American Literary Tradition," in *Critical Essays on Frederick Douglass,* ed. William L. Andrews (Boston: G. K. Hall, 1991), 209, 208. McDowell is quoting James Olney, "The Founding Fathers—Frederick Douglass and Booker T. Washington," in *Slavery and the Literary Imagination,* ed. Deborah E. McDowell and Arnold Rampersad (Baltimore: Johns Hopkins University Press, 1989), 81. See also Henry Louis Gates Jr., "From Wheatley to Douglass: The Politics of Displacement," in *Frederick Douglass: New Literary and Historical Essays,* ed. Eric J. Sundquist (Cambridge: Cambridge University Press, 1990), 47–65.
89. Rogers, *World's Great Men of Color,* 2:85.
90. Edna Worthley Underwood, *The Penitent* (Boston and New York: Houghton Mifflin, 1922), [v]. (Page numbers of this work will hereafter be cited parenthetically in text.) Underwood completed only one other volume of the projected trilogy, which does little besides recapitulate the ideas developed in the first. See Underwood, *The Passion Flower* (Boston and New York: Houghton Mifflin, 1924). I have found only one other novel about Pushkin written in English, by the Englishman James Cleugh, *Prelude to Parnassus: Scenes from the Life of Alexander Sergeyevich Pushkin* (London: A. Barker, 1936). This novel does not share the racial fixation of the texts I analyze here. One French novel of the 1940s based on Pushkin's life has also appeared in English translation: Lydia Lambert, *Pushkin, Poet and Lover,* trans. Willard R. Trask (New York: Doubleday, 1946); it does not focus on race.
91. John Oliver Killens, *Great Black Russian: A Novel on the Life and Times of Alexander Pushkin* (Detroit: Wayne State University Press, 1989). The novel was published posthumously; Killens died in 1987.
92. Bernard W. Bell, *The Afro-American Novel and Its Tradition* (Amherst: University of Massachusetts Press, 1987), 248.
93. Bell, *Afro-American Novel,* 248–52.
94. By contrast, African American texts tend not to emphasize the hybrid nature of Pushkin's background, though they acknowledge it by referring freely to both his "Russianness" and his "Africanness."
95. Given the book's blatant racism, it is surprising to note that it was well reviewed by at least one major black newspaper. Apparently the mere fact of Underwood's emphasizing, rather than ignoring, Pushkin's racial identity was what recommended the book to this reviewer ("Mrs. Underwood throws a

shaft of light on a bundle of things of interest to us, Negroes, as a race . . . One of the vital things she brings to light is [Pushkin's] racial identity"). The reviewer urges readers to "Get it, at any cost," calling *The Penitent* "a book that colored people especially must read. It is the first noted work that has appeared anywhere on the noble life and character of the distinguished Negro poet of Russia" (Walrond, "'The Penitent,'" 3). See also Amanda Reed, "Corona Girl Figures in Great Historical Novel, Featuring Alexander Pushkin, Negro Poet of Russia," *Negro World* 13, no. 9 (October 14, 1922): 3. This article profiles Underwood's young black secretary, of whom Underwood is said to be "immensely proud." Underwood herself published translations of Pushkin's works in the black press, including one of "The Moor of Peter the Great" which was preceded by a biographical sketch of the poet that rather markedly deemphasized his race. See Underwood, "Alexis Sergiewitch Pushkin," 53–54.

96. Killens, *Great Black Russian,* 29–30. (Page numbers of this book will hereafter be cited parenthetically in the text.)

97. The expression "white Russian" would have been meaningless to Pushkin as a designation of social class. The application of this label to tsarist troops during the Revolution and to anti-Communist émigrés probably encouraged the American tendency to interpret nonracial color vocabulary in terms of American racial divisions, as did the use of the word "Reds" to designate Communists and leftists in general during the Cold War. Paul Robeson, for example, was called "a dangerous Red . . . and a dangerous Black" (quoted in Essence R. McGill, "Afroslavs: Tracing the Role and Influence of Afro-Americans in the Communist Party Movement" [master's thesis, Harvard University, 1997], 65). See also the title of Homer Smith's *Black Man in Red Russia* (Chicago: Johnson Publishing, 1964).

98. A particularly telling example of Pushkin's willingness to draw on all facets of his ancestry in constructing his persona is found in the poem "My Genealogy," in which he accords equal emphasis to his boyar and African origins. See Pushkin, *Polnoe sobranie sochinenii,* 3:261–63.

99. F. M. Dostoevsky, "Pushkin (A Sketch)," in *The Diary of a Writer,* trans. Boris Brasol (Salt Lake City: Gibbs M. Smith, 1985), 967, 980.

100. Quoted in Irina Paperno, "Pushkin v zhizni cheloveka serebrianogo veka," in *Cultural Mythologies of Russian Modernism,* ed. Boris Gasparov, Robert P. Hughes, and Irina Paperno (Berkeley: University of California Press, 1992), 21.

101. Dostoevsky, "Pushkin (A Sketch)," 979.

102. Ibid., 977.

103. Gnammankou, "New Research on Pushkin's Africa," 221 (italics mine).

Liza Knapp

Tsvetaeva's "Blackest of Black" (*Naicherneishii*) Pushkin

IN HER MEDITATIONS on Pushkin in poetry and prose,[1] Marina Tsvetaeva (1892–1941) refers to Pushkin's African heritage and to the blackness she associates with him as determining features of "her" Pushkin and, in turn, of her understanding of what it means to be a poet.[2] Although she points out that Pushkin did not bear some of the physical characteristics associated with an African heritage—her Pushkin was "light-haired and light-eyed"—Tsvetaeva still considers Pushkin a black poet. Her understanding of what this meant is based on other things (*Proza* 2:250). Tsvetaeva's assertions of Pushkin's blackness, her intuitions about the role it played in his poetics, her defiant warnings to the political and literary powers that be of all times that "Black cannot be repainted / White" (*Chërnogo ne perekrasit' / V belogo; Stikh* 3:149), set her at one end of the spectrum, at the other end of which is Vladimir Nabokov, another Russian writer to explore the significance of Pushkin's African heritage at length.[3] Nabokov all but reduces Pushkin's African heritage to an ethnographic and scholarly curiosity—a "taxonomic problem"—and expresses some scorn at Pushkin for having made a fuss over his ancestor, Abram Gannibal.[4] In contrast, Tsvetaeva regards Pushkin's African heritage and his blackness as extremely significant in human, poetic, and political terms.

Tsvetaeva's understanding of Pushkin and his blackness evolved over time, in response to the events of her life and of the world around her. It culminated in her most sustained treatment of this subject, which is to be found in her cycle of poetry "Verses to Pushkin" (1931) and in her prose work "My Pushkin" (1937), an excerpt of which is reprinted in an appendix to this volume. In this essay, I will examine some of the earlier manifestations of Tsvetaeva's interest in Pushkin's racial identity before turning to the later works.[5]

Tsvetaeva's early poem (1913) "A Meeting with Pushkin" (*Stikh* 1:147–48) is set in the Crimea, a locale that evokes Pushkin, whom she calls the "curly-haired magus of these lyrical environs." The Crimean setting has particular implications within the context of Pushkin's life and works. While in the Crimea, on the margins of the Russian Empire, Pushkin found relative personal and creative freedom. But in *Eugene Onegin* (1.50) the narrator, while in the Crimea, dreams of escape to the greater creative freedom to be found "under the sky of [his] Africa." In Tsvetaeva's poem, she imagines an encounter with Pushkin and describes their immediate sense of kinship as they wander together through the Crimean landscape. Although not mentioned directly, Pushkin's African sky and the promise of freedom it represented hovers over Tsvetaeva's poem. The Pushkin that Tsvetaeva wanders with in her fantasy is described as being "curly-haired" and "swarthy," two attributes that appear often when an author wants to draw attention to his African heritage. Tsvetaeva's poem seems to respond to Anna Akhmatova's early poem about Pushkin, which begins "The swarthy youth wandered . . ." Akhmatova describes a swarthy young Pushkin wandering dreamily in the park of Tsarskoe Selo. (Although it is clear that Pushkin is seeking refuge in the park, Tsarskoe Selo still is closely associated with the imperial court and all that it represents.) Akhmatova uses this poem to lay her claim to poetic kinship with Pushkin, on the grounds that she, with her proprietary feelings about Tsarskoe Selo, cherished his footsteps there. Tsvetaeva's poem, in which she establishes *her* common ground with Pushkin in the Crimea, has the effect of liberating Pushkin from Tsarskoe Selo (and Akhmatova) by moving him closer, actually and metaphorically, to his African sky and by establishing her hold on him.

Tsvetaeva expressly notes that she does not lean *on* his "swarthy arm" as she walks (*ne opiraias' o smugluiu ruku*). But at the end of the poem, they laugh together and run down the mountain hand in hand (*za ruku*) in a more egalitarian posture. These details show that the Pushkin she communed with in her poetic fantasy world treated her as a kindred spirit ("he would know from the first glance" who she was) and, significantly, without any patriarchal or sexist condescension: they walk hand in hand as equals. This poem sets the tone for Tsvetaeva's subsequent evocations of a Pushkin whose own yearnings for his African skies made him into a poet who in Tsvetaeva's vision stood dramatically and emphatically for freedom and the eradication of patriarchalism, racism, sexism, imperialism.

When the Communist revolution claimed that it united and embraced all people regardless of race, class, nationality, or ethnicity, Tsvetaeva was skeptical. On the one hand, Tsvetaeva yearned for liberty, equality, and brotherhood and sisterhood, all of which were associated in her mind with *her* African Pushkin. On the other hand, as she looked around her in the new Communist regime, she found it stifling and alien. Something had gone wrong and she used Pushkin to prove it. In her prose memoir "My Jobs" ("Moi sluzhby"; 1918–19), Tsvetaeva describes her travails as she works as an employee of the new Communist government in order to receive government rations to feed herself and her children. Although Pushkin appears mostly through hints and associations, Tsvetaeva makes his presence felt in this essay and, in the process, makes it clear that Pushkin represents for her the true spirit of revolution, which this revolution had failed to embody.

In "My Jobs" Tsvetaeva describes working in the Moscow office of the "Narkomnats," an acronym for the Narodnyi Komissariat po delam natsional' nostei (People's Commissariat for Nationality Affairs). As the name suggests, this commissariat was to address the issue of nationality, which was a prickly subject in the Communist regime. Workers, including Tsvetaeva, sat at various tables clipping and annotating newspaper articles about different nationalities. The project was, apparently, related to utopian Communist dreams of the International.

Within the Russian context, the idea of transcending nationality had been associated with Pushkin, in part because of the influence of Dostoevsky's Pushkin speech of 1880. In this speech, written for the inauguration of the Pushkin monument in Moscow, Dostoevsky presents Pushkin as a messianic figure. He argues that Pushkin's particular Russian genius for intuitively transcending and uniting the spirits of various nations and peoples has the power to make Russia into an internationalizing, universalizing phenomenon.[6] The extent to which Dostoevsky's vision of Pushkin is true to the spirit of Pushkin is, of course, open to debate. However, Dostoevsky's idea had broad appeal. Traces of his suggestion that the Russian poet was an internationalizing force surfaced in many widely different variations in twentieth-century interpretations of Pushkin, including ones as different from Dostoevsky's and from each other as Tsvetaeva's and that of the cultural ideologists of the early Soviet state.

Tsvetaeva describes her boss as a starry-eyed Communist who believes in the mission of the Narkomnats. His desire to eradicate nationality further manifests itself in his enthusiasm for Esperanto. He dreams of this universal language taking over the world. For Tsvetaeva, this is the logical course for a philologist with Communist convictions. (After she calls him an Esperantist, she notes in parentheses: "i.e., a communist from Philology" [*Proza* 1:56].) Yet this man earns Tsvetaeva's respect because he, unlike many Communists, is without (partisan) political convictions and does "not distinguish red from white," "right from left," or "man from woman" (*Proza* 1:57). In other words, although misguided in some ways, he still has a sense of an egalitarian love that transcends whatever arbitrary divisions separate human beings. For Tsvetaeva, this love is the essence of true revolution.

Tsvetaeva notes that her boss even rejects the Communists' slogan "in the beginning was the deed" in favor of "in the beginning was the word" (*Proza* 1:57). For Tsvetaeva, this belief in the word is a positive sign, but she has severe misgivings about the poetic potential of Esperanto. The language does not live up to its name. When Tsvetaeva, moved by the root of the word

"Esperanto," recites a Lamartine poem about "hope" ("*Espère, enfant, demain! Et puis demain encore* ..."), her boss recognizes the power of poetry—of Tsvetaeva's "word"—and wishes that he could harness Tsvetaeva to his cause: "Oh, what an Esperantist you would be" (*Proza* 1:56).

Despite her fondness for her Communist boss, Tsvetaeva maintains a bitterly ironic attitude toward the official attempt of the Communist revolution to eliminate racial, class, and national boundaries among people. She ends "My Jobs" with a description of a reading she gives along with Anatoly Lunacharsky, the people's commissar of enlightenment. She proudly relates having read lines from her "Fortuna," in which she refers to vengeance taken for "the triple lie of Freedom, Equality and Brotherhood" (*Proza* 1:70). For Tsvetaeva, when "Freedom, Equality and Brotherhood" becomes an official slogan, it becomes a lie. This was the message she intended to convey to Lunacharsky and others.

And yet individual strangers can behave as brothers and sisters to each other, and these are moments Tsvetaeva highlights in her description of Moscow during civil war and famine. In "My Jobs" an important role is played by one of Tsvetaeva's coworkers, whom Tsvetaeva dubs the "white negro." This moniker may have been initially inspired by her curly hair, each "ovine" ringlet of which embodied a "challenge," and by her "impassioned mug" (*zadornaia morda*; *Proza* 1:59). Here, as in the case of Pushkin who was the measure of all Negroes for Tsvetaeva, a "negro" is someone who lives in passionate defiance of authority. Tsvetaeva's "white negro" is seventeen, prone to falling in love, devout, and less cultured than Tsvetaeva. Her father is a porter who works in a building frequented by Lenin.[7] The "white negro" confides that she has daydreamed about shooting Lenin during one of his visits to her father's building as an act of retribution for Lenin's burning of churches (*Proza* 1:60–61). Afraid of the consequences (especially of what would happen to her family), Tsvetaeva's friend does not actually carry through her plan to assassinate Lenin. But at least in her aspirations, this "white negro" lives up to the nickname Tsvetaeva has given her: Tsvetaeva's vision of being a "negro" means defying the powers that be and living in a state of rebellion against oppression. It means living in imitation of *her* Pushkin.

By referring insistently to the woman she befriends as her "white negro," Tsvetaeva wants to suggest that she herself crosses the (here quite metaphorical) boundary of race in forming her friendships. Tsvetaeva delights in championing her "white negro" and, at the same time, in showing that the official Communist attempt to eliminate racism, classism, and nationalism is a farce. She and her "white negro" represent the true spirit of "revolution" (and poetry) because they are free. They form an alliance, a sisterhood that transcends race, class, and all such boundaries. In the culmination of one episode, the "white negro" shares a loaf of bread with Tsvetaeva (*Proza* 1:59), an act that acquires great significance in the context of the Moscow famine and in the context of Tsvetaeva's cult of poets. In fact, later, in "My Pushkin," Tsvetaeva describes how her early knowledge that Pushkin was fatally wounded in the stomach made her acutely aware of the *stomach* of the poet. She notes that in her own subsequent dealings with poets, she cared for the stomach "which is so often empty and in which Pushkin was killed" "not less than for the soul."[8] Tsvetaeva's "white negro," in sharing her bread with Tsvetaeva and her children, shows what Tsvetaeva considers the right attitude toward poets, whereas the failure of the Communist regime to tend to the empty stomach of the poet was a sin Tsvetaeva never forgave.

In "My Pushkin," Tsvetaeva declares: "In every Negro I love Pushkin and I recognize Pushkin" (*Proza* 2:253). Although Tsvetaeva does not say so explicitly in "My Jobs," the "white negro" she befriends is a representative of Pushkin. More generally, Pushkin lurks beneath the surface of the discussion of nationality, race, language, revolution, and poetry throughout "My Jobs." Pushkin figures directly in Tsvetaeva's essay in a seemingly offhand but very significant way. Moved by the fact that the office where she, her "white negro," the Esperanto enthusiast, and others work is located in the Moscow house which had been used by Tolstoy as a model for the Rostov house in *War and Peace*, Tsvetaeva starts thinking about Natasha Rostova. Tsvetaeva cannot forgive Tolstoy for what happens to Natasha at the end of the novel. In earlier parts of the novel, Natasha embodies the "spirit of poetry," according to Tsvetaeva. But Tolstoy then changed Natasha from "Psyche" into a hag, married to Pierre Bezukhov, and going around waving her baby's diapers. If only, Tsvetaeva muses, Natasha Rostov could have met Pushkin, then her fate would have been different . . . Tsvetaeva is convinced that Natasha would have fallen in love with Pushkin right away, since Natasha "heard lots of stories about the poet and blackamoor [*arap*]."[9] Here Tsvetaeva sets forth the two essential components of Pushkin's identity that in her mind were mysteriously joined: his poetry and his African heritage. Tsvetaeva considered poetry to be the "free element" (see below), and she considered Pushkin's African heritage to be what kept him spiritually free, even in the midst of the oppressive political circumstances in which he lived.

As Tsvetaeva knew well, in his own writings on this subject Pushkin suggests that his African heritage and the political destiny of his ancestor Abram Gannibal had a profound effect on his own attitudes toward the tsarist regime and its attempt to control various aspects of his personal and literary life. (For Tsvetaeva, as she wrote "My Jobs" and found herself a servant of the state— if not a gentleman of the bedchamber, like Pushkin—these issues of the poet's cooperation with the state were very relevant. She would naturally look to Pushkin for guidance in this regard.)

Pushkin's ancestor, as Peter the Great's "nursling" and foster child, found himself in an anomalous position in the Russian power structure. Perhaps Pushkin best sums up the essence of Gannibal's position and his legacy to Pushkin in the poem "My Genealogy." In "My Genealogy," Pushkin depicts the Russian gentry as toadying to the tsar. He ends in a defense of his African ancestor, "my black grandpa, Gannibal." Although—or because—he was an *arap*, Gannibal had the spiritual freedom needed to *not* be a slave of the tsar and his regime. Pushkin plays on linguistic and perhaps cultural expectations: although Gannibal ostensibly was "purchased," he is not for sale. Even more pointedly, Pushkin declares that his ancestor was an *arap* but not a slave, these words in Russian forming a word play and rhyme: *arap* and *a ne rab*. (These words rhyme in Russian because the "b" at the end of *a ne rab* is devoiced and sounds like a "p"). Pushkin thus reverses the expectation that an *arap* (blackamoor) should be a *rab* (slave) by opening up the *arap* and transforming the word into a negation of slavery (*a ne rab* [but *not* a slave]). In this regard, Pushkin denies the rumors that his grandfather was actually a slave, and he subverts both the cultural expectation and the possible expectation that the Russian language seems to promote because the words rhyme with each other.

Given the way that Tsvetaeva read Pushkin and poetry in general, one can assume that the Russian word *arap* (blackamoor) conjures up its Pushkinian rhyme, *a ne rab*. For Tsvetaeva, embedded in the *arap* (blackamoor) was the ability *not to be a slave*.[10] Tsvetaeva adds to whatever romantic associations would go along with Pushkin's being "a poet and an *arap* (blackamoor)"; she conveys her conviction that Pushkin would have preserved Natasha's status as the "spirit of Poetry" intact. Whereas Tolstoy's scenario—marriage to Pierre Bezukhov—resulted in what Tsvetaeva saw as a hateful, oppressive existence, Pushkin, as blackamoor and poet, would have granted liberty to Natasha.

Much as Pushkin is presented as the figure who had the power to save Natasha from her oppressive fate ("if only . . ."), Pushkin is likewise the force that *could* save Russia. But the Soviet regime has failed to embody what he represents. Had the Revolution been different and had it understood and embraced Pushkin in his two combined natures of poet and *arap,* and had it taken to heart what he stood for, then it might well have transcended racial, national, and class divisions and brought about liberty, equality, and fraternity. But, as it was, Tsvetaeva saw it as a failure. In "My Jobs" the "white negro"— with her rebellious demeanor, her daydreams about shooting Lenin, and her acts of kindness to a starving poet—is the closest embodiment of Pushkin that Tsvetaeva meets.

Tsvetaeva's "Verses to Pushkin" were written in Paris in 1931, during Tsvetaeva's years of emigration, when she felt alienated from both the Soviet regime in Russia and the Russian émigré establishment in Paris. In these poems, Tsvetaeva reacted against the way Pushkin was being appropriated and co-opted both by the Soviet literary establishment in Russia and by the émigré establishment. Of these poems, she herself commented: "They are frightfully harsh, frightfully freedom-loving, have nothing in common with the canonized Pushkin and have everything counter to the canon. *Dangerous* verses . . . They are *inwardly* revolutionary, in such a way those in Russia never even dreamed of."[11] In these "inwardly revolutionary" poems, she attacks both the political authorities (the regime of Nicholas I of Russia and, by extension, any state that oppresses poets) and the literary authorities who, in Tsvetaeva's view, were violating Pushkin by making a "mausoleum" out of him (*Stikh* 3:149). In particular, she felt that these authorities were denying a vital part of Pushkin, the very part that she championed and the part she felt was most kindred to her as a poet.[12] She attempts in these angry verses to reinstate in her poetry the Pushkin that "they" were effacing: her black Pushkin.

In these poems Tsvetaeva accuses the oppressive authorities, literary and political, of trying to tame Pushkin's "African passions" (*Stikh* 3:151), of physically keeping him away from "his Africa." In essence, they were trying to "repaint black white" (*Stikh* 3:149). Peter the Great appears as Tsvetaeva's ally in the battle for Pushkin, a battle conceived by Tsvetaeva as both sides literally pummeling each other using Pushkin as a weapon (*Stikh* 3:154). In Tsvetaeva's poems, Peter the Great, who murdered his own biological son for being too timid, regarded "*the Negro*" (by which she means Pushkin's ancestor, Abram Gannibal) as his "true son" (*Stikh* 3:152). And had Peter and Pushkin been contemporaries, the poet's biography would have taken a very different course: as Pushkin's personal censor (the role actually assumed by Nicholas I), Peter—unlike Nicholas—would have granted Pushkin permission to travel "to his African wilds" and he would have allowed him other forms of freedom (*Stikh* 3:151). In describing Pushkin in these verses, Tsvetaeva repeatedly uses phrases that evoke his African origins: she mentions his "grin of a Negro," his "Negro's teeth" (*Stikh* 3:153). And Tsvetaeva revels in the irony and poetic justice of what resulted from Peter's having taken "that little African boy" under his tutelage: Russia, which is referred to in the previous stanza as "white Russia," "received light from the grandson of a *Negro*" (*Stikh* 3:151, Tsvetaeva's emphasis). As Tsvetaeva attempted to "beat" (or pummel) her enemies "with Pushkin" (*Stikh* 3:149), she beat them with the black Pushkin they had refused even to see.

As Peter Scotto has shown, Tsvetaeva in "Verses to Pushkin" was in part responding to the attempt of the émigré Russian literary establishment in Paris to deny her Pushkinian heritage. In particular, Vladislav Khodasevich, a powerful figure in the Russian emigration, criticized her for refusing to adhere to what he and many others saw as the Pushkinian poetic doctrine of moderation: she had refused to live in the "world of measure."[13] Tsvetaeva echoes this episode in the opening poem of "Verses to Pushkin," in which she portrays critics as "whining" the following in regard to her verse: "Where in-

Liza Knapp

deed is the Pushkinian sense of measure [moderation]?" (*Stikh* 3:149). Tsvetaeva answers by reminding them of the Pushkinian "sense of the sea." (Here she engages in wordplay by countering *chuvstvo mery* ["sense of measure"] with *chuvstvo moria* ["sense of the sea"].)

Among the evidence of Tsvetaeva's abandonment of the "world of measure" that Khodasevich cited were the following lines from "The Poets" of 1923 (*Stikh* 3:68):[14]

> Что мне делать, певцу и первенцу,
> В мире, где наичернейший — сер!
> Где вдохновенье хранят, как в термосе!
> С этой безмерностью
> В мире мер?!

> What am I to do, a singer and first-born,
> In a world where the blackest of black is gray!
> Where inspiration is kept, as in a thermos!
> With this measurelessness
> In a world of measure?!

In her analysis of this poem, Olga Hasty notes that it is a response to Pushkin's own "The Poet."[15] Thus the very poem that Tsvetaeva's critics considered anti-Pushkinian was one in which she herself had been expressing her kinship to Pushkin.

Of Tsvetaeva's complaint about a world in which black is turned gray, Hasty writes:

> In Tsvetaeva's poetic system "blackness," when applied to the art of poetry, is an emblem of purity. This purity is projected in a broad range of examples, including, predictably, Pushkin's negritude, the elevation of the denigrated poet, and the virtue vouchsafed a text by the fertile blackness of its rough draft (*chernovik*). The antipode to this "blackness" is gray—that Hamlet of the color charts, which, neither black nor white, is situated somewhere in-between.[16]

Thus blackness for Tsvetaeva evokes both Pushkin and the creative process.

Tsvetaeva describes the poet's state of living at odds with a world in which the blackest of black is but gray. To denote this blackness, Tsvetaeva uses the word *naicherneishii*, a hypersuperlative long form of an adjective of color, a member of the class of adjectives for which comparative and superlative degrees are problematic. As these markers indicate, this is the essence and epitome of blackness—but only the poets see it; the rest of the world registers it as merely gray. Here Tsvetaeva uses the adjective *ser*, with the short form denoting an ephemeral, subjective state—it is not really, essentially gray; it just appears that way in this temporal realm, in this "world of measure." In her play with the way these adjectives are formed and with the way morphology signifies, Tsvetaeva shows her poetic mastery of the system of language and how she uses it to push beyond to some deeper meaning—the long, elegantly archaic, Slavonic *naicherneishii* (most black, blackest of black) suggests some metaphysical category, while the brutally truncated *ser* is brief and ephemeral. This stanza amounts to a spirited poetic embrace of Pushkin's blackness, which Tsvetaeva felt was being denied, or turned gray, by both the Soviet regime and the Russian émigré establishment.

Given the fact that her critics considered anti-Pushkinian the very poem in which she had evoked Pushkin's blackness, Tsvetaeva, true to form, came back in "Verses to Pushkin" with a strong counterattack in which she intensifies her embrace of Pushkin's African heritage and makes his blackness even more absolute.[17] In "Verses to Pushkin" Tsvetaeva further explores the significance of Pushkin's blackness and Africanness and overtly accuses her (and Pushkin's) adversaries of a kind of racism as they tried to deny Pushkin's African heritage and, in general, "paint the black [Pushkin] white."

In her prose essay "My Pushkin," written in Paris in 1937 for the centenary of Pushkin's death, which was being celebrated in Paris as well as in Russia, Tsvetaeva explains the genesis of her understanding of Pushkin, and specifically of a black Pushkin. In this regard, "My Pushkin" provides a gloss on the evocations of Pushkin in her earlier work. Tsvetaeva lays great emphasis on the fact that her sense of kinship with Pushkin predates her learning to read—and that her acquisition of literacy, consequently, occurred under the aegis of her already present love for Pushkin, a love imbued with his blackness and African heritage.

As she explains in "My Pushkin," Tsvetaeva's first awareness of Pushkin stemmed from two representations of him that were part of the daily landscape of her childhood: a picture of Pushkin's duel hanging in her house (see figure 75), and the Pushkin monument standing not far from her house in Moscow. She begins by describing the picture of the mortally wounded Pushkin which she observed from a young age in her mother's room. She emphasizes the fact that even before reading the words of Pushkin, she absorbed the image of his death. In her evocation of her childhood, Tsvetaeva hints that this image of Pushkin's death to some degree replaced the icons that Russian mothers taught their children to venerate. The iconic significance of the mortally wounded Pushkin (his passion) and the fact that it, to some degree, presented an alternative to Christianity is further emphasized when Tsvetaeva reports that her mother reveled in the fact that Pushkin, mortally wounded though he was, still chose to go ahead and take his shot at his enemy d'Anthès rather than forgive him. By approving this act of Pushkin's and thereby failing to preach Christian meekness and forgiveness, Tsvetaeva's mother "return[ed] Pushkin with all of us to his native Africa of revenge and passion." Tsvetaeva's mother did "not suspect what a lifelong lesson, if not of revenge then of passion, she was giving the four-year-old, barely literate, me" (*Proza* 2:250).[18] To Tsvetaeva, her mother's interpretation of Pushkin's behavior at death reveals that she did not approve of the attempt to Russify and de-Africanize the famous descendant of Gannibal: she wanted to return to him the "African sky" and all it represents, if only in death. Moreover, in this way, Tsvetaeva sets forth as her mother's legacy to her a vengeful and passionate "African" alternative to Orthodox meekness and Russian nationalism. This "African passion" was to play a significant role in Tsvetaeva's self-representation.

From this early stage (even before she read his works), Tsvetaeva came to identify Pushkin with his death. In fact, Tsvetaeva regarded him as a martyr, in the same way Christ is traditionally regarded.[19] Bearing witness to Pushkin's martyrdom determined Tsvetaeva's emotional and spiritual makeup. She declares, referring to this painting: "the *sister* in me began with Pushkin's duel" (*Proza* 2:249, Tsvetaeva's emphasis).[20] Tsvetaeva countered Saint Paul's brothers and sisters in Christ with her sisterhood to Pushkin and, by extension, to all poets, regardless of race and national origin.

Tsvetaeva describes how her early knowledge of the fact that Pushkin was wounded in the stomach left her with a "sacred" feeling about the word "stomach." Even a simple mention of somebody having a stomachache, much less a bullet wound in the stomach, would "fill her with a wave of convulsive sympathy that excluded all humor" (*Proza* 2:249). Here she shows that from early childhood she developed the sense of compassion (in its etymological sense of "suffering with") for Pushkin that she would retain—and that would be an essential part of her humanity—throughout the rest of her life. Indeed, the extent to which her cult of the martyred Pushkin became a religion that mimicked features of Christianity is made clear in her declaration that "All of us were wounded in the stomach by that shot." One hears echoes here of Christian formulations such as "Christ died for us" and of the general idea of Christians sharing Christ's passion. Perhaps she even hints that Pushkin lovers have stigmata in the stomach?

In "My Pushkin" Tsvetaeva recreates the pattern of associations inspired by her childhood exposure to the image of Pushkin's death: *russkii poet—negr, poet—negr, i poeta ubili* ("the Russian poet is a Negro, the poet is a Negro and the poet was killed"; *Proza* 2:250). The facts that Pushkin was a Russian poet and a Negro and that the poet was killed all led the child Tsvetaeva to draw natural conclusions from these givens. A pattern emerged in her mind, which, alas, experience seemed to confirm. And the adult Tsvetaeva notes, enclosed in parentheses: (*Bozhe, kak sbylos'! Kakoi poet iz byvshikh i sushchikh* ne *negr, i kakogo poeta—*ne *ubili?* [Tsvetaeva's emphasis]) ["(Good lord, how it has come to pass! What poet of the past or present is *not* a Negro, and what poet has *not* been killed?)"]. In this parenthetical remark, Tsvetaeva gives her response to the question that her Russian contemporaries were facing as they watched so many of their poets die young, in eerie imitation of Pushkin. (Among these were Blok, Mayakovsky, and Esenin.) What answers could be found in Pushkin's death?[21]

In responding to this question, Tsvetaeva goes to the heart and soul of her understanding of the meaning of Pushkin's blackness. "Good lord, how it has come to pass! What poet of the past or present is *not* a Negro, and what poet has *not* been killed?" This remark about all poets being Negroes also brings to mind Tsvetaeva's earlier statement in her "Poem of the End" ("Poema kontsa") that *V sem khristinneishem iz mirov / Poety—zhidy*! ("In this most Christian of worlds, / Poets are Jews"; *Stikh* 4:185). Instead of the more neutral *evrei*, she uses the derogatory term *zhid*, as if to emphasize her point about how Jews and poets are treated in the Christian world. Earlier in the same poem Tsvetaeva had used the idiom *Vechnyi zhid* ("Eternal Jew"), declaring it to be "one-hundredfold more worthy to become a Wandering Jew" than to live in this life. Her claim that poets are *zhidy* thus harks back to this line about the Wandering Jew. Her references to Jews recall the fact that Jews were forced to live outside of the center of town (a detail relevant to this poem and its partner, "Poem of the Mountain," where the two lovers feel excluded from life in the center and wander the mountainous outskirts).[22] But Tsvetaeva goes beyond residential marginalization. Earlier in the "Poem of the End" she speaks of life being "a pogrom for everybody who's not vermin" (*Stikh* 4:185). In this poem, these references to Jewish pogroms may seem gratuitously hyperbolic self-dramatization in the midst of her personal romantic tragedy—is she simply appropriating and co-opting the tragic experiences of the Jews and using them to her own personal ends? Is this an inappropriate use of analogy? On the other hand, her likening *the poet* to Jews—and to blacks (in "My Pushkin")—whose very lives are in jeopardy, fits into a complex system of associations she develops not so much about her own personal troubles as about her romantic and tragic vision of the poet and the mission of poetry.[23] The poet was, in her view, an outsider whom the dominant group threatened to exterminate but who wielded a spiritual authority that transcended all. This vision of the poet was vital to her understanding of Pushkin and of herself and of all poets.

Whereas the picture of Pushkin's duel hanging in her mother's room evoked Tsvetaeva's profound compassion and sisterhood, the Opekushin Pushkin monument outside, in her mother city of Moscow, was more awe-inspiring, triumphant, and defiant. Although Tsvetaeva does not refer overtly to the history of this monument, it may be relevant to note that it was erected in Moscow after a long campaign waged by devotees of Pushkin acting independently rather than under the auspices of the autocratic regime. Within the Russian context, the erection of this monument could even be seen as a defiant attempt to limit imperial control over all the various aspects of literature and the writer's destiny.

> And I preferred [a walk] to the Pushkin monument, because, opening and even in my hurry ripping the suffocating white Karlsbad "jacket" I'd gotten from Grandfather, I liked to run toward it/him [the monument] and, once there, to walk around it/him, and then, raising my head, to look at the blackfaced, black-handed giant, who wasn't looking at me, and who was unlike anyone or anything in my life. (*Proza* 2:251)

The Pushkin monument represents a kind of ultimate other to the child Tsvetaeva. One of the numerous oppositions operative in this description is that of white and black. The white of her jacket (and by extension, her own "whiteness") is opposed to the black of Pushkin. Significantly, as she runs toward the black Pushkin monument, she frees herself from her "suffocating white Karlsbad 'jacket' . . . from Grandfather." She even does violence to the jacket by ripping it, so desperate is she to liberate herself from its constraint. In her desperate, almost violent, desire to rid herself of this jacket can be read a desire to dissociate herself from the legacy of her grandfather, her family and heritage, and to affiliate herself with Pushkin—or, better, become his sister.

Tsvetaeva then goes on to explain what her "choice" of the Pushkin monument signifies. After describing a game she liked to play which consisted of comparing a small white china figurine to the big black statue, Tsvetaeva writes: "The Pushkin monument was my first encounter with black and white: so black [masc.]! so white [fem.]!" (*Pamiatnik Pushkina byl i moei pervoi vstrechei s chërnym i belym: takoi chërnyi! takaia belaia!*; *Proza* 2:252). And she explains that when faced with the choice between the white china figurine and the big black Pushkin, she chose the latter:

> Since *black* appeared in the form of a giant, and *white* in the form of a comical figure, and since one absolutely had to choose, I then and there and forever chose black [masc. animate], not white [masc. animate], black [neuter], not white [neuter]: black thoughts, black fate, black life. (*Proza* 2:252)

In rejecting the white doll (and the life in a Doll's House it represents), Tsvetaeva imitates Pushkin's Tatiana, who did not play with dolls (*Eugene Onegin* 2.27).[24]

Tsvetaeva's choice of black is further outlined:

> From the Pushkin monument stems my mad love for blacks, stretching through my whole life, to this day a gratification of my whole being when, by

chance, in the car of a tramway or somewhere else I find myself next to a black. My white wretchedness side by side with black divinity. In each Negro I love Pushkin and recognize Pushkin, the black Pushkin monument of my preliterate childhood and that of all Russia. (*Proza* 2:253)

The whole thrust of this section of "My Pushkin" is to establish the supremacy of the black Pushkin monument over all that Tsvetaeva knew as a child and to assert the lasting effect of these childhood impressions. For example, she juxtaposes her "household gods" to the Pushkin monument, with the latter overpowering the former. The household gods, who, for example, could be moved about, were dusted with rags before Easter and Christmas, whereas the Pushkin monument was immobile and was washed by rain and dried by the winds. The Pushkin monument provided her with her "first vision of inviolability and immutability," and her household gods paled in comparison.

The section of "My Pushkin" describing her childhood rapture over the Pushkin monument ends with the seemingly elliptical mention that "at the Patriarchs' Ponds, there were no Patriarchs." This is why she preferred the Pushkin monument—Pushkin was definitely present at the Pushkin monument, whereas the Patriarchs were absent from the Ponds that bore their name—no church patriarchs actually still lived there. But Tsvetaeva's comment about the absence of the patriarchs only confirms what was hinted at as the little Tsvetaeva ran to Pushkin, liberating herself along the way from the white jacket her grandfather had bestowed on her: Tsvetaeva is dissatisfied with her own patriarchal heritage. Not just her little white doll, but even all the white patriarchs of Tsvetaeva's world—the patriarchs of the church, the patriarchs of her family—fail to measure up to the black Pushkin monument. And clearly her devotion to the Pushkin monument and all it stands for in her mind provides Tsvetaeva with an alternative to submitting to patriarchal authority.

For Tsvetaeva, Pushkin represented rebellion not only against patriarchal authority, but also against imperial authority. In fact, as she describes it in "My Pushkin," the Pushkin monument embodies Pushkin's own struggle to overcome imperialism. Tsvetaeva sees the chains at the base of the monument as being symbolic of Emperor Nicholas's attempt to control and enslave the poet. The chains, interspersed with rocks, which surround the statue, form the "circle of Nicholas's arms, never embracing the poet but also never letting go. The circle, created with the words: 'You are no longer the former Pushkin, you are now *my* Pushkin' and broken apart only by d'Anthès's bullet" (*Proza* 2:254). Although the chains thus remind Tsvetaeva of the "gloomy" part of Pushkin's existence, Tsvetaeva envisions a way of subverting these chains and what they represent: "On these chains I, with all of the children of Moscow, swung, without suspecting what we were swinging on. It was a very low swing, very hard, very iron. '*Empire*'?—*Empire.*—Empire—the Empire of Nicholas

I." (*Na etikh ia, so vsei detskoi Moskvoi, proshloi, sushchei, budushchei, kachalas'—ne podozrevaia na chem. Eto byli ochen' nizkie kacheli, ochen' tverdye, ochen' zheleznye.—'Ampir'?—Ampir.—Empire—Nikolaia 1-ogo Imperiia!; Proza* 2:254.) The iron chains form a "Style Empire" swing, and for Tsvetaeva the oppressive aesthetic of "Style Empire" embodies all that the empire of Nicholas I stands for. Are the children of Moscow, as they swing on these imperial chains at the feet of the black Pushkin monument, being unwittingly filled with the spirit of rebellion against oppressive authority?[25]

Tsvetaeva suggests that the black Pushkin monument ideally fosters a spirit of rebellion against oppression in the past, present, and future children of Moscow. This is fitting because Pushkin himself believed that this spirit of freedom was part of his own genealogy. Tsvetaeva believed that Pushkin, like his ancestor the *arap*, ultimately refused to be the tsar's slave—even though Pushkin lost his life as a result of what she perceived to be the machinations of the tsar and his henchmen.

This struggle between freedom and Pushkin on the one hand and oppression and temporal authority on the other—and Pushkin's ultimate victory—was literally inscribed on the monument, which was one of the major "texts" through which the young Tsvetaeva came to know Pushkin. On the base of the monument, lines from Pushkin's own "Monument" poem had been carved when the monument was erected in 1880, but not as Pushkin had written them.[26] Ironically, they appeared in a version that had been altered by Zhukovsky. To appease tsarist censorship, Zhukovsky in publishing the poem had gotten rid of Pushkin's declaration that he had "praised freedom in his cruel age," and replaced it with a declaration about having made himself "useful" through his poetry. Tsvetaeva found Zhukovsky's additions about the social utility of poetry to be thoroughly "non-Pushkinian and anti-Pushkinian." Tsvetaeva took this violation of Pushkin's poetry as a grave affront to all that Pushkin stood for. Zhukovsky had tried to make a slave out of Pushkin. At last, in 1937, Zhukovsky's version was erased from the monument and Pushkin's original version—celebrating freedom in his cruel age—was inscribed on the Pushkin monument. Tsvetaeva found some consolation in this, for now her beloved Pushkin monument more truly represented the rebellious and liberty-loving spirit of Pushkin.

As Tsvetaeva herself well knew, the *true* monument to Pushkin was the one he himself erected—out of words. In his poem of 1836, "I have erected a monument to myself . . ." Pushkin had already declared his poetry to be a monument "not made by human hands" (*nerukotvornyi*) that he erected to himself in an indirect defiance of imperial monuments and imperial power. (Pushkin pronounces *his* monument to be greater than the Alexander column, erected to honor Tsar Alexander I.) Pushkin's poem declares the supremacy of poetry over any other "monument" or memorial. And yet, if Tsvetaeva chooses to focus such attention on the Pushkin monument in Moscow, it is because she is convinced that this monument, although erected "by human hands" out of cast iron and granite, is a worthy tribute to Pushkin and in the spirit of his "Monument" poem and of the whole corpus of poetry he calls his "monument" to himself.

For Tsvetaeva, the Pushkin monument forcefully reflects Pushkin's African heritage, most obviously through its physical blackness, which for her was richly significant. But how, in Tsvetaeva's view, did Pushkin's African heritage manifest itself in his poetry? Here the connection is less overt, but nonetheless present. For Tsvetaeva (as discussed above), there were two intimately related facets of Pushkin: he was a poet and he was of African descent. These two features mysteriously combined to form the essence of the Pushkin she loved. In her commentary on the edition of Pushkin she knew as a child, she discusses an edition intended for municipal schools. She disliked the contents of this edition because it presented a "rendered-harmless, tamed Pushkin," although she liked the picture on the cover, which was Pushkin as "a Negro boy, supporting his cheek with his fist": "For that matter, to this day, I consider this childhood Negro portrait to be the best of the portraits of Pushkin, a portrait of his distant African soul and of his still-dormant poetic one. A portrait reaching into two distances—backward and forward, a portrait of his blood and of his coming genius." Pushkin's poetic genius and his African blood were inextricably and mystically linked in Tsvetaeva's mind.

In "To Yazykov," a poem written in 1824 (during the same Mikhailovskoe period as Tsvetaeva's beloved "To the Sea"), Pushkin himself, by association, links poetry-writing with his African heritage, in a way that may well have become a source for Tsvetaeva's intuitions on this subject. Pushkin writes his fellow poet Yazykov and, in the name of the important kinship of inspiration between poets, invites him to come to his family estate of Mikhailovskoe.[27] Pushkin alludes to the fact that he himself is not free to come to Yazykov because of the conditions of his exile. Mikhailovskoe is presented as the retreat Abram Gannibal had used on retiring from the machinations of Peter's successors, their courts and regimes. Pushkin tells Yazykov that he awaits him in the place where his ancestor "thought" of "his distant Africa." His ancestor's thoughts of "distant Africa" in the poem are opposed to the political world of the court (from which Gannibal has escaped). In fact, the structure and metaphors of the poem point to an equation (and a genetic relation) of Pushkin's ancestor's dreams of his Africa to Pushkin's own poetic composition. Mikhailovskoe provides a congenial setting for both dreams of Africa and writing poetry. By extension, because of the *rodnia po vdokhnoven'iu* ("kinship by inspiration") that relates all poets, Yazykov and other poets partake of these distant African dreams, especially, but not only, if they visit Pushkin at Mikhailovskoe. Tsvetaeva seems to have taken quite literally Pushkin's suggestion, stated most directly in this poem, that his writing poetry was the direct legacy of his African great-grandfather's homesick yearning for Africa. Poetry becomes equated with a spirit of exile and otherness. Tsvetaeva clearly believed that Pushkin's invitation to Yazykov to partake of "dreams of Africa" (or poetic inspiration) extended to her too. As part of her imitation of Pushkin, she attempted to create her own Africa and metaphorically to experience his blackness.

In her essay "Mother and Music," Tsvetaeva herself associates her own poetic inspiration with blackness. "Mother and Music," written in 1935, is closely related to "My Pushkin" because both are largely autobiographical works that chart Tsvetaeva's creative development in childhood and give her poetic genealogy: both Pushkin and music were forces in Tsvetaeva's childhood that prepared her to become a poet. These forces are part of her matrilineal heritage; Pushkin's African heritage also came from his mother. Interestingly, music and Pushkin entered Tsvetaeva before she acquired full literacy, and they formed a "preliterate" foundation that determined her understanding of the nature of words and the uses of language.

In "Mother and Music," Tsvetaeva describes her childish perceptions of her mother's black grand piano in much the same manner as she describes the black Pushkin monument in "My Pushkin." (In "My Pushkin," she even signals a link between the two when she notes that "the Pushkin monument was black like the piano" [*Proza* 2:253].) Both when she describes the monument in "My Pushkin" and when she describes the piano in "Mother and Music," Tsvetaeva reproduces the mental and emotional operations of the child (and future poet) as she apprehends these mystical black forces, which were part of the "cast of characters" of her childhood.[28] Consciousness of herself and self-understanding came to Tsvetaeva through her study of, and interaction with, these two powerful and mysterious and nonverbal black beings. In "Mother and Music," Tsvetaeva describes seeing her face reflected in the black piano: "And there, from the very dark bottom, a round, five-year-old inquisitive face approaches, without any smile, pink even through the blackness—like that of a Negro, dipped in the dawn, or like roses, in an inky pond. The piano was my first mirror, and my first awareness of my own face was through blackness, a translation of it into blackness, as into a dark, but comprehensible, language. So it has been all my life, in order to understand the simplest thing, I have had to dip it into verse, and see it *from there*" (*Proza* 2:187–88).[29] In this passage, Tsvetaeva links blackness and verse—the two components of "her" Pushkin, the *arap* (blackamoor) and the poet—in a way consonant with the associations she assigns to these two entities. By becoming black like Pushkin, she finds her poetic voice.

Significantly, Tsvetaeva begins to learn this "dark language" (later the medium of her poetry) before fully acquiring literacy, before being fully introduced to language as a system, and before acquiring complete mastery of the arbitrary conventions and ruling paradigms of her verbal culture. In fact, her point in all these Pushkin-related texts is that her whole subsequent relationship to language was influenced by her early exposure to Pushkin, his African origins, and his blackness. She suggests that this "dark language" of poetry was one that was able to embrace and depict a more transcendent and primal reality. By studying her own reflection in her mother's black piano, by contemplating a depiction of Pushkin's duel (and of his "return to native Africa of revenge and passion"), and by fathoming the Pushkin monument, the preliterate Tsvetaeva trained to become the poet she became.

In the final sections of "My Pushkin," Tsvetaeva describes the exposure to Pushkin's words that followed her earlier exposure to various images of him. She notes her love for various parts of Pushkin's oeuvre, which she initially read on the sly by stealing into her half-sister's room. She ends "My Pushkin" with a story about her inspired childhood reading of Pushkin's "To the Sea." Given the "marine" associations of Tsvetaeva's first name, this poem was especially kindred to her.[30] She believed it contained some special message to her about her identity and destiny. The first line of this poem reads: *Proshchai, svobodnaia stikhiia!* ("Farewell, free element!"). Tsvetaeva relates how in her semiliterate mind, she equated the "free element" (the sea to which Pushkin says farewell) with poetry—her mistake stemmed from an inspired childish intuition about the nature of poetry and, more obviously, was based on the near-identity of *stikhiia* (element) and *stikhi* (verse). Tsvetaeva perhaps assumed that words related in look or sound ought to bear some more profound relation. As readers of her poetry are well aware, she delights in exploring connections of this sort. The mystical connections she maps between words belong to the "dark language" of poetry—which she believed she acquired from Pushkin, who, in turn, acquired it from his African heritage— more than to the system of language.

In the finale to "My Pushkin" Tsvetaeva writes: "And I will say more: the illiteracy of my childish equation of the element with verse turned out to be an insight: 'the free element' turned out to be verse, and not the sea, verse, that is the only element from which one never ever parts" (*Proza* 2:279). In calling her "illiteracy" "insight" (and in privileging the illiterate and free child over the civilized adult), Tsvetaeva moves further into the network at the heart of her thinking about Pushkin, herself, and the meaning of poetry. Quite simply, the poet takes liberties with language. In Tsvetaeva's mind, Pushkin was not only a poet who valued and sang about "freedom" in his "cruel age," but one who applied a freedom to his poetry. The freedom sung in the poetry thus is also an important part of the poetics: in consciously affiliating herself with Pushkin and thus embracing his heritage, Tsvetaeva articulates a "dark language" in which signs can be interpreted more freely but not arbitrarily.

Tsvetaeva's poetic language is a language in which binary oppositions often play a crucial role. Relevant here is her comment: "I can be kept going only by contrasts, that is, by the all-presence of everything."[31] Under the pen of Tsvetaeva, binary oppositions are used not so much to divide and sustain arbitrary and often oppressive distinctions, but rather to question, transcend, or to destroy these divisions (and the isms they embody), especially if she believes them to be only temporal and especially if these oppositions in any way threaten to separate her from what she loves.

In her essay "The Poet and Time"—yet another work where Pushkin figures prominently in her thinking about the nature of poetry—Tsvetaeva asserts that the inscription "In the future there will be no borders" found on contemporary border posts has already come true in art (*Proza* 1:369). Tsvetaeva deems race, along with other demarcations such as "territoriality," "ethnicity," "nationality," and "class consciousness," to be "the first or seventh layer of skin, to climb out of which is the poet's main goal" (*Proza* 1:372). Having no mother language, and aware that heaven (where the poet's ideal reader may be found) is "all-lingual," Tsvetaeva's poet writes in a "dark but comprehensible" language. Tsvetaeva's language of poetry perhaps fleetingly resembles the Esperanto of her boss at the Narkomnats ("the Communist from Philology") in its intent ultimately to speak to all nations, races, and ages, but it differs from it profoundly in most other ways, a fact brought home even to the Esperantist boss when Tsvetaeva recites a couple of lines of Lamartine to him. In Tsvetaeva's view only poetry, the free element, transcends time and space, and only poetry has universal authority.

While Tsvetaeva's poet ultimately seeks to leave race, nation, and even gender behind, it was not in her nature, developed, as it was, in the presence of Pushkin, simply to ignore history. She still believes that the poet must bear witness to her age. Thus, when in "My Pushkin" she declares the Pushkin monument in Moscow to be "a memorial against racism, for the equality of all races, for the supremacy of each race, if only it has produced a genius" and "living proof of the baseness and deadness of racist theory" (*Proza* 2:253), she is testifying against the racist theory of Hitler. (She was writing in 1937.) In Tsvetaeva's "My Pushkin," the Pushkin monument becomes more than a monument to a very black Pushkin, it becomes a monument *against* Hitler.

Tsvetaeva thus wrestled with the binary opposition between black and white, even insisting that of course one *has* to choose, and she chooses . . . Pushkin. But in the process of making her choice, she does something more than romantically choose black over white, she critiques the very way in which these categories—and by extension other categories—are thought about and put into words.[32] In *Figures in Black: Words, Signs, and the 'Racial' Self*, Henry Louis Gates Jr. argues that profound answers and questions about race lie in *how* the racial self is translated into words and in the "critique of the structure of the sign." Tsvetaeva fiercely rejects received ideas about blackness signifying "absence," but she also goes beyond simply asserting blackness to be a "trope of presence."[33] Gates stresses the fact that "in literature, blackness is produced in the text only through a complex process of signification." In her texts on Pushkin's racial self, Tsvetaeva reminds "white Russia" of Pushkin's blackness and what it signifies, but she does so in a poetic style that defies convention. Tsvetaeva was inspired by Pushkin's blackness to challenge and subvert received ideas not just about race but also about language. Tsvetaeva's poetic examination of Pushkin's racial self thus becomes what she considered the Pushkin monument to be: a powerful monument against racism and for the human spirit.

Notes

1. Citations of Tsvetaeva's poetry, abbreviated "*Stikh*" with accompanying volume and page numbers, refer to Marina Tsvetaeva, *Stikhotvoreniia i poemy v piati tomakh*, ed. A. Sumerkin and V. Shveitser, 5 vols. (New York: Russica, 1980–90). Citations of Tsvetaeva's prose, abbreviated "*Proza*" with accompanying volume and page numbers, refer to Marina Tsvetaeva, *Izbrannaia proza v dvukh tomakh, 1917–1937*, ed. A. Sumerkin, 5 vols. (New York: Russica, 1979). All further references to these works will be included in parentheses in the text. All translations are mine.

2. What Pushkin meant to Tsvetaeva has been discussed in many studies. Of particular interest here for the attention given to Pushkin's African heritage are the studies by Peter Scotto, *The Image of Pushkin in the Works of Marina Tsvetaeva* (Ph.D. diss., University of California at Berkeley, 1987); Stephanie Sandler, "Embodied Words: Gender in Tsvetaeva's Reading of Pushkin," *Slavic and East European Journal* no. 34 (1990): 139–57; Lily Feiler, *Marina Tsvetaeva: The Double Beat of Heaven and Hell* (Durham, N.C., and London: Duke University Press, 1994); Paul Debreczeny, *Social Functions of Literature: Alexander Pushkin and Russian Culture* (Stanford, Calif.: Stanford University Press, 1997); and Irina Paperno, "Pushkin v zhizni cheloveka serebrianogo veka," in *Cultural Mythologies of Russian Modernism from the Golden Age to the Silver Age*, ed. B. Gasparov, R. Hughes, and I. Paperno (Berkeley and Los Angeles: University of California Press, 1992), 19–51, which includes discussion of the response of several poets (including Tsvetaeva) to Pushkin's African heritage.

3. Nabokov's "Abram Gannibal," originally an appendix to his translation and commentary of *Eugene Onegin*, has been reprinted in Vladimir Nabokov, *Notes on Prosody and Abram Gannibal* (Princeton, N.J.: Princeton University Press, 1964).

Liza Knapp

4. Nabokov, *Notes on Prosody*, 158.

5. For the most part, I treat Tsvetaeva's works in the order in which they were written. Whereas the earlier works such as "A Meeting with Pushkin" (1913) and "My Jobs" (1918–19) depict Tsvetaeva as a (young) adult responding to Pushkin, in the later works such as "Mother and Music" (1934) and "My Pushkin" (1937) Tsvetaeva returns to her childhood—and the black Pushkin of her childhood—to find the keys to her understanding of the "dark language" of poetry. The older Tsvetaeva got, the further back into her childhood she reached for an understanding of "her" Pushkin.

6. For an excellent discussion of Dostoevsky's promotion of Pushkin as an internationalizing force, see the notes for the "Pushkin Speech" in F. M. Dostoevskii, *Polnoe sobranie sochinenii v tridtsati tomakh*, ed. V. G. Bazanov et al. (Leningrad: Nauka, 1984), 26:441–92.

7. The father of the "white negro" has a position in Lenin's court analogous to that of the *arap* in tsarist times. See the second definition of *arap* in note 9.

8. The "white negro" obtains this rationed bread from a coworker with official connections; he expects to "buy" her affections with this bread; she takes the bread (which she shares with Tsvetaeva) but proves that her affections were not for sale.

9. *Arap* is the term Pushkin uses for his ancestor, Gannibal. Dal' defines this word as follows: "by nature or by tribe, a black-skinned, black-bodied person from warm countries, especially Africa; a Moor, a Negro" (Vladimir Dal', *Tolkovyi slovar' zhivogo velikorusskogo iazyka*, 4th ed. [St. Petersburg and Moscow: M. O. Vol'f, 1912], s.v. *arap*). The dictionary records a second meaning for *arap*, referring to a type of servant at court with door-keeping duties; it is noted that this service could also be performed by a white servant.

It should be noted that Abram Gannibal, Pushkin's ancestor, was by no means an *arap* in the second meaning of the term: he rose to the rank of general in the tsarist army. However, this secondary meaning of *arap* haunted his descendant, who was humiliated by the Tsar when he was named a gentleman of the bedchamber, an honorific version of office fulfilled by an *arap*.

Pushkin uses this term, along with *negr* (Negro), in reference to his ancestor. See J. Thomas Shaw's article reprinted in this volume.

10. In this regard, her reading of Pushkin resembles that of Dostoevsky, who boldly declared: *Pushkin pervyi ob'iavil, chto russkii chelovek ne rab i nikogda ne byl im, nesmotria na mnogovekovskoe rabstvo* ("Pushkin was the first to declare that the Russian person is *not a slave* and never was one, despite the many-century-long slavery"; Dostoevskii, *Polnoe sobranie sochinenii*, 26:115; Dostoevsky's emphasis).

11. Letter to Teskova, January 26, 1937, in Marina Tsvetaeva, *1969. Pis'ma k A. Teskovoi*, ed. Vadim Morkovin (Prague: Academia, 1969), 149.

12. For a discussion of these poems, see Scotto's *The Image of Pushkin*.

This dissertation also contains a very informative discussion of how Tsvetaeva's works on Pushkin respond to critical debates in émigré circles, and especially the attempts of Tsvetaeva's detractors to deny her her Pushkinian patrimony.

13. Scotto, *Image of Pushkin*, 15–24.

14. Discussion in Scotto, *Image of Pushkin*, especially 24.

15. Olga Peters Hasty, *Tsvetaeva's Orphic Journeys in the Worlds of the Word* (Evanston, Ill.: Northwestern University Press, 1996), 128.

16. Hasty, *Orphic Journeys*, 128.

17. In this regard, she imitates Pushkin himself, who wrote one of his strongest affirmations of his own African heritage (as well as his Russian heritage) in "My Genealogy," a poem composed in response to a piece that Bulgarin wrote in which he made fun of Pushkin's African ancestor. See Shaw's article in this volume for a discussion of Pushkin and Bulgarin.

18. Relevant in this "return" is the story of Pushkin's ancestor Abram Gannibal who, in Pushkin's view, lived a kind of dual life. He was christened with Peter the Great as his godfather, educated in France, participated in imperial affairs and Russian life, but yet he still longed for his "native Africa," especially under the rule of Peter the Great's descendants.

19. See Paperno, "Pushkin v zhizni," on the tendency to mythologize Pushkin's life and death during the Silver Age.

20. Similarly, Pushkin himself referred to slaves of African descent in America as his "brothers." He identifies, on the basis of their common African heritage, with the slaves' suffering. See Shaw's article in this volume for mention of this letter.

21. Tsvetaeva's meditations on this subject followed in the wake of two important works on this subject: D. S. Mirsky's "Two Deaths: 1837–1930" and Roman Jakobson's "A Generation That Squandered Its Poets." On how Tsvetaeva responded to these, see Viktoriia Shveitser, *Byt i bytie Mariny Tsvetaevoi* (Paris: Syntaxis, 1988), 402.

22. For other commentary on these lines, see David Bethea, "'Mother(hood) and Poetry': On Tsvetaeva and the Feminists," in *For SK: In Celebration of the Life and Career of Simon Karlinsky*, ed. Michael S. Flier and Robert P. Hughes (Oakland, Calif.: Berkeley Slavic Specialities, 1994), 51–70, especially 54.

23. In this regard, Tsvetaeva's reference to the pogroms differs quite a bit from Sylvia Plath's controversial reference to her personal "Auschwitz" in her poem "Daddy."

24. Debreczeny writes that "her white doll of course represented everything that was expected of a good little girl, including playing the piano and looking forward to a happy life conforming to the conventional female role; but instead she chose blackness and unhappiness." See Debreczeny, *Social Functions*, 64.

25. In "Natalia Goncharova," Tsvetaeva's essay about the twentieth-century Russian artist who was the namesake and a distant relative of Pushkin's wife, Tsvetaeva describes how the artist's grandmother as a young woman would ride on a swing in order to escape from suitors (and from marriage in general). (Tsvetaeva describes how she and Goncharova, meeting in Paris as adults, learned that they grew up next door to each other, the Tsvetaev house having formerly also belonged to the Goncharov family. In fact, the swing was in the yard that became the Tsvetaevs'.) Tsvetaeva quickly adds that her own poetry provided her with a similar escape from life. "Weren't my verses written at age fifteen the same thing as Goncharova's grandmother's swing?" asks Tsvetaeva (*Proza* 1:289). Swinging, then, for Goncharova's grandmother and for Tsvetaeva is an act of rebellion against traditional expectations. Likewise, in "My Pushkin" Tsvetaeva implies that swinging on the chains of the Pushkin monument definitely figured into her own escape into poetry and into her hatred of oppression.

Eventually, it seems, Goncharova's grandmother got off her swing and got married. (But, by Tsvetaevan association, it would seem that Natalia Goncharova's art was the legacy of her grandmother's swinging: the granddaughter inherited from her grandmother a spirit of creative rebellion.)

26. For a discussion of the role of this poem by Pushkin in the erection of the Pushkin monument, see Marcus Levitt, *Russian Literary Politics and the Pushkin Celebration of 1880* (Ithaca, N.Y.: Cornell University Press, 1989), 23–26.

27. For a discussion of this poem, see Shaw's article in this volume.

28. Again, in "My Pushkin," she relates the piano and Pushkin monument by noting that "the Pushkin monument was a fixture of our everyday life, part of the cast of characters of childhood, just like the piano or the policeman Ignatiev outside the window" (*Proza* 2:251).

29. Paperno comments on the relevance of this passage. She notes that Tsvetaeva's act of looking into the piano, and seeing herself looking "like a Negro" in the "inky pond," "gives birth to the poet in her." She sees in "dark language" a possible reference to Pushkin's poem "Verses composed at night during insomnia . . ." where Pushkin declares his desire to understand "the dark language" (Paperno, "Pushkin v zhizni," 35).

As John Malmstad points out, the lines from "Verses composed at night during insomnia" about the "dark language" were favorites of Andrei Belyi and figured prominently in his thinking about Pushkin and the language of poetry. Malmstad notes, however, that the line about the "dark language" amounted to one of Zhukovskii's "corrections" of Pushkin. Pushkin's original was not reinstated until the 1920s, but many, including Belyi, continued using the old versions of these poems. See John Malmstad, "Silver Threads among the Gold: Andrei Belyi's Pushkin," in *Cultural Mythologies of Russian Modernism,* ed. Gasparov, Hughes, and Paperno, 474.

30. Many of Tsvetaeva's lyrics treat her "marine" origins and suggest that she is a creature associated with the sea.

31. This line is quoted by Hasty in her preface, which discusses the relationship between Tsvetaeva's understanding of the word and of the nature of the poet. See Hasty, *Orphic Journeys,* xiii.

32. In his analysis of Frederick Douglass's *Narrative,* Gates shows how Douglass "has subverted the terms of the code he was meant to mediate" by challenging oppositions such as that between "slave-son" and "master-father." He concludes that "Douglass has subverted the terms of the code he was meant to mediate; he has been a trickster. As with all mediations, the trickster is a mediator and his mediation is a trick—only a trick—for there can be no mediation in this world. Douglass's narrative has aimed to destroy the symbolic code that created the false oppositions themselves." See Henry Louis Gates Jr., *Figures in Black: Words, Signs, and the "Racial Self"* (New York and Oxford: Oxford University Press, 1987), 93–94.

33. Gates, *Figures in Black,* 235–76.

Alexandar Mihailovic

"Sometimes I Feel Like a Motherless Child": Paul Robeson and the 1949 Pushkin Jubilee

> The patriarch of the forest
> will outlive my forgotten time,
> Just as he outlived the age of our fathers.
> —Pushkin, "Whether I wander along
> the noisy streets . . . ," 1829

THE HISTORIAN Martin Duberman observes in his 1989 biography of Paul Robeson that he had "scant interest in recording his thoughts and feelings," so we have no ready memoiristic window onto his own thoughts, and there is much about the African American social activist and performer's emotional life that remains a mystery to us.[1] Certainly Robeson's response to the injustices of Stalinism during the late 1930s and the postwar years was at best equivocal and at worst mute, muffled by his pronouncements of unwavering support of Soviet policy. Was Paul Robeson an unequivocating apologist for the Soviet regime? If not, can we find in his work any criticisms, however veiled, of Stalinism and its legacy? To be sure, with the recent appearance of the first volume of Paul Robeson Jr.'s memoiristic biography, some additional light has been shed on what the Henry James biographer Leon Edel calls the "passional life," the wellspring of intellectual yearnings and motivating forces in an artist's creative work. We see this hidden vein in Paul Jr.'s recollection of his father's reaction to Stalin's repressive domestic policy. According to this account, Robeson was fully aware that injustices had taken place. As early as 1938 he admitted to his son that "'terrible' things had been done, and that innocent people had been 'sacrificed to punish the guilty.'" In the same conversation Robeson emphasized to his son (then enrolled in a school for the children of the Soviet diplomatic corps in London) that it was also important to understand that dissent could not be brooked in the Soviet Union, which was experiencing "the equivalent of war." Robeson explained to his son that "sometimes . . . great injustices may be inflicted on the minority when the majority is in the pursuit of a great and just cause."[2] That Robeson could never bring himself to write these comments, and could express such misgivings only in the context of a spoken, and clearly pained justification—you can almost feel the self-inflicted sting and wince of the comment about "great injustices" visited out of necessity upon a minority—tells us a great deal about his profound ideological dilemmas.

A few years after the appearance of Duberman's biography, and in an apparent rebuttal to its claim about the enigmatic aspects of Robeson's life, Paul Jr. wrote an essay about his father in which he quotes from some of the artist's unpublished notes. One statement in particular stands out. In 1936 Robeson jotted down a remark about Pushkin that is as cryptically autobiographical as it is observant of the historical significance of the Russian poet himself. "It is interesting," Robeson writes, "that Pushkin, the shaper of the Russian language, like Chaucer and Shakespeare rolled into one, was of African descent. So the Russian language as spoken today passed through the temperament of a man of African blood . . . Pushkin means more to me than any other poet."[3] The personal identification with Pushkin is, to use one of Pushkin's own turns of phrase, a window that Robeson cuts open to look out upon the territory of cultural identity. Perhaps it is even the kind of window or access onto Robeson's own inner life that Duberman senses is too deeply hidden in his writing and performative art to be easily excavated.

Robeson's attempts to negotiate a passage between the demands of his American identity and his progressive conscience are writ large in the events of his life after the end of the Second World War, and provide a necessary starting point in considering his reading of the Russian poet. By all accounts, the beginning of the Cold War was a pivotal if difficult time for Robeson. Always controversial for his pro-Soviet views—which sometimes went well beyond expressed sympathy for the suffering of the Russian people during the German invasion—Robeson was often gloomy and depressed during the years of the Truman and Eisenhower administrations. With increasing frequency he voiced his dissatisfaction with the domestic political situation during his concert tours abroad, where he felt less inclined to muffle his views. After the war, Robeson gradually transformed his concerts into vehicles for protest against American foreign and domestic policy, a newfound emphasis often encouraged by his audiences and political representatives of the host country themselves. A particularly powerful example of Robeson's blending of culture and politics and his sometimes uneasy relations with his hosts is his participation in the sesquicentennial jubilee commemorating Pushkin's birth, an official Soviet celebration which took place in Moscow in 1949. Robeson appeared at the jubilee with artists and writers from many countries. After giving a short speech in Russian, Robeson sang for the audience and lingered in Moscow long enough to write articles on Pushkin and music for *The Literary Gazette*, *Komsomolskaia Pravda*, and *Soviet Music*. Hostile American responses to Robeson's interest and support for the Soviet cause only sharpened his sense of commitment to it and further developed his own view of what it meant to be an American. Robeson's published essays and public speeches are often no less personal than they are political statements. Bearing in mind that Robeson regarded Russian music and literature as parallel to the cultural legacies of many African nations, one would think that he would have viewed the African-Russian Pushkin as the ne plus ultra of the salvific and progressive Otherness of Russian culture. And yet Robeson's statements about the Russian poet do not corroborate what would seem to be this logical extension of his views. In order to get a better sense of how Robeson attempted to negotiate a way between the Scylla of his American identity and the Charybdis of his political beliefs, we need to retell the story of his involvement in Russian and Jewish cultures in the former Soviet Union from the 1930s up to the time of the 1949 sesquicentennial. Two public statements made by Robeson in 1949 are especially important in the present discussion: the June 6 speech he gave in Moscow and the June 19 speech he gave at the Welcome Home Rally for him in Harlem. These texts represent in some sense the key to both Robeson's understanding of Pushkin and his general political orientation during that year. Robeson's Moscow speech in particular represents the culmination of years of political and artistic maturation; it was born after a long gestation of ideas that he explored, adopted in a programmatic way, and subsequently ramified and refined.

Almost from the beginning of his study of the Russian language and culture in 1931, Robeson sensed a special affinity between them and African American culture. That year he stated to the press that he found his voice very much suited to Russian music, perhaps because there seemed to be a "kinship between the Russians and the negroes. They were both serfs, and in their music there is the same note of melancholy touched with mysticism."[4] On January 18, 1932, at New York's Town Hall, Robeson performed Russian songs for the first time in his career. The response of Russians in the audience was enthusiastic. After the concert the singer told a reporter that "I have found a music very closely allied to mine, which I also find a more natural means of expression than English," adding that "certainly many Russian folk songs seem to have come from Negro peasant life and vice versa." Over the next four years up to the singer's first trip to the Soviet Union, several Russians noted Robeson's superb command of the language. In a letter to the famous anarchist Aleksandr Berkman, Emma Goldman praised Robeson for speaking the language beautifully, like "an educated Russian." In her diary entry from that time, Robeson's wife Essie wrote that "[Paul] feels that he can become an official, and important interpreter of Russian music, and literature. He feels he understands it, and is close to it, and he loves the language."[5] That same year, Robeson told the *Manchester Guardian* that he wanted to continue studying Russian literature in order to add Pushkin to a theatrical repertoire of famous blacks which also included Toussaint L'Ouverture and Alexandre Dumas, taking on the poet as part of his cultural project to popularize the images of famous blacks.[6] By 1936 Robeson fully espoused the notion that Pushkin represented the spiritual nexus between black and Russian cultures, a figure whose "African temperament" served as the die that had been cast for the development of the modern Russian tongue. Robeson's identification of Pushkin as the consummate embodiment of cultural internationalism was inevitable given his interest in artistic multiculturalism and his growing familiarity with Russian literature over the previous five years.

On the surface, Robeson's first trip to the Soviet Union, in 1936, did little to change his ideas about Russia's place in world culture. Nonetheless, during his stay in Moscow that summer, Robeson does seem to have become more aware of the diversity within Russia itself, moving away from a reductive view of it as a "serf" culture animated by a soulful melancholy. Recalling that time in an unpublished letter written years later to two Russian friends, Robeson mentions the fact that he saw Solomon Mikhoels's famous interpretation of King Lear at the State Jewish Theatre, a performance he compares to that of the African American actor Ira Aldridge in the nineteenth century.[7] In the letter Robeson goes on to describe his friendship with Mikhoels, whom he met in 1936 through the famous film director Sergei Eisenstein. Eisenstein served as a kind of unofficial host for the American artist.[8] Eisenstein arranged for a screening of several Soviet films for Robeson, one of which was Grigory Aleksandrov's *Circus* (1936), about a white American woman with a black child fleeing the United States for the Soviet Union. The child was played by Jimmy Patterson, the son of the African American expatriate Lloyd Patterson. In the same letter Robeson comments on the young Patterson's "touching" performance in the film and Mikhoels's small role in it. He also tells of meeting Mikhoels again in 1943 when the Russian Jewish actor came to New York together with the Yiddish poet Itsak Feffer as representatives of the Jewish Antifascist Committee, the foremost Jewish organization in the Soviet Union spreading awareness of the Nazi genocide and working toward war relief of refugees and displaced persons. Robeson describes discussing with Mikhoels in New York the similarities between black music and Jewish music, and the "richness of the different cultures of the Soviet republics, as shown in the film *Circus*," which ends with Jimmy Patterson being serenaded by a multiethnic circus audience in response to a disruption by his mother's racist and abusive business manager. Mikhoels appears briefly on screen singing in Yiddish to Patterson, apparently as a symbolic representative of the Jewish Autonomous Region of Birobidzhan, which had been officially established the year before *Circus* was filmed.

Circus apparently made a deep impression upon Robeson. After his 1936 trip, Robeson included "Native Land" (also known as "Wide Is My

Motherland"), the film's theme song, in his repertory. The song (composed by Isaak Dunaevsky with text by the poet Vasily Lebedev-Kumach) celebrates the vastness and human inclusiveness of the Soviet Union and the justness of Stalin's "pan-national" law.[9] "Native Land" is considered a classic among a particular category of patriotic songs from the Soviet era. As one Russian critic has recently noted with considerable insight, Dunaevsky's songs in particular were shrewdly composed pastiches of melodies echoing Cossack, Ukrainian, Jewish, gypsy, and Russian folk music—and, one might add, the *romans,* the approximate Russian counterpart in the nineteenth century to the German *Lied*—in order to appeal to as wide an audience as possible.[10] As a knowledgeable musicologist and ethnographer as well as performer, Robeson could not have failed to appreciate the ethnically diverse melodic composition of a song such as "Native Land." Certainly the vision of a hybrid culture was very appealing to him, and in this regard it is significant that Robeson widely performed "Native Land" in a composite version of an abridged Russian text together with an English translation. As he asserted in a 1935 interview published in the *Californian Eagle* (an African American newspaper), "as a race we must develop a sense of dignity," which "can only come through a knowledge of all black peoples . . . It is foolish to admit to one cultural background and leave the other out completely. As American Negroes we are a people of mixed culture."[11] Robeson evidently became increasingly drawn to what can only be called multiculturalism, a more thoroughgoing understanding of the similarities and parallels between completely separate cultures. The affinities he now saw between black, Jewish, and Russian cultures became a radical affirmation of such cultural convergences. For Robeson, Pushkin represented just such an embodiment of "mixed culture." As we shall see later, the American singer and activist was eager to find in the Russian poet's work an anthemlike assertion of multicultural values that echoed his interpretation of Dunaevsky's song.

Before examining in detail Robeson's 1949 speech on Pushkin, we must delve into the intervening events in his biography insofar as they further shaped his notions of ethnic, political, and civic identity. At a legislative hearing in 1946 in California, Robeson testified under oath that he was not a member of the Communist Party. As he relates in his autobiographical essay *Here I Stand,* he would soon view this statement with regret, regarding it as a capitulation to an utterly unjustified demand for the surrender of his constitutional rights. Subsequently, he would refuse to give courtroom testimony or to sign affidavits regarding his links to the party.[12] In 1947 Robeson's name was repeatedly mentioned by prosecutors and witnesses at the Hollywood Ten trial, partly as a result of which most of his American concert bookings were canceled through the end of the following year.[13] In April 1947, the House Committee on Un-American Activities (HUAC) cited Robeson together with many others as "one invariably found supporting the Communist Party and its front organizations."[14] That same week, when asked point-blank by reporters about his political affiliations, Robeson replied:

> There are only two groups in the world today—fascists and anti-fascists. The Communists belong to the anti-fascist group and I label myself an anti-fascist. The Communist Party is a legal one like the Republican or Democratic Party and I could belong to either. I could just as well think of joining the Communist Party as any other. That's as far as you'll get in any definition from me.

To another, more liberal, journalist Robeson gave a much more pointed response: "If Communism means pointing out to the people that their lives are being dominated by a handful, I guess I'm a Communist."[15] The year 1948 was, of course, a particularly trying one for prominent Americans with leftist sympathies: that summer the House Committee on Un-American Activities campaigned to make compulsory the registration of all American citizens with current or prior Communist Party membership.[16]

The following year proved to be the true beginning of Robeson's political travails in the United States. On April 20 of that year, he made a series of controversial comments at the Paris World Peace Conference. Participating in the conference under the auspices of the American delegation headed by W. E. B. DuBois, in his speech Robeson expressed a Communist internationalist view of the exploitation of the working class in the United States, stressing that it had geopolitical ramifications because it cut across racial lines. America's wealth, he stated, was built "on the backs of the white workers from Europe . . . and on the backs of millions of blacks. And we are resolved to share [this wealth] equally among our children."[17] The speech is most famous, however, for a statement purportedly included in it that Robeson in fact never made. The Associated Press misquoted Robeson as provocatively asserting that African Americans should ally themselves with the Soviet Union in its continued support of progressive movements in Africa because "it is unthinkable that American Negroes could go to war on behalf of those who have oppressed us for generations against the Soviet Union which in one generation has raised our people to full human dignity." The putative statement—a garbling of a critical remark in the speech about American policy toward African nations as formulated by the U.S. representative to the United Nations, Edward Stettinius Jr.—was immediately seized upon by the American press and later adduced by the House Committee on Un-American Activities as a key piece of evidence testifying to the singer's putatively treasonous inclinations.[18] The shower of vitriolic criticism from home only strengthened Robeson's resolve to speak his mind more boldly in order to clarify his views. To this end he conferred at the Paris conference with Aleksandr Fadeev (the head of the Soviet delegation) and Pablo Neruda, who were both slated to appear at the Pushkin celebration in Moscow several weeks later. In Paris Robeson privately stated to Fadeev that "you can count on me as a faithful soldier, one who won't let you down in battle."[19] In his capacity as general secretary of the Writers Union and president of the All-Union Pushkin Committee, Fadeev would play a highly visible role at the Pushkin anniversary, delivering the keynote address at the Bolshoi Theater.[20] Several days after the Paris World Peace Conference, Robeson left France to do a concert tour of Scandinavian countries, Czechoslovakia, and Poland and arrived in Moscow on June 4. According to the schedule of public presentations at the Pushkin sesquicentennial (preserved in the archive of the All-Soviet Society of Cultural Relations Abroad [VOKS]), Robeson delivered his speech on June 6.

Robeson's strongly worded promise to Fadeev suggests that he felt that a great deal was at stake in his participation in the Pushkin sesquicentennial, and that his comments there would reflect a level of political commitment no less than those he made at the Paris Peace Conference. In this respect, it must be said that Robeson's June 6 tribute to Pushkin is undoubtedly anticlimactic and disappointing. Nonetheless, the speech is significant for much of what it leaves unsaid or hinted at, and furthermore contains statements that, when scrutinized from the official Soviet perspective, are more idiosyncratic and subversive than meets the eye.

Any discussion of Robeson's June 6 speech in Moscow needs to be prefaced with a discussion of the authenticity of the published piece. Did Robeson himself write it, or was it ghostwritten by a publicist or journalist, a common practice in the publication of supposed first-person statements by sympathetic visiting foreigners which persisted well into the Brezhnev era? Here a number of considerations point to the speech's authenticity. A partial videotape of his speech is extant in the Russian state film archive in Krasnogorsk.[21] Unfortunately, the sound quality is extremely poor. The only audible segment of the film—consisting of one sentence—does, however, coincide exactly with the published text. The fact that the two published versions of this speech (the first appearing in a special supplement to the journal *New Time* (*Novoe vremia*) and the second a year later in one of the proceedings volumes of the conference) differ somewhat in phrasing suggests that the Russian texts are alternate editorial tinkerings with a spoken statement. The volume presents a longer text of the speech, with differences in wording from the first that do not always represent clear-cut stylistic improvements. Apparently, the transcriber or translator of the speech went back to the original speech, using the abridged version from *New Time* as a kind of template. We know from at least one stenographic record (kept in the Russian State Archive of Literature and Art in Moscow) of a public discussion that took place between Robeson, Il'ia Erenburg, and Yury Zavadsky on June 10, 1949, that Robeson had on at least

"Sometimes I Feel Like a Motherless Child"

one occasion alternated between speaking in Russian and using a translator.[22] It is possible that he resorted to such a combination in his speech several days later. Even more tellingly, the first printed version of Robeson's public statement about Pushkin is paragraphed into small segments, suggesting the dynamics of an actually given speech. Although editorial comments in Stalin-era publications should always be taken with a grain of salt, the prefatory remark by *New Time*'s editor about Robeson's *vzvolnovannyi* ("agitated") delivery[23] does seem to be a genuine report of the public reading of the printed text. Perhaps the most significant proof of the published speech's authenticity, however, is the fact that it echoes Robeson's own oeuvre much more than it does conventional notions about Pushkin in vogue at that time in the Soviet Union. Furthermore, Robeson's Russian correspondence and stenographic records of statements he made in Moscow during the same trip are strikingly similar in phrasing, sometimes to the point where entire sentences from these other occasions seem to be echoed in the Pushkin speech.[24] The following discussion relies on the speech as printed in the proceedings volume because it seems to be the fuller text.

The celebration of the 150th anniversary of Pushkin's 1799 birth had already been under way for several weeks when Robeson arrived in Moscow. Both the published and archival documents relating to the anniversary celebrations exude a powerful infusion of Stalinist xenophobia and chauvinism that far exceeds the ideological militancy of even the 1937 centennial commemoration of the poet's death. As N. F. Bel'chikov stated during the introductory session of the 1949 commemoration, the "correct and fruitful path of studying Pushkin's historical uniqueness and his independence from foreign influences" has been pointed out only by the Party; in a similar vein, that same year the renowned if ideologically dogmatic Pushkinist and Stalin Prize recipient Dmitry Blagoi asserted that "in his literary development Pushkin not only caught up with, but surpassed western Europe." In his presentations at the conference, Blagoi characteristically resorted to Stalinist shibboleths extolling the virtues of centralized state socialism; thus, for example, he emphasized the overweeningly individualistic and Western attitudes and non-Russian provenance of negative heroes such as Aleko in *The Gypsies* (*Tsygany*) and the potentially liberating force of Peter the Great's autocracy in *Poltava*.[25] As Marcus Levitt cogently puts it in his study of Russian official celebrations of Pushkin from the nineteenth century to the late Soviet period, the 1949 jubilee was especially distinctive in attempting to "cleanse" the poet of "alien ideologies" and, "like the Russian people who had single-handedly withstood the German invasion, glorif[y] [him] for his indigenous greatness."[26]

But more than just patriotic saber-rattling resounded in the preparations and actual celebration of the commemoration of Pushkin's birth. For one thing, an element of anti-Semitism had already tainted Soviet journalistic and textbook writing about the impending anniversary. Already in a 1946 *Soviet Culture* (*Sovetskaia kul'tura*) article titled "In Defense of Pushkin," the poet Nikolai Tikhonov called the Jewish literary critic Isaak Nusinov "a vagabond without a passport" who was trying to "westernize" Pushkin in his writing about the Russian poet.[27] Nusinov was arrested during the Pushkin sesquicentennial year and executed shortly thereafter.[28] A 1949 teacher's guide for dealing with the subject of the anniversary stipulated that lectures about Pushkin must be directed against the "bourgeois 'ideas' of rootless cosmopolitanism," an injunction that was repeated in the preface to the proceedings volume in which Robeson's speech was published a year later.[29] Virtually all of the Soviet participants at the conference and a surprising number of foreign guests (including even Robeson's friend, the West Indian writer Peter Blackman)[30] emphasized the quintessential Russianness of Pushkin and the ontological negative capability and universality of spirit that his Slavic nation represents. This notion of course originates in Dostoevsky's famous speech at the 1880 Pushkin celebration. In the particular form it took at the 1949 sesquicentennial, this idea at best was raised to the level of a paradox and at worst was undercut by a crippling contradiction: it irreconcilably prizes the diversity of world culture while embracing the exceptionalism of Russian culture insofar as only it can truly appreciate multiculturalism. Blagoi is especially adroit in transposing Dostoevsky's conception of Pushkin's Russian universalism to a Soviet setting, and even goes so far as to use some of the same arguments and examples advanced by Dostoevsky (most notably the antihero Aleko in *The Gypsies*) without once explicitly referring to the nineteenth-century novelist. At the 1949 celebration, the Russian exceptionalism of Dostoevsky's Pushkin was crossbred with Stalinist state paternalism in matters of ethnic identity and culture, echoing the growing anti-Semitism in Soviet institutions that culminated in the fabricated 1952 "Doctors' Plot" against the Soviet leader.

Needless to say, such a monstrous cross-pollination of ideas was quite different from the vision of the diverse political and cultural life that Robeson had in mind. We can see that such a constellation of prejudices would have been intolerable to Robeson given that his closest Russian friends (such as Eisenstein, Mikhoels, and Feffer) and future daughter-in-law were Jewish. Indeed, none of the published Russian accounts of Robeson's concerts in Moscow that summer broach the subject of the parallels between Russian and African American music that Robeson found so interesting and productive, an omission paralleled by the scrupulous avoidance in the Pushkin sesquicentennial of any discussion of the African, non-Russian component of the poet's ancestry. The fact that both the official biography of Robeson prepared by VOKS for his appearance at the celebration[31] and the published proceedings of the sesquicentennial repeatedly refer to Jim Crow laws and lynchings in the

United States but never make a connection to Pushkin's own mixed ethnicity seems to be a strange omission and, from the political perspective of internationalism, a missed opportunity. Ethiopia (in ancient times known as Abyssinia, and until only very recently assumed to be the homeland of Pushkin's ancestor Abram Gannibal) was in fact one of the two countries in Africa with which the Soviet Union had diplomatic relations in 1949.[32] The Kremlin was very interested in encouraging the growing anticolonialist stance of Haile Selassie, the Ethiopian ruler who later became a symbol for the Rastafarian movement. At the height of the purge of Jewish political and artistic figures, however, the pressure to portray Pushkin as ethnically and racially pure was too strong to be affected by such considerations. To his credit, Robeson completely ignores the Russian nationalist component of the contemporary Soviet view of Pushkin, and in fact he never uses the adjective "Russian" in his speech. As we shall see, his Pushkin is less Russian, more truly multicultural, and therefore personal to him.

In this public statement Robeson quotes from two famous Pushkin poems, "Ia pamiatnik sebe vozdvig nerukotvornyi" ("I've raised a monument to myself not made by hands") and Vnov' ia posetil" ("I visit yet again . . ."). There is certainly much about Robeson's short speech that is completely consistent with the orthodox Soviet view of Pushkin's achievement. Addressing members of the Soviet cultural elite, Robeson unequivocally states "we know that the land of the Soviets stands at the head of the struggle [*stoit vo glave*] for the freedom of all nations," adding that it was the Soviet Union in all its might that destroyed fascism, and that progressive Americans are resolved to fight for peace and the friendship of the Soviet people, who are building *mnogoobraznuiu chelovecheskuiu zhizn'* ("a diverse human existence") based on the ideas of Lenin and Stalin and who represent the *nadezhda vsego mira* ("hope of the entire world").[33] Relying on a particularly obnoxious Soviet cliché about Pushkin—one that was emphasized by the president of the Soviet Academy of Sciences, Sergei Vavilov, at the opening of the 1949 celebration and which was reiterated well into the Brezhnev era[34]—Robeson refers to the poet's 1836 ode "I've raised a monument to myself not made by hands" as an example of the poet's anticipation of socialist reality with its ideal multiethnic audience of the future, one in which no stigmatizing significance is attached to a listener's native culture or skin color: "[Pushkin] belongs to the peoples he himself spoke about in his 'Monument,' those who decades later became one multinational nation, consisting of equal and fully developed citizens of the different Soviet republics."[35] Robeson is referring to the famous third stanza of the poem:

Word about me shall spread throughout Russia far and wide,
And each person will call out my name in his native tongue:

> The proud grandson of the Slavs, the Finn, and now the wild Tungus, and that friend of the steppes, the Kalmyk.

At least one Soviet scholar has argued that Pushkin's famous anthem was not truly understood or appreciated until the 1937 centenary, when the meaning of its social promise had finally become manifest in reality. Certainly the poem's vision of a multiethnic community must have been very appealing to Robeson. Similar ideas are expressed in Dunaevsky's "Native Land," the anthemlike Russian song from Robeson's repertory at that time. Robeson's belief that the Soviet people do not acknowledge any genuine difference in the color of one's skin seems to be a distant echo of the line in "Native Land" that "for us there is neither black nor light-skinned" (*Net dlia nas ni chernykh ni tsvetnykh*). But Robeson's attempts at accommodation with Soviet attitudes was problematic from the perspective of his belief in the importance of cultural difference, of ethnic identity as a hyphenization rather than assimilation—the latter a specter that lurks behind the assertion of difference as being of no importance. Judging by his 1942 recording of "Native Land," Robeson seems to have sensed this disparity already, and actually changes the line in Lebedev-Kumach's text about the unimportance of race into a statement asserting the importance of difference within a political union: "Side by side, the black, the white, the yellow." His manuscript notations on his score of Dunaevsky's song (dated from the 1950s) also seem to suggest that he continued to associate the song with racial issues.[36]

Robeson was far too intelligent not to sense these tensions, which are evident even in the apparently orthodox first half of his speech. Here Robeson is strangely elliptical and oblique in his reference to Pushkin's African heritage, only stating that "we, the representatives of black people, are proud of him [*gordimsia im*], revere his memory and love his great works." Here Robeson is speaking with a deliberate ambiguity, asserting the progressive content of Pushkin's works at least as much as the matter of his solidarity with the African nations through his lineage. The issue of pride in Pushkin and what nation is the legitimate modern-day possessor of it becomes even more diffused when Robeson states later that had "Pushkin been alive today, he would have been proud of the Soviet people, just as you are." Like his hosts at the conference, Robeson voices a curious mix of views, emphasizing the political primacy of the Soviet Union while promoting Pushkin as a figure of cross-cultural significance.

And yet Robeson goes further, portraying Pushkin as a figure who cannot be reduced to any single culture either in his time or in ours. In this respect we see clear links to Robeson's speech several weeks earlier in Paris, and in fact Robeson in his Pushkin speech seems to echo and refer to the speech he delivered at the World Peace Conference:

"Sometimes I Feel Like a Motherless Child"

> I came here from progressive America, from millions of oppressed blacks and the working masses of many countries. I recently appeared at many meetings in Europe and America, at meetings that were dedicated to the fight for peace.... Soon I will return to America in order to appear as a witness at a hearing against twelve leaders of the American Communist Party, who are being brought to trial for their devotion and loyalty [*predannost'*] to the American working class. We representatives of progressive Europe and America will fight for peace regardless of the cost!

As in his Paris speech, Robeson stresses both the solidarity and internationalism of the workers' grievances; at the same time, here he also reiterates his sense of moral obligation to fight for that equality not on the international stage, but in the United States. At this point in his career Robeson was remarkably uninterested in the concrete manifestations or cultivation of a workers' international, which he viewed at this stage more as an ideal or principle to which to aspire than as an actual program. As Robeson describes it, descendants of the African diaspora and people living in the third world must first effect change in the countries of their birth, a struggle that would naturally give way to or result in the consolidation of the Workers' International.

Bearing in mind that for Robeson the personal was very much the political, perhaps we can find the key to unlock the motivating force behind these statements in his reference to the other, even more autobiographical poem in Pushkin's late work, "I visit yet again . . ." Like "I've raised a monument," this piece comes from a loosely connected series of strangely elegiac and seemingly prescient poems Pushkin wrote in the last two years of his life. The occasion of Pushkin's bucolic poem "I visit yet again . . ." is his return to the family estate at Mikhailovskoe. The poet's feelings about the place are, at best, ambivalent. Recollecting his two-year exile there (from 1824 to 1826) in stark contrast to a happier, more recent period of exile on the Black Sea, he experiences no sense of homecoming upon his return, only intimations of his own mortality. The poet contemplates three pine trees which have grown in his absence and the thicket of bushes and saplings that surrounds them; he muses that although he will never live to see them flourish, his grandson perhaps will think of him as he passes their fully grown shapes at night.

A brief discussion of the poem which Nabokov calls "Mikhailovskoe revisited" goes a long way in explaining Robeson's choice of it in his speech.[37] Sensing the hybrid genre sources of the 1835 poem, the renowned Pushkin scholar B. V. Tomashevsky insightfully characterizes it as a meditative lyric in the form of a dramatic monologue.[38] Other, more politically minded Soviet scholars have seen the poem as subtly expressive of Pushkin's yearning for freedom from the stifling surveillance and patronage of the court of Nicholas I, and his musings about the posthumous appreciation of him by future generations as prophetic not only of his imminent death (later rumored to have been precipitated by court intrigue) but also of the eventual arrival of ideal readers raised in the socialist state.[39] Although Robeson in his capacity as an interpreter of Russian songs may have first learned of the poem from Prokofiev's lugubrious setting of it for the 1937 Pushkin centenary celebration (titled, after Briusov's Pushkin edition, "Pine Trees" ["Sosny"], op. 73), there is no evidence that he ever performed it. In any event, Prokofiev—evidently intent on rendering an elegiac Tchaikovskian *romans*—retains only the first ten lines of the poem, leaving out the poet's more hopeful ruminations about the survival of his image in posterity.[40] It is precisely this latter part of the poem that interests Robeson, and in his Pushkin speech he states that he remembers with particular fondness one moment in the poem in which the poet greets with bittersweet optimism the budding thicket as a new generation whose robust full growth he will never live to see (*Zdravstvui, plemia mladoe, neznakomoe. Ne ia / Uvizhu tvoi moguchii pozdnii vozrast*). With these two lines Pushkin begins the final strophe of the poem. The first and last strophes complement each other with an exquisite symmetry. Both segments are of exactly the same length (ten lines long), and in the first one the poet dwells as much on his fear of loss, forgetfulness, and oblivion (referring to his exile in Mikhailovskoe as two "unnoticed" [*nezametny(e)*] years) as he earnestly hopes, in the last strophe, for the fond remembrance of him by his descendants. These two meditations on, respectively, the past and the future frame the more Wordsworthian and sprawling middle strophes, where the poet dwells on the present with his close observation of the surrounding countryside. In his 1958 Russian recording of the poem, Robeson tellingly retains only the first and last strophes of the poem, creating a more explicit causal link between the poet's meditations on the compounded exiles that have distorted his life and the hope that his ancestors will appreciate him in a way that many of his contemporaries do not. He pauses for fifteen seconds before beginning the last segment of the poem, which he begins with an emphatic, almost melodramatic reading of the poet's two-line greeting to posterity.[41] According to one Russian researcher on Robeson, the singer repeated the first of these two lines on several occasions during his 1949 stay in Moscow, during which he also referred to Pushkin as a *rodnik vdokhnoveniia* ("source of inspiration") for him.[42] In some sense, Robeson clearly felt that these lines underscored his spiritual kinship to Pushkin in particular and Russia in general at a time when he was becoming increasingly estranged from American culture. The images in these lines are certainly echoed in much of Pushkin's post-Decembrist verse of resignation in the face of personal and political adversity, perhaps most obviously in "Whether I walk along the noisy streets . . ." (*Brozhu li ia vdol' ulits shumnykh* . . .) with its arresting metaphor of the ancient oak as a patriarch who outlives the paltry life spans of the multiple generations of its human observers. The melancholy statement in that poem that it is time for the grown man to age and for the *mladenets* ("baby") to blossom (*Mne vremia tlet' / A tebe tsvesti*) only serves to underline the powerful emotional significance of the vegetative metaphor as a symbol for human transience in Pushkin's work.

But in what specific sense were the two lines from "I visit yet again . . ." so resonant for Robeson? In his speech at the Pushkin jubilee, his citation of them seems unmotivated and disconnected in the context of his otherwise forceful and clear-cut presentation. The answer lies in Robeson's biography. He came to Moscow at a time when he found social and intellectual contact abroad increasingly more congenial than life in the United States, where many were already beginning to mount a campaign based on his public statements in which his right to be called an American was challenged. In his memoiristic essay *Here I Stand* and in numerous interviews during the 1930s and 1940s Robeson repeatedly stresses the importance of citizenship as the linchpin of constitutional freedoms and the full realization of civil rights. Asked by one journalist in 1937 about his son's enrollment in a Soviet school and his own sense of what it meant to be American, Robeson replied:

> I do want Paul Jr. to return to America often enough to become familiar with its traditions as far as the Negro is concerned because he is, first of all, an American. My reason for coming back here to live is that I have realized that the more I live abroad, the more convinced I am that I am an American and this is where I belong—my roots are here—the material for my career is here.[43]

By 1949 with the first wave of McCarthy's witch hunts already cresting, Robeson had become only more convinced of this notion of his civic duty, which would become one of the major leitmotifs of his later life. As much as he valued his trips to Europe and viewed himself as a mid-twentieth-century citizen of the world, he always regarded the growing political necessity of extended leaves in Europe as instances of exile, and the thought of what would become of his family in these increasingly straitened circumstances was never far from his mind. Both issues—exile from native soil and the lives of one's offspring and how they would remember their progenitor—are powerfully at the forefront of the two Pushkin poems that Robeson cites. Certainly the generational aspects of family life must have been very much at the forefront of his mind that summer when his son married. As a dissenting African American, Robeson's exile was compounded twice over: he was a descendant of the historical exile brought on by the collective trauma of slavery—with its harrowing memory of the middle passage—and a spiritual expatriate in the land of his birth. Robeson would seem to have chosen Pushkin's meditation in verse on his return to Mikhailovskoe as a major point of reference in his 1949 Pushkin speech precisely for its resonance with both his existential condition and the transitional and sometimes painful situation he was experiencing at that time. Robeson, like Pushkin in his poem about revisiting Mikhailovskoe, struggles with the idea of a compounded exile.

Robeson's fixation on Pushkin as the objective correlative of his own conflicted cultural and political identity took a more radical turn in his next public speech, delivered upon his return to the United States from Moscow on June 19. Speaking in Harlem that day at the Welcome Home Rally for him (arranged by the Council on African Affairs), Robeson reflected on the Pushkin celebration as an expression of cultural solidarity between the African and Soviet peoples, sprinkling his comments with references both to the recent fall of European fascism and the posthumous memorialization that Pushkin describes. It was a busy, eventful, and somewhat unpleasant day for Robeson and his wife. Their son had been married earlier that day, and after the private ceremony they had had to endure hecklers and aggressive members of the press who crowded outside their son's apartment. The fact that Paul Jr. married a white Jewish American woman only served to further enrage the conservative American mainstream, which was already so incensed by his father's comments in Paris that in one instance armed guards had to be posted outside a summer camp in upstate New York for children of leftist families who openly supported the idea of a civil rights movement.[44]

If we examine Robeson's Moscow speech in light of his "Welcome Home" statement two weeks later we see that his earlier reference to Pushkin's purportedly prophetic ode is not the Soviet boilerplate that it appears to be, is no less highly marked and original than his response to "I visit yet again . . ." and points to a disjunction between his own political views and the ideological status quo at the Pushkin jubilee. Robeson's own sense of defiance, outrage, and embattled isolation in his native land of the United States is sharply etched in the speech he gave later that day:

> Here is a whole nation which is now doing honor to our poet Pushkin—one of the greatest poets in history—the Soviet people's and our proud world possession. Could I find a monument to Pushkin in a public square of Birmingham or Atlanta or Memphis, as one stands in the center of Moscow? No. Perhaps one to Goethe, but not to the dark-skinned Pushkin.[45]

Here Robeson is surely bearing in mind Pushkin's famous description of the raising of a monument to himself, appreciated only by the multiethnic audience of posterity; moreover, his reference to this central image of Pushkin's poem is animated by the shrewd parallel he draws between the absence of full civil rights in his own country and the alienation and lack of recognition that the poet felt in the society of Nikolaevan Russia. Furthermore, in tandem with the subtext of Pushkin's poem, Robeson's reference to a German poet on the one hand and an African-Russian one on the other—an opposition that his 1949 audience would immediately associate with the battle lines drawn during the Second World War—suggests yet another parallel, to the unacknowledged and unappreciated contribution of African American servicemen to the war effort. In Robeson's hands, Pushkin becomes the emblem of the African who is (in all senses of the term) unrecognized in America. The Pushkin subtext in his "Welcome Home" speech points up what might be called Robeson's tragic optimism, his sense that the true appreciation of himself and his people will indeed occur, but very possibly after his death and perhaps even then only in the very distant future. The speech reflects a complex thought-structure which testifies both to Robeson's prodigious skills as a rhetorician and to his nuanced understanding of the conflicting feelings, intimations, and ultimate acceptance of mortality that underlie Pushkin's "I've raised a monument," ones to which the Soviet triumphalist view (of the poem as a vision of the socialist state to be) were largely deaf. The speech also demonstrates the extent to which he probably perceived the figure of Pushkin as a highly personal reflection of himself. In its own way, this perception was no less prophetic of Robeson's political travails during the 1950s and 1960s and the posthumous reassessment of his legacy during the late 1970s in light of the civil rights movement than were Pushkin's own ruminations about his immanent death and eventual canonization. As Robeson had put it to a friend during his stay in Prague earlier that summer for a series of concerts: "I don't know if I'll live to see the end of the struggle. I've overcome my fear of death. I never think about death now."[46] Robeson seems to have been aware of the irony behind the poet's apparent immodesty in "I've raised a monument" (insightfully pointed out by Nabokov), the sense in which the acceptance of death in the poem undercuts the poet's wish for a glory, a fame that of course he will never live to see.[47] Robeson could not have chosen better vehicles to express his contemplation of mortality during a time of injustice than the two poems by Pushkin he refers to in New York and Moscow.

But there is more to Robeson's New York speech than a simple autobiographical meditation. What is most striking about the statement quoted above is the obvious fact that Robeson describes Pushkin as a black man—at the Harlem rally as "*our*" poet—whereas two weeks earlier in Moscow he glossed over the poet's mixed ancestry. It would be too facile and unfair to Robeson to explain this difference with the argument that he attempted earlier to appease his Russian hosts with a vision of a "colorless" Pushkin, appeasing a crypto-racist point of view. Robeson's comments on Pushkin in Moscow were completely sincere and idealistic, assuming that race in the Soviet Union doesn't matter. But what occurred in the time between the two speeches changed Robeson's opinion: on the eve of his June 16 departure for New York, he was finally allowed by Soviet authorities to meet with his arrested friend Itsak Feffer, the Yiddish-language poet who, together with Solomon Mikhoels, served on the Jewish Antifascist Committee. Using hand motions, Feffer indicated to Robeson that the hotel room was bugged. When Robeson asked him about the fate of their mutual friend Mikhoels, Feffer drew a finger across his throat. Mikhoels had been murdered by the Soviet secret police the previous year. On June 14 at the Tchaikovsky conservatory Robeson gave a concert which became famous for his performance of the Yiddish "Song of the Warsaw Ghetto Rebellion," a provocative choice of repertory given the recent and highly deliberate nonintervention of Soviet troops during the Nazis' suppression of the Polish underground's uprising in Warsaw near the end of the war, and the growing rumblings of a new purge in the Soviet Union which was clearly anti-Semitic in character. Many commentators on Robeson's life—among them the biographer Martin Duberman and the singer's son—see in his public dedication of the Warsaw Ghetto song to his friends the actor Solomon Mikhoels and the poet Itsak Feffer a direct and heroic defiance of official Stalinist anti-Zionism.[48] But the evidence here for Robeson's objection to Stalinist policy on a philosophical level is equivocal at best. It is more likely that Robeson based his provocative dedication simply on the heartfelt principle of fidelity to like-minded comrades and friends, which he most famously expressed during his testimony before the House Committee on Un-American Activities. In her memoirs about life during the Stalin era, his contemporary, the Russian Jewish pianist Maria Yudina—an artist who, like Robeson, found her faith in the state socialism of the Soviet Union severely challenged in light of the purges—memorably expressed this continued faith in kindred spirits during a time of betrayed political ideals with the statement "for me prayer means personal relations."[49] The black Pushkin of Robeson's "Welcome Home" speech is a response to the somewhat hazy political idealism of his Moscow speech and the subsequent wake-up call of the singer's exposure to institutional anti-Semitism in the Soviet Union, where the supposed irrelevance of race conceals at best an indifference to cultural realia and at worst a profound racism; it was a response to what had happened to two valued friends, those with whom he had his own "personal relations." Robeson wanted to acknowledge finally that it is far better to assert difference than to adhere to the fiction that it does not exist.

By closely examining Robeson's Pushkin sesquicentennial speech and his subsequent Harlem speech, we also understand a great deal about his conception of civic duty and citizenship. When Robeson himself was finally called to appear before the HUAC Committee in 1956, he took the Fifth Amendment while echoing his statements from nine years before about his membership in the party: "As far as I know [the Communist Party] is a legal Party, a

Party of people who have sacrificed for my people."[50] When taunted with the question why he did not become a Soviet citizen during one of his trips to Russia, Robeson shot back with the answer "because my father was a slave . . . and my people died to save this country, and I am going to stay here and have a part of it just like you. And no fascist-minded people will drive me from it. Is that clear?"[51] This statement is important for two reasons. First, it reveals the extent to which Robeson viewed himself as an American striving to fulfill the promise of his country's democratic ideals. Second, it manifests Robeson's anxiety that the generational continuity of his family will be cut short by injustice, a preoccupation which (as we have seen) he perceives as sharing with Pushkin. In another exchange with committee members at the 1956 hearing, Robeson called them the "true un-Americans" who should be ashamed of themselves.[52] Similarly, two years later in *Here I Stand*, Robeson states "our [U.S.] government may properly instruct its employees as to what they may or may not say when travelling abroad, but people who go abroad as private citizens are not servants of the State Department . . . No job holder in Washington has the legal or moral right to demand that any American traveler advocate the viewpoint of that official in order to get a passport."[53] As the labor historian Mark D. Naison insightfully notes, throughout his involvement with labor organizations Robeson defined labor itself as the true "criterion for citizenship."[54] Like any managerial organization, the government must be completely subordinate to the needs of its "workers," and not the other way around. According to Robeson, the administrative bodies of government and state cannot constitute and should not attempt to displace one's ethnic identity, a form of consciousness which is, by its very nature, peripheral to the workings of the state. In this regard, Robeson's son Paul Jr.—for all his own controversial views and highly public disagreements with Martin Duberman and Lloyd Brown, the two most prominent biographers of his father[55]—is undoubtedly justified in arguing that his father was adamantly opposed to any notion of a collective American identity represented by the ideal of the "melting pot."[56]

But there is more. Underpinning the singer and activist's heightened awareness of Pushkin was a corollary view that he hinted at in his public statements during the 1950s: that the standard Soviet view of international labor underestimated the significance of race and cultural difference all too easily. Already in 1949 Robeson had begun to become involved in public debates about oppressive political conditions in sub-Saharan Africa. Official Kremlin policy at that time toward Africa dictated aggressive and paternalistic Soviet involvement. Robeson's views on third world development were essentially irreconcilable with Soviet policy in Africa as articulated by his contemporary Andrei Zhdanov, a pillar of the Soviet ruling elite during the late 1940s and founder of the Communist Information Bureau (or Cominform). In his inaugural speech at the secret first meeting of the Cominform in Warsaw in 1947,

Zhdanov went so far as to reject the idea of a "third world" altogether, arguing that its social struggles in fact differed in no substantial way from those in other parts of the world and that the notion of politically progressive nonaligned movements was a logical impossibility in developing or preindustrial countries.[57] Soviet attitudes toward the labor movement in the entire third world were in fact too blinkered by the expectation of unconditional loyalty to the Soviet bloc to establish fruitful links to the independent political culture that was developing in many countries, especially in Africa. Robeson, in a speech titled "Forge Negro-Labor Unity for Peace and Jobs" (delivered in 1951 at a New York gathering of the Council on African Affairs), pointedly states that trade unions represented a progressive force in Africa no less than elsewhere in the world, calling them "the backbone of the people's struggle."[58] Robeson's opinion about the role of labor in African countries ran counter to current Soviet policy, which emphasized the unreliability of independent labor organizations in Africa as opposed to their counterparts in industrialized nations, where popular fronts comprised of various left-leaning organizations were *perceived* to be more feasible than those on the subcontinent. As late as the early Gorbachev era, independent, nonaligned movements in African countries were viewed with great suspicion in Soviet diplomatic circles.[59] In sharp contrast, Robeson considered alignment among political movements in various countries to be ideally more a matter of confluence and coincidence than planned coordination and orchestration. We now see that Robeson's more overtly political writings are very much of a piece with his work on comparative musical ethnography, in which he highlights the felicitous parallels and uncanny similarities among historically disparate cultures and downplays the notion of direct indebtedness. Direct indebtedness, be it political, economic, or artistic, is a manifestation of imperialism.

When the State Department stripped Robeson of his passport from 1950 through 1958, the singer found that even the labor organizations that had supported him earlier were now aloof.[60] As his concert bookings dwindled with his inability to travel abroad and schedule performances in formerly friendly venues, Robeson slipped into a period of artistic stagnation and personal despair. Interestingly, at a 1955 press conference in front of the U.S. district court in Washington, D.C., Robeson ended his statement on the continuing legal battle to have his passport returned with the comment that he had tentative plans to play the title role in Mussorgsky's opera *Boris Godunov*.[61] Although these plans never came to fruition, a recording of Robeson's stunning and highly controlled performance of Boris's final "Prayer and Death" (with Lawrence Brown on piano) does survive from this period, as does a truncated version of the piece from his May 9, 1958, concert at Carnegie Hall.[62] Robeson had first expressed interest in performing segments from the opera in 1932, and in 1935 he stated that he found Mussorgsky's music to be especially "vital."[63] What then explains his delay of two decades in recording his interpretation of the role? Why was Robeson suddenly more attracted to playing a ruler rather than a laboring Everyman?

I believe that the answer to these questions about the timing of Robeson's renewed interest in the opera is hinted at in his pointed 1955 characterization of it as "Mussorgsky's adaptation of Pushkin's *Boris Godunov*." Both the opera itself and the palimpsest of Pushkin's play within it exercised a powerful attraction for Robeson. The embattled isolation of Boris in his final scene—his sense of alienation from and betrayal by both those immediately around him and the Russian people or *narod* itself—clearly struck a chord in Robeson during the time when even many of his like-minded compatriots shunned him. A citizen like Robeson, stripped of the *labor* of his artistic activity, is destined to perish spiritually. We hear this despair in the tightly controlled, almost muted basso profundo of Robeson's interpretation of Boris's "Prayer and Death," in which the singer shuns the eloquent melodramatics of Chaliapin's classic performance for a suffering resignation and a heartfelt plea for absolution. The heightened awareness of empire's abuse of power helps us to understand more clearly Robeson's growing interest from 1949 (the year of his exposure to the undemocratic cast of Soviet socialism) to the early 1960s in Mussorgsky's *Boris Godunov,* an opera based on a Pushkin play that portrays the downfall of a morally compromised autocrat who in the end begs for forgiveness from his son, imploring him not to ask by what means he obtained the throne (*Proshchai. Moi syn, umiraiu, / Seichas ty tsartvovat' nachnesh'. / Ne sprashivai, kakim putem ia tsarstvovat' priobrel*). That particular statement of Boris (which represents a conflation and condensation of several different lines in the play, having the effect of foregrounding the tsar's guilt) evidently fascinated Robeson, who sings it as a positive example of modernism in music in a filmed interview he gave in Moscow in September 1958, shortly after his passport was returned to him.[64] While removing much of the ambiguity about Boris's literal guilt, Mussorgsky amplifies upon the poignancy of mortality already present in Pushkin's meditations on generational strife and stymied inheritance. In this regard, Robeson's perception of Pushkin's poetry as a contemplation of mortality and legacies is particularly relevant. The two Pushkin poems that Robeson cited in his June 6, 1949, speech at the Pushkin sesquicentennial in Moscow ("I've raised a monument to myself not made by hands" and "I visit yet again . . .") powerfully foreground the anxiety of how future generations remember their ancestors. Needless to say, this same preoccupation is abundantly in evidence in the play *Boris Godunov*, which is a profound meditation on dynastic succession and mentoring, and what happens when attempts are made to disrupt, falsify, or corrupt these links. In this light, Boris's conceit that the Russian populace should be treated like children in need of perpetual discipline is on the same level of hubris as the Pretender

Dmitry's attempt to usurp power by falsely claiming a blood relation to the throne. As Boris notes with revealing chagrin at the end of the play, the *narod*, like a son, cannot be placed in continuous servitude (*syn u otsa ne vechno v polnoi vole*). Godunov suffers his fatal breakdown shortly after making this statement, as if in punishment for indulging in the notion. For Pushkin, the fact that Boris thinks this immoral thought and uses it as a touchstone for his statecraft is more significant than the mystery of whether or not he actually killed Dmitry, the true successor to the throne. Robeson's statement at the 1949 Paris Peace Conference (quoted earlier) that "we are resolved to share [wealth] equally among our children" dovetails very well indeed with Pushkin's own metaphorical thinking about collective and individual suffering. Robeson was drawn to Pushkin's play because of its foregounding of matters of conscience, of the taking and fatal breaking of oaths, whether they be monastic (as in the case of Pimen and his novitiate Grigory, the False Dmitry) or political, as in the case of Boris and, of course, Robeson himself in his legal battles during the 1950s, which culminated in June 1958 with the Supreme Court deciding (in a 5–4 split decision) that Robeson and others cross-examined at the HUAC hearings several years earlier should have their passports restored to them and that they be allowed to travel abroad.

By far the most curious feature of Robeson's recording of Boris's final speech is his substitution of the infinitive *prostit'* ("to forgive") for the singular and plural forms of the verb's imperative (*prosti . . . prostite*) that we find in both Pushkin's play and Mussorgsky's libretto. What was Robeson—whose Russian was quite good—thinking of by tinkering with a doubly canonical text, and repeating the verb a third time, as if to emphasize his departure from it? The notion of forgiveness—the act of forgiving, *to* forgive—clearly preoccupies him. But who is in need of forgiving, or who needs to forgive, is not immediately clear. A contemplation of Robeson's life up until that point offers several highly suggestive possible answers. Because of the entertainment industry's unofficial boycott of Robeson during the time his passport was suspended, the singer recorded the Mussorgsky piece in an independent studio in 1956. Earlier that year news had seeped into the press about Khrushchev's "secret" anti-Stalinist speech at the Twentieth Party Congress, in which the Soviet leader excoriated many of the injustices of the previous regime. By all accounts, Robeson was deeply conflicted and nonplussed by the revelations, and refused to comment about them even to his closest friends.[65] The combined pressures and contradictions in Robeson's life certainly begged the question of forgiveness on at least two different levels: of institutional injustice and racism in a political system that Robeson professed to support, and of the singer himself for denying the existence of it while his own family was beset by the same intolerance of ethnic diversity. Robeson's 1956 performance of Godunov is a profoundly personal one, an attempt to come to terms with guilt and to arrive at some form of forgiveness both of self and of others. The circumstances of Robeson's life during the 1950s pushed him to take a new and less overtly political direction in his music, one in which ethical self-reflection played as large a role as activism. His art evolved as a result of what Mussorgsky himself in an 1872 letter to his mentor Vladimir Stasov describes with strange glee as the experience of "being caught in a vise," of being at the mercy of adversity or fate. Far from being disasters, such pivotal events represent opportunities for growth, for what Caryl Emerson (explicating Mussorgsky's strange adaptation of Darwin) describes as the "key to survival": the use of "one's creativity and inventiveness to escape."[66] Robeson's interpretation of Pushkin through Mussorgsky is a sharply etched testimony of an artist's attempt to maintain a thoroughgoing integrity during a Time of Troubles. Both Pushkin's *Boris Godunov* and Mussorgsky's adaptation of it foreground the trap of power that is accountable only to itself, that both destroys the immediate family of the state elite and traumatizes the community at large. In the colonial and postcolonial eras, that community is in fact the world at large.

Robeson's recording of *Boris Godunov* represents the culmination of his interest in Pushkin's work as a vehicle for both self-examination and political criticism, first evident in his two 1949 speeches asserting that modern-day Africans and African Americans had reason to be proud of Pushkin as a poet of African ancestry, in addition to feeling solidarity with the poet on account of his progressive ideals. Such a notion was completely out of place in a celebration which (to use a turn of phrase from the inaugural speech of Sergei Vavilov, the president of the Soviet Academy of Sciences) pointedly saw in Pushkin's poetry "a scathing slap in the face of Russia's enemies"[67] and which viewed any attempt to explain his greatness in terms of affinities with other cultural traditions as an assault; in this respect the fear of contamination from "cosmopolitan" (i.e., Jewish) influences was clearly part of a larger xenophobia raging in Soviet ideology at that time. The exploration of the cultural significance of Pushkin's African ancestry became fully acceptable in Soviet scholarship only in the 1970s and 1980s with the development of a socialist regime in Ethiopia under Haile Mengistu, that is, only after the putative homeland of Pushkin's great-grandfather had been drawn firmly into the political orbit of the Soviet Union.[68] In this regard, Robeson's speech is so anomalous that one almost wonders, in retrospect, how it was permitted to be published together with the other pieces in the volume. Certainly Robeson's deceptively blithe and ahistorical statement that "the Soviet Union gave Pushkin to the world" reflects a notion of a stubborn cultural continuity that runs against the grain of the rigid orthodoxy of Soviet Hegelianism and the crypto-Russocentrism that pervaded the 1949 Pushkin celebration. We come to a better understanding of this seemingly naive statement if we bear in mind that Robeson sought for the future in the past, in the eventual reawakening of remote antecedents, be they in the form of the collective solidarity of African Americans with contemporary Africa in its attempt to overthrow colonialism or in the individual African American's struggle to know about his or her own ancestors in all their cultural difference. Robeson's preoccupation with the ramifications of ancestry brings to mind T. S. Eliot's famous line from the *Four Quartets* (another poetic meditation on genealogy, one that was contemporary with the singer) that "In my beginning is my end." The political conclusions that Eliot draws from contemplating the transatlantic migration of his seventeenth-century English ancestors to North America are, of course, quite different from those that the singer asserts as the son of William Robeson, a fugitive slave who was descended from enslaved Africans brought to the New World during the same historical period.[69]

Robeson's 1936 assertion that Pushkin meant more to him than "any other poet" is merely one of several indicators of the special and highly charged emotional regard that he had for the Russian writer's work. In his 1949 speech he emphasizes how *tronut i vzvolovan* ("touched and moved") he felt at finding himself on Soviet soil, "in the country where Pushkin was born."[70] Nonetheless, Robeson's reading of Pushkin shifted from his initial appreciation of the poet in the mid-1930s to a reassessment of him at the beginning of the Cold War; his 1949 meditation on the poet was in fact a highly personal statement, one in which the singer conflated details from his own life with his discussion of the cultural significance of Pushkin's African heritage. That Robeson voiced these personal preoccupations at a state occasion in the Soviet Union renders them all the more salient. In various statements and performances from the 1930s through the 1950s, Robeson characterizes the circumstances of Pushkin's life as being similar to his own; he viewed both himself and his predecessor as being misunderstood and unappreciated in their lifetimes, suffering from periods of exile which were internal as well as external. For Robeson, the image of Pushkin is the objective correlative of his own situation, in which the civic ideal of participatory citizenship is tragically deferred as a legacy for future generations. Furthermore, in his speech Robeson indirectly registers his growing unease with the anti-Semitic character of the nationalism that had already fully become a fixture in Stalinist ideology. That Robeson even hinted at such views on a state occasion dedicated to the most canonical of Russian writers reveals in him reserves of ideological independence that are unexpected in one who otherwise never wavered in his public support of the Soviet Union. Comparing his comments about Pushkin at the sesquicentennial with those he made at the Welcome Home Rally in New York two weeks later, we realize that Robeson's recent exposure to the Russocentric and "anti-cosmopolitan" Soviet Pushkin helped to crystallize further in his mind a more radically multicultural view of the poet, one in which Pushkin's blackness played a role equal to his

Russianness. Robeson's meditations on Pushkin at the beginning of the Cold War reflect a renewed appreciation of the reality of cultural difference. Underpinning the singer and activist's heightened awareness of Pushkin was a corollary view that Robeson seems to have recognized in his political unconscious but which he studiously avoided pursuing in all of his subsequent public statements: that the standard Soviet view of international labor glossed over the significance of race and cultural difference all too easily.

Robeson himself memorably portrayed the painful yet ultimately liberating effects resulting from the recovery of an ancestral past in the 1936 film *Song of Freedom,* in which he played a London dockworker who struggles to shake off colonialist prejudices as he discovers that he is the scion of a west African dynasty. No doubt Robeson was initially drawn to Pushkin's poem about returning to Mikhailovskoe precisely because of the poet's hopeful appeal to future generations of his family. Pushkin's muted indignation at the possible sentence of perpetual exile held over him by those in power is vividly evident in this poem, a fact that explains Robeson's attraction both to it and to the gospel song he often performed in concert:

> Sometimes I feel like a motherless child
> A long way from home
> Sometimes I feel like I'm almost gone

The song—which Robeson always made more despairing by secularizing, omitting the last line "True believer / Way up in the heavenly land"[71]—comes close to what the singer must have felt at the end of his stay in Moscow in 1949, a time when, for the first time in his life, people he cared about became victims of Stalinist injustice. In that light, Pushkin's poem about the bitterness of returning "home" seems all the more apt to the singer's painful situation at the beginning of the Cold War, when he was confronted by politics of repression both in the United States and the Soviet Union, the only country where Robeson said he felt "like a real human being." Robeson's qualified critical stance toward Soviet ideology also brings into sharper focus for us the extent to which Soviet notions of state were, in the end, irreconcilable with many of his core beliefs.

Notes

1. Martin Bauml Duberman, *Paul Robeson: A Biography* (New York: Alfred A. Knopf, 1989), 558.
2. Paul Robeson Jr., *The Undiscovered Paul Robeson: An Artist's Journey 1889–1939* (New York: John Wiley and Sons, 2001), 306.

3. Quoted by Paul Robeson Jr., in his essay "Paul Robeson and Black Culture," in *Paul Robeson, Jr. Speaks to America* (New Brunswick, N.J.: Rutgers University Press, 1993), 75. Robeson's son indicates that the statement comes from a page of notes "inserted into a Russian edition" of Pushkin. In one set of liner notes, Robeson Jr. states that "Alexander Pushkin, the Afro-Russian 'Shakespeare of Russia,'" was his father's "favorite poet" ("Pages from an Odyssey: Notes by Paul Robeson, Jr.," *The Odyssey of Paul Robeson,* Omega Classics OCD 3007, 1).

4. Quoted in Duberman, *A Biography,* 149.

5. Duberman, *A Biography,* 156. Robeson resumed seriously studying the language during the summer of 1936 before placing his son in a Soviet Model school (David Levering Lewis, "Paul Robeson and the U.S.S.R.," in *Paul Robeson: Artist and Citizen,* ed. Jeffrey C. Stewart [New Brunswick, N.J.: Rutgers University Press, 1998], 218). As is evident from the few comments between songs at his June 14, 1949, concert at Tchaikovsky Hall, Robeson's Russian had become reasonably proficient by the end of the next decade. During his stay in Moscow that summer, one journalist reporting on a Robeson concert wrote that the singer spoke Russian "rather well" in some comments he made to the audience after his friend Sergei Eisenstein's introduction (*Sovetskoe iskusstvo,* June 28, 1949, 3).

6. Duberman, *A Biography,* 166.

7. Russian State Archive of Literature and Art (RGALI; Moscow), collection 2693 (S. M. Mikhoels), inventory 1, no. 264: "Pis'mo Robsona Polia Dolinskomu M. i Chertoku S. 28 fevralia 1958." The letter is in Russian and is a typed carbon copy. Another part of this letter (not cited in this article) has been published in a recent memoir about Mikhoels (M. Geiser, *Mikhoels: Zhizn' i smert'* [Moscow: Glasnost', 1998], 234]. Mikhoels's *King Lear* premiered in 1935. The actor's daughter mentions in her memoirs that the production continued to be performed by Mikhoels in repertory through January 18, 1944 (Natalia Vovsi-Mikhoels, *Moi otets Solomon Mikhoels: Vospominaniia o zhizni i gibeli* [Tel Aviv: Iakov, 1984], 108).

8. For Russian descriptions of this trip, see Vladimir Zimianin, *Pol' Robson* (Moscow: Molodaia Gvardiia, 1985), 127; and Viktor Grokhov, *Robson* (Moscow: Sovetskii pisatel', 1952), 145.

9. The complete version of Lebedev-Kumach's poem, with its reference to Stalin, was rarely performed. For the full text, see V. I. Lebedev-Kumach, *Izbrannye* (Moscow: Sovetskii pisatel', 1949), 7–8. Robeson seems to have relied on the abbreviated version sung in the film *Circus*. His performance of the song is currently available only on the CD collection *Paul Robeson: Songs of Free Men,* track 10, 1997, Sony Classical MHK 63223.

10. E. Petrushanskaia, "'Pesnia dostaetsia cheloveku': O 'misticheskoi' prirode sovetskikh massovykh pesen," *Literaturnoe obozrenie* 2 (1998): 57.

11. "An Interview with Paul Robeson," *The California Eagle*, June 12, 1935, 12.

12. Paul Robeson, *Here I Stand* (Boston: Beacon, 1971), 38–39; Zimianin, *Pol' Robson*, 178.

13. Duberman, *A Biography*, 338.

14. Ibid., 317.

15. Ibid., 318.

16. Zimianin, *Pol' Robson*, 181–82.

17. Duberman, *A Biography*, 342.

18. Quoted in Duberman, *A Biography*, 342. No full English text of the speech is known to exist: the film recording of the event seems to be lost (see Duberman, *A Biography*, 687–88). A Russian translation of the speech was published in a proceedings volume of the Paris conference: *Pervyi vsemirnyi kongres storonnikov mira. Parizh-Praga, 20–25 aprelia 1949-go goda. (Materialy)*, (Moscow, 1950), 58–59. Susan Robeson's memoir *The Whole World in His Hands: A Pictorial Biography of Paul Robeson* (Secaucus, N.J.: Citadel, 1981) contains an especially poignant account of this episode in her grandfather's life (164).

19. Zimianin, *Pol' Robson*, 190.

20. Marcus C. Levitt, *Russian Literary Politics and the Pushkin Celebration of 1880* (Ithaca, N.Y.: Cornell University Press, 1989), 167.

21. Krasnogorsk film archive, no. I-7389-X.

22. RGALI (Moscow), collection 3002 (B. M. Filippov), inventory 2, item 198: "Stenogramma vechera v TsDRU. Pol' Robson v gostiakh u masterov iskusstv," p. 1.

23. "K 150-letiiu so dnia rozhdeniia A. S. Pushkina: Rechi na iubileinykh zasedaniiakh v Moskve," appendix to *Novoe vremia*, no. 25 (June 15, 1949): 16.

24. Slight variations of virtually all of the statements in the Pushkin speech about the solidarity of the American working class with the Soviet Union appear as well in the transcript of the public meeting in Moscow of Robeson with the writer Il'ia Erenburg ("Stenogramma vechera v TsDRU. Pol' Robson v gostiakh u masterov iskusstv," RGALI [Moscow], collection 3002 (B. M. Filippov), inventory 2, item 198, pp. 1–2), and in a note that Robeson sent to the Soviet Writers Union (RGALI, collection 631, inventory 14, item 1051, p. 3). The former document is dated June 10, 1949, five days before the first publication of Robeson's Pushkin speech in *Novoe vremia*. The consistency of Robeson's statements during his 1949 Russian trip suggests that he worked from the same set of notes for his speaking and writing engagements.

25. S. I. Vavilov et al., eds., *A. S. Pushkin 1799–1949: Materialy iubileinykh torzhestv* (Moscow and Leningrad: AN SSSR, 1951), 43–44; D. Blagoi, "Istoricheskaia poema Pushkina ('Poltava')," in *Pushkin: Issledovaniia*

i materialy. Trudy tret'ei vsesoiuznoi pushkinskoi konferentsii (Moscow/Leningrad: AN SSSR, 1953), 243–44.

26. Levitt, *Russian Literary Politics*, 167.

27. Louis Rapoport, *Stalin's War against the Jews: The Doctors' Plot and the Soviet Solution* (New York: Free Press, 1990), 84.

28. Dates for Nusinov's death vary from 1949 to 1950 (Rapoport, *Stalin's War,* 126; Geiser, *Mikhoels: Zhizn' i smert'*, 313; see also A. M. Kuznetsov's commentary to a collection of letters from that period, "Iz perepiski M. V. Iudinoi i M. M. Bakhtina (1941–1966 gg.)," *Dialog, karnaval, khronotop* 4 [1993]: 44). In 1940, Nusinov served on the faculty committee assembled for the dissertation defense of the famous Russian literary critic Mikhail Bakhtin. In 1944 Bakhtin contacted Nusinov (who was favorably disposed to Bakhtin's work) in the hope that the latter could help him publish his thesis. Their contact ended shortly before Nusinov's execution. For a sympathetic and insightful biographical account of Nusinov, together with bibliographic and archival references, see N. Pan'kov, "M. M. Bakhtin: Ranniaia versiia kontseptsii karnavala," *Voprosy literatury* 5 (September–October 1997): 95–96.

29. *A. S. Pushkin k 150-letiiu so dnia rozhdeniia (sbornik materialov v pomoshch' kul'tprosvetrabotnikam)* (Simferopol': Krymizdat, 1949), 9; Vavilov et al., eds., *A. S. Pushkin 1799–1949*, 9.

30. Vavilov et al., eds., *A. S. Pushkin 1799–1949*, 373.

31. State Archive of the Russian Federation (GARF; Moscow), collection 5285 (VOKS), inventory 8, item 332, pp. 211–13.

32. Anatolii Gromyko, *Afrika v mirovoi politike* (Moscow: Nauka, 1986), 166.

33. Vavilov et al., eds., *A. S. Pushkin 1799–1949*, 62.

34. Archive of the Academy of Sciences, Russian Federation (Moscow Division), collection 596 (S. I. Vavilov), inventory 1, item 213: "Vystuplenie na pushkinskikh torzhestvakh v sviazi s 150-letiem so dnia rozhdeniia pisatelia. Iuin' 1949," pp. 3, 34–35.

35. Vavilov et al., eds., *A. S. Pushkin 1799–1949*, 62.

36. Robeson, *Paul Robeson: Songs of Free Men,* track 10. Robeson's score of "Native Land" is kept at the RGALI Archives in Moscow (collection 995, inventory 3, item 14: "Sbornik pesen iz repertuara P. Robsona. Rukopisi s pravkoi P. Robsona, 1950–1960 gg."). The first page of the score has an enigmatic two-line notation by the singer:

(?) mozhet byt' ?)
stikhi ot (*Otello*)

Perhaps Robeson saw a connection between the apparent antiracism of Dunaevsky's song and Othello's final, presuicide speech (which Robeson was especially famous for in productions of the play) with its famous line "Speak of me as I am" (*Othello* 5.2.342).

37. Aleksandr Pushkin, *Eugene Onegin*, trans. Vladimir Nabokov, 4 vols. (New York, 1964), 2:219.

38. B. Tomashevskii, *A. S. Pushkin* (Moscow and Leningrad: AN SSSR, 1956–61), 2:101.

39. N. V. Izmailov, "Liricheskie tsikly v poezii Pushkina 30-kh godov," in *Pushkin: Issledovaniia i materialy,* vol. 2 (Moscow and Leningrad: AN SSSR, 1958), 38–39.

40. For a useful discussion of Prokofiev's setting of this poem, see A. N. Sokhor, "Lirika Pushkina v tvorchestve sovetskikh kompozitorov," in *Pushkin: Issledovaniia i materialy,* vol. 5 (Moscow and Leningrad: AN SSSR, 1967), 245–46.

41. Archive of Sound Recordings (Moscow), "Paul Robeson: Pushkin (1958)."

42. Zimianin, *Pol' Robson,* 190. This phrase reappears as the title of the article about Pushkin which Robeson wrote for the *Literary Gazette* in Moscow that summer but which never appeared in print. A copyedited manuscript of this piece is extant in the newspaper's archives (RGALI, fund 634, inventory 3, item 168, pp. 39–41). The content of the piece is very close to his June 6 speech.

43. Quoted in Allison Blakely, *Russia and the Negro: Blacks in Russian History and Thought* (Washington, D.C: Howard University Press, 1986), 150.

44. The most detailed account of the sequence of events that day are in Duberman, *A Biography,* 355–56. Also see Susan Robeson, *The Whole World,* 165–71. David Horowitz tells of his leftist parents taking him as a child to hear Robeson perform and describes the politicized summer camp he attended at that age in his autobiography *Radical Son: A Generational Odyssey* (New York: Free Press, 1997), 53–54, 65. Horowitz vividly brings to life the way in which Robeson was regarded by many at the beginning of the McCarthy era as a symbol of the African American struggle.

45. *For Freedom and Peace. Address by Paul Robeson at Welcome Home Rally. New York, June 19, 1949* (New York: Council on African Affairs, 1949), 9.

46. Dorothy Butler Gilliam, *Paul Robeson, All-American* (Washington, D.C.: New Republic, 1976), 139.

47. Vladimir Nabokov on the last stanza of the poem: "The last quatrain is the artist's own grave boast repudiating the mimicked boast. His last line, although ostensibly referring to reviewers, slyly implies that only fools proclaim their immortality" (Pushkin, *Eugene Onegin*, trans. Nabokov, 2:310). One suspects a droll pun in the word "grave," characteristic of Nabokov.

48. Duberman, *A Biography,* 352–54; Paul Robeson Jr., "Paul Robeson's

Censored Moscow Concert," liner notes for *Paul Robeson: Live Concert from Tchaikovsky Hall in Moscow. Recorded 6/14/49,* Fenix PR7000.

49. Russian State Library (RGB), collection 527 (M. V. Iudina), cahier 7, item 8, p. 9. For a discussion of Iudina's unpublished memoirs (all of which are kept in the manuscript division of the Russian State—formerly Lenin—Library in Moscow), see my study *Corporeal Words: Mikhail Bakhtin's Theology of Discourse* (Evanston, Ill.: Northwestern University Press, 1997), 14–15, 89–90.

50. Duberman, *A Biography,* 440.

51. Ibid., 441.

52. Ibid., 442. For a later reiteration of this assertion, see Robeson's *Here I Stand,* 64–65.

53. Robeson, *Here I Stand,* 66.

54. Mark D. Naison, "Paul Robeson and the American Labor Movement," in *Paul Robeson: Artist and Citizen,* ed. Stewart, 185.

55. The polemic between Paul Jr., Duberman, and Lloyd Brown has been bitter and at times vitriolic. In his biography of the singer Duberman openly if cordially acknowledges these disagreements with Robeson's son, stating that "sons and scholars often have separate agendas" (*A Biography,* 557). More recently, Duberman (who has written widely on the gay rights struggle) replied to Lloyd Brown's accusation that Duberman's biography asserted "homosexual values" (Duberman, "Writing Robeson," *The Nation,* December 28, 1998, 35). An angry exchange of letters among the three resulted from Duberman's criticism of Brown ("Robeson: How to Write a Life?" *The Nation,* February 1, 1999, 2, 23).

56. Robeson Jr., *Paul Robeson, Jr. Speaks to America,* 72–73.

57. Roger Edward Kanet, "The Soviet Union and Sub-Saharan Africa: Communist Policy toward Africa, 1917–1965" (Ph.D. diss., Princeton University, 1966), 181, 184.

58. Paul Robeson, *Forge Negro-Labor Unity for Peace and Jobs* (New York: Council on African Affairs, 1950), 8.

59. A view stressed by Anatolii Gromyko (see his *Afrika v mirovoi politike,* especially 165–70).

60. See Naison, "American Labor Movement," 190–92.

61. UCLA Film and Television Archive, item 19201: "People in the News: Robeson Continues to Fight for Passport [Washington, D.C.; Paul Robeson, U.S. District Court]," August 16, 1955.

62. Paul Robeson, *Odyssey of Paul Robeson,* track 7.

63. Robeson Jr., *Undiscovered Paul Robeson,* 200, 216.

64. Gosfilm Archive (Moscow), no. 0-21474, reel 23.

65. Duberman, *A Biography,* 416–17.

66. Caryl Emerson, *The Life of Musorgsky* (Cambridge University Press, 1999), 14–15.

67. Archive of the Academy of Sciences, Russian Federation (Moscow Division), collection 596 (S. I. Vavilov), inventory 1, item 213: "Vystuplenie na pushkinskikh torzhestvakh v sviazi s 150-letiem so dnia rozhdeniia pisatelia. Iuin' 1949," p. 3.

68. Aleksei Bukalov, "'Pod nebom Afriki moei," *Aziia i Afrika segodnia* 6 (1984): 45–49; Aleksei Bukalov, "Bereg dal'nyi': Pamiati A. S. Pushkina," *Aziia i Afrika segodnia* 2 (1987): 38–41. See also Nikolai Khokhlov, "Nashi Gannibaly," *Druzhba narodov* 5 (1978): 227–34.

The editorial presentation of these articles and the circumstances surrounding their conception eloquently testify to the politicization of Gannibal as a topic of discussion and research in the Soviet Union during the time of Mengistu's socialist regime (1974–1991). The editor's preface to Khokhlov's article explicitly refers to Ethiopia embarking on "the road of revolutionary transformations," a fact adduced as facilitating Soviet-African friendship, particularly in regard to Pushkin's ancestry (227). According to one article devoted to Gannibal, Bukalov worked as a Soviet diplomat for three years in Ethiopia (Nadezhda Braginskaia, "Otkuda rodom Gannibal," *Novoe russkoe slovo* [New York], June 6, 1996, 16).

69. In his recent book on Robeson, Lloyd Brown discusses the ancestry of William Robeson in greater detail than Duberman does in his biography (Lloyd L. Brown, *The Young Paul Robeson: "On My Journey Now"* [Westview, 1997], 6).

70. Vavilov et al., eds., *A. S. Pushkin 1799–1949*, 62.

71. "Sometimes I Feel Like a Motherless Child," in *Joe Davis Folio of 50 Favorite Negro Spirituals*, ed. Joe Davis (New York: Joe Davis, 1932), 15.

Caryl Emerson

Artur Vincent Lourié's *The Blackamoor of Peter the Great*: Pushkin's Exotic Ancestor as Twentieth-Century Opera

"MY DEAR ANNUSHKA," Artur Lourié wrote in March 1963 to Anna Akhmatova, from whom he had parted forty years before,

> recently I read somewhere that when D'Annunzio and Duse met after twenty years' separation, they knelt down before one another and wept. And what can I tell you? My "glory" has also lain in a ditch for twenty years, that is, ever since I arrived in this country [the United States]. At first there were moments of great and brilliant success, but the local musicians took all possible measures to ensure that I would not gain a foothold. I wrote a huge opera, *The Blackamoor of Peter the Great,* and dedicated it to the memory of our altars and hearths. It is a monument to Russian culture, the Russian people and Russian history. For two years now I have been trying unsuccessfully to have it staged. But in this country nobody needs anything and the road is closed to a foreigner. All this you foresaw forty years ago: "the bread of a foreign land is as bitter as wormwood." The Blackamoor is my second big composition on a Pushkinian subject: in Paris I wrote an opera-ballet, *Feast in the Time of Plague,* which was accepted at the Opéra right before the war but has never been performed on stage in full, only in excerpts. In general I live in utter emptiness, like a phantom. All day long your photographs gaze at me. I embrace and kiss you tenderly. Take care of yourself. I await news from you. A.[1]

A clandestine correspondence did develop between composer and poet—but on the *Blackamoor* opera, no news was forthcoming. Lourié and Akhmatova died within half a year of each other, in 1966, she in Soviet Russia and he at his residence in Princeton, New Jersey. Evidence suggests that Akhmatova was skeptical toward the final Pushkin project of her distant friend. In his reminiscences of the poet, Anatoly Naiman writes that near the end of her life, Akhmatova "described with amusement how 'Arthur had sent a request from America': could she use her connections to get his ballet *The Negro of Peter the Great* produced in the Soviet Union? 'Over there [Akhmatova observed] he couldn't think of anything more intelligent than a ballet about a negro amongst whites'—this was the time of the race riots."[2] Akhmatova's casual remark betrays, to be sure, the conventional flattened view of Western culture available to Soviet citizens at that time. The West did indeed know "race riots." But there was also a long, sophisticated twentieth-century tradition of representing blackness in art that could not have wholly passed Lourié by: the passion for "la negritude" that seized Paris in the 1920s, the discovery of jazz, the splendors of the Harlem Renaissance. Nevertheless, from a Russian perspective, Akhmatova's misgivings about this project were understandable. Why might this aging, disillusioned, émigré composer, in racially tense and increasingly conservative postwar America, turn to Pushkin's historical romance about the "civilizing black man" in Peter the Great's near-savage court?

The present essay takes on that question, as well as others even more speculative. A half-century after its inception, this opera, of which Lourié wrote to Akhmatova with such bitter resignation, remains an unperformed archival curio. For many Russian artists of Lourié's displaced generation, especially those of elitist temperament who did not (or could not) adjust to the manners and marketing procedures of the New World, America was a promised land only in the most attenuated sense. It was a country of physical safety but aesthetic invisibility, reassuringly distant from the fronts of war but, as they saw it, almost entirely devoid of culture. Only the rare creative artist, like Vladimir Nabokov, could adapt and move forward. Many moved backward. Arthur Lourié was one: he ended his career in America by producing a Russian symbolist opera—arguably the only one of its genre, a half-century after symbolism had been snuffed out on Russian-Soviet soil.

ARTUR VINCENT LOURIÉ, 1891–1966

Emigration was not kind to this gifted but now scarce-remembered composer, who became a footnote in the life of his more famous contemporaries.[3] A composition student of Glazunov's (and classmate of Prokofiev's) at the St. Petersburg Conservatory between 1912 and 1916, a regular at the Stray Dog cabaret, Lourié enjoyed local fame among the stellar poets of his generation for his wit, superb piano skills, aristocratic demeanor, and fastidious, decadent dress.[4] He was among the first to set Anna Akhmatova's early verse to music.[5] In her lyrical tributes to the Silver Age, Akhmatova alludes sporadically to their intimacy (begun in 1913, "the final year of the nineteenth century," and resumed in 1921); the relationship broke off abruptly in 1922, however, when Lourié, then head of the Music Division of the Commissariat for Popular Enlightenment, defected to Berlin while on a business trip.[6] He left behind in Bolshevik Russia an ex-wife and young daughter. Seventeen letters to Akhmatova entreating her to join him in emigration apparently went unanswered. Lourié was promptly blacklisted in Soviet musical circles, his name written out of books and his family put under suspicion.[7]

In 1924 Lourié settled in Paris, where he found work as a musical arranger and public spokesman in the household of Igor Stravinsky. Two of Stravinsky's experimental works from that decade, the austere secular oratorio *Oedipus Rex*, performed in Latin, and the opéra bouffe *Mavra* based on Pushkin's "Little House in Kolomna," had disappointed Parisians who were eager for another display of savage primitivism in the vein of *Le sacre du printemps*. Lourié defended the composer's turn to neoclassical and eclectic styles.[8] He praised these two pieces, and *Mavra* in particular, as a contribution to the cosmopolitan Glinka-Tchaikovsky line of "inclusionary" Russian nationalism—a line that in literature had long been associated with the effervescent and receptive pan-European genius of Alexander Pushkin.[9] In Lourié's view, the path chosen by Stravinsky was one of the few routes of creative rebirth available to opera, a genre that had been in decline since Wagner. That two exiled Russians should cultivate this renascence is not surprising. For Stravinsky and Lourié, a displaced condition was a national trait, almost a national virtue. They believed that Russia was at her strongest when translating, combining, and interbreeding with those beyond her borders. Her most gifted and visionary minds (like Pushkin and Peter the Great) had always preferred to borrow eclectically from the outside world rather than distill some arbitrary list of native traits into an "essence." By definition, authentic Russianness was a hybrid.[10]

Lourié's own music is an exotic mix of periods and styles. His early work was indebted to Debussy, Scriabin, and, briefly, to the futurist Nikolai Kul'bin, a rarefied Russian modernist composer who worked with microtones and an altered piano.[11] During his Paris period, Lourié, who had been baptized a Roman Catholic in 1912 while still in St. Petersburg, befriended the neo-Thomist philosopher Jacques Maritain.[12] The sacred musical genres of the Roman church (primarily masses and motets) were to leave a strong trace on the composer's work, albeit filtered through the dense bass sonorities reminiscent of Russian liturgical chants. As one astute critic has observed, however, Lourié's creative evolution is unusual for European composers in the twentieth century.[13] It is the converse of, for example, Schoenberg or Berg, who began as Mahlerians in the tradition of Wagner and then developed a theory that would legitimate their break with this lush, late brand of Romanticism. Lourié, in contrast, *began* his musical life as a self-conscious "theoretical" radical; then, after flirting with Stravinskian neoclassicism, he polemicized against musical serialism and argued for a return to subjectivity and lyricism in art.[14] Lourié ended his career by writing religious music in the spirit of the great Italian masters: Monteverdi, Gabrieli, Palestrina. In the most ambitious stage project of his final years, his gargantuan, highly stylized *Blackamoor* opera, the composer incorporated all these musical tonalities and dramatic traditions.

When the Germans invaded Paris in 1940, Lourié and his wife (by now his third: a countess by birth and the great-granddaughter of Vasily Zhukovsky) abandoned everything and fled south of the Pyrenees. Through the intervention of Serge Koussevitzky, the immensely successful conductor of the Boston Symphony, the couple finally arrived in the United States. In the 1940s, struggling to survive professionally in New York City, Lourié made overtures to Vladimir Nabokov, hoping first to engage him as librettist for a musicalization of Dostoevsky's *Idiot* and then, at the end of the decade, for an opera based on Pushkin's *Blackamoor.* (The Koussevitzky Foundation, a mainstay of support for Lourié's music, had commissioned a symphony; Lourié proposed an opera instead.) Nabokov declined both offers. As the novelist remarked in 1943 to his close friend Mstislav Dobuzhinsky, the émigré artist and scene designer who had conveyed Lourié's request: "I cannot abide Dostoevsky"; and as regards his émigré-composer compatriot, Nabokov added: "Judging from an article of his on music . . . Lourié and I have completely different views on art."[15] In 1949 Dobuzhinsky again approached Nabokov on Lourié's behalf, this time over *Blackamoor.* Acknowledging that librettists "usually commit blasphemous deeds," Dobuzhinsky nevertheless insisted that Nabokov alone was competent to "embroider something on this fragment of Pushkinian canvas." This time Nabokov pleaded overwork. He was also reluctant, it appears, to elaborate creatively on an unfinished literary text; the scrupulous Nabokov did not wish to second-guess Russia's great poet. As Nabokov wrote to his friend Dobuzhinsky, Pushkin's intention to end his *Blackamoor* on a plot symmetry—an illicit black baby born to Ibragim's mistress in Paris, an illicit white baby born to Ibragim's wife in Russia—was an elegant hypothesis but one that could be confirmed only indirectly, by memoiristic testimony.[16]

This noncollaboration is one of the great might-have-beens in the history of Pushkin in music. Had the project gone forward, the émigré writer and the émigré composer most certainly would have disagreed on the appropriate aesthetic treatment of Pushkin's black ancestor. The lofty, epic-heroic tone of Lourié's operatic plot—in keeping with Pushkin's own mythologization of his great-grandfather's royal lineage and distinguished service to tsar and country—is utterly at odds with Nabokov's 1962 statement on the topic, "Pushkin and Gannibal." In that dazzling and ungenerous piece, the young

Ibragim is demoted from the "native prince" of the myth to routine North African slave booty; his baptism becomes a piece of licentious carnival by the curio-collecting tsar; his years of study in Paris are revealed as impoverished and undistinguished; his humanist values are exposed as fantasy; and his temperament is confirmed as "sour, groveling, crotchety, timid, ambitious, and cruel."[17]

The task of a *Blackamoor* libretto eventually went to Lourié's final companion and muse, Irina Graham. Her sentimental tastes and lyrical gifts could not have been further from Nabokov's. As Lourié confessed to her in 1949, while recruiting her services, "I had thought to attract Sirin [Nabokov], he liked the topic, but he's very busy and what's more I no longer think I could have gotten along with him: he's very capricious and I am capricious, and what I need is cooperation."[18] What Lourié reaped was adoration. Graham, a young freelance journalist of Russian-Italian parentage, born in Genoa, raised in Harbin, married to an American engineer in Shanghai, and eventually employed by the Tolstoy Foundation, fell deeply in love with Lourié and his music.[19] With her devoted assistance, Lourié produced two versions of the *Blackamoor* opera.

The first version was the result of a frantic six-week collaboration by post between New York and San Francisco, where Graham was based with her husband (then shuttling between the West Coast and the Chinese mainland) in the spring of 1949.[20] The urgent tone of their correspondence reflected a most unrealistic deadline; the opera had been scheduled for Tanglewood's 1950 season, a target that could not conceivably be met.[21] The second version, begun after Graham was widowed later that year, took ten years to complete and was considerably more "grand" and ambitious. Graham moved permanently to New York City in 1957, supporting herself (and subsidizing the Louriés) by a dozen different jobs. It appears that the revisioning of the opera was a very domestic affair; sitting alongside the composer at the piano, Graham generated the new libretto in pace with the music. (By her own account, she had a pleasant natural alto and "sang through all the parts: the bass Peter, the baritone Ibragim, the contralto Lastochka, the lyrical soprano Natasha, and the dramatic soprano Countess.")[22] A piano-vocal score was finished in 1956 and the full orchestral score in 1961. But by that time, as evidenced by the composer's lament to Akhmatova two years later, both the Pushkin jubilee enthusiasm of 1949 and any possible funds for staging the opera had faded away.

In 1961 Lourié and his wife Ella settled into Jacques Maritain's house in Princeton, in accordance with a generous item in the late philosopher's will. The composer's final years were marked by resignation, piety, residual dandyism in attire, and—according to the Mandelstam scholar Clarence Brown, who knew the elderly couple well—a musical profile so low as to be imperceptible.[23] Although modestly successful in Europe, Lourié's music had not found an audience in America. Lourié continued to compose in his pan-European style; in addition to motets, he planned an opera on Apuleius's *Golden Ass* with a libretto in Italian provided by Graham. But he no longer hoped for publishers or performances.[24] The composer died in 1966 in Princeton and was laid to rest in the cemetery behind St. Paul's Church on Nassau Street. By the time of his death, the stressful New World menage à trois with Irina Graham had become an awkward parody of those brilliant triangular affairs practiced and celebrated by poet-artists—Akhmatova and Lourié among them—during the fabulously distant Silver Age.

In 1991, with Soviet taboos crumbling, the Russian violin virtuoso Gidon Kremer undertook single-handedly to honor Lourié with a centennial.[25] Irina Graham had supplied him with all extant archival materials. An American documentary film, *In Search of Lost Orpheus,* was produced on Lourié's life; dormant scores were revived; and commemorative performances were mounted in St. Petersburg, Cologne, and Boston. These included the premiere, in Cologne on December 9, 1992, of a full concert performance in Russian of *The Blackamoor of Peter the Great.* In 1990, what appears to be a libretto toward that concert premiere was published (English text only), edited by the German musicologist and Lourié specialist Detlef Gojowy.[26] There the matter rested. We can dream about a premiere under Valery Gergiev in the new St. Petersburg Mariinsky Theater. As of 2004, however, the opera has been neither published nor staged. A production was reputedly being considered under the direction of the venerable Gennady Rozhdestvensky, the seasoned conductor who briefly served as musical director of Moscow's Bolshoi Theater in 2000, but it seems unlikely that this expensive, lavish opera will be mounted soon in that financially troubled house.

An echo of the *Blackamoor* project did make its debut on compact disc in 1996. Alongside works by Igor Stravinsky and Alfred Schnittke in a miscellany assembled by Gidon Kremer entitled *Out of Russia,* there is a twenty-minute reduction in eleven episodes of musical material from *Blackamoor,* dated 1961 and bearing the curious subtitle "The Blackamoor of Peter the Great (Symphonic Prose)."[27] From the label it is unclear whether Lourié himself or some later arranger undertook this transposition from operatic score into instrumental "prose." Either way, this pastiche of truncated orchestral episodes, largely dance scenes, is at present our sole recorded sample of the opera that Lourié, after forty years in emigration, intended as his tribute to Pushkin, Peter the Great, and Peter's City.

Irina Graham died in 1996. Thanks to her persistent efforts, a Lourié archive exists today in the New York Public Library for the Performing Arts at Lincoln Center. It contains a full, undated orchestral score of *The Blackamoor of Peter the Great* in manuscript, its libretto handwritten in Russian with inserts in French, Italian, Latin, and Greek.[28] According to the curator of the archive, interest in the Lourié manuscripts is brisk among musicologists. In 1999 a brief essay appeared in the Russian press on Lourie's "American diaries" from 1942 to 1962 (the *Blackamoor* years), which had been archived in Paris by the family of Lourié's friend Louis Laloy; these diaries, which confirm the composer's abiding fidelity to Silver Age culture throughout the American years, await more detailed study.[29] The present essay is thus no more than a placeholder, designed to alert students of Russian culture to this ambitious Pushkin project unperformed in its composer's lifetime, as yet unstaged, and the target of only scattered scholarly attention.

THE OPERA'S PLOT: GENESIS AND INITIAL SHAPE

In a series of increasingly impatient letters to Irina Graham on March 2, 14, and 19, 1949—the composer really did wish her to produce a finished libretto within the month—Lourié sketched out his initial ideas.[30] "Don't worry about what others have done," he wrote to her on March 2,

> just seek something new and bold, like what Alexander Sergeevich would have written, had he reworked his prose into an opera libretto . . . what's important is that nothing sound calculated or didactic; the result should be a weaving-together of purely musical forms, that is, each moment of the action must find its own expression in musical form: arias, duets, trios, choruses, marches, sarabands, minuets, serenades, imagine whatever you like and it will be clear—only no rhetoric, what's necessary here is precisely an uninterrupted visual and aural impression . . . There's no need for a lot of words in the libretto. No more than in Pushkin's little dramas.

At this early point, it seems, Lourié envisaged no change in Pushkin's plot. He assumed that a competent Russian audience would be intimately familiar with Pushkin's texts, and thus a musical setting did not need to tell the story; it needed only to enhance and illustrate this story at select points, using the rich resources of music.

"So what's with my *Blackamoor*?" Lourié wrote Graham twelve days later.

> If you were here, closer by, we would have solved the problem long ago, the libretto would have been almost finished . . . I've already done one choral piece . . . but the arias, where are the arias? Where can we get them from? We don't need many arias. For the leading roles, one aria each per scene is sufficient . . . We can begin with the scene at the Countess's, awaiting the birth of

the child. Fortunes are told, bets are laid: what will it be, white or black? But can we raise such a commotion, with champagne and frolicking, in the very house of the Countess during her childbirth? I think we can; it's in keeping with the tastes of the epoch. And then (scene with the blackamoor)? With the courier from Peter (the offer to return) and from the Duke, an offer to remain. The meeting with Peter at the border—here an insert, "the window onto Europe." We must absolutely have a scene on the ship—on the masts—the report to the tsar. The foreign monkey [*zamorskaia obez'iana*, Peter's name for the Parisian dandy Korsakov] fits in here. Dinner at the boyar's . . . [You write of] "African passion combined with melancholy." This is all splendid, but texts, texts, texts!

The theme, Lourié assured Graham in this March 14 letter, was ready-made (he had none of Nabokov's scruples about supplementing Pushkin's fragment or second-guessing the poet). "Here's the whole plot, the way Pushkin thought it out. In the first act, in Paris, the Countess gives birth to a black child for which a white one is substituted. In the second and third acts, in Petersburg, the wife gives birth to a white child for which a black one is substituted. There it is, a libertine opera in the taste of the eighteenth century, all in a single formula."[31]

This crystalline plot, as Lourié thrust it at Graham in the spring of 1949, displays something of the symmetrical justice of *Eugene Onegin*. But its action is more violent, its loves more crudely expressed, the confrontations more unforgiving. The use of interracial childbirth as the revelatory event anchoring the plot fore and aft has the additional tantalizing appeal—or terror—of one's innermost private life involuntarily made public through an "incarnated" product. Such birth scenes might be said to function as criminal trials do in a novel, but at a level far more efficient, illicit, unburdened with words, irrational, "operatic." No wonder Lourié felt little need to highlight Ibragim's blackness as a special trait—and all the more so in his adoptive America, with its restless postwar climate and distinctive racial bigotries and sentimentalisms. Given his aristocratic temperament, Lourié doubtless wished to avoid the innocent, but ill-informed and essentializing, appropriation often encountered in black American celebrations of the octoroon Pushkin. Lourié was in pursuit of more transcendental imagery. On March 19 he wrote to Graham: "Think how to ensure that the problem of the Negroes glints through, but of course without didacticism and without any social moral."[32]

The anxious tone of these initial letters suggests that Graham was losing heart. Lourié wrote to her caressingly on March 23, offering a conflation of orientalist myths (Asian, African, Turkish):

So you see—no special experience is necessary at all. None of the professional librettists could have done any better, of that I am convinced. The boyars' scene is splendid! It doesn't matter that there's no quartet . . . [But] I think in the Assemblée there must be more singing than recitative. The Assemblée should have nothing of the routine boyars' Russia about it. After all, something wholly different and new is happening there. Primitive, savage Europeanization. Something for which no words can be found. Pushkin does not define that primeval energy, but one can sense it in the air. Some sort of Asia in conjunction with . . . Protestantism . . . The blackamoor is something subtle and mysterious, it seems to me, there's nothing animal about him at all. His cruel elemental impulses are subordinated, already bridled . . . And what if, in that scene, the blackamoor were to sing, [set as] a Turkish song, "Oh, Maiden Rose, I Am in Fetters"?[33] I agree that anything especially "Negro" in *Blackamoor* would be untrue.

The recently discovered diaries for 1949 confirm this resurgence of Lourié's Eurasianism, a quarter-century after Stravinsky had espoused the doctrine and catered to the Parisian vogue for a savage, virile Russia of the steppe.[34] In the postwar 1940s, however, Lourié was evoking not some prehistoric *Rite of Spring* but the moment of Russia's entry into the modern age. The image of the black man in this drama is not thrillingly savage or "primitive." Quite the contrary; the most savage under-civilized place in Lourié's opera is white, pre-Petrine Russia, and to modernize such a resistant place Tsar Peter must have recourse to methods that are also savage. As Lourié counseled Graham, Ibragim's blackness was almost incidental and should not be emphasized. He is an Othello before the fall: exotic, subtle, articulate, highly skilled, the best combination of a "man of nature" and a cosmopolitan man of the world. Ibragim's person in the opera is in no way burdened with the ferocious prejudice common to North American culture, with its history of race-based slavery and its predisposition to pass judgment based on color alone.

This initial version of the opera from 1949 is probably not recuperable. But from Lourié's fervent commentary to Graham and from what we know of the composer's own musical preferences, we can speculate on the musicodramatic vision that had animated it. The initial concept might well have resembled that of Stravinsky's *L'Histoire du soldat* or *Mavra*, in which a series of rhythmically diverse, eclectic musical genres (from folk song to jazz and fox-trot) are packed into close proximity—their intensity relieved, when necessary, by set pieces of more somber cast: processions, madrigals, and other such blocks of massed sound. In this "weaving together of purely musical forms," characters burst onto the scene already possessed of a strong profile, in a singing or dancing rhythm. Vocal interactions are essentially clashes, which resolve unexpectedly (if they resolve at all) with their genre edges still palpable. No single mood controls the field for long. In *Mavra*, the result is irrepressible, flirtatious, Mozart-like but within a modernist tonal envelope—

a perfect fit with the pace and wit of "Little House in Kolomna," and as close to the quicksilver feel of Pushkin as we are likely to have in music.

In 1949, however, Lourié was working with a very different text of Pushkin's than the self-referential, parodic whimsy that had caught Stravinsky's ear in the 1920s. Lourié's life and world after the Second World War contrasted starkly with that now-distant Parisian scene. We can assume that the full-length opera libretto he and Graham eventually created out of Pushkin's narrative was in many ways continuous with their earlier, more crisp and compact version, but that ultimately they invested it with other tensions. Dominant everywhere in the revised *Blackamoor* opera are strangeness and incompatibility, the coexistence and nontranslatability of worlds, with juxtapositions that prove threatening rather than wondrous. There are few mediators between these worlds. Of the two most important arbiters, one is the black man Ibragim. The other is Eros, a marble statue which (always significantly in Pushkin) comes intermittently to life.[35] Only once in the opera does Eros appear on stage in blackface; for most of the action, these two forces—Eros and blackness—are in subtle and desperate competition.

FINAL SHAPE OF THE OPERA

Graham speaks of a huge correspondence with Lourié during this whirlwind first phase of composition, the spring of 1949. After citing six letters, however, she concludes vaguely: "And what was the result? In place of the composer's original concept for a short two-act opera ('the music was to last overall no more than an hour,' he wrote), there emerged an opera in three acts, twice as long as the one he had planned for." It is not clear what provoked the decision to revise, but apparently two years after mapping out the compact chamber work (1952), Lourié began to reshape it into a grander opera. For the literary side of this task, Irina Graham provided an explanatory note in 1972, which listed the poetic sources for the revision. In addition to Pushkin (complete), she noted "verses and lines from Lermontov, Tiutchev, Baratynsky, Griboedov, Blok, Vyacheslav Ivanov, Gerard de Nerval and Baudelaire translated into Russian to fit the meter of the music, Shakespeare's song from *As You Like It* in Pasternak's translation"—and, among historical documents—"medieval texts translated from Old French, archaic verses of the Petrine and pre-Petrine epoch, and the authentic speech of Peter I, taken from his official regulations and letters."[36] In her note, Graham insists that this raid on the world's great poets, however elusive and decontextualized, was a deliberate attempt to overcome the routine problem with opera libretti created out of Pushkin's themes and texts. "Alongside Pushkin's verses, the texts of other authors . . . seem insipid and flat," she observed; "they sound like ditties and evoke ridicule or dissatisfaction on the part of critics and audience." The verbal texture of *The Blackamoor of Peter the Great* was to be a high-class hybrid, not just a pastiche. All lines would be the lines of masters; no mere filler would link bits and pieces of "real Pushkin" solely for the sake of moving forward the story. Lourié and Graham did not wish their listeners to wince over their product the way Pushkin lovers are still wont to do, fairly or unfairly, over the patchwork libretti of Mussorgsky's *Boris Godunov* or Tchaikovsky's *Eugene Onegin*.

But a deeper poetics, it seems, was at stake. For the symbolist creator, the reality of this world is dependent upon (and responsive to) the reality of the next. The space we inhabit now is saturated with artistic texts from all periods and cultures, which resound in us simultaneously; a minuscule allusion is sufficient to summon a line, a poem, a context, a persona into luxuriant being. Symbolist artworks demand of their audience a high level of cultural knowledge as well as phenomenal powers of recall and conjuration, for the experience of living thickly inside a culture, reverent toward its traditions and alert to the art that fills it, itself constitutes the appeal—and at times the very plot—of the work. In no way are "new" events or "original" utterances more vigorous, relevant, or wisdom-bearing than a reminiscence. To be literate means to recognize the full recuperability of the past. And thus it is in this libretto: everything is there, all times are interconnected, nothing is meaningless or free.

Those familiar with the six-plus chapters of Pushkin's *Blackamoor*—and also with the liberties routinely taken in other operas built off Pushkin's texts—will be struck by the close correspondence between the action of the source text and that of the 1961 libretto. Pushkin's relatively infrequent instances of direct dialogue are inserted verbatim into the score, although at times moved partially into French. Lourié's additions to Pushkin are largely of the intermezzo sort, which serve to interrupt and stylize the story line rather than to change it grossly; the large number of processions, choruses, ballets, pantomimes, troupes of bacchantes and harlequins, and meditative arias set to bits of verse by other poets or to other poems by Pushkin impart to the whole the transhistorical gloss of an oratorio or a "play within a play." For this particular transposed tale, it turns out, stylization is especially appropriate. The key biographical events in Pushkin's *Blackamoor* are already "aestheticized" or moved into myth: the black baby/white baby legend, for example, is a conflation of two separate incidents happening to two different couples in the Pushkin family genealogy, and the mandated marriage of a royal favorite to a Russian boyar's reluctant daughter did not in fact happen to Ibragim but to another member of Peter's court. As one recent critic has observed, the "hero" of Pushkin's *Blackamoor* is not Ibragim and not even Peter I but the Petrine epoch itself, a dynamic self-made era in which anecdotes were "true" if their tellers believed them and if they could potentially have occurred.[37] Such periods of history, in which stylization, allegorization, and fabrication have the force of truth, open up intriguing and even liberating potentials for the projection of character on the operatic stage. Grand opera has long been censured for its paradoxical treatment of human personality—which, in order to "carry" on stage, must be internalized, heightened, and flattened all at the same time. Historical figures answering for real-life events are especially vulnerable during such operatic deformations and heightenings. But Lourié, with his keen dramatic sensibilities, must have sensed that Pushkin, even when writing as a historian, intuitively recorded and balanced the facts of the world as a poet. Here as in the *History of Pugachev*, symmetries glint beneath each documented particular. "The plot," as Lourié had written to Irina Graham, "is ready-made."

THE BLACKAMOOR OF PETER THE GREAT: SYNOPSIS AND COMMENTARY

The account of the 1961 opera provided here follows the most complete summary of the plot in print: Detlef Gojowy's 1990 pamphlet *The Blackamoor of Peter the Great* (containing an "Outline," a more complete narrative "Synopsis," and an English-language libretto). The copy of the pamphlet deposited in the Lourié archive at Lincoln Center contains several handwritten corrections, most likely pertaining to the premiere.

The Blackamoor of Peter the Great
An Opera in Three Acts (nine scenes)

Paris and Sankt Piterburkh [*sic*], beginning of the eighteenth century.

Cast of characters:
Peter the Great, Emperor of Russia	bass
Ibragim Gannibal, the Blackamoor, his godson	baritone
Eleonora, mistress to Ibragim	soprano
The Count, husband to Eleonora	tenor
Duke Philippe d'Orleans, Regent of France	bass
Eros (a dancer on the stage)	mezzo-soprano in the orchestra
Korsakov, a Russian officer, educated in Paris	tenor
Princess Natasha Rzhevskaia	soprano
Prince Rzhevsky, Natasha's father	bass
Dura, jester to Prince Rzhevsky	mezzo-soprano
Nana, a dwarf, Natasha's nurse	contralto
A captive Swede, Natasha's music master	tenor
The innkeeper	contralto

The supporting or ornamental cast (brilliantly, exotically dressed) includes altar boys, cavaliers, dancers and corps de ballet, maskers, sultans, monks, midgets, Ethiopian royalty, Spanish grandees, Chinese emperors, cavaliers, maskers, shipbuilders, sailors, guests of the Emperor, grenadiers, a marshal of ceremonies, nurses, maids, two executioners, and two nuns.

The following account of the opera's action is culled from the libretto, the full score, and the narrative summary, and contains my commentary.

Act One opens on a series of set pieces and stylized musical genres prefiguring the major themes. A Hymn to St. Benedict the Moor, choreographed in the style of seventeenth-century Spanish or Italian religious dances, is followed by three Pushkinian epigraphs sung by a chorus offstage. During a brief Pantomime, Eros, made up as a blackamoor, rushes in from the wings pursued by women. A backstage chorus sings the final stanza of Pushkin's adolescent lyric from 1814, "Mon portrait": *Vrai démon pour l'espièglerie! Vrai singe par sa mine! Tu es vilain, vilain!* (Omitted from the operatic setting are the poem's two concluding lines, where *par sa mine* rhymes with the final word, *Pouchkine.*)[38] Eros moans in fear and pain.

Scene I. The Letter. Eleonora's salon in Paris. In distress, Eleonora reads a letter announcing her husband's imminent return. When Ibragim enters, she addresses him as "monster"—and to his sympathetic ministrations she replies: "You have ruined me! My husband will kill me!" When Ibragim offers to challenge the Count to a duel, Eleonora is appalled: "He is so kind, so considerate, and yet I dared to be unfaithful to him, I betrayed him for you, a monster!" Ibragim takes her tenderly in his arms. In desperation, she blurts out a plan that might save her honor.

The second episode of the scene, the Countess's confinement, is entitled *Gossip*. Cavaliers and ladies come and go; the men are playing cards and laying bets on the color of the child. The women disapprove of such callousness (*Kakoe nizkoe kovarstvo!* ["What base perfidy!"] a chorus of ladies sings, addressing the men with a famous phrase from the first stanza of *Eugene Onegin*); "will you men always slander us?" Ibragim is escorted on stage by two maid-ballerinas. He sings an abject aria begging forgiveness of his wronged and suffering mistress. A maid runs on stage with a white baby; a second maid runs out of Eleonora's bedroom with a black baby; Ibragim blesses the departing infant and then rushes distraught into the bedroom.

Scene 2. The Masked Ball. A ballroom at the Palais Royale. Ibragim is surrounded by dancing maskers, who sing of the Arabian deserts he is willing to exchange for the snowy light of Russia. Eleonora (in medieval costume), the Count (as a white unicorn), and the Regent enter and watch a ballet, "The Birth of Eros," performed in four phases: the dance of the Night with the Wind, the appearance of the Silver Egg in the lap of Darkness, the breaking of the Egg, and the Dance and Aria of Eros ("Amour"). After the ballet is over, the Regent mentions to Ibragim a letter he has received from Tsar Peter, inviting his godson to return home. But the Regent advises the blackamoor to remain in France ("You were not born a subject of Peter... You are a stranger to the half-savage ways of Russia!"). Ibragim answers that Russia remains his primary allegiance and that his destiny is linked with Peter's. Were he fated once again to see his ancestral southern homeland, even there, "under the skies of his Africa," he would sigh and pine for dreary Russia. (Here the signature line from *Eugene Onegin*, chapter 1.50, *pod nebom Afriki moei*, is put into the hero's mouth; for Ibragim, like the stylized narrator of Pushkin's novel in verse and like Pushkin himself, admits the mournful pull of this great, gloomy northern land even as he entertains dreams of release from it.) Against the background of a chorus celebrating, in French, the pleasures of love, Ibragim decides to return to Petersburg.

Scene 3. Les Adieux. Eros appears in front of the curtain and announces himself the manager of the scene ("Whoever you are, I am your master, I shall be with you forever! My eye is keen..."). The curtain rises on Ibragim and the Count playing chess; Eleonora is at the harpsichord. She sings an Italian aria and Ibragim a madrigal. As soon as the Count exits, Ibragim breaks the news of his departure, reminding his mistress of the trials they have undergone and of the terrible birth of their son ("Our happiness cannot last..."). After a conventional farewell duet, Eros and the chorus comment wryly: *Ne dolgo zhenskuiu liubov' / pechalit khladnaia razluka: / Proidet liubov', nastanet skuka, / Krasavitsa poliubit vnov'!* ("Chilly separation does not sadden woman's love for long; love will pass, boredom will set in, the beauty will fall in love again!")

Act Two is the site of Peter's superhuman will—and also of the maturation of Eros, the single most stubborn threat to that will. *Scene 4*, at the Inn, opens with a lullaby-lament (from Blok's 1916 poem "The Hawk" ["Korshun"]), sung over a cradle, on the theme of Russia's fate: "Ages pass, war is rumbling, rebellions rage, villages go up in flames: how long will the mother grieve, how long will the hawk hover overhead?" Peter I sits in the corner, smoking his pipe and reading newspapers by candlelight as Ibragim enters, a Russian fur coat over his French uniform. The reunion between tsar and godson is warmly affectionate. Ibragim informs Peter of events in France; Peter, in turn, tells the repatriated blackamoor of the new capital he created *iz t'my bolot* ("out of the murky dark of swamps")—and you know, he remarks to Ibragim, "this new city appeared to me in a dream." Peter then delivers his lengthy tribute to his capital, an arioso setting of the first eighty-four lines of *The Bronze Horseman* (*Mednyi vsadnik*). Ibragim rejoices with his sovereign. "Let me now show you my *paradis*," Peter sings as they prepare to set out, "a city where the forest once stood."

Scene 5. On the Dockyards. Shipbuilders are constructing a frigate;

below it, at a worktable, Ibragim is busy with a compass. Peter, hatless, hammer in hand, dressed in the red jacket of a shipmate, appears and disappears on the mast of the ship. A chorus sings a lament on the theme of betrayed love. Korsakov appears, in powdered wig, embroidered coat, and velvet breeches, looking around in astonishment. He sings in a mixture of French and Russian. "This barbaric place . . . ," he remarks to Ibragim. "But who is your tailor? . . . Do you at least have an opera house . . . Ah, our dear Paris! Do you remember our Paris?" The two friends sing a duet in French (in the score, Ibragim is given the choice of singing his lines in French or in Russian); they recall their "perfumed paradise," now "more distant than India or China."

Korsakov delivers to the tsar his dispatches from France by clambering up the ship's mast; Ibragim, meanwhile, drills a group of peasant-sailors. "*Entre nous*," Korsakov notes, "our emperor is a very strange man . . . " Having promised to appear at the Palace for a festival honoring the arrival of a Greek statue from the south, Korsakov exits. Peter descends from the ship. In the guise of a dictation to his secretary-scribe Ibragim, he sings an extensive aria on the burdens of statecraft: "The two necessary conditions for governing are civil order and defense. Contempt for war often results in total ruin, as the fall of the Greek monarchy shows us . . ." A cannon shot announces the rising of the Neva. At this point a tulle curtain falls, with Falconet's monument to Peter the Great reflected on it; in honor of Peter, a chorus sings scattered lines from *The Bronze Horseman*. Prominently inserted into their praise, however, is Evgeny's ominous threat to the statue, which signals his descent into insanity: *Dobro, stroitel' chudotvornyi! Uzho tebe!* ("Fair enough, miracle-working builder! I'll show you!"). This web of Petersburg symbols thickens and is literally layered on stage, as past and future are glimpsed through the translucent curtain of the present.

Scene 6. The Festival. A hall in Peter's palace, full of guests. The tsar is playing a game of dice with an English shipmaster, English couples dance a jig, Guards officers sing a boisterous military song. Korsakov, astonished by this informality and lack of hierarchy, tries (unsuccessfully) to attract Peter's attention. As grenadiers carry in a Greek statue of Eros, the tsar welcomes his guests with a ceremonial speech. From this point on, the capricious and sinister power of "Amour" becomes ever more pervasive. Korsakov glimpses the young beauty Natasha Rzhevskaia and, smitten, asks her to dance; the two exchange subdued love murmurings. Peter finally takes notice of Korsakov—now that the latter has committed a breach of court etiquette—and delights in sentencing him to mock punishment with the words: "The drunkenness of Bacchus be with you!" Peter and Ibragim laugh, forcing the Frenchified dandy to drink the Goblet of the Great Eagle. Inebriated and humiliated, Korsakov staggers off.

At a signal from her father, Natasha asks Ibragim to dance. At this point the statue of Eros comes to life on its pedestal. (At this point the Lincoln Center copy of the libretto contains a handwritten addendum in the margins: "The movements of Eros are seen only by Ibrahim.") The statue sings to the hero: "Don't approach her! Don't! She is encircled by a magic ring!" When the startled Ibragim looks up at the voice, Eros has again become lifeless marble. Natasha and the blackamoor dance. Tsar Peter, meanwhile, is examining a map of America; leafing through a folio with his usual keen curiosity, he sings a canticle about Cerberus, three-throated hound of hell, a shameless copulator who devours the world's finest fruits. (Could this map and hellish song be an echo of Lourié's attitude toward the New World?)

The tsar then takes his godson Ibragim aside and asks if Natasha appeals to him. A marriage will be arranged, Peter promises, so that he will not be so alone, so unprotected in society and bereft of noble connections. As in Pushkin's account, Ibragim hesitates: "But how do I dare? I'm a blackamoor, alien to everyone . . ." Peter will have none of that. "Nonsense, in what way are you not a fine suitor? (*chem ty ne molodets*?) Besides, I'll be the matchmaker." At this news, bacchantes rush in and dance; upon their exit, Ibragim sings a blissful serenade: "Is the hope of happiness really possible for me?" As the second act ends, then, the lines are drawn. Tsar Peter, confident in his power to impose a city upon nature, now intends to impose his will upon Eros as well. Ibragim—hard worker and hero-worshiper—cannot resist believing that in this as in all other brave and "unnatural" acts, his benefactor will succeed.

The three scenes of *Act Three* are set in the Rzhevsky household. *Scene 7* takes place at table. Family and guests, dressed in the required European fashion, are being entertained by Dura (the Fool), the dwarf Nana (who bursts out of a huge baked pastry), harlequins in animal masks, gypsies, and a dancing bear. The entertainment here is as traditionally grotesque and "Muscovite" as Peter's company in the previous scenes had been mercantile, forward-looking, and devoted to practical, profitable labor. The Fool mimics the "foreign monkey" Korsakov (*Monsieur . . . mamzelle . . . L'assemblée . . . pardon . . .*), to everyone's delight.

Unexpectedly, and accompanied by a chorus singing in Greek, the Emperor's sleigh drives into the courtyard. As the Rzhevsky household hurries to honor its guest, Peter discusses the Russian defeat at Narva with Natasha's dance-master, the captive Swede. Taking up his violin, the Swede then plays a tune while Peter (somewhat incongruously) dances with the daughter of the house. During their brief dance, the Emperor and Ibragim's destined bride exchange disturbingly suggestive lines. "I must avoid you!" Natasha cries to her partner, "your deceits are known to me"; in response, the tsar declares himself a captive of her beauty. In this strange episode, where a blackamoor is the intended legal bridegroom but the tsar and his courtiers retain every right to tempt, confuse, and seduce a susceptible maiden named Natasha, it is difficult not to see an allusion to Pushkin's risk-laden courtship of the beautiful Natalia Goncharova and their fateful marriage.

The imperial theme returns. In a self-assured aria to the Swede, Peter—never one to regret a vigorous enemy—recalls his victory over Charles XII at Poltava ("Your sovereign once taught me a different sort of dance. He was our cruel teacher in the science of glory! . . . I raise this goblet to my teachers!"). But Natasha is full of foreboding. Her father bids the tsar farewell and sends his daughter to her room. He then announces to the Swede and Nana that the Emperor has betrothed Natasha to the blackamoor. Rzhevsky pleads Ibragim's noble birth and godson status, but in vain. A horrified trio ensues, which is overheard by Natasha listening in at the door; at their words "Into the claws of that black devil? . . . it's unthinkable!" she faints. Natasha is carried out, the household is in commotion, but "the Emperor's will reigns" and the verdict stands. Harlequins dance while the chorus sings the final couplet from "The Tsar's Blackamoor Had a Notion to Get Married," Pushkin's 1824 verse experiment in the folk style: *A kak on arap chernshenek / A ona-to dusha beleshen'ka* ("How black-black the blackamoor is, and she's a white-white soul").[39] Ibragim enters humbly. To ensure that the Rzhevskys' jeering servants will not understand him, he sings an aria in Italian, consecrated to his newly legitimate love.

Pushkin's final completed chapter (that is, 6) ends soon after this forced betrothal. In cool, nonjudgmental prose we read that Natasha is raving over her absent beloved, Valerian, and rebelling against her fate: "One hope alone remained to her: to die before the hateful marriage came to pass" (*PSS* 8:32). In the fragment of chapter 7 that Pushkin added a year later (1828), a man we assume to be Valerian mysteriously turns up at the Rzhevsky house and is received by the captive Swede, who has just packed away his flute and is retiring for the night. The final two scenes in Lourié's opera speculate on possible futures for this truncated final scene in Pushkin.

The necessary economy of a libretto prompted certain changes. Korsakov was substituted for the lover Valerian—a conflation of characters that considerably alters the symbolism of the whole. The Valerian of Pushkin's text is a member of an old boyar family, one of Natasha's own circle, the son of a seditious *strelets* (musketeer) and thus himself a potential threat to the throne. (The illicit lover who is also a political rebel is an ancient plot, of course, in both neoclassical drama and in Russian historical narrative; Pushkin himself used it in his 1822 fragment "Vadim.") By contrast, the operatic Korsakov is a dandy, a Frenchified "monkey" who has turned the head of an otherwise obedient girl. In the opera, it seems, it is the special province of foreigners to arouse and command Eros. Tightening the noose on his hapless lovers, Lourié structures the two scenes of his finale as a hallucinating vortex.

When collapse comes, we are thrown back into a Russia that is unprecedentedly primitive and violent.

Scene 8, entitled "The Magic Lantern," takes place in the bedroom of the house of Ibragim. It opens on a wedding lament, a complex musical genre familiar to Russian folklore and to the twentieth-century Russian stage (consider, for example, the stylized lament that opens Stravinsky's *Les noces*—which, under cover of ritualized grief, conceals liberation and a female coming-of-age). But in Lourié's opera there is nothing ceremonial or conventionalized about this lament. Natasha really is desperate. Her maids undress her, mourn with her, and sing: "Oh, unhappy bride, look at your girlfriends, listen to what they say: Shove the blackamoor off your wedding bed!" In an arioso recalling the birth of Eros from the union of Night and Wind, the dwarf Nana sings of the groaning of the wind, its dark and alien language, and the songs it transmits to us of our "ancient native chaos," words "born from flame and light."

Suddenly the windows brighten with a flare. The figure of Korsakov in powdered wig and white satin coat appears briefly. He sings of his lady's smile and eyes, which have slain him—but only Natasha hears and sees the vision. She ecstatically recalls the minuet she had danced with Korsakov, and then bitterly recalls that her father had felt no pity for her. The dwarf responds by paraphrasing the concluding lines of Pushkin's *Gypsies: spasen'ia net ot bed i vsiudu strasti rokovye . . . i ot sudeb zashchity net . . .*" ("there is no salvation from calamity, fatal passions are everywhere . . . there is no defense from fate"). Ibragim enters and bows deeply to his wife. Natasha and Nana cling to each other, terror-stricken.

Scene 9, the finale, is subtitled "Puppet Show." A stage direction instructs "all participants in the scene to behave like puppets." The setting is the Swede's room (as in Pushkin's fragment of chapter 7), lit only by candlelight; he is dismantling his flute. Suddenly Eros appears at the door dressed in a cloak, tricorn hat, and Hessian boots. The Swede greets him as an old friend. Eros inquires about the scandal in the blackamoor's house—and the Swede comments ruefully on a scene that then begins, woodenly, to be acted out on stage. Natasha and Korsakov enter, singing of life's golden cup and nights of love: "So," the Swede sings, "the foreign rascal made the blackamoor a cuckold before his wedding!" Nursemaids carry in an empty cradle ("is it some black imp wailing in his cradle?" they sing. "Or is it a lamb, bleating before being roasted?") A midwife carries in a white baby. "Accursed wedding! Devilish wedding!" the Swede remarks, continuing to annotate the performance. "That black devil thought to make a black child by his wife, but the young wife bore him a white baby!" Ibragim enters in despair, singing: "I was fooled by hope, death smirks at my anguish, my life has no meaning." To which Eros responds: *Mea culpa, mea maxima . . .*

The penultimate episode of the Puppet Show is authentic Guignol, full of capricious and fathomless violence. "The tsar was furious, for he was the matchmaker!" the Swede barks out. Peter enters, shouting: "That simpleton, allowing a wench to deceive him! And where's Korsakov, that dandy? Show him no mercy!" Korsakov rushes on stage and flings himself at the tsar's feet, begging pardon. Two executioners grab the miscreant, but Peter stays their hand: "Wait!" he sings. "Marry him to Dura!" The Fool promptly snatches up Korsakov, whirls him about like a rag doll and throws him on the bed, promising to lord it over her new husband and bring back the whip. Eros looks on and comments: "What a ghastly sight."

The final episode is brief, but in its somber movement invokes a major motif in Russian political history: generations of cast-off tsarinas, disobedient wives, and inconvenient female elements interred behind convent walls. Natasha enters in a nun's habit, singing mournfully of her imprisonment, her tears and sleepless nights. Eros asks: "Where is our fair rose?" In response, the Swede takes up his flute and plays. On an emptied and darkened stage (whose very bleakness is a trademark closure in the classic tradition of Russian historical opera), only the silent marble Eros remains.

Thus is this dancing, corporeal Eros revealed as a vital character in the opera. It both acts and tells, predicts and punishes, opening and closing the work with its conjuring wand. Such a personification became as central to Lourié and Graham's dramatic concept as a demonic presence was to Prokofiev's *Fiery Angel*. Pushkin, of course, had not embedded any such meta-symbolic presence in his *Blackamoor* family romance; there, as in his prose overall, everything is clear and dry. But through singing, dancing, incarnating, orchestrating, grand opera inevitably heats up and heightens all stories realized on stage. Multileveled symbolist opera of the sort Lourié was attempting is even more ambitious. It must make manifest the absolute authenticity of another plane of reality. But this second plane, while real, is selective. On the symbolist stage, not everyone sees everything that happens. The world that embraces us is at the same time our own projection. Since each individual psyche creates its own time and space, the intersection of these private visions is always disorienting and something of a miracle—terrifying to some, for others triumphant, and for most of the world, invisible.

What guarantees the integrity of the whole? The narrating function in Lourié's opera is assumed by dancing bacchantes and pagan choruses, who deliver an undercurrent of advice and prophecy. At crucial moments, the story is stage-managed by a protean Eros. Sometimes Amour is an arch-hero in the baroque buffo tradition, teasing the lovesick during an intermezzo. Sometimes it is a statue, which comes to life to warn Ibragim that even his benefactor, the matchmaker-tsar, cannot control or pair off at will all the elemental energies of the cosmos. If Eros/Amour appears at the beginning in frightened blackface in an Orphic pantomime, by the ninth scene—a coda and extension of Pushkin's plot—Amour is dressed dashingly as an officer of the Guards. And by the final curtain, the statue of Eros is on display alone, in the garb of that scapegrace adolescent Pushkin at the Lycée, in tricorn hat and military boots. Thus does the opera interweave painful allusions to Pushkin's carefree bachelor youth and final troubled married year with the threatening statuary of *The Stone Guest* and *The Bronze Horseman*. Lourié, recoding all of this in the Dionysian spirit of the Silver Age, assigns to the realm of Eros those creative impulses and human affinities that are constrained by imperial will—but not forever, and never without cost.

It would seem, then, that Lourié and Graham envisaged an intimate family tragedy unfolding within an essentially "imperial opera." For all Lourié's declared intent not to emphasize racial factors, the blackness of Ibragim indisputably became the mark of his outsideness and thus of his spiritual closeness to the great innovator and "outsider" tsar, Peter the Great. Both men are restless, endowed with intelligence and vision, ambitious to reconfigure the traditional culture of Muscovy. Tsar Peter is permitted, at some level, to succeed. But Ibragim, on his plane, does not succeed. With the tsar's blessing—indeed, with the tsar's nonnegotiable mandate—he is given in marriage. Since this hybrid mating project is in defiance of nature (or at least is perceived as unnatural by Russia's conservative boyar class), it must collapse as soon as any power stronger than Peter challenges it. That power is Eros—organic, spontaneous, unpredictable, and largely unknowable—which respects neither politics nor progress.

The fate that Lourié metes out to his two main heroes, then, is a variant on one of the foundational Petersburg myths: the struggle between indestructible tsar and his perishable, vulnerable subjects. For this reason *The Bronze Horseman* sits at the center of the opera, foreshadowing and backshadowing the plot. Its poor clerk Evgeny wishes for nothing other than invisibility and a measure of domestic bliss; when he blames the founder of Petersburg for the loss of his Parasha, a statue comes to life to punish him for his rebellion. In *The Blackamoor of Peter the Great*, the cast of characters is similar—but the rivalries and fault lines are differently drawn. Like Evgeny, Ibragim dreams of a normal, unmarked family life. But unlike Evgeny, he is "marked" by his color; his private life leaves traces, his progeny can be tracked. Also unlike Evgeny, Ibragim is Peter's enthusiastic ally and intimate. He "belongs" to the tsar and has no desires apart from his. As in Pushkin's Petersburg poem, an animated statue will thwart these desires. But the statue of Eros in the opera, unlike the Bronze Horseman by the Neva, is indifferent to civic responsibility, heroism, the cost of achieving empire, or the fate of Russia. Its power, capricious like that of the flood, is mythical and pan-human. It works not with epic duty, but with appetites and aesthetic effects.

As a final exercise in appreciation of this complex opera, we will now revisit three key episodes, with special attention to their Pushkinian starting points. Each illustrates a different principle of transposition that integrates Lourié's *Blackamoor* into Russian musical history, into the mystique of Petersburg, and—subtly, for we are dealing here with a reticent and delicate biography—into the myth of Pushkin. The first episode takes place in Paris (act 1, scene 1), where Eleonora gives birth to a black baby. The second is Peter's reunion with Ibragim and the tsar's vision of a mature St. Petersburg (act 2, scene 4). And finally there is the Puppet Show epilogue. Its fully incarnated Eros and stylized tragedy reach beyond the bounds of Pushkin's text and, as in the bittersweet symmetries of *Eugene Onegin*, serve to balance the whole.

THREE EPISODES AND A MORAL

Lourié, like all composers who adapt a literary narrative for the operatic stage, had to work within certain genre constraints. In conventional opera, dramatic confrontations must be arranged at close distance, in face-to-face duets and trios, not in the more detached—and for Pushkin, more compatible—realms of mistimed letters and private longing. (Consider Tchaikovsky's bold plot adjustments in the final scene of his *Eugene Onegin*, which so alter the personalities of the two principals.) This necessary manufacture of passionate encounters and playably dramatic ensembles out of Pushkin's cool narration is deftly illustrated in Lourié's first scene, a setting of the Paris chapters. In Pushkin, the comely but shy young African Ibragim is anything but operatic; he is so courteous, so modest, so convinced that "nature had not created him for reciprocal passion" (*PSS* 8:5) that at first he scarcely believes he is loved. Countess D. is the initiator. Since "love without hopes or demands touches the feminine heart more truly than all the calculated wiles of seduction" (5), matters take their natural course. The love affair is mutual and self-respecting. Indeed, against a background of cynicism and societal dissipation (Pushkin emphasizes this aspect of early eighteenth-century Paris), the exotic couple strikes a note of normalcy and constancy. But fear of gossip, ridicule, and the inevitable shame awaiting her at the end of her pregnancy unhinges the Countess: "at times she would complain to Ibragim in tears, at times reproach him bitterly" (6). As her confinement nears, "Ibragim came to see her every day. He watched her spiritual and physical strength gradually wane. Her tears and horror burst forth" (6). After the birth and exchange of infants, however, "everything returned to normal" (7). Such a hybrid liaison might seem scandalous to some—but to the two lovers, Pushkin gives us to believe, it was serious, natural, no longer marked by color but by mutual concern and compassion. Ibragim "loved passionately and was loved in return" (7). The poet had a personal stake in the reality of such deeply rooted reciprocal love.

Opera, of course, cannot abide the return of normalcy, which is so devoid of dramatic potential. But how then might the plot sustain the anger, irrationality, and sense of injury that is necessary (at least at peak moments) to the grand stage? Lourié and Graham do not grant these desperate moods to the hero—whom it is almost impossible to provoke. (In this regard, Ibragim's evolution on stage is deeply unlike Othello's during his final days; in fact, Ibragim does not develop psychologically at all.) Alongside their desire to dismiss the "especially 'Negro'" element in *Blackamoor*, composer and librettist take care to elevate and refine Ibragim's character at every point. No matter what is occurring on stage, he is always a site of self-control, loyalty, and dignity. In arias as well as in choral commentary, his double displacement—Africa to Russia, Russia to France—is continually emphasized. The resulting image, however, is not that of hapless exile or outcast but that of a man at home everywhere rather than nowhere, a man whose passion is native but whose behavior is finely disciplined by civilization. The unmanageable blackness of Ibragim is transferred to the periphery, to jealous societal gossip, where, if anything, this exotic detail adds stature to his conquest. It is a group of card-playing cavaliers betting on the color of Eleonora's baby, and not Ibragim himself, who sing the famous lines from Pushkin's 1820 lyric, "Yur'evu": *Potomok negrov bezobraznyi / Liubezen iunoi krasote / Besstydnym beshenstvom zhelanii* ("The hideous descendant of Negroes pleases young beauty by the shameless madness of his desires").

In contrast to the attractive, versatile blackamoor—who all but falls victim to his own loving and solicitous demeanor—only one side of Eleonora's personality (excessive even by opera's norms) is displayed in the opening scene. In hysterics from start to finish, she welcomes Ibragim with the words, *Vy chudovishche!* ("You are a monster!"). She accuses her lover of infidelity and indifference, all the while praising her noble husband. Ibragim's response comes in an aria of excruciating sympathy, where he takes upon himself all the blame for the anguish of her position. This polarization, with accusatory rage from the woman and self-abasement from the man, is dramatically very effective—and sets the stage for Ibragim's departure. That act of abandonment is somewhat calculated and drily cruel in Pushkin (whose Ibragim contemplates leaving Paris soon after the birth of his son), but appears far more justified here.[40]

Scene 3, "Les Adieux," inevitably recalls Tchaikovsky's operatic Onegin and Tatiana in their final rapturous meeting. The parting lovers in Lourié's opera also deviate profoundly from the restrained tone of the original. In his *Blackamoor* chapters, Pushkin permits Ibragim to slip away from Paris and then write a letter (that most excellent resolution) to his abandoned mistress from the safety of Russia. The opera, however, obliged to compress and confront in person, embeds a portion of Ibragim's letter to Eleonora in an on-the-spot love duet, as a quasi-parlando—and not wholly persuasive—vindication of his decision to leave. In Lourié's *Blackamoor* as in Tchaikovsky's *Onegin*, epistolary candor is transposed into a face-to-face lovers' confession. As body acts on body and the duet warms up, there is always a risk of coarsening the sentiments.

Arguably, Tchaikovsky's operatic *Onegin* does coarsen Pushkin's delicate final canto, requiring responses from Tatiana that are wholly out of keeping with the distanced dignity of her person at the end of Pushkin's novel in verse. Lourié's *Blackamoor* cannot be so charged. For it is not constructed, as is Tchaikovsky's opera, to mirror a realistically inflected psychological novel. Thus horizontal continuity of character is not presumed; pragmatic conversation between the principals is not the norm. Lourié's plot is fueled by fragments of metaphysical poetry, and by the primacy of vertical links reminding us of the simultaneous coexistence of times. In part because of these stylized non-prosaic modes of musical encounter, and in part because of the frequent intermezzi, both outrage and lust soon fade away. The Countess quickly mellows. After the dance of the Birth of Eros, individuals are no longer fully answerable for their actions or fates; some higher force moves them, and this gives a dreamy, pan-mythological sheen to the vocal ensembles. Eleonora's final madrigal opens on a question: "why does the young Desdemona love her blackamoor the way the moon loves the misty fog?" Ibragim answers that there is no law governing the moon, the eagle, or a maiden's heart. The opera infuses this sublunary parting song—a quotation from the Improvisatore's first performance, in chapter 2 of Pushkin's *Egyptian Nights*—with abstract and existential significance. In such ensemble scenes, Lourié reflects both the musical conventions of medieval French and Italian courtship, so precious to him, and the dynamics of love in the symbolist era.

Our second episode identifies another route by which Lourié and Graham integrated their opera into Russian cultural history. Perhaps surprisingly, given the centrality of music to the aesthetics of the Silver Age, there is no single agreed-upon exemplar of a full-scale Russian symbolist opera.[41] An assumption of the present essay is that Lourié's *Blackamoor* might qualify as that opera. Its dense web of allusions, its expectation of a highly literate audience, its willingness to grant stylized, timelessly vertical relations as much reality as time-bound plot intrigue, and Lourié's own remarks to Akhmatova that his work was a "monument to Russian culture . . . dedicated to the memory of our altars and hearths," all suggest a symbolist's commitment to what might be called a cumulative or "agglutinative" understanding of tradition. Nothing is pushed out; everything is added on, stitched in, remembered; sons don't kill their fathers but rather cite them and praise them. We saw this synthesizing impulse at work as Lourié and Graham wove a libretto out of individual lines by world-class poets and constructed a musical fabric out of self-contained song and dance genres (pantomimes, ballets, madrigals, chorales, puppet shows). An operatic symbolist would also exploit allusions to signature scenes in the canonic nineteenth-century operatic repertory—Glinka's *Ruslan and Ludmila,* Tchaikovsky's *Eugene Onegin* and *Queen of Spades,* Mussorgsky's *Boris Godunov.* That these four operas are also built off Pushkin texts makes them even more appropriate for Lourié. As a sample of what such analysis might uncover, I offer here a reading of scene 4 (the opening of the second act) that attempts to account for associations too obvious, it would seem, to be unplanned. The subtext presumed is that most famous and quotable of Russian operas, Mussorgsky's *Boris Godunov,* whose act 1, scene 2 ("An Inn at the Lithuanian Border") glints through this portion of Lourié's score.

Lourié's scene 4 opens in an inn on the border, with an innkeeper singing a folk song in expectation of a traveler from abroad. The main characters are the Russian tsar and a protean border figure (a "hybrid") of uncertain nationality—who thus can function as the perfectly flexible collaborator and translator. But unlike the canonized hostility between resident authority and roaming pretender in the analogous place in Pushkin's play or Mussorgsky's opera (with its dim-witted police-state coloration and its clear message that Grishka Otrep'ev wants out of Muscovy at any cost), in Lourié's *Blackamoor* we have that unheard-of alternative, travelers moving in the other direction, back into Russia—and happily. At this later historical moment, significantly Petrine and not Muscovite in the shadow of Ivan the Terrible, there is real possibility for cooperation and integration between East and West, between home and abroad. The hybrid outsider no longer challenges the state. On the contrary, both tsar and subject wish to refashion Old Russia into something as cosmopolitan as themselves; thus the long, hopeful "imperial" inserts from *The Bronze Horseman,* sung by the tsar in arioso. Such coziness between ruler and godson—which the astute Nabokov debunked as a banal embroidery on historical fact—is very much in the statist, pro-Petrine spirit of Pushkin's *Blackamoor.*

Where Lourié and Graham depart from Pushkin's original, however, is in a second and far less lyrical arioso given to Peter in the same scene. After his ecstatic Petersburg vision, the tsar turns severe. *Lukav narod nash i leniv!* ("Our people are sly and lazy!") he confides to Ibragim in despair. "They are like children who will not study, who will not learn their letters unless forced to do so by their teacher . . . No matter how well I might carve with my chisel, I cannot beat sense into my people with this cudgel!" The effect of this bit of invective is dire. The prototype suddenly moves from Pushkin's good-natured Tsar Peter, secure enlightened Westernizer, to the operatic Boris Godunov in extremis, bitter about his subjects' ingratitude, cynical toward his subordinates, surrounded by potential traitors, expecting the worst.

Ibragim, by temperament a conciliator, refuses to believe the situation is so hopeless. He consoles Peter: "Sire, the truth is on your side" (*Gosudar', za vami pravda*), "you will soften all hearts with knowledge." But Peter remains in Godunov's irritable mold, the energetic but disillusioned modernizer of a savage state. In a later arioso in the Assemblée scene, the tsar elaborates further on the unreliability and naïveté of the Russian people. The text leaves one on edge. Historically, Peter's task has been seen as a continuation of Godunov's—except that there is, at this later imperial period in which the opera is set, no pretender and no dynastic threat. Bustling St. Petersburg is a commercial triumph. Even the captive Swede is reconciled to the fact of Poltava, and Peter is secure enough to celebrate not only his own victories but also the lessons he learns from his foes. In this opera, Peter has no enemies. Ibragim is his loyal ally. Some other destabilizing factor, beyond the political or the social, will upset them both.

What this factor might be is suggested textually at one startling point in the opera, where Pushkin's *Bronze Horseman,* the imperial and mythopoetic theme, is conjoined to Pushkin's *Eugene Onegin* with its currents of mistimed love, broken hope, and renunciation. Peter—a tsar not devoid of poetry—finishes his quotation from Pushkin's poem ("and the Neva, sensing spring days, rejoices!") in a meditative mood. He then extemporizes:

> Промчалось много, много дней
> С тех пор, как юная Россия
> И с ней Петрополь в смутном сне
> Явилися впервые мне;
> И побежденную стихию
> Я сквозь магический кристалл
> Еще неясно различал . . .

Many, many days have passed / since that time, when young Russia / and with her, Petropolis, in a hazy dream / first appeared to me. / And I did not yet clearly discern the conquered elements through my magic crystal . . .

The conjunction of these two wholly separate, equally famous Pushkinian passages—one addressing the beloved image of Tatiana at the end of Pushkin's novel in verse and the other evoking the untamed elements to be banished from Peter's City—is almost comically blunt, the sort of move that only opera can make with impunity.[42] Let us take it seriously. What might Pushkin's "magic crystal" signify in the context of *The Blackamoor of Peter the Great*? Exactly what it signifies in *Eugene Onegin,* I suggest: that life's novel is open, but that the recombinations of human fates within that novel are severely limited. A kaleidoscope will refract events into patterns—but only as mirror images, fixed parts with their fates reversed. Eleonora and Ibragim, high-society lovers, launch the plot in Paris by maintaining appearances and spiriting their illicit black child away; Korsakov and Natasha close down the plot in St. Petersburg as helpless puppets, their private life wholly exposed, on tones of ridicule and forced renunciation. Peter's imperial will becomes that fate "from which there is no defense." Lourié, having saturated his opera with impetuous intermezzos and formal entr'actes, ends it with his heroes and heroines literally "pulled by strings"—perhaps to underscore this gradual, inexorable constriction.

Our third episode, the Puppet Show of the final scene, is best understood from the perspective of this growing unfreedom. As an ending device for the *Blackamoor* opera, puppet theater is rich. On the one hand, the institution has enormous resonance in Russian culture, from fairgrounds and hawkers' booths through symbolist theater (Aleksandr Blok's "Fair Show Booth" ["Balaganchik"]) and into the emigration, with Stravinsky's stylized, tragic-carnival *Petrushka*. That the devilish buffoon "Petrushka," the eternally defeated, alternately bullying and bullied outsider, should be evoked in an opera about Peter the Great might give us pause. For Lourié's opera does not indicate clearly where progress and virtue lie. As the composer explained in his letter to Irina Graham, the *Blackamoor* plot must portray a "primitive, savage Europeanization," "Asia in conjunction with Protestantism." In such processes, there would be little unambiguous enlightenment. The ultimate conflict in the opera is between two sorts of darkened force: Peter's will, and unbridled nature that would resist that will.

Those two forces are locked in a fatal embrace. Untamed Eros subverts Peter's matchmaking efforts just as the untamed elements subvert Peter's city. But Peter, both as equestrian statue and as emperor, can be only temporarily submerged—not subdued. This article of faith is surely the cornerstone of the Petersburg myth. In the final puppeteering scene Peter again reasserts control, condemning and then capriciously sparing Korsakov, forcing the potent to wed the impotent and the comely to mate with the grotesque, sending (in fine Muscovite fashion) the wayward wife to a convent. The meaning of Natasha's anxious little dance with Tsar Peter in the third act now becomes clear. From the point of view of boyar Russia, Peter is a changeling. He can assume any form, Eros among them. But ultimately, his energy is punitive. Ibragim, vehicle of civilization, imperial scribe and royal beneficiary, will lose his personal happiness but he will not, we must assume, lose faith in Peter's power or vision. The Puppet Show at the end confirms what the blackamoor sings in the fourth scene (from Yazykov's poem "Ala," which Pushkin placed as the epigraph to his historical romance): "Russia—transfigured by the iron will of Peter!"

How might this "blackamoor project" contribute to the realm of Pushkin in music, a domain already burdened with masterpieces? An inventory from 1974 lists 500 works by Pushkin that had given rise to 3,000 musical compositions by over a thousand musicians.[43] In such lists, the Lourié-Graham *Blackamoor of Peter the Great* must figure as one of the very few full-length twentieth-century operas on a Pushkin text.[44] The advantages enjoyed by Lourié as a post-symbolist, pan-European émigré composer were considerable. He could draw on the culture of the Silver Age's Pushkin scholarship as well as on a wide range of post-Wagnerian musical syntax. (A case could even be made that the classical genius of Pushkin requires post-Romantic musical forms for its full realization, just as the surreal "Petersburg" genius of Gogol, at its unnerving zenith in "The Nose," required Shostakovich.)[45] In its matrix of themes and allusions, *Blackamoor* is a thoroughly Russian artwork—yet its composition was not molded by Soviet constraints; here Lourié, however bitter the air of his exile, must have appreciated the diaspora's freedom from harassment and Stalin-era censorship. The "Petrine" core of Lourié's *Blackamoor*, that energy which wills progress and yet delivers violence, might even be seen as a prefiguration of the Revolution itself.[46]

But most centrally, the opera is a superb condenser of Alexander Pushkin. It is arguably the sole musical-dramatic work built off one of his texts that integrates successfully the dominant myths of Pushkin's personal life (rebellion and Eros), his fatal—and perhaps fated—marriage, his political ambivalence (vexed, complex relationships with tyrannical and visionary tsars), his exotic "cosmopolitan" ancestry (Ibragim the Blackamoor), and his role as singer of the Russian Empire's greatest metropolis. In *The Blackamoor of Peter the Great,* Artur Lourié's tributes to the Golden and the Silver Age are almost perfectly fused. How reassuring that he found the resources to compose it during a time he could only have considered an Age of Bronze.

Notes

1. Letter cited in Ol'ga Rubinchik, "V poiskakh poteriannogo orfeiia: Kompozitor Artur Lur'e," *Zvezda* 10 (1997): 198–207, especially 206. For more on the Lourié-Akhmatova relationship, see B. Kats and R. Timenchik, *Anna Akhmatova i muzyka* (Leningrad: Sovetskii kompozitor, 1989), 8, 30–36; and Felix Roziner, "The Slender Lyre: Artur Lourié and His Music," trans. Peter Lubin, *Bostonia* 8 (Fall 1992): 36–37. The line of poetry to which Lourié alludes, "*Polyn'iu pakhnet khleb chuzhoi*" ("the bread of a foreign land

is as bitter as wormwood") is from Akhmatova's lyric in *Anno Domini* (1922), "*Ne s temi ia, kto brosil zemliu . . .*" ("I am not among those who abandoned their native land . . ."). Akhmatova never answered this 1963 letter from Lourié, although she did write a lyric in response, "Cherez 23 goda" ("After 23 Years"), dated May 13, 1963.

2. See Anatoly Nayman, *Remembering Anna Akhmatova,* trans. Wendy Rosslyn (New York: Henry Holt, 1991), 80. Nayman then added: "Reminiscences about the composer Arthur Lourié usually came to Akhmatova by association with someone else: with Mandelstam, with Olga Sudeykina . . . or the Stray Dog cabaret" (80). Such secondariness has indeed been Lourié's fate.

3. For a basic biography of Lourié, see Roziner, "Slender Lyre," 34–40; and Rubinchik, "V Poiskakh," 198, 200. Lourié was born Naum Izraelevich Lur'ia, the first of five children of a well-to-do Petersburg timber merchant (the descendent of Spanish Jews and an agnostic) and an Orthodox Jewish mother. Akhmatova affectionately referred to Lourié as her "Tsar David," but according to Benedikt Livshits, the composer was less enthusiastic about his origins. He reconstructed his name in honor of Schopenhauer (Arthur) and Van Gogh (Vincent), and he was contemplating adding both "Percy Bysshe" and "José-Maria" when World War I intervened (several letters from 1913 were signed "Percy"). See Larisa Kazanskaia, ed., "'Moi pervyi drug, moi drug bestsennyi . . .': Pis'ma Artura Lur'e Ivanu Iakovkinu (1912–1915)," *Muzykal'naia akademiia* 1 (1999): 188–98, especially 193–96. In Russian sources he is referred to as "Artur Sergeevich Lur'e."

4. For Lourié's relationship with the artistic avant-garde of the 1910s (and especially the futurist composer Nikolai Kul'bin), see Larisa Kazanskaia, "'Khrabreishii boets za ideäly molodogo russkogo iskusstva': Nikolai Ivanovich Kul'bin i russii muzykal'nyj avangard," *Muzykal'naia akademiia* 1 (1998): 144–58, especially 154–55. One of Lourié's teachers recalled in her memoirs: "An original fellow, very gifted and not at all stupid, but a person of fashion, thoroughly given over to 'Decadence'" (155).

5. In 1914 Lourié wrote a song cycle, "Prayer Beads. Ten Songs to Poems of Akhmatova"; Akhmatova in turn mentions him in over a dozen poems. See Lourié's 1963 retrospective article, "Detskii rai," on life among the futurists in the 1910s and 1920s, included in R. Timenchik's appendix "Lur'e" in his edition of Anna Akhmatova, *Poema dez geroia* (Moscow: MPU, 1989), 338–52, especially 341–50. After World War I, Lourié moved in with Akhmatova and Ol'ga Glebova-Sudeikina at no. 18 Fontanka.

6. See Rubinchik, "V poiskakh," 202, and also Kazanskaia, ed., "Moi pervyi drug," 188–90. Boris Pasternak was on the same steamship out of Petrograd in August 1922. Lourié's wife Yadwiga Tsybul'skaia (b. 1888 near Odessa, a Polish Catholic by birth, and an accomplished pianist) did not remarry after her husband's departure. After her death in 1930, their fifteen-year-old

daughter Anna Arturovna received a letter from her father inviting her to join him in Paris. The young *komsomolka* was instructed to answer that a relationship between them was possible only if he returned home.

7. Lourié's daughter was denied access to higher education, and for years the composer's father had to report to Lunacharskii each time he received news from his truant son. The "traitor"-composer was either wholly ignored by Soviet scholarship or, when reference could not be avoided, vituperatively abused. See Richard Taruskin, *Stravinsky and the Russian Traditions: A Biography of the Works through Mavra* (Berkeley: University of California Press, 1996), 2:1586–87, especially n116.

8. See Taruskin, *Stravinsky*, 2:1585–91. Lourié's article "Dve opery Stravinskogo," which Taruskin considers "a document of unsurpassed importance" in grasping Stravinsky's evolution, was published in the Eurasianist journal *Versty*, no. 3 (1928): 109–22. An earlier polemic, "Muzyka Stravinskogo," had been published in *Versty*, no. 1 (1926). Lourié's personal relationship with Stravinsky ended unhappily in the 1930s, apparently over his opposition to Stravinsky's second marriage (see Roziner, "Slender Lyre," 38).

9. Lourié expanded on this thesis in his "biographical chronicle" of his close friend and mentor Serge Koussevitzky, published in 1931. Identifying the two conventional strands in Russian music (the "Slavophile" Mussorgsky and the "Westernizing" Tchaikovsky), Lourié remarks that "Russian musicians have long since devoted their mature efforts to the latter, have striven to overcome the 'provincialism' of Russian music and the exoticism which is particularly characteristic of it. They have desired to stand on a level with the general development of western European music . . . That is why Tchaikovsky, in spite of his love for and subjection to the canon of western Europe, is not less of a Russian musician than Moussorgsky, as many people in Europe mistakenly suppose him to be" (Arthur Lourié, *Sergei Koussevitzky and His Epoch: A Biographical Chronicle*, trans. S. W. Pring [New York: 1931; AMS Press reprint, 1971], 77–78).

10. Such is the thesis of Richard Taruskin's magisterial set of "historical and hermeneutical essays," *Defining Russia Musically* (Princeton: Princeton University Press, 1997). Lourié figures in that study only in passing (399–400), but he could easily serve as yet another exemplary composer.

11. For more information on Kul'bin and his colleagues in the Russian musical avant-garde and their relations with Kandinsky, Schoenberg, and the polymath futurists, see Kazanskaia, "Khrabreishii boets."

12. According to Kazanskaia in "Moi pervyi drug," the Polish Catholic family of Lourié's wife was an important spur toward his baptism in St. Petersburg in the fall of 1912. Nikolai Kul'bin's daughter Nina Kovenchuk reports that during those years "Artur Lourié invariably appeared with a rosary in his hands" (190).

13. "A Note on the Music of Artur Lourié," signed K. B. [Keith Botsford, publisher and editor-in-chief of *Bostonia* magazine], in Roziner, "Slender Lyre," 40. "The fact is, Lourié . . . was experimenting throughout his musical life, but experimenting *against the grain*" (40).

14. The essays from the 1930s and 1940s have been collected and published in French as Arthur Lourié, *Profanation et sanctification du temps. Journal musical. Saint Pétersbourg—Paris—New York, 1910–1960* (Paris: Desclée de Brouwer, 1966). By the end of the 1920s, brief essays by Lourié had begun to appear in the American journal *Modern Music:* "The Crisis in Form" (vol. 8, no. 4 [May-June 1931]: 3–11); "An Inquiry into Melody" (vol. 7, no. 1 [December-January 1929–30]: 3–11); "Neogothic and Neoclassic" (vol. 5, no. 3 [March-April 1928]: 3–8). Tonality and melody, Lourié insisted, are inevitably personal and thus always disclose a truth for which the creator is morally responsible; they are our sole bulwark against the "impersonal esthetics and forcible objectivism" of abstract, twentieth-century musical form ("An Inquiry into Melody," 4, 9).

15. Nabokov turned down Lourié's Dostoevsky commission in a letter from Cambridge to M. V. Dobuzhinsky, May 15, 1943. See "Perepiska Vladimira Nabokova s M. V. Dobuzhinskim" (compiled, introduced, and annotated by V. Stark), *Zvezda* 11 (1996): 92–108, especially 101.

16. "Perepiska Vladimira Nabokova," 103. In his letter to Nabokov at the end of January 1949, Dobuzhinsky recalls hearing somewhere that Pushkin had intended to end his *Blackamoor* on a plot symmetry (the poet confided this plan to his friend A. N. Vul'f, who later recorded it in his memoirs; see J. Thomas Shaw, "Pushkin and Africa," in *Pushkin Poems and Other Studies, Part II* [Los Angeles: Charles Schlacks Jr., 1996], 92–121, especially 102, of which a shorter version is reprinted in this volume). Nabokov answers Dobuzhinsky (February 20, 1949) that he "had not found confirmation of your information about Pushkin's proposed plan"—but then adds in a conciliatory tone: "I would very much like to see *The Blackamoor* with your costumes and stage sets."

17. Vladimir Nabokov, "Pushkin and Gannibal: A Footnote," *Encounter* 29, no. 1 (July 1962): 11–26, especially 26. The revised essay was included as an appendix in the original hardcover edition of Nabokov's four-volume translation and commentary to *Eugene Onegin* (Princeton: Princeton University Press, 1964): 3:387–447. It is not included, however, in the two-volume Princeton paperback of the Nabokov *Onegin,* which omits all appendixes. Nabokov intended his exhaustively researched "footnote" to sober down the idolaters of Pushkin's *Blackamoor,* in which (Nabokov writes) "a greatly glamourized Ibrahim is given fictitious adventures in France and Russia—all this is not in the author's best vein" (24–25). Nabokov also thoroughly discredits the fabular "German biography" (written by a son-in-law of Gannibal and

known to Pushkin in Russian dictation). For a defense of Pushkin's *Blackamoor* as an exercise not in biography or history (genres made factually responsible only later, in the 1830s) but as a Russian version of a Walter Scott-style novel, see N. N. Petrunina, *Proza Pushkina (puti evoliutsii)* (Leningrad: Nauka, 1987), 49–53. For a sensible Soviet-era take on Nabokov's essay, see I. L. Feinberg, ed., *Abram Petrovich Gannibal, praded Pushkina: Razyskaniia i materialy* (Moscow: Nauka, 1986): "This highly tendentious view—suffering not only from one-sidedness but also simply false—emerges in Nabokov because, as a biographer, the historical approach was alien to him; and for this reason his superficial judgment of Gannibal contains neither historical nor psychological truth. Of course Nabokov is very talented, but arrogant and very subjective. Everything he writes, however, is very interesting" (23). Nabokov's essay first appeared in Russian translation in *Legendy i mify o Pushkine* (St. Petersburg: Akademicheskii proekt, 1995), 5–53.

18. Lourié continues disingenuously in his letter to the love-struck young woman (the correspondence appears to predate their intimate relations): "I hope you and I will work out, and I prefer you to Sirin" (letter to Irina Graham, March 2, 1949, in Irina Grem, "Arap Petra Velikogo," *Novoe russkoe slovo* [January 8, 1993, 21]).

19. For a brief biography of Graham, see the headnote to Irina Grem, "Orficheskii rekviem," *Neva* 3 (1996): 27–82, especially 27. Not surprisingly, Graham, who had slipped into the time-honored Russian role of female servitor-muse to a great and helpless talent, expressed a jealous antipathy to Anna Akhmatova, whom she referred to as a "witch." In Akhmatova, Graham wrote, "the woman eclipsed all else. There was no authentic humanity in her, as there was, say, in Tsvetaeva, whom I love and grieve for . . . in Tsvetaeva there was none of this Akhmatovian 'self-fulness' [*samost'*] and narcissism" (Grem to Kralin, December 28, 1972, cited in Mikhail Kralin, *Artur i Anna: Roman* [Leningrad: Oformlenie Paukevich T. A., 1990], 38). Predictably and sadly, Graham herself became a target of caprice and disgust for Ella Lourié, who accused her of breaking up the family when she "traveled every day to Princeton, so as not to abandon my poor Pussycat [i.e., A. S.]" (letter to Kralin, June 25, 1973, in *Artur i Anna,* 90). Most predictably of all, Graham ended by casting the net of blame over her partner. "Of course," she wrote to Kralin in a letter of November 14, 1973, "A. S. was a remarkable artist, he wrote marvelous music, he was brilliant, intelligent, clever, full of charm . . . but no matter how angelic the garb I dressed him up in, as a person he was . . . strange. This person, who spoke so much about humanity, about evil and good, about the struggle between evil and good, about suffering, etc., lacked, in my opinion, any concept of elementary morality. Perhaps in some sense A. S. was . . . immoral [*amoralen*]. How else could he have made use of the feelings of a woman—such as myself—solely in his personal interests . . . ?" (*Artur i Anna,* 89, ellipses in original).

20. See Graham's reminiscences about this period late in life in Roziner, "Slender Lyre," 41–42; see also Grem, "Arap Petra Velikogo," 21. In this second of two brief commemorative articles in *Novoe russkoe slovo*, Graham published six of Lourié's letters to her (February 19 to March 23, 1949), a period of intense work on the initial version of *Blackamoor*.

21. See L. Z. Korabel'nikova, "Amerikanskie dnevniki Artura Lur'e (k probleme muzykal'noi emigratsii 'pervoi volny')," in *Keldyshevskii sbornik: Muzykal'no-istoricheskie chteniia pamiati Yu. V. Keldysha*, ed. M. G. Aranovskii et al. (Moscow: Gosudarstvennyi institut iskusstvoznaniia, 1999), 232–39, especially 234. According to an entry in Lourié's diary for 1949, Dobuzhinsky was greatly enthusiastic about this project and even offered his own services as librettist. "Dwarfs must absolutely crawl out of pies," he counseled the composer (233).

22. See Graham's letter of March 17, 1973, to Mikhail Kralin, in *Artur i Anna*, 56. There she also reveals her own eclectic musical preferences ("Only Glinka, Mussorgsky, Borodin, and Scriabin. In general, my god is Mozart. Then come Schubert, Schumann, Chopin; Bach, of course. And of course, my adored old Italian masters of the 16th and 17th centuries").

23. Beginning in 1958, Clarence Brown served as intermediary for the exchange of letters and mementoes between Lourié and Akhmatova. Brown recalls the composer's aristocratic dislike of self-promoting Russian émigrés, his preoccupation with pious themes, and his refusal to write his memoirs. I thank Clarence Brown for sharing his recollections (as well as a tape of a discussion with Lourié from 1965).

24. Keith Botsford notes: "Lourié, who had been a pioneer in serial and microtonal music, was out of touch with one part of the musical establishment (the Germanic, Viennese part) and equally out of tune with the folkloristic impetus of a music that was deliberately seeking to be 'American'" (K. B., "Note on the Music of Artur Lourié," 39). Part of the problem was surely Lourié's aristocratic disdain of seeking a market. Dependent upon Koussevitzky for performances, Lourié was left in a vacuum, without agents or sponsors, upon the latter's death in 1951. In 1992 his Princeton attorney Joseph Lynch recalled: "He had the most interesting opinions on art, politics, history. He was devoted to Pushkin, and used to talk to someone in the Slavic Department about him. Only once did he play something for me. He asked how I liked it, and I replied that it was melodic, that it sounded romantic. He was so insulted by my ignorance that he never played anything for me again . . . He did not seem to have much respect for the other musicians in Princeton. He was, I think, homesick for Russia" (Roziner, "Slender Lyre," 38–40, 87). In a similar vein, the devoted Irina Graham had written to Mikhail Kralin on October 17, 1972: "A. S. enjoyed considerable fame in Europe; his name is mentioned in all musical dictionaries (Oxford University Press in England, The Grove Dic-

tionary in America, Riemann in Germany, Larousse in France, etc.). A. S. was not fortunate in America, since he behaved modestly and with a noble demeanor, as befits a genuine artist; he didn't push himself forward anywhere, he did not trumpet himself, he never engaged in self-advertisement nor fawned in front of anyone. What is more, the enemies of melody—that is, the influential musicians (and critics) who themselves did not possess a melodic gift and who produced by reflex, in the pseudo-light Stravinsky style, a heap of cacophonous notes signifying nothing—deliberately silenced him. But recognition will come, in this I believe, and I search constantly for performers of A. S.'s music" (Kralin, *Artur i Anna*, 16).

25. Rubinchik, "V poiskakh," 198. "It was a great discovery for me to come across the work of this completely forgotten Russian composer, Artur Lur'e," Kremer remarked in an interview for *Russkaia zhizn'*. "I want to mount a defense for this highly gifted person . . ."

26. Lourié, Arthur, and Irina Graham. *The Blackamoor of Peter the Great*. Opera in Three Acts [libretto]. Studien zur Musik des XX. Jahrhunderts in Ost- und Ostmitteleuropa. Edited by Detlef Gojowy. Osteuropaforschung. Schriftenreihe der Deutschen Gesellschaft für Osteuropakunde Herausgegeben von Eberhard Reissner. Band 29 (Berlin: Arno Spitz, 1990), 131–77.

A copy of this English-language libretto—incomplete if calibrated with the full score, in places awkwardly Englished, and corrected by an unidentified hand—is deposited in the Lourié archive at Lincoln Center (JPB 92-61 no. 68: "Librettos, synopses, and other papers concerning the vocal works of Arthur Lourié, ca. 1920–ca. 1966"). For additional Lourié scholarship by Gojowy dating from the 1970s and 1980s, see Taruskin, *Stravinsky*, 2:1585–86n115. Gojowy is the author of the one monograph to date on Lourié, *Arthur Lourie und der russische Foutourismus* (Laaber, 1993).

27. Gidon Kremer (violin), Philharmonia Orchestra, Christoph Eschenbach, *Out of Russia*, Teldec 4509-98440-2, recorded in London, April 1996. *The Blackamoor of Peter the Great* is billed as an "Orchestral Suite based on original orchestration and vocal passages adapted from the opera," with the following parts: (1) Introduzione: Lento; (2) Game of Dice: Allegro; (3) Introduction to the Ballets: Lento; (4) Ballet No. 1: The Dance of the Night and the Wind; (5) Ballet No. 2: The Appearance of the Silver Egg; (6) Ballet No. 3: Hymn to Eros (instrumentation by Schnittke); (7) Ballet No. 4: Amor's Aria; (8) Toccatina; (9) Dance of the Skomorochs (Harlequins); (10) Les Adieux: Prélude de Concert; (11) Coda. The suite was premiered by the Boston Symphony in 1992, under Gidon Kremer. I am indebted to Carol Ueland, who came across this CD and first alerted me to the existence of Lourié's *Arap* opera.

28. *Arap Petra Velikogo*: Opera v trekh deistviiakh (deviati kartinakh) po Pushkinu / Libretto Iriny Grem; [muzyka] Artur Lur'e. Full orchestral score

in manuscript, 646 leaves, undated, with the vocal text handwritten in Russian, select arias in French and Italian (some choral inserts in Greek and Latin). On deposit in the Lourié archive (JPB 92-61 no. 85), Music Division, New York Public Library for the Performing Arts at Lincoln Center, New York City. The archive also contains undated scraps of preliminary text (lines of poetry in various languages, scribbles, doodles), apparently in Lourié's hand.

29. Among other details, we learn that Lourié was planning to set verses by Osip Mandelstam for the Epilogue of *Blackamoor* ("these lines contain a synthesis of the entire opera"); that he sympathized with Shestov and Gershenzon and deeply admired James Joyce; and that as late as 1962 he was planning an opera-ballet (unrealized) entitled *Petersburg*, on Blok's poems "Snezhnaia Maska" ("Snow Mask") and "Dvenadtsat'" ("The Twelve"). See Korabel'nikova, Amerikanskie dnevniki," 234–36.

30. Six letters from Lourié, including these three, were published as part of the centenary celebration in the New York-based *Novoe russkoe slovo* in Grem, "Arap Petra Velikogo," 21. Occasional reference is made to further personal correspondence deposited in the Lincoln Center archives, but no letters are catalogued there.

31. Ibid., 21.

32. Ibid.

33. "O deva-roza, ia v okovakh," is a lyric by Pushkin (1823) with southern/"Eastern" motifs; in his earliest drafts, Lourié planned to interpolate poetry (from Pushkin's era as well as his own Silver Age poets) into the opera as sung numbers.

34. See Korabel'nikova, Amerikanskie dnevniki," 234: "[Diary entry for] 8 March 1949: At night I read Khlebnikov. Youthful reminiscences swept over me, and again there wafted a wind from Asia. How I loved that wind in past years! Everything European in me is dead, decadent, bifurcation, disintegration, doubts, skepticism and apathy, as with everyone. Everything Asiatic is alive, authentically living, joyous and bright. What a strange vision: Christ in Asia!"

35. For the classic statement of this theme in Pushkin's life and work (the statue come to life on a "punitive campaign"), see Roman Jakobson's "The Statue in Pushkin's Poetic Mythology," originally published in Czech in 1937, available in English in Roman Jakobson, *Language in Literature*, ed. Krystyna Pomorska and Stephen Rudy (Cambridge: Harvard University Press, 1987), 318–65. Lourié might have borrowed the idea of a Greek statue at Tsar Peter's rough-and-tumble court from Merezhkovsky's 1905 novel *Anti-Christ: Peter and Alexei*, although in the Merezhkovsky novel the statue is of Venus. I thank Alexander Dolinin for suggesting this highly probable allusion to one of the symbolist period's most influential novels.

36. Graham's "preliminary note" to the opera is attached to a letter to Mikhail Kralin dated October 17, 1972 (Kralin, *Artur i Anna,* 17–19).

37. For a fine reading of Pushkin's *Blackamoor* that treats these historical incompatibilities, see Svetlana Evdokimova, *Pushkin's Historical Imagination* (New Haven: Yale University Press, 1999), chapter 5, "Forging Russian History: *The Blackamoor of Peter the Great.*" In Pushkin's historical writing, Evdokimova notes, storytellers and societies evolve but often—oddly—the characters do not. They can function as composite "emblems" of their time, the end result of popular rumor and solidified anecdotes told about them. "The reader, therefore, cannot probe the inner world of Ibragim, who speaks infrequently in the novel. Unlike Grinev from *The Captain's Daughter,* who undergoes certain development in the course of the novel, Ibragim does not change in any significant way and enters the novel as an already mature character. Rather than portraying an inwardly complex and growing human being, Pushkin introduces a protagonist whose very career is a commentary on historical process" (151).

38. Pushkin's final quatrain reads: *Vrai démon pour l'espièglerie, / Vrai singe par sa mine, / Beaucoup et trop d'étourderie. / Ma foi, voilà Pouchkine.* For aid in identifying this and other poetic quotations and allusions in the libretto (as well as for many illuminating comments on the whole), I am indebted to Boris Gasparov, Alexander Dolinin, and William Mills Todd, who kindly read early drafts of this study. The libretto still awaits detailed documentation of each poetic allusion.

39. Pushkin's uncompleted fragment "Kak zhenit'sia zadumal tsarskii arap," an imitation in the folk style, was written in 1824 but not published until 1894. In translation it reads: "The tsar's blackamoor took a notion to get married, / He walks among the boyar women, / He gazes at the young boyar daughters, / The blackamoor has chosen a young lady for himself, / The black raven has chosen a white swan, / How black-black the blackamoor is, and she's a white-white soul." See Shaw, "Pushkin and Africa," 101–2, n. 12.

40. Boris Gasparov suggested, in a personal correspondence, that the transformation of Pushkin's docile French Countess into the rather vicious Eleonora of the opera could be an allusion on Lourié's part to Pushkin's preoccupation, in the 1820s, with the profligate and dazzling Polish beauty Karolina Adamovna Sobanska, who was dallying as well with Adam Mickiewicz and with General Witt of the Russian secret police. In a draft of a letter to Sobanska (February 2, 1830, in French), Pushkin asks permission to call her Ellénore, after the heroine of his favorite novel, Benjamin Constant's *Adolfe.* This particularly abrasive love of Pushkin's was much alluded to by symbolist and acmeist poets.

41. For the argument, see Simon Morrison, *Russian Opera and the Symbolist Movement* (Berkeley: University of California Press, 2002). Morrison

considers several candidates for a symbolist opera (Tchaikovsky's *Queen of Spades* [1890], Rimsky-Korsakov's *Legend of the Invisible City of Kitezh and the Maiden of Fevronia* [1905], Scriabin's aborted project *Mysterium,* and Prokofiev's *Fiery Angel* [1923/27]), but endorses none wholly. A successful incarnation of the "musical symbol" eluded both poets and composers, since it "oscillates between temporal and narrative layers: the past and present (and future), the natural and supernatural, the internal and external, the real (*realia*) and more real (*realiora*)" (17–18). Such a task—if realizable at all—was at odds both with theatrical representation and with twentieth-century modernist aesthetics.

42. The relevant portions from each are as follows, in prose translation: from *The Bronze Horseman*, ll. 86–92: "Be beautiful, city of Peter, and stand unshakeable like Russia, so that even the conquered elements may make their peace with you"; and from *Eugene Onegin,* chapter 8, 50: "Many, many days have rushed by / Since that time, when young Tatiana / And with her, Onegin, in a dim dream / First appeared to me— / And the distant horizon of my free novel / I still discerned unclearly / Through my magic crystal."

43. N. G. Vinokur and R. A. Kagan, comps., *Pushkin i muzyka* (Moscow: Sovetskii kompozitor, 1974). The vast majority of settings are of lyric poems, but the falling-off of Pushkin as a source text for opera in the twentieth century (and his replacement by Gogol, Dostoevsky, and even Tolstoy) is an interesting question, related surely to the shifting status of opera in the modern period.

44. Felix Roziner, studying the *Blackamoor* score in the company of Irina Graham in the early 1990s, called it "quite possibly the best Russian opera of the twentieth century." See Roziner, "Slender Lyre," 34.

45. Gogol's Ukrainian fantasies found delightful embodiment in operas by Tchaikovsky and Rimsky-Korsakov, but the tone and terror of the Gogolian fantastic—as in "The Nose"—is only approached by Shostakovich and, later, by Rodion Shchedrin's "opera scenes in three acts," *Dead Souls* (1977), and by Yury Butsko's "opera-monologue for baritone in two acts," *Notes of a Madman* (1963).

46. See Lourié, *Koussevitzky,* 73–74, where Lourié repeats this symbolist maxim in its pure Blokian form: "The revolutionary explosion of 1918 hurled us definitely and with terrible force into the twentieth century, into a world with new standards of measurement, into a new order of things . . . What sort of role does music play in this process? It is very difficult and rather awkward to speak of it 'professionally.' You see, this historical process in its entirety was 'music.' It was the agitated element, dark and turbid, which cast up on the shores of life that which was hidden in the abyss of its chaos let loose." It is also the case, of course, that Pushkin saw Peter the Great as a revolutionary, the Marat as well as the Robespierre of Russian history.

Ludmilla A. Trigos

Appendix A: Creativity and Blackness—a Note on Yury Tynianov's "The Gannibals"

Yury Tynianov (1894–1943), Russian formalist critic, scholar, and film scenarist, brought to his writing of historical fiction extensive scholarship and a profound understanding of Russian literature and culture of the eighteenth and nineteenth centuries. Tynianov had studied under the famous professor S. N. Vengerov and had at an early point in his career carved out his territory in the study of early nineteenth-century literature, specifically concentrating on Pushkin and his contemporaries to illustrate his theory of their interactions (as "literary battles") in the development of Russian literary language and style. Though he shifted his focus from formalist literary studies per se to historical prose in the mid-1920s, he continued his scholarly work up until his death, writing articles on literary evolution, genre, and his favorite triad of authors—Alexander Pushkin, Vilhelm Kiukhel'beker, and Aleksandr Griboedov. He concurrently served as editor and member of the editorial board for a variety of publications, including the "Poet's Library" series (Biblioteka poeta), until the beginning of the 1940s.

Tynianov began writing the novel "The Gannibals" ("Gannibaly") in July 1932, three years before he commenced work on his biographical novel about Alexander Pushkin. In December 1932 he confided to his close friend, Kornei Chukovsky, his plan to write a novel about Pushkin's ancestors, but it remains a little-known fact that Tynianov originally intended to portray Pushkin's ancestors at all.[1] "The Gannibals" was to serve as an "epic prologue" to the biography of Pushkin that Tynianov had planned.[2] The fragments of the "Gannibals" novel remained unpublished until the 1960s; the introduction finds its first English translation in this volume. He completed outlines, a draft of the first chapter, and a lyrical "author's introduction" before putting the text aside.[3] By the spring of 1933, Tynianov had already moved on to work on the Pushkin novel. One of Tynianov's students, N. Stepanov, speculated that Tynianov's decision to shift his focus to Pushkin himself (rather than devote an entire novel to his Gannibal forefather) can be explained by the author's de-

Appendix A

clining health (that is, he chose to concentrate his remaining energies on his primary focal point, Pushkin). Stepanov also suggests that the Pushkin text made the Gannibal volume superfluous.[4] It is our misfortune that Tynianov did not manage to complete more than the fragments we have, since they show tremendous artistry and promise.

In his work, Tynianov counters the construction of an "official Pushkin," a process that Soviet critics undertook in the 1920s; this tendency became especially apparent after 1922, when Tynianov wrote his article "Sham Pushkin" ("Mnimyi Pushkin") attacking not only the already existing mythic image of Pushkin, but also the lack of a critically rigorous approach of many Pushkinists in their attribution of newly discovered poetry to him, as well as in their analysis of his oeuvre.[5] Most of all, Tynianov objected to the blurring of the boundary between literary scholarship (which must be precise and rigorous and focus on the works themselves) and the study of the personality and psychology of the author, more appropriate to fictional representations of authors.[6] Both Monika Greenleaf and Angela Brintlinger have noted Tynianov's use of Pushkin as a background in his scholarly work on Pushkin's contemporaries; Brintlinger also points out that Pushkin served as "a foil" to the other characters in Tynianov's fiction.[7] Indeed, scholars have long commented on the close and interdependent relationship between Tynianov's scholarly research and his fictional works. I would argue here that Tynianov's earlier combating of a "sham Pushkin" shades into the realm of his historical fiction. Tynianov continued his lateral approach to Pushkin with the introduction to his fictional project on Pushkin's African ancestor. This work served as a bridge—from his earlier assays in the genre of biographical novel where Pushkin played a minor, though important role—to his later unfinished novel, dedicated specifically to Pushkin.

In "The Gannibals," Tynianov provides the reader with a revivified version of Pushkin by exploring the influence of "Gannibality" (*gannibal'stvo*, as I am translating it here) on Russian cultural history. For Tynianov, "Gannibality" serves as a life force, a positive, creative energy which invigorates the stultifying elements of Russian culture and life. The lyrical introduction thus postulates crucial links between creativity and blackness in Pushkin's oeuvre. Tynianov penetrates to the essence of what Pushkin's African heritage meant to the poet and taps in to several important ideas about Pushkin's blackness which were in the air in the Soviet Union in the 1930s. Tynianov was one of the first writers during the Soviet era to acknowledge explicitly and to celebrate the destabilizing effect of Pushkin's African heritage upon traditional assessments of Pushkin's Russianness. In addition, he was one of the few to assert the positive, synthetic influence of the Gannibal element upon Russian culture, by highlighting the multiethnic composition of the allegedly pure Russian nobility from its beginnings.

Appendix A

Tynianov begins his introduction with a story about Abyssinia in days gone by, setting the stage for his story about Pushkin's great-grandfather, Abram Petrovich Gannibal. Providing a swift summary of Abram's life, Tynianov highlights the significant events: Abram's unwilling passage from Abyssinia to Turkey as a captive, his journey to Russia and then France where he became a "French engineer and French soldier," his marriage to a captive Swede, children, and then "fourteen Abyssinian and Swedish sons became Russian nobility. And thus, the story is about Russia."[8] Tynianov's opening invokes a central motif which surfaces in the literature dealing with Pushkin's African ancestry: the reconciliation of the non-Russian and Russian elements of Pushkin's heritage, specifically its racial aspects. As Tynianov depicts it, Gannibal was fully incorporated into Russian society (as were many other non-Russians during the time of Peter the Great), except for his dark blood (*temnaia krov'*), which remains a "brand" (378). Tynianov highlights the problematic aspect of that partial incorporation; Petrine society viewed Gannibal as different, "not one of their kind," because of his race. At first Tynianov seems to suggest that it is only the physical marks of Gannibal that keep him from being perceived as fully "Russian." Yet Tynianov also seems to make a distinction between the character traits of the Russian-Abyssinian nobility and the pure Russian nobility. Tynianov characterizes "Gannibality" as ebullient, passionate, and larger than life; for him, the Gannibal nature manifested itself in all of life's extremes. Tynianov seems to look upon these qualities with a benevolent eye because of their life-affirming capacity. The "full measure of human madness" of the Gannibals challenges the stultifying categories and conventions of society. Indeed, in Gannibal's and Pushkin's defense, Tynianov undermines the idea of pure "Great Russian" nobility by emphasizing the multicultural aspects of the Russian empire and its nobility:

> So quickly, easily and freely did they enter the Russian nobility that the Abyssinian and Swede's grandson fought for the rights of the Russian nobility during the reign of Nicholas I. And it was accomplished because that very Russian nobility was also Swedish and Abyssinian, and German, and Danish . . . The nobility conceived and constructed a national Great Russian state descended from Great Russians, Poles, Kalmyks, Swedes, Italians, and Danes. (378)

Tynianov asserts that Pushkin's mixed ancestry was no different from that of any other "Great Russian," except that it was more superficially apparent because of race. Tynianov thus calls into question the closed or canonical definitions of ethnic purity and with them the myth of the "Great Russian" state.

For Tynianov, Pushkin's life and work cannot be understood without a knowledge of his Gannibal roots for a variety of reasons. Tynianov portrays

Appendix A

Pushkin's decision to cast Gannibal as his primogenitor as falling in line with the construction of genealogies by other members of the Russian nobility, including even that of Tsar Ivan IV. In some ways, then, Pushkin's act of self-definition is not as unusual as it seems; he, like other Russian nobles, participates in the construction of his genealogy, picking and choosing "appropriate" ancestors. Yet Tynianov goes to great lengths to put Pushkin's ancestry into this multiethnic context in order to probe the resonance of Pushkin's choice of Gannibal. The first explanation Tynianov gives gets to the essence of Pushkin as an evolving personality and as an artist. As Tynianov puts it: "He was Pushkin until 1820, Gannibal from 1820 to 1830. The letters and deeds of his Gannibal uncles, Benjamin and Paul, have been preserved. In them one senses the completely open, hot mouths and clenched fists of the people and also the expansive elegance of the gesture. In their spirit and writing, Alexander Pushkin's letters much more closely resemble theirs than the conceited, lisping, trembling prattle of his father and uncle Pushkin" (380). Tynianov thus attributes Pushkin's creative energy and forcefulness to qualities inherent in the Gannibal personality.

In the introduction to "The Gannibals" Tynianov raises the question of why Pushkin would choose to emphasize his Gannibal origins. Beyond the obvious (physical) explanation which Tynianov provides, that Pushkin "could not hide the Gannibals" (380), lies another reason. Tynianov posits that Pushkin actively began his self-mythologization in 1820 (in his poem "To Yur'ev," published 1829), by openly identifying himself with the Gannibal line.[9] Yet Tynianov acknowledges that the differences Pushkin inherited from his African ancestor transcended the mere physical. Tynianov writes, "The fact that Gannibal was 'not of our kind,' that he was also a valet and confidant [to Peter the Great] and a Russian nobleman from African princely origins . . . places him in the first rank of ancestors" (381). Indeed, Pushkin makes an active attempt to differentiate himself from the rest of the Russian nobility. Though he could have chosen to emphasize the lineage of his Pushkin ancestors (who were members of the old boyar nobility) and downplay the Gannibal family tree, he did not ultimately do so. Tynianov points to the privileging of Gannibal as also apparent in Pushkin's poem "My Genealogy" to highlight the importance of an oppositional element for Pushkin. By equating Gannibal's difference with opposition and placing him at the head of his genealogy of family rebels, Pushkin illustrates the two essential aspects of his African heritage as he saw them. Tynianov brings the circle to a full close when he equates Pushkin's blackness and oppositional stance with his artistry: "The bureaucrats said, 'He is not our kind,' the same thing that the faithless wife said about his black ancestor. 'He isn't our kind,' said the half-English Lord Vorontsov. And the average landowners said, sweating, 'Yes, yes, he is not our kind, he's a scapegrace [*kromeshnik*], Pushkin, the writer'" (381–82). The essential interplay becomes one between difference and creativity, blackness and the very act of writing.

Appendix A

"So he [Pushkin] searched for and found his family. And thus also he searched and found, and discovered his homeland" (381). With this expansive gesture, Tynianov encapsulates Pushkin's personal search for identity with his literary activity. By equating Pushkin's literal journey through the other "Russian" (*rossiiskie* and not *russkie*) lands with his poetic discovery of those very lands, Tynianov bestows full responsibility upon Pushkin for the incorporation of those exotic lands and their people into Russian culture: "In 1821 the Caucasus was discovered by poetry, in 1822—the Crimea, in 1824—Bessarabia. In prose, Bashkiria was discovered, the conquest of the Kamchadals and Yukagirs was prepared" (382).

Tynianov's vision of Pushkin recalls and expands the rhetoric of Dostoevsky's 1880 Pushkin speech. In Tynianov's imagery, Pushkin becomes a cultural "conqueror," discovering and laying claim to the lands he portrays in Russian literature. We see Pushkin's ability to incorporate other peoples into his oeuvre and thus transform them; they become something knowable, an integral part of Russian culture. Pushkin's talent echoes Gannibal's ability as a conqueror of the Russian nobility's closed society during Petrine times: "the blackamoor of Peter conquered the drawing rooms and gave offense to the daughters of the old aristocracy" (382). Pushkin's artistic conquest and Gannibal's sexual conquest become one and the same in Tynianov's view. In both cases, their deeds exhibit creative aspects. In Pushkin's artistic imagination and appropriation, he creates his own version of the lands and peoples he depicts; in Gannibal's procreation, he creates new versions of himself, but with a difference because of an admixture of new blood.[10] Tynianov extends the metaphor even further by extrapolating the knowledge of Pushkin in his time as part of his conquest and, thus, transforms him into a cultural warrior for freedom and difference: "And other people's grandchildren read him. Such is the earthly fate of every great person up until now: to think that he toils for himself under the sun and fights for his people, but he toils and fights for other people's grandchildren" (383). Echoing Dostoevsky, Tynianov closes with an affirmation of the universality of Pushkin's oeuvre and the claim of Pushkin's benefit to other non-Russian peoples.

As I suggested earlier, Tynianov transposes the Gannibal theme into his unfinished novel *Pushkin*. I will confine my remarks to the most striking and symbolically significant examples of the link between Gannibal and his descendant. The first occurs in the scene in which we are introduced to the infant Alexander Pushkin during the family gathering in honor of his christening. Pushkin's uncle, Petr Abramovich Gannibal, who was not invited to the party, visits the Pushkins to see his new nephew for the first time. He literally designates little Alexander the heir to the Gannibal line: "My honest Annibal word—he's a little lion cub, a little blackamoor [*arapchonok*]! Dearie! The great Annibal! He takes after his grandfather! Look! I accept him! Some

373

Appendix A

wine!"[11] The Gannibal christening supersedes the traditional Orthodox Christian rite. The supremacy of the mother's line, of the Gannibal origins, is confirmed, much to the chagrin of Pushkin's parents, Sergei Lvovich and Nadezhda Osipovna. In an effort to assert his patrimony, Sergei Lvovich claims: "I dare to believe that my son is not . . . a lion cub . . . and not a little blackamoor [*arapchonok*], but a Pushkin, like I am" (28). In asserting their respective rights and claims, Sergei Lvovich and Petr Abramovich almost come to blows as a result of the dispute and the scene ends in a scandal, with Petr Abramovich storming out of the house in a fury. In Tynianov's portrayal, Nadezhda Osipovna reacts aversely to her uncle's affirmation of little Alexander's Gannibal lineage and his dismissal of the patrimony of Sergei Lvovich. Petr Abramovich's act results in an important emotional change in Nadezhda Osipovna; from this point on in the novel, she immediately becomes repelled by the infant and wants little to do with him: "Then she looked upon her child as if he was someone else's" (29). In this crucial scene, Tynianov forces us immediately to confront the issue of Pushkin's African ancestry, asserting its relevance and influence upon Pushkin's overall psychological development, but especially upon his evolution as an artist.[12]

In the second and final example, Tynianov exploits the connection between Gannibal and Pushkin for its creative potential. Here he represents two moments during Pushkin's youth when the Gannibal alliance was made. First, while strolling in the gardens at the Lycée in Tsarskoe Selo, Pushkin and his companions discover a monument commemorating the Battle of Navarino and honoring Brigadier Gannibal (his uncle, Ivan Abramovich Gannibal, though young Alexander thinks it refers to his grandfather). He decides one day to bow—albeit surreptitiously—to the monument, acknowledging his kinship (despite what Tynianov depicts in the novel as "the family's silence" about the Gannibals). Later, we learn from Tynianov that Pushkin loved toying with his name and the names of his friends. He also enjoyed fiddling with his signature, using his initials, his Lycée room number, and various other ciphers. During this play, he has a revelation: "Once, having recopied some of his poems, he recalled, glancing at his manuscript, his grandfather's pockmarked monument, and signed his name: 'Annibal.' The diversity of names and signatures was surprising to him: each time it seemed to him, not only the name—but he himself—took on a new appearance" (247). Thus, Pushkin's new creative outlook comes as the result of the inspiration of his Gannibal roots; this "new appearance" enables him to go beyond his ordinary realm and to imagine other possibilities. Thus in both works, the introduction to "The Gannibals" and the biographical novel *Pushkin,* the identification with Gannibal evidently served as a significant and formative moment in Pushkin's adolescence, and it helped shape his creative persona.

While discussing his own choice of topics in literature and criticism, Ty-

Appendix A

nianov wrote in his autobiography, "Most of all, I was not in agreement with established assessments."[13] I would suggest that in his fragmentary sketches of "The Gannibals" and in his unfinished novel *Pushkin,* Tynianov's enterprise was to challenge and broaden conventional perceptions of Pushkin, his heritage and his legacy. In so doing, Tynianov acknowledged Pushkin's racial difference as a significant source of his creativity.

Notes

1. See *Iurii Tynianov: Biobibliograficheskaia khronika* (St. Petersburg: Arsis, 1994), 48.

2. N. Stepanov, "Neosushchestvlennyi zamysel," *Nauka i zhizn',* no. 10 (1964): 121.

3. N. Stepanov, untitled, in *Iurii Tynianov: Pisatel' i uchenyi* (Moscow: Molodaia Gvardiia, 1966), 134–38.

4. Stepanov, in *Iurii Tynianov: Pisatel' i uchenyi,* 138. Certainly at that early stage Tynianov most likely did not realize it, but he would later be battling against time and progressive chronic illness in an unsuccessful attempt to complete his magnum opus before his untimely death. Dictating pages while in his hospital bed, Tynianov managed to complete parts 1 and 2 of his novel *Pushkin,* encompassing the period up to Pushkin's southern exile.

5. See Iurii Tynianov, "Mnimyi Pushkin," in Iurii Tynianov, *Poetika. Istoriia literatury. Kino* (Moscow: Nauka, 1977), 78–92.

6. Angela Brintlinger discusses Tynianov's essay in great detail. See her *Writing a Usable Past: Russian Literary Culture, 1917–1937* (Evanston, Ill.: Northwestern University Press, 2000), 47–51.

7. See Monika Greenleaf, "Tynianov, Pushkin and the Fragment: Through the Lens of Montage," in *Cultural Mythologies of Russian Modernism: From the Golden Age to the Silver Age,* ed. Boris Gasparov, Robert P. Hughes, and Irina Paperno (Berkeley: University of California Press, 1992), 264–92; and Brintlinger, *Writing a Usable Past,* 42. Brintlinger provides a thorough discussion of the fictional Pushkins in Tynianov's trilogy of biographical novels (especially 42–61).

8. Iurii Tynianov, "Gannibaly. Vystuplenie," in *Iurii Tynianov: Pisatel' i uchenyi,* 204–10. This introduction receives its first English translation in this volume (see "Introduction to 'The Gannibals,'" 377–83). All references will be made to this translation and will be cited parenthetically in the text.

9. See J. Thomas Shaw's article in this volume for Pushkin's other references to his African ancestry from his works written in the 1820s.

10. It seems that Tynianov here refers not to the historical fact of Gannibal's descendants (who were fathered on Christina von Schöberg, a Swedish

Appendix A

noblewoman) but to the fictional Ibragim in Pushkin's unfinished novel *The Blackamoor of Peter the Great,* who was to marry into the Rzhevsky family, members of the old boyar class.

11. Iurii Tynianov, *Pushkin* (Leningrad: Khudozhestvennaia literatura, 1976), 27. Hereafter page numbers of this work will be cited parenthetically in the text.

12. Though an analysis of the psychological implications of Nadezhda Osipovna's animosity is beyond the scope of this article, it should be noted that her dislike of her son plays a significant role in Tynianov's depiction of Pushkin's childhood in his unfinished novel *Pushkin.*

13. Iurii Tynianov, "Avtobiografiia," in *Iurii Tynianov: Pisatel' i uchenyi,* 19.

Translated and with notes by Ludmilla A. Trigos

Appendix B: Introduction to "The Gannibals" by Yury Tynianov

This time the story is about Habesh, of old Abyssinia, about its northernmost part—the country of Tigré, where people speak in the language Tigrinya. About the mountainous part of Tigré which is called the country of Hamasen. In this land Hamasen there is a river called the Mareb. On the banks of this river stood—perhaps to this day still stands—a sycamore tree which the Arabs call "daro." One hundred years ago its branches spread out for thirty-six meters. The crown of the tree covered a circle of six hundred meters. In its shade rested the Hamite warriors, numbering some fifteen hundred and more. On its highest branches roosted golden Abyssinian doves. Two hundred years ago, if you went from Habesh to the Turkish city of Massawa without fail you would go past this tree. Then the doves sent people on their way with a tale. It's a story about a man, an Abyssinian, who passed by this tree unwillingly. He was taken into Turkish slavery. So the story goes about ancient Turkey, which in the seventeenth and eighteenth century was no less important for Europe than Russia, and for Russia was no less important than Europe.

Then he ended up in Russia and in France. He became a French engineer and French soldier. Again he went to Russia, married a captive Swede, a captain's daughter. Children came, and fourteen Abyssinian and Swedish sons became Russian nobility.

And thus, the story is about Russia.

The tale is about how no one stays in one place for long on this wonderful earth.

The family tree begins in Abyssinia. But the Turks, the powerful and wealthy Turkish merchants want to conquer the land of Habesh, because of what the word "Habesh" means: sweet-smelling extracts and fragrances. The inhabitants of this land are called "kash" or "habashat"—the gatherers of sweet-smelling extracts and spices necessary and pleasing to human inhalation. The Turks in the seventeenth century kept moving from the seaside closer and deeper into Abyssinia. They took the Abyssinians into captivity and

Appendix B

sold them into slavery. So the family tree, the human seed, was torn from Habesh and went by sea to Istanbul to the Sultan's palace. Thus afterward he was quickly stolen for the Russian consul.

And only his dark blood hinders him later from tracing his family to some other person, descending "from the Germans" during the times of Yaroslav or Alexander Nevsky. The dark blood remains noticeable, a brand. The first wife of the Abyssinian Negro, a Greek woman, did not want to marry him, "because he was not one of our kind." And he soon wore her out. The dark blood remained in the lips, the flared nostrils, the prominent brow, resembling an Abyssinian tower, as well as in the cry, the joke, the mischief, the dance, the song, the anger, the liveliness, the Russian serf harems, the ferocity, the murder and love, which resemble complete human madness. Thus began the lively, ferocious, Russian "Gannibality" [*gannibal'stvo*]—bigamists, jokers, rebels—the Russian Abyssinian nobility.

So quickly, easily and freely did they enter the Russian nobility that the Abyssinian and Swede's grandson fought for the rights of Russian nobility during the reign of Nicholas I. And it was accomplished because that very Russian nobility was also Swedish and Abyssinian, and German, and Danish. The genealogies are interesting not because they are true, but precisely because they were conceived and invented as the times demanded.

The nobility conceived and constructed a national Great Russian state descended from Great Russians, Poles, Kalmyks, Swedes, Italians, and Danes.

And these same noble surnames were well conceived. The Italian "Villa-Nuova" and Casa-Nuova became Vilanovsky and Kasanovich or Kasanovsky; the German "Gundret-Markt" is Markov; Doctor Pagenkampf is Pogankov, the Czech count Garrakh is Gorokh and later also Gorokhov and from his name came Gorokhovaia Street in Petersburg where Oblomov and Rasputin lived. The Italian Basko became Baskov, and in Petersburg there is Baskov Lane. The Italian Vavili became Vavilin, Chicheri—Chicherin. And the Danish Kos-von Dalen became the Russian Kozodavlev.

The families were noble (or earlier, boyar) not because they were genuinely Russian, but they became genuinely Russian, Great Russian, because they were or wanted to be boyars, and later, noblemen.

That's how it had been since olden times.

Markgraf Meissen came in 1425 to Russia and became Prince Myshnitsky and then Myshetsky, and much later, under Nikon, his direct descendant Prince Andrei Myshetsky became the elder Dosifey, the ardent leader of the Russian Schism.

And the ancestors did not stay in one place, the ancestors wandered, setting off for wherever it was better. The great expanses of land were always changing hands. Only when the noblemen felt settled did it begin to seem to

Appendix B

them, and did they make others believe, that they had always been in Rus', somewhere not far from Moscow.

And the Tatar Baran became Baranov, until the time of Ivan IV, the Terrible, when he went to the Estonians, to the Baltics. There his children, grandchildren and great-grandchildren became German barons and Lutherans: Von Barangof. And then already during the reign of Nicholas I, they left again for Russia and these Germans, perhaps not even knowing about the ancient change, according to the law of consonance once again began calling themselves the Russian nobles Baranov. Because on this earth nothing settles for long—there are exchanges of places, just like exchanges of people. The wind carries one family to Russia and an excess tosses another one out of Russia.

And when the aristocracy or the nobility experienced difficulties, even genuine Russians stopped calling themselves by Russian names—and so it was in different times. For example, under Tsar Ivan IV and Simon Bekbulatovich in Moscow they started concealing their Russian names: Fedor, Petr, Matvei—and called themselves Bulat, Murat, Akhmat. From thence came the Bulatovs and the Akhmatovs, not Tatars, but Great Russians. The Russian Ivan IV, the Terrible, told his consuls: "I am not Russian, I'm from German stock." But the German Alexander III, a Romanov, with the beard of a Bavarian crown prince, liked his artists to cultivate a boyar style.

The obscure Great Russian noble state accepted and banished people, it dug around in papers, rustled orders, real and fake, watched over regions, groped about in beds. That's why a genealogy was necessary, but in the genealogy the first pages were the easiest, then it got harder. Illegitimate children were placed on the same footing as legitimate, just as Pagenkampf became Pogankov. But the state stood on guard over every bed. And the thick-lipped "Gannibality"—the bigamists with very red, very thick blood—ran and sat out their entire lives away from their legal wives, away from both unhappiness and the tsarist courier.

Twice the family collided with the Pushkins: first toward the end of the eighteenth century and toward the beginning of the nineteenth century, having worn out and having caught a chill thoroughly at birth, light as a feather, prattling, conveying their light noble bodies along country roads and capital city avenues, but also getting stuck, lightly settling themselves like fluff wherever life was comfortable. Only two firm and terrible foundations preserved these people to the end of the eighteenth century. First, they thought that the family line had fallen on hard times and was dying out, that it was necessary to convey to the drawing rooms witty words and refurbished waistcoats, or else everyone would completely forget who those noble Pushkins were. These gullible, extravagant, garrulous people were astonishingly miserly, so that everything they got their hands on would suddenly disappear. And they were

Appendix B

miserly: they brutally bargained for every penny with the coach driver, and looked at him like a dark enemy who was undermining the fortune of the unsteady family of the noble Pushkins. However, after clambering onto the open carriage, they smiled easily and blissfully and thought themselves better than all the pedestrians. And second—a dark, miserly jealousy of their wives, a jealousy having come as the inheritance from their forefathers, a miserliness to that final possession over which they were masterful, to the extent which they still sometimes were tempted to be masterful. And misfortune pursued them. The fathers were wife-killers and the children became improvident. Then follows a history of offenses, prison terms, villages in a state of neglect, bankruptcies, fights, marital wailing, and French prattle over the heads of the pedestrians. The story narrows to the confines of the parlor with its faded wallpaper, it penetrates to the cage of the French parrot.

The story narrows the quantity of characters—it becomes about only one person and suddenly expands beyond all boundaries. And this person claims all the scores of his family and all the prison terms and all the oppositions and offenses, the bankruptcies and ruins, the jealousy and miserliness. He calls by name the Abyssinian tenderness and ferocity.

In his youth they noticed his unusual coldness. He was Pushkin until 1820, Gannibal from 1820 to 1830. The letters and deeds of his Gannibal uncles, Benjamin and Paul, have been preserved. In them one senses the completely open, hot mouths and clenched fists of the people and also the expansive elegance of the gesture. In their spirit and writing, Alexander Pushkin's letters much more closely resemble theirs than the conceited, lisping, trembling prattle of his father and uncle Pushkin.

The man was on the periphery of his family, which, wearing thin, went to pieces and was coming to ruin already for a hundred years, but even here one still met with monsters—a new breed—"Gannibality." The man was about to leave, completely alone—he was an aristocratic scapegrace. He hungrily sought out friends, family, a wife, a homeland—as a foothold, as a condition and nourishment of life. He found them, discovered and conquered with poetry and prose, that is, with the imagination and with travels, with the military methods of his time.

The story is about Russia.

The discourse is about a man who took upon himself all of the scores of his family and the scores of all the old masters. (In the nineteenth century, to take on yourself anyone else's scores was sometimes called "to receive your inheritance.") The nineteenth-century man who was obligated to present aristocratic credentials could not hide the Gannibals. They were too much in everyone's mind; their memory was in the flared nostrils, in the prominent brow, etc. With Pushkin one could do whatever you wanted: the Pushkins had a little bit of everything. But already at the same time the descendant also se-

Appendix B

lects such Pushkins who are on the periphery, completely apart, in opposition. For this, it is true, he had to go into the family history, to the lateral line of Pushkins.

Bypassing his sharp-nosed, sensual father and potbellied, prattler-poet uncle, who had only minor debts, he selected his own genealogy. Not one of the Pushkins named by him in his biography, not Gavrila Grigor'evich (an agent of Tsar Dmitry), nor his [older] brother Sulemsha, nor the *okolnik*[1] Matvei Stepanovich, a signatory to the document of the abolition of the *meshchanstvo,* nor his son Fedor Matveevich—the schismatic and *strelets*[2]— belongs to the direct line of Pushkin's forefathers. He collected offshoots of the family tree. Perhaps he would have renounced his direct great-grandfathers and grandfathers if they had not been murderers, "ardent and cruel" people.

From 1818 he proclaims, proud and bragging, that he places himself beyond the limits of ancestral appraisals:

Descendant of ugly Negroes . . .

The nobility, like servants, were invited to "jump on the hobbyhorse."

His great-grandfather Abram's first wife did not want to marry him "because he's not our kind." The fact that Gannibal was "not our kind," that he was also a valet and confidant [to Peter the Great] and a Russian nobleman from African princely origins—for the average conception of nobility in Nikolaevan times—place him in the first rank of ancestors. Here everything came in handy—Pushkin's argument with Bulgarin about Abram Petrovich Gannibal was an affair of intimate and vital significance for both of them. An argument about whether or not he was the orderly or valet of Peter should not be forgotten among the latter scores, leading to the duel and death.

So he searched for and found his family.

And thus also he searched and found, and discovered his homeland.

He was the first to see and speak out—he conquered Russia. But, truly, there were such periods—and they returned, they repeated themselves— when Great Russian places (not those near Moscow, not Tula, not Ryazan) were called Russia and Rus'. He, perhaps, at first would also have been glad to have called the Moscow area Russia, even though it, the Moscow area, didn't exist at the time. The old blackamoor's estate, Makarovo, was a complete wasteland.

And for a long time, he painfully insinuated himself into the family of middle nobility, but where could one hide the prominent brow, like a tower, and the turned-up nose of a quadroon, the thick lips, trembling in anger, the love for a woman resembling genuine human madness, the unprecedented poetry and the coldness of the builder of great schemes?

The bureaucrats said, "He is not our kind," the same thing that the faithless wife said about his black ancestor. "He isn't our kind," said the half-

Appendix B

English Lord Vorontsov. And the average landowners said, sweating, "Yes, yes, he is not our kind, he's a scapegrace—Pushkin, the writer."

And he hauled off all over Russia, not the Moscow region, not "Rassia," not Rus'.[3] In 1821 the Caucasus was discovered by poetry, in 1822—the Crimea, in 1824—Bessarabia. In prose, Bashkiria was discovered, the conquest of the Kamchadals and Yukagirs was prepared. He discovered with poetry and conquered with journalistic prose.

At the same time the conquest not only of the real, his surroundings, but also of the past, was accomplished. A comrade of the Pretender, Gavrila Pushkin continued his opposition against Moscow in the seventeenth century; the blackamoor of Peter conquered the drawing rooms and gave offense to the daughters of the old aristocracy. The conflict with the Russian peasantry ended with the incomplete and flimsy victory over Pugachev, and he unleashed the partisan Dubrovsky against the prominent nobility. The expansion lay ahead—the conquest of the Caucasus in historical prose.

Having looked around, he named the peoples that he still had not conquered and had not articulated in poetry and prose—these peoples which it still lay ahead to unite in poetry and prose. Maybe he did not think that he would manage, and wanted a poetic myth so that they recognized him, named him, reading not about themselves, but, of course, reading themselves.

. . . and the Finn, and now the wild Tungus and the Kalmyk, friend of the steppes. And the Bashkirs today sing Tatiana's letter to Onegin.

He had friends, many friends. They exiled him, banished him; he served his time, and survived. He conquered his homeland. It was a gypsy encampment, the dry Crimean earth, Mikhailovskoe, the village[4] of the old blackamoor. His old friends were dispersed, God knows where they were sent, thrust to the ends of the earth, underground. He found a wife. New friends appeared. And he achieved very much, he repaid many of his family's offenses and many resettlements. The "Kalmyk" and the "Tungus" remained silent.

He had a measure of time, because he conquered and named many spaces. He lived so that at twenty years each of his muscles was twenty years old and at twenty-five years his heart was exactly twenty-five years.

He never got to go abroad; he wanted to feel at least Asia beneath his feet, but when he stepped on Asian soil, it turned out to be Russian.

By his thirties he wanted to settle down. Then his home became a Petersburg apartment near Pevchensky Bridge, not far from the Winter Palace.

He surpassed all other Russian poets. For him, poetry stopped being what it had once been. He started to publish a journal and wanted to publish a newspaper.

And the courtiers nearby said about him: "He is not our kind." His wife betrayed him "because he is not our kind." He died from a wound.

I don't want to speak about how his family became desolate after this

Appendix B

man. However his clan, his family tree continued and continues. One grandson runs a cooperative near Moscow. His other descendants are already half non-Russian, they spilled out of Russia. Perhaps an American merchant would have avoided his quadroon grandfather, but his grandchildren are satisfied and remember him because the grandfather is not around and he is famous. In Bonn, Germany, the police chief is one of his grandchildren. There are others—foreign dukes; and also owners of a diamond mine in Africa from whence two hundred years ago came Avraam, later calling himself Gannibal.

And other people's grandchildren read him. Such is the earthly fate of every great person up until now: to think that he toils for himself under the sun and fights for his people, but he toils and fights for other people's grandchildren.

Here the sun beats down on the steppes—not resembling anything other than the sun. Here graze the cattle. Here the Bashkir sings in his own elusive language Tatiana's letter to Onegin.

[1932]

Notes

The "Introduction to 'The Gannibals'" is a translation of a manuscript from the Iurii Tynianov archive that was edited by N. L. Stepanov and published in *Iurii Tynianov: Pisatel' i uchenyi* (Moscow, 1966), 204–10. Special thanks to Ronald Meyer and Nicole Svobodny for their comments on this translation.

1. *Okolnik*: From the *okol'nichi*, a member of social group second in status to the boyars during the Muscovite period. (Compare *Oxford Russian-English Dictionary*.) For more information on the less well-known branches of Pushkin's family tree, see S. B. Veselovskii, *Rod i predki A. S. Pushkina v istorii* (Moscow: Nauka, 1990).

2. *Strelets*: In Muscovite Russia in the sixteenth and seventeenth centuries, a member of the military corps instituted by Ivan the Terrible and enjoying special privileges (*Oxford Russian-English Dictionary*, 2nd ed., 782).

3. "Rassia": In the Russian original, Tynianov spells the word "Russia" (spelled *Rossiia* in Russian) as *Rassiia* to indicate a dialectical pronunciation rather than the more common pronunciation.

4. "Village": In the original, the word is *kival'* (or *kebele*), which in the Amharic language of Ethiopia means "village." (Note provided in the original edition.)

Translated and with notes by Ellen Nidy

Appendix C: Excerpt from "My Pushkin" by Marina Tsvetaeva

It begins like a chapter from the favorite bedside novel of all our grandmothers and mothers—*Jane Eyre*—The secret of the red room.

In the red room was a secret cabinet.

But before the secret cabinet there was something else, there was the painting in mother's bedroom—"The Duel."[1]

Snow, the black branches of saplings, two black figures supporting a third, under his arms, to a sleigh—and one more, someone else, walking away, back turned. The one being carried away is Pushkin, the one walking away is d'Anthès. D'Anthès challenged Pushkin to a duel, that is, he lured him into the snow, and there, among the black, leafless saplings, killed him.

The first thing that I learned about Pushkin is—that they killed him. Then I learned that Pushkin was a poet, and d'Anthès was a Frenchman. D'Anthès developed a hatred for Pushkin, because he himself couldn't write poetry, and challenged him to a duel, that is, lured him into the snow and killed him there with a pistol shot in the stomach. So I learned for a fact at three years old that poets have stomachs, and—I'm remembering all the poets I've ever met—I worried no less about this *stomach* of a poet, which is so often not-full and in which Pushkin was killed, than about his soul.[2] The *sister* in me took its start from Pushkin's duel. I'll go even further—for me, there is something sacred in the word stomach—even a simple "I have a stomachache" floods me with a wave of shuddering sympathy that excludes all possibility of humor. With that shot they wounded us all in the stomach.

Goncharova wasn't mentioned at all, and I learned about her only as an adult. A lifetime later, I fervently hail my mother's silence. The petit-bourgeois tragedy attained the grandeur of myth. And, in essence, there was no third party in this duel. There were two: anyone and one. That is, the eternal personae of Pushkin's lyric poetry: the poet and the mob.[3] The mob, this time in the uniform of a cavalry guard, killed—the poet. And a Goncharova, like a Nicholas I, can always be found.[4]

Appendix C

◊   ◊   ◊

"No, no, no, you just imagine!" said mother, completely unable to imagine this *you*. "Fatally wounded, in the snow, and he didn't refuse his shot! He took aim, he hit, and he even said to himself: 'Bravo!' " said in a tone of such admiration that it would have been more natural to her, a Christian, if she'd been saying: "Fatally wounded, bloody, but he forgave his enemy! He threw down his pistol and held out his hand." With this, with us all, she was obviously returning Pushkin to his native Africa of revenge and passion and did not suspect what kind of lesson—if not of revenge, then of passion—she was giving four-year-old, barely literate me, for my whole life.

Mother's bedroom was black and white, without a single colorful spot, the black and white window: the snow and the branches of those saplings, the black and white painting—"The Duel," where on the whiteness of snow a black deed was committed: it's a perpetually black deed, the killing of a poet— by the mob.[5]

Pushkin was my first poet, and my first poet—was killed.

Since then, yes, ever since Pushkin was killed right before my very eyes in Naumov's painting—daily, hourly, continuously being killed through my infancy, childhood, youth—I divided the world into poet—and everyone else, and I chose—the poet, as a defendant I chose the poet: to defend—the poet—from everyone, no matter how they were dressed or what they were called.

There were three such paintings in our Three Pond Lane house: in the dining room, "The Appearance of Christ to the People,"[6] with the never-solved mystery of the incredibly small and incomprehensibly near, the incredibly near and incomprehensibly small Christ; the second, above the music bookcase in the salon—"The Tartars"[7]—Tartars in white robes, in a stone house without windows, among white pillars, killing the chief Tartar ("The Killing of Caesar"); and—in mother's bedroom—"The Duel." Two killings and one appearance. And all three were terrifying, incomprehensible, threatening, even the baptism with the never-seen-before black curly-haired, aquiline-nosed, naked people and children filling the river so full that not a drop of water remained, was no less terrifying than the other two—and they all prepared a child extremely well for its fated terrifying epoch.

Pushkin was a Negro. Pushkin had side-whiskers (NB! only Negroes and old generals have them), Pushkin had hair that stuck up and lips that stuck out and black eyes, with bluish-whites, like a puppy's—black, as opposed to the obviously light-colored eyes of his numerous portraits. (Since he was a Negro—black.)[8]

Pushkin was just as much a Negro as that Negro in the Alexander arcade, next to the white, standing bear, above the eternally dry fountain where

Appendix C

mother and I used to walk to have a look: hadn't it struck up? Fountains never strike (and how would they do that?), the Russian poet is a Negro, the poet is a Negro, and the poet—they struck down.

(God! how it came true! What poet, past or present *isn't* a Negro, and what poet—*didn't* they strike down?)

But before Naumov's "The Duel"—for every memory has its own *before*-memory, ancestor-memory, forefather-memory, just like a fire escape you back down, not knowing if there will be another step—which there always turns out to be—or the sudden night sky, in which you continually discover ever newer and newer highest and farthest stars—but before Naumov's "The Duel" there was another Pushkin, a Pushkin—when I still didn't know that Pushkin was Pushkin. Pushkin not as a memory, but as a state of being, Pushkin—forever and from forever—before Naumov's "The Duel" was the dawn, and growing out of it, disappearing into it, splitting it with his shoulders, as a swimmer does a river—a black man higher than all and blacker than all—with his head inclined and his hat in his hand.

The Pushkin monument was not Pushkin's monument (possessive), but simply Pushkin-Monument,[9] one word, containing the equally incomprehensible and separately nonexistent concepts of monument and Pushkin. That which is eternal, in the rain and in the snow—oh, how I see those shoulders weighted down with snow, African shoulders weighted down with and overcome by all the Russian snows!—with shoulders going into the dawn or into the blizzard, whether I am coming or going, running away from or running up to, standing with the eternal hat in hand, is called "Pushkin-Monument."

The Pushkin monument was the goal and the end of walks: from the Pushkin monument—to the Pushkin monument. The Pushkin monument was also the goal of races: who could run to the Pushkin-Monument faster. Only Asya's[10] nanny, out of simpleness, sometimes shortened it: "And we'll sit for a while by Pushkin," which invariably provoked my pedantic correction: "Not by Pushkin, but by Pushkin-Monument."

The Pushkin monument was also my first spatial measure: from the Nikitsky Gates to the Pushkin monument was one verst, that same eternal Pushkin verst, the verst of "The Demons," the verst of "A Winter Road," the verst of Pushkin's whole life and of our childhood primers, striped and sticking out, incomprehensible and accepted.[11]

The Pushkin monument was—everyday life, the same kind of persona in a child's life as the piano, or the policeman Ignatiev outside the window—who stood, by the way, almost as immutably, only not so high—the Pushkin monument was one of two (there wasn't a third) daily, unavoidable walks—to Patriarch Ponds—or to Pushkin-Monument. And I preferred—to Pushkin-Monument because I liked opening up and even tearing open my white, from grandfather, from Carlsbad, strangling "cardigan" on the run, running to him,

Appendix C

and reaching him, walking around him, and then, lifting my head, looking at the black-faced and black-handed giant, who did not look at me, who did not resemble anything or anyone in my life. And sometimes simply hopping around him on one foot. And I ran, in spite of Andriusha's[12] lankiness and Asya's weightlessness and my own pudginess—better than them, better than anyone: from a pure sense of honor, to run up to and then simply to burst. It pleases me that this very Pushkin monument was the first victory in my race.

There was also another game, my game, with the Pushkin monument, namely to put next to his pedestal a little white porcelain figure, the size of a little finger, a child's little finger—they used to sell them in china shops, whoever grew up at the end of the last century in Moscow knows—there were gnomes under mushrooms, children under umbrellas—to put next to the gigantic pedestal one of those little figures, and, running my eyes gradually from the bottom all the way up the whole granite cliff, until my head was on the point of falling off, to compare—the height.

The Pushkin monument was also my first encounter with black and white: such black! such white!—and since *black* was represented by a giant, and *white*—by a comical little figure, and since it was absolutely necessary to choose, it was right then that I chose forever the black and not the white, black, and not white: black thoughts, black fate, a black life.

The Pushkin monument was also my first encounter with numbers: how many of these little figures did I need to stand one on top of the other to get a Pushkin monument? And the answer was the same as it is now: "However many you stand . . . ," with the proudly modest addition: "But what if it were a hundred of *me*, then—*maybe*, because after all, I'm still growing . . ." And, at the same time: "And if a hundred little figures were placed one on top of the other, would it make—me?" And the answer: "No, not because I'm big, but because I'm alive and they're porcelain."

So, Pushkin-Monument was also my first encounter with matter: cast iron, porcelain, granite—and my own.

The Pushkin monument with me under it and the little figure under me was also my first visual lesson of hierarchy: in front of the little figure I was a giant, but in front of Pushkin I was—me. That is, a little girl. But one who would grow up. I was to the little figure—that, which Pushkin-Monument was—to me. But what then, to the little figure was—Pushkin-Monument? And after agonizing thought—a sudden dawning: but he is so big for her, that she simply doesn't see him. She thinks—*a house*. Or—*thunder*.[13] And *she* to him—is so small, that he also—simply doesn't see her. He thinks—simply a flea. But me—he sees. Because I am big and pudgy. And soon I would grow up more.

My first lesson in numbers, my first lesson in scale, my first lesson in matter, my first lesson in hierarchy, my first lesson in thought, and the main

Appendix C

thing, the visual confirmation of all my subsequent experience: out of a thousand little figures, even one placed on top of the other, you can't make Pushkin.

. . . Because I liked to walk away from him along the sandy or snowy promenade and to return to him along the sandy or snowy promenade—toward his back with the hand, toward his hand behind his back, because he always stood with his back turned, *away* from him—his back is turned and *toward* him—his back is turned, his back is turned to everyone and everything, and we were always walking toward his back, since the boulevard itself, with all three of its promenades, led to his back, and the walk was so long that every time we and the boulevard would forget what kind of face he had, and every time his face was new, although just as black. (I think with sadness that the last trees *before* him didn't even know what kind of face he had.)

I loved the Pushkin monument for its blackness—the opposite of the whiteness of our household gods. Their eyes were completely white, but Pushkin-Monument's were completely black, completely full. Pushkin-Monument was completely black, like a dog, even blacker than a dog, because even the very blackest of them always has something yellow above the eyes or something white below the neck. The Pushkin monument was black like a piano. And if they had never told me at all, later, that Pushkin was a Negro, I would have known that Pushkin was a Negro.

It is also from the Pushkin monument that I got my mad love for black people that's lasted my whole life: to this day I feel a fullness in my entire being when by chance, in a streetcar, or somewhere else, I find myself next to—a black person. My white emptiness side by side with black divinity. In every Negro I love Pushkin and recognize Pushkin—the black Pushkin monument of my preliterate infancy and of all Russia.

. . . Because I liked it that we were going or coming, and he—was always standing. Under the snow, under the flying leaves, in the red sky, in the blue, in the murky milk of winter—always standing.

But our gods were moved sometimes, although rarely. At Christmas and Easter our gods were brushed off with a cloth. That one, though, was washed by the rain and dried by the wind. That one—always stood.

The Pushkin monument was my first vision of inviolability and immutability.

"To Patriarch Ponds or . . . ?"

"To Pushkin-Monument!"

At the Patriarch Ponds—there were no patriarchs.

A wonderful thought—to place a giant among children. A black giant—among white children. A wonderful thought to doom—white children to black kinship.

Those who grew up under the Pushkin monument will not prefer the white race, and I—so obviously prefer—the black. The Pushkin monument, surpassing events, is a monument against racism, for the equality of all races, for the primacy of each one—as long as it yields a genius. The Pushkin monument is a monument to black blood flowing into white, a monument of the confluence of bloods, as there is confluence of rivers, a living monument to the confluence of bloods, to the mixing of national souls—of the most distant and seemingly—most unmixable. The Pushkin monument is a living proof of the baseness and deadness of racist theory, living proof—of its opposite. Pushkin is the *fact*, which overturns the theory. Racism, before it was born, was overturned by Pushkin at the very moment of his birth. But no—earlier: on the day of the wedding ceremony of the son of the Negro of Peter the Great, Osip Abramovich Gannibal, with Maria Alexeevna Pushkina.[14] But no, still earlier: on a day and hour unknown to us, when Peter first rested his black, bright, cheerful and terrifying gaze on the Abyssinian boy Ibragim. That gaze was a command to Pushkin *to be*. So children who grew up under the Petersburg Falconet Bronze Horseman,[15] also grew up under a monument against racism—and for genius.

It's a wonderful thought, to make the great-grandson of Ibragim black. To cast him into iron, as nature cast his great-grandfather into black flesh. Black Pushkin is a symbol. It's a wonderful thought—with the blackness of a sculpture to give Moscow a patch of the Abyssinian sky. For the Pushkin monument obviously stands "under the sky of my Africa."[16] It's a wonderful thought—with an inclination of the head, a step forward of the leg, a removal from the head and a placing of the hat of a *bow* behind the back—to give to Moscow, under the legs of a poet, the sea. For Pushkin stands not over a sandy boulevard, but over the Black Sea. Over the sea of the free element—Pushkin of the free element.[17]

A dismal thought—to place a giant among chains. For Pushkin stands among chains, his pedestal encircled ("fenced") by rocks and chains: rock—chain, rock—chain, rock—chain, all together—a circle. A circle of Nikolaevan arms, which never embraced the poet and never released him. A circle that began with the words: "You are no longer the former Pushkin, you are *my* Pushkin"[18] and opened only with d'Anthès's shot.

I swung on these chains with all of childhood Moscow of the past, present, future—without suspecting, on what. They were very low swings, very hard, very iron.—"*Empire*"?—*Empire*.—Empire—the Empire of Nicholas I.

But with the chains and the rocks—a wonderful monument. A monument to freedom—to captivity—to element—to fate—and to the ultimate victory of genius: to Pushkin, who rebelled out of the chains. We can say it now, when the humanly disgraceful and poetically incompetent erroneous substitution of Zhukovsky:[19]

> And for a long time by the *people I will be loved*
> For I awakened good feelings with my lyre,
> *For by the charm of living verse I was useful.*

Appendix C

with such a non-Pushkinian, anti-Pushkinian introduction of *utility* into *poetry*—a substitution that disgraced Zhukovsky and Nicholas I for almost a century and was their disgrace for all eternity, that sullied the Pushkinian pedestal since the year 1884—the placing of the monument—and was finally replaced with the words of *Pushkin's* "Monument."[20]

> And for a long time *I will be loved by the people*
> For I awakened good feelings with my lyre
> *For in my cruel century I glorified freedom*
> And called for mercy for the fallen.

And if I haven't named the sculptor Opekushin until now, that's only because great glory is anonymous. Who in Moscow knew that Pushkin was Opekushin's?[21] But no one has ever forgotten Opekushin's Pushkin. Our imaginary ingratitude is the best gratitude to the sculptor.

And I'm happy that I succeeded in one of my youthful verses in producing once again his black offspring—in the words:

> And there, in vast fields
> Serving the *heavenly* tsar—
> The cast-iron great-grandson of Ibragim
> Sparked the dawn.

Notes

1. Tsvetaeva is referring to the Russian painter A. A. Naumov's (1840–98) painting titled "Pushkin's Duel," which depicts the duel in which Pushkin was fatally wounded.

2. The Russian word for "stomach," *zhivot,* meant "life" in Old Church Slavonic, and Tsvetaeva here is clearly playing with both meanings of the word.

3. This is an important play on words which is untranslatable into English. The Russian word for "mob" (or "rabble") is *chern'*, which has the same root as the Russian word for "black," *cherny*. Tsvetaeva is setting up the opposition between white and black, which is central in her mythopoetic approach to Pushkin. In her discussion of Naumov's painting, she emphasizes the contrast between the white snow and the black trees. Here the color black represents the evil of the deed directed against the poet. Later in the essay, Tsvetaeva views the color black favorably: it is used to represent Pushkin himself because he is of African descent. It also symbolizes passion, while the color white symbolizes emptiness.

Appendix C

4. Natalia Nikolaevna Goncharova (1812–63) was Pushkin's wife. A society beauty who was popular in the court of Tsar Nicholas I (reigned 1825–55), it was her rumored liaison with Baron Georges d'Anthès that led to Pushkin's duel. Tsvetaeva viewed her as rather frivolous and vapid. Under Tsar Alexander I, Pushkin had been exiled to the Crimea and the Caucasus from 1820 to 1824 and to his family estate, Mikhailovskoe, from 1824 to 1826 for writing political poetry. Tsar Nicholas allowed him to return to St. Petersburg, but acted as his censor and kept a close watch on him by insisting he and his wife be involved in all the social activities of the court.

5. See note 3.

6. Tsvetaeva is referring to a painting by the Russian painter A. A. Ivanov (1806–58).

7. Some scholars believe Tsvetaeva's use of Tatar (or "Tartar") imagery is a reference to what she considered philistine revolutionaries, i.e., Bolsheviks, bureaucrats, and tyrants.

8. Pushkin had light-colored hair and light-colored eyes. (Tsvetaeva included this footnote in the original text.) Tsvetaeva makes the point in her footnote that although she considers Pushkin to be black, he actually had light coloring.

9. The Pushkin monument is a full-size statue of the poet sculpted by A. M. Opekushin in 1880. It stands in Pushkin Square, at the end of Tverskoi Boulevard in Moscow.

10. "Asya" is the diminutive of the name Anastasia. She was Tsvetaeva's younger sister by two years.

11. There a fantastic verst
  Protruded before me . . ." ("The Demons").

Pushkin is talking here about a mile marker.

> Neither light, nor black huts . . .
> Wilderness and snow . . . To meet me
> Only striped versts
> I found myself alone . . . ("A Winter Road")

The preceding is Tsvetaeva's footnote in the original text. These are two poems by Pushkin ("The Demons," 1830; "A Winter Road," 1826). Tsvetaeva cites excerpts from each in her footnote. A verst is both a physical milepost and a specific unit of measurement equivalent to 3,500 feet.

12. "Andriusha" is the diminutive of the name Andrei. He was Tsvetaeva's half-brother by her father's first marriage and was two years older than her.

13. Tsvetaeva as a child is playing with the rhyme in Russian of *dom*,

Appendix C

"house," with *grom,* "thunder." I've retained the literal meaning and sacrificed the rhyme.

14. Pushkin's great-grandfather, Abram Petrovich Gannibal, was supposedly of Ethiopian descent and was brought to Russia by Peter the Great. His son, Osip Abramovich Gannibal, married Maria Alekseevna Pushkina as his second wife.

15. The "Bronze Horseman" is a famous sculpture in St. Petersburg that depicts Peter the Great on a rearing horse with his hand gesturing to the Neva River. The monument was commissioned by Catherine II in 1766 and created by the French sculptor Étienne-Maurice Falconet. The monument served as the inspiration for Pushkin's narrative poem *The Bronze Horseman* (1833).

16. A reference to the line from *Eugene Onegin* in which Pushkin refers to his African origins.

17. Tsvetaeva is referring to Pushkin's poem "To the Sea," the first line of which is "Farewell, free element." The poem and this first line become an important leitmotif in this essay. Pushkin wrote it in 1824 when he was leaving Odessa, his place of exile on the Black Sea.

18. Tsar Nicholas I reportedly said this to Pushkin when he summoned the poet back to St. Petersburg in 1826.

19. The poet V. A. Zhukovsky (1783–1852) made some changes in Pushkin's verse in order to please the tsar.

20. The verse is from Pushkin's poem "Exegi Monumentum." Tsvetaeva's date of 1884 is incorrect. The monument was erected in 1880 as part of a celebration in which Dostoevsky gave his famous speech on Pushkin. Pushkin's original text was restored on the monument in 1937, the year of Pushkin's centennial and the same year Tsvetaeva wrote this essay.

21. See note 9.

*Translated by Catharine Theimer Nepomnyashchy and
Slava I. Yastremski with notes by Slava I. Yastremski*

Appendix D: Excerpt from *Strolls with Pushkin* by Abram Tertz (Andrei Sinyavsky)

Pushkin's Poet (in his most extreme and, I repeat, loftiest manifestation) has no face—and this is very important. What happened to all the grimaces, the fidgetiness, and the chatter to which we've grown so accustomed? Where has all trace of Pushkin gone, leaving behind this figure that can't even be called a personality, to such an extent has all personality been trampled out of it along with everything human? If *this* is a state, then what we see before us is some sort of idol; if *this* is movement, then we are observing a tempest, a flood, madness. Just try to approach the Poet—Hello, Aleksandr Sergeevich!—he won't answer, he won't even understand that you are talking to him—to him, to this effigy that sees no one, hears nothing, holding a stone lyre in his hands.

> The poet strummed his inspired lyre
> With his vacant hand.[1]

Allegories and cold conventionalities are necessary to mark, even if only through ellipsis, this sojourn in the spirit of Poetry, which is inaccessible to language. We have reached the highest point we can attain in describing it; here all life ends, and only muted symbols try to convey the message that it is better to remain silent at these heights.

"For what reason was he given to the world, and what did he prove by his presence?" Gogol asked about Pushkin, with his characteristic meticulousness in posing metaphysical questions. And he answered himself: "Pushkin was given to the world in order to prove by his presence what the poet as such is and nothing more—what the poet is when considered not under the influence of any specific time or circumstances, nor as conditioned by his own personal character, but as a man, independently of everything; so that, if some higher anatomist of the soul wished someday to dissect and explain to himself what the essence of a poet is . . . , then he could satisfy him-

Appendix D

self by looking at Pushkin" ("What Is, Finally, the Essence of Russian Poetry, and Wherein Lies Its Uniqueness," 1846).

"Independently of everything . . ." Yes, Pushkin showed us the Poet in manifold and exhaustive variations, including independently of everything, of the world, of life, of himself. Reaching this point we stop, deafened by the silence that suddenly falls, powerless in any way to express and restate in words the pure essence of Art, which barely allows a cloak of phenomena to be thrown over it.

> Like a deity, it does not need
> The outpourings of earthly raptures.[2]

In the meantime, however, on the earth the completely normal author lives and languishes, wandering about with nothing to do, only occasionally going insane or falling into a stupor of a higher order. He fidgets and fusses and suffers and knows the beautiful and frightening secret of his connection with the Poet, and he wants to name it in human language, to find an approximate synonym. He recalls various peculiarities of his biography, among which his attention is attracted by a bloodline that is for some reason especially dear to his heart—the Negro branch,[3] which was grafted onto the genealogical tree of the Pushkin family.

Negro is good. Negro is No. Negro is the sky. "Under the sky of my Africa."[4] Africa *is* the sky. An exile from the heavens. More likely a demon. Not of this world. A priest. Like his second, celestial homeland, only more accessible, flowing in his veins, subterranean, hot, boiling up like the netherworld, and bursting out in his face and in his character.

This is now the absolutely real, immediately recognizable Pushkin (not the Poet), only slightly exaggerated, combining in himself human and poetic features in that very thick mixture that gives birth to a new quality, the indissoluble unity of marvelous exotica, of spiritual ardor and attractive ugliness, which is more appropriate to the rank of the artist than the standard mask of the singer with a reed pipe. Pushkin's irreproachable taste chose a Negro for a coauthor, having figured out that the black, monkeylike physiognomy would suit him better than the angelic face of Lensky, that it really was his true face of which he could be proud and which enhanced him in the same way as lameness did Byron, ugliness—Socrates, more than could all the Raphaels in the world. And besides, goddammit, there was a huge amount of irony in that face! . . .

Oh, how Pushkin seized upon his Negroid appearance and his African past, which he loved perhaps more dearly than he did his aristocratic ancestry. Because besides the blood kinship, here was a spiritual kinship as well. A kinship in fantasy. There were many noblemen, but there was only one Negro. In all of immense, pale mankind there was only one poet, bright as an ember.

Othello. A poetic negative of a man. Italics. Graphite. Special, unlike anyone else. Such a one didn't even need a Demon. He was himself a Negro.

In those days children probably didn't read Mayne Reid[5] and Jules Verne and didn't play games in which they pretended to be in exotic countries with hot climates. But Pushkin already had his own personal (you can't have it!) Africa. He played at Africa just as a boy of today, while playing cowboys and Indians, might suddenly realize that he himself is a real Indian,[6] and he finds it funny, and for some reason he feels sorry for himself, and everything quivers inside from a bittersweet feeling of happiness—he has to bump along with his quite ordinary mama on a summer carriage ride through Razuvaevka[7] (on the Moscow-Tashkent line) while he is an Indian and won't forget it to the end of his days. Like being carried on the wings of fate, evidence of a past life lost in time, a premonition that, though you are a legitimate son, all the same you're a foundling, an abandoned child, an uninvited guest, a prisoner of the Caucasus in this vale of tears, and God knows how you got here, and nobody knows or remembers about you, but you have your own ideas. You are stronger, you are older; you're closer to the animals, to savage tribes and forests. A wild genius. A steaming, blood-soaked piece of poetry with an opening into chaos. And you look out from under your brow, like a Moor on the prowl, remaining calm until the hour strikes for you to take on any city that comes your way. "Give 'em hell!"—you'll bare your teeth, just try me, the crowd will part, and calmly and quietly, all keyed up, you will bear your inscrutable face through the parted crowd. "At the sight of Ibrahim,[8] they all begin to whisper: 'The Moor! The tsar's Moor!' He hurriedly led Korsakov through this motley crowd of servants." "He felt that to them he was a kind of rare beast, a peculiar, alien creature, who had accidentally been transplanted into a world that had nothing in common with him. He even envied people whom no one noticed, and considered their insignificance a blessing."

Pushkin wrote this when he had already grown tired of the spectacle, fame, and slander that swirled in his wake and secretly yearned for happiness "on the common path." Since youth he had regarded his black otherness in society, inherited from his grandfather Ibrahim, with great enthusiasm, rightly viewing his wild pranks as a sign of the elemental force raging within him. Whereas the white bones of his aristocratic kin gave Pushkin legitimacy in the national family, in history, his Negro blood took him back to the primordial sources of art, to nature and myth. The black race, the experts tell us, is more ancient than the white one, and inspired by it the poet plunged into Dionysian games, wedding in a single guise Africa and Hellas, art and animal instinct.

> And I, the eternally idle scapegrace,
> The ugly descendant of Negroes,
> Nurtured in savage simplicity,

Appendix D

> Not knowing the sufferings of love,
> I, through the shameless frenzy of my desires
> Find favor with young beauties;
> With an involuntary flame in her cheeks,
> A young nymph, herself not understanding why,
> From time to time sneaks a glance at the faun.[9]

And here again his black grandfather, Ibrahim, came in handy. How convenient that he happened to be called Hannibal! A whole geyser of visions spouted forth from this name. The path that the Negro boy Pushkin took to come to us led there, there—back to prehistoric antiquity, to goat-legged gods and maenads. Pushing the pudgy boyars to the far end of the table, "My black grandfather, Hannibal" became the central hero of his genealogy—the poet's first and most important ancestor.

Besides the famous name and black face, he bequeathed to Pushkin one more treasure: Hannibal was Tsar Peter's favorite and godson, standing at the beginning of the new, European, Pushkinian Russia. *The Blackamoor of Peter the Great* relates in detail how the tsar arbitrarily married the Moor off into the boyar aristocracy, grafting him to a good Russian stalk (probably hoping to get a rare plant—Pushkin). What was immeasurably more important, however, was that, thanks to Hannibal, the dark-complected physiognomy of the grandson unexpectedly radiated a striking resemblance to Peter. Since being Peter's godson was as good as being Peter's son, through his black grandfather the poet managed to become related to tsars and advance into the ranks of proud firstborns, the successors of the great skipper.

> The skipper was that famous skipper
> Who moved our land,
> Who powerfully set a stately
> Course with the rudder of our native ship.
>
> And he was Hannibal's father . . .[10]

Having secured such relatives, he could boldly say to himself: "You are a tsar, live alone . . ."[11] The path from the Negro led to the sovereign. Pushkin solved the vital problem of the relationship between the poet and the tsar, which tormented him for so long, with the equation: the poet is a tsar.

Appendix D

Notes

This excerpt and the following notes were reprinted with minor changes in transliteration from Abram Tertz (Andrei Sinyavsky), *Strolls with Pushkin*, trans. Catharine Theimer Nepomnyashchy and Slava I. Yastremski (New Haven: Yale University Press, 1993), 118–22.

1. *The poet strummed his inspired lyre:* These are the opening lines of the poem "The Poet and the Crowd" (1828).

2. *Like a deity, it does not need:* These lines are from the poem "A Conversation between the Bookseller and the Poet" (1824).

3. *The Negro branch:* Pushkin's great-grandfather on his mother's side was Abram Gannibal (Ibragim Hannibal; 1697?–1781). According to legend, he was the son of an Abyssinian prince. In 1705 he was stolen from the palace of a Turkish sultan where he was living as a hostage and presented to Peter the Great. In 1717 Peter sent him to France to study the military arts. In 1723 Hannibal returned to Russia, where he received the rank of engineer-lieutenant of an artillery company in the Preobrazhenskii Regiment. In 1762 he retired with the rank of commander in chief of fortifications.

4. *Under the sky of my Africa:* This line is from *Eugene Onegin*, 1.1.

5. *Mayne Reid:* A British writer who lived and worked as a journalist in the United States. He fought in the Mexican-American War of 1846–48 and wrote adventure novels about Indians, Mexican rebels, hunters, and young people traveling to exotic countries in search of rare animals, flowers, and plants. Together with Jules Verne, Captain Mayne Reid has been the most popular writer among Russian children since 1860, when his novels (*The Headless Horseman, Osceola the Seminole, The Quadroon, The Plant Hunters*, and *The Cliff Climbers*) were translated into Russian.

6. *A real Indian:* When Russian children play cowboys and Indians, the roles are reversed in comparison with American culture: the Indians are the good guys. The cult of the noble savage was popularized in Russia by the works of such writers as James Fenimore Cooper and Sinclair Thompson (*The Little Savages*), as well as Mayne Reid.

7. *Razuvaevka:* A Russian town on the Moscow-Tashkent railway line where Sinyavsky spent summers with his grandparents when he was a boy.

8. *At the sight of Ibrahim:* The unfinished historical novel *The Blackamoor of Peter the Great* was Pushkin's first attempt at writing prose. It tells the story of how Peter married his godson Ibrahim Hannibal to a girl from an old Russian aristocratic family, the Rzhevskys.

9. *And I, the eternally idle scapegrace:* These lines are from the poem "To Iur'ev" (1820).

10. *This skipper was that famous skipper:* These lines are from the "Post Scriptum" to the poem "My Genealogy" (1830).

11. *You are a tsar, live alone:* This line is from the poem "To the Poet" (1830).

Index

Abo Peace, 66, 69
Abramovich, A. L., 151
Abyssinia: and "Abyssinian" as terms, 6, 254; as Gannibal's homeland, 6, 32, 178, 243, 377–78, 380, ("established") 22, (later disproved) 31, 52, 311; Pushkin as descendant of kings of (Nabokov's view), 24; tribes of, 6–7
Africa: British influence in, 37n26; Council on African Affairs, 320; countries honoring or claiming Pushkin, 26; mythical, to Pushkin, 136, 138, 232; northern and southern Africans classified, 80; Russian knowledge of, relations with, 6–7, 9–13, 197, 201. *See also* Abyssinia; Cameroon; Ethiopia
African-American Museum (Cleveland), 249
African Americans: anthology of writings (*Wheatley, Banneker, Horton*), 234; contemporary thinking of, 125; culture of, 259–60; newspapers published by, 251, 263, 275n55, 306; Pushkin as model for, 227–28, 234–35, 236–45, 248–50, (as Father figure) 262, 267–68, (and relevance of heritage) 256; Russian view of, 10; and Soviet Union, 25–26, 242–43, 249, 258, (Robeson misquoted on) 307. *See also* Harlem Renaissance; Negroes
Ahmed III, sultan of Turkey, 47, 53
Aidline-Trommer, Elbert, 244, 260, 273n36
Aivazovsky, Il'ia: *Farewell, Free Elements!*, 180 (and fig. 16); *Pushkin on the Shores of the Black Sea*, 192n42 (and figs. 63 and 64)
Akhmatova, Anna, 280, 332–34, 336, 337, 354, 362n19

Aksakov, Ivan S., 41n76
Aksakov, Sergei, 199
Albedelias family, 65
Aldridge, Ira, 222n21, 305
Aleksandrov, Grigory: *Circus* (film), 25, 305
Alekseev, M. P., 198, 219n1
Alexander I, tsar of Russia, 231, 232, 263, 292, 391n4
Alexander Nevsky, Saint, 378; Order of, awarded to Gannibal, 6, 70
Alexander Pushkin Poetry Prize, 237–38. *See also* Pushkin Prize
Algeria, 10
All-Union Pushkin Committee, 308
American Revolution, 126. *See also* United States
Amo, Anthony William, 157
Amsterdam News, 253
Anabia, Louis, 38n39
Anikushin, M., 185 (and fig. 45)
Anna, empress of Russia, 65, 84
Anna Leopoldovna, regent of Russia, 6, 66
Annenkov, P. A.: *Pushkin in the Alexandrine Era*, 30
"Annibal." *See* Gannibal
Anti-Semitism. *See* Jews and Jewish culture
Anti-Slavery Record, The (newspaper), 251
Anuchin, Dmitry N., 23, 35n8, 51, 143, 254–55; "A. S. Pushkin: An Anthropological Sketch," 21–22, 80
Apraksin, Aleksei, 71
Apraksin, Elena Mikhailovna (née Princess Golitsyna), 71
Apraksin, Fedor Alekseevich, 71
Apraksin, Petr Alekseevich, 71
Apraksin, Petr Matveevich, 70–71
Apuleius, Lucius: *Golden Ass*, 337

399

Index

"Arab" as term, 15, 148n25, 177
Araps. See Blackamoors
Armistead, Wilson: *A Tribute for the Negro,* 250–51
Arndt, Walter: *Pushkin Threefold,* 194n60
Asanti, Molefi Kete, 234, 241
Associated Press, 307
August II, king of Poland, 58
Augustine, Saint, 234

Baker, Lee D., 8
Bakh, R. R., 188n10 (and fig. 50)
Bakhtin, Mikhail, 125, 328n28
Baldwin, James: "Here Be Monsters," 125
Bantysh-Kamensky, D. N., 58
Bantysh-Kamensky, N. N., 61
Baratynsky, E. A., 341
Barkov, I. S., 102
Barsukov (friend of Pushkin family), 177
Bartenev, P. I., 20–21
Barthelemy, Anthony Gerard, 155
Batiushkov, K. N.: *Assays,* 159
Battle: at Chesmensky, 13; of Lesnaia, 47; of Navarino, 74, 79, 91, 374; of Poltava, 67, 202
Baudelaire, Charles-Pierre, 341
Bayley, John, 219n1
Beard, symbolism of, 112–14
Beaumont, Gustave de, 229
Behn, Aphra, 11
Belashova, E. F.: *Pushkin as a Boy,* 191n39 (and fig. 56)
Bel'chikov, N. F., 309
Belidor (engineer and teacher), 61
Belinsky, Vissarion, 3, 19, 221n16
Belkin, D. I., 159–60, 161
Belobrov, V., 31
Belyi, Andrei, 300n29
Benet, William Rose, 241
Benkendorf, Count A. K., 17, 91, 92, 93, 98n14
Berg, Alban, 334
Berkman, Aleksandr, 304
Bernal, Martin, 156, 158
Best, George, 157–58
Bestuzhev-Riumin, Count Aleksei P., 66, 69, 74
Bethea, David, 100
Bezliudnyi, A., 184 (and fig. 39)

Bitov, Andrei, 175, 178
works: *Pushkin House,* 174; "Pushkin's Photograph," 174, 190n21
Black(s): actor playing Othello, 222n21; black baby motif, 48, 139, 150–67, 258, 342, 352; black U.S. press, 251; domestic servants, 12–13, 220n2; Russian view of, 10–11, 197, 201. *See also* Blackness; Negroes; Racism
Blackamoors (*araps*), 7–8, 12, 148n25; *arap* defined, 298n9; Pushkin as, 284, (denies identification with) 112; Pushkin quoted on, 15
Blackman, Peter, 310
Blackness: denial of, 8, 22, 23, 143, 243, 254–56, 287, (by Pushkin) 101; essence of, as expressed by Tsvetaeva, 286–87, ("dark language") 294–96; Pushkin's feelings about, *see* Pushkin, Alexander Sergeevich; Pushkin's treatment of theme of, 132–33; Russian conception of, 7–8, 10–11, 15–20, 23; as term, 9; and The Black Man, 124; theories about origin of, 157. *See also* Africa; Negroes
Black Russians (documentary), 3, 34n
Black Scholar (periodical), 256, 257
Blackwood's Magazine, 252
Blagoi, Dmitry, 309, 310
Blakely, Allison, 246n12
Blok, Aleksandr, 289, 341
works: "Fair Show Booth," 357; "The Hawk," 345
Blok, Ivan Leont'evich, 78n77
Blumenbach, Johann Friedrich, 10, 156
Bolshevik Revolution, 195n62, 263. *See also* Communist Revolution; Russian Revolution (1917)
Bontemps, Arna, 236, 241
Boston Symphony Orchestra, 335
Botsford, Keith, 363n24
Bour, General, 50
Bowser, Aubrey, 258
Braithwaite, William Stanley, 241
Brancoveanu, Constantin, 54
Brasol, Boris, 254
Brawley, Benjamin, 253
Brezhnev, Leonid, 29, 174, 308
Brintlinger, Angela, 370
Briullov, A. P., 181, 184 (and fig. 42)

Index

Briullov, Karl, 39n45
Briusov, Valery, 314
Broitman, L. I., 77n62
Brown, Clarence, 336
Brown, Lawrence, 320
Brown, Lloyd, 319
Brown, William Wells, 251
Bruce, James, 10
Bruni, F. A., 184 (and fig. 11)
Bukalov, Aleksei, 331n68
Bulgakov, Mikhail: *The Last Days*, 28
Bulgarin, Faddei, 123, 153, 163, 267; attacks Pushkin, 17–18, 86, 89–93, 164, 165, 381; Pushkin's response, 90–94, 135, 142, 232
Burnashev, V. P., 143
Bynner, Witter, 241
Byron, George Lord, 116, 125, 126, 131, 139, 239; Pushkin as Byronic figure, 123, 127, 130, 180, 271n19

Californian Eagle (black newspaper), 306
Cameroon, 31, 46, 52, 273n28
Capitein, Jacobus, 157
Carrera, Valentine: *Alexander Pushkin*, 244
Catherine I (Ekaterina Alekseevna), empress of Russia, 4, 34n1, 50, 59, 62, 63
Catherine II (the Great), empress of Russia, 6, 13, 72, 74, 84, 392n15
"Caucasoid" Africans, 80, 175, 177, 178
Censorship: Stalin-era, 358; tsarist, 82, 98n14, 228, 231, 285, 292, 391n4, (Pushkin's letters to wife opened) 124, 142
Census Bureau, U.S., 43n95
Central House of Artists (Moscow), 187n2
Chaadaev, P. Ya., 271n15
Chaliapin, Fyodor, 321
Charles XII, king of Sweden, 49, 59
Chateaubriand, François de, 229
Chaucer, Geoffrey, 303
Chekov, Anton, 122, 262
Chelishchev, P.: *Pushkin Taking a Stroll*, 181 (and fig. 25)
Cherkasov, I. A., 7, 68
Chernetsov, G. G., 181 (and figs. 20a and 20b)
Chestnutt, Charles, 248
Chirikov, S. G., 178–79, 181 (and fig. 14)

Christian church, 65, 200, 287–88, 289
Christina Eberhardine, queen of Poland, 58
Chukovsky, Kornei, 30, 369
Cold War, 278n97, 303, 324, 325
Coleridge, Samuel Taylor, 199–200, 206
College of Foreign Affairs, 69
Colored American, The (newspaper), 251, 275n55
Communism, 25, 26, 243; Cominform, 319; Communist Party, 306–7, 309, 318–19, (American) 278n97, 312
Communist Revolution, 280–83. *See also* Bolshevik Revolution; Russian Revolution (1917)
Constant, Benjamin, 366n40
Cooper, James Fenimore, 229, 397n6
Crisis, The (journal), 250
Cugoano, Quobna Ottobah, 38n40, 157

Danilov, Igor, 45n116
Dante Alighieri, 119
D'Anthès, Georges, 10, 186, 218, 287, 291, 384
Davis, Paul, 194n60
Dawe (English painter), 190n18
Debreczeny, Paul, 187n5, 219n1, 299n24
De Brini, Major General, 66
Debussy, Claude, 334
Decembrist Uprising (1825), 84, 153, 180, 192n43, 223n33, 275n57, 314
Defoe, Daniel, 10
Del'vig, Baron A. A., 89, 91–92, 101, 183
De Nerval, Gerard, 341
Derzhavin, Gavrila Romanovich, 180
De Valiere (chief of French artillery), 60
De Vivien, Jean, 182 (and figs. 28 and 66)
Dioper, Andrei, 5, 64
Dioper, Evdokia. *See* Gannibal, Evdokia Andreevna (first wife of Abram)
Dmitriev, I. I., 135, 142, 176, 215
Dmitry, tsar of Russia, 381
Dobuzhinskii, Mstislav, 335; *Pushkin and the Decembrists*, 192nn39,43 (and fig. 65)
Dobychin, Leonid, 191n50
Dodonova, G. B.: *Pushkin-Lycéeist*, 192n39 (and fig. 60)
Dolgoruky, Prince Vasily L., 60, 61–62, 63, 64

Index

Dolia. See Volia/dolia
Dolinin, Alexander, 365n35
Dombes, Prince of, 59–60
Domogatskii, V. N., 195n62
Dostoevsky, Fyodor, 21, 94, 122, 124, 136, 262, 367n43; Pushkin speech by (1880), 19–20, 248, 267, 268, 281, 298n10, 310, 373, 392n20; *The Idiot,* 335
Douglass, Frederick, 249, 250, 262, 265; *Narrative,* 301n32
Duberman, Martin, 302, 303, 318, 319
DuBois, W. E. B., 136, 235, 240, 307
Ducis, Jean-François, 198–99, 214
Duddington, Natalie, 244
Dumas, Alexandre, 305
Dunaevsky, Isaak: "Wide Is My Motherland" or "Native Land," 25, 305–6, 311
Dunbar-Nelson, Alice, 244, 245, 255
Duras, Claire de: *Ourika,* 11

Edel, Leon, 302
Eeckhout, Gerbrand van den, 189–90n15
Egorov, Boris, 146n15
Egypt, 10, 80
Ehrenburg, Il'ia, 308
Eisenhower, Dwight D., 303
Eisenstein, Sergei, 305, 310
Ekaterina Alekseevna. *See* Catherine I
Elagina, Avdotia P., 182 (and figs. 34a and 34b)
Eliot, T. S.: *Four Quartets,* 324
Elizabeth I, empress of Russia, 6, 7, 51, 66–67, 68; death of, 72; and Gannibal, 69, 70, 74, 79, 84, 85, 150, 153
Emerson, Caryl, 323
Empedocles, 102
Encyclopédie ou dictionnaire raisonné des sciences, des arts, et des métiers, 7
Enlightenment, the, 7, 10, 102, 146n13, 156, 271n15; in Russia, 159
Equiano, Olaudah, 11–12, 157
Eremin, M., 230
Esenin, Sergei, 289
Ethiopia, 6, 7–8, 37n29; claims Pushkin, 26, 31, 32; and "Ethiopianness" of Pushkin, 34n; Russian/Soviet relationship with, 37n26, 311; socialist regime, 323
Ethiopian Observer, 26

Euripides, 102
Evdokimova, Svetlana, 161–62

Fadeev, Aleksandr, 307–8
Falconet, Étienne-Maurice, 392n15
Fanon, Frantz, 124
Fascism, 311
Fate as concept. *See Volia/dolia*
Favorsky, Vladimir: *Pushkin as a Boy at the Lycée,* 191n39 (and fig. 52)
Feffer, Itsak, 305, 318
Fiquelmont, Countess Dolly F., 16, 24, 142, 143, 176, 180
Fontenelle, Bernard de, 162
Foreign Quarterly Review, 271n19
France, 4, 7, 102; Gannibal's studies and military service in, 4, 46, 47, 59–61, 63, 79, 84, 137; military training in, 58, 60–61, 62; Shakespeare produced in, 198–99; war with Russia, 89; war with Spain, 60, 207. *See also* French Revolution
Freedom as concept. *See Volia/dolia*
Freedom (black newspaper), 263
Freedom's Journal (black newspaper), 251, 275n55
French Revolution, 11, 128, 156
Freud, Sigmund, 110, 112, 124
Friendship University (Moscow), 26
Frost, Robert, 241
Fugard, Athol: *The Blood-Knot,* 229

Gabrieli, Giovanni, 335
Galaktionov, S. F., 181, 184 (and fig. 43)
Gal'berg, S., 181 (and fig. 21)
Galla tribes, 7, 178
Gannibal, Abram Petrovich (Pushkin's great-grandfather): African heritage, 7–8, 22, 24, 177–78, 196–97 (*see also* country of origin, *below*); autobiography or memoirs, 13, 34n1, 47, 72; biographies, 20, 31, 49, ("German biography") 6, 35n12, 39n54, 48, 55–56, 58, 62, 72–73, (great-granddaughter's) 34n1, 61, (Pushkin fictionalizes as *The Blackamoor of Peter the Great*) 14 (*see also* Pushkin, Alexander Sergeevich: works), (Pushkin's biographical notes) 84, 93, 230–31, 249–50; birth and baptism, 49–51, 54–55, 57–58, (tricentennial of birth) 31;

402

Index

character and personality, 20, 73, 137, 158n27, (cruelty to first wife) 5, 74, 148n27, 171n38, 218; as child, sold into slavery, 3, 46–47, (sojourn in Turkey) 47, 51, 52–54, 55–56; country of origin, 3, 6, 26, 33, 311, (established) 31, 45n116, 46; education, 4, 55, 58, 59–63, 168n10 (*see also* military service, *below*); exiled to Siberia, 4–5, 47, 63–64, (illegally returns) 65, 84, 153, 231; final years and death of, 5–6, 46, 47, 50, 84; force of legacy of, 29, (as joke) 31; in France, 4, 46, 47, 59–61, 63, 79, 84, 137; as gift to and protégé of Peter the Great, 3–4, 12, 46–62 passim, 74, 79, 122, 283–84, (after tsar's death) 4–6, 63, (alternate version of story) 17, 91, (Pushkin's version of story) 83–84; land holdings, 5–6, 66, 69, 70–72, 74, 150, 153 (*see also* Mikhailovskoe, estate at); marriages and children, 5–6, 13, 64–70 passim, 74, 141, 202, (first wife's infidelity) 5, 64, 148n27, 154, 217–18, (will) 71, 74; memorial to, 49; military service, 4, 6, 46, 47, 58–64, 79, 84, (retires from, returns to) 5–6, 64–72, ("Victory of Gannibal") 13, (wounded) 60, 201; portraits, 22, 57, 59, 177; princely ancestors, 122–23, (as "kidnapped prince") 12, 51; Pushkin as descendant of, 122, (identifies with) 202; renewed public interest in, 31; siblings, 55, 56, 83–84, 160; social aspirations, 80 (*see also* Social class); Soviet "whitewash" of, 23; surname adopted by, 123, (first use of) 5, 49, 64, (Pushkin cites as "Annibal") 83–84, 86

Gannibal, Agrippina (daughter of Abram), 67

Gannibal, Aleksei Petrov (alleged brother of Abram), 56

Gannibal, Anna (daughter of Abram), 67

Gannibal, Anna Semenovna (great-granddaughter of Abram), 34n1, 61

Gannibal, Benjamin (grandson of Abram, Pushkin's uncle), 372

Gannibal, Christina Regina ("Krestina" Matveevna) (née von Schöberg, second wife of Abram), 5, 65, 67, 69–70, 74, 375n10

Gannibal, Elizabeth Abramovna (daughter of Abram), 67

Gannibal, Evdokia Andreevna (née Dioper, first wife of Abram), 5, 35n6, 64–65, 71, 74, 148n27, 149n37, 154, 171n38, 217–18

Gannibal, Evdokia (or Poliksena) Abramovna (daughter of Abram), 67, 154, 218

Gannibal, Isaak (or Savva) Abramovich (son of Abram), 67, 177

Gannibal, Ivan Abramovich (eldest son of Abram), 13, 65–71 passim, 79, 84; at Navarino, 74, 80, 91, 374

Gannibal, Maria Alekseevna (née Pushkina, daughter-in-law of Abram; Pushkin's grandmother), 13, 71, 218, 389

Gannibal, Nadezhda (Pushkin's mother). *See* Pushkina, Nadezhda Osipovna

Gannibal, Osip Abramovich (son of Abram; Pushkin's grandfather), 13, 67, 71, 74, 154, 218, 389

Gannibal, Pavel Isaakovich (grandson of Abram; Pushkin's uncle), 29, 372

Gannibal, Petr Abramovich (son of Abram), 7, 13, 29, 34n1, 35n12, 58, 67, 72, 73, 373–74

Gannibal, Poliksena Abramovna (daughter of Abram). *See* Gannibal, Evdokia (or Poliksena) Abramovna

Gannibal, Sofia Abramovna (daughter of Abram), 35n12, 51, 67, 72; descendants of, 70

Gannibal, Yakov Abramovich (son of Abram), 67

Gannibal family: and "Gannibality," Tynianov's novel about, 369–75, 377–83; Pushkin meets members of, 13, 29, 153, 202

Gasparov, Boris, 366n40

Gates, Henry Louis, Jr., 9, 125, 234, 251, 262, 296–97

Geitman, E. I., 178–79, 181, 182, 186, 191nn29,39 (and fig. 1)

Geitman, F., 99

Gendel'man, E. A.: *Pushkin-Lycéeist*, 192n39 (and fig. 61)

Gergiev, Valery, 337

Gippius (or Hippius), Gustav A., 182, 187n6 (and fig. 29)

Glazunov, Aleksandr, 333

Glinka, Mikhail, 334; *Ruslan and Ludmila*, 355

403

Index

Gnammankou, Dieudonné, 31, 52, 191n32
Gnedich, N. I., 80–81, 178–79, 181
Goethe, Johann Wolfgang von, 125, 239, 258, 316
Gogol, Nikolai, 184, 262, 367n43; quoted on Pushkin, 3, 19, 248, 393–94; sketches Pushkin, 190n21 (and fig. 51); "The Nose," 358
Gojowy, Detlef, 337, 343
Goldman, Emma, 304
Golikov, I. I., 50
Golitsyna, Princess Anna Borisovna, 71
Golitsyna, Princess Elena Mikhailovna, 71
Golitsyn princes, 56
Gol'mer (subordinate to Major General de Brini), 66
Golovin, General A. I., 71
Golovin, Count Fedor Alekseevich, 51, 54, 57
Goncharov, I. A., 194n59, 262
Goncharova, Natalia (Pushkin's wife). *See* Pushkina, Natalia Nikolaevna (née Goncharova)
Gorbachev, Mikhail, 320
Gorky, Maksim, 262
Graham, Irina, 336–38, 339–43, 351–58 passim
Grech, Nikolai, 89, 98n15
Greek War for Independence, 15, 91, 96n4, 126, 230
Greenleaf, Monica, 370
Gregoire, Henri, 251
Griboedov, Aleksandr, 176, 180, 341, 369; *Woe from Wit,* 12
Grigor'evich, Gavrila, 381
Grigoriev, Apollon, 19
Gronniosaw, James Albert Ukawsaw, 38n40
Guber, P., 225n56
Guizot, François, 201, 213, 223n30

Habesh, 6, 377–78
Haile Mengistu, 323
Haile Selassie, 311
Hakluyt, Richard, 157
"Hamitic" Africans, 6, 22, 80, 177, 178, 254, 377
Hannibal (Carthaginian general), 5, 52, 144n2
Harlem People's Bookshop, 249

Harlem Renaissance, 25, 226–27, 233–41, 243–44, 248–49, 260, 261, 333
Harlem Writers' Guild, 263
Hasan (Turkish vizier), 53
Hasty, Olga, 286
Haynes, Elizabeth Ross, 256
Hazlitt, William, 222n23
Henning, Hillarius Hartman, 69–70
Herder, Johann Gottfried von, 156, 201
Hippius. *See* Gippius
Hitler, Adolf, 296
Hollywood Ten trial, 306
Holstein, Casper, 237, 242
Homeric universe, 102
Horowitz, David, 329n44
House Committee on Un-American Activities (HUAC), 306–7, 318–19, 322
How Tsar Peter Married Off His Blackamoor (documentary), 32–33
Hudlin, Warrington, 240
Hughes, Langston, 25, 236, 249

Inquisition, the, 156
In Search of Lost Orpheus (documentary film), 337
Islam, 46
Itkin, A. Z.: *Pushkin-Lycéeist,* 191–92n39 (and figs. 57 and 58)
Iuon, K. F., 184 (and fig. 41)
Ivan IV (the Terrible), tsar of Russia, 372, 379, 383n2
Ivan VI, tsar of Russia, 66
Ivanov, Vyacheslav, 341
Izmailov, N. V., 219–20n1

Jakobson, Roman, 225n51
James, Edwin, 145n9
Jewish Antifascist Committee, 305, 318
Jewish Autonomous Region of Birobidzhan, 305
Jews and Jewish culture, 22, 289, 304, 306; and Soviet anti-Semitism, 310, 311, 318, 323, 324
Johannes, Haile Gebré, 44n99
John of Novgorod, Saint, 102
Johnson, Charles S., 236, 238
Johnson, James Weldon, 236, 241
Johnson, Samuel: *The History of Rasselas, Prince of Abyssinia,* 10, 52
Journal of Negro History, 235, 239

Index

Joyce, James, 365n29
Jung, Carl, 125

Kalashnikov, Olga, 258, 266, 267
Kantemir, Antioch, 159
Karamzin, Nikolai Mikhailovich, 109, 128, 139, 215
　works: *History of the Russian State*, 107; "Il'ia Muromets," 111
Karamzina, Sof'ia Nikolaevna, 150
Karatygin (actor), 37n31, 179
Kent, George E., 238
Khodasevich, Vladislav, 28, 29, 285–86
Khokhlov, N. P., 51
Khomiakov, Aleksei, 8
Khomutova, Anna, 16
Khrushchev, Nikita, 322
Khvostov, Count, 181
Killens, John Oliver, 241, 246–47n33, 250, 263, 265–67
Kiprensky, O. A., 181, 182–84, 185, 186, 190n15 (and fig. 36)
Kiukhel'beker, Vilhelm, 101, 369
Kokovstov, M. G., 10
Komsomolskaia Pravda (periodical), 303
Korf, Baron, 68
Korf, M. A., 16
Kornovsky, S. D., 16
Korovin (student in Paris), 61
Kotóko (African tribe), 46
Koussevitsky, Serge, 335, 363n24
Kovenchuk, Nina, 360n12
Kozlov, A. A., 185 (and fig. 10)
Kozlov, V. V., 185 (and fig. 46)
Kravchenko, A. I.: *Pushkin*, 184 (and fig. 40)
Kremer, Gidon, 337
Krivtsov (friend of Pushkin), 208
Kronstadt Canal, 69, 70
Krylov (friend of Pushkin), 181
Kul'bin, Nikolai, 334
Kustodiev, B. M.: *Pushkin in Petersburg*, 185
Kuz'min, N. V., 185 (and figs. 70 and 71)

Ladoga Canal, 64, 70
Laloy, Louis, 338
Law, John, 60
Layton, Susan, 17
Lazhechnikov, I. I., 97n10, 176, 194n58

Lebedev-Kumach, Vasily, 306, 312
Lelong family, 73
Lenin, V. I., 172, 174, 262, 282, 284, 311
Lerchenfeld-Kofering, Maximilian von, 10
Lermontov, Mikhail, 94, 341; *Masquerade*, 217
Le Tourneur, Pierre, 199, 220n5, 223n30
Levendal, Governor (of Revel), 66
Levitt, Marcus, 21, 23, 24, 309
Life of Alexander Pushkin, The (comic book), 249
Lincoln University (Pennsylvania), 249
Lindsay, Vachel, 241
Linev, I., 173, 181, 193n54 (and fig. 8)
Liprandi, I. P., 202
Literary Gazette, 89, 229, 303
Living Pushkin (documentary), 32
Locke, Alain, 241, 248, 259, 261
Lomonsov, M. V.: "A Hymn to the Beard," 112
Lopukhina, Evdokia, 64
Lotman, Yury M., 7–8, 23–24, 146n15, 179–80
Louis XIV, king of France, 38n39, 59–60
Louis XV, king of France, 60, 61, 159
Lourié, Artur Vincent, 359n3
　works: "American Diaries," 338; *The Blackamoor of Peter the Great* (opera), 332–58; *Feast in the Time of Plague* (opera-ballet), 332; "Prayer Beads" (song cycle), 359n5
Lourié, Ella, 336, 362n19
Loury, Glenn C., 133
Lovejoy, A. O., 156
Luberas, General Johann-Ludwig, 67–69
Lukin, Petr, 55
Lumumba, Patrice, 26
Lunacharsky, Anatoly, 282, 360n7
Lurie, Felix, 45n116
Lutova, Svetlana, 45n116
Lynch, Kara, 34n
Lynch, Joseph, 363n24

McCarthy, Joseph, and McCarthy witch hunts, 315, 329n44
McDowell, Deborah E., 262
Mahler, Gustav, 334
Maine, Duke of, 59–60, 61
Maistre, Xavier de, 182 (and fig. 30)
Makarov, A. V., 35n2, 59, 60

405

Index

Makarov, M. N., 176; "A. S. Pushkin in Childhood," 135
Maksimovich, M., 148n24
Malinovsky (Pushkin's boyhood friend), 101
Malmsted, John, 300n29
Manchester Guardian, 304
Mandelstam, Osip, 365n29
Maritain, Jacques, 334, 336
Martin, Pierre-Denis the Younger, 47, 59
Masiutin, V. N., 194n62 (and fig. 72)
Mathé, V. V., 183–84 (and fig. 38)
Matveevich, Fedor, 381
Mayakovsky, Vladimir, 289
  works: "Jubilee," 28; "My Discovery of America," 242
Menshikov, Prince, 4–5, 63
Merezhkovsky, Dmitry, 267
Meyer, Ronald, 74n
Michelangelo, 146n15
Mickiewicz, Adam, 366n40
Mikhailovskoe, estate at, 43n98, 382; granted to Gannibal, 66, 70, 84, 150, 153, 231; Pushkin exiled to, 13, 82–85 passim, 107, 128, 139–40, 150, 153–54, 202–3, 239, 293, 314, (returns from) 154, 208, 391n4, 392n18, (revisits) 313, 316, 325
Mikhoels, Solomon, 25, 305, 310, 318
Miltiades, 127
Minikh, Count B. Kh., 5, 6, 64, 65–66, 72
Mirsky, Prince D. S., 177, 180, 194n60, 249, 250, 255
Mochalov, Pavel, 199, 221n16
Modzalevsky, B. L., 73, 144n2
Mokritsky, A. N., 184 (and fig. 12)
"Mongoloid" features, 175
Montagu, Duke of, 157, 162
Montesquieu, Charles Louis de, 159, 162
Monteverdi, Claudio, 335
"Moor" as term, 199–200, 201
Moore, Thomas, 145n3
Morales, Gera Leopoldovich Zacharin, 34n
Morali ("Moor Ali"), ship captain, 96n4, 202
Morning Star, The (almanac), 148n24
Moscow Herald, 198, 201, 214
Moscow News, 21
Moscow Telegraph, 173, 214
"Mulatto" as term, 80
Murav'ev, Governor M. N., 49
Murray, Daniel, 251–52

Musin-Pushkin, Count Platon Ivanovich, 60, 61
Mussorgsky, Modest, 360n9; *Boris Godunov,* 320–23, 342, 345
Mustafa II, sultan of Turkey, 53
Myshetsky, Prince Andrei, 378

Nabokov, Vladimir, 24, 279, 317, 333, 339; discredits "German biography," 6, 136, 361–62n17; refuses Lourié's opera, 335, 336
  works: "Adam Gannibal," 75n16, 177–78; "Pushkin and Gannibal," 51–52, 335–36; translates and edits *Eugene Onegin,* 94n1, 145n2, 149n42
Naiman, Anatoly, 332
Naison, Mark D., 319
Napoleon Bonaparte, 139
Nashchokin, Pavel, 18, 93–94, 105
National Urban League, 235
Naumov, A. A.: "Pushkin's Duel," 384–86 (and fig. 75)
Nazism, 26, 305, 318
Negroes: "Moors" distinguished from, 199–200, 201; "la negritude" (Paris, 1920s), 333; "Negro" and "Negroid" as terms, 80; "Negroid" characteristics, 24, 27, 42n85, 122, (seen in Pushkin) 175–79, 181, 184–86, 197, 255, 394; "scientific study" of, 7; as "species," Voltaire on, 150; "white," 282–83. *See also* African Americans; Blackness; Slavery
Negro Worker (journal), 26
Negro World (journal), 255
Neill, Michael, 223n35
Nenasheva, A. M.: *Pushkin-Lycéeist,* 192n39 (and fig. 59)
Newman, Karen, 157–58
New Negro, The (manifesto), 259
New Time (Russian journal), 308–9
New York Public Library, 248, 337
Nicholas I, tsar of Russia, 11, 240, 285, 291–92, 313, 317, 389–90; censorship by, 98n14, 285, 391n4; and Pushkin, 144, 153, 208, 298n9, (allows return from exile) 391n4, 392n18, (and Bulgarin's attack on Pushkin) 91–92; and Pushkin's wife, 28, 218; secret police of, 17
Nietzsche, Friedrich, 124

406

Index

Njeri, Itabari, 122
"Noble savage," 200, 228, 230
Norov, A. S., 10
Northern Bee, The (periodical), 17, 163
Northern Flowers (almanac), 89
Northern Herald, The (periodical), 149n41
Northern War, 8, 59, 62, 70
Novikov, I. A., 138
Novosel'e (almanac), 184
NTV (Russian TV station), 32
Nubia, 10
Nusinov, Isaak, 310
Nystad, Peace of (1721), 58

O'Bell, Leslie, 10
Obolenskaia, Iu. L., 194n62 (and fig. 73)
Olenin, A. O., 98n15
Olenina, Anna, 87, 98n15, 148n24, 176, 224n40
Olga Nikolaevna, Grand Princess, 11
Opatovich, S. I., 35n6, 148n27
Opekushin, A. M., 180, 185, 289, 390 (and figs. 18 and 44)
Opportunity: A Journal of Negro Life, 226, 227, 235–44 passim, 248–49, 255
Orleans, Duke of, 159, 160–61
Orlov, General, 112
Orthodox Church, 49–50, 53, 55, 173
Osipova, Praskovia A., 13, 202
Othello, 228, 340, 353; Pushkin compared to, 10, 155, 217–19; Russian performances of *Othello,* 198–219; as theme for Pushkin, 82, 88–89, 125, 148n24, 164, 196–219
Our Pioneer (journal), 45n116
Ovid, 125; *Metamorphoses,* 203, 216
Oxley, Thomas, 261

Palazzi (death mask by), 181
Palestrina, Giovanni, 335
Panaev, I. I., 143
Paraskevy Church, 49, 50
Parfenov, Leonid, 32
Paris Conference (1948). *See* World Peace Conference
Park, Mungo, 10
Parris, Guichard, 241–44
Parry, Albert, 239
Pasternak, Boris, 341, 359n6
Patterson, Lloyd, and son Jimmy, 305

Patterson, William L., 26
Paul I, tsar of Russia, 72, 78n77
Pavlinov, P. Ia., 195n62 (and fig. 74)
Pavlova, E. V., 182, 187n6, 188n10, 191n39
Pericles, 15, 127
Peter I (the Great), tsar of Russia: and Africa, 9; African boy (Gannibal) as gift to and godson of, 3–4, 7, 12, 17, 46–63 passim, 66, 74, 83–84, 91, 285, (matchmaking) 161, (naming) 144n2, (relationship as analogy to Pushkin's situation) 153; Alexander I compared to, 231; black servants of, 12; death of, 4, 5, 63, 79, 149n37; and plot against Turkey, 8, 53; portrayed with blackamoor, 57, 59; Pushkin's portrayal of, 140–42; and race, 162; and slavery, 85; wife of, 5, 64; wins victory over Swedes, 49–50, 54, 57, 59, 70
Peter (Alekseevich) II, tsar of Russia, 4, 63
Peter III, tsar of Russia, 6, 72, 74
Peterson, Dale, 259
Philippe, Duke of Orleans and Regent, 60, 61
Plácido (Gabriel de la Concepción Valdés), 234
Plath, Sylvia, 299n23
Pletnev, P. A., 222n23
Poe, Edgar Allan, 250
Pogodin, Mikhail, 201
Pogodin, N. A., 182
Poletika, P. I.: "The State of the Society in the United American States," 228–29
Polevoi, N. A., 173
Popkin, Richard, 156
Popov, O., 31
Preobrazhensky Regiment, 4, 56, 59, 62, 64
Prince, Nancy, 38n44
Prokofiev, Sergei, 333
works: *Fiery Angel,* 350, 367n41; "Pine Trees," 314
Puschin, Ivan, 101, 176, 180, 194n59, 266
Pushkin, Alexander Sergeevich: African origin of, 3–4, 7, 19, (negative aspect) 40n59, 158, 218, (pride in) 93, 99, 178, 180, 182, 228, 229, (relevance of) 8–9, 21–22, 94, 279 (*see also* blackness of, *below*); American and British attention to, 252–68; anniversaries or celebrations of birth and death, 21, 24–26, 28, 31–33,

407

Index

194n62, 235, 241–42, 249, 303, 308–18, 323–24, 336; biographies of, 7–8, 32, 44n99, 238, 249, (Tynianov's biographical novel) 369–75; blackness of, 7, 15–22, 28–29, 33, 142–43, (denied) 8, 22, 23, 101, 143, 243, 254–56, 287, ("Ethiopianness," "Africanness") 34n, 268, (mother's opinion) 276n80, (Pushkin's anxiety over) 100, 107, 115, 118, 119, 122, (Pushkin's interest in, sensitivity to) 13–15, 40–41n68, 132–38, 201–2, 206, (and race) 122–23, 254–68, 389, (viewed as black poet) 279–97; death (1837), 10–11, 18, 287–90, 291; death masks of, *see* portraits of, *below;* debauchery of, 107, 137, 366n40, (Don Juan list) 100, 116, 130; descendants of, (illegitimate child) 258, (great-granddaughter) 43n95; education of, 10, (at Lycée) 16, 99–100, 101, 104, (self-taught) 238–39; exiled, 100, 118, 128, 180, 231, 391n4 (*see also* Mikhailovskoe, estate at); family relationships, 92, 276n80, 374, (meets Gannibal relatives) 13, 29, 153, 202; as Father of Russian Literature, 261–62; marriage, 81, 108, 143, 154, 348, 351, (jealousy of wife) 218, (letters to wife) 124, 135, 142, 176, (search for bride) 99, 202, 208, 216, (wife's beauty and connections) 81, 119; monument to (1880), 180, 187, 281, 289–93, 296, 386–90; nanny of, *see* Rodionovna, Arina; nicknames, 23–24, 170; parents, 15, 32, 81, 84, 276n80, 372, 374, (mother defamed) 91–92, 123; physical appearance, 22, 32, 172, 175–86, ("blackamoor profile") 87, 147n24, 197, 230, ("monkey and tiger") 16, 24, 100, 118, 175, 176, 179, ("Negroid" characteristics) 175–79, 184–86, 197, 255, 394 (Pushkin's concern about his "ugliness") 135, 142, 176, 197 (*see also* blackness of, *above*); portraits of, 172–73, 175, 178–86, 238, 293, (death masks) 32, 172–74, 178, 181, 185, 193n54, 194n62, (duel portrayed) 287, 289, 384–85, 386, (self-portraits) 106, 117–18, 119, 122, 184, 185–86, 187n6; public image of, 80–81, 143, ("canonization") 3, 8, 93n54, (as cultural icon) 18–22, 172–74, 195n62, (declines) 18, (as national poet) 18–19, 21, 25, 26, 27, 29, 122, 187n5, 249, 268, (twentieth-century) 23–31, (post-Soviet) 32–34, 193n54; (public fascination with) 20, 23, 43n95, 79; "Russianness" of, 18, 94, 136, 143, 253, 258, 310, 370; and slavery, *see* Slavery; and social class, 17–18, 96n4, 99, 122–23, 124–28, 137, 141–42, 232, (Bulgarin's attack on Pushkin) 90–94, 123, 142, (wife's family connections) 81; Soviet view of, 27–28, 29
works:
"An Assembly at the Time of Peter I," 81, 86
"Áttempts to Reflect Several Nonliterary Accusations," 163
"The Bad Day Has Ended," 97n8
"Beginning of an Autobiography," 154, 201, 217
Belkin Tales, 152
The Blackamoor of Peter the Great, 73, 82, 85, 99, 150–52, 232–33, 256; blackness/Othello motif in, 134–35, 139–40, 142–43, 144, 197, 202–7, 216–17; inaccuracies in, 20, 48–49; operatic version, 332–58; self-portrait drawn in ms. of, 118; story line, 14, 57, 97n13, 139–41, 160–62, 224n42, 396; "telltale baby," 48, 162, 165–67; translated as "The Negro of Peter the Great," 238–39; writing abandoned, 86, 137, 151–52, 153, 159, 163–64, 196, 208
Boris Godunov, 98n14, 137, 152, 220n5; Mussorgsky's setting for, 320–23, 342, 345, 355
The Bronze Horseman, 102, 118, 143, 162, 245n10, 345, 351, 356, 367n42, 392n15; arioso setting for, 345, 346, 355; significance of horseman, 117
The Captain's Daughter, 125, 143, 144, 168n6, 366n37; review of, 244
"Chapter IV from a Historical Novel," 81, 86
"A Comparison," 112
"A Conversation between the Bookseller and the Poet," 153, 166, 397n2
"The Demons," 391n11
"Desire for Fame," 149n36

408

Index

Dubrovsky, 152
Egyptian Nights, 97n13, 153, 164–65, 213–14, 216, 219, 354
Eugene Onegin, 81–85, 102, 129–30, 134, 152, 163, 230–31, 356, 367n42; biographical footnote to, 10, 13, 73, 83–84, 86, 93, 99, 137; Nabokov translation, 94n1; Tatiana as heroine of, 135, 224n42, 225n53, 290; Tchaikovsky's setting for, 342, 352, 353–54, 355; Whittier quoted on, 252
Ezersky (unfinished), 97n13, 171n40, 213, 216, 219
"The Faun and the Shepherdess," 118–19
Feast in Time of Plague, 147n23
The Fountain of Bakhchisarai, 129, 131
The Gypsies, 129, 131, 138, 217, 225n53, 309–10, 349
The History of Peter the Great, 76n14, 168n6
The History of Pugachev, 124, 143, 168n6, 343
"It's time, my friend, it's time," 130
"I've raised myself a monument not made by hands," 30, 311, 313, 317, 321
"I visit yet again," 311, 313, 315, 321
"John Tanner," 127, 230
Journey to Arzrum, 163
"The light of day grew pale," 238
The Monk, 101–11, 117, 119
"Monument," 292–93, 311, 390
"My Genealogy," 81, 82, 278n98, 284, 372; as answer to Bulgarin, 17, 89–94, 135, 142, 143, 163; "Post Scriptum" to, 90–91, 232, 397n10
"My Portrait," 100, 102, 112, 122
"Nachalo," 168n10
"The Nereid," 88
"Ode to Freedom," 257
"Oh, Maiden Rose," 340
"Onegin's Journey," 202
"On Nationalism in Literature," 220n5
Othello as theme, 82, 88–89, 164 (see also *Poltava,* below)
"The Poet," 286
"The Poet and the Mob," 233, 397n1
Poltava, 81, 82, 88, 93, 152, 163, 170–71n30, 224n43, 309; "Objections to the Critics of," 202–3, 208, 216, 217; Othello theme in, 148n24, 169n12, 196, 197–98, 204, 208–13, 219
The Prisoner of the Caucasus, 80–81, 99, 178
"Rebuttal to Criticisms," 148n24
"Rusalka," 106–7, 110, 111, 112
Ruslan and Ludmila, 100, 103, 105, 106–18, 197; Glinka's setting for, 355
The Stone Guest, 97n8, 102, 106, 351
"Table Talk," 12, 81, 82, 89, 216–17
"To Dawe, Esq.," 81, 86–87, 147n24, 230
"To an Infant Child," 138
"To My Inkwell," 105
"To Natalia," 100–1, 102
"To Ovid," 97n8
"To the Poet," 397n11
"To the Sea," 293, 295, 392n17
"To Yazykov," 81, 84–86, 90, 201, 231, 293–94
"To Yur'ev," 81, 87–88, 93, 118, 119, 120n3, 134, 137, 197, 229–30, 372, 397n9
"Vadim," 348
"Verses Composed at Night," 300n29
"When the Tsar's Moor Thought of Getting Married" ("How the Tsar's Blackamoor Thought to Marry"), 96n6, 168n12, 202, 348
"Whether I wander along the noisy streets," 302, 314–15
"A Winter Road," 391n11
Pushkin, Catherine (great-granddaughter), 43n95
Pushkin, Elizaveta (sister-in-law), 177
Pushkin, Lev A. (grandfather), 218
Pushkin, Lev Sergeevich (brother), 15, 176, 177, 183, 203
Pushkin, Sergei Lvovich (father), 372, 374
Pushkina, Nadezhda Osipovna (née Gannibal, mother), 73, 84, 93; Bulgarin vilifies, 91–92, 123; relationship with son, 92, 276n80, 374; skin color of, 15, 32, 90, 177, 220n3
Pushkina, Natalia Nikolaevna (née Goncharova, wife), 81, 99, 119, 142, 208, 300n25, 348, 384; Nicholas I and, 28, 218; painting of, 180–81; Pushkin's letters to, 124, 135, 142, 176
Pushkina, Olga Sergeevna (sister), 73
Pushkin House, 73, 174

Index

Pushkin Journal, 220n1
Pushkin Prize, 238, 243, 246n29, 249
Pushkin Square, Pushkin's statue on, 185

Racial hybridity, 21, 33, 263, 334, 355
Racism: anti-Semitism, *see* Jews and Jewish culture; denial of blackness as, 22, 287; the Enlightenment and, 10; Hitler's, 296; nineteenth-century political, 18, 21; Pushkin and, 122–23, 254–68, 389, (American discourse on) 250, 256, 266; racial exogamy and monstrous births, 158; racial "superiority," 155–57; in Russia, 158–59, (Peter the Great and) 162, (racial stereotypes) 15; in Soviet society, 25–26, 33, 317–18; Underwood's novel dealing with, 263–65; in U.S., 8–9, 43n95, 229, 255, (laws concerning) 252–53, (lynchings) 310–11, (race riots) 333, (segregation/Jim Crow laws) 244, 253, 310–11, (struggle against) 243. *See also* Slavery
Radishchev, Aleksandr, 10
Raeff, Marc, 36n23
Raevsky, Alexander Nikolaevich, 88, 138, 217
Ragusan Republic, Ragusans, 53, 56
Raguzinsky, Efim Ivanovich, 55, 56–57
Raguzinsky, Savva. *See* Vladislavich-Raguzinsky, Savva Lukich
Rak, V. D., 220n1, 223n30
Rastafarian movement, 311
Reid, Mayne, 395
Repin, Il'ia: *A. S. Pushkin* (fig. 35); *Farewell, Free Elements!,* 180 (and fig. 16); *Pushkin at the Lycée Examination,* 180 (and fig. 17); *Pushkin Declaiming to the Decembrists,* 180; *Pushkin on the Banks of the Neva,* 191n26
Rezanov (student in Paris), 61
Rimsky-Korsakov, Nikolai, 367nn41,45
Robeson, Paul, 26, 45n115, 263, 278n97, 302–25; "Welcome Home" speech, 316–17, 318, 324; *Here I Stand,* 306, 315, 319
Robeson, Mrs. Paul (Essie), 304, 316
Robeson, Paul, Jr., 302, 303, 315, 316, 318, 319
Robeson, William, 324

Rodionovna, Arina ("nanny"), 13, 153–54, 180, 266; influence of, 260–61
Rogers, J. A., 255–62 passim
Rogervik construction works, 70
Romanticism, 126, 139, 156, 180, 200; break with, 334; German, 18; and Shakespeare, 204, 214
Rosset-Smirnova, A. O. *See* Smirnova, A. O.
Rostopchin, Countess, 177
Rostovsky, Dmitry: *Chet'ii Minei,* 102
Rotkirkh, Adam (or Adolf) Karpovich, 13, 35n12, 48, 51–52, 55–56, 58, 63, 72–73
Rotkirkh, Ivan, 72
Rotkirkh, Vladimir, 73
Rousseau, Jean-Jacques, 201, 228, 230, 232, 239
Rozhdestvensky, Gennady, 337
Russia: blacks and blackness as viewed in, 7–8, 10–11, 15–20, 23, 197, 201; culture of, 135–36, (Golden Age) 226, 227, (Silver Age) 333, 338, 351, 354, 358, 365n33; expansion of empire, 9, 19, 20; "Great Russian" nobility, 29, (Gannibal and) 371, 372, 373, 378; Pushkin as cult figure, 122, 172, 173–74, 226–27, 258, 370; Russian opera, 354–55; Shakespeare criticism in, 200–1; -U.S. relations, 35n27, 228–29, 235; U.S. slavery as viewed in, 230; wars, 89, 91 (*see also* Sweden); "white Russian" as term, 278n97. *See also* Soviet Union
Russian Antiquity (periodical), 148n27
Russian Archive (almanac), 202
Russian Gazette, The, 149n42
Russian Revolution (1917), 25, 195n62, 278n97, 280, 284. *See also* Bolshevik Revolution; Communist Revolution
Russian State Archive of Literature and Art, 308
Russkaia starina (journal), 35n6, 40n61
Russkie vedomosti (journal), 42n80
Ryleev, K. F., 202–3

Said, Edward, 170n25
St. Petersburg Art Square monuments, 185
Sancho, Ignatius, 12, 157
Sandiford, Keith A., 157
Scarborough, W. S., 257, 258–59, 260
Schiller, Friedrich, 52

Index

Schlegel, August-Wilhelm, 200, 201, 214–15, 206
Schnittke, Alfred, 337
Schoenberg, Arnold, 334
Schomberg Collection, 248, 249
Schoonebeck, Adrian, 57
Schuyler, George, 254
Schwartz, Maurice, 244
Scott, Sir Walter, 125, 152, 163
Scotto, Peter, 285
Scriabin, Aleksandr, 334, 367n41
Seltzer, Isadore, 194n60
Semenova, Ekaterina, 221n13
Semenovsky Regiment, 71
"Semitic" type, 6, 22, 177, 178, 254
Serfdom, Russian, 10, 96n4, 257, 260–61. *See also* Slavery
Serov, V. A.: *Pushkin in the Park,* 191n39 (and fig. 53)
Sessarakoo, Prince William Ansah, 38n40
Shadr, I. D., 185 (and fig. 47)
Shakespeare, William, 125, 239; Pushkin compared to, 136, 258, 303
  works: *As You Like It,* 341; *Hamlet,* 220n5; *Measure for Measure,* 220n5; *The Merchant of Venice,* 200; *Othello,* 10, 89, 157, 164, 168–69n12, 196–219, 228, 239, (French translation of) 201, 223n30; *The Tempest,* 165–66; *Titus Andronicus,* 155
Shaw, J. Thomas, 7, 18, 133–34, 178, 219n1, 227, 231
Shchedrin, Rodion, 367n45
Shevyrev, S. P., 198, 201, 214
Shostakovich, Dmitry, 358
Shtein, V. F.: *Pushkin as a Boy,* 191n39 (and fig. 54)
Shukhaev, V. I., 186 (and fig. 49)
Shuvalov, Count P. I., 72
Simmons, Ernest J., 235, 243, 254, 255
Sinyavsky, Andrei. *See* Tertz, Abram
Skudnov, M., 193n56 (and fig. 68)
Slavery, 11–12, 155–56, 177; abolitionist movement, 11, 157, 250, 251, 252, 258; in America, 8, 10, 15, 95–96n4, (compared to Russian serfdom) 36n21, 85, 128, 228, 230, 235, 257, 265–66, (Pushkin's interest in, stance toward) 126, 128, 228–29, 230, 232, 257; "Gannibal" sold into, 46–47, 377–78, (Pushkin denies) 284; Pushkin's definition of, 233; Pushkin uses *rab* as term for slave, 85–86, 90, 132, 231, 284; Russia not involved in, 9, 201; Russian view of, 168, 228. *See also* Serfdom, Russian
Smirdin, A. F., 184
Smirnova, A. O., 22, 143, 149n41
Smirnova, O. N., 149n41
Smith, Homer, 25, 243, 275n50
Sobanska, Karolina Adamovna, 366n40
Social class, 90–94, 96n4, 123–28, 137, 141–42, 232; blackness and, 17–18; family connections and, 81; Gannibal and, 80, 122–23, 371, 372, 373, 378; Russian nobility, 29, 99, 122, (surnames adopted by) 378
Sokolov, P. F., 181 (and fig. 23)
Somov, Konstantin, 186; *Pushkin at Work,* 179 (and fig. 15)
Somov, Orest, 89
Soviet Academy of Sciences, 311, 323
Soviet Culture (periodical), 310
Soviet Music (periodical), 303
Soviet Union, 281, 284, 322; and Africa, 26, 307, 311, 323; collapse of, 30, 31, 33, (Soviet icons vanish) 188n9; Jews in, *see* Jews and Jewish culture; propaganda of, 235, 249, 257, 305–6, 310; Pushkin in culture of, 23–30, 102, 153, 258, 260, 284, 310, 317, 323, 370, (as cult figure) 172–74, 195n62, (jubilee celebrating) 303, 309–12, (post-Soviet) 31–34, 193n54, (Soviet Pushkin studies) 128. *See also* Russia; Stalin, Joseph, and Stalinism; VOKS (USSR Society for Cultural Relations)
Spafarius, Nikolai Gavrilovich Milescu, 53–54, 55–56
Spain, 201; French war with, 60, 207
Stalin, Joseph, and Stalinism, 172, 174, 183, 185, 193n54, 194–95n62; anti-Stalinism (Khrushchev), 322; "Doctors' Plot" against, 310; Robeson and, 302, 309, 311, 318, 324
Stalin Prize, 309
Stasov, Vladimir, 323
State, U.S. Department of, 319, 320
Stepanov, N., 369
Sterne, Lawrence: *Letters,* 12

411

Index

Sternstet, Baron, 68
Stettinius, Edward, Jr., 307
Stocking, George, 155–56
Stolbov, G. A.: *Africa,* 192n39 (and fig. 62)
Stravinsky, Igor, 335, 337, 341;
　works: *L'Histoire du soldat,* 340; *Mavra,* 334, 340–41; *Oedipus Rex,* 334; *Petrushka,* 357; *Le sacre du printemps,* 334
Supreme Court, U.S., 322
Svinin, Pavel, 10
Sweden: Battle of Lesnaia with (1708), 47; Peter I wins victory over (1704), 49–50, 54, 57, 59, 70; Russian border with, 67, 69, 74; Russian fortifications against, 62; war with (1741–42), 66

Taburin, V., 193n56 (and fig. 67)
Talleyrand, Charles-Maurice de, 128, 145n11
Tania (gypsy), 176
Tanner, John, 41n68, 85. *See also* Pushkin, Alexander Sergeevich: works
Tchaikovsky, Pyotr Ilich, 334, 367n45
　works: *Eugene Onegin,* 342, 352, 353–54, 355; *Queen of Spades,* 355, 367n41
Teletova, Natalia, 45n116
"Telltale baby," 64–65, 157, 342; black baby motif, 48, 139, 150–67, 258, 342, 352
Tertz, Abram (Andrei Sinyavsky), 128–29, 174, 195n65; *Strolls with Pushkin,* 29, (excerpt from) 393–96
Themistocles, 15, 127
Thompson, Sinclair, 397n6
Tikhonov, Nikolai, 310
Tillman, Katherine, 252, 253
Timiriazev, I. S., 16
Tiutchev, Fedor Ivanovich, 34
Tocqueville, Alexis de: *De la démocratie en Amérique,* 127–28, 229
Toker, Leona, 24
Tolstaya, Tatiana: "Limpopo," 30, 33
Tolstoi, Petr Andreevich, 52–53, 54, 55, 56
Tolstoi, Count V. V., 100
Tolstoy, Leo, 94, 122, 191n50, 262, 367n43; *War and Peace,* 283, 284
Tolstoy Foundation, 336
Tomashevsky, B. V., 106, 313
Toomer, Jean, 248, 260
Toussaint L'Ouverture, François, 305

Trediakovskii, Vasili, 221n16
Trench-Bonett, Dorothy, 256, 257–58, 261
Trommer. *See* Aidline-Trommer, Elbert
Tropinin, V. A., 173, 181, 182, 195n62 (and figs. 31, 32, and 33)
Troyat, Henri, 179, 258
Trubetskoi, P. P., 194n56 (and fig. 69)
Truman, Harry S, 303
Tsarskoe Selo, 13, 100, 280; Lycée, 10, 100, 374
Tsiavlovskaia, Tatiana G., 138, 139, 140, 154, 175
Tsiavlovsky, M. A., 163
Tsvetaev, Andrei (Andriusha), 387
Tsvetaeva, Anastasia (Asya), 386
Tsvetaeva, Marina, 28, 279–97, 362n19
　works: "Fortuna," 282; "A Meeting with Pushkin," 279–80; "Mother and Music," 294; "My Jobs," 280–83, 284; "My Pushkin," 29, 279, 283, 287–91, 294–96, 300n25, (excerpt from) 384–90; "Natalia Goncharova," 300n25; "Poem of the End," 289; "The Poet and Time," 96; "The Poets," 286; "Verses to Pushkin," 279, 284–85, 287
Tsyvul'skaia, Yadwiga, 359n6
Tunisia, 10
Turgenev, Aleksandr, 10, 37n31, 145n11, 169n16
Turgenev, Ivan S., 94, 176, 262
Turgenev, Nikolai, 10, 169n16
Turkish empire, 3, 55, 57; Gannibal's sojourn in, 47, 51, 52–54, 55–56; Greek struggle against, *see* Greek War for Independence; invades Africa, takes slaves, 46–47, 52, 178, 377–78; Peter's plot against, 8, 53; Russian ambassadors to, 53, 67–68
Tynianov, Yury, 28, 29, 51
　works: "The Gannibals," 369–75; *Pushkin,* 373–75

Ul'ianov, N. P.: *Pushkin and His Wife before the Mirror at a Court Ball,* 180 (and fig. 19); *Pushkin in the Lyceum Gardens,* 191n39 (and fig. 55)
Underground Man, 124
Underwood, Edna Worthley, 238, 239–41, 243, 250, 263–65
Uniate Church, 50

Index

United States: Pushkin as viewed by, 252–68; Pushkin's comments on, 127; racism in, *see* Racism; relationship with Russia, 37n27, 228–29, 235; Russian view of Constitution of, 228; slavery in, *see* Slavery
Ustrialov, N. G., 50
Utkin, N. I., 183 (and fig. 37)
Uvarov, Count S. S., 98n15

Vauban, Sébastien de, 63
Vavilov, Sergei, 311, 323
Veliaminov, I. A., 198, 199, 214
Venetsianov, A. G., school of, 182 (and figs. 26a and 26b)
Vengerov, S. N., 369
Verne, Jules, 395
Viazemsky, Prince Petr A., 11, 15, 126, 230, 233
Vigel', F. F., 16, 88, 138, 217
Vil'boa, Field Marshal A. N., 72
Vilno archive, 49–50
Vinogradov, V., 177
Vitali, I. P., 181 (and fig. 22)
Vladislavich-Raguzinsky, Savva Lukich, 53, 54, 55, 56, 63
VOKS (USSR Society for Cultural Relations), 242–43, 308, 310
Volia/dolia, 128–33, 136, 141, 144
Volkonskaia, Princess Agrafena, 74
Vol'pert, L. I., 208, 219n1
Voltaire, François de, 89, 100, 102, 125, 162, 179, 239, 258
  works: *Candide*, 10; *Philosophy of History*, 150, 168; *Zaire*, 216
Von Schöberg, Christina Regina. *See* Gannibal, Christina Regina
Von Schöberg, Juliana and Anna, 65
Von Schöberg, Matthias, 65
Vorontsov, Chancellor M. I., 68, 69
Vorontsov, Count M. S., 127–28, 138, 372, 382
Vorontsova, Countess Elizaveta Ksar'evna, 138, 139, 140, 154
Vorontsova, Sophia, 138, 139

Vrangel, N. N. and P. N., 70
Vul'f, Aleksei, 151, 154
Vysotsky, Vladimir, 32–33

Wagner, Richard, 334, 358
Walker, Clint, 39n46
Walrond, Eric, 255
War of the Spanish Succession, 207
Warsaw ghetto rebellion, 318
Weekly Progress (newspaper), 249
Wheatley, Phyllis, 157
"White negro," 282–83
"White Russian," 278n97
Whittier, John Greenleaf, 252, 258
Williams, Francis, 157
Wintz, Cary, 233–34
Witt, General (of secret police), 366n40
Wolff, Tatiana, 145n11
Wood, Clement, 241
Workers International, 313
World Peace Conference (Paris, 1949), 307–8, 312, 322
World War II, 317; Germans invade Paris, 335
Wright, Thomas, 181 (and fig. 24)

Yazykov, Nikolai Mikhailovich, 357
Yiddish Art Theater, 244
Yudina, Maria, 318
Yur'ev (Pushkin's friend), 119
Yurov, Aleksei, 59
Yuzefovich, M. F., 176

Zagoskin, Mikhail Nikolaevich, 163
Zamiatin, Evgeny: *We*, 27, 29
Zavadsky, Yury, 308
Zelensky, B. A., 185 (and fig. 48)
Zenger, N. G., 73
Zhdanov, Andrei, 319–20
Zhukovsky, Vasily, 94, 176, 181, 182, 292, 389–90; sketch, *Pushkin in His Coffin*, 185 (and fig. 13); "Twelve Sleeping Maidens," 114
Zinov'eva-Annibal, L. D., 70
Zotov, Lt. Capt. Konon, 35n2, 57

413

Contributors

David M. Bethea is Vilas Research Professor of Slavic Languages at the University of Wisconsin, Madison. The author and editor of various studies of classical and modern Russian poetry, he has edited the following works on Alexander Pushkin: *Pushkin Today; Realizing Metaphors: Alexander Pushkin and the Life of the Poet; Publications of the Jubilee Pushkin Conference at Stanford, 1999;* and *The Pushkin Handbook.* At present he is working on a creative biography of Pushkin.

Richard C. Borden is the author of *The Art of Writing Badly: Valentin Kataev's Mauvism and the Rebirth of Russian Modernism* and has translated Leonid Dobychin's *The Town of N* and *Encounters with Lise.* He has written numerous articles on twentieth-century Russian literature. He lives in London.

Caryl Emerson is A. Watson Armour III University Professor of Slavic Languages and Literatures at Princeton University, where she chairs the department and holds a coappointment in comparative literature. She has published on Bakhtin, Pushkin, Tolstoy, Dostoevsky, Russian music (especially opera), and the future of the humanities.

Henry Louis Gates Jr. is W. E. B. DuBois Professor of the Humanities and chair of the department of African and African American studies at Harvard University. He has written numerous works of literary and cultural criticism, most recently *America Behind the Color Line: Dialogues with African Americans.* His work has appeared in publications including the *New York Times,* the *New Yorker,* and *Time* magazine.

Richard F. Gustafson is an emeritus professor of Russian at Barnard College, Columbia University. He has written studies of Fet and Tolstoy, as well as numerous articles on Pushkin, Gogol, Tyutchev, and Solovyov.

Contributors

Olga P. Hasty is a professor of Russian literature at Princeton University. She is the author of *Marina Tsvetaeva's Orphic Journeys in the Worlds of the Word* and *Pushkin's Tatiana* and is coeditor and cotranslator of *America through Russian Eyes*.

Liza Knapp is the author of *The Annihilation of Inertia: Dostoevsky and Metaphysics* and the editor of *Dostoevsky's The Idiot: A Critical Companion*. She has published articles on Tsvetaeva, Chekhov, Gogol, and Tolstoy, and is the coeditor of the MLA *Approaches to Teaching Anna Karenina*. She taught at the University of California at Berkeley before moving to Columbia University, where she is an associate professor of Russian literature.

Anne Lounsbery is an assistant professor of Russian literature at New York University. She has published articles on *Dead Souls'* representation of the reading public, Joseph Brodsky as American poet laureate, and the symbolic geography of Russia. Her forthcoming book, *Public Anxieties: Nikolai Gogol, Nathaniel Hawthorne, and Authorship in Russia and America, 1820–1860* (Harvard University Press), is a comparative study of how Russian and American models of authorship developed in response to print culture.

Ronald Meyer is publications officer at the Harriman Institute, Columbia University. He is the editor and translator of Anna Akhmatova's *My Half-Century: Selected Prose*. His other translations include works by Babel, Chekhov, Dostoevsky, Gogol, Lipkin, Sobol, and Palei.

Alexandar Mihailovic is director of the Russian program and a professor of Russian and comparative literature at Hofstra University. He is the author of *Corporeal Worlds: Mikhail Bakhtin's Theology of Discourse* and editor of *Tchaikovsky and His Contemporaries: A Centennial Symposium*. His current project is entitled "Thunder Rogues: Militarism and the Politics of Nostalgia in the Work of St. Petersburg *Mit'ki*."

Catharine Theimer Nepomnyashchy is Ann Whitney Olin Professor of Russian Literature at Barnard College and director of the Harriman Institute at Columbia University. She is the author of *Abram Tertz and the Poetics of Crime* and of numerous articles on Soviet and post-Soviet literature and culture, Russian journalism, and Pushkin, as well as cotranslator of Abram Tertz's *Strolls with Pushkin*.

Ellen Nidy received her B.A. in Slavic languages and literatures from the University of California at Berkeley and her M.A. in Russian literature with an emphasis in literary translation from Columbia University. She is currently managing editor of Rizzoli International Publications in New York.

Catherine O'Neil is an assistant professor of Russian at the University of Denver. She is the author of *With Shakespeare's Eyes: Pushkin's Creative Appropriation of Shakespeare,* as well as several articles about Pushkin and Western literature. She is comanaging editor of the journal *Pushkin Review.*

J. Thomas Shaw is an emeritus professor of Slavic languages at the University of Wisconsin, Madison. He is the author of various studies of Russian poetry, including *The Letters of Alexander Pushkin* (1963), *Pushkin's Rhymes: A Dictionary* (1974), *Pushkin: A Concordance to the Poetry* (1985), and *Studies in Pushkin's Rhyming: Theory from Practice* (2002). At present he is working on *The Rhyming in Pushkin's Post-Lyceum Poetry: A Comparative Computer-Assisted Study.*

Nicole Svobodny received her Ph.D. from Columbia University. Her dissertation is entitled "'But Who's His Father?': Alexander Pushkin's *Little Tragedies* and the Self-Creation of a National Poet." She has taught at Columbia University and Pennsylvania State University. She is currently a senior editor with Harcourt Achieve.

Natalia Konstantinovna Teletova is docent at the Repin Institute of Painting, Sculpture and Architecture in St. Petersburg and is one of the foremost experts in Russia on Pushkin's forebears. Her many publications on Pushkin and his ancestors include *Zabytye rodstvennye sviazy A. S. Pushkina* and "K nemetskoi biografii Gannibala."

Ludmilla A. Trigos is an independent scholar. She received her Ph.D. in Russian literature from Columbia University. She is currently completing her book *Ardent Dreamers in the Land of Eternal Frost: The Decembrist Myth in Russian Culture.* She has taught at Barnard College and at Columbia, New York, and Drew universities.

Slava I. Yastremski is an associate professor of Russian and director of the Russian studies program at Bucknell University, where he helped to develop and teaches in programs in comparative humanities and film studies. Yastremski is the author of numerous articles on Russian poetry, film, and literature of the twentieth century, and has translated eight books, including Olga Sedakova's *Poems and Elegies* (Bucknell University Press) and Igor Klekh's *A Land the Size of Binoculars* (Northwestern University Press).